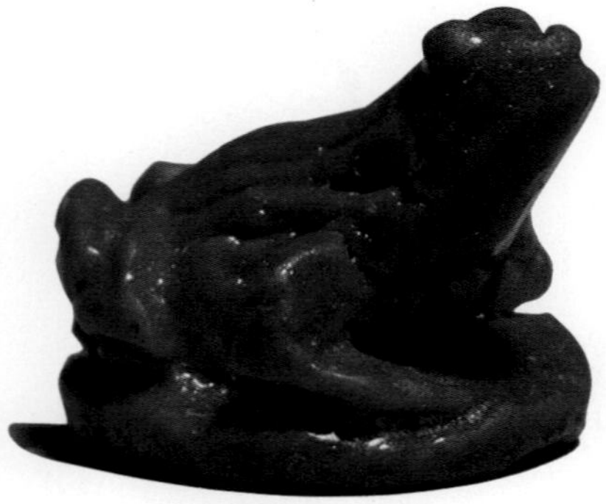

GIFTS OF THE NILE

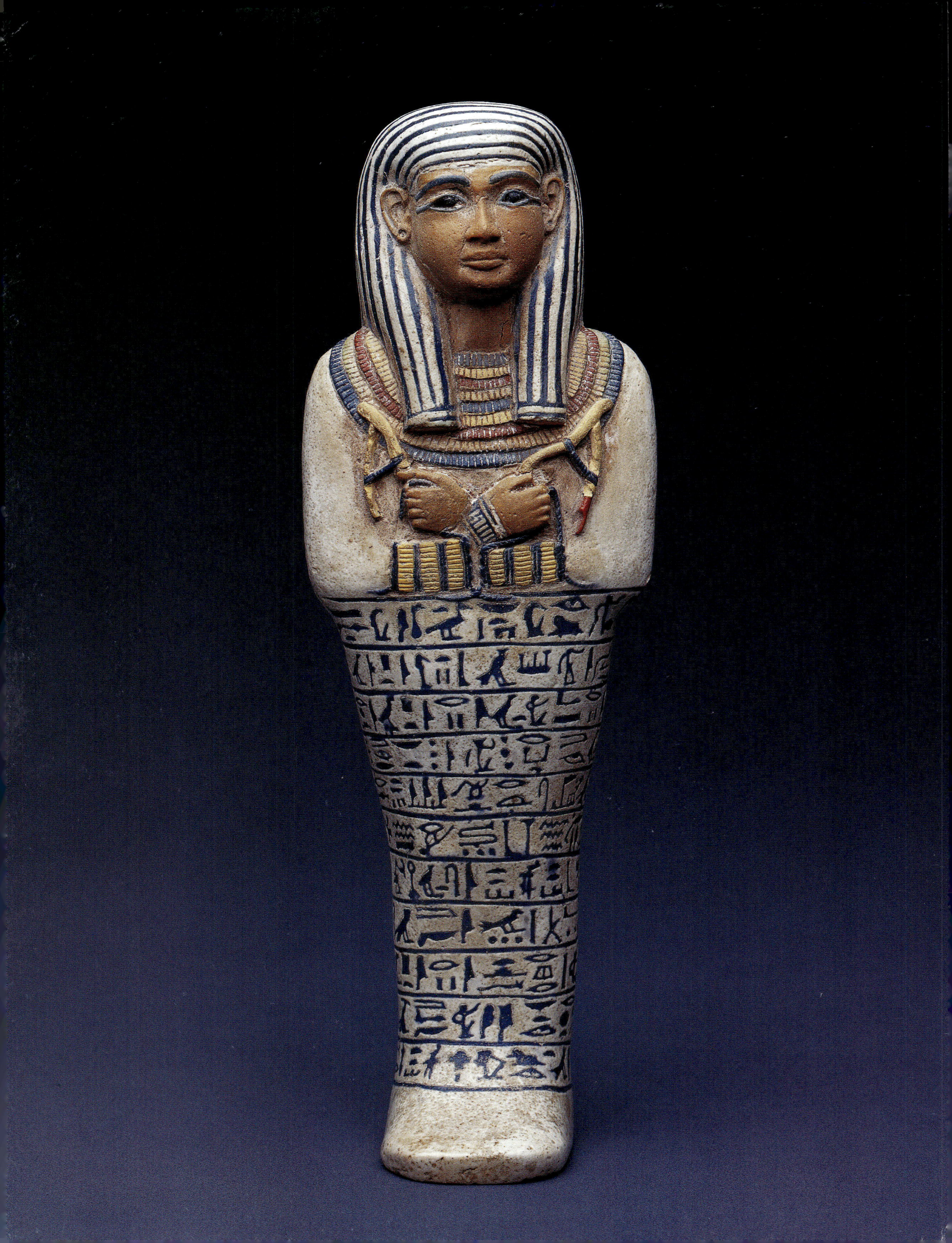

GIFTS OF THE NILE

ANCIENT EGYPTIAN FAIENCE

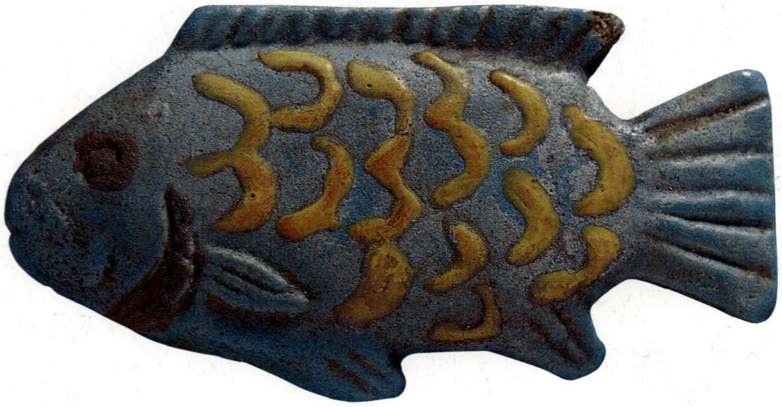

Edited by Florence Dunn Friedman
with the assistance of Georgina Borromeo
Technical Editing by Mimi Leveque

With 483 illustrations, 224 in colour

T & H

THAMES AND HUDSON

For my husband

First published on the occasion of the exhibition 'Gifts of the Nile: Ancient Egyptian Faience', organized by the Museum of Art, Rhode Island School of Design, Providence.

Numbers in square brackets [ ] refer to catalogue entries.

Illustrations. Page 1: [70] frog-shaped bead, The Cleveland Museum of Art.
Page 2: [150] the shabti of Lady Sati, Brooklyn Museum of Art. Page 3: [118] fish amulet, Museum of Art, Rhode Island School of Design, Providence. Page 5, below left: [61] inlay in the form of the composite hieroglyph, "The Horus (or falcon?) of Gold," The Metropolitan Museum of Art. Page 5 above right: [160] pectoral inscribed for Panhesi, Staatliche Museen zu Berlin - Ägyptisches Museum und Papyrussammlung. Pages 8–9, [103] broad collar, Museum of Fine Arts, Boston.
Pages 10–11: [74] Bes-image holding a ring, The Metropolitan Museum of Art. Page 12: [125] conical rhyton or drinking cup, The British Museum, London.
Page 13: [78] bowl with fish and lotus motifs, Staatliche Museen zu Berlin - Ägyptisches Museum und Papyrussammlung.

First published in Great Britain in 1998 by Thames and Hudson Ltd, London

British Library Cataloguing-in-Publication Data
A catalogue record for this book is available from the British Library

ISBN 0-911517-65-0

Printed and bound in Singapore

CONTENTS

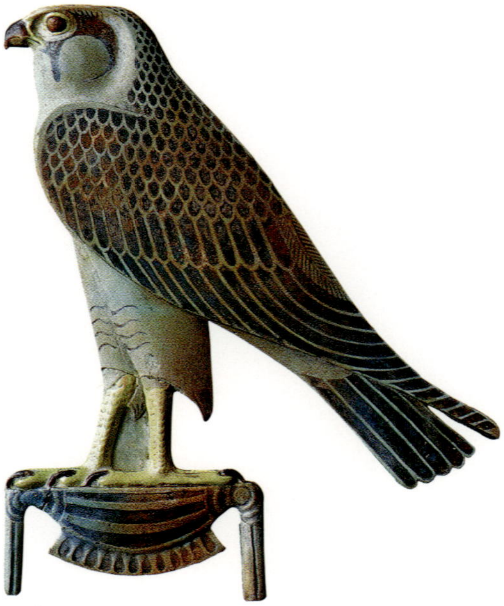

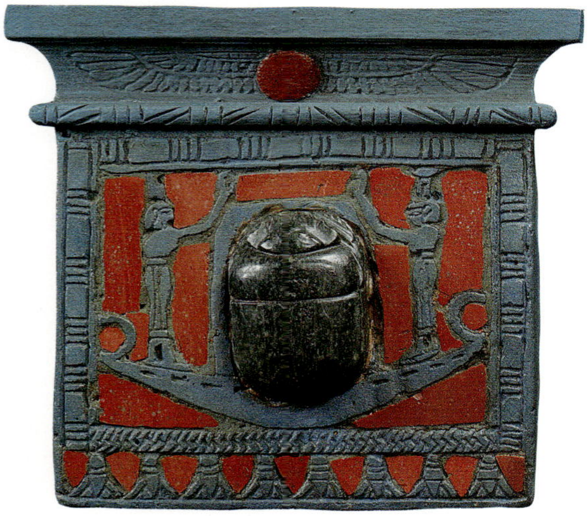

THE PLATES

ACKNOWLEDGMENTS

by Florence Dunn Friedman

Mounting an exhibition, like producing a play, is a team effort in which many are due credit. My thanks go first to Peter Lacovara and Yvonne Markowitz at the Museum of Fine Arts, Boston, for several years ago suggesting faience as the idea for an exhibition; and to Nicholas Reeves who, eager to see such an exhibition realized, generously introduced me to the largely unknown faience treasures at the Myers Museum at Eton College. My deepest appreciation goes to Roger Mandle, President of the Rhode Island School of Design, who has enthusiastically supported the exhibition, and Doreen Bolger, Director of the RISD Museum, who championed the project from the first and who has been enormously helpful at every point in the project, as has Richard Benefield, Assistant Director. My thanks also go to Robert Bergman, Director of the Cleveland Museum of Art, and Edmund P. Pillsbury, Director of the Kimbell Art Museum, who are hosting this exhibition.

I am extremely grateful to the major consultants on this project, Dorothea Arnold, Metropolitan Museum of Art, and Leonard Lesko, Brown University, who committed their time and expertise to make this exhibition happen; and to the catalogue essayists Robert S. Bianchi, Diana Craig Patch, Peter Lacovara, and Paul T. Nicholson. Many thanks also to Mimi Leveque, technical editor, author of the Glossary, and director of the many replication experiments that have benefited our understanding of faience production. Special gratitude to Robert Segal, the designer of the exhibition, with whom I enjoyed many hours of planning and computer design; Trina Avery and Judy Singsen, for editorial assistance; Frank Muhly, director of the video; Stephen Thompson, research assistant; Laurel Barker, curatorial assistant, and Raquel Benros, curatorial secretary; Ann LaVigne, translator; Maya Benton and Lisa Bordoff, Brown University interns; Alex Teeters, Howard Miller, and Jonathan Van Gieson for typing assistance; the Wilbour Library and Arabella Berkenbilt for bibliographic support; Masi Oka for computer aid in times of crisis; to Michael Fredericks and Del Bogart, photographers, and John Ross, research photographer; Shawn Kenney, Illustrator; Ellie Vuilleumier and Tara Emsley, RISD Registrars; E.D. Tully, Carolyn Riccardelli, and Wei Fang, conservation interns; Larry Bush, Head of RISD Ceramics, and Neal Forrest of Nova Scotia, for our first faience replication experiment.

Curators and staff at museums and collections in the United States and Europe were extremely hospitable, taking time to discuss issues with me or otherwise provide assistance. To them I offer much gratitude: Robert A. Lunsingh Scheurleer and Willem M. van Haarlem at the Allard Pierson Museum, Amsterdam; Ian Wardropper and Mary Greuel at the Art Institute of Chicago; Morris Bierbrier, Jeffrey Spencer, Carol Andrews, Clare Messenger, Tania Watkins, and Evelyn Wood at the British Museum; Richard Fazzini, Donald Spanel, Madeleine Cody, and Diane Bergman and Mary Gow at the Brooklyn Museum of Art; Arielle Kozloff, Larry Berman, Beth Whitten, Pat Griffin, and Jeffrey Strean at the Cleveland Museum of Art; William Peck at the Detroit Institute of Arts; Eleni Vassilika, Penny Wilson, and Julie Dawson at the Fitzwilliam Museum; Karol Wight at the J. Paul Getty Museum; Noël Adams and Julia Schottlander, London; Dorothea Arnold, Diana Craig Patch, Marsha Hill, James Allen, Catharine H. Roehrig, Adela Oppenheim, and Earl Hazell at the Metropolitan Museum of Art; and technicians Sergio Salerno and Don Fortenberry; Rita Freed, Peter Lacovara, Yvonne Markowitz, Joyce Haynes, and Sue D'Auria at the Museum of Fine Arts, Boston; Christiane Ziegler, Elizabeth Delange, and Geneviève Pierrat-Bonnefois at the Musée du Louvre; Stephen Spurr and Nicholas Reeves at the Myers Museum, Eton College; Elizabeth Goring and Rosalyn Clancey at the National Museums of Scotland; Mogens Jørgensen at the Ny Carlsberg Glyptotek, Copenhagen; Barbara Adams and Rosalind Janssen at the Petrie Museum of Egyptian Archaeology, University College London; Hans D. Schneider at the Rijksmuseum van Oudheden, Leiden; Dietrich Wildung and Hannelore Kischkewitz at the Staatliche Museen, Berlin; Sylvia Schoske and Alfred Grimm at the Staatliche Sammlung, Munich; David Silverman, Jennifer Wegner and Brigit Crowell who facilitated work at the University of Pennsylvania Museum of Archaeology and Anthropology; and Ellen Reeder, Stephen Harvey, and Barbara Fegley at the Walters Art Gallery. A special debt of gratitude goes to private collectors Dr. and Mrs. Jerome M. Eisenberg, Dr. Benjamin Harer, Alan May, Dr. Leo Mildenberg, George Ortiz, and Prof. William Kelly Simpson, all of whom were generous with their time as well as their beautiful objects; and to Alex Kaczmarczyk and Pamela Vandiver, for their useful comments on objects and technology.

The exhibition is also much indebted to the laboratory analyses of Ann Heywood and Mark T. Wypyski, at the Sherman Fairchild Center for Objects Conservation at the Metropolitan Museum of Art; Henry Lie and Eugene Farrell at the Straus Center for Conservation at the Harvard University Art Museums; and Richard Newman at the Department of Objects Conservation and Scientific Research at the Museum of Fine Arts, Boston. To all of these scientists I offer my appreciation.

The exhibition itself would not have been realized without the help of Stephen Wing, Frank Sousa, David Newton, Dan Reed, and Scott Benson, Preparators at the RISD Museum; Michael Franco, Don Jones, Cheryl Comai, and Ronn Smith, RISD's Office of Institutional Advancement; Ann Hudner and Monica Smith, RISD's Office of Communications; and Becca Friedman, Marsha Dunn, Janice Yellin, Laura Siegel, Peter Sharrer, Robert Haber, and Maria and Ralph Heroux.

We offer much appreciation for the generous support of the National Endowment for the Humanities, Carl and Carolyn Haffenreffer, and the National Endowment for the Arts, with additional funding from the Joukowsky Family Foundation, Textron Inc., and many other anonymous supporters who made this exhibition and catalogue possible. This exhibition is supported by an indemnity from the Federal Council on the Arts and Humanities. And finally, my thanks to everyone at Thames and Hudson, especially Sarah Vernon-Hunt, for undertaking the publication of this book.

Most importantly, I thank Georgina Borromeo, Assistant Curator of Ancient Art at the RISD Museum, without whom this exhibition and catalogue would not have been possible.

CHRONOLOGY

The dates used here are based on the chronology in Baines and Málek 1980, pp. 36–37. Details are given only for those pharaohs mentioned in the text.

Predynastic		**5500–2920 BC**
Badarian		5500–4000
Amratian (Naqada I)		4000–3500
Gerzean (Naqada II)		3500–3100
Late Predynastic (Naqada III)		3100–2920
Early Dynastic Period		**2920–2649**
1st Dynasty		2920–2770
2nd Dynasty		2770–2649
Old Kingdom		**2649–2134**
3rd Dynasty		2649–2575
Djoser (Netjerykhet)	2630–2611	
4th Dynasty		2575–2465
5th Dynasty		2465–2323
Raneferef	2419–2416	
6th Dynasty		2323–2150
7th/8th Dynasties		2150–2134
First Intermediate Period		**2134–2040**
9th/10th Dynasties		2134–2040
11th Dynasty (Theban)		2134–2040
Middle Kingdom		**2040–1640**
11th Dynasty		2040–1991
12th Dynasty		1991–1783
13th Dynasty		1783–after 1640
14th Dynasty		
Second Intermediate Period		**1640–1532**
15th Dynasty (the Hyksos)		
16th Dynasty (the lesser Hyksos)		
17th Dynasty		1640–1550
New Kingdom		**1550–1070**
18th Dynasty		1550–1307
Thutmose III	1479–1425	
Hatshepsut	1473–1458	
Amenhotep II	1427–1401	
Thutmose IV	1401–1391	
Amenhotep III	1391–1353	
Akhenaten	1353–1335	
Smenkhare	1335–1333	
Tutankhamun	1333–1323	
Ay	1323–1319	
Horemheb	1319–1307	
19th Dynasty		1307–1196
Ramesses I	1307–1306	
Seti I	1306–1290	
Ramesses II	1290–1224	
Merneptah	1224–1214	
20th Dynasty		1196–1070
Ramesses III	1194–1163	
Third Intermediate Period		**1070–712**
21st Dynasty		1075–945
Siamun	978–959	
22nd Dynasty		945–712
Shoshenq I	945–924	
Shoshenq II	909–883	
Shoshenq III	835–783	
23rd Dynasty		828–712
Iuput II	731–720	
24th Dynasty		724–712
25th Dynasty (Nubia + Theban area)		770–712
Kashta	770–750	
Piye	750–712	
Late Period		**712–332**
25th Dynasty (Nubia + all Egypt)		712–657
Taharka	690–664	
26th Dynasty		664–525
Psametik I	664–610	
Apries	589–570	
Amasis	570–526	
27th Dynasty (Persian)		525–404
28th Dynasty		404–399
29th Dynasty		399–380
30th Dynasty		380–343
Second Persian Period		**343–332**
Graeco-Roman Period		**332 BC–AD 395**
Ptolemaic Period		332 BC – 30 BC
Ptolemy I	304–284	
Roman period		30 BC–AD 395
Meroitic Kingdom		**300 BC–AD 350**

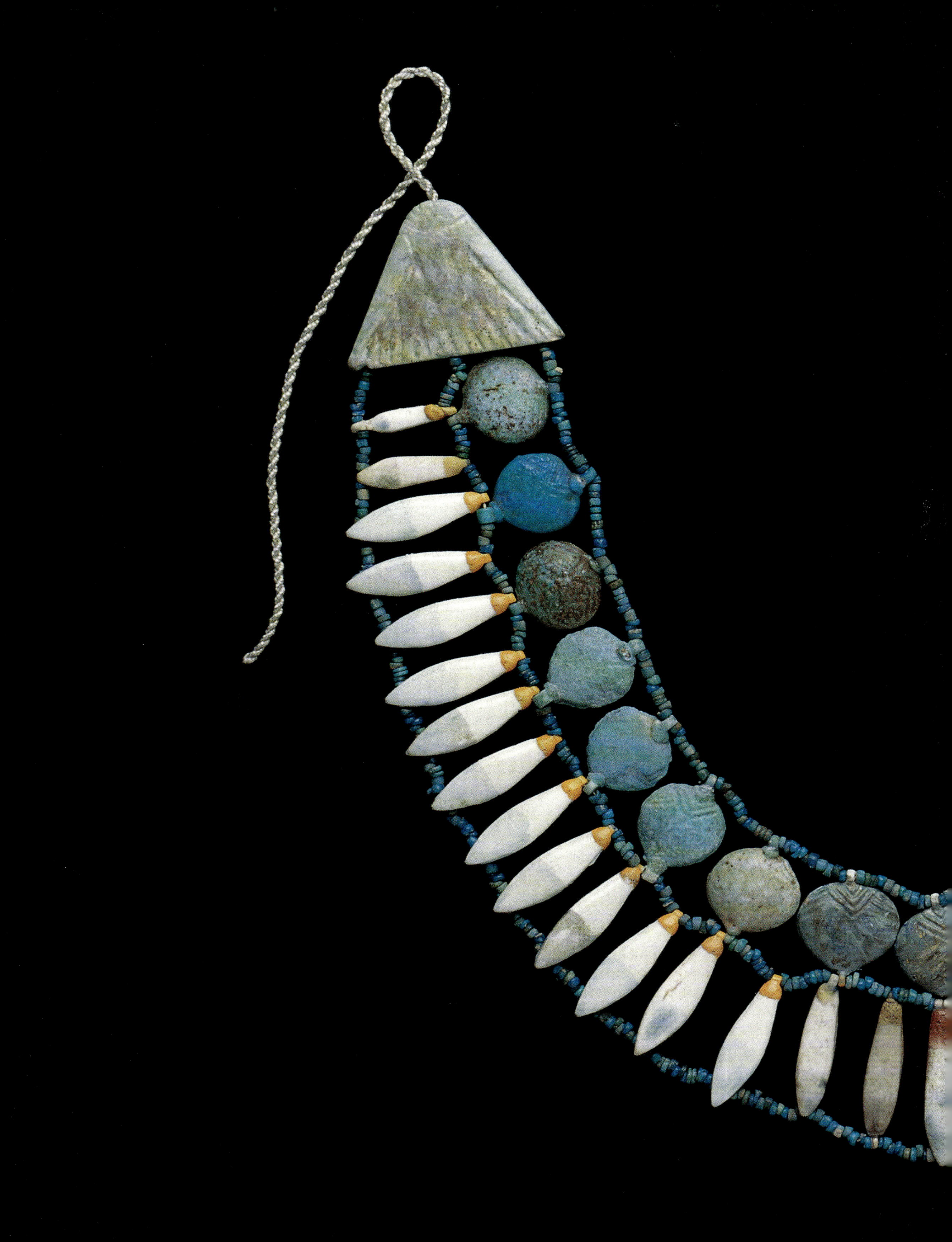

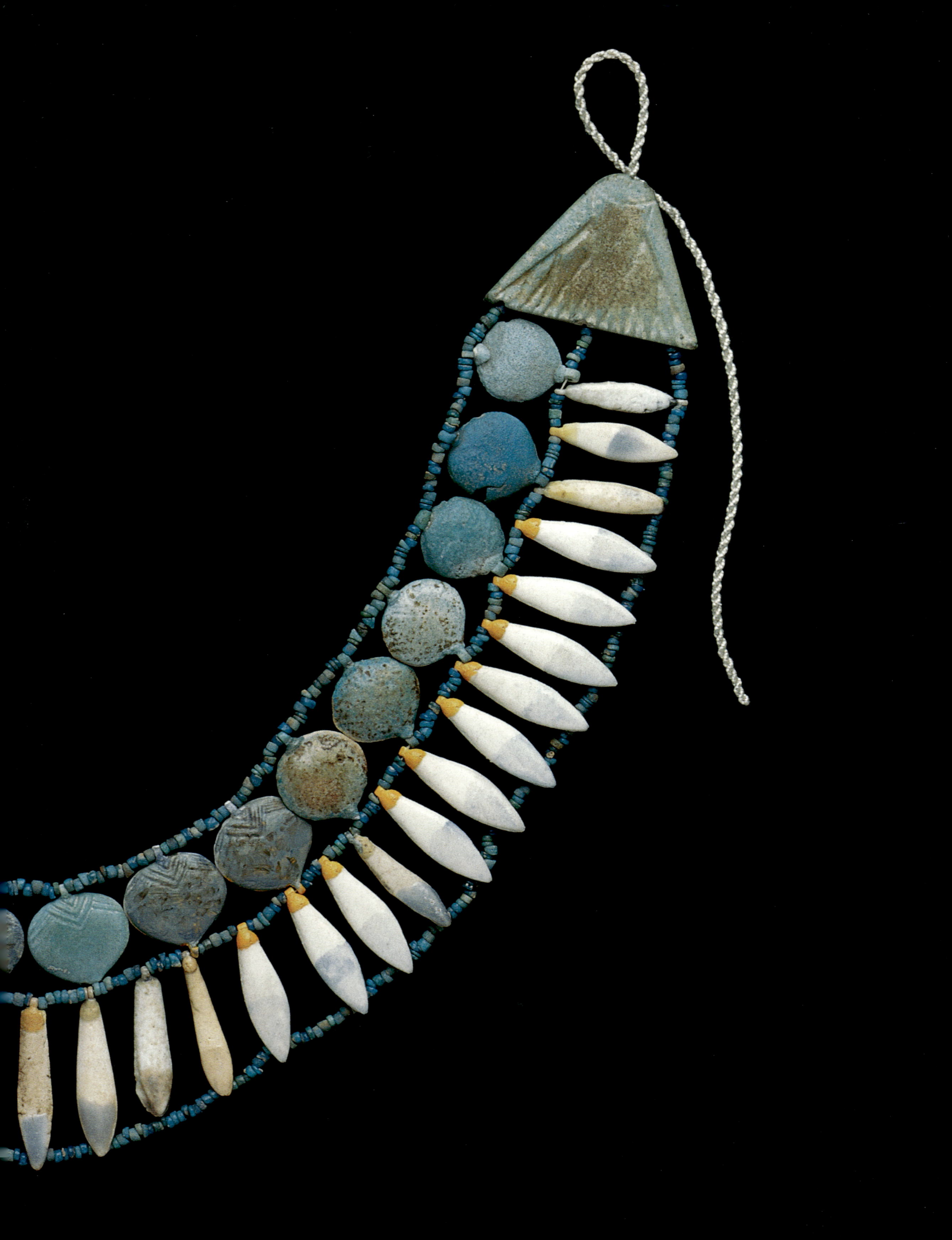

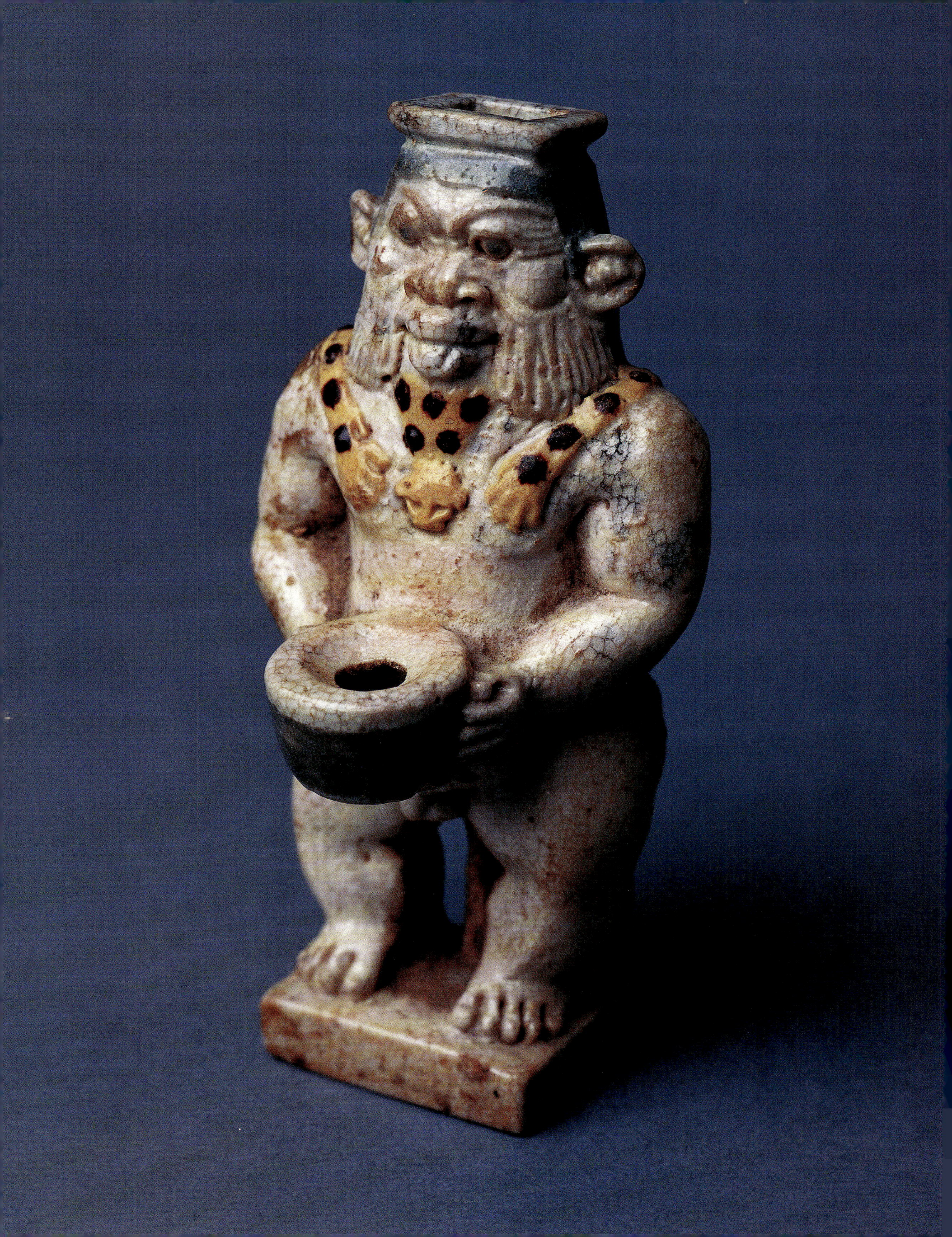

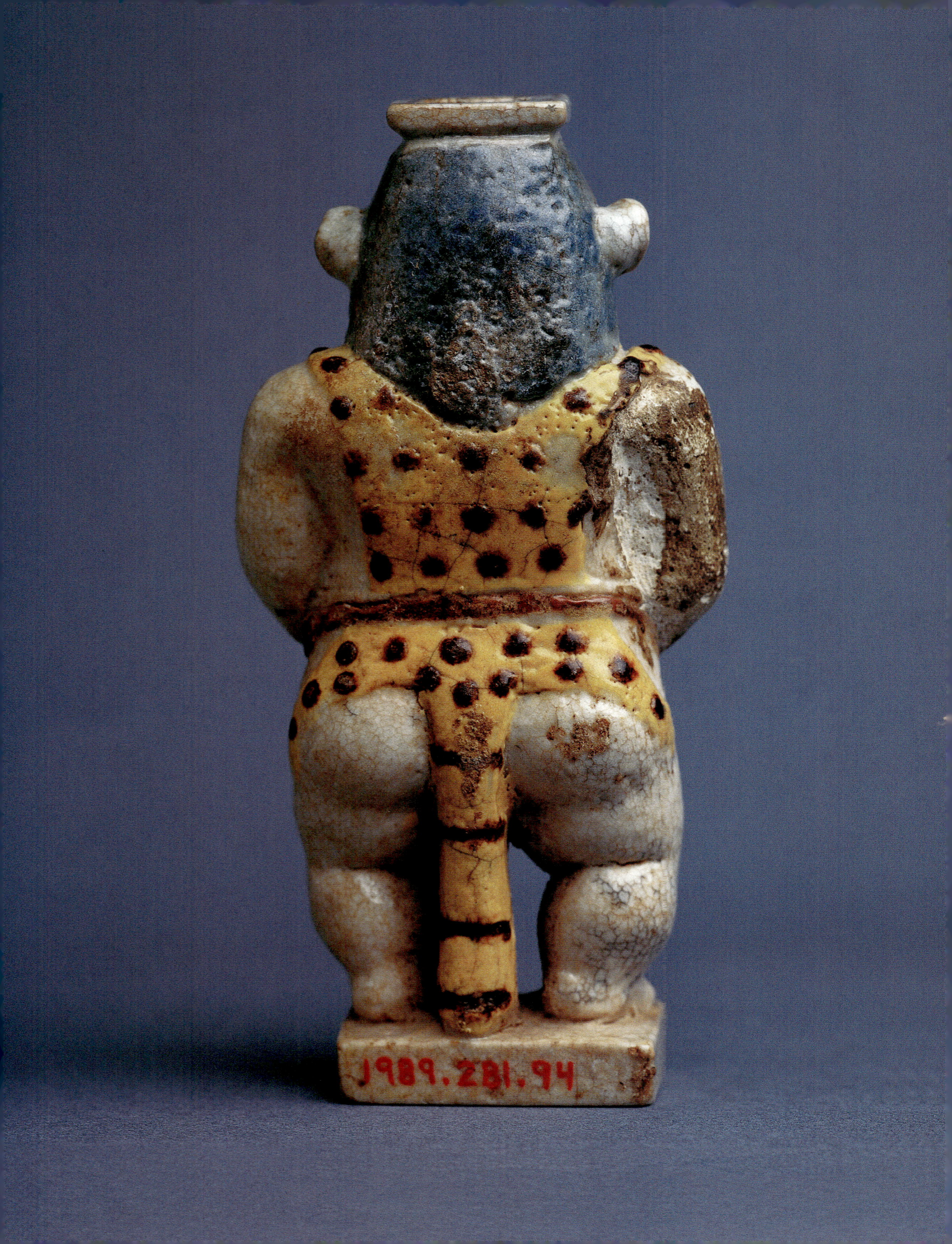
1989.281.94

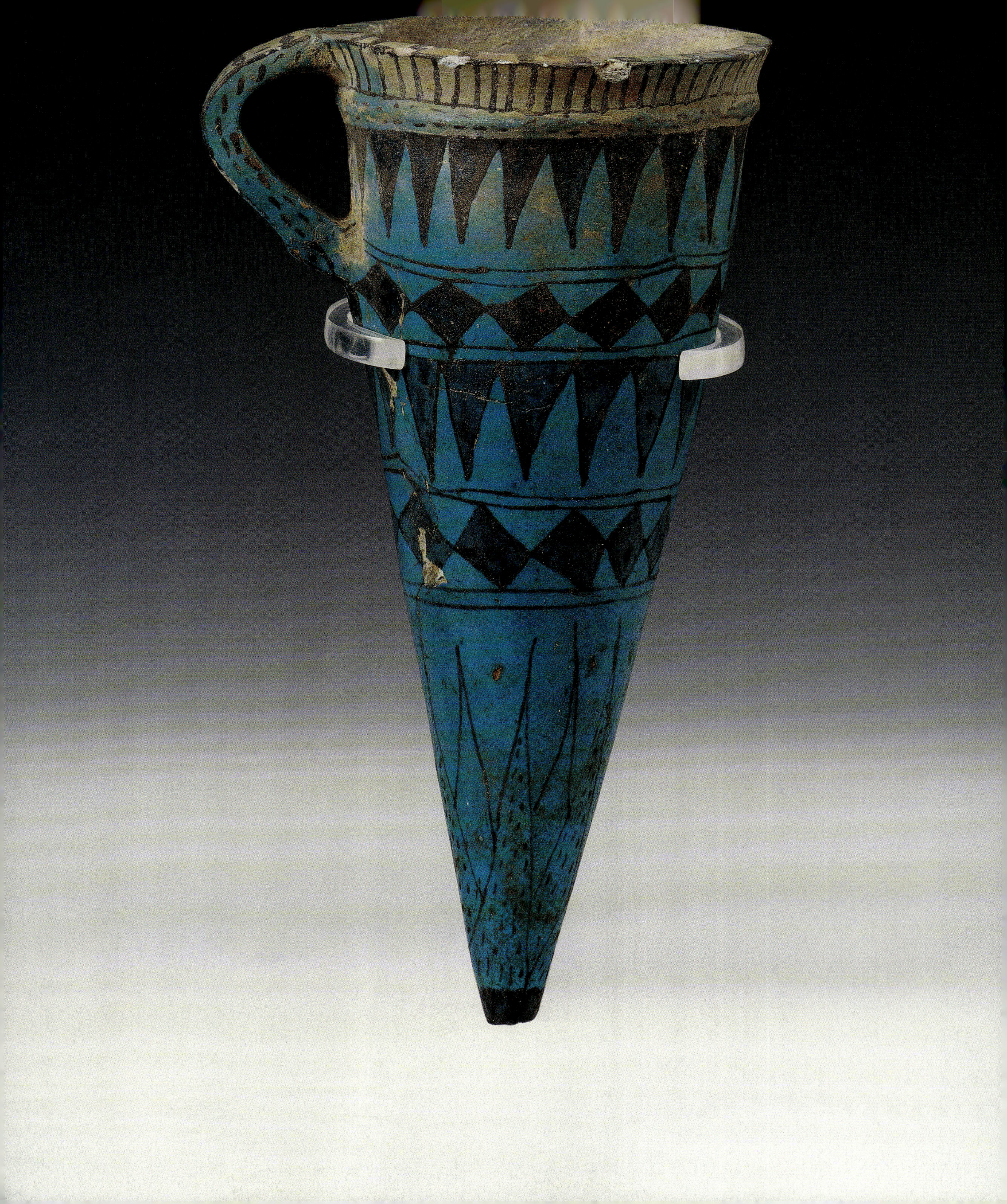

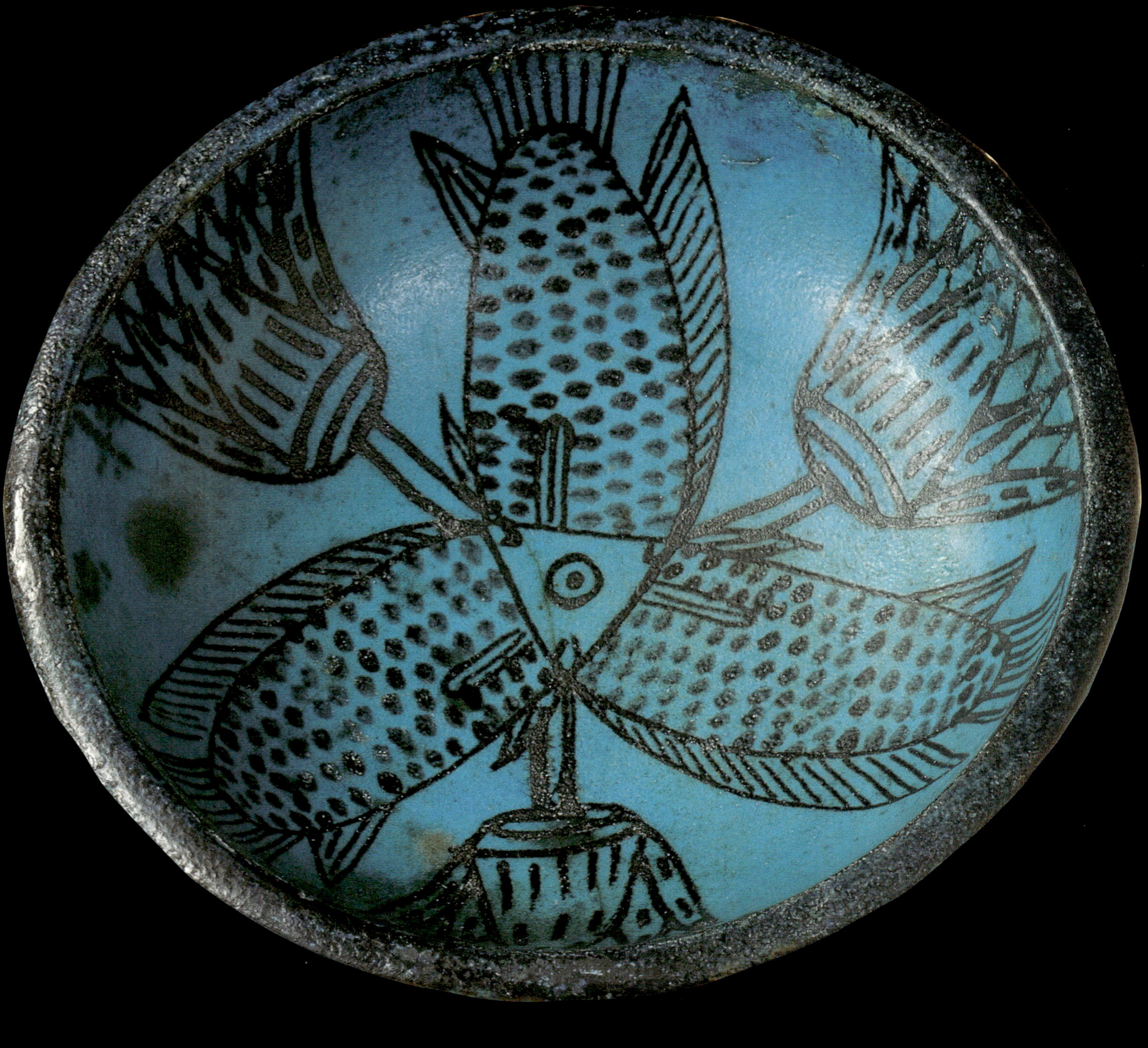

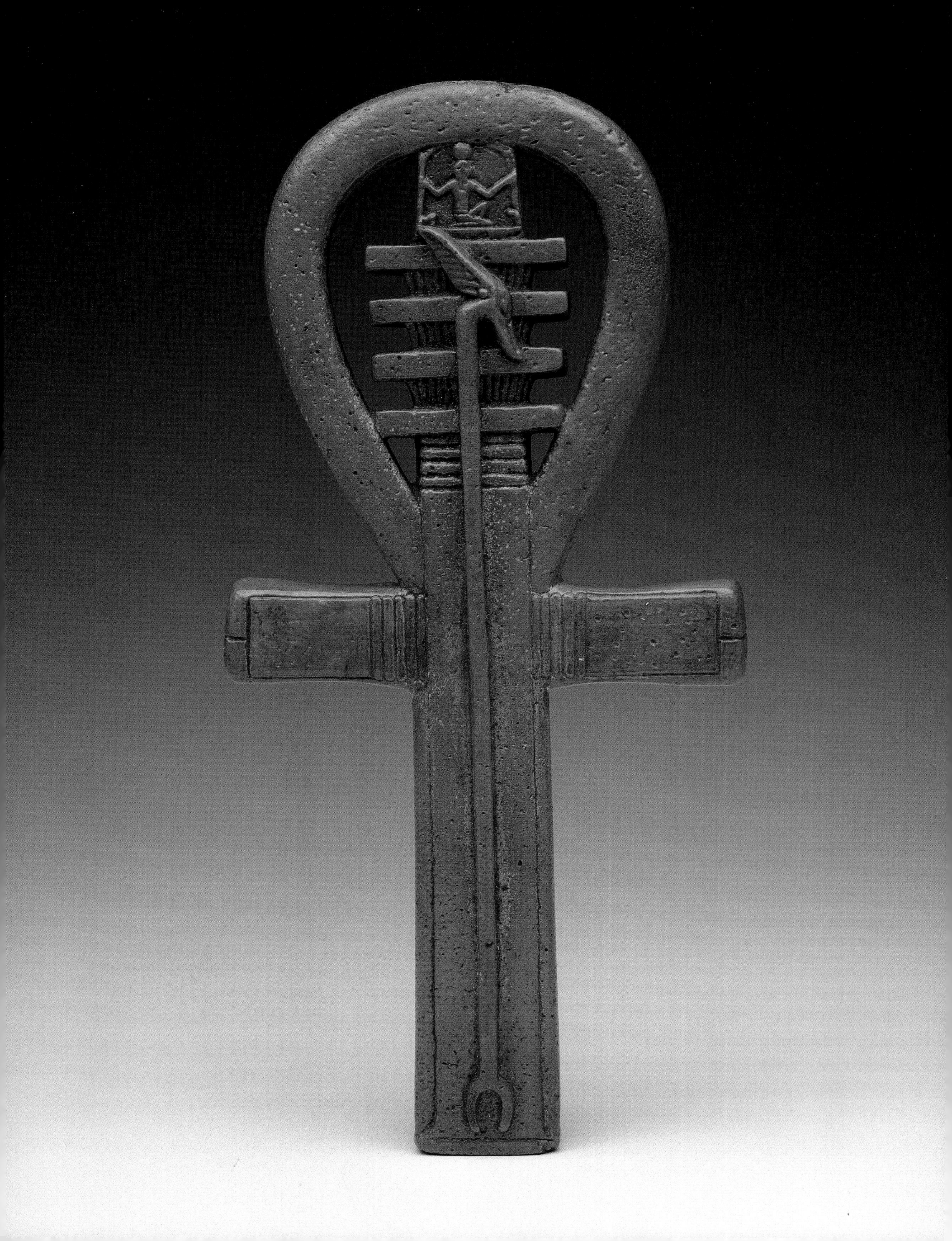

FAIENCE: THE BRILLIANCE OF ETERNITY

Florence Dunn Friedman

One of the ancient world's most beautiful forms of ceramic is today called Egyptian faience.[1] To the ancient Egyptians, however, it was known as *tjehnet*, meaning that which is brilliant or scintillating, like the light of the sun, moon, and stars.[2] As these heavenly bodies shimmered by day or night, so faience was seen to glisten with a light that in Egyptian thought was symbolic of life, rebirth, and immortality.[3] Egypt produced some of its finest small-scale masterpieces in faience, such as the apple-green sistrum from Providence ([91], p. 102) or the unique—and somewhat enigmatic—blue object of Akhenaten from Copenhagen (fig. 1). Over 200 faience works, ranging in date from the late Predynastic to the Roman period, have been selected from public and private collections throughout the United States and Europe for this exhibition, the first interpretive study of its kind. Its purpose is to explore the meaning of faience within Egyptian culture, as well as to examine how it was made, and for—and by—whom.[4] It is also an exhibition intended for the sheer pleasure of viewing beautiful works of art.

While faience was used in many strata of society,[5] it was essentially a luxury product. The human and animal sculptures, vessels, jewelry, amulets, and inlays shown here were primarily for the elite. Unlike other elite materials such as gold or semiprecious gems, however, faience was not rare or of high value in itself but was made of common materials. Its main ingredient is quartz, obtained from sand, flint, or crushed quartz pebbles, to which was added an alkali (e.g., plant ash or natron), a bit of lime, and ground copper as a colorant. When fired, the quartz body developed its typical blue-green glassy surface that time has sometimes dulled.

The palette would eventually expand to include a broad range of blues, greens, white, yellows, reds, and even marbleized browns, blacks, and other hues. But in the late Predynastic Period, when faience first appeared, it was blue-green. Apparently deemed magical, this color was regarded in the following millennia as symbolizing life and good health,[6] attributes of rebirth probably already inherent in the earliest faience grave goods, which took the form of beads[7] ([1], [2], p. 74). As early as the Old Kingdom, the hieroglyphs for *tjehnet*–faience included a pectoral with pendant beads,[8] suggesting the association of these shiny blue-green objects with a wish for continued life.

In search of blue-green surfaces, the Egyptians also glazed steatite, a soft stone that hardened on firing ([9], p. 68). But stone had to be carved, while faience, whose ingredients when mixed with water form a malleable paste, could be hand-modeled or better yet molded. Folding the colorant into the paste meant that, on firing, it would glaze automatically.[9] The faience paste must have seemed magical: it entered the kiln dry, dull, and almost colorless but emerged after firing brilliantly transformed. Nicholson's essay below explains the process in more detail, and it is illustrated in part in fig. 4.[10]

Faience may originally have been developed as an inexpensive substitute for lapis, a violet-blue rock found mainly in distant Afghanistan,[11] or for turquoise, a highly prized blue to blue-green mineral from the Sinai that occurs as veining in rock.[12] The Sinai was later sacred to the goddess Hathor, who held the titles Mistress of Turquoise and Mistress of Faience.[13] Abundant votive offerings (requests or thanks to a deity) were left at Hathor shrines throughout Egypt,[14] and the cow, lotus, and other iconography of this goddess of love, fertility, and music decorate many faience works, from bowls ([76–78], pp. 112–13) to sistra (ritual rattles) ([91], p. 102). But faience was not merely a cheap substitute for lapis, turquoise, or any other material,[15] as Patch and Bianchi note in their essays below. Its inherent associations with light, rebirth, and fertility, through Hathor, gave it a meaning that far transcended its mundane composition.

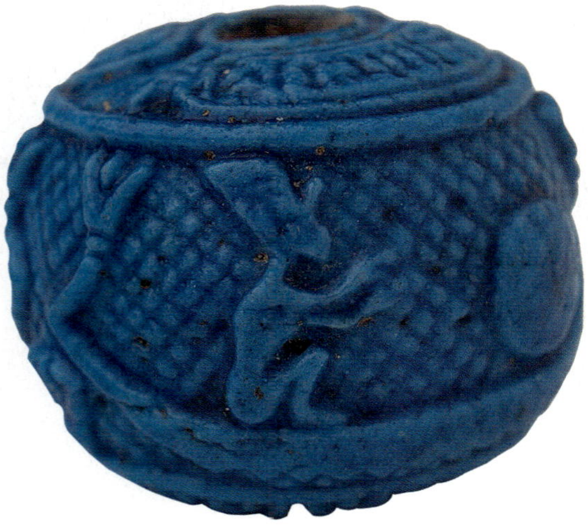

Fig. 1 Object inscribed for Akhenaten and Nefertiti. Dynasty 18, Ny Glyptotek Copenhagen. AEIN 1588.

Opposite
[119] AMULET COMBINING ANKH, DJED, HEH, AND WAS-SCEPTER SIGNS. Dynasty 25 to Late Period, *c.* 700–500 BC; H. 23.5 cm.

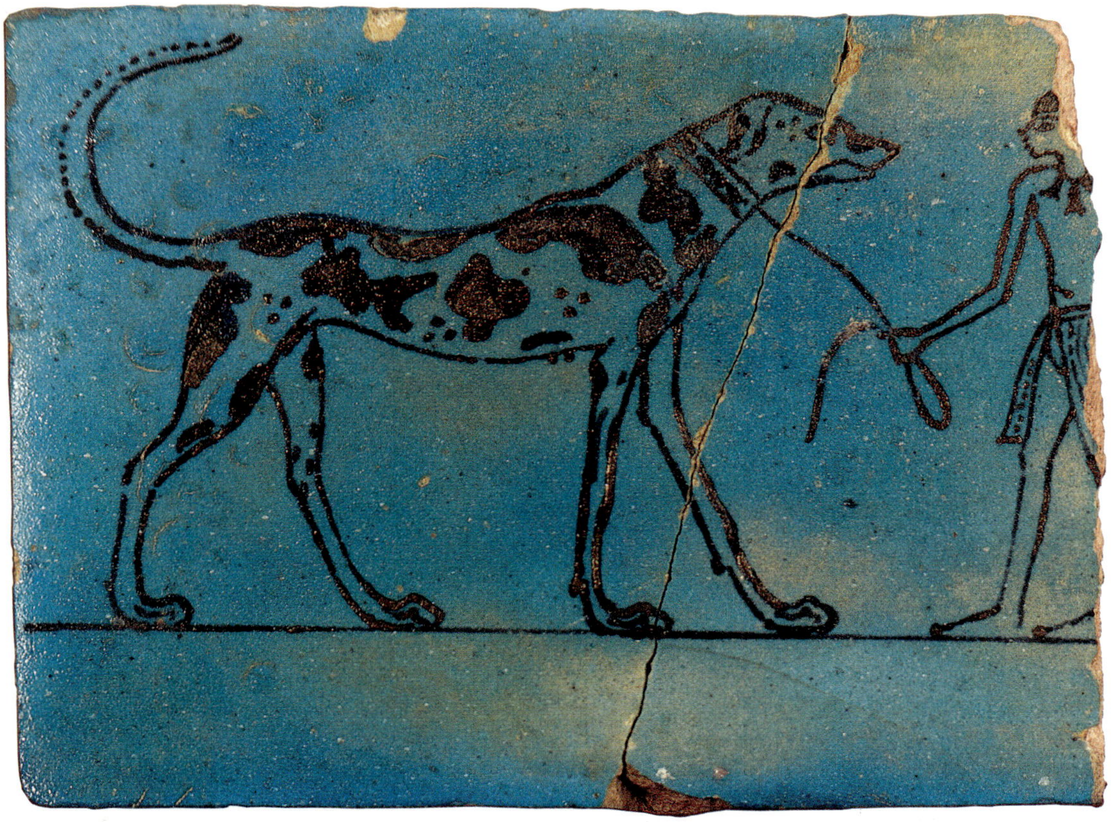

Fig. 2 Faience plaque or tile of a man with piebald dog. Dynasty 18, The Nicholson Museum. R.116.

Yet one might ask why the Egyptians created a new glazed ceramic when clay had already been in use for thousands of years.[16] Though it requires much preparation, clay is easier to work and more easily modeled or molded, and it has the tensile strength to be pulled up on a wheel, which faience does not unless clay is added (as was sometimes done in the Graeco-Roman Period).[17] Faience's major advantage, besides easy preparation, is that it could be glazed, something Egyptian craftsmen either could not or would not do to their clay pottery until Roman times.[18]

In the first two dynasties (also known as the Archaic Period, *c.* 2920–2649 BC), faience was used extensively for religious and funerary purposes in the form of small votive temple offerings, decorative temple wall tiles, and royal tomb objects. Hand-modeled votives, such as model vessels, human figures, and small animals, especially baboons ([3], [4], p. 69) appear at temple sites from Tell Ibrahim Awad in the East Delta[19] in the north, to Abydos,[20] Hierakonpolis,[21] and Elephantine[22] in the south. [23] An Archaic baboon,[24] 23 cm (9 in) high, from the Osiris Temple at Abydos and possibly representing the early deity The Great White One (Hedj-Wer), is evidence of larger, hollow, mold-made technology (fig. 3). It is likely that the small votives, stylistically varied within the same site and probably made over several centuries ([5–10], pp. 68–69) were manufactured in workshops attached to the temple shrines. But it is also possible that they were made in more centralized localities and exported throughout Upper (southern) and Lower (northern) Egypt. The faience wall tiles ([15], [16], pp. 72–73), also from temples at Abydos, Hierakonpolis, and Elephantine, with their varied designs (such as palm tree, leaf, and reed) and methods of attachment (rear or side holes, with high or low bosses), raise the same issue of local or distant manufacture centers.[25]

Royal tomb objects of faience early reveal a desire to imitate other materials, for instance the use of spiral veining that resembles stone.[26] Such swirled mixtures of faience paste are precursors to the marbleized faience found from the Eighteenth Dynasty (such as [90], p. 118, though of Near Eastern manufacture) to Ptolemaic times. Faience copies of clay and stone forms also appear by the First Dynasty in non-elite tombs,[27] and some faience vessels even imitate coiled basketry[28] ([92], p. 120). Yet faience remained largely an elite product, as is especially evident in inlay manufacture, which found its finest expression under Amenhotep III (for instance [23], [24], pp. 80–81).

Inlay within faience, though not difficult in principal, is one of the most technically exacting forms of faience production to do well. The earliest known example of this technique is a vessel belonging to Egypt's first king, Aha, which has one colored faience paste inlaid into a faience body of another color ([13], p. 75). The technique was soon extended to inlaying faience into other materials. An item of royal wooden furniture, possibly a box, has triangles of molded faience paste and wood inlaid to create a design resembling bound rush (fig. 5).[29] Such imitative practices found their most dramatic expression in the 36,000 mold-made faience tiles arranged in panels and imitating bound reeds that lined several underground chambers of King Djoser's Third Dynasty Step Pyramid complex at Saqqara ([17–20], pp. 66, 72). Until recently, faience was thought to be absent from much of the Old Kingdom Pyramid Age, but new examples have come to light from Fifth Dynasty royal funerary monuments at Abusir, where blue faience was sometimes originally surrounded by gold ([21], p. 80).[30] Faience inlays imitating materials like carnelian or lapis ([23], p. 81) were used for millennia, for reasons both practical (it is easier to squeeze faience paste into a channel than to cut stone to fit) and symbolic (relating to notions of rebirth), as discussed by Patch. It is likely that such faience inlays were intended not merely to decorate objects but also to enhance their meaning. Inlays were also used in larger-scale architectural contexts. Perhaps inspired by Fourth Dynasty experiments with paste inlays in the limestone tomb reliefs of Prince Atet and his wife Nefermaat (fig. 6), craftsmen centuries later possibly made architectural examples for Eighteenth Dynasty walls in the temple at Luxor[31] and continued the tradition in the famous prisoner tile inlays in Ramesses III's palace and mortuary temple ([52–54], pp. 92–93).[32]

It seems certain that faience workshops existed by the First Dynasty (*c.* 3100 BC), when many forms of craft specialization appear to have been established in urban centers.[33] Yet despite extensive faience production, we know little about where or by whom it was made. There is new evidence of a workshop of the Old Kingdom/early First Intermediate Period at Abydos, to add to

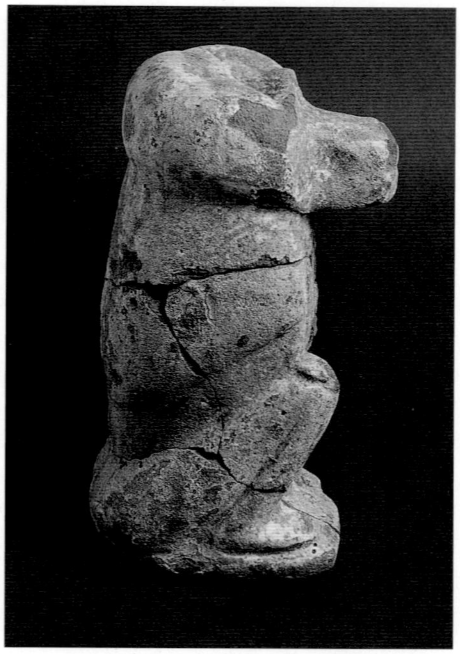

Fig. 3 Faience baboon, possibly representing the early god Hedj-Wer, from the Osiris Temple, Abydos. Dynasties 1–2, The Fitzwilliam Museum, Cambridge. E.23.1903.

a late Middle Kingdom one at Lisht; and recently kilns have been found at New Kingdom (Eighteenth Dynasty) Amarna, while there is evidence of other workshops, especially during the Late Period and Roman Period, as discussed by Nicholson (pp. 56ff.). But there must have been other, now-lost workshops, for example at Memphis or Saqqara during the Archaic Period and Old Kingdom,[34] or, later, at Tuna el-Gebel, from where so much Third Intermediate Period faience has come (such as [46], p. 95; [108], p. 123; [114–17], pp. 126–27).

Standard Egyptian practice would suggest that more than one person worked on different aspects of a single faience product. Yet while tomb paintings detail the division of labor for many crafts, such as pottery, metalwork, leather, jewelry, woodworking, and stone carving, there are, oddly, no sure representations of faience manufacture (though see p. 56 and fig. 31). Considering the vast amount of faience discovered, from tiny, mass-produced beads to a royal *was*-scepter over 2 m (7 ft) high (fig. 36),[35] one might wonder if its depiction was prohibited. It has been suggested indeed that faience working was deliberately shrouded in mystery because of its inherently magical and religious significance, accounting for its absence from the visual record.[36]

Faience production was probably combined with other crafts in order to economize on manpower and fuel sources. The same kilns could have been used for faience, pottery, and Egyptian blue, a non-glazed matte material ([181], p. 167) related to faience that first appears in the Early Dynastic Period,[37] and glazed steatite. This suggestion is supported by the recent finds of kilns at Amarna, noted above, where pottery, glass, and perhaps faience were made in the same workshop complex, as Nicholson describes. In earliest times it is even possible that copper smelting took place nearby, with its byproducts used to color the faience. Undoubtedly there were experts who specialized, for instance, in polychrome inlay ([150], p. 153; [160], p. 161, [194]; p. 174) and who also may have worked on wood, ivory (both elephant and hippo), and bone carving, crafts requiring similar meticulous cutting into soft materials. These workshops must have been hot, dusty, and, with the challenge of controlling firing temperatures, even dangerous. That mistakes occurred in firing is clear from objects such as the slumped sistrum ([189], p. 168) or the pile of melted bowls ("wasters") ([180], p. 171).

Although the step-by-step process of faience production is absent from the visual record, we can suggest a division of labor both from depictions of other craft activities and from what we can surmise of faience manufacture from our own replication experiments at RISD. First, high-quality materials had to be obtained, for the quartz body could vary from fine bright white to dull grey, and assuredly faience suitable for the king and court would require the finest crushed quartz pebbles. Laborers then prepared the faience quartz paste, adding water to achieve the correct consistency; a craftsman possibly hand-formed or mold-made the objects, while a more skilled artisan, perhaps the designer, may have added the final tooling before the piece dried completely. A separate individual would have been in charge of the kilns, with the task of maintaining the firing temperature on which

Fig. 4 Making faience.

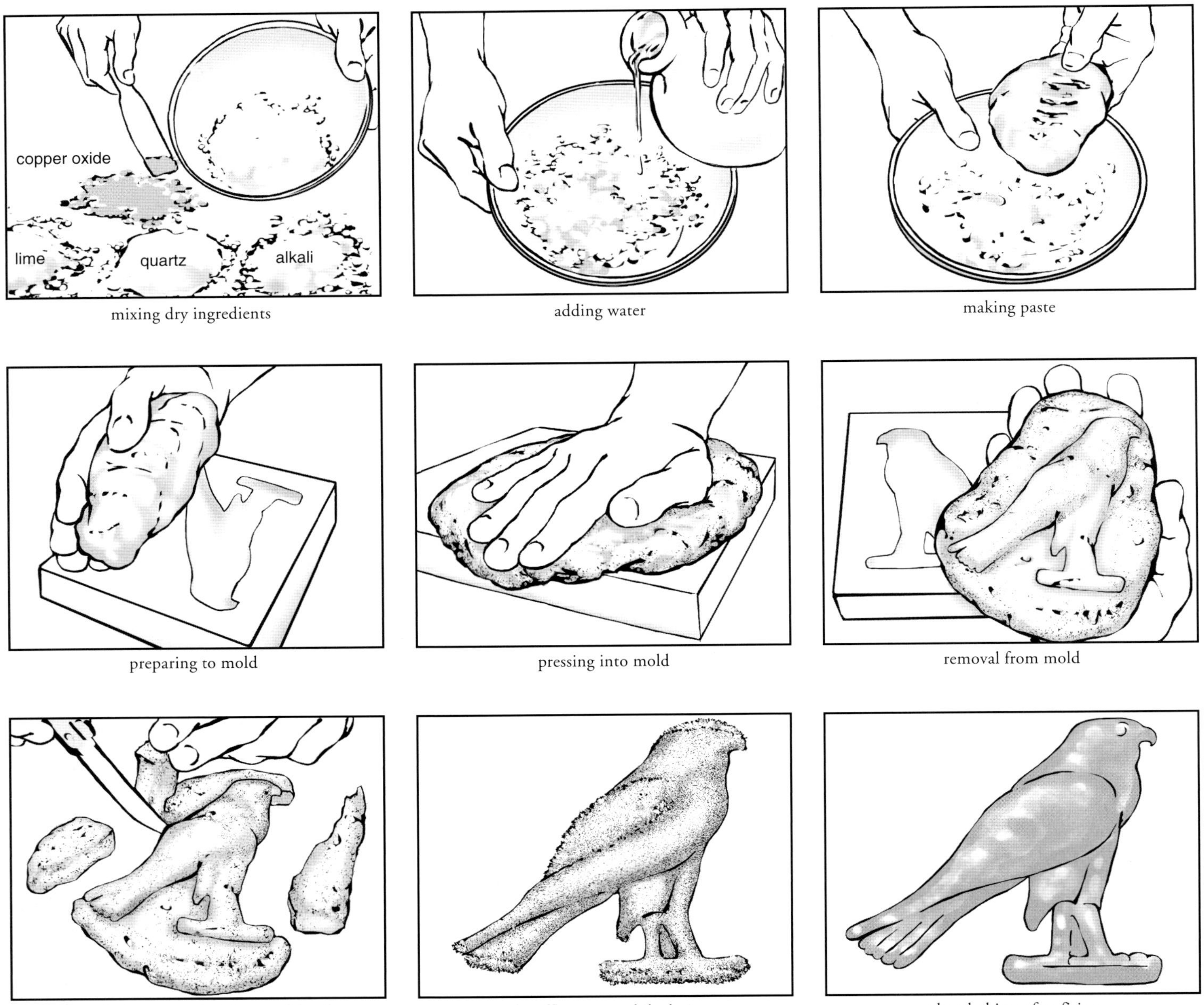

mixing dry ingredients · adding water · making paste · preparing to mold · pressing into mold · removal from mold · removal of excess and addition of details · salts efflorescing while drying · glazed object after firing

the final success of all ceramics depends. Some multiple media objects, such as the sidelock of hair of gilded faience over wood from the statue of a princess ([192], p. 176) required the talents of craftsmen in both faience and carpentry.

Those who made faience were, like most ancient artists and artisans, anonymous. A few names are recorded, however, for instance Rekhamun, whose Nineteenth Dynasty faience stela names him as "the maker of faience for the god Amun" ([166], p. 156).[38] Objects of faience were made within the strict canonical guidelines that were applied to other Egyptian art, and design or execution were rarely subject to the whims of an individual, as Bianchi discusses. Yet it cannot be denied that certain personalities, especially royal ones, were behind innovations. During the reign of Thutmose IV, faience has an uneven, bubbly surface (see fig. 14), resulting from poor firing. But under his son and successor, Amenhotep III, this gives way to unparalleled work that exhibits a new, wider palette of colors and an unequalled skill in polychrome inlays ([23], [24], pp. 80–81)—innovations undoubtedly influenced by the recent introduction of glass technology (and perhaps glass workers) into Egypt. The interest of Amenhotep III and his son and successor, Amenhotep IV/Akhenaten ([32–42], pp. 84, 86, 88–90) took faience to new heights. Amenhotep III, who also commissioned exceptional glass in the period, was clearly interested in exploring the possibilities of faience and in securing the skills of Egypt's finest craftsmen.

Faience's cultural significance is not always clear, and fashion alone may have dictated its use in some instances, as opposed to the owners' conscious awareness of the symbolic meaning of the

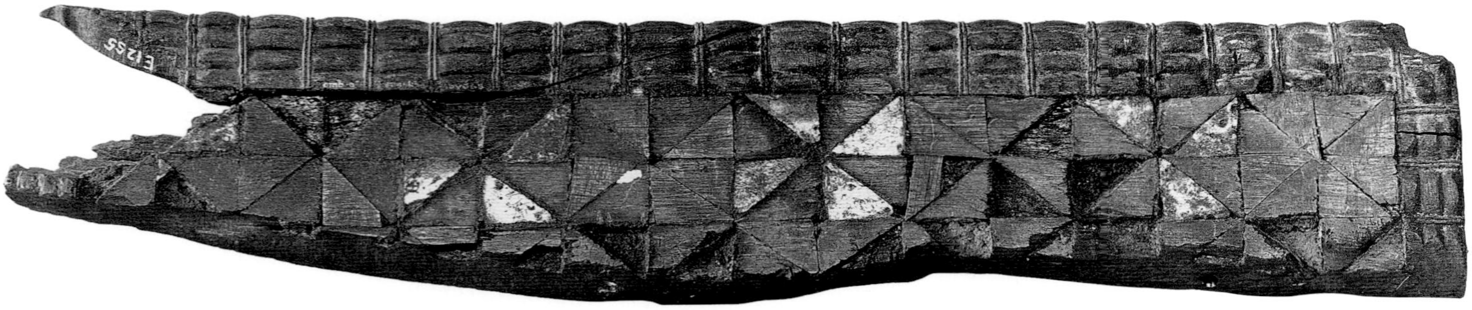

Fig. 5 A fragment of wooden furniture
inlaid with faience, from Tomb U (Semerkhet) at Abydos. Dynasty 1,
Ashmolean Museum, Oxford. 1896-1908 E. 138 + E. 1255.

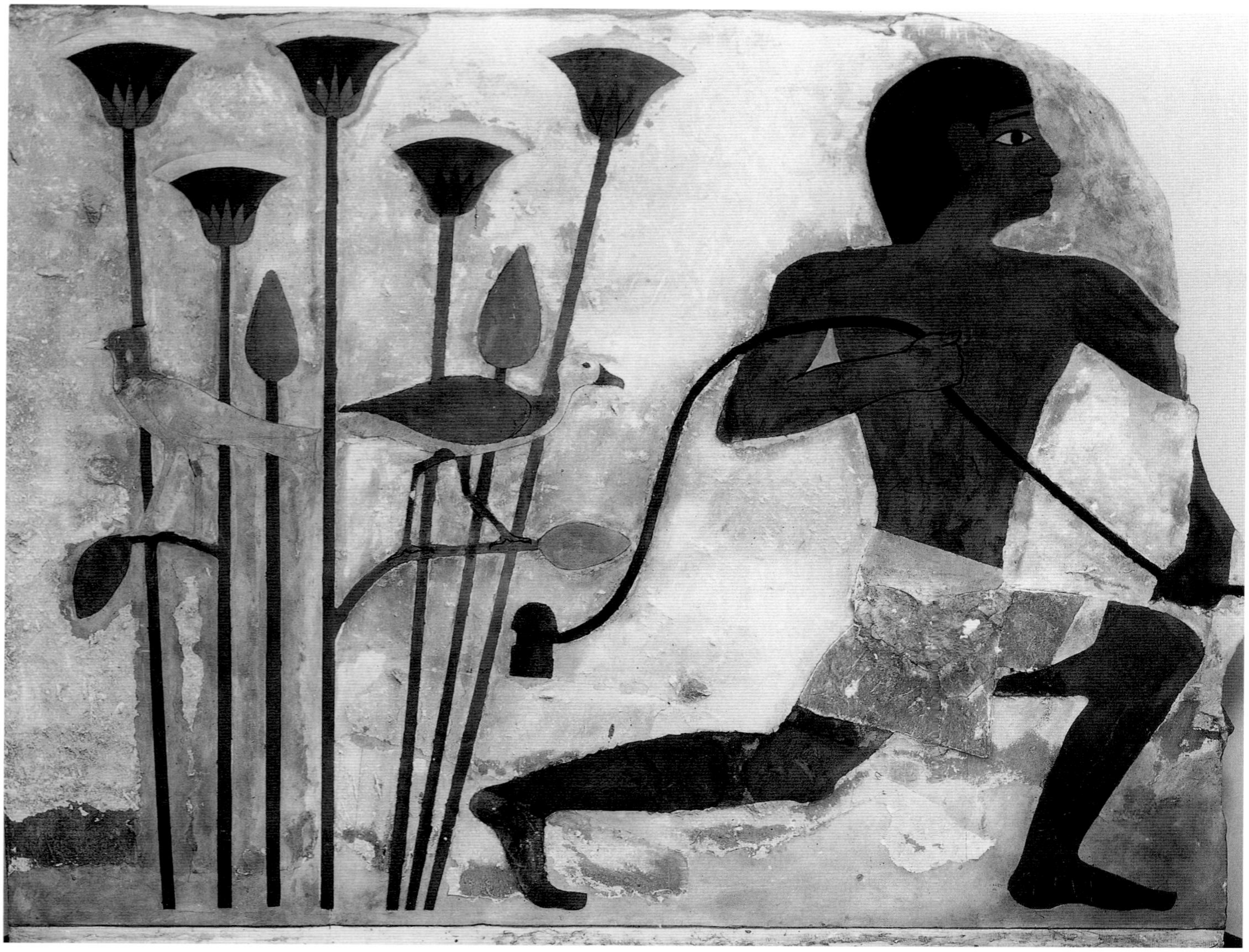

Fig. 6 A fragment of a limestone relief
with paste inlays, from the lintel of the false door of the tomb of Nefermaat at Meidum. Dynasty 4,
Ashmolean Museum, Oxford. 1910.635.

material. For meaning, however, we look to archaeological, visual, and written evidence to aid our interpretations. The engaging Middle Kingdom hippos ([142–45], pp. 148–49), for instance, come from both houses and tombs, suggesting they were not only protective talismans for the dead (as they certainly were) but also fashionable knickknacks for the home.[39] In representations depicting lotus chalices, including ones of faience imitating stone or metal prototypes ([114–17] pp. 126–27), the vessels are shown with contents ranging from sacred libations for Hathor to vegetables and flowers,[40] illustrating the fact that faience object types could serve multiple purposes. Written evidence is especially important. A faience mummy pectoral in the form of a winged Isis ([159], p. 158), for example, assumes new meaning when we consider that the Egyptians described the human chest as *tjehen*-resplendent.[41] Bianchi looks at some of the symbolic meanings of faience based on texts and other sources; Patch explores the archaeological context of faience, with special emphasis on the New Kingdom when the tomb evidence is most plentiful. And Lacovara looks at the Nubian contribution to faience and related glazed materials.

Replication experiments by Mimi Leveque have been exciting aids in suggesting ancient methods of faience manufacture, and laboratory analyses have been another tool for understanding and interpreting the works. We are fortunate in having new analyses from scientists at the Sherman Fairchild Center for Objects Conservation at the Metropolitan Museum of Art. Their examination of the blue Sphinx of Amenhotep III ([22], pp. 78–79) supports the interpretation proposed here of its original function. Analysis of a small tile from the mortuary temple of a Fifth Dynasty king by the Straus Center for Conservation at the Harvard University Art Museums revealed an early use of calcareous (calcium-rich) gesso as a soft backing for gilding in a faience object ([21], p. 80), a fascinating example of Old Kingdom craft experimentation.[42] And ongoing research at the Department of Objects Conservation and Scientific Research at the Museum of Fine Arts, Boston, is revealing differences in technique and composition between Nubian and Egyptian faience ([153], p. 155).

We have divided the faience objects into groups, relating to earliest uses, royal life, women's life and female-related themes, daily life and devotion, and funerary traditions, with a final section dedicated to faience technology. Within these fluid and overlapping categories we examine the objects' archaeological context, though this is often lacking since many were purchased on the art market or were donated without provenance. We also consider how religious, literary, and other forms of inscriptional evidence use terms for faience that may illuminate the meaning of a given work. Laboratory analyses shed more light on forming or glazing technologies.

Despite the marshaling of archaeological, textual, and laboratory data, scholars may still hold differing opinions, so that not all interpretations offered in this volume will necessarily accord. But we hope to show some of the methods by which conclusions were drawn so that viewers can participate in what we feel is an exciting and ongoing process of discovery about ancient Egyptian culture seen through one of its most beautiful ceramic creations.

1 The term is a misnomer arising because the material was once confused with brightly glazed Italian majolica from Faenza, a tin-glazed earthenware also called faience produced since medieval times.
2 Aufrère 1991, ch. 18, esp. pp. 523–26; 531–33.
3 Kings and gods could partake of *tjehnet*'s life-giving light through epithets. King Ay, successor to Tutankhamun at the end of the Eighteenth Dynasty, called himself *tjehnet khaw*, "shimmering of (glorious) appearances (like the sun)," and *tjehnet khepheru*, "shimmering of manifestations" (von Beckerath 1984, p. 232). Such royal epithets appear from the Eighteenth Dynasty (Aufrère 1991, p. 532). *Tjehnet* as an epithet of brilliance was bestowed on many gods, including Hathor, Thoth, and Horus, whose light-filled appearances were likened to celestial light.
4 Faience was used beyond the bounds of Egypt, most notably in the ancient Near East in modern-day Iraq and Iran, as well as Greece, especially the East Greek island of Rhodes. It is also found in the form of small beads in prehistoric northern Europe, Britain and Ireland (Kozloff in Kozloff and Bryan 1992g, p. 397, n. 23).
5 Cf. the green glazed vases from non-elite tombs at Tarkhan (Petrie 1914a, p. 10).
6 For the multiple meanings of *w3ḏ*, see Vergès 1992, pp. 17–18. Goresy and Schliegl in DuQuesne 1996, p. 63, maintain that faience before the Late Period was always blue, which has since corroded to green.
7 E.g., Naqada I–II beads from Naqada (Ashmolean Museum, Oxford 1895.880a) and spherical Naqada II faience beads with gold leaf from el-Amrah (Ashmolean Museum, Oxford E.E.36). Note also a Naqada I amulet of a falcon, probably faience, from Naqada (Ashmolean Museum, Oxford 1895.142; see Vandiver in Kaczmarczyk and Hedges 1983, p. A-140, fig. 29a; fig. 30b; fig. 29c.
8 *WB* V, p. 390; Aufrère 1991, p. 522.
9 This self-glazing or "efflorescence" technique is the most common, the others being application and cementation (see the essay by Nicholson and the Glossary).
10 For faience materials and technology, we are especially indebted to the pioneering work of Kaczmarczyk and Hedges, with its invaluable Appendix by Vandiver (Kaczmarczyk and Hedges 1983), and the exhibition and catalogue *Bleus Égyptiens*, in Geneva (Vergès 1992). New analysis and replication experiments on Egyptian faience and Egyptian blue (*Türkis und Azur Forschungsprojekt zur Kieselkeramik*) are in progress at the Staatliche Museen Kassel in Germany.
11 Lapis, perhaps obtained through trade, is already found in the Early Dynastic Period, for instance a female figurine from Hierakonpolis (H. 8.9 cm/3½ in) in the Ashmolean Museum, Oxford (E.1057; 1057a).
12 Ann Bomann's recent excavations reveal the presence of "industrial mineral and stone working" in the eastern desert as early as Predynastic and Early Dynastic times (*KMT* vol. 7, no. 1, 1996, p. 8).
13 In Late Period and Ptolemaic texts Hathor was called *Tjehnet*, the "Scintillating One," who gleamed like the sun's eye (Aufrère 1991, p. 533; *Wb* V, p. 394, 2); the Eye of the Sun is known as *Tjehney* (Scintillating One) from the Twenty-First Dynasty (*Wb* V, p. 394).
14 See, e.g., Valbelle and Bonnet 1996 on the Hathor sanctuary at Serabit el-Khadim.
15 An offering of minerals in a New Year's text from Dendera pairs gold with silver and lapis with turquoise, while faience is separately carried, an act that may signify faience's distinct and inherent value (Aufrère 1991, pp. 522; 533). Nonetheless, Egyptian texts sometimes make clear that "real lapis" and not faience is being used.
16 The term "ceramic" includes not only clay but other non-clay materials like faience.
17 They may have tried adding clay even in Predynastic times but found that its presence hindered glazing.

18 Some examples of earlier glazed clay exist but the practice was apparently not fully developed until the Roman occupation after 30 BC. Egyptian Nile silt clay is also a muddy, dull color that even when glazed does not produce the white reflective body valued in faience.
19 Van Haarlem 1995. The faience was usually separated from other materials like clay, though Room B contained a mixture of the two; a similar separation of material is evident at Elephantine (van Haarlem, pers. comm.).
20 Petrie 1903, pp. 24–28; pls.V–X.
21 Adams 1974, pp. 20–30 (nos. 97–148), pls. 13–22, which include models and fragments of statues and figurines that as at other sites are predominantly faience but also include clay and limestone.
22 Dreyer 1986 (votives) pp. 68–83, pls. 11–41; (tiles) pp. 89–93, pls. 47–54.
23 Concerning dating, Kemp's remarks on the Elephantine material are pertinent: "...whilst the Early Dynastic Period is the date for the origination of the style and repertoire of forms, it is not necessarily the date for the manufacture of every piece" (Kemp 1989b, p. 74).
24 Fitzwilliam Museum E.23.1903. I thank Eleni Vassilika for bringing this piece to my attention.
25 On the tiles, see Friedman in Der Manuelian 1996, p. 343, ns. 36–38.
26 On First Dynasty Abydos Temple material, e.g., Ashmolean Museum, Oxford E.35: model cylinder vase with spiral veins imitating stone; or E.56 a swirl-designed bead, both from the Osiris Temple at Abydos, Chamber M 69. Similar swirled faience is found at Tell Ibrahim Awad (van Haarlem, pers. comm.).
27 Petrie 1914b, p. 10; pl. IV 3:8.
28 E.g., Petrie 1914b, pl. IV 4:7; drawing on pl. V, 13 (2057), today in Manchester Museum.
29 Ashmolean Museum, Oxford E.138; E.1255; from Abydos, reign of Semerkhet; probably from a wooden box (Killen 1994b, pp. 21–22; p. 23, fig. 24).
30 Verner 1994, e.g., p. 139, though the gilding has disappeared. Gilding around a parallel faience piece is known from analysis of the Raneferef inlay [21], recalling Late Period and Ptolemaic texts that pair *tjehnet* with gold as though they were two complementary aspects of light: the sun's light being gold, the moon's being *tjehnet*'s (Aufrère 1991, pp. 525, 526; and cf. 522–24).
31 Lanny Bell, pers. comm., suggests that the empty sockets in some walls at Luxor, still with plaster adhering, were once filled with faience inlays, probably from the reign of Amenhotep III.
32 Use of non-faience inlays in stone goes back, however, to palettes (e.g., Ashmolean Museum, Oxford 1895.84-7) and figures (e.g., Ashmolean Museum,Oxford 1895.132) of the late Predynastic Period.
33 Bard 1994, pp. 5–6.
34 First Dynasty Memphis must have accommodated the craftsmen, artisans, and architects who worked on the Saqqara mastabas (Vercoutter 1993, p. 71), including their faience luxury products ([14]; or Petrie Museum UC. 30426, 30427 from Saqqara tomb superstructure, Tomb 3504); one could suggest similar scenarios at Hierakonpolis (cf. Vercoutter 1993, p. 73) and Abydos.
35 Victoria and Albert Museum 437-1895, made in cylindrical segments; see the essay by Nicholson, p. 61 and fig. 36.
36 Brigit Crowell, pers. comm., also citing Strauss in Arnold et al. 1978, p. 43, who notes that the protective power of faience amulets, for example, was understood as implicit in the material itself. Faience, she states, was even pulverized and eaten as a health remedy. In terms of visual evidence, a possible scene of faience manufacture is found in the Twenty-Sixth Dynasty Tomb of Ibi, illustrated in the essay by Nicholson, p. 56, fig. 31.
37 See Petrie Museum of Archaeology, University College London UC. 15345-6 from the Umm el-Qaab cemetery—an Egyptian blue vessel already evidencing sophisticated body formation.
38 See [166] for other named workers and the possibility of placing them within a workshop order.
39 Kemp and Merrillees 1980, pp. 167–68.
40 Pinch 1993, p. 307.
41 Aufrère 1991, p. 533.
42 On the First Dynasty wooden furniture fragment cited in n. 29, linen, presumably covered with gesso, is used as a ground for gold leaf (Killen 1994b, p. 22). On another Fifth Dynasty inlay from Abusir, plaster is already used (Lacovara in Der Manuelian 1996), a practice known for the Middle Kingdom and standard for the New Kingdom, as in the Eighteenth Dynasty furniture of Yuya and Thuya, parents of Amenhotep III's Queen Tiye (Davis 1907, p. 47, pl. XXXVIII).

Faience's symbolic properties

Let us now consider the ancient Egyptian word *tjehnet*, generally translated "faience."[35] From the Middle Kingdom[36] through the Ptolemaic and Roman Periods,[37] several texts repeatedly mention *tjehnet* as an ore in phrases such as "true *tjehnet*," "all the *tjehnet* from Punt," and "*tjehnet* from Libya."[38] The latter two phrases, consisting of the noun *tjehnet* plus a toponym introduced by the genitive, follow the pattern seen elsewhere for raw materials from foreign regions. Because of this standard pattern, such phrases have been taken to mean that the Egyptians obtained a raw material that they termed *tjehnet* from various places. However, due to the restricted terminology of the ancient Egyptian lexicon, the interpretation of *tjehnet* in such passages remains enigmatic, as also are apparent mentions in somewhat cryptic form in at least one medical text.[39] Whether *tjehnet* can refer to a basic mineral component from which faience was made or to a mineral or some other substance like lapis lazuli or turquoise, some property of which recalls characteristics of faience, is unknown.

Before discussing some of faience's symbolic aspects, we must address the commonly held opinion that *tjehnet* was an inexpensive material used as a substitute for costlier lapis lazuli or some other semiprecious stone because it could be mass-produced.[40] Modern notions of an economic hierarchy of raw materials are irrelevant here for several reasons. First, *tjehnet* is often used in a given item together with any number of semiprecious stones and gold[41] in weights so small as could hardly have affected the overall cost of the bauble in question. Second, any prejudice against *tjehnet* as a deluxe material has as little merit as a dismissal of clay on the same grounds. In the Eighteenth Dynasty, often considered the apogee of ancient Egyptian culture and wealth, Amenhotep III commissioned representations of himself in unfired clay (fig. 7).[42] It would be ludicrous to argue that the pharaoh used clay because he could not afford a "more expensive" material. Rather, in ancient Egyptian culture clay was regarded as imbued with the essence of life—a primeval medium from which creation arose.[43] Thus, in a sculptural program which stressed youthful images as a visual manifestation of Amenhotep III's symbolic rebirth associated with his jubilees, clay was chosen for a head not for economic reasons but because of its symbolic properties.

Similar considerations apply also to *tjehnet*. Etymologically, *tjehnet* is related to words connoting luminosity and scintillation. The ancient Egyptians thus associated *tjehnet* with brilliance and appreciated its sparkling qualities. But ancient Egyptians were not interested in "art for art's sake," as already noted, and the luminous qualities of *tjehnet* were not prized simply on aesthetic grounds. That *tjehnet* was primarily valued for the symbolic properties associated with its connotative meanings of "luminosity" and "scintillation" becomes clear when one considers its predominance in the mythological topography associated with Osiris and the dead in general.[44]

Shabtis (funerary figurines that accompanied the dead) are frequently made of faience, particularly during the Late Period, and are often associated with the spell "a chapter for causing the shabti of *tjehnet* to descend into the *Duat* [the Under- or Netherworld]."[45] On another level, *tjehnet*'s luminosity is associated with the sun god himself, one of whose epithets was *tjehen*,[46] so that shabtis made from *tjehnet* become solar symbols. Prayers on some Late Period faience shabtis are introduced by the word *sehedj*, traditionally translated into English as "the one who causes [some one or thing] to be illuminated = the inspector." But since the word *sehedj* is often followed immediately by that for the deceased identified as Osiris, the phrase is perhaps better translated as "the illuminated[47] Osiris," meaning that because the shabti is made of *tjehnet*, the deceased has already become assimilated with the solar deity, Re. The metamorphosis of the deceased from Osiris, upon death, into Re, upon resurrection, appears at least as early as the Old Kingdom Pyramid Texts and is much later made manifest in the architecture of the Ptolemaic Temple of Hathor at Dendera, where the terrestrial Osiris becomes solarized during the Festival of Khoiak.[48]

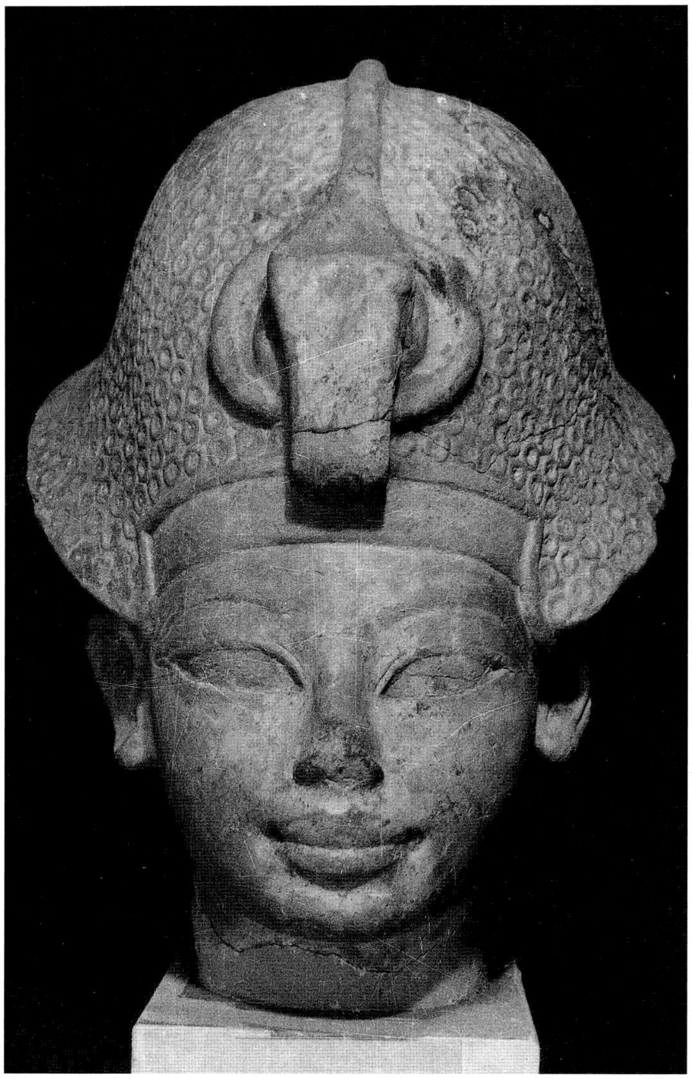

Fig. 7 A clay head of Amenhotep III. Dynasty 18, The Egyptian Museum, Cairo. JE 38597.

"Brides of the dead" and Hathor

Tjehnet's symbolic properties were doubtless responsible for its selection as the material for many of the so-called "brides of the dead"[49] ([64], p. 104) that first appear in the Middle Kingdom and continue into the Second Intermediate Period.[50] Because these curious figurines have been found in tomb, temple, and domestic contexts, they can be interpreted in several different ways, but here it is their funerary associations that concern us.[51] The figures are shown effectively naked[52] and invariably wear a wig, linked with the goddess Hathor whose erotic connotations are well documented. Series of dots on the lower abdomen and thighs represent tattoos, almost exclusively associated with women in ancient Egyptian culture and also imbued with erotic overtones.[53] Such figures often also have gossamer, diaphanous garments, again depicted as networks of black dots, that recall the fishnets worn by female rowers in the employ of pharaoh Khufu as described in the Westcar Papyrus.[54] Their jewelry usually takes the form of a girdle of cowrie shells, commonly regarded as vaginal symbols, slung around the hips.[55]

Another significant feature of these figures is the implied physical handicap that magically denies them the use of their feet—their legs have been purposely truncated at the knees, depriving them of mobility. Their arms and hands are symbolically atrophied, being held close to the sides of the body. As a result, these figurines can ritually neither walk nor use their hands in accordance with their own desires. The lack of self-volition intentionally incorporated into these figurines reinforces the sexual connotations of their coiffure, tattoos, garments, and accessories, causing them to become virtual sex objects.

In ancient Egyptian society the separation between sex and procreation may not have been as distinct as it is today. And because of the polyvalence of visual motifs in ancient Egyptian culture, such a figure can have a wide range of associations ranging from physical sex,[56] including conception and childbirth, to symbolic fecundity and metaphysical regeneration or resurrection in the broadest sense. In a funerary context, then, these figurines were intended to quicken the deceaseds' procreative powers and enable them to become identified with Osiris.[57] Following his murder and dismemberment, Osiris had his sexual prowess restored by Isis, enabling him to father his posthumous heir, Horus; revivified, Osiris became lord of Westerners.[58] The presence of such figurines in tombs imparts Osirian qualities to the deceased—including women[59]—who are identified with Osiris.

Faience enhances the erotic overtones of these figurines in another way too. A seductively attractive woman's silky smooth skin was habitually linked to *tjehnet*,[60] as the passage "do not be taken in by a [woman with a] body of *tjehnet*" in The Instructions of Ptahhotep warns. On yet another level, the predominantly bluish-green[61] hues of faience suggest youth, vigor, and joy—qualities that enhance both the erotic and regenerative aspects of the figurines.[62] The connections with resurrection are further heightened by *tjehnet*'s inherent solar characteristics, which have been noted above.

Some of these "brides of the dead" are shown wearing a so-called Hathor wig,[63] the distinctive curls of which fall over each breast. The eroticism of luxuriant female tresses is well known in ancient Egyptian contexts, as is their association with numerous goddesses,[64] foremost among them Hathor herself.[65] In these Hathoric contexts, particularly common during the Middle Kingdom, hair is often a symbol of resurrection because of its ability to grow after having been cut. The interpretation of certain vignettes among the scenes decorating the walls of Middle Kingdom tombs, as well as of one type of contemporary amulet, relies on this symbolic meaning of hair.[66]

It is in the theology of the goddess Hathor, which finds its greatest textual expression on the walls of the Temple of Dendera, that all the seemingly disparate themes discussed so far come together wonderfully. The texts reveal that Hathor here represents the unbridled fecundity necessary to insure the continuity of cosmic cycles, and such associations can be extended to the brides of the dead. Doubtless the Egyptian elite would have understood this plurality of meanings and appreciated how the confluence of themes enhanced an object's significance in its ritual context.

Many of the same themes are evident in a group of bowls associated with the god Nun [76–78].[67] Investigations by Barbara Porter suggest that some of these vessels, found in the Deir el-Bahri/Asasif cemetery of Western Thebes, may also be connected with the cult of Hathor in the same valley.[68] The primeval swamp that is their principal decoration is related to the fecundity of Hathor as a cosmic goddess responsible for creation. As the texts from the Dendera Temple make abundantly clear, Hathor is simultaneously the begetter of the cosmos and the guarantor of resurrection;[69] the bowls make such themes manifest.

That faience objects had an intrinsic symbolic value and were not crafted primarily as utilitarian items is further demonstrated by examining two additional kinds of objects—balls ([190], p. 172) and sistra (sacred rattles) ([91], p. 102). Balls have survived in a variety of materials, but the only evidence for ball games purely as sport in ancient Egypt[70] consists of a group of scenes, mostly of Middle Kingdom date, that have been interpreted as depictions of women juggling.[71] Identifying contemporary examples of faience balls with such scenes is tempting, but the assumed fragility of the material (see below) might suggest that they were not intended for actual use.[72] They do appear to imitate known leather examples in the way their polychromatic design mimics sewn leather segments. Balls of leather or other suitable materials may have been associated either with an ancient Egyptian ritual version of skittles or with a bat-and-ball game whose aim was to drive away evil. If faience balls were used in such rituals they were perhaps intended to shatter when hit, their destruction being symbolic of the destruction of Apophis (the snake of the Underworld, linked with forces of chaos).[73] Ancient Egyptian material culture contains examples of numerous other objects created for the sole purpose of being ritually destroyed, including the so-called Reserve Heads made of limestone of Old Kingdom date.[74]

There is no direct evidence that the balls discussed here were ritually destroyed, however, and it is possible that they were actually tossed around during rituals. Faience's durability has often been called into question, doubtless because of its modern associations with glass and glazes. However, the discovery of identical component parts for chariots made of faience and more "durable" materials—metal and stone—force us to reconsider faience's fragility.[75] On the other hand, the ritual nature of several kinds of faience objects implies they were never intended to function as practical items of daily use. Faience sistra are significant in this regard. Such "musical instruments" appear to have been exclusively non-utilitarian, because they could not produce their characteristic *sesheshet*-sound when shaken.[76] They are, then, better regarded not as musical instruments but as references to the ritual pulling up of papyrus stems in order to shake them in association with celebrations of the refuge of Hathor and her infant son in the papyrus swamp.[77] The characteristic apple-green color of these particular objects certainly reinforces this association ([91], p. 102).

Faience in inlays and as imitation of other materials

Ancient Egyptian faience can both be embellished with secondary materials and serve as a secondary material itself. Examples of the former include a squatting cynocephalous ape with eyes of inlaid rock-crystal (fig. 8);[78] a statuette of the god Montu (fig. 9), inscribed for Pharaoh Shabaka of the Twenty-Fifth Dynasty, with bronze feathers as an attribute;[79] and a Bes-image[80] with silver earrings and a gold nose ring.[81] Of many examples of faience as a secondary material we can mention a limestone stela[82] of late New Kingdom date into which a faience bovine has been inset.

This multimedia technique is as old as Egyptian civilization itself,[83] but its symbolic value is often overlooked. Monumental inlaid architectural elements, foremost among which are temple doorways, may be embellished with a host of secondary materials, including faience.[84] Since the inlays symbolically represent all the minerals contained in the earth,[85] such inlaid doorways reinforce the interpretation of the temple as a manifestation of the primeval mound from which creation arose. Religious treatises, from the earlier Pyramid Texts to the later Book of Respirations, contain passages suggesting that naturally occurring minerals could transform the deceased into a wholly "mineralized" divinity.[86] This finds an echo in the parallels between the dismembered body parts of Osiris and various minerals of the earth. When his body was reassembled, Osiris metaphorically became possessed of the entire mineral wealth found beneath the earth's surface. All the properties of these minerals could then be magically summoned and concentrated within the body of the reassembled Osiris in order to ensure his efficacious resurrection. In another myth, both the mineral and vegetal wealth of Egypt were gathered together

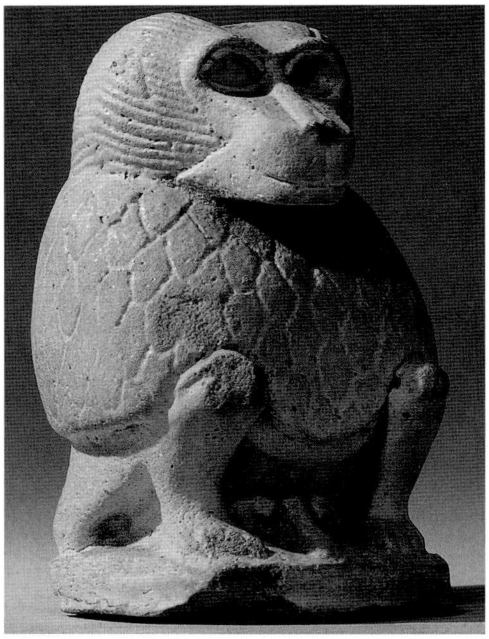

Fig. 8 A faience ape or baboon with eyes of inlaid rock crystal. The Metropolitan Museum of Art, New York. 66.99.131.

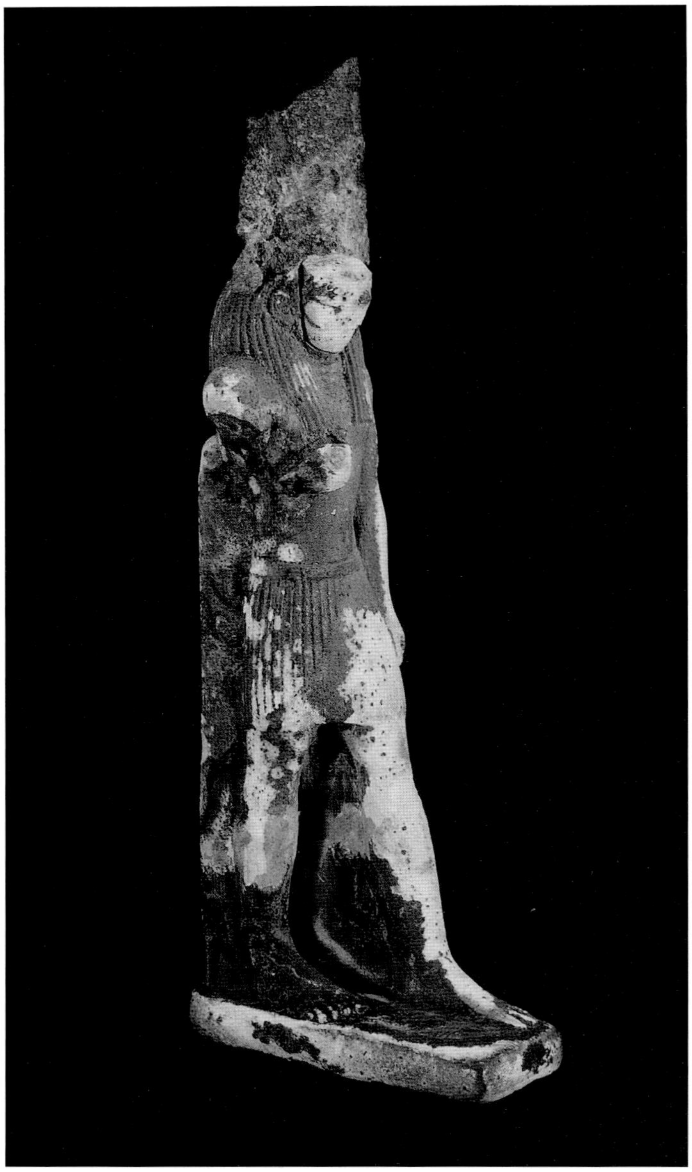

Fig. 9 Statuette of the god Montu. Dynasty 25, The British Museum, London. EA 11334.

into the *wadjet,* or sacred eye, of the god Horus, as a symbol of the triumph over death ([106], [107], p. 123; [161], p. 161).[87] It is no doubt for such reasons that almost all *wadjet*-eye amulets are made of faience, a material inextricably linked to ideas of regeneration.

Manufacturing faience was a highly traditional craft and its component elements did not change over time.[88] Consequently, the dating of an object is generally based on archaeological context or stylistic analysis, especially since it cannot be scientifically dated using thermoluminesence or carbon-14. It is equally difficult to distinguish faience manufactured in Egypt from that made elsewhere in the Mediterranean basin during the course of the second and first millennia BC. Other Bronze Age civilizations prized Egyptian faience, as shown by the foundation plaques found at Mycenae inscribed with the name of Pharaoh Amenhotep III,[89] which seem to have been valued by the Mycenaeans for their symbolic properties, just as the Minoans of Crete valued objects in Egyptian faience.[90] There was also a reciprocal borrowing of forms, and many faience vessels are Egyptian imitations of Aegean shapes, including rhyta ([124], p. 135) and stirrup jars ([123], p. 137).[91] At least one commentator has suggested that these vessels were manufactured in Egypt in faience because of the material's symbolic value.[92]

More significant, however, is the Egyptian tradition of translating into faience, either partly or wholly, objects customarily made in some other substance. This practice is well established by the Old Kingdom, as the fragmentary wooden vessels inlaid with faience and other materials reveal.[93] The inlays imbue these vessels with symbolic properties, enhancing their funerary function and complementing the regenerative connotations of the sycamore[94] core. Other objects translated into faience from different materials include the shafts of model scepters or columns in the foundation deposit of King Mentuhotep II, now in Luxor Museum.[95]

More intriguing is a faience helmet, without a known findspot and now in New York, for which there are neither any known parallels nor representations in two-dimensional art (fig. 10).[96] The helmet is assumed (because of the nature of its stains) to have been found on the mummy of an individual named Hor-Psametik, for whom it is inscribed. The green color of the faience strongly suggests that it is an imitation of a bronze original, although this color is also consistent with the overtones of rebirth complementing its supposed funerary function. As we have seen, however, faience is sufficiently durable for this helmet to have been worn in life. If this is correct, it is one of only a handful of examples of ancient Egyptian regalia to have survived and may more profitably be regarded as parade armor than as an actual battle helmet. Faience's symbolic value is in no way compromised by this function, since the Egyptian military is closely associated with the deities of the land, many of whose characteristics are resident in faience. On the basis of the color of its fabric and the name of its owner, which incorporates a nomen common to several pharaohs of the Twenty-Sixth Dynasty, a date in that dynasty can be suggested that places it squarely among works created during the first half of the first millennium BC.

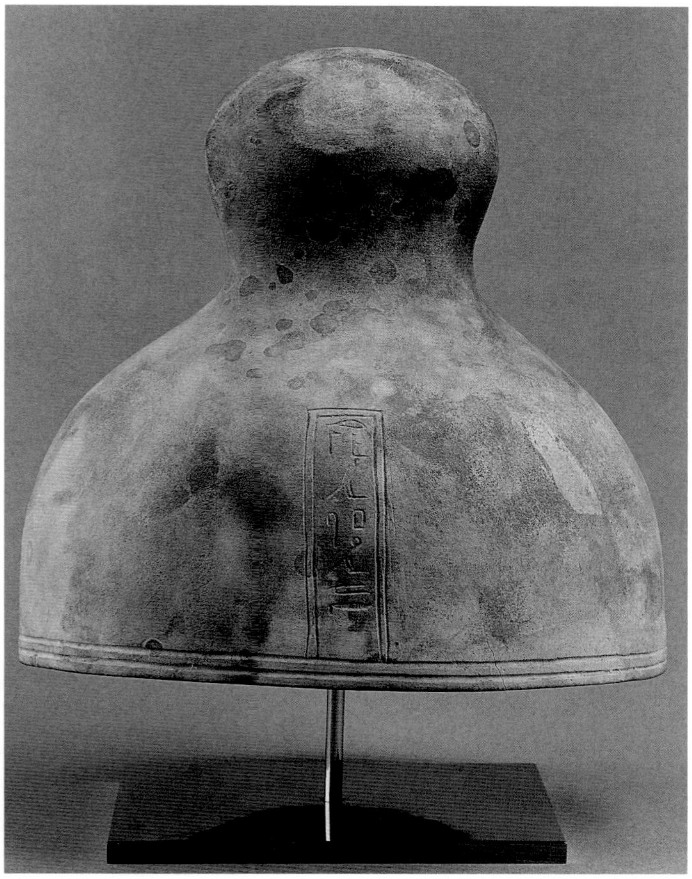

Fig. 10 A faience helmet inscribed with the name Hor-Psametik. Possibly Dynasty 26, The Metropolitan Museum of Art, New York. 41.2.9.

Numerous faience objects[97] in an Egyptianizing idiom from this same period have been uncovered at sites such as Rhodes[98] and Perachora,[99] and in several Etruscan tombs.[100] Many of these objects are scarcely distinguishable from those found in Egypt, and were presumably crafted there. It is risky to speculate about whether such pieces retained the pharaonic symbolism associated with the elite craft of Egyptian faience, but it seems unlikely that these meanings were transferred unchanged to neighboring civilizations.

Ptolemaic and Roman faience

The faience of the Ptolemaic[101] and Roman periods presents us with an interesting situation. I have argued elsewhere that the complexes of funerary objects that characterize almost every major phase of Egypt's history from the Predynastic Period on are virtually absent from the material record of these two epochs.[102] And yet, as the temple texts of these periods reveal, pharaonic intellectual discourse continued, and at an accelerated pace.[103] While Ptolemaic Egypt was made up of two societies—the native Egyptian and the immigrant Hellenic—that were separate and unequal,[104] the evidence is mounting that the Greeks were in fact borrowers of things Egyptian, which they cloaked in a Classical mantle. The theology and image of the god Serapis are a case in

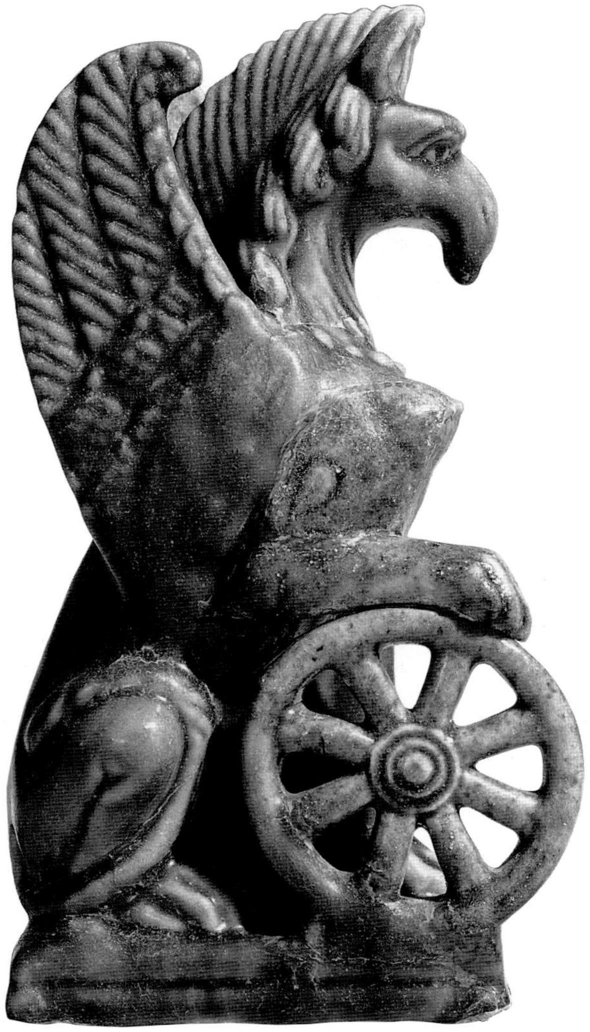

Fig. 11 Faience statuette of the griffin Nemesis. Roman, Imperial Period, Brooklyn Museum of Art. 53.173.

point.[105] Derchain's suggestion that there were intellectual crossovers,[106] particularly among the Greek-speaking population of Egypt, is thus appealing, but more research is necessary. At present, I believe that most faience vessels created in Egypt during the Ptolemaic Period are indebted to Classical traditions for two reasons. The first is that the motifs decorating these vessels, and their interpretations,[107] appear to rely more heavily upon Greek and Roman than on pharaonic imagery. The second is based on the form these vessels take. As a general rule Classical vases are open-form, and such open-form vessels are exceedingly rare in the collections of the Graeco-Roman Museum in Alexandria,[108] which contain no parallels for the ovoid goblets known only from one example each in Brooklyn[109] and Thessalonike.[110] Others, such as the vessel in Brussels with images of Bes—that quintessentially Egyptian deity[111]—as appliqués,[112] hark back to Egyptian concepts, however transmuted.

Faience production of the Roman Imperial Period can be divided into two categories: statuettes and vases. Several types of statuette retain their pharaonic significance, as is certainly the case with the faience statuette of the griffin Nemesis (fig. 11) in the collections of the Brooklyn Museum of Art,[113] as Quaegebeur demonstrated.[114] It is also true of the frogs[115] in glazed terra-cotta and figures of a Bes-like[116] demon in Naples, which find their closest parallels in similar figurines in the Egyptian Museum, Cairo,[117] generally dated to the second century AD and including sphinxes of pharaonic style. Given the syncretism of the period, other statuettes in a decidedly Classical idiom, such as an Aphrodite Anadyomene also in Brooklyn,[118] may also have been imbued with faience's symbolic overtones of rebirth.

Faience vases of the Roman Imperial Period, which display a variety of shapes and decoration ([141], p. 142), have been conveniently collected under one heading by Grimm,[119] but his study is more concerned with issues of the provenance and dating of the vases[120] than with an interpretation of their motifs and significance. Their apparently Classical iconography may well mask pharaonic concepts, but to demonstrate this hypothesis would require an intensive investigation of all the motifs employed against the extensive preserved literary record.

Conclusion

The deluxe faience objects discussed in this essay were manufactured in institutionally affiliated workshops under the direction of administrators, for the most part nameless, who received wages well above those of the laborers under their direction. These administrators, hired by members of an elite that was dominated by the pharaoh, were responsible for the manufacture of canonically sanctioned objects imbued with symbolism and meanings that were developed and understood by the elite.

Raw materials for faience were obtained, it is argued here, not from entrepreneurs but rather from regions directly under the control of pharaoh, by strictly regulated and religiously sanctioned operations. There is some evidence from texts to suggest that a material also termed *tjehnet* by the ancient Egyptians was obtained from Punt and Libya, but the exact nature of this substance remains unknown, as does that of the *tjehnet* appearing in at least one medical text.

The modern notion that faience was an inexpensive material is here called into question by suggesting that it was employed for its symbolic values; this in turn explains why objects traditionally crafted in other materials, such as pottery, were often translated into faience. Moreover, contrary again perhaps to general belief, the durability of faience is indicated by its use for chariot parts that were also made in either stone or metal.

We have demonstrated that the properties inherent in the root meaning of the word *tjehnet*, which include "scintillation" and "brilliance," were at the core of its symbolic associations. Foremost among these is solar imagery, but that imagery is complemented by the predominantly blue-green hues of this material, which connoted rebirth, regeneration, and related concepts. In ancient Egyptian religion and iconography one and the same motif could have several interpretations.

As a result of its associations with luminosity, *tjehnet* figures prominently in the mythological topography of the Underworld and imbues faience shabtis with solar associations, reinforcing concepts of resurrection in the hereafter. Many of these same connotations can be attached to the "brides of the dead" of Middle Kingdom date, and were readily transferred to the goddess Hathor in her role as a cosmic genetrix in association with the New Kingdom bowls.

Faience seems to be the material of choice for some nonutilitarian objects used in cult rituals, such as balls and sistra, and perhaps also a parade helmet of Twenty-Sixth Dynasty date. Together with other materials, faience was also used to embellish architecture, particularly doorways, as well as statues, vases, and stelae, among other things. Objects so embellished were anciently thought to become "mineralized," metaphorically incorporating into their fabric the totality of the earth's mineral wealth, which was thereby concentrated in the object and enhanced its efficacy.

One of the cornerstones of ancient Egyptian civilization is its dependence upon ritual and symbol. There is perhaps no better way for a modern audience to gain an appreciation of that fact than by contemplating the technically accomplished craft productions displayed here, in conjunction with an understanding of the elite's role in Egyptian society and the meanings which that elite associated with these scintillating faience objects.

1 Baines 1989, pp. 471–82; Baines 1990, pp. 1–23.
2 On the question of artists, see in general the comments by Wilson 1947, pp. 231–49, and the continuing discussion about craftsmen and "creativity" in essays such as Barta 1970, with additional comments by Ritner 1993, pp. 31–32, about issues raised by te Velde 1970, pp. 175–86. On the anonymity of these craftsmen within the context of craft-productions in general, see Valbelle 1990, pp. 59–60.
3 The complexities of dealing with the sophisticated polyvalence inherent in ancient Egyptian symbols may be appreciated by consulting just these few essays dealing with the meaning of the color red: Derchain 1975a, p.74; Wild 1960, p.55 (j); Goyon 1975, pp. 380–83; and Morenz in Firchow 1955, p. 243.
4 Yoyotte 1983, pp. 463–65.
5 The opinion of Junge in Eton-Kraus and Graefe 1990, pp. 26–38, is at variance with those who subscribe to the received meanings of canonical images in ancient Egyptian art, as defined and discussed by Davis 1989, p. 208, and reviewed by Bianchi 1992, pp. 328–30.
6 Altenmüller 1991, pp. 17–27.
7 Baines 1985a, p. 8, allows some degree of individual initiative on the part of the craftsmen, but nevertheless supports the basic premise that artistic freedom was in fact subordinated to the socially important purpose that the representation served.
8 Davis 1989, p. 8, regards the pharaoh as principal in the process, a conclusion reaffirmed by Kozloff and Bryan 1992, p. 7, in their remarkable study of Amenhotep III and his monuments.
9 Valbelle 1990, pp. 38–39, demonstrates that by far the greater proportion of these craftspeople were men.
10 Valbelle 1990, pp. 38–39.
11 Valbelle 1990, pp. 42–44.
12 Arnold 1996, pp. 41–46.
13 The conclusion is implied by Valbelle 1990, pp. 35, 37, and 59–60.
14 Foster 1979, p. 26. Few today would subscribe to the theory of origin of ancient Egyptian faience proposed by J[ean] C[apart] 1936, pp. 484–87.
15 Bierbrier 1982, pp. 13–14, *passim*, for a general overview of the issue; Gitton 1976, pp. 65–90, with additional discussions by Gitton 1979, pp. 327–31, for a specific case; and Robins 1993, pp. 126–29, for this issue as it relates to women in general.
16 Rothenberg 1988.
17 Castel and Soukiassian 1989.
18 Examples include that undertaken during the reign of Ramesses IV of the Twentieth Dynasty for *bekhen*-stone in the Wadi Hammamat (Peden 1994b, pp. 24–28) and that in the same dynasty during the reign of Ramesses VII for galena (Peden 1994a, pp. 101–6). I am not aware of any textual evidence suggesting that an ancient Egyptian individual exploited those resources for his/her own advantage as an entrepreneur, a circumstance one would expect to find commemorated in at least one graffito in such places as the Wadi Hammamat, the region of Aswan and the First Cataract, Gebel Tier, and the like. And whereas many component elements of faience, namely sand, limestone chip, natron, and copper (if needed for color and regardless of how minute a quantity) are readily available in the Egyptian landscape, the limestone and copper, even if recycled scrap, could only have originally been obtained by royal decree. Whether natron could be gathered by an entrepreneur remains unknown. That the load carried by Khun-anup's donkeys in the Tale of the Eloquent Peasant (Lichtheim 1973, pp. 169–84) included natron is not evidence that Khun-anup himself gathered the natron, since the load also included staves from the Cattle-Country, perhaps to be identified with the Farafra Oasis, as well as the skins of both leopards and wolves. The narrator of the tale does not mention how Khun-anup acquired such a motley assortment of goods, but one suspects he is merely a driver transporting goods rather than selling his own property. If it were otherwise, he would have been a man of substance and the subsequent petitions against Nemtynakht would be difficult to explain if one continues to regard the narrative as the Egyptian exemplar of the vindication of the weak against the powerful.
19 Keimer 1944, pp. 135–47.
20 *Inter alia*, Newberry, 1893, plate IV, in the topmost register of the north wall of the main chamber of Tomb 15.
21 Aufrère 1991, pp. 59–92.
22 Helck in Verhoeven and Graefe 1991, pp. 159–64.
23 Cauville 1987b, pp. 73–117.
24 Pusch in Eggebrecht et al. 1993, pp. 126–43.
25 Nenna and Seif el-Din 1993, p. 595, identify seven kilns here that they insist were for the manufacture of faience objects and not, as others have maintained, for the manufacture of glass.
26 Smith 1981, p. 91, commenting upon the find made in 1975 by Abdulla Sayid.
27 Bernand 1981, pp. 7–8.
28 Bulté 1991.
29 Castel and Soukiassian 1985, pp. 290–91.
30 Perhaps all the inscriptions associated with craftsmen should be compared to ascertain whether the office of overseer/administrator of faience workers was held by individuals responsible for other craft specializations as well. This is certainly the interpretation of a passage in Badawy 1961, p. 271, "I know how to make [things of paste and inlaid things], without letting the fire melt them, nor do they wear off in water either." See, also, Barta 1970, pp. 120–22, for other suggestions for emending the lacunae in this passage, many of which concur in broad strokes with those of Badawy.
31 Valbelle 1990, pp. 59–60.
32 Valbelle 1990, pp. 59–60.
33 The entire passage from the Wisdom of Ptah may be translated as follows, "Never does one reach the limit of one's craft [i.e. the limits of craft are never exhausted]. There does not exist a craftsman who is fully equipped with respect to his mastery." Compare Lichtheim 1973, p. 63, 1.
34 Badawy 1961, p. 269.

35 Lucas and Harris 1962 (1989), pp. 155, 156–67, *passim*; and Erman and Grapow (eds.) 1931, p. 390, nos. 11–16, and p. 391, nos. 1–20.
36 *Inter alia*, Coffin Texts VI, 212–13; and Newberry 1920, p. 160.
37 Mariette 1870–1880 (1874), pl. 87.
38 Aufrère 1991, pp. 521–23.
39 Kurth 1989, pp. 81–83.
40 Raven 1988, pp. 238–39.
41 Andrews 1990, p. 21 (a broad collar of Senebtisi of Middle Kingdom date) and pp. 138–39 (a pectoral of pharaoh Sheshonq II of Third Intermediate Period date).
42 Cairo, The Egyptian Museum JE 38597: Kozloff and Bryan 1992, p. 254, fig. 46a.
43 Raven 1988, pp. 240–41.
44 Aufrère (XV/2) 1991, pp. 523–24.
45 Schneider 1977, pp. 235–45.
46 Raven 1988, pp. 238–39.
47 Raven 1988, pp. 238–39.
48 Cauville 1990, pp. 68–84.
49 I wish to acknowledge a grant from the Alfred C. Kinsey Institute for Sex Research, Inc., Bloomington, Indiana, that enabled me to investigate aspects of the corpus of ancient Egyptian erotica, of which brides of the dead are a part.
50 Bourriau 1988b, pp. 125–26, for their findspots, dating, and suggested interpretations.
51 Bianchi in Fazzini et al. 1989, no. 26.
52 Here I employ the word as defined in this overtly erotic sense by Clark 1959, pp. 23–54.
53 Bianchi in Rubin 1981, pp. 21–28.
54 Janssen 1995–96, pp. 41–47.
55 Andrews 1990, p. 254, fig. 46a.
56 Nevertheless, Derchain in Martin 1981, p. 169, argues that love for the sake of love is alien to the Egyptian material cultural record, as it is currently understood.
57 The Chapel of Ptah-Sokar at Abydos: Porter and Moss 1939, p. 24, (218)–(219): Sety and El Zeini 1981, pp. 140–53, esp. figs. 11-11 and 11-16.
58 Cauville 1990, pp. 68–84, where the ritual is represented in much greater detail than on the walls of the Temple of Abydos, demonstrating once again how vital the inscriptions on the walls of the Ptolemaic and Roman temples are for a better appreciation of the subtleties of ancient Egyptian theological discourse. No comparable corpus of inscriptions has survived from the earlier pharaonic periods. See, too, Meeks and Favard-Meeks 1996, pp. 66–69.
59 Robins 1993, p. 175.
60 Derchain in Martin 1981, p. 74.
61 An interesting issue regarding the modern designation of an ancient Egyptian color as blue or green is raised by Goresy and Schiegl in DuQuesne 1996, pp. 63–64. They argue that deterioration over time has transformed the polychromatic hue of objects that were originally blue into hues we now call green. They further argue that green was not a component of ancient Egyptian faience until the Late Period. Ancient Egyptian color terminology is too broad an issue to discuss in depth here. Suffice it to say that the Egyptians seem to have had only five color words, corresponding to English "white," "black," "red," "green," and "of variegated hue." Within this limited range, colors from the lower to middle bands of the modern spectrum—green, blue, indigo, and violet—were commonly referred to in ancient Egyptian texts as "green." This division of the spectrum into five color words conforms to the lexicon of other cultures whose members also designate perceived colors with five color words. In each such culture, there is invariably a word rendered into English as "green," but not a word rendered as "blue," as discussed by Harden 1988, pp. 165–66, who earlier explains the differences between these two colors (Hardin 1988, pp. 156–62). This apparent lack of precision in the ancient Egyptian lexicon thereby compounds the complexities raised by Goresy and Schiegl. For a summary of the lexical issues, see Baines 1985a, pp. 282–97. To my knowledge, no one has conclusively demonstrated that other ancient Egyptian words, for example *hsbd* (Erman and Grapow (eds.) 1931, p. 334, nos. 1–13), generally translated into English as "lapis lazuli," were used in a strictly lexical sense as words for colors.
62 Derchain in Martin 1981, p. 74.
63 Evers 1929, pp. 28 and 185, observes that such a headdress appears for the first time during the second half of the Twelfth Dynasty. Tefnin 1983, pp. 98–100, concurs, adding that there are no attested examples of this wig in the Old Kingdom. Fazzini 1988, p. 17, suggests that this "Hathoric" wig is rarely represented on mortals after the close of the New Kingdom. Fazzini's reluctance to identify this wig exclusively with Hathor is well taken.
64 Derchain in Martin 1981, p. 59.
65 Hornblower 1929, p. 40, ignores the polyvalence inherent in ancient Egyptian motifs when he automatically associates representations of this wig with Hathor, as Fazzini 1988, p. 17, correctly realizes. The plurality of meanings of any given motif in ancient Egyptian art precludes a dogmatic approach to visual motifs.
66 Nactergael 1981, p. 587, citing Staehelin 1978, p. 83.
67 Strauss 1974.
68 Personal communication based on her work on the material excavated by the Metropolitan Museum of Art at Thebes confirms this. Because of the polyvalent nature of ancient Egyptian visual motifs, many of the suggestions adduced by Strauss 1974 for the symbolism of these vessels still pertain in the context of Hathor.
69 Cauville 1990, pp. 7–11.
70 Decker 1992, p. 113.
71 Decker 1992, p. 113.
72 Decker 1992, p. 113, where Decker does, however, entertain the possibility that such faience balls, if used at all, were manipulated only by "experts."
73 Ritner 1993, pp. 136–42.
74 Tefnin 1991.
75 Pusch in Eggebrecht et al. 1993, pp. 132–33, figs. 129 and 131. I thank Anja Herold of that expedition for discussing this matter with me during a recent visit to Hildesheim.
76 Manniche 1991, p. 63.
77 Manniche 1991, p. 63.
78 The Metropolitan Museum of Art 66.99.131: Chase and Pease 1942, pl. 33, no. 11.
79 The British Museum EA 11334.
80 Romano 1980, pp. 39-56, but see now the comments both by Meeks in Luft 1992, pp. 423–36; and Malaise in Israelit-Groll 1990, pp. 680–729.
81 The British Museum EA 37401.
82 Tübingen, University Collection 1716: Brunner-Traut and Brunner 1981, pp. 100–01, and color pl. 11.
83 One cites in this regard a painted terra-cotta head, apparently of a deity, from Merimda-Benisalama, to which tufts of hair may originally have been attached. The piece, perhaps the terminal for a staff of another material, is provisionally dated to the end of the fifth millennium BC and is now in Cairo, The Egyptian Museum JE 97472; Saleh and Sourouzian 1987, p. 39, no. 1.
84 Early examples include the use of faience tiles in the funerary complex of Djoser at Saqqara, some of which are in Cairo, The Egyptian Museum JE 68921, and the use of paste inlays in the Tomb of Nefermaat, now also in Cairo, The Egyptian Museum JE 43809: Saleh and Sourouzian 1987, nos. 17 and 25a-b, respectively. For a brief discussion of this architectural practice together with the pertinent bibliography, see Arnold 1994, p. 36.
85 Aufrère (CV/1) 1991, p. 168.
86 Aufrère (CV/1) 1991, pp. 329–47; and compare Beinlich 1984, but see the comments on these same scenes by Pantalacci 1987, pp. 108–23.
87 Aufrère (CV/1) 1991, pp. 199–224; see, too, Meeks and Favard-Meeks 1996, pp. 72–74.
88 Foster 1979, p. 10.
89 Cline 1988, p. 254.
90 Vermeule in Brovarski et al. 1982b, p. 152.
91 Vermeule in Brovarski et al. 1982b, pp. 154–58.
92 Vermeule in Brovarski et al. 1982b, p. 152, "...Egyptian versions...which may

also have sacral and royal connotations...."
93 Borchardt 1909, pp. 59–66, and frontis.
94 *Inter alia*, Hermsen 1981. It appears to me that this same symbolism is inherent in the choice of sycamore for the panels on which some of the Fayum portraits and early Christian icons are painted.
95 Romano 1979, pp. 16–18, no. 16.
96 The Metropolitan Museum of Art 41.2.9: Bull 1942, pp. 41–42.
97 Webb 1978.
98 It remains to be seen whether the faience inlays recovered from Rhodes in the form of hieroglyphs that appear to spell the name of one of the Saite pharaohs (Apries? or Necho?) of the Twenty-Sixth Dynasty are of ancient Egyptian manufacture or an imitation thereof (Skon 1977, p. 10).
99 James in Dunbabin 1940, pp. 461–516.
100 Hölbl 1979, is a useful compendium of such finds.
101 Nenna and Seif el-Din 1993, pp. 565–98, offer a sober assessment of what is known of the faience vessel industry in Ptolemaic and Roman Egypt.
102 Bianchi 1996a, pp. 191–202.
103 Sauneron 1982.
104 Bianchi in Johnson 1992, p. 15, citing Samuel 1989.
105 Bianchi in Johnson 1992, pp. 23–214.
106 Derchain 1990, pp. 9–30, inspired in part by a head displaying signs of age in the collection of Christos G. Bastis, New York: Bothmer in Hall 1987b, pp. 93–94, on loan to the Brooklyn Museum of Art (L76.9.3).
107 Such as the vase with garland and dolphins in the collection of Jack A. Josephson and its parallel in the Stanford Place Collection, now on loan to the Metropolitan Museum of Art in New York (L1997.4 unpublished). To these should be added the *oinochoai*, or so-called queen's vases, such as the fragment in New York, The Metropolitan Museum of Art 26.7.1016. See Bianchi et al. 1988a, pp. 223–25, no. 116; and pp. 174–75, no. 68, respectively, for the Josephson vase and Metropolitan Museum's queen vase fragment. According to Nenna and Seif el-Din 1993, p. 569, at least 200 *oinochoai* are represented by the individual pieces or discrete sherds in the collections of the Graeco-Roman Museum in Alexandria, Egypt, which contains on estimate more than 1,300 separate vessels represented in whole or in part.
108 Nenna and Seif el-Din 1993, p. 581.
109 Brooklyn, The Brooklyn Museum of Art 76.40 (without a known findspot): Parlasca 1984, p. 302. A sherd in Amsterdam, Allard Pierson Museum 7567, decorated with a *biga* in pursuit of a cat seems, nevertheless, to relate to the subject matter of the Brooklyn vase.
110 Thessalonike, Archaeological Museum 2829: Andronicos 1975, p. 283, which was discovered in a tomb in Thessalonike dated to the second century BC.
111 According to Dasen 1993, there is little evidence to suggest any influence of the Bes-images on the majority of phenomenologically similar images in Greece. Since this seems to be the case, one can suggest that the Bes-image retained its uniquely ancient Egyptian associations.
112 Brussels, Musées Royaux d'Art et d'Histoire E4424: Bianchi et al. 1988a, p. 226, no. 118. Nenna and Seif el-Din 1993, pp. 583 and 585, report that there are fragments of at least four more similar vessels in the collections of the Graeco-Roman Museum in Alexandria, Egypt.
113 Brooklyn, The Brooklyn Museum 43.173: Riefstahl 1968, no. 91.
114 Quaegebeur 1983, pp. 41–51.
115 Naples, Archaeological Museum 76/166, one of a pair decorating the impluvium in the House of the Tragic Poet: Ward-Perkins and Claridge 1976, p. 103, no. 105; and La Rocca et al. 1976, p. 325, for a discussion of that house.
116 Naples, Archaeological Museum 22583: Ward-Perkins and Claridge 1976, p. 103, no. 194. This particular figure is one of several like images found at various find-spots throughout Pompeii not only within the Temple of Isis but also from the House of the Mosaic Columns (La Rocca et al. 1976, pp. 19, 54, and 159), where several were employed as decorative elements at the corners of the garden. It is interesting to compare these images with a Bes-image from the west wall of the smaller of two rooms at the west end of the Temple of Isis at Pompeii, now Naples, Archaeological Museum 8916: Ward-Perkins and Claridge 1976, p. 103, no. 188.
117 *Inter alia*, Cairo, The Egyptian Museum, exhibition numbers 5650-5652: Maspero 1915, p. 548, "Armoire J," were the objects described as manufactured of "terre émaillée bleu."
118 Brooklyn, The Brooklyn Museum, 44.7: Riefstahl 1968, no. 88. To these objects in blue in Brooklyn should be added three additional pieces in New York, The Metropolitan Museum of Art: 26.7.1019, a figure of a ram with a manger: Arnold 1995, p. 54, fig. 74; and Grimm 1972, p. 92; and 26.7.1020-1021; two tragic masks: Metropolitan Museum of Art 1952, p. 219, no. 27.
119 Grimm 1972, pp. 71–100.
120 Nenna and Seif el-Din 1993, pp. 589–90 and 593, review the thorny issues involved in dating these types of vessels.

BY NECESSITY OR DESIGN: FAIENCE USE IN ANCIENT EGYPT

Diana Craig Patch

Brief historical survey

The earliest faience objects are beads and occasionally amulets found as jewelry in Predynastic burials. During the Early Dynastic Period, new types appear in temple and shrine contexts, while beads and amulets continue to adorn the dead, appearing even in royal burials. Figurines from temple levels at Abydos, Elephantine, and Hierakonpolis, for instance, were often modeled in faience.[1] Other small faience objects were probably votive pieces too, as suggested by their find-spots. Tiles ([15], [16], pp. 72, 75), possibly used to decorate shrines, and vessels ([13], p. 75), also appear at this time.

In these early periods, no single type of object seems to have been made exclusively in faience. Given the increase in number and range of faience objects it seems that craftsmen were experimenting with the material: the variety of types and their variability imply that the early temple figurines, for example, were produced in many different workshops. The manufacture of faience at several sites suggests that it was widely accepted in Upper Egypt for certain functions early in Egyptian history,[2] and its use for votive statuettes at three widely separated temple sites demonstrates that its suitability for sacred objects can be traced at least to the start of the Pharaonic Period.[3] For the next three millennia, faience remained the preferred material for most small votive objects.

In the Old Kingdom, faience was used for the same types of objects as before, although—with the exception of beads—they are relatively rare.[4] The enormous number of faience tiles in Djoser's Third Dynasty Step Pyramid complex at Saqqara ([17–20], pp. 66, 72), however, suggests two new developments. First, faience is certainly being manufactured in bulk in a manner not seen previously, except perhaps for beads ([1], [2], p. 74); and second, faience now decorates funerary structures as well as cultic ones (though in Djoser's intensely religious precinct, the distinction between the two realms may well have been blurred).

Finds from graves in Middle Egypt of the First Intermediate Period demonstrate that beads and amulets continued to be made in faience and glazed steatite, although hard semiprecious stones were predominantly used. Blue glaze was extremely common as the finish for small amulets. By the Twelfth Dynasty the variety of faience objects increased once again and included statuettes of all sizes and shapes, some with detailed black-outlined decoration. Most figurines depict animals, especially hippos, apes, cats, lions, and crocodiles but occasionally also hedgehogs, calves and jerboa ([98], [99], p. 129; [142–47], pp. 148–49). While earlier human and animal figures are found in public shrines and cult temples, their Middle Kingdom counterparts come from private tombs in cemeteries throughout Egypt, including those of Heliopolis, Lisht, Beni Hasan, Abydos, and the west bank at Thebes. These extensive groups of Middle Kingdom figures seem to be more than simply votive, and their role in funerary cult may have been a strongly magical one.[5]

Although stone remains the predominant material for beads and amulets in the Middle Kingdom, faience is increasingly important, particularly for funerary jewelry. An exquisite faience broad collar was found around the mummy of Wah; and Lady Senebtisi's funerary garment was made completely of faience except for a single carnelian amulet, while green faience beads were a major component of one of her broad collars.[6] Turquoise and carnelian are also employed extensively in funerary jewelry, as is gold leaf over a wood or paste core. Everyday jewelry is made of gold, silver, carnelian, amethyst, turquoise, and feldspar, but rarely faience, which seems to be reserved for burials.

New object types, often on a significantly larger scale than before, are added to the faience repertoire in the New Kingdom. Statues, shabtis, game boards, sistra, headrests, model furniture, and large containers, including canopic jars, are found in Eighteenth Dynasty contexts, usually funerary ones. It was also only in the Eighteenth Dynasty that faience became popular for such small items as containers, game pieces, and inlay. By the middle of the dynasty, small faience objects were usually made in molds, a technique allowing the rapid production of identical pieces—particularly useful for beads and amulets. This increased use of mold technology may well account for the expansion in the numbers and types of faience objects in the second half of the New Kingdom period. Shrines have yielded many beads, amulets, and small items sacred to the resident deity made almost exclusively in faience.[7] Faience was also frequently chosen to make model equipment for burials and foundation deposits, in contrast to the clay, stone, and metal used in earlier times. Artisans also perfected decorative techniques, as seen in spectacular multi-colored faience shabtis ([150], p. 153), kohl tubes, and jewelry ([31], p. 87), and faience elements became common in decorative inlay.[8]

Toward the end of the New Kingdom, the Egyptians mastered the construction of faience objects on an even grander scale, such as the lion-shaped newel posts from the throne dais of Ramesses II's palace at Qantir, which are almost 70 cm (27½ in) tall.[9] Multicolored tiles from the same site demonstrate a new skill in producing detailed scenes in faience ([50], p. 80).[10]

Faience continued to be a dominant material for certain object types after the New Kingdom. In the Third Intermediate Period, the number of faience amulets and small statuettes representing deities increased significantly,[11] although about half of the smaller amulets dated to the Twenty-First through the Twenty-Fifth Dynasty and later are still made of stone and metal, especially those depicting hieroglyphs or sacred objects. Shabtis are the most common faience objects after beads and inlays from the Third Intermediate Period on. The availability of mold-made shabtis ([150–52], pp. 152–53, 155) certainly facilitated the belief that the deceased needed an "answerer" for every day of the year, plus overseers to direct them.

Faience was also used exclusively for decorated chalices ([114–17], pp. 126–27), openwork spacers and rings, pectorals, sistra, large amuletic or votive symbols,[12] and tiny multicolored ring beads for elaborate outer mummy garments. Other types of containers, including canopic jars, as well as small statues, were also made in faience, often similar to those in the New Kingdom faience repertoire,[13] and mostly for cultic or funerary use. Similar categories of Ptolemaic faience objects attest to their continued popularity.

Characteristics and qualities of faience

Why was faience chosen to make a particular item in preference to another material? It has generally been accepted among Egyptologists[14] that faience was used primarily as an inexpensive alternative to more costly substances, [15] and not because of any of its inherent characteristics such as brilliant color, reflectivity, or plasticity. Indeed, faience probably was inexpensive to make. [16] Most of its components—sand, quartz, lime, and an alkali—are common, easily found materials. Copper, which produced the usual brilliant turquoise color, was probably the most costly of the ingredients, because it was mined at some distance from the Nile Valley. Yet the use of copper scraps from local metal-working shops would have added little to the cost.[17] This ready availability of faience's ingredients, added to the abundance of objects made of it, especially in later Pharaonic times, has led many to assume that producing faience must always have been inexpensive and that it was therefore principally used as a substitute for more expensive stones.

But do these assumptions stand up to scrutiny?[18] Recent research indicates that the use of molds—the faience manufacturing technique most often associated with inexpensive production—was a relatively late development.[19] Many earlier techniques did not allow such rapid fabrication and it seems reasonable to assume that the more complex the production of a faience object, the fewer examples could be made and the less likely they were to be widely available, regardless of the cost of the raw materials. Scarcity of an object, therefore, need not be related to its cost,[20] and if molding only became common later, then assumptions based on faience production and availability are not necessarily valid.

Raw material cost and ease of production were only two of the considerations affecting the choice of faience to make an object: the type of object in question is also important. Molding not only increased availability, but it also allowed an exactness of repetition and a symmetry of color and shape impossible with natural stones and vital for such objects as beaded collars or tiny ring beads.

Faience's versatility and malleability certainly explain its choice for many types of objects. Inlaying a thin band of color into a strip of a different color, an effect favored by late Eighteenth Dynasty kings ([23], [24], pp. 80, 81), is difficult with other materials.[21] Another attractive quality of faience was certainly the ease with which it could be modeled and carved to create objects with intricate patterns, such as elaborately decorated chalices or openwork rings ([114–17], pp. 126–27; [108], p. 123).

Sources of information

We must next ask whether an object would have been made in faience had another material been available. If we accept the assumption that faience objects were easy and inexpensive to make, we should expect large numbers of faience objects to be found in the homes and tombs of the less wealthy, which in turn should be small and simply constructed. Such owners of faience should also possess fewer objects in more expensive materials, such as precious metals, rare stones, ivory, or imported wood. Conversely, burials of members of the elite should contain proportionately fewer faience items than the non-elite but more inscribed objects, as these entailed the added expense of a scribe. Further, because of the close association between wealth and rank, those who regularly used faience should lack titles indicating high rank or considerable responsibility.

In general, studies identifying different socioeconomic groups in ancient Egypt have centered on their occupations: pharaoh, official, scribe, priest, craftsman, and peasant. But wealth had less to do with a person's type of work than with his rank among those of the same occupation. Thus, "chief priest," "chief craftsman," and "chief scribe," were more likely to have considerable income than a priest, craftsman, or scribe of lower rank.[22] For the purposes of comparison we must therefore look at faience objects belonging to individuals whose socioeconomic status has been determined by more than simple occupational titles: we must assess their rank titles, if any, as well as the types and quantities of valuable substances, including inscribed material, in their tombs.

The best information on the status of individuals tends to come from their tombs, because it was here they attempted to ensure the survival of their identity and genealogy. Funerary remains also tend to dominate the archaeological record, while evidence of daily life is relatively scarce. There are some data from settlements, but most publications concentrate on domestic architecture rather than artifacts: with the exception of Deir el-Medina and Amarna, small remains, if recorded at all, are seldom completely published.[23] Continuing work at Amarna and Memphis should eventually shed light on faience use in daily life for comparison with mortuary contexts.[24]

When studying data from burials it is important to identify tombs that are undisturbed, that can be clearly attributed to a specific socioeconomic group, and that have been published in sufficient detail to identify the types, quantities, and materials of grave goods. It is also necessary to compare tombs that are roughly

TABLE I FAIENCE OBJECTS FROM THE TOMB OF TUTANKHAMUN

Jewelry
Beads: ex. CCN 85, CCN 256, CCN 4t, CCN 525
Collars: ex. CCN 53a; CCN 21u
Amulets: ex. CCN 256rrr; CCN 620(18–20)
Rings: ex. CCN 53b, CCN 620:66
Bracelets: ex. CCN 620(40-41), CCN 620(38)

Vessels (67)
Heset: ex. CCN(31-32)
Nemset: ex. CCN 54zzz
Hes jars: ex. CCN 461t
Drop-shaped jar: ex. CCN 399a
Cups: ex. CCN 54qq
Oviform jars: ex. CCN 620(29–30)

Ritual Equipment
Objects representing forelegs of bovids: ex. CCN 261f
Figurines of deities: ex. CCN 261g
Wands: ex. CCN 620(9–10)
Shabtis and their tools: ex. CCN 459h
Was scepter: ex. CCN 629(14–17)

Furniture
Headrest: ex. CCN 403b
Inlay: ex. CCN 12a

Games
Gaming pieces: ex. CCN 12e

(CCN = Carter Catalogue Number)

contemporary, to eliminate variations through time in both the available technology and the cultural reasons for using faience. Burials of the Eighteenth Dynasty best satisfy these criteria[25] and here we focus on those of Tutankhamun from the Valley of the Kings; Kha, an Eighteenth Dynasty minor official buried at Deir el-Medina; and several burials from an early Eighteenth Dynasty cemetery at Abydos. This material is supplemented with evidence from other contemporaneous tombs and then contrasted with information from a series of houses at Amarna.

Tutankhamun: faience in a royal burial

Tutankhamun's burial is a good place to begin a study because both his social status and the condition of his tomb (KV 62) and its equipment are known. His tomb was disturbed twice after it was sealed, with the loss of up to 60% of his "best loose" jewelry, linen, cosmetics, and vessels in precious metals.[26] The remainder of the grave equipment was well preserved when Carter opened the tomb in 1922, although not arranged precisely as originally buried. Although the loss of the cosmetics and linens does not affect this study, the absence of many metal vessels and elaborate jewelry must qualify our comparison of items made of faience with similar ones in more costly materials.

Tutankhamun's cartouches have been identified on statues, stelae, and personal equipment at various sites throughout Egypt, attesting to his position as a pharaoh who reigned for at least nine years.[27] Other evidence clearly indicates that he ruled in the final years of the Eighteenth Dynasty, shortly after Akhenaten's death. As pharaoh, Tutankhamun had the highest rank in late Eighteenth Dynasty society, and he presumably therefore had access to any materials available. Because of his youth when he inherited the throne, his advisors may unofficially have wielded more political power than he,[28] but there is no reason to suppose that they would have denied him access to any materials for his personal or funerary equipment.

Luxury[29] materials, such as gold, silver, lapis lazuli, turquoise, ivory, and glass, were readily available during Tutankhamun's reign. The relative stability of Egypt's borders and the international alliances established under Amenhotep III continued into Tutankhamun's time,[30] so that the king had access to many materials through government-sponsored expeditions and an extensive trade network.[31] It is thus reasonable to assume that cost was not an issue when Tutankhamun or his officials selected his burial equipment. So if faience was regarded as inexpensive and nonexclusive, few, if any, faience objects should be found in Tutankhamun's tomb.

The reality is quite different, however. Howard Carter listed over one hundred objects either wholly faience or having substantial faience components.[32] Five major categories were found: jewelry, ritual equipment, vessels, furniture, and games.

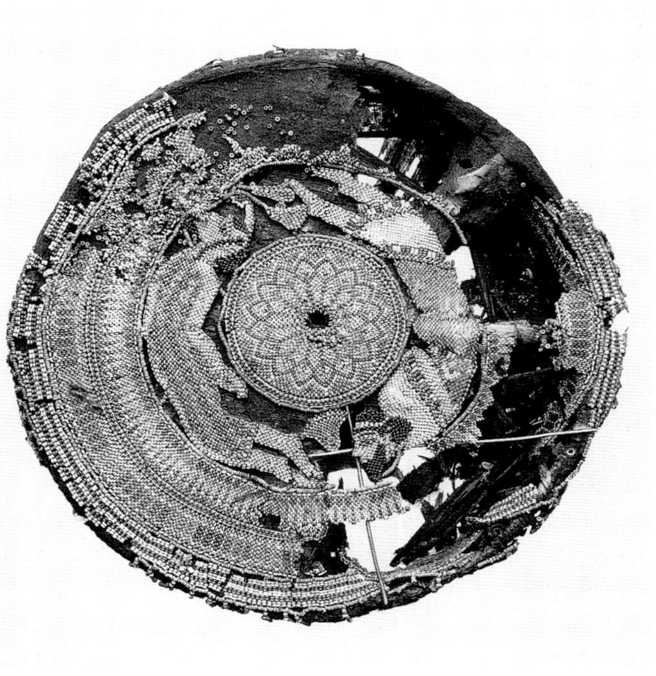

Fig. 12 A hassock (CCN 354) from Tutankhamun's tomb illustrating the small ring beads that form the decoration. *Photo by the Egyptian Expedition, Metropolitan Museum of Art, New York.*

Two arguments can be made to support the hypothesis that the presence of these faience objects can be attributed to their inexpensiveness and easy availability. First, the considerable use of faience might reflect the haste required for the burial of a king who died young. Tutankhamun, somewhere between 18 and 26 when he died, would have been expected to live two to three decades longer,[33] and in the rush to assemble his burial equipment[34] officials could well have opted to produce some items in readily available faience (the Egyptians were not above shortcuts for their burial equipment).[35] But if such haste had been necessary, we would expect to find specific objects only in faience that were made in more exclusive materials for other pharaohs. Second, some faience objects may have been added after the robberies to replace missing items originally fashioned in precious materials; here again, the choice of faience would relate to its ease of manufacture and availability at short notice. But had this been the case, a variety of object types should have been found, and arranged in an orderly manner since they would have remained undisturbed until Carter's excavation. Study of the types of faience objects in Tutankhamun's tomb (Table I) reveals that the range is narrow in relation to the variety of objects found there; in addition, most are quite small. It seems that the reasons for the use of faience are more complex than generally supposed.

Technological rather than economic considerations seem to be behind the use of faience in Tutankhamun's jewelry. Most of this faience takes the form of beads, for instance in the broad collars (such as CCN[36] 53a) which imitated floral necklaces and were used only once, for the funerary meal and burial. These required leaf and flower beads in a variety of colors and with a uniformity in size and shape for which faience is well suited.[37] The tiny disk or ring beads on the skull cap (CCN 256:4t), sandal (CCN 147a), and hassock (CCN 354) (fig. 12) would have been all but impossible to produce in hard stone, although they were not necessarily inexpensive to make in faience, given their size and variety of colors. Some of Tutankhamun's bangles (CCN 620:40-42) had inscriptions inlaid with faience of a second color, an effect that would have been quite difficult using two types of stone. The rarity of examples of inlaid bichrome faience—they seem to belong to or have been gifts from royalty[38]—testifies to difficulty of manufacture, not inherent cheapness.

Simple bezel rings were issued in large numbers but only in honor of celebrations or festivals—they were never intended for daily wear. Thus, the rings in Tutankhamun's tomb (CCN 53b and CCN 620:66a–w) were apparently not manufactured specifically for his adornment, and their presence among his possessions suggests that he, like many Egyptians, had kept them as mementos or commemoratives.[39] Again, therefore, the use of faience seems not to have been influenced by cost.

But why was faience used for *shebyu*-collars (CCN 21y, 44bb-dd, 255, 256a, 525), which are regarded as items of award jewelry and usually made of gold, and a pectoral (CCN 256rrr)? Choker-like necklaces of blue faience disk beads, well documented in Eighteenth Dynasty contexts, have consistently been identified as imitations of *shebyu*-collars or necklaces.[40] Tutankhamun had at least seven faience versions[41] and their presence in a royal tomb seems inconsistent with our current understanding of their function: why would Tutankhamun need inexpensive imitations of gold award necklaces when he could easily have obtained the real thing? However, gold *shebyu*-collars are found in several burials of individuals of different socioeconomic status.[42] The idea that Tutankhamun's faience collars are mere imitations of gold prototypes is especially problematic in the light of a singular example (CCN 256) found around the neck of the gold mask covering Tutankhamun's mummy[43] and made of three strands of disk beads of yellow and red gold regularly interspersed with blue faience disks.[44] Since the entire necklace could easily have been made of gold, the distinctive combination of gold and faience was obviously a deliberate choice. Perhaps faience's brilliant blue color or intense luster added meaning, though if color were the main concern, one would expect to see lapis lazuli, a material frequently used in Tutankhamun's jewelry, and often in combination with gold.[45]

Tutankhamun's other major piece of faience jewelry is a large *wadjet*-eye pectoral (CCN 256rrr).[46] Another *wadjet*-eye pectoral (CCN 256vvv) of similar design but made from gold inlaid with stones and glass indicates the availability of alternative materials, so that the use of faience for this pectoral may relate to the eye's symbolic meaning.[47] While it is conceivable that faience was used for the pectoral because it could be crafted faster than one of inlaid stones, the numerous carved and inlaid bracelets and pectorals among Tutankhamun's equipment make this explanation unlikely.

Most of the non-jewelry faience objects from Tutankhamun's tomb consist of ritual equipment. Faience containers, generally libation vessels, are nearly all of the so-called *heset* and *nemset* form; the remainder are simple cups and bag-shaped vessels (fig. 13).[48] Because most glass and metal vessels were stolen from the tomb it is difficult to know whether faience here replaced more expensive materials.[49] Many of the faience vessels, however, were found in a box (CCN 54) and Carter's photograph shows neatly stacked vessels covered with fragments of other burial goods placed there after the second robbery,[50] indicating that the faience vessels were part of the original tomb equipment and not substitutes for missing glass and metal containers.[51] Whether the faience vessels served the same function as the glass and metal ones is not known, but the stone containers in the tomb probably had different uses from the faience vessels.[52]

Other faience objects include model food offerings, figurines of deities, amulets, shabtis and their tools, wands or throwsticks, and decorative elements for furniture. Identical or similar objects are often found in two and even three different materials. Shabtis were made in several types of stone and wood as well as faience, while many of their implements were in copper and wood in addition to faience. A faience papyrus scepter (CCN 261f) has smaller parallels in gold inlaid with feldspar.[53] The wands or throwsticks (CCN 620:9–10) have counterparts in wood decorated with faience and gold leaf. The model food offerings, largely forelegs of bovids,[54] do not appear in other materials, nor

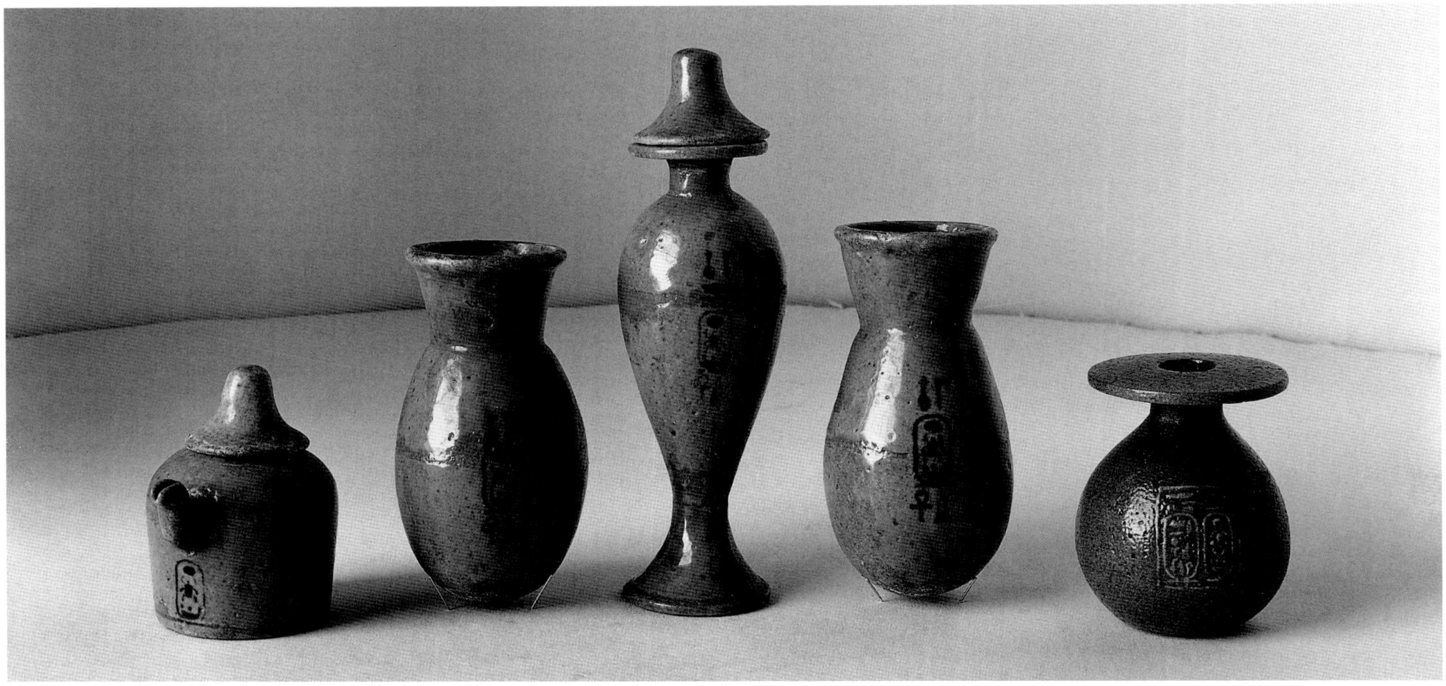

Fig. 13 Faience vessels from Tutankhamun's tomb: (left to right) CCN 620 (33), (30), (31), (29) and 399A. *Photo by the Egyptian Expedition, Metropolitan Museum of Art, New York.*

do the figurines of Thoth and Horus, although numerous statuettes in the tomb are made from other materials.[55]

Thus the faience objects in Tutankhamun's burial cannot be grouped into a single object type, nor is a single explanation sufficient for their manufacture in this material. Certain objects, principally jewelry or decorative forms, were made from faience for technological reasons. Of the remaining object types, few were made solely in faience, suggesting that affordability, availability, or speed of production were not the reasons for using faience.[56] Pinch has suggested that faience jewelry was deposited in royal tombs because the objects' intrinsic material value was unimportant in religious contexts.[57] This interpretation certainly has its attractions; it does not, of course, explain why some examples of an object were manufactured in faience while others were not.

Faience objects from other royal tombs

The surviving funerary equipment from two other Eighteenth Dynasty royal tombs provides further insights into the inclusion of faience in royal burials. Davis recovered a variety of objects in diverse materials from Tomb 55 in the Valley of the Kings (KV 55), but only a few were of precious materials such as gold and silver.[58] Although the identity of the person or persons buried in the tomb remains uncertain, there is general agreement that they were royal.[59] Items listed in Davis's publication can be categorized as amulets or ritual objects,[60] vessels,[61] "small caskets,"[62] statues of deities,[63] throwsticks,[64] and model food.[65] The categories of faience objects overlap with those in Tutankhamun's tomb.[66] Because there is no evidence that the KV 55 burial preparations were hurried, the tomb's remains provide further evidence for dismissing speed of manufacture as an explanation for the faience objects among Tutankhamun's burial items.[67]

Parallels can also be found between material from both KV 55 and Tutankhamun's tomb and the faience objects from the tomb of Thutmose IV (KV 43) (fig. 14), further indicating that faience was perfectly acceptable in the uppermost socioeconomic stratum (Table II).[68] Although detailed object comparisons between KV 55, Thutmose IV's and Tutankhamun's tombs are impossible because of extensive disturbance in the first two, the similar types of faience objects in all three demonstrate that Tutankhamun's faience was not anomalous (Table II).

The excavation reports for all three tombs mention the poor quality of some of the faience.[69] Poor quality in objects for which high quality could easily have been achieved strongly hints that the particular substance used was the important aspect of an item, especially when the same type appears in other materials. Pinch's[70] suggestion, mentioned above, that quality may not influence the effectiveness of certain types of votive items again seems relevant.

Faience use among non-royal socioeconomic classes

The tomb of Yuya and Thuya, the parents of Queen Tiye, provides an interesting contrast to the royal tombs.[71] Yuya was of the highest class of officials, a status reinforced by his relationship to Queen Tiye, the wife of Amenhotep III, and this royal connection accounts for the location of his tomb in the Valley of the Kings (KV 46).[72] Although the tomb had apparently been systematically looted of its most valuable objects, including metal, glass, linen, and ointment containers, the indications are that Yuya and Thuya's burials were originally rich ones.[73] Because the tomb had been looted, the information from the burials is, of course, less complete, and the knowledge that many pieces are missing prohibits an assessment of the variety among any given object type. Nevertheless, had faience objects ever been among the

TABLE II FAIENCE OBJECTS FROM THREE EIGHTEENTH DYNASTY ROYAL TOMBS

Tutankhamun	**KV 55**	**Thutmose IV**
CONTAINERS	CONTAINERS	CONTAINERS
heset		*heset*
nemset		*nemset*
small cups	small cups	small cups
bag-shaped jars		bag-shaped jars
drop-shaped jars	drop-shaped jars	
	ankhs	
	cosmetic jar (*female*)	
		kohl tube
JEWELRY AND AMULETS	JEWELRY AND AMULETS	JEWELRY AND AMULETS
shebyu-collars		
wadjet pendant	*wadjets*	
papyrus scepters	papyrus scepters	
rings		
	serpent's heads	
STATUETTES OF DEITIES	STATUETTES OF DEITIES	
Thoth	Thoth plaque	
	Bes-images	
DECORATIVE BEADING		
RITUAL EQUIPMENT	RITUAL EQUIPMENT	RITUAL EQUIPMENT
model food (forelegs)	model food (grapes)	model food (lotus)
throwsticks/wands	throwsticks/wands	throwsticks/wands
	bookrolls	bookrolls
	mooring pole?	
		ankhs
SHABTIS, IMPLEMENTS		SHABTIS, IMPLEMENTS
FURNITURE	FURNITURE	
headrest	small boxes	
GAMES		
gaming pieces		

tomb's furnishings one would expect to find fragments of faience, as in the royal tombs. But the only faience pieces mentioned by the tomb's excavator, Davis, are a *djed*-pillar amulet and a kohl tube inlaid with Amenhotep III's name—there are no signs of the vessels, shabtis, or other ritual items found in the royal tombs. The *djed*-pillar amulet has a parallel among the material from Tutankhamun's tomb and the inlaid kohl tube must have been made by a master craftsman, which, in conjunction with the name of Amenhotep III, indicates that it was probably a royal gift.

The paucity of faience recovered from this tomb could be taken as support for the hypothesis that faience was used as an inexpensive substitute: these elite individuals used it rarely because they could afford higher-quality materials. In Yuya and Thuya's tomb, however, faience was not used to imitate more costly materials—but painted wood and painted pottery were.[74]

In 1906, Schiaparelli discovered the undisturbed tomb of Kha and his wife Merit at Deir el-Medina.[75] Kha had the title "The Overseer of Works in the Great Place [Valley of the Kings]" (*jmy-r k3t m s.t ꜥ3*), indicating that he supervised the work in royal tombs, a position with similar responsibilities to those of an architect today.[76] Inscriptions in the tomb and on funerary equipment show that he worked during the reigns of Amenhotep

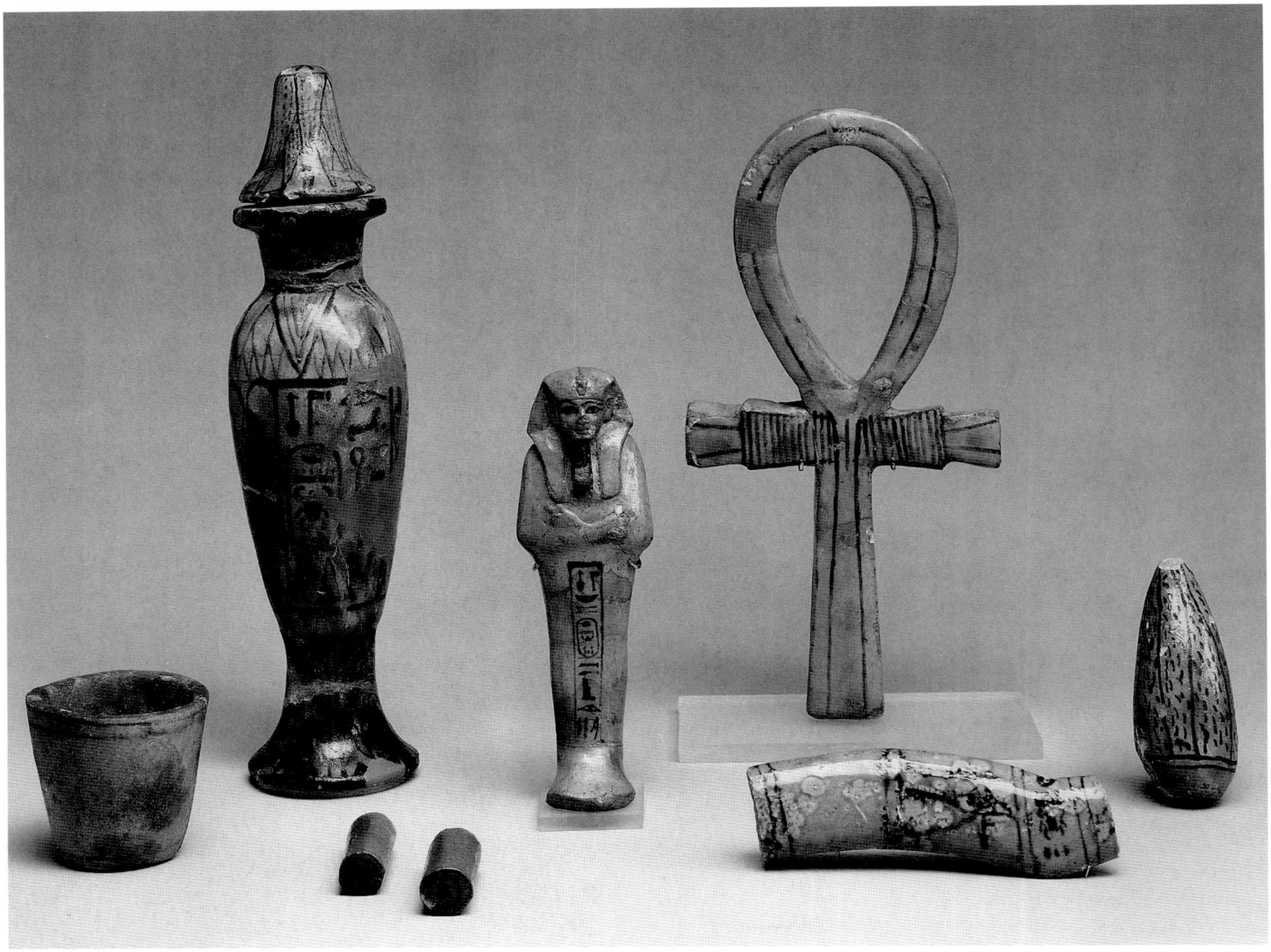

Fig. 14 A group of faience vessels and other votive objects from the tomb of Thutmose IV. Left to right: cup; *hes* jar; papyrus rolls; shabti; *ankh*; fragment of throwstick; and lotus bud. *Photo courtesy the Metropolitan Museum of Art, New York (left to right: 30.8.42; 30.8.37AB; 30.8.33; 30.8.34; 30.8.27; 30.8.29; 30.8.31; 30.8.35), Theodore M. Davis Collection. Bequest of Theodore M. Davis. 1915.*

II, Thutmose IV, and Amenhotep III.[77] X-rays of his unwrapped mummy reveal that he was buried wearing a number of pieces of gold jewelry, including a necklace of large disk beads that has been called a *shebyu*-collar, a chain, earrings, rings, and bracelets.[78] Kha and his wife were well equipped in death and several items of their funerary assemblage were made from precious metals, including silver, electrum, and gold.[79]

Kha did not belong to the elite stratum of Eighteenth Dynasty society: his title is not that of a high official. Within his village of Deir el-Medina, however, he held a supervisory position among the workmen,[80] and the gold jewelry on his mummy and his inscribed gifts from Amenhotep II and Amenhotep III[81] are strong indications that he enjoyed a successful career. Kha's accomplishments enabled him to acquire a decorated tomb chapel with a pyramidion and multiple coffins.[82] His burial chamber was also decorated, and among his funerary equipment was an inscribed wooden statue and one of the earliest known copies of the Book of the Dead.[83] Thus, the style and contents of his tomb, together with his title, place him somewhere in the upper half of ancient Egyptian society, but not among its highest officials.[84]

Given Kha's socioeconomic position and income, we might expect fewer of his funerary objects to be made of expensive materials and those that are present should be small, but he should possess numerous faience pieces. In fact only about 10% of the tomb's contents (excluding food items) are metal (bronze razors, adzes, chisels, sieves, a lamp, and vessels). Several containers, however, were made of silver and one was electrum, while gold leaf adorned Kha's second coffin and his cubit rod.

Jewelry accounts for the major use of precious metal in the tomb, almost exclusively adorning the mummies of Kha and Merit since no collection of personal items was found. In addition to his gold, Kha wore three stone funerary amulets—a scarab, a *tyet*, and a snake's head—the last two probably in carnelian.[85] Merit wore a faience bead collar, a girdle of gold wallet-type beads and glass or faience ring beads, and a pair of gold earrings.[86] Other goods in precious materials were two glass cosmetic containers, a set of alabaster ointment containers, 16 alabaster storage jars of various shapes and sizes, and an ebony box with ivory inlay.[87]

The list of faience objects is shorter than we might expect, and what there is falls into two categories: jewelry and vessels. In addition to the items among Merit's jewelry, the only other faience objects were two rings, two armlets, a pilgrim flask, and a decorated jar and bowl. Kha and Merit's faience funerary equipment has more in common with the objects in Yuya and Thuya's tomb than with the royal ones.[88]

Most objects in Kha and Merit's tomb are made of wood, basketry, pottery, and linen. Much of the equipment could well have come directly from among their household goods, although the flimsiness of some of it suggests it was created specifically as burial equipment.[89] Because Kha appears financially comfortable but not wealthy, and because he probably arranged that the objects in his burial should be decorated to imitate other materials (painted pottery jars), why were these objects, especially the toilet equipment, not made in faience rather than wood or bone?

Some insight is provided by the type of faience objects in the tomb. The rings are of the same commemorative sort as those found in Tutankhamun's tomb; the armlets are styled like *awaw*-bracelets, suggesting they are faience copies of so-called award jewelry. The shallow bowl is a well-known vessel type made only in faience and usually decorated with designs depicting a watery environment ([76–78], pp. 112–13); such bowls are now considered ritual funerary equipment.[90] An unusual ripple-necked jar is decorated with lotus petals, a decorative element symbolizing rebirth.[91] Faience was used for the tiny beads in the girdle for technical reasons, like the beads on Tutankhamun's hassock, skull cap, and sandals. Only the faience pilgrim flask might be considered an imitation of an object from daily life, since such vessels are often made in pottery. It is unlikely, however, that faience was more easily obtained than pottery, and it is far more probable that the piece had a ritual purpose, like many other faience vessels. In summary, therefore, the faience objects in Kha's tomb, with the possible exception of the tiny ring-beads, appear to have ritual or commemorative associations.

In 1902, Mace excavated the large "Cemetery D" at Abydos, along the western edge of the cemetery zone north of the wadi. A sizeable number of its burials date to the early Eighteenth Dynasty,[92] and it contained a series of graves, several large mastabas, and numerous reused shaft tombs, whose contents indicate that they belonged to members of Egypt's middle or lower class. Although none of these tombs is intact and they are thus not ideal candidates for this study, they are included here because no other sizeable, well-published group of relatively undisturbed tombs dates to this period and is clearly associated with such classes.[93]

Several Cemetery D tombs contained objects unquestionably of early New Kingdom date, and this extremely limited chronological range suggests that each tomb group should be considered a component of a single burial or nearly contemporary burials of closely related individuals. Two such tomb groups, D102 and D116, are dated with confidence to the early Eighteenth

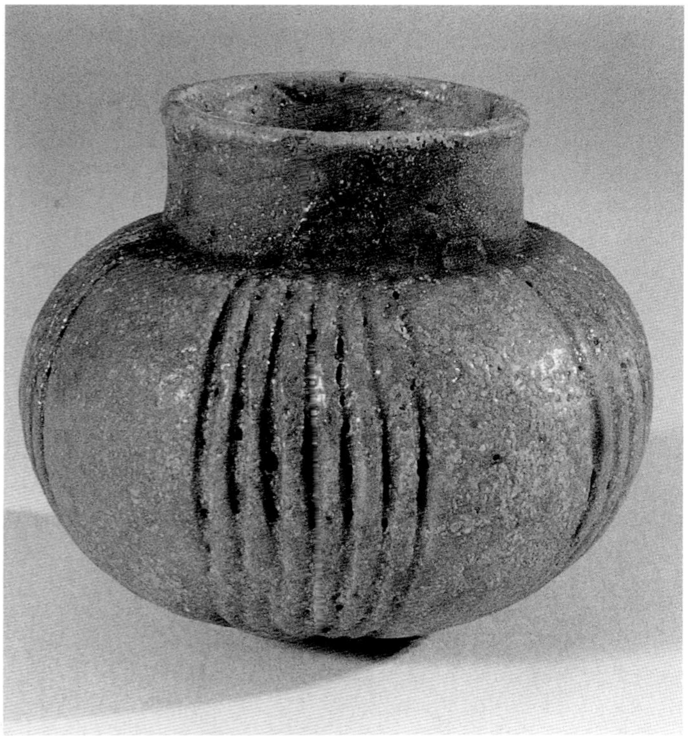

Fig. 15 A small faience jar from tomb D116 at Abydos (CMNH 1917-535). *Photo courtesy the Carnegie Museum of Natural History, Pittsburgh.*

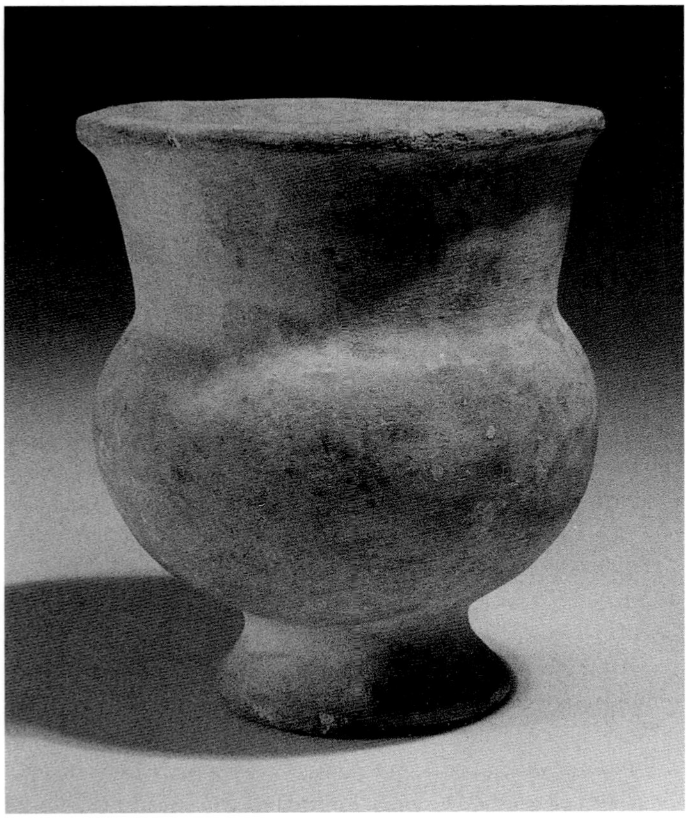

Fig. 16 A footed jar in Egyptian blue from tomb D116 at Abydos (CMNH 1917-476). *Photo courtesy the Carnegie Museum of Natural History, Pittsburgh.*

TABLE III FAIENCE EQUIPMENT IN TOMBS BELONGING TO SEVERAL DIFFERENT SOCIOECONOMIC LEVELS

Highest Level	**Middle Level**	**Middle or lower level**
TUTANKHAMUN	KHA and MERIT	CEMETERY D
VESSELS	VESSELS	VESSELS
nemset *heset* bag-shaped drop-shaped simple cups	decorated bowl decorated ripple-necked jar pilgrim flask	small jar (D116) lotus vessel (D116) footed jar (D116) footed bowl (D102)* carved kohl pot (D116)#
JEWELRY	JEWELRY	JEWELRY
shebyu-collars *wadjet*-pendant amulets rings	*awaw*-bracelets rings	*shebyu*-collar (D102) leopard necklaces (D116) rosette bead necklaces (D116) amulets (D102, D116) scarabs (D102, D116)
RITUAL EQUIPMENT		
forelegs (model food) throwsticks or wands figurines of deities		
SHABTIS AND THEIR IMPLEMENTS		
RING BEADS IN DECORATION		
HEADREST		
GAMES		GAMES
gaming pieces		gaming piece (D116) depicting Bes-image

* Egyptian blue # glazed steatite

Dynasty by the presence of scarabs bearing royal names of Hatshepsut and Thutmose III[94] and by the forms and decoration of the associated pottery. Analysis of these two burials suggests that the owners did not belong to the elite class. Neither was associated with a large mastaba like other occupants of the cemetery; instead, they were found in reused Middle Kingdom shaft tombs. In addition, these burials contained little inscribed material. Lacking titles, we cannot identify the rank of either individual;[95] indeed, the scarcity of inscribed material is one indicator that they were not members of a high socioeconomic group. Inlaid stone eyes were recovered, showing that at one time coffins or funerary masks were present, but no coffins were found.[96] Both tombs contained metal objects.

Evidence from these tombs indicates that the owners belonged to a lower socioeconomic class, but that they were not poor.[97] Over a hundred objects were found in each tomb, including jewelry, amulets, cosmetic equipment, tools, and vessels. Certain objects were made in substances believed costly for ancient Egyptians, including bronze, gold, silver,[98] and alabaster, and a variety of more exotic materials, such as ivory[99] and turquoise,[100] suggesting that the individuals had at least some discretionary income, though there is no sign they had titled positions as Kha did. Abydos at this time was a provincial center, unlike Thebes, Kha's home, which was the capital city. Thus the occupants of Cemetery D could be provincial members of the same socioeconomic group as Kha, but would not have had the opportunity to acquire more luxurious materials or to receive gifts like Kha because he lived in the city.

The faience objects in tombs D102 and D116 consist of amulets, beads, and small vessels, the designs on two of which are generally considered to have symbolic meaning.[101] Three faience vessels,[102] a small ointment jar and a footed jar from D116 (figs. 15, 16),[103] and the open bowl from D102 are undecorated. Most of the faience in these tombs takes the form of jewelry, principally beads, scarabs, and other amulets. D116 contains two examples of a rare necklace form made from multicolored faience beads (fig. 18),[104]

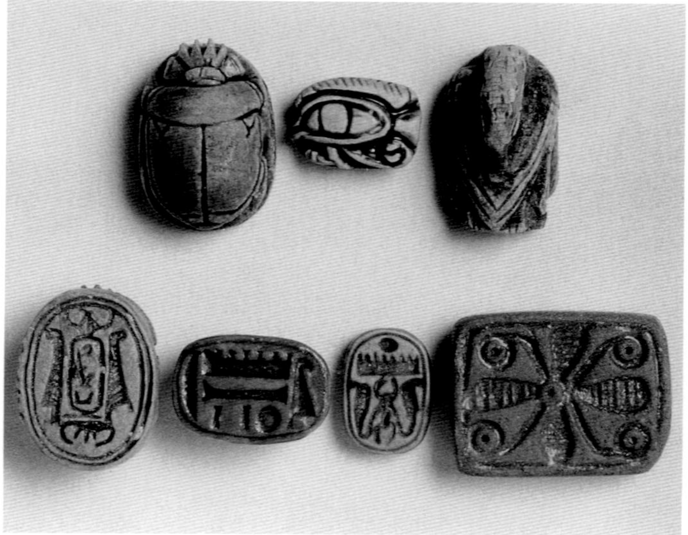

Fig. 17 A group of six scarabs and amulets from the early Dynasty 18 tombs in Cemetery D at Abydos (left to right top to bottom: CMNH 1917-78, 1917-328, 1917-287, 1917-60, 1867-7b [not from Cemetery D], 1917-206, 1917-63). *Photo courtesy the Carnegie Museum of Natural History, Pittsburgh.*

which may have been more than simple ornaments. Part of a *shebyu*-collar in blue faience disk beads was found in D102,[105] and D116 also contained two rosette bead necklaces, another unusual type. In both tombs the scarabs and amulets were largely made of faience, not glazed steatite. Two categories of faience objects can be recognized in the D tombs: items that clearly possess symbolic or ritual meaning, including some containers, amulets, a gaming piece, unusual necklace forms, and a *shebyu*-collar; and small undecorated vessels probably for cosmetics. These are the same categories found in other tombs studied. In D102 the scarabs were made of several different materials—faience, glass, and carnelian.[106] The use of several different materials for the same object was observed in Tutankhamun's tomb too.

As in Kha and Merit's funerary equipment, the small number of faience objects from the two Cemetery D tombs challenges the hypothesis that the lower the socioeconomic class the more faience would be found among the funerary goods.[107] Even more interesting is the similarity in types of faience objects from Kha and Merit's tomb and those in the Cemetery D tombs (Table III). One possible explanation for this is that their owners belonged to the same socioeconomic group, though one lived in a province and the other in the capital. If so, then members of the same class must have had extensive cultural contacts in New Kingdom Egypt. Alternatively, the faience objects may be similar because faience was used for specific purposes consistent throughout the culture, regardless of socioeconomic class. This explanation seems more likely, especially because certain types of faience appear in the tombs of every socioeconomic category studied.

The settlement at Amarna

A brief look now at Eighteenth Dynasty Amarna allows a general comparison with information derived from the burials.[108] In this settlement the larger house compounds produced the largest number of recorded objects, and these were made of the greatest variety of materials. Three of the large structures can be associated with titled individuals,[109] and of the largest groups of objects from such structures two came from these three units. The data thus suggest that large houses with compounds, sometimes with additional buildings, belonged to members of the elite.

Overall the number of faience objects recovered from the section of the settlement reviewed was low. In relation to the total number of objects found in any one structure the number of faience items varies widely, from 0% in a small house with only five finds to 73% of the fifteen objects from another small house. Some of the smaller structures have the largest percentages of faience objects, and assemblages from the largest house structures or complexes contained only between 22 and 33% faience objects.

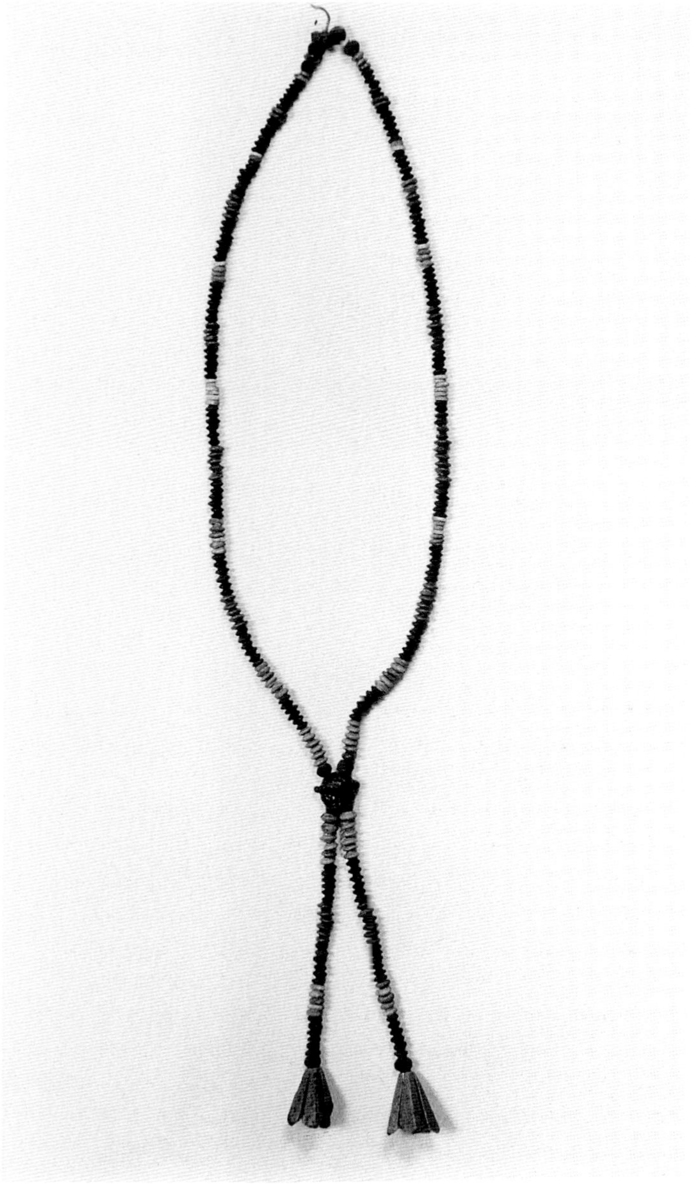

Fig. 18 Multicolored faience bead necklace with a leopard-head spacer (CMNH 1917-30). *Photo courtesy the Carnegie Museum of Natural History, Pittsburgh.*

TABLE IV SELECTION OF AMARNA HOUSES AND THE FAIENCE FINDS

HOUSE NUMBER	TYPE	DESCRIPTION	Number of objects	Number of faience objects	Variety of materials	% objects in faience	% faience objects not jewelry	Necklace elements	Rings	Scarabs	Armband	Inlay	Grapes	Snakes	Throwsticks	Vessels	Tile	Figurine	Foundation deposit	Other	Unknown
M50.4	House	very small house	18	5	12	28	16	1	1							2					1
M50.6	House	very small house	8	4	3	50	0	2	2												
M50.2	House	small house	6	1	3	17	0		1												
M50.3	House	small house	38	12	10	32	5	7	3	1				1							
R45.1	House	small house	21	6	8	29	5		2	1											1
M50.7	House	small house	30	7	14	23	3	3	3								1				
N47.7	House	very small house with enclosure	4	3	2	75	50	1				1				1					
N47.8	House	very small house with enclosure	31	21	7	68	0	13	3	5											
N47.4	House	small house with enclosure	11	3	5	27	18					1			1				1		
M50.1/51.1	Farms	small house with large enclosure	5	0	2	0	0														
N48.9	Houses	very small house-attached	37	17	12	46	5	5	7	3		1						1			
M50.10	Houses	very small house-attached	26	3	11	11	0		1			2									
P47.23	Houses	small house-attached	36	15	9	42	19	5	5			1				2	1				3
N48.8	House	small house-attached	15	11	5	73	13	6	3			1								1	
N47.5	House group	very small houses-attached	13	4	7	31	15		1			1				1					
P48.1	Small house group	very small houses-attached	55	18	12	33	9	4	6	1	1	2			1		1	1			
M50.11	Farm/house	small houses-attached	26	10	9	38	19	4	1	1		2						1?		1	
P46.1	Small house group	small houses-attached	82	15	16	18	7	4	4	1		1				2	1	1			1
M50.5	Houses	small house, 1 very small attached building	8	2	4	25	13	1				1									
Q47.3	House	small house, 1 attached	35	13	14	37	9	4	4	1		2				1					
N47.3	Farm	2–3 houses with large enclosure	26	8	7	31	19	1	1		1	1	2		1	1					
M47.3	Farm	house, outbuildings	131	10	11	8	4	1	3	1		1	1			1		1			1
M.50.8	Farm	house with enclosure	24	8	9	33	4	5	1	1			1								
P.48.2	Farm	house with enclosure	148	46	17	31	4	29	6	5		1	1	1			1	1			1
P47.1	House	house with enclosure many attached buildings	176	55	21	31	4	30	12	4		4	1			2			1		
Q46.1	Large farm	very large house with enclosure, outbuildings	107	24	14	22	12	4	7			6	1			1	1		1		3

In all but one case, up to 80% of the faience objects recorded are pieces of personal ornamentation, most of them commemorative rings or elements of broad collars (Table IV).

Many of the objects in the remaining 20% are inlay or architectural elements, such as a bunch of grapes or snakes' heads; only a few belong to other object categories. These remaining faience finds are, however, quite interesting. Non-jewelry items include the same object types seen elsewhere in ritual contexts—such as tombs and shrines—including vessels, figurines, throwsticks, tiles, and items associated with foundation deposits. Most were fragmentary and usually only the larger buildings on the site yielded more than one type. But in proportion to their areas, the smaller and larger structures seem to produce about the same low number of non-jewelry items, which are therefore likely to be accidental occurrences.

In summary, the same kinds of faience object types are found in this settlement as in the tombs studied—mostly jewelry of some kind. The smaller house structures and compounds yielded more pieces of jewelry than the larger ones, but on the whole these are collar elements and rings and they may have been found at their site of manufacture.[110] Non-jewelry faience finds are relatively rare and in general seem to be object types found elsewhere in ritual contexts.

Conclusions

Several conclusions can be drawn from this review of the types of faience objects from ancient Egypt. First, the range of objects fashioned from faience is restricted, consisting basically of jewelry, inlay and small architectural ornaments, small vessels, gaming pieces, statuettes, sistra, and headrests. The earliest objects made from faience (or its counterpart, glazed steatite) are beads and small amulets. In each subsequent chronological period, artisans added new object types to the existing repertoire, until the New Kingdom when the broadest range of types is found. Faience continued to be important for both ritual and funerary items into the Roman Period.

During the Early Dynastic Period, most faience items are found in cultic contexts. By the First Intermediate Period and particularly by the Middle Kingdom, items made for personal use become common in burials and many pieces clearly had a function connected with funerary ritual. Faience remained important in cultic contexts throughout Egyptian history.

A study of faience objects from mortuary contexts demonstrates that faience was probably not used as an inexpensive replacement for more costly materials. It appears to be more common in royal tombs than in those of individuals of any other socioeconomic level. Also, within a single context a given object type is often found in several different materials, of which faience is only one, again suggesting that faience was chosen deliberately. Although faience is often said to be used to imitate more expensive items, graves with faience objects often contain far more obvious imitations, commonly made from painted wood. Apparently faience was not a material that the poorer members of society were forced to use, but rather was chosen for certain funerary and cultic items.

Most faience pieces have come from cemeteries and temples, largely due to the course of archaeological excavation in Egypt, and so our understanding of how faience was used in ancient Egypt is currently distorted. However, a brief study of debris from a residential area in a large metropolitan settlement, Amarna, shows that the types of objects found there parallel those known from ritual contexts. Most of these faience pieces are jewelry, followed by architectural elements; when these categories are excluded, what little significant material that remains is probably not helpful in understanding the settlement's function.

Thus, the data indicate that faience was used by the ancient Egyptians principally in temple and tomb—that is in ritual contexts. All socioeconomic strata, including royalty, chose faience for certain pieces of funerary equipment. The range of object types is narrow and most can be assigned an amuletic function. Faience (or glazed steatite) was used not because of its inexpensiveness or easy availability—that is in imitation of more precious substances—but because of its color and finish; the choice of faience was integral to the function of the finished product.[31] The fact that numerous faience pieces have amuletic functions would explain why the king had so many more, and mostly ritual in nature, than any non-royal individual: he required far greater protection. Shrine and temple equipment would have been made in faience not only because of the ease with which it could be molded but also because of the magical quality of the material.

1 These figurines are widely believed to be of Early Dynastic date, but none appear in an unequivocally dated context. Kemp 1968, pp. 138–55.
2 Probably even Lower Egypt, since similar finds appear at Tell Ibrahim Awad; van Haarlem 1995, pp. 45–52.
3 Predynastic sites have not yet produced enough examples to confirm this statement. The presence of faience amulets among funerary equipment does show, however, that its use for ritual items was already established.
4 The Old Kingdom brings a change in this category as well: instead of the few cylinders or disk-style beads found in single-strand necklaces, much more complex pieces of personal ornamentation are now made from faience. Most noteworthy are the funerary collars, for example Impy's from Giza (see Andrews 1990, fig. 100) and bead net dresses (see Jick in D'Auria et al. 1988, no.9).
5 See Bourriau 1988a, pp. 110–27 and Bourriau in Quirke 1991, pp. 11–12.
6 Wah's collar (MMA 40.3.2); Senebtisi's falcon collar (MMA 08.200.30) and funerary garment (MMA 08.200.42).
7 For a thorough study of material from Hathor shrines, see Pinch 1993.
8 For example in the Ramesside Period, JE 62014.
9 For example, MMA 35.1.23, although large objects such as this newel post or the *was*-scepter of Amenhotep II (Petrie 1896, pl. 78) (fig. 36 here) are rare.
10 See also for example, MMA 35.1.5; .16; .21; .104.
11 The cemeteries of Illahun, Matmar, and Mostagedda illustrate this point.
12 For example, see the *w3s* scepter (MMA 26.4.46) and *djed* pillar (MMA 26.7.1039) similar in concept to the *ankh* vases and papyrus scepters in the royal tombs of the Eighteenth Dynasty.
13 For example, the small statuette of Amenhotep III as a sphinx [22] and a portion of one dating to the Sixteenth Dynasty (MMA 1990.25).
14 For example, Aldred 1971a, p. 35; Andrews 1990, p. 59; Donatelli in Roveri 1988a, p. 198; Hayes 1953, p. 24; James 1979, p. 213; Smith 1942, p. 24.
15 These materials would most likely be turquoise, feldspar, and lapis lazuli, blue and green stones commonly used in the manufacture of personal arts.
16 See Kaczmarczyk and Hedges 1983, pp. 118 and 195.
17 Nicholson 1993, p. 21.
18 See, for example, Hayes 1953, p. 24.
19 Vandiver in Olin and Franklin 1982, pp. 176. This does not imply that molding was unknown in early times. The faience tiles from Djoser's burial complex were probably initially shaped in molds, but this was not the most common manufacturing method until the New Kingdom; see Nicholson 1993, p. 21; Vandiver in Olin and Franklin 1982, pp. 174–75.
20 See Kemp 1989b, pp. 232–34.
21 That inscribed inlaid objects often belong to members of the royal family, to be given as royal gifts, or to be very elaborately made shabtis, suggests that this method of manufacture was anything but simple. See, for example, Brovarski in Brovarski et al. 1982, p. 222, no. 277; Kozloff and Bryan 1992, no. 70, p. 328 and nos. 100–02, pp. 398–400.
22 The letters of Hekanakhte, for example, show that identifying economic status solely with occupation can lead to serious misapprehension of a person's wealth; Baer 1963, pp. 1–19; James 1962.
23 Memphis, Lisht, and Buhen.
24 New Kingdom material from Memphis now being prepared for publication may greatly change our ideas about faience use in daily life (Lisa Giddy, pers. comm.).
25 Although the tombs studied range chronologically over almost two hundred years, I feel that comparisons of the burial equipment are nonetheless valid.
26 Reeves 1990a, pp. 95–97 and 150. He bases the words in quotes on Carter's evaluation of the jewelry remaining in the tomb and the condition of jewelry boxes.
27 For a brief summary of this documentation, see Reeves 1990a, pp. 26–29.
28 Grimal 1992, p. 241. Although rank and power are often tied together, the correlation is not absolute; see Quirke 1991, pp. 123–39, for a discussion of power during the late Middle Kingdom and Second Intermediate Period.
29 For ancient Egypt, the offering lists ranking materials are accepted as a source for what the Egyptians considered precious. Gold, silver, and lapis are consistently at the top of the lists.
30 Aldred 1975, pp. 66–71; Kozloff and Bryan 1992, p. 57.
31 Certainly the paintings of tribute from Egypt's southern empire in the tomb of his Viceroy Huy suggest that precious materials were freely available to the

Egyptian state under Tutankhamun.

32 This count is based on the material in Murray and Nutall 1963. One cannot be more accurate since some objects made from faience pieces are listed as a single item—for example, groups of beads are counted as one item—and others are object types for which no material information is provided but are usually made in faience. Neither problem imposes serious restrictions on the argument here.

33 Patch 1994, n. 65.

34 Reeves 1990a, p. 208.

35 Such as the usurpation of costly items from other royal individuals and the use of discarded temple equipment to replace items that should have been commissioned in the king's name (for examples, see Patch 1994, pp. 68–69; Reeves 1990a, pp. 131 and 151).

36 CCN=Carter Catalogue Numbers.

37 Andrews 1990, pp. 122–23.

38 See n. 8.

39 Eaton-Krauss in Brovarski et al. 1982, p. 244; Hayes 1990 (1959), pp. 250–51. Their commemorative nature is supported by the recovery of most examples not from burials but from the royal settlements of Amarna and Malkata; see Boyce in Kemp 1989, pp. 160–68.

40 Hayes (1990 (1959), p. 179) calls faience examples exceedingly common. Some scholars consider the faience strings of disk beads as inexpensive imitations of the gold *shebyu*-collars; see Eaton-Kraus in Brovarski et al. 1982, pp. 238–39 and Andrews 1990, p. 183.

41 Several of these faience disk-bead necklaces from Tutankhamun's tomb are currently displayed in Room 9 of the Cairo Museum, including two strands (T 762 and 765) of disks made from yellow, red, white, and blue faience beads, two strings (T 760 and 761) of blue beads, and a double strand (T 975) of smaller beads in black and white. Regrettably, the author was unable to link the T numbers on the exhibition labels securely to the Carter Catalog Numbers (CCN).

42 Some *shebyu* are made completely in gold; see, for example, the Seventeenth Dynasty mummy in Petrie 1909a, p. 9, pl. 29; Kha in Aldred 1971a, p. 228, pl. 117; Psusennes I in Montet 1951, pp. 135–38, nos. 482–84, pls. 107–09; and Stierlin and Ziegler 1987, pl. 11.

43 For a good description and illustration see Edwards 1976, p. 11, fig. 3.

44 Edwards 1976, p. 11, fig. 3.

45 Certainly the necklace type was an important part of the funerary equipment: at least seven were buried in the tomb and the most elaborate was integral to the mask placed upon the royal mummy itself. The presence of CCN 255 (a similar necklace on the inner coffin) or 256a, however, makes it difficult to accept the notion that the use of faience in this necklace type reflected the need for low-cost or rapid production. Why faience *shebyu*-collars were created has not been addressed adequately. If the gold *shebyu*-collar is an award, as seems clear, then what does a faience one represent? Is it a replacement for a gold one that had been acquired but then expended, perhaps on furnishing a tomb? If so, that might explain the presence of faience *shebyu*-collars (MMA 26.8.66-.69) in the tomb of the three princesses from the time of Thutmose III, but not the faience award jewelry (MMA 36.3.154) in the tomb of a child called Amenhotep: surely he was too young to have acquired award jewelry. A fragment of the same type of disk-bead necklace was recovered from D102 in a cemetery at Abydos. The individual whose tomb this is seems to be from a socioeconomic class with not much opportunity to receive award jewelry. Also, groups of beads of appearance very similar to these collars are found as votive gifts at the Hathor shrine at Deir el-Bahri; see Pinch 1993, p. 265, pl. 57b.

46 Edwards 1976, pp. 41–42, fig. 27.

47 Edwards 1976, pp. 41–42 states that these two pieces differ in their symbolism.

48 *Heset*: example: 620:30; *nemset*: example 399a; bag-shaped example: 620:29; cup example: 54t, drop-shaped or *henket* example: 54w.

49 Some forms of faience vessels were made in more expensive materials as well, in particular the lotus-form chalices; see Brovarski in Brovarski et al. 1982a, p. 146, no. 145 and JE 39872=CG 53260 in Freed 1987, no. 22, p. 155.

50 Reeves 1990a, p. 200.

51 Empty boxes whose labels or packing contents indicate that vessels of these materials were present at the time of burial but disappeared during the robberies.

52 Reeves 1990a, pp. 198–200.

53 Carter 1927, II, p. 259, a and b.

54 Examples CCN 367r.

55 Reeves 1990a, pp. 130–35.

56 In fact, the variety of materials used to make any specific object type needs further study. Economy may be the rationale for the faience gaming pieces, although not everyone agrees with this interpretation. Tait 1982, pp. 28–29 questions whether these eight pieces were ever meant to go with the ivory gaming box (CCN 345) with which they were found. Carter (1927, III, p. 132) suggested that the box's original playing pieces were of gold and silver, and were thus stolen. Tait suggests that the roughness of these gaming pieces, in conjunction with other gaming material, may imply that they were substitutes for the original pieces stolen during the robberies (p. 45), but Reeves 1990a, p. 161, does not agree with this view.

57 Pinch 1993, p. 277.

58 Davis 1910.

59 Bell 1990, pp. 97–137.

60 40 *wadjet*-eyes (JE 39644: SR 2677), 13 papyrus scepters (JE 39644: SR 2718), one mooring pole? (JE 39644: SR 2723), and 16 book-rolls (JE 39645: SR 2695); see Bell 1990, pp. 103.

61 Libation vases shaped like *ankhs* (JE 39643: SR 2687), truncated cone cups (JE 39652: SR 2674; MMA 30.8.52), water jars (JE 39653: SR 2673), jar stands (JE 39654: SR 2688), cosmetic jar in the shape of a woman (JE 39655: SR 2684); see Bell 1990, pp. 103–05.

62 Small boxes (JE 39650: SR 2675; MMA 30.8.50; JE 39651: SR 2676); see Bell 1990, p. 104.

63 Thoth plaque (JE 39639: SR 2693), Bes statues holding vessels (JE 39660: SR 2686 and JE 39659: SR 2682), and serpents' heads (JE 39646: SR 2695); see Bell 1990, pp. 103 and 105.

64 17 throwsticks (JE 39663: SR 2724); see Bell 1990, p. 105.

65 15 bunches of grapes (JE 39661: SR 2679); see Bell 1990, p. 105.

66 Bell suggests (p. 136) that KV 55 was originally sealed during the reign of Tutankhamun, which would explain the similarity in object types between the two tombs.

67 Bell 1990, pp. 136–37.

68 Carter et al. 1904. Parallels with Tutankhamun can be found among shabtis, their equipment (pl. XV), and faience vessel types (pls. XVI–XXI). In fact, faience vessels seem to be consistently *heset*, *nemset*, small cups, and bag-shaped jars in all three royal tombs. Also, the "throwsticks" and *ankh*-vase are quite similar in KV 55 and Thutmose IV (pls. XXV and XXIV [40] respectively). The published descriptions for these three tombs suggest that more thorough publication would reveal more parallels.

69 Hayes 1990 (1959), p. 148.

70 Note 57; see also Pinch 1993, p. 344.

71 Davis 1907.

72 Grimal 1992, p. 221; Reeves 1990b, p. 149.

73 Reeves 1990b, pp. 148–53.

74 Davis 1907, pls. 27–29.

75 Schiaparelli 1903–1927.

76 Delange in Eggebrecht 1987, p. 348. Note that Bierbrier (1982, p. 18) translates the same title as foreman, a common title in the administrative structure of Ramesside Deir el-Medina.

77 Vandier d'Abbadie 1939, p. 18; Roveri 1988a, p. 18 includes the reign of Thutmose III as well.

78 Curto and Mancini 1968, pp. 77–81.

79 Schiaparelli 1903–1927.

80 Steinmann 1984, pp. 30–40.

81 These include an electrum cup, a cubit rod covered in gold foil, and a Book of the Dead papyrus; see Donatelli in Roveri 1988a, fig. 223; Roccati 1988, p. 27;

Roveri 1988a, pp. 18; Schiaparelli 1903–1927, p. 172.
82 Delange in Eggebrecht 1987, p. 348.
83 Roveri 1988a, p. 18.
84 B. Lesko's recent comments on socioeconomic status at Deir el-Medina interpret the status of the workers similarly; see B. Lesko in Lesko 1994 pp. 23–25. Also see Leospo in Roveri 1988a, p. 150.
85 Curto and Mancini 1968, pp. 78–79.
86 Curto and Mancini 1968, p. 79 called her necklace "hard stone," but the reconstruction of the elaborate floral collar from the x-ray information indicates that the beads are probably faience; see Rosati in Roveri 1988a, fig. 321.
87 Schiaparelli 1903–1927.
88 As remarked by Reeves 1990b, p. 149.
89 Curto in Roveri 1988c, fig. 149.
90 Milward in Brovarski et al. 1982a and b, pp. 141–43, nos. 138–39; Porter in D'Auria et al. 1988, pp. 138–39, no. 76.
91 Turin 8481. Such decoration on *heset* and *nemset* jars and ritual vessels of other shapes seems to be atypical. Room 12 in the Cairo Museum contains cases in which most faience vessels, as well as other ritual objects, are decorated with lotus and papyrus elements. Containers from KV 55 and Thutmose IV (KV 46) and the large *ankh*s were also decorated with lotus or papyrus elements. Tutankhamun's faience ritual vessels were undecorated, possibly reflecting the speed of the tomb's preparation or it could point to a change in style.
92 Randall-MacIver and Mace 1902. A basic difficulty with this material is that the Eighteenth Dynasty burials reused Twelfth Dynasty shafts and were in some cases disturbed during the Third Intermediate Period: some mixing of material may have occurred during this reuse or later looting. The author, however, feels that overall the material from these shaft tombs can be readily distinguished; in addition, the excavators seem to have recognized some physical separation between the initial use of the shaft and the secondary ones.
93 The author undertook a detailed study of the early Eighteenth Dynasty material from this cemetery while working at the Carnegie Museum of Natural History in Pittsburgh. The information presented here comes from that work and the author gratefully acknowledges the Carnegie Museum of Natural History's permission to use it. See also Patch 1988 and Patch 1990. Photographs of the Carnegie material were taken by Melinda O. McNaugher.
94 CMNH (Carnegie Museum of Natural History) 1917-58, 60, 64, 69, 74, 191, and 206. D102 also had a bead (CMNH 1917-217) bearing the name of Amenhotep I, a scarab (CMNH 1917-192) inscribed for Thutmose I, and a design amulet (CMNH 1917-201) bearing Princess Neferure's name.
95 And of the few stelae or statues from the small Eighteenth Dynasty burials none was associated with D102 or D116.
96 Although the cemetery zone of Abydos is in the low desert and extremely dry, preservation of wood and basketry is generally poor because of certain insect species that consume organic material.
97 Likewise, these tombs revealed no evidence of any royal gifts such as found in the burials of Kha and Yuya.
98 D116: CMNH 1917-49 and 52, 1917-62. D102: CMNH 1917-148 and 158.
99 D116: CMNH 1917-1, 1917-8 and 10.
100 D102: CMNH 1917-144.
101 A glazed steatite kohl pot with decorations of apotropaic deities and symbols and a lotiform chalice. Nearby tombs of comparable style and contents contained similar faience object types. For example, D111 had a bowl with decoration symbolizing a watery environment and a lotus-form chalice came from D115; both vessels have religious symbolic value.
102 Egyptian blue and glazed steatite are added here because they are closely related materials.
103 The footed jar has a close parallel in alabaster among the cosmetic equipment.
104 These necklaces were strands of multicolored disk beads looped through a leopard-head bead separator with the ends finished in jasmine flower tassels; one had gold foil beads as well (Patch 1990, pp. 50–51; Eaton-Krauss in Brovarski et al. 1982, pp. 240–41, no. 320).
105 See discussion under Tutankhamun's collars.
106 CMNH 1917-201, 217, and 177, respectively.
107 As with Yuya and Thuya's tomb, the record of faience objects in D102 and D116 is probably relatively complete. If numerous faience objects had been among the original tomb furnishings, then at least fragments of these objects should have been recovered. One could argue that Mace would not have collected faience fragments from small tombs like these, only complete pieces, and that this would skew the amount of faience reported in the publication. Still, if faience usage increased as socioeconomic level dropped one would at least expect to find a wide variety of faience object types from tombs throughout the cemetery, even if a full complement of object types made in faience was not collected from a single grave. This is not the case, however: the objects consistently made in faience in these early Eighteenth Dynasty tombs are small vessels, amulets, scarabs, and jewelry. This practice is reinforced by the point that Mace was able to recover gold, silver, and electrum jewelry as well as a variety of objects in bronze and other materials. Given the survival of such a varied group of materials, including objects in precious metals and ivory, faience objects would probably have been recovered if they had been present.
108 Borchardt and Ricke 1980. The author analyzed a number of entries in this publication. Each entry generally describes what appear to be a single domestic unit, although in several cases the entry covers a group of closely related structures. The group studied was not a random sample, but every attempt was made to include a variety of structures. The data from which my conclusions are drawn appear in Table IV.
109 Nos. 21, 25, and 26 in Table IV.
110 In his study, Boyce notes that most faience collar elements come from areas in the settlement related to faience manufacture and occupied by groups of small houses; see Boyce in Kemp 1995, pp. 160–68.
111 The intense bright blue color found on faience has long been popular in the Middle East. Why this blue was a potent protective device in ancient Egypt has often been discussed. For recent treatments, see Vergès 1992, pp. 15–20; Aufrère 1991, pp. 492–505 and 534–37.

NUBIAN FAIENCE

Peter Lacovara

Manufacture of glazed materials in Nubia dates back as early as the A-group Period (around 3100 BC). While faience beads found in prehistoric and A-Group contexts seem to be Egyptian imports, Nubian craftsmen were producing objects of glazed quartz. A blue-glazed quartz lion's head of *c.* 3000 BC (fig. 19) was found in an unusually rich grave at Sayala by archaeologists of the First Archaeological Survey of Nubia,[1] and a similar example was discovered in an A-Group grave by the Joint Scandinavian Expedition during the Third Survey.[2] Although the latter pendant is not reported as having blue glaze, it may well originally have been glazed as this surface coating is very fugitive and can often only be detected with the aid of a lens. Blue-glazed quartz (imported from Nubia) was found also at Hierakonpolis, where other A-Group remains have been discovered. How this Nubian glazed quartz was produced in the absence of a tradition of faience manufacture is unclear. Perhaps imported beads and other faience items were ground to a fine powder which was used to coat the surface of an object and then fired. Faience beads are not as common in A-Group contexts as in later Bronze Age Nubia, and only a few faience vessels of Archaic Egyptian type were discovered at Qustul.[3]

Increased contact with Egypt is evident in the large amount of faience imported into Nubia during the Middle and New Kingdoms. Elaborate beadwork appliqués on leather garments, characteristic of Nubian costume, have been found in C-Group and Early Kerma burials (dating to the second half of the third millennium BC). Designs most often consist of diamond, zigzag, or lozenge motifs, executed in combinations of white, blue, red, and yellow faience beads;[4] similar motifs are found on contemporary Nubian pottery. Beadwork necklaces and diadems are also associated with Bronze Age Nubian burials, along with faience scarabs, seals, and amulets. Although the beadwork is used

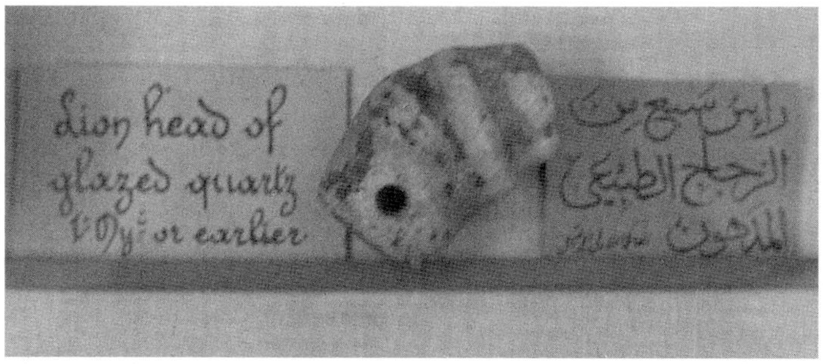

Fig. 19 Blue-glazed quartz lion-head bead. A-Group, *c.* 3000 BC. The Egyptian Museum, Cairo. *Photo courtesy Peter Lacovara.*

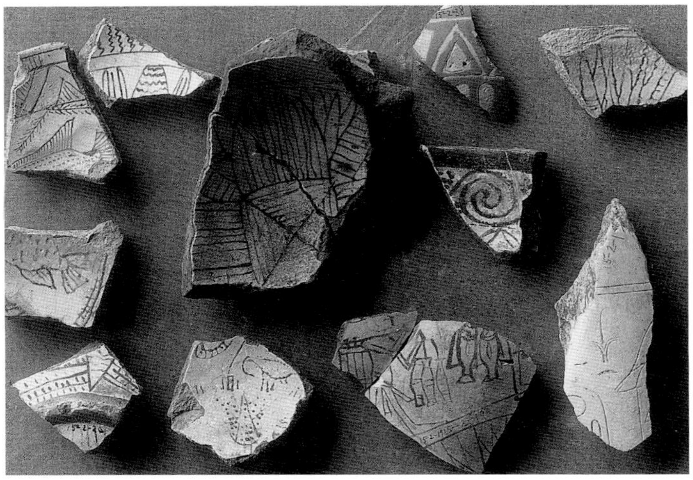

Fig. 20 Imported Egyptian faiences from Kerma. Classic Kerma Period, *c.* 1600 BC. *Photo courtesy Museum of Fine Arts, Boston.*

in uniquely Nubian designs, the faience beads themselves appear either to have been imported from Egypt or possibly came from the Egyptian forts in the Second Cataract region.

A large amount of faience is associated with both the Middle and New Kingdom occupation of these frontier garrisons. Bowls, cups, scarabs, amulets, beads, figurines, and shabtis have been found in both graves and dwellings associated with the fortifications. Whether this material was originally shipped upriver from Egypt or made within the forts remains unknown. Certainly there appears to have been a local pottery industry, so it is possible that faience was also produced there. Unusual features, such as a faience mummy mask from Mirgissa, may point to local innovation.

For most of the Bronze Age, the pre-eminent state in the Nile Valley aside from Egypt was the Kingdom of Kush in the Third Cataract area. In all likelihood this kingdom was centered at the site of Kerma, in the Dongola Reach, which was first excavated by George A. Reisner in 1913–16. He discovered both a vast cemetery site and a large town, and noted an abundance of faience: "I have never seen a site where there was so much broken faience littering the surface as at Kerma. Every traveler has been struck by that fact; for the bright bits of blue against the grey desert catch and hold the eye."[5] The importance of the Kerma kingdom grew as Egyptian control over Lower Nubia weakened in the Late Middle Kingdom and Second Intermediate Period. Its zenith, known as the "Classic Kerma" phase (*c.* 1700–1550 BC), is marked by the construction of the great royal tumuli K IV and K III. This period

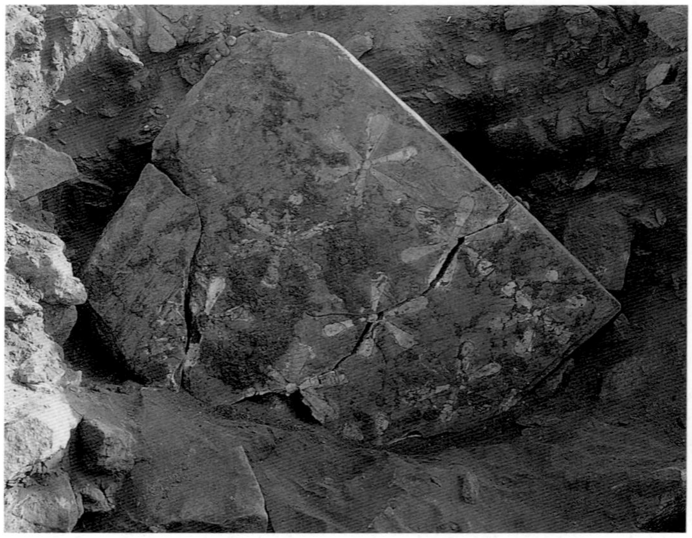

Fig. 21 Roofing slab from Kerma. Classic Kerma Period, *c.* 1600 BC.
Photo courtesy Museum of Fine Arts, Boston.

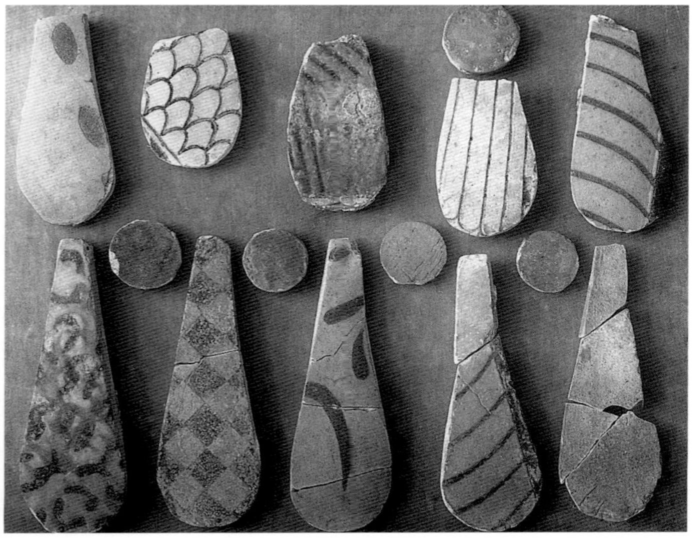

Fig. 22 Cut tiles for roofing slab from Kerma. Classic Kerma Period, *c.* 1600 BC.
Photo courtesy Museum of Fine Arts, Boston.

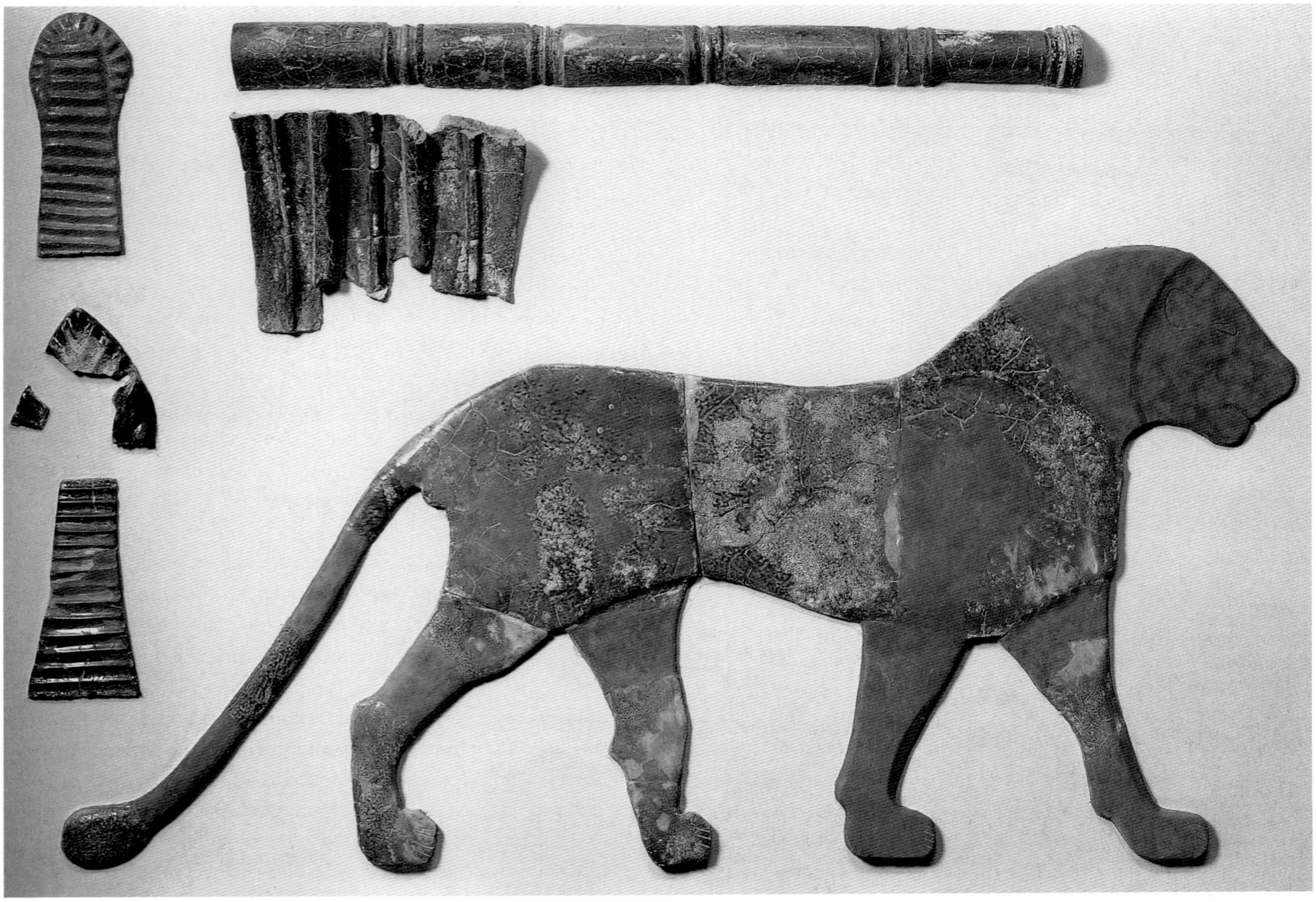

Fig. 23 Faience tile lion and architectural inlays from Kerma.
Classic Kerma Period, *c.* 1600 BC. *Photo courtesy Museum of Fine Arts, Boston.*

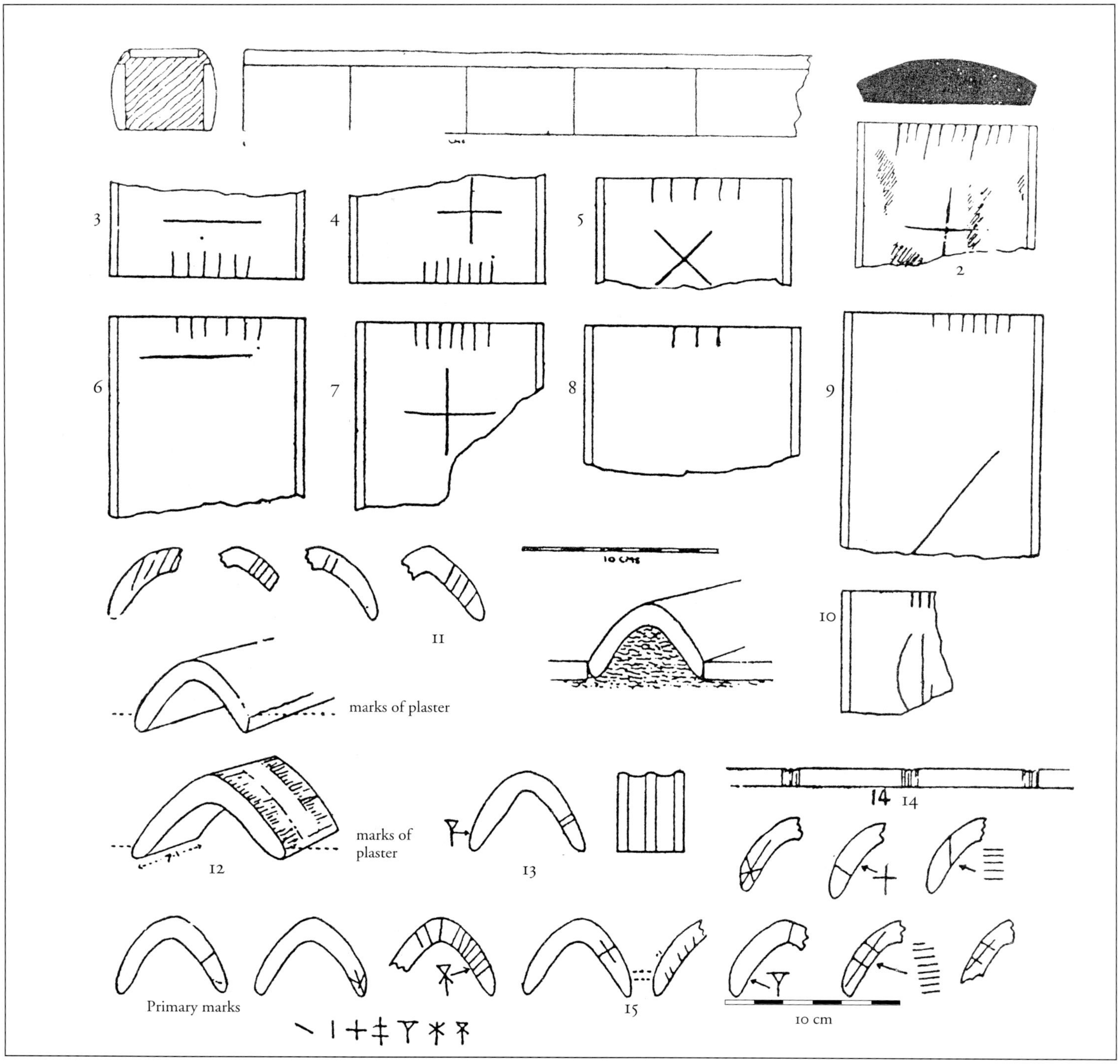

Fig. 24 Faience tiles from Kerma showing sections and markings. Classic Kerma Period, *c.* 1600 BC.
Courtesy Museum of Fine Arts, Boston.

is also characterized by the appearance of the monumental mud-brick funerary chapels, K XI and K II, the Upper, or Eastern, *Defuffa*, associated with the tumuli. A similar massive cult building, K I, the Lower, or Western, *Defuffa*, was located in the center of the town site. It is in these structures that most of the faience was found, the character and origin of which have been matters of great speculation.

Much of the faience from the site derives from broken vessels. As Reisner noted, the pieces are typical of faiences found in Middle Kingdom Egypt (fig. 20), with particularly close parallels to those found at Lisht by the Metropolitan Museum Expedition. Despite this striking similarity to the Egyptian forms, the existence of kilns and other evidence of manufacture, including the presence of wasters, might be taken to suggest local production. However, analysis has shown that the composition of the vessel fragments differs on the whole from the large glazed tiles and larger vessels found at the site that do appear to be of Nubian manufacture.

Such importation of vast quantities of faience fragments, including wasters, is puzzling; but, just as with fragments of Egyptian sculpture found at Kerma, the sherds may have been used as raw materials. This was certainly the case for the ceiling tile from the funerary chapel K XI.[6] Here, a sandstone slab was inlaid with a rosette decoration similar to that found in Egyptian tombs (fig. 21). The petals of the rosettes were formed of fragments of faience vessels ground down, fitted together with dowels, and cemented into place (fig. 22). It is obvious that the craftsmen were working with a mixed bag of raw material, since plain and patterned fragments were often used together. This practice appears just before the end of the "Classic" Kerma Period—a date coincident with the manufacture of the vessels from which the fragments came. As with other materials, the numbers of Egyptian imports seem to decline after this, an indication perhaps of the beginning of hostilities between the Theban, Hyksos, and Kerma kingdoms.

It is also during this period that local production of faience blossoms. Faience tile inlays in the funerary chapel K II are evidence of the emergence of this home-grown industry (figs. 23 and 24):[7] analyses of the tiles have shown a distinctly different composition in their glaze and bodies.[8] Experimentation with applying a vitreous glaze to quartz crystal, milky quartz—including to sculpture (fig. 25)—and even carnelian appears to be a local innovation. However, there is no evidence for glazed quartzite or pottery.

Analysis by Pamela Vandiver and Alex Kaczmarczyk of local and imported faiences shows a small overlap in their compositions. Likely explanations include the grinding down and reuse of Egyptian faiences as raw material for local production, and/or the importation from Egypt of the constituent elements.[9] In this context, it should be noted that a sherd of an imported ceramic jar from Cemetery M has a hieratic inscription that appears to read *sht hm3t*, a name associated with the Wadi Natrun,[10] the main source for the natron in Egyptian faience.

With the Egyptian re-conquest of Nubia in the Eighteenth Dynasty, faience manufacture returns to Egyptian traditions. Material from the New Kingdom forts, fortified towns, and temples is indistinguishable from that of contemporary Egypt. Although the shabtis are typically Egyptian they are of specific individuals resident in Nubia and so were in all likelihood produced locally.[11]

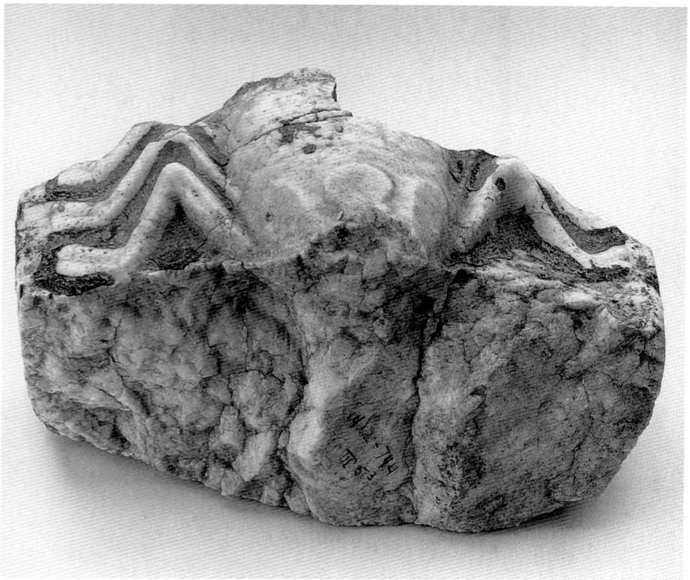

Fig. 25 Glazed milky quartz scorpion from Kerma. Classic Kerma Period, *c.* 1600 BC. *Photo courtesy Museum of Fine Arts, Boston.*

With the end of Pharaonic control of Nubia in the Third Intermediate Period local faience production re-emerges, although many imported Egyptian vessels also turn up at sites such as Gebel Barkal and the surrounding cemeteries at el-Kurru and Nuri. Royal shabtis, the most obvious instances of native manufacture, have been found at the site of Sanam,[12] suggesting they may have been made throughout the kingdom. Large inlay compositions may also have been produced locally, as well as a series of elaborate faience pectorals. Other faience ornaments, including splendid sets of horse trappings and a number of *menat* necklaces, are also indigenous, as are inscribed foundation deposit plaques and cups. On the other hand, the mummy bead nets found in a number of Napatan Period burials throughout Nubia are very similar to contemporary Egyptian examples and may be imports. A yellow faience cosmetic spoon in the form of a swimming girl probably derives from Egyptian prototypes, but has proportions and a hairstyle characteristic of later Kushite art.[13]

While faience is found later, in Meroitic cemeteries, it is often very rough and low-fired. The growing importance of the glass industry, particularly at Meroë, seems eventually to eclipse the long faience tradition in Nubia.

1 Firth 1927, p. 38, pl. 18.
2 Nordström 1972, p. 124.
3 Williams 1986, p. 128, pls. 60–61.
4 Cf. Säve-Söderbergh 1989, pp. 81–83, 131; Junker 1925, pp. 19–20, pl. 3
5 Reisner 1923b, p. 134.
6 Reisner 1923a, pp. 266–67.
7 Reisner 1923b, pp. 147–53.
8 Vandiver et al. forthcoming.
9 Vandiver et al. forthcoming.
10 Dunham 1982, p. 69.
11 O'Connor 1993, pp. 140–41.
12 Haynes and Leprohon 1987.
13 Wenig 1978, p. 177.

MATERIALS AND TECHNOLOGY

Paul T. Nicholson

Faience was widely used in ancient times and is probably familiar to many visitors to museum collections of Egyptian antiquities today. Despite this, few people have a clear idea of what faience is or how it was made. Our subject here is more correctly called "Egyptian faience," to differentiate it from a type of pottery, formerly known as faience but now called majolica, that was made in Faenza in Italy, and elsewhere, from late medieval times.[1] The richly colored glazes of this pottery, often blue in colour, seemed closely related to the frequently blue, vitreous material discovered by (or sold to) European visitors to ancient Egyptian sites.

Composition

First and foremost, faience is a glazed non-clay ceramic material. Vandiver and Kingery[2] have described it as "the first high-tech ceramic" to emphasize its status as an artificial medium. It is composed mainly of crushed quartz or sand, with small amounts of lime and either natron or plant ash. This body is coated with a soda-lime-silica glaze that is generally a bright blue-green color due to the presence of copper.[3] A similar high silica composition was described in AD 1301 by Abu'l-Qasim,[4] and its use in Iran in the 1960s[5] is testimony to its longevity.

To understand the material more fully, we will examine the raw materials at the human level, since the ancient craftsmen who worked with them were not chemists, at least in our sense of the term, but skilled artisans who knew how to transform one group of materials into another. Although we know very little about faience making in ancient Egypt, we do know that many crafts in which matter is transformed from one state to another carry an air of mystery and ritual; for example, the making of iron in parts of Africa is strongly associated with sexuality and birth, and both ancient and modern texts show that glass making and working were also surrounded by ritual.[6]

The basic raw material of faience is silica (SiO_2), which, as Vandiver[7] notes, can comprise up to 99% of the body. Egypt is rich in readily accessible silica—the sand of the desert—but it is likely that some sources were considered superior to others. Sand is rarely pure silica: it is generally mixed with numerous impurities such as chalk, limestone, or iron. Some of these, for instance iron, are not beneficial to faience production and can discolor the glaze.

There is some evidence to suggest that a high-grade form of silica was produced by crushing quartz pebbles (see below) which would be largely free of impurities, resulting in a clean, dazzling white body material. It is believed that faience, particularly in the earliest times, served as a substitute for the semiprecious stones used in jewelry, so that the ability of fine quartz to reflect light through the glaze, reproducing the brilliant effect of such stones, would be highly regarded. Indeed, faience frequently has two distinct body layers: a coarse, often discolored core covered by a brilliant white layer over which the glaze was applied (fig. 26). This may well argue for the more limited availability (or more laborious production) of the finer material.

Evidence for the crushing of quartz pebbles comes from the 1891–92 excavations at Amarna by Sir Flinders Petrie. Among the debris from faience/glass factories Petrie discovered quartz pebbles, some cracked and with drips of glaze, that he assumed had originally formed a furnace floor[8] ([173–75], p. 166). He noted that repeated heating and cooling of the pebbles, some of which are now in the Petrie Museum,[9] would lead to cracking, enabling them to be more easily crushed as a high-quality source of silica.

Lime, or calcium oxide (CaO), forms between 1 and 5% of the composition of faience. It is found naturally in limestone or chalk, but it is not known whether the Egyptians exploited this for the lime for their faience, or whether it was added inadvertently as an impurity in the sand.[10] Between 0.3 and 5% of the faience body consists of alkali, primarily soda (Na_2O), for which there are two main sources. The better known is natron, a naturally occurring mixture of sodium carbonate and sodium bicarbonate with sodium chloride and sodium sulphate, found most famously in Egypt's Wadi Natrun. Less well known, but similarly effective, is the ash of certain salt-loving (halophytic) plants, particularly those of the *salicornia* family. The source of the alkali can be determined chemically by examining the quantity of magnesia: high magnesia indicates a plant ash source. Other components of faience occur only in small amounts and are added either accidentally as impurities or deliberately to impart color to the glaze.

What then, are the functions of the three main ingredients? Silica, the bulk of the body, is the material from which the object

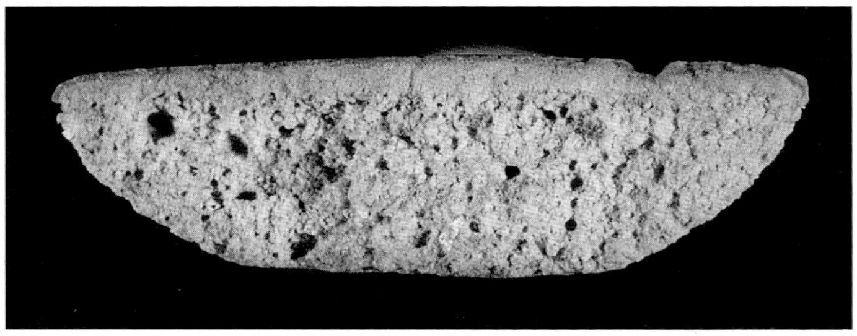

Fig. 26 Section through a faience inlay. A layer of fine white quartz lies directly below the glaze (top) while the rest is coarser body material. Length 19 mm (¾ in). *Photo Gwil Own, courtesy of the Egypt Exploration Society, Amarna object No. 8430.*

shape is formed and is also the source of its optical properties. Depending on the brilliance of the quartz body, and whether a layer of more finely ground quartz has been applied, the material will scatter light in different ways. Unlike potter's clay, silica/sand is not easy to form unless it has been very finely ground, and though the addition of water helps shaping, the finished object will crumble if the particle size is too great. The addition of lime and soda help to cement the quartz grains together in drying, thus lending the object greater mechanical strength than it might otherwise have.

Faience is closely related to soda-lime-silicate glasses, which share the same three major ingredients, though in different proportions. In a glass the silica comprises most of the mixture and is known as the "network former" while the sodium and calcium act as fluxes ("network modifiers"). These latter ingredients help to reduce the melting temperature of the silica and combine with it to make a non-crystalline material. In faience, the proportions of the ingredients are different, and the higher proportion of silica, probably combined with a lower firing temperature and shorter firing duration, produce a crystalline material.[11] However, the network modifiers are generally sufficient to develop some degree of interstitial glass (see below, n. 28), which fuses the mass together.

Shaping technology

Under the microscope it can be seen that, unlike faience, the microstructure of clay is one of small platelets which, once wetted, readily slide over one another allowing the material to be easily shaped. As the clay dries out, water is lost by evaporation, and with it the plastic properties of the clay. This process is exploited in pottery making: the plastic form dries, shrinking as it does so, until it is quite rigid. It could easily be returned to the plastic state by the addition of further water, but if the potter is satisfied the piece is put into the kiln and fired. At temperatures of around 600°C the edges of the clay platelets begin to fuse in a process known as sintering; once cooled the addition of water will no longer render the clay plastic:[12] it has changed in state from clay to ceramic.

Silica behaves in a different way. The particles are angular and do not slide readily over one another even when wetted. Instead, the typical faience mixture is *thixotropic*: behaving as a solid at first and then becoming soft and flowing as it begins to be shaped. However, if shaping is too rapid the material cracks or splits, so that its working properties are much less attractive than those of potting clay. This disadvantage makes faience's long and continued use in Egypt alongside clay ceramics all the more intriguing.

The difficulties of shaping the faience material and handling it for insertion into the kiln should be borne in mind. However, recent experiments by Mimi Leveque and others have shown that, if very finely ground, the faience paste adheres well and only the most coarse bodies are potentially friable. A number of agents have been suggested as possibly assisting in the binding process, notably gum-Arabic, clay, and lime.[13] Both Lucas and Noble[14] failed to find traces of clay in most pharaonic faience, while gum proved too sticky for the removal of objects from their molds.[15] Leveque, however, has found a small amount of gum-Arabic to give good results, and this draws attention to the need for new studies of faience and highlights the shortcomings of the earlier work. Lucas, for example, assumed that the faience was fired and then glazed, rather than both processes being a single operation, which seems, in fact, to have been the case.[16] Also, although he found that 5 to 10% of natron gave the best results, he had to account for the lower percentages found in the analyses by loss and chemical combination in firing.

The methods used to shape faience varied over time (Table V), but can be grouped into two broad categories: *modeling*, shaping the object by hand, and *molding*, using a mold, form, or template to provide the shape. In both cases, details can be added by subsequent carving with a variety of tools. Faience does not reach a "leather-hard" stage as clay does, rather it attains an optimal degree of dampness when the paste is perfect for modeling or tooling. As it dries, the surface can be rewetted to allow further work. Carving or abrading dry faience is possible, but the material easily cracks and chips, requiring great skill on the part of the craftsman. Where the salt efflorescence is disturbed by carving, the reworked areas will have less glaze unless it is added either by direct application or by cementation (see glazing methods below).

Peltenburg[17] regards faience making as an essentially cold technology, more akin to stone working than to glass making, which he relates to metallurgy. Although not a clear distinction, it does draw attention to the fact that the faience body shape is formed cold, unlike shapes in glass. Since Predynastic times the Egyptians had been carving and glazing soft stones such as steatite (which changes to the harder enstatite in firing) as well as quartz. But while there are certainly parallels between the abrasion of stone and the abrasion of a siliceous aggregate, it seems that the situation is more complicated and that there is a link with "hot technology" as well as cold. In the New Kingdom, glass and faience production seem to be going on in the same workshops, suggesting that the Egyptians viewed the two materials as closely related, although this might have as much to do with their raw materials as with the application of heat. It has even been suggested that glass was added to certain faience objects[18] (see below), although Shortland (pers. comm.) suggests that such glass as is found results from the interaction of the raw materials, and not due to its addition.

Molding is a sophisticated technique which can allow complex shapes to be made without extensive secondary working, although faience does not take as crisp an impression as clay would. Most of the faience molds discovered in Egypt are single-sided, made of porous clay, but there is also evidence for multiple-part molds. Unlike clay ceramics, complex faience objects can successfully be constructed dry and joined with a slurry of faience paste. This allows the molded parts to be assembled when they are stiff enough to handle without breaking. The molds were made by impressing a model of the object into wet clay to give a negative of the required item. Any solid material could be used for the model, e.g., clay, wax, or wood, or a completely finished object in another material of which a faience copy is desired. Rings originally made in metal can be copied in faience in this way. A finished faience object can also be used to produce the mold for others.[19] The clay mold was fired to make it durable, then the faience paste was pressed into it and quickly removed for drying or re-working before firing.

TABLE V METHODS OF FAIENCE MANUFACTURE OVER TIME (Modified from Vandiver 1982, p. 172.)

Period	Body Manufacture	Glazing Process	Factory Evidence
Predynastic (5500–2920 BC)	Modeling a core for grinding Surface grinding Free-form modeling (rare)	Application (?) Cementation (?) Efflorescence (?)	None
Early Dynastic (2920–2649 BC)	Modeling Surface grinding	Efflorescence	None
Old Kingdom (2649–2134 BC)	Painting with slurry Layering (rare)		
First Intermediate (2134–2040 BC)	Core forming (rare) Marbleizing (rare) Molding (?)		Abydos
Middle Kingdom (2040–1640 BC)	Modeling Molding on a form	Efflorescence Cementation	Lisht Kerma
Second Intermediate (1640–1532 BC)	Core forming Marbleizing Layering Painting with colored quartz slurry Incising Inlaying Resisting Painting with pigment wash	Application	
New Kingdom (1570–1070 BC)	Molding on a form Pressing into openface molds Forming over a core Joining of molded parts with quartz slurry Layering Incising Inlaying with quartz slurry Painting with pigment wash Throwing (?)	Efflorescence Application Finely powdered glass, added to body or inlay to extend color range (?)	Amarna Lisht
Late Period (1070 BC–AD 395)	All New Kingdom techniques, plus throwing	Application Efflorescence	Memphis Naukratis

Molds could be reused to produce large numbers of the same artifact, and in this way mold technology facilitated mass production of such faience objects as amulets, rings, and inlays. Objects can provide evidence for the use of techniques of mass production that are common in pottery manufacture, such as forms over which open bowls were shaped or the use of templates which allowed rapid outlining.

One further technique is throwing on a wheel. This was certainly established by the Graeco-Roman Period, when large amounts of clay seem to have been added to the faience body, and may have developed as early as the New Kingdom, though evidence for this is as yet equivocal. The result of this technology was the production of vessels more closely akin to those produced by potters, and presumably an increase in the rate of production.

Glazing methods

Vandiver[20] divided the various faience glazing techniques into three broad categories: efflorescence, cementation, and application (fig. 27). Recognizing the different techniques is not easy, and their characteristic features can overlap; they may also be used in combination with one another.

Efflorescence is a so-called self-glazing method[21] in which the glazing materials, in the form of soluble salts, are mixed with the raw crushed quartz and alkalis of the body. As the water in the body evaporates, the salts migrate to the surface to form a kind of scum.[22] The precipitated salts comprise sodium and to a lesser degree potassium carbonates, sulphates, and chlorides from the natron or plant ash.[23] In firing this precipitated layer melts and fuses to become a glaze, the thickness of which varies according to

Fig. 27 Three methods of faience glazing. Each can be used alone or in combination. (After Vandiver 1983, p. A145.)

A. EFFLORESCENCE OF GLAZE
Effloresced salts form glaze on surface during firing

Glaze thickness depends on:
a. concentration of salts in paste
b. drying rate (dependent on ambient climate, coarseness of particles, and their capillary forces)
c. firing temperature
d. length of firing

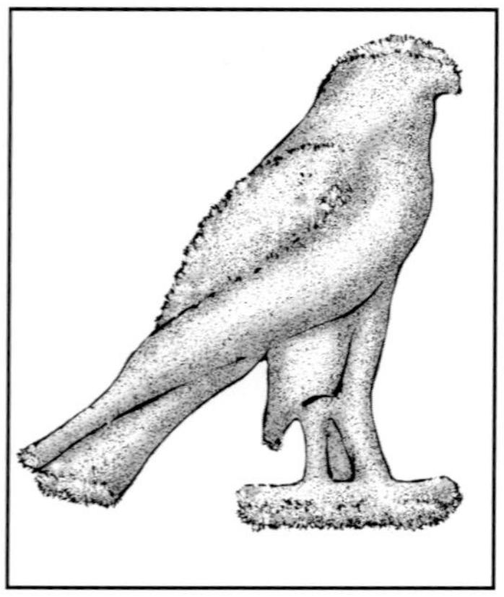

drying body with efflorescing salts

B. CEMENTATION OF GLAZE
Glaze forms directly on surface from contact with glazing powder during firing

Glaze thickness depends on:
a. coarseness of particles
b. firing temperature
c. length of firing
d. concentration of salts in glazing powder

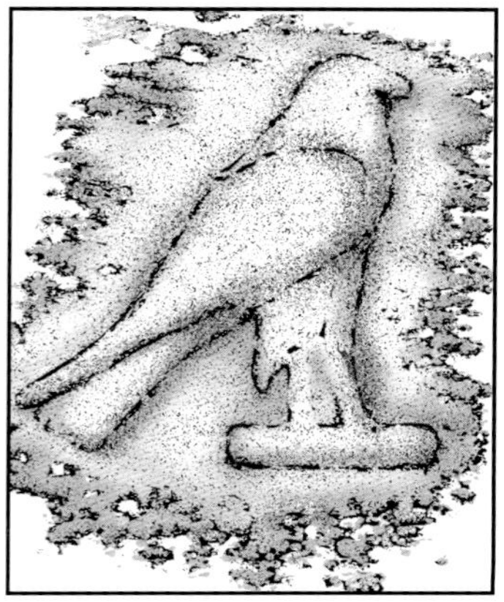

quartz body covered with glazing powder

C. APPLICATION OF GLAZE
Applied glaze slurry forms glaze during firing

Glaze thickness depends on:
a. body porosity
b. water concentration of slurry
c. number of layers applied
d. firing temperature
e. length of firing

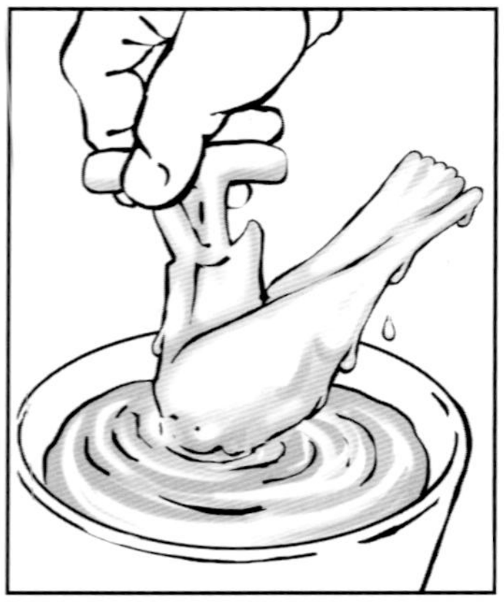

dipping object into glaze

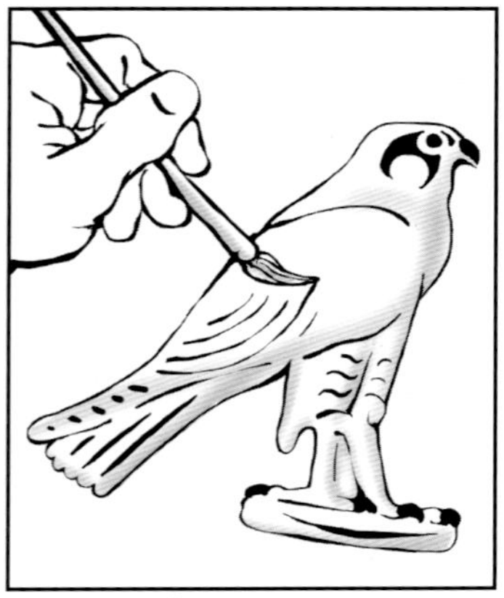

painting object with glaze

the amount of efflorescence that developed during drying. Rapid drying produces the greatest thickness of deposited surface salts, and thus the thickest glaze.[24] Artifacts glazed by efflorescence may show traces of stand marks, where the piece was set down to dry, cracking, and a glaze that is thinnest toward the edges and in concave areas. Glaze does not form where evaporation was impossible, such as the underside of a piece in contact with the drying surface. During firing the piece is usually put on some kind of support, and this frequently leaves some trace in the glaze. However, Vandiver[25] notes that an object placed on a non-wetting support may be free of firing marks, and thus confusion with the cementation glazing method is possible.

A broken section across a faience object glazed by efflorescence generally shows a narrow, well-defined interface between the glaze and the underlying body. This is because where drying has been rapid the greatest concentration of salts has built up on the surface, and when fired at fairly low temperatures the glaze sinters[26] without soaking into the body. However, where overfiring occurs the glaze becomes less viscous and so soaks into the surface of the object. The same effect is achieved by adding more flux[27] to the ingredients.

Examination under the scanning electron microscope (SEM) of pieces glazed by efflorescence shows extensive interstitial[28] glass in the body, resulting from the presence of the alkali salts. Salts that do not reach the surface fuse in the body and have the effect of hardening it further (fig. 28).

A second self-glazing technique is that known as *cementation* or, sometimes, the "Qom technique," so named from its discovery in use at the village of Qom in Iran in the 1960s.[29] In this method an artifact is buried in a vessel containing glazing powder with a high flux content which, on firing, becomes fused to the surface of the object by a chemical reaction. However, the exact nature of this process is not fully understood.[30]

Cementation produces a glaze that is characteristically even all over, since the object was completely surrounded by the glazing powder and no drying marks occur. Small objects glazed in this way[31] do not usually have firing marks, though larger pieces may. The glaze is sometimes thicker on the underside of the object, simply because of gravity. In broken section the interface between glaze and body is thick and well defined, but SEM examination shows little interstitial glass, since the glaze has had to penetrate the body from the outside, rather than growing from the inside as in efflorescence (fig. 29). This technique seems not to have been used before the Middle Kingdom.

The third method is that of *application.* This technique was formerly assumed to be the only one used for glazing faience[32]—

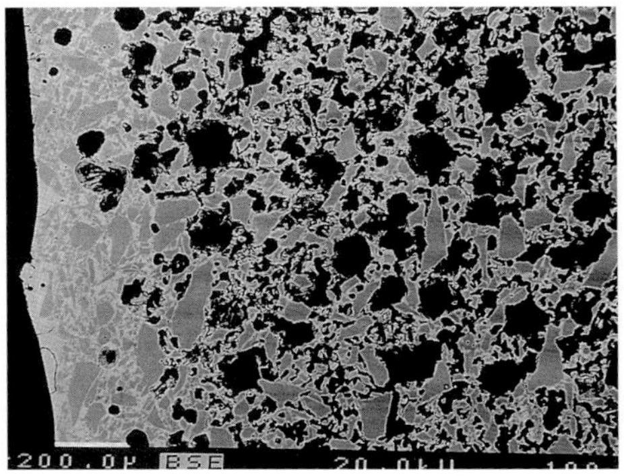

Fig. 28 Scanning electron microscope photograph of a section through faience glazed by efflorescence; a Dynasty 18 vessel (UC.30153). Glaze and interstitial glass show as pale gray, quartz as dark gray, and voids as black. *Courtesy Petrie Museum of Egyptian Archaeology, University College London and Prof. M.S. Tite.*

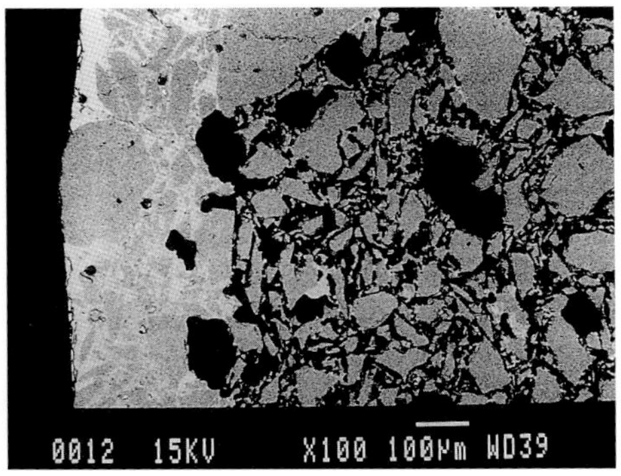

Fig. 29 Scanning electron microscope photograph of a section through faience glazed by cementation; a Dynasty 21 shabti (BRML 16323). Glaze shows as white, quartz as dark gray, and voids as black. *Courtesy the Trustees of the British Museum and Prof. M.S. Tite.*

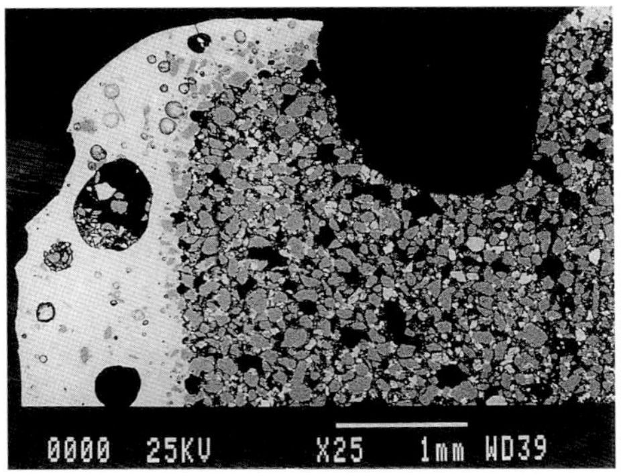

Fig. 30 Scanning electron microscope photograph of a section through faience glazed by application; a Late Period shabti (BRML 16322). Glaze shows as white, quartz as dark gray, and voids as black. *Courtesy the Trustees of the British Museum and Prof. M.S. Tite.*

an erroneous if understandable view, given knowledge of pottery glazing processes,[33] and one that must be borne in mind when consulting early accounts of faience technology or descriptions of faience objects.[34] In this method the glazing materials, comprising silica, lime, and alkali, are ground to a small particle size and mixed with water to form a slurry that is applied to the unfired quartz core. They may be ground together in their raw state, or be partially fritted and then ground, as in the making of a pottery glaze. The object can be dipped into the slurry or the slurry can be poured over the object. Brushing is also a possibility, although Vandiver[35] found traces of it only on polychrome faience of the New Kingdom. When glazing pottery it is common to fire the clay body and then apply the glaze before a second firing, but for faience a primary firing has been found unnecessary, and firing temperatures tend to be low enough to prevent the glaze becoming too liquid.

Applied glazes characteristically vary in thickness and may preserve traces of kiln supports. The glaze covers the object entirely, unless intentionally limited, and drips and flow lines may be visible. The interface of body and glaze in this method is not well defined, and since there may be little interstitial glass the body itself may be quite soft (fig. 30).

As with many technological processes, we should remember that craftsmen do not necessarily work to hard and fast formulae, and we should not be surprised to find a combination of techniques in a single piece. For example, Vandiver and Kingery[36] report that a faience chalice of the New Kingdom was formed from a body that produced an effloresced glaze. However, carving the relief decoration into the surface inevitably cut through some of the effloresced salts. The chalice then had only partial glazing, and in order to correct this, the finished piece was coated in a slurry of the body material. In other words, a new layer of efflorescent material was added to the piece, essentially applying a glaze to an effloresced piece.

Glaze composition can be quite variable.[37] This may be related to changes in the formation of the body and variations in glazing method arising regionally and/or chronologically, and according to the status of the workshop. Those workshops enjoying royal patronage presumably had better access to the best raw materials and, more importantly, greater freedom to experiment, while smaller local concerns may have tended toward conservatism.[38]

Decoration

Although faience is itself decorative in character, it was commonly enhanced by some additional means. Perhaps the commonest form of decoration is the application of details in a black manganese, or iron oxide, paint. This is applied before firing and once fired is permanent. It was used to add facial and other details to shabtis, and to paint designs onto faience bowls.

More complicated designs might be executed in color, not by painting but by inlaying. Shaped faience "tiles" were commonly used as inlays themselves, but it was also possible to inlay one color of faience paste into another to make a compound tile or object. This technique reached its height in the New Kingdom when the color palette expanded and craft technology developed. The inlaying of faience paste seems to take two forms. In the first, the body material is prepared and then has a channel incised into it to receive paste of another color. The body is allowed to dry slightly before the new paste is applied and as a consequence it is common to find a slight crack around the inlay. This may be deliberate policy by the craftsman to enhance the outline of the inlay. The efflorescence technique is used for such inlays.

In the second method the inlay seems to have been added earlier, before significant drying took place. The effect produced is much more akin to painting—indeed the inlays may have taken the form of slurry—and there is no void around the different colors. In firing the glaze merges so there can be a blurring of the color boundaries. This can be used to good effect in vegetation, and some of the tiles produced in the Amarna Period depicting natural scenes are of a high quality. The fact that the two techniques were in use at the same time suggests that they had different purposes.

A related technique is the making of small faience objects, such as daisies of one or two colors, and inserting them into a background, such as a green tile. Daisy tiles are commonly found with many of the daisies missing, suggesting that they were usually added after firing using gypsum or similar cement. These too are characteristic of the New Kingdom, especially the Amarna Period.

Related materials

Glassy faience[39] has long been recognized as a misnomer,[40] as it is a kind of imperfect glass and has no distinct glaze layer, being instead homogeneous throughout. The material is usually an apple-green or pale turquoise blue color with a matte surface, though glossy examples are known. It is frequently marked with brown spots that may have been deliberately produced. Lucas[41] noted that experimental work showed it to be especially well suited to sculpting, since before firing it has "something of the plasticity of clay," unlike glass which cannot easily be worked cold. The material was originally thought to have been an invention of the Twenty-Sixth Dynasty, but by the 1960s it was known from contexts as early as the Twenty-Second Dynasty, when it seems to have served some of the functions of glass, which was rare at this time. Most recently it has been identified from the Middle Kingdom at Lisht.[42] It has also occasionally been reported for vessels of the Ptolemaic Period. It is mostly used for detailed, decorative pieces. Glassy faience should not be confused with the material recently described as vitreous faience.[43]

Egyptian blue frit is another related material that is sometimes confused with faience. It is the product of a solid-state reaction similar to that used in the first stages of Egyptian glass making. Recent work[44] has divided frit into two groups: blue frits, in which the main crystalline phase is a calcium-copper tetrasilicate known as "Egyptian blue" ($CaO.CuO.4SiO_2$) in a very limited matrix of glass; and turquoise blue frits in which the dominant phase, other than quartz, is a calcium silicate known as wollastonite ($CaSiO_3$). There are coarse and fine variants of the two depending on their stage of production—the coarse usually representing incompletely prepared material. The finer material was regularly used as a pigment as well as for making objects. Its texture may be so fine that it is virtually indistinguishable from glass, especially if the latter is weathered. Despite the possible confusion with glass, the frits are easily distinguished from faience in a broken section by their lack of a core—they are homogeneous throughout and have no separate glaze layer.

The Greeks referred to the material as *kyanos*,[45] while Vitruvius refers to it as *caeruleum*[46] and reports that it was invented at Alexandria, though in fact it is of much greater antiquity and is known as early as the Fourth Dynasty.

Firing

Recent experiments attempting to replicate ancient faience production have brought about a greater understanding of firing techniques.[47] Studies have shown that faience is fired in the range of 800–1000°C. Modern electric kilns and replica faience pastes were used, however, and although the firing temperatures recorded are unlikely to be significantly different from ancient ones, experiments using replica kilns are needed to assess the role of kiln atmosphere in firing and also to explore the difficulties likely to arise in firing this material by traditional means.

Until recently very few kilns were known archaeologically. However, excavations at Abydos and Amarna have now supplemented the picture gained from earlier excavations at Lisht, Memphis, and Naukratis (see below). These new discoveries also help in the difficult question of fuel. Charcoal fragments were found in the recent work at Abydos and Amarna, although the structures with which the fuel is associated at Amarna are more likely to be for glass production. The Amarna charcoal has recently been shown to be from sycamore fig (*Ficus sycamorus*).[48] It is not known whether it was produced deliberately, or was simply the byproduct of incomplete combustion of wood used as fuel, but its condition suggests the latter.[49]

Whether or not charcoal was produced deliberately, it is likely that a certain amount of wood and domestic rubbish was burned in the kilns; certainly animal bone fragments are found in the ash at Amarna. This is a likely recourse in a country as deficient in timber as Egypt, and considerable pains were probably taken to economize on fuel. Petrie[50] states that Graeco-Roman kilns at Memphis burnt straw as fuel. However, although straw may have been a component, it burns quickly and it seems unlikely to have been the main source as huge quantities would be needed for a long firing. Dung is another possible fuel, perhaps in combination with wood, but once again experimental work is necessary.

The objects to be glazed would have to be protected from the smoke and ash particles of the fire in some way. In efflorescence and application glazing the pieces probably stood in deep trays or saggars, possibly with lids. In cementation glazing they would be buried in glazing powder, itself contained in some kind of vessel. To prevent an all-over glazed object from adhering to its saggar, to the kiln, or to neighbouring objects it would have been necessary to rest it on some kind of support. This could have taken the form of small cones or bars of clay, possibly rich in alumina to help prevent sticking. Numerous small marl clay balls discovered at Lisht may have served this purpose, perhaps covering the bottom of a tray, much as modern potters use alumina powder to prevent pots sticking to kiln shelves. A number of marl clay hemispheres were also found at Lisht ([172], p. 166).

Textual and documentary evidence

The Egyptians referred to faience as *tjehnet*, a word related to those for "shining" or "gleaming," emphasizing the position of faience as an artificial semiprecious stone. This does not necessarily mean that it was inferior to lapis lazuli or turquoise, although the term "genuine lapis" is sometimes used.

Excavations at Lisht (see below) revealed the burial of one Debeni, overseer of faience workers. Other funerary texts also relate to such individuals, for instance the Nineteenth Dynasty funerary papyrus of Qn-hr[51] (also called "Qennou") which refers to him as the *ỉmy-r irw hsbd*, the director or overseer of faience makers. Note that this title includes the word *hsbd*, which strictly means lapis lazuli, but which by the New Kingdom had come to refer to faience also.[52] Rather confusingly, the word can also refer

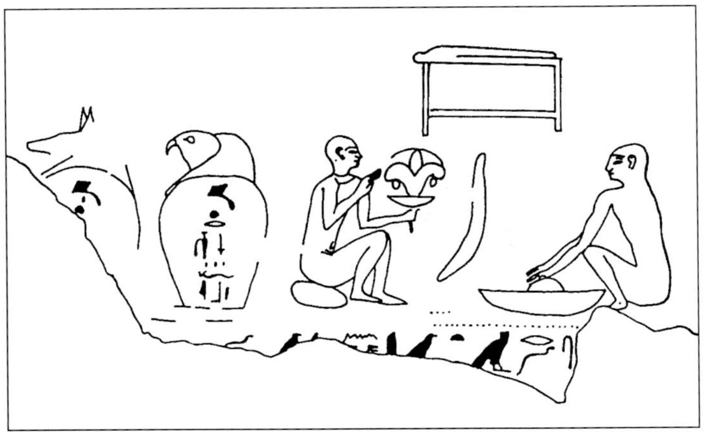

Fig. 31 A scene from the tomb of Ibi (Aba), chief steward of the divine adoratress in the time of Psametik I (664–610 BC) at Thebes (TT 36). It may show a workman (right) mixing faience ingredients while another (left) finishes a more complete piece. (After Davies 1902, pl. 25.)

to glass; here we surely see the Egyptians thinking of these materials in terms of their brilliance, like semiprecious stones, rather than their actual composition. In the Royal Museum of Scotland are two Nineteenth Dynasty faience stelae, one of which ([166], p. 156) belonged to Rekhamun,[53] who held the title "faience maker of Amun," again with the *hsbd* element.[54] This title is not common, though it is less rare than sometimes thought.

There are many scenes in Egyptian painting and reliefs of potters at work that can be used to flesh out archaeological and scientific analysis, but only one scene may, possibly, show faience makers.[55] This comes from the tomb of Ibi (Aba) chief steward of the divine adoratress in the time of Psametik I (Twenty-Sixth Dynasty) at Thebes (TT 36)[56] and shows one man apparently grinding or rolling something while another seems to be making a jewelry element (fig. 31). Since there is no identifying text, however, it is not possible to be sure exactly what is represented.

Technology through time

Predynastic and Early Dynastic

The Predynastic Period was a time of experimentation. From *c.* 5000 BC stones were glazed using the application method, and the glazing of crushed quartz (i.e. faience) as an artificial medium presumably developed from this. Forming a core and shaping it by abrasion has much in common with the making of stone artifacts. Neither metal nor glass technology had been developed during the Predynastic Period and the advantages of shaping a fairly complex piece from plastic materials and working it to final shape rather than carving it from stone must have been greatly appreciated. Further, the glaze applied to solid stone, particularly steatite, is often less bright than that on faience, and the granular surface of the crushed quartz lends an added brilliance to the pieces.

It is still not clear which glazing techniques were in use at this time, though application glazing is particularly likely. It is possible that efflorescence and even cementation were also practiced,[57] although there is no firm evidence for the latter before the Middle Kingdom. The objects made were small on the whole—mainly beads and amulets. As might be expected at such an early stage, the material is by no means standardized, and examination of faience from the Naqada cemetery has shown that composition of pieces varied even within the same grave.[58] With the Early Dynastic Period, the size of faience objects increased somewhat, although beads and amulets were still the most common products. Small figurines, some showing considerable detail, were produced.

Old Kingdom and First Intermediate Period

The Old Kingdom is the period for which we have our earliest factory evidence. This comes from excavations at Abydos by the joint University of Pennsylvania Museum-Yale University-Institute of Fine Arts, New York University expedition under Dr. Matthew Adams. Near the modern village, not far from the Archaic Period Khentiamentiu temple, part of a settlement dating back to at least the mid-Old Kingdom (and extending into the early Middle Kingdom)[59] has been unearthed. Apparent factory remains consist of several very clear circular features, thought to be the remains of kilns. Some have a lining made from broken bricks and sherds of pottery, and all are fire-reddened. There is no sign of any superstructure. Lenses of ash and re-linings suggest that some of these features were used several times[60] (figs. 32 and 33).

If there were indeed no superstructures, then these features are perhaps to be regarded as shallow pits beneath what were, in effect, bonfires. This "open-firing" technique is well known from ethnographic studies of pottery manufacture, but would need certain refinements for the firing of faience. For example, faience amulets and beads found at Abydos would have had to have been placed inside something to protect them from the ash and fuel piled around them. Some kind of lidded vessel would be the most obvious solution, and the excavators suggest that domestic pottery jars may have been used for this purpose since many hundreds of fragments of such jars were found in the area.

Numerous small clay balls (*c.* 0.75 cm (⅓ in) in diameter), yet to be analyzed, were also discovered which may be the precursors of those known from Lisht and perhaps even Amarna. Their function is not clear, though evidence from Lisht and Amarna suggests that they were used as a surface on which beads were fired. A clay disc from Abydos with finger impressions each roughly the size of one of the clay balls is perhaps connected with them. Small balls of white chalky material may be unfired faience material, and a program of analysis is planned to investigate them.

It is clear from both the "kilns" as well as beads and amulets found with evidence of manufacturing mistakes that faience was produced at Abydos, and the results of future excavations may throw much light on manufacturing processes at this time. Questions of how the industry was organized and for whom its products were intended must remain open. It is perhaps significant that the installations for this industry were not connected to any house or workshop structure. Its location on the desert edge may reflect its status as a small-scale industry unconnected with the temple, although it may simply be a consequence of the technology—industries involving smoke are often relegated to such places. However, the presence of such an

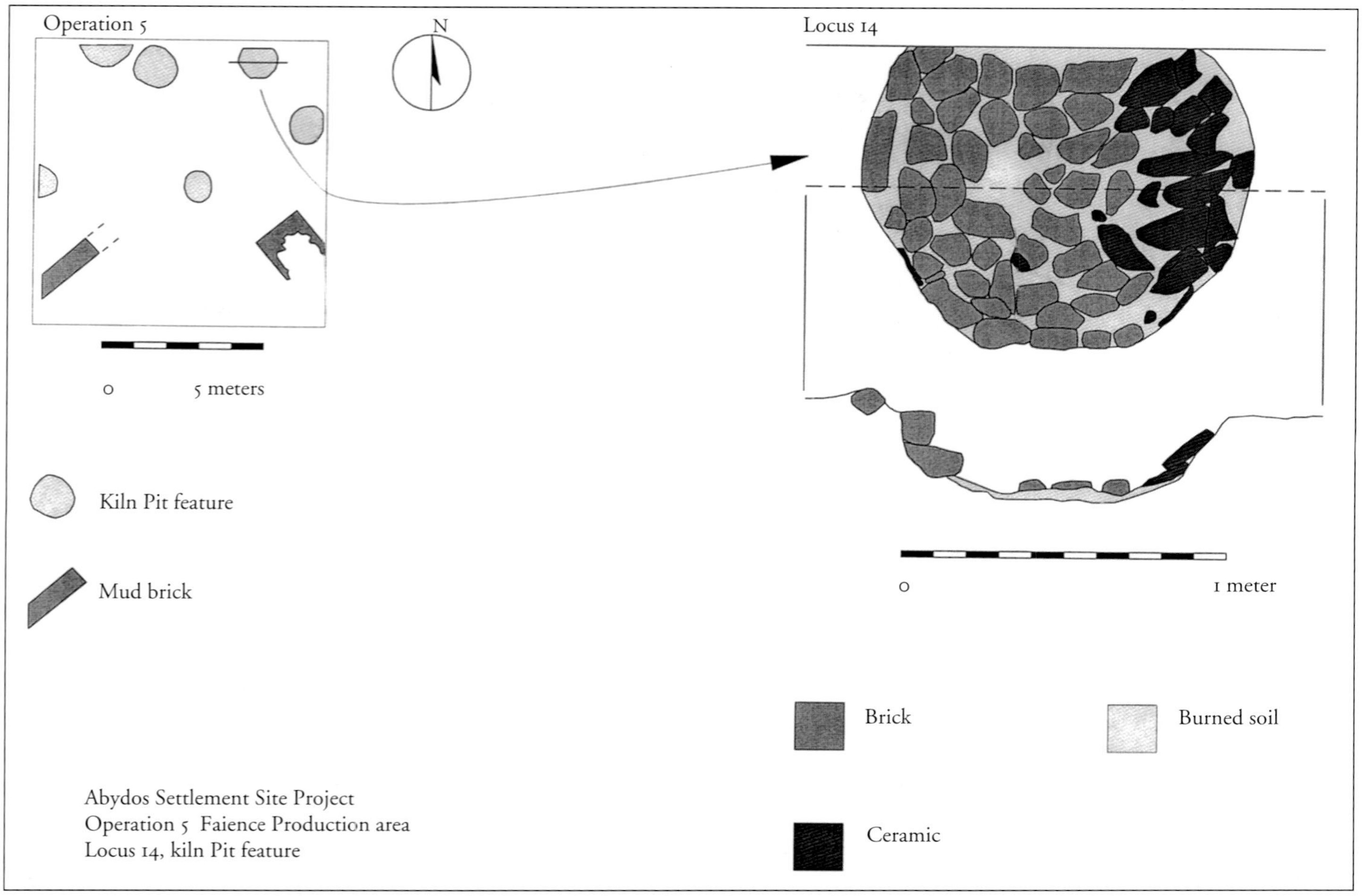

Fig. 32 One of the kiln pits discovered at Locus 14 of the Abydos excavation by the Joint University of Pennsylvania Museum-Yale University-Institute of Fine Arts, New York University. *Copyright: University of Pennsylvania Museum, reproduced courtesy of Dr. Matthew Adams.*

establishment on a site already of great religious significance might suggest that it was in some way related to cult activities and was perhaps attached to a temple.

For many years scholars regarded Old Kingdom faience production as quite limited in scope and scale, the exception being the mass production of the thousands of tiles used in the Step Pyramid complex of Djoser at Saqqara ([17–20], pp. 66, 72). Lauer[61] regarded these tiles as molded, despite the fact that their width varies considerably. This is not so surprising, however, since approximately 36,000 tiles were required[62] and many molds must have been needed. Vandiver suggests a technique which is perhaps better described as "controlled forming," consisting of rolling the paste between two parallel sticks: this determined the thickness and length of each tile, while the width might vary. The back of each tile is extensively ground to leave a pierced boss through which wires would have been threaded as an aid to mounting the tiles in large panels. There is often very little glaze at the rear of the tiles, which suggests that they were glazed by efflorescence.

However, Djoser's tiles are no longer seen as the peak of Old Kingdom faience production following discoveries made by the Czech archaeological mission at Abusir. Inlays and tiles of especially fine workmanship were found in the Fifth Dynasty pyramid temple of Raneferef;[63] some had added decoration in gold leaf which was itself incised. A number of tiles had a coarse paste for the body with a finer white layer underlying the glaze. This technique had been developed for figurines at Hierakonpolis in the Early Dynastic Period and became common in later times.

The inlaying of one faience paste into another seen in some of the Raneferef pieces may have an antecedent in the inlays in the tomb of Nefermaat at Meidum, where colored paste was inlaid into stone (see fig. 6). Much has been made of this technique as an ancestor of faience working, but it is probably more important for introducing the concept of inlaying paste than for any development in the material technology. The paste forming these inlays was neither fired nor effloresced, and its importance should not be overstated.

It is likely that the Raneferef pieces were glazed by efflorescence; indeed all the faience of the Early Dynastic through to the end of the First Intermediate Period examined by Vandiver[64]—the glazing technique of which could be ascertained—proved to have been glazed by this method. However, it was not glazing that was the focus of experiment in the Old Kingdom, but rather techniques of shaping. These built on the methods of the Predynastic Period and made extensive use of modeling and surface grinding, but forming on a core and, probably, molding were also introduced.

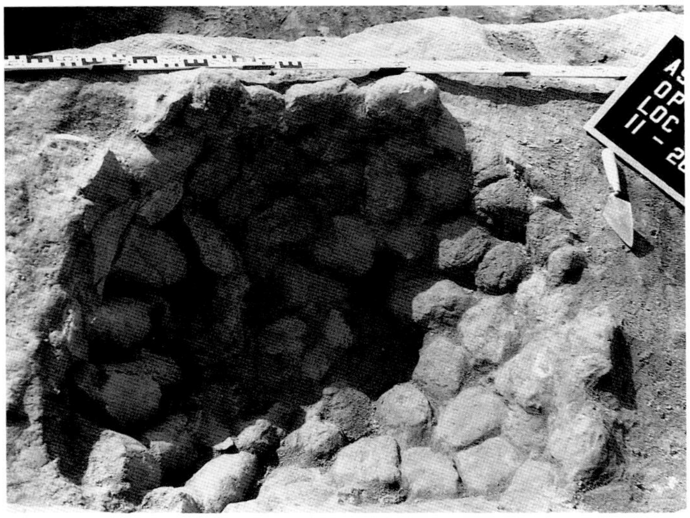

Fig. 33 A kiln pit discovered at Locus 14, Abydos, after excavation (looking south). The bowl-shaped construction is clearly visible, lined with bricks and fragments of pottery. Maximum dimension 1.2 m (4 ft). *Copyright: University of Pennsylvania Museum, reproduced courtesy of Dr. Matthew Adams.*

Evidence from Abydos suggests the production of faience went on relatively unhindered during the troubled times of the First Intermediate Period (2134–2040 BC). This should probably not surprise us, since industries do not necessarily cease during times of political upheaval, and as yet we know so little about industrial organization that it is impossible to say what level of industry is represented or who controlled it. Demand for amulets in the late Old Kingdom and First Intermediate Period seems to have been great and local rulers prided themselves on furthering crafts.[65]

Middle Kingdom and Second Intermediate Period

Stable conditions after the First Intermediate Period and the extensive use of amulets and magical figurines all seem to have been a stimulus to the development of the craft. There followed a period of the greatest diversity and experimentation in faience making since the Predynastic. It is perhaps no coincidence that for the first time we have evidence of an overseer of faience workers. Debeni's partly gilded and inscribed coffin, dating to the Thirteenth Dynasty, was found in tomb shaft 879 at Lisht. This is well known as the provenance of the famous Lisht Dolphin Jug[66] imported to the site from Southern Canaan.

Debeni held the title "Overseer of faience workers." Together with a mention of a similar worker on the stela now in Edinburgh ([166], p. 156)[67] this is a rare reference to such a craftsman. It has been suggested that the tomb is related to a workshop discovered nearby, but chronological distinctions are not sufficiently fine to make this a certainty.[68] The presence of this official may be significant in assessing the status of the industry, and could imply that production for the royal household was underway at Lisht, although not necessarily only at the one location so far identified.

Shaft 879 lay immediately north of the main part of a building labeled AI.3, and just a little north of what is believed to be a kiln. The building which houses the kiln is situated immediately south of the probable line of the south wall of the pyramid enclosure of Amenemhet I, and was located by the 1907–34 expedition of the Metropolitan Museum of Art. In the 1920–21 season a so-called "glaze factory" was unearthed in buildings AI.2 and AI.3. It was in this area that the numerous pieces of faience, mostly beads, and many hundreds of small marl clay balls were found ([172], p. 166), along with the clay hemispheres and possible kiln supports similar to those mentioned above.

Most significant was the discovery of the kiln. Photographs of this structure exist, but it was not particularly well recorded and it has been questioned whether or not it is in fact a later grain silo, cutting into the Middle Kingdom layers. However, recent research by Dr. Dieter Arnold and Felix Arnold suggests that it may indeed be a kiln. It consists of a semicircular structure of about 1.5m (5 ft) external diameter, built into the corner of a room and filled with a deep ashy deposit.[69]

It is clear that faience was being produced at Lisht in the Middle Kingdom, although the precise technology is not yet known. Examination by the author of faience objects from the site suggests that application glazing was used as well as efflorescence. Pieces are mostly beads, and possible elements from flails and amulets. Cementation has not been identified with any certainty.

In addition to modeling, regular use was made in the Middle Kingdom of forming on a core and shaping over a form or *patrix* (a variant of molding). Shapes approximating to a sphere were sometimes modeled around a ball of straw, a notable example being the popular hedgehog figurines ([98], p. 129) which seem to have had some magico-religious significance. Hippopotamus figures were also popular at this time, and are frequently decorated with designs of aquatic plants applied before firing in a manganese-based paint ([142–45], pp. 148–49).

Middle Kingdom faience vessels tend to have thick walls, although they need not be clumsily executed and some, such as the bowls with Nilotic scenes, are very accomplished. The use of a thin quartz layer on a coarser body also becomes widespread, leading to some extremely fine, bright glaze effects. Closed-form vessels such as jars were now also made in faience, and, as with the bowls, they drew on shapes well known in pottery. Decorative techniques developed, too, notably the mixing of two different colored body pastes to give a marbleized effect—a rarity in the preceding period but now more common ([90], p. 118) of New Kingdom date), as is the incising and inlaying with faience of another color ([23], p. 81, also New Kingdom). Glazes are commonly applied to a body that has a fine white layer on a coarser body, and the resulting effect can be of the highest quality. The glazes themselves are produced by efflorescence and cementation, the first time the latter technique is securely attested. The earliest firm evidence for this technique comes from the reign of Senusret I of the Twelfth Dynasty.

At Kerma in the Sudan there is evidence for the application of glazes as a slurry[70] and Reisner's account also suggests glazing by efflorescence. Reisner believed that some of the faience vessels were wheel-thrown, while others had been formed around a core. If this is correct, this is probably the earliest evidence of the regular throwing of faience vessels. Although widely (and probably

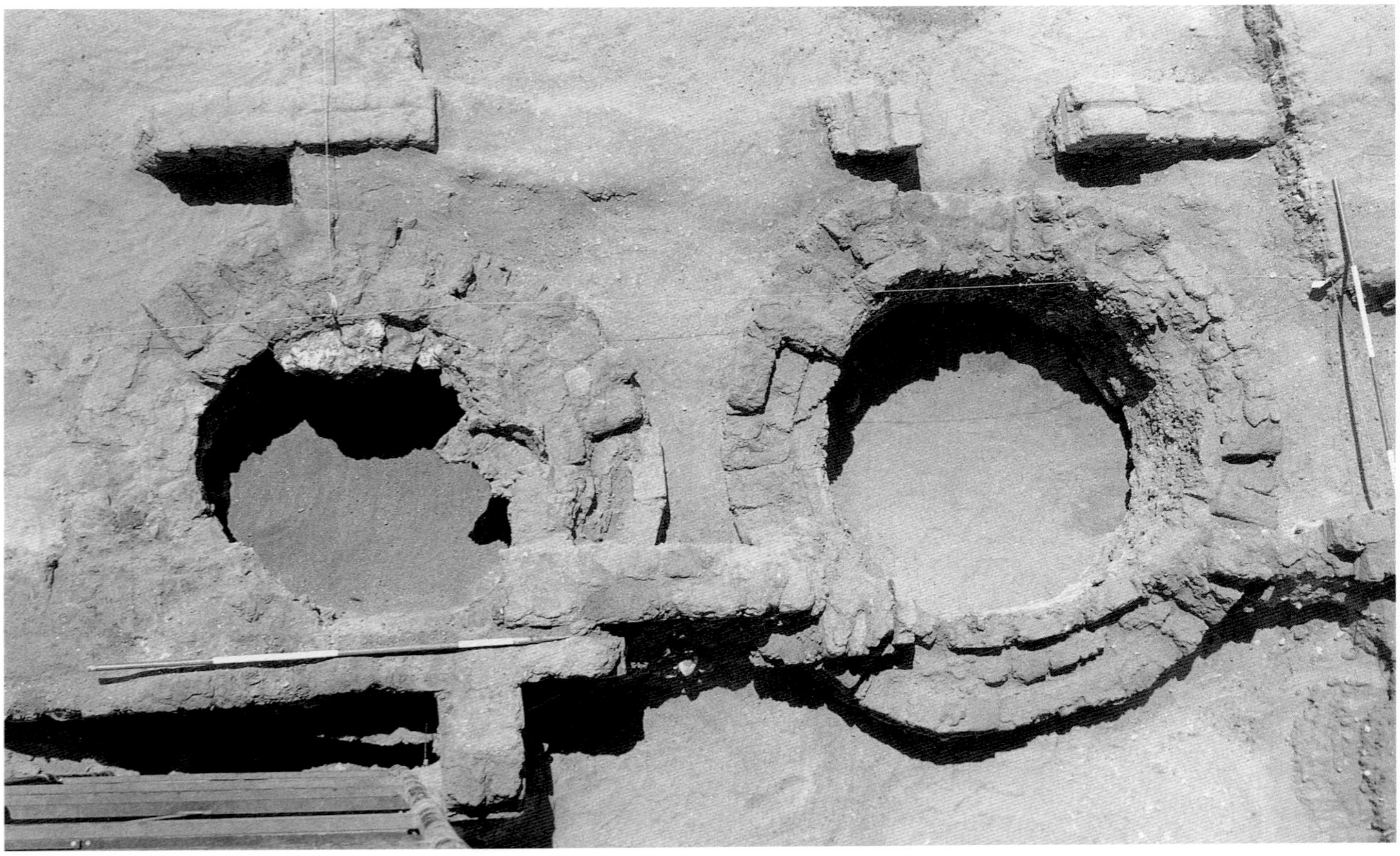

Fig. 34 The two large furnaces discovered at Amarna site O45.1. These were probably used to make glass rather than faience, but it is difficult to distinguish evidence for the production of different vitreous materials at this time. The ranging rods are 2 m (6½ ft) in length; north is at the bottom of the photograph.
Figs. 34 and 35, courtesy of the Egypt Exploration Society.

correctly) regarded as a factory site, Kerma has no *in situ* factory evidence. Glazed quartz pebbles are believed to have served as supports for the firing of the numerous, sometimes elaborate, tiles from the site. Inlaying of one faience paste into another is also well attested here. No kilns have been certainly identified; the most probable example, which was "too damaged to be drawn,"[71] seems to have been made from a truncated pottery vessel, or perhaps from a clay cone fired *in situ* like the many so-called bread ovens from Amarna and elsewhere. Reisner suggested that it was heated from the outside, which would imply that it served as a kind of saggar or separator, protecting the glazes from ash damage.

Although faience develops rapidly and is widely used at this time, it should not be assumed that the practice of glazing stone died out. Scarabs became important during the Middle Kingdom and most are of stone, perhaps because their hieroglyphs were more legible than in faience and because stone is more durable. The development of somewhat harder faience bodies may in part be an attempt to improve its durability and to make it appear more like stone.

New Kingdom

This period not only builds on the developments of the previous one, but it is also a time of innovation, experimentation with

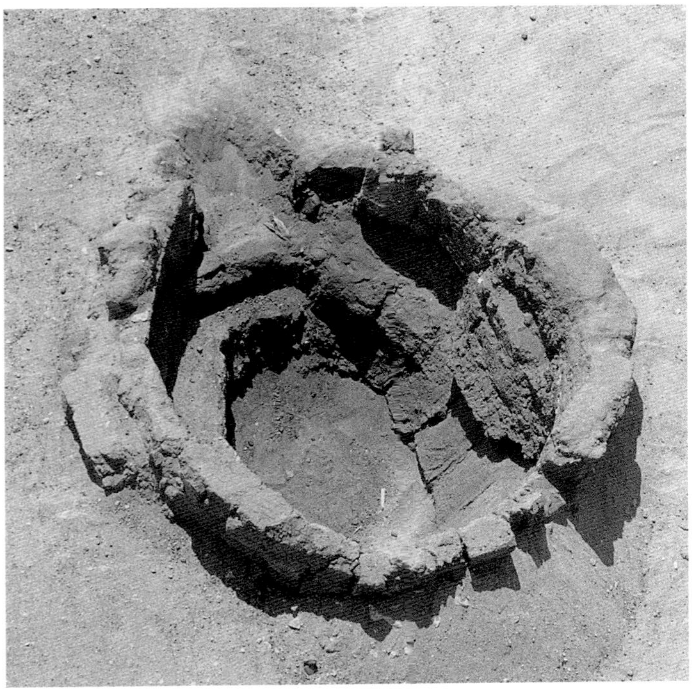

Fig. 35 A kiln or furnace at Amarna site O.45.1. The vertical bricks in its lower course are known from pottery kilns, but it may also have been used to fire faience.

combinations of new materials, and influence from foreign ideas. It is at this time that glass first appears in Egypt as a deliberate product, and seems to be allied with faience production as part of a "vitreous materials industry." We know of these links as a result of the discovery of well-preserved factory evidence at a number of sites, and the co-existence of the two crafts seems to have led to experimentation not only in production techniques but also in the range of colors used. The royal court of the Eighteenth Dynasty seems to have been much influenced by relations with the Egyptian empire, where more colorful decorations seem to have been prominent.

Among the innovations is the open face mold, as attested by many thousands of finds, not least from the 1910–21 Metropolitan Museum of Art excavations at Malkata, the palace of Amenhotep III at Thebes. Such molds allowed the production of large numbers of rings, amulets, and beads which probably made faience available to a much wider section of society than previously. Although the finds by both the Metropolitan Museum of Art and later by Waseda University are not so well known as those from Amarna, the site has yielded several molds still filled with unfired faience paste, now in the Metropolitan Museum of Art ([186], p. 166).[72] (See Wypyski's analysis in Appendix.)

The making of faience finger rings ([106], [107], p. 123) was facilitated by the development of a more robust body containing extensive glass in the matrix to fuse it more firmly. Glass making is itself attested at Malkata, as well as at Amarna, the Egyptian capital for most of the reign of Akhenaten. Amarna has been fundamental to our understanding of faience and glass technology following Petrie's work in 1891–92. His publication[73] provides a thoughtful discussion of faience production, although the distinction between excavated evidence and interpretation is not always clear and certain details are lacking. For example, he mentions finding three or four glass factories and two large glazing works,[74] but precise locations for these are not given, nor their proximity to one another. It is also unclear whether there were also more minor workshops not covered in the account.

The area marked on Petrie's map[75] as "moulds" probably locates at least one of these glazing works and refers to the many thousands of fired clay molds[76] used for forming faience objects, notably amulets and inlays ([185], p. 167). Petrie[77] thought these molds were pressed against a lump of faience paste and the raised image so produced was then sliced off and left to dry. He believed that the objects would next be dipped in powdered glass and fired in order to glaze them—in other words an applied glaze. Although he found molds with paste in them, he assumed that this was the remains of the fine quartz body only and not the residue of efflorescence which may in fact be more likely (the efflorescence method was unknown to him). Analysis of residue from actual Amarna pieces is needed to clarify this view, however.

While Petrie located no kilns at Amarna,[78] a recent geophysical survey by Mr. I. Mathieson on behalf of the writer succeeded in locating kilns or furnaces near Petrie's "moulds" area. This site, O45.1, is on the western fringe of the city close to the limit of modern cultivation and not far from the Small Aten Temple. It has yielded evidence of what is believed to be a workshop producing glass, faience, and pigments.[79] The furnaces may have been in an open courtyard with small rooms on the western side, but further excavation is needed to confirm this. Because the large kilns seem to have been subjected to temperatures higher than those needed to produce faience they are currently believed to be for glass (fig. 34). A third, less highly vitrified kiln probably served for pottery and perhaps for faience (fig. 35).

Our difficulty in separating the various crafts involving firing siliceous materials, at least in the New Kingdom, is perhaps an artificial one stemming from a modern terminology that seeks to separate closely related crafts. The Egyptians had not long had the use of glass and were employing it not only as a material in its own right, but as a substance to add to faience in order to produce new colors.[80] Similarly, some of the colorants of glass also became widely used, notably cobalt, antimony, and lead,[81] which occur from the reign of Thutmose III, the pharaoh generally credited with establishing glass production in Egypt.[82] Thus the Egyptians might have regarded glass and faience making, and possibly pigment production, as part of an ancient "vitreous materials" industry, and while it is important to differentiate the technological processes of each, we should not be surprised to find a range of products made in the same workshop using the same kilns/furnaces and possibly by the same group of craftsmen.

Numerous pieces of evidence from the Amarna excavations are at present difficult to interpret, among them calcareous plaster trays, usually with impressions of textiles on their upper surfaces ([176], p. 166). These may have served as drying trays for faience objects, particularly inlays, which often have textile traces on their undersides.[83] Equally mysterious are small, flattened clay balls, to which adhere tiny faience beads of just 2–3 mm in diameter, these are not the calcareous "marl clay" balls already referred to but are of "Nile silt" clay. In some cases the beads seem to have been pressed in fairly deeply, in others they adhere to the balls only by their edges. Numerous pieces of coarse yellowish plaster, often with layers of crystalline blue pigment adhering to them, are also of unknown function. The pigment has not yet been analyzed but may be Egyptian blue. Many other enigmatic objects from the excavation need further study before their function becomes clear. For the moment all that can be said is that, at least at Amarna, glass and faience making seem to be closely linked and that this link probably extends to other pyrotechnical industries too.

In the New Kingdom, at Amarna as elsewhere, faience paste was also used to cement together faience elements, such as ring shanks and bezels. Elements of a ring are often of various colors, likewise the suspension loop of an amulet is a different color from the amulet itself. The making of these suspension loops is not fully understood; their tiny size, often less than 2 mm in diameter, means that there is effectively no core—the entire body consists of the glaze. In this respect the loops are actually glass objects, albeit with the composition of faience glaze rather than true glass. Larger items might also be made of separate faience elements: the famous *was*-scepter from Naqada[84] was made by joining together various sections (fig. 36). Similarly, the faience lotus chalices ([114–17], pp.

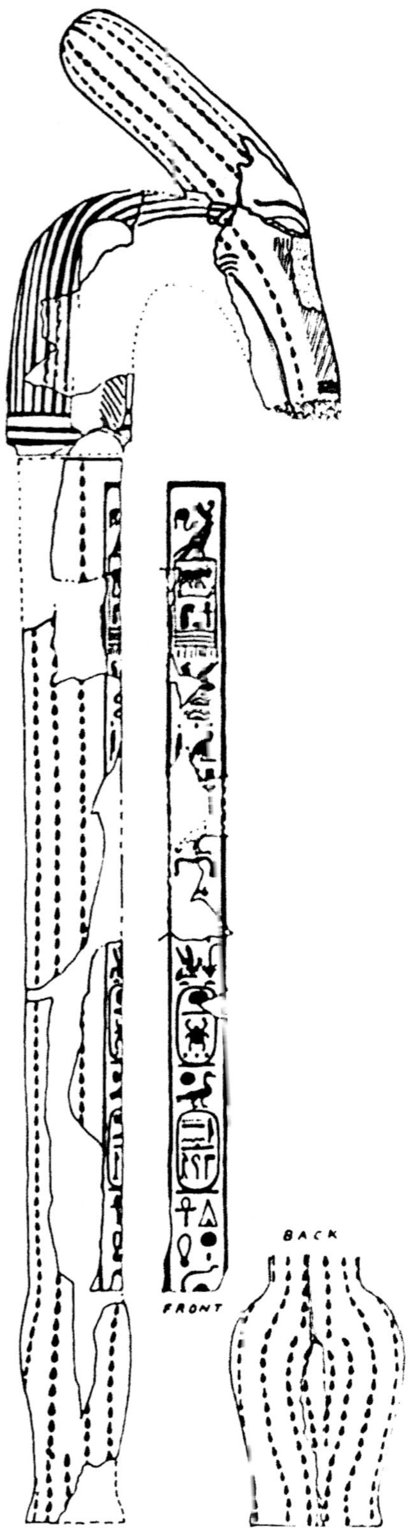

Fig. 36 A *was*-scepter discovered by Petrie in 1894 at Naqada. Made in sections, this is one of the largest faience objects known, at 215.8 cm (85 in) in length. Victoria and Albert Museum 437-1895. (After Petrie 1896, pl. 78.)

126–27) characteristic of the New Kingdom usually have a join at the junction of the bowl and stem-foot.[85]

Forming over a shaped *patrix* (former) and around a core continued, as did incising and inlaying. Inlaying reaches its height at this time and was achieved by the two techniques described above (p. 54). These techniques can produce the effect of a painted tile ([42], p. 90), accentuated by the bleeding of copper-based colors into the background color, which is often white. A kind of halo effect is thus produced around areas of the tile, notably foliage ([33], p. 88). Vandiver[86] was unable to determine the glazing method used to produce this type of tile, although those with shrunken inlay seem to have been produced by efflorescence and that cannot be ruled out here. Polychrome tiles showing prisoners ([52–54], pp. 92–93) and inlays of fish and birds (such as [118], p. 128) produced at this time are truly remarkable pieces of craftsmanship—with our present knowledge of faience making they would be extremely difficult to replicate today.

The use of faience in architecture must not be underestimated. In addition to tiles and hieroglyphic inlays, there were also complicated floral inlays and three-dimensional pieces such as the famous grape clusters from Amarna. These were mold-made and could be either flat-backed, for attachment to a wall or beam, or fully three-dimensional, made by joining two flat-backed pieces together. It has been suggested that the clusters were hung from the ceilings of buildings, reproducing the effect of a vineyard ([36–38], p. 89). Hamza[87] rightly singles out the polychrome tiles from the late New Kingdom site of Qantir in the Eastern Delta as examples of master craftsmanship. These combine numerous colors of paste in a single tile, often depicting their subject in remarkable detail. Of particular quality are figurative tiles representing bound captives, which were part of royal architectural structures like a throne dais. Similar tiles are known from the mortuary temple of Ramesses III at Medinet Habu ([52–54], pp. 92–93).

Excavations at Qantir in 1928 conducted by the Egyptian Department of Antiquities[88] unearthed more than ten thousand fired clay molds of the kind known from Amarna and Malkata, most of which still bore traces of the colored faience paste they had contained.[89] Numerous faience tiles were also unearthed and cylindrical vessels and "lumps of the favourite blue colour" (i.e. Egyptian blue pigment) were found. While Hamza's statement[90] that "the objects discovered make it certain that we are face to face with a faience and glazing factory of great size" may well be correct, he goes on to make it clear that these objects were not found in their primary context. Rather, "the original workrooms had actually vanished, but the debris was full of hundreds of fragments which illustrate the finished objects and furnish us with almost every stage and detail of the mode of manufacture."[91] Recent excavations by the Roemer-Pelizaeus Museum[92] have found similar remains in such a dump context. Interestingly, they have been able to associate many of them with glass production, while it seems that some of Hamza's description probably refers to Egyptian blue. The evidence suggests that this workshop of the Nineteenth and Twentieth Dynasties probably had similar craft affinities to those at Amarna, again illustrating our difficulties in differentiating between what are now regarded as distinct crafts.

No kilns have yet been located at Qantir, but a series of cylindrical clay tubes believed to be the nozzles of bellows were discovered.[93] This identification is quite plausible, though again it is not possible to say to which of several industrial processes they belonged. The text implies that they were found in primary contexts[94] but unfortunately there are no plans or photographs upon which to base a judgment. Egyptian faience produced at manufacturing sites such as these was exported around the Mediterranean[95] and is well known from Cyprus and Crete as well as parts of the Greek mainland, where it was widely imitated.

Post-New Kingdom

By the time of Egypt's Third Intermediate Period (1070–712 BC), the technology of faience production had become widespread, and it can be difficult to differentiate Egyptian imports from locally made copies at sites around the Mediterranean.

Antimony and cobalt, introduced in New Kingdom times, almost disappear as constituents of faience in the Third Intermediate Period. Interestingly, this is also a period of little glass production. Although it does not die out, as was once thought, it is certainly true that it was much reduced in scale, and that most of the products were of lower quality. Cooney[96] has suggested that the production of the material known as "glassy faience" (see above, p. 55) may account for the decline in glass production. Although widely used, particularly for the making of shabtis, this material is not well defined, falling into a kind of negative category of materials that cannot safely be described as either faience or glass. It should be noted also that this glassy faience is known at least as early as the Middle Kingdom[97] and should therefore not be thought of as a late development in faience manufacture.[98]

The Greek settlement of Naukratis (modern Kom Gi'eif) in the Delta, which dates back to at least 630 BC, is a key source for understanding the technology of the Late Period.[99] Here Petrie discovered a so-called "scarab factory" making Egyptian as well as Egyptian-style faience artifacts. Unfortunately, however, the details of this are not well recorded and the publication concentrates more on the finds themselves than on their context. More recent excavations have unearthed pottery kilns at the site.[100]

The revivalist spirit of the Twenty-Fifth and Twenty-Sixth Dynasties was accompanied by a renewed attention to traditional methods of faience making. A distinctive apple-green color was introduced, and there was a preference for high-quality matte faience rather than the earlier shiny glazes. The quality of some of these matte pieces, such as sistrum handles ([91], p. 102), is exceptional, with every element of the wigs and jewelry worn by the deities executed in minute detail. And when a high glaze was required, the faience makers were capable of producing excellent work of almost glass-like quality ([130], p. 132). Yellow glazes became possible again through the reintroduction of antimony as a colorant, a move perhaps not unrelated to the increase in the circulation of glass at this time.

Techniques found in the New Kingdom continued, but methods borrowed from pottery manufacture were added to the repertoire, including throwing vessels on the wheel and applying glaze as a slurry. Kaczmarczyk and Hedges[101] have suggested that the black glazes common in the Late Period, produced by the use of reducing kiln conditions, were derived from contact with Greek mercenaries and traders who were increasingly important in Egyptian life and who were familiar with the manipulation of kiln conditions for their Attic pottery. Some support for this is to be found in the more widespread use of reducing kiln conditions in Lower Egypt, close to the Greek settlements, while Upper Egypt continued to produce black by using manganese. The reduction technique was already known in Egypt in Predynastic times, but had not been widely used on pottery subsequently. Kaczmarczyk and Hedges[102] also propose a link with the metal industry, in that their analyses show low concentrations of tin in faience in those areas where the bronze also has a low tin concentration.

Relatively little attention has been paid to post-Pharaonic faience, although the work of Nenna and Seif el-Din[103] should be noted. Relief decoration is common on Ptolemaic and Roman faience bowls and vases, and the effect is often enhanced by two-tone glazes. A good example is the bowl in the Metropolitan Museum of Art ([170], p. 163), which may have been made in Alexandria, for which we have the closest parallels.[104] The two-tone effect here is very clear: the dark blue seems to be applied as an inlay over the turquoise body colour, and when examined has a slightly matte appearance.

Such vessels were among the products of the Graeco-Roman faience workshop at Memphis, excavated by Petrie.[105] This site has sometimes been overlooked because it was described as being for the production of "glazed pottery," but finds, now in the Petrie Museum, demonstrate that faience was made here. However, the forming and firing techniques used to make faience vessels at this time clearly owed much to pottery technology: some of the vessels are wheel-thrown, and saggars were commonly used in firing.

Misfired vessels were also discovered, some with kiln supports still attached, showing how they were stacked in the kiln ([179, 180], pp. 170–71). Cylindrical vessels seem to have served as saggars for firing the objects, and Petrie[106] compares them with vessels of the same shape that he regarded as stands for glass-fritting pans at Amarna, again emphasizing the links between these pyrotechnical industries.

Six unequivocal kilns found at Memphis were square, or more accurately rectangular, with internal sides measuring between 106 and 211 cm (42 and 83 in). The draught or stoke hole was more than halfway up the profile and it was reported that the kiln walls were heavily slagged above, but not below, this level—a pattern consistent with heating by an updraught kiln. No traces of a perforated floor or chequer were discovered, leading Petrie[107] to suggest that stacks of saggars some 10 ft (*c.* 3 m) high were made and the fuel thrown between them, with the result that the lower pots received a lower firing temperature than the upper ones.

According to Petrie the fuel was straw (which was found carbonized in the slag), and there was no trace of wood or charcoal. Since the precise nature of the "slag" is not given, it is unclear whether the straw is in fact from a plaster layer in the kiln or was in reality the fuel. Unfortunately, we cannot be sure whether all these kilns were contemporary, which makes any assessment of the scale of the industry uncertain. However, the number of misfired vessels from the site combined with the number of kilns (assuming some at least were contemporary) argues for a degree of sophistication. Petrie also found traces of the manufacture of a blue colorant, which he believed was also roasted in sealed vessels in the kiln, having found "pills" of the material at the site. This may argue for a link with the pigment industry, or may simply be for coloring this late faience, as Petrie assumed. There is no suggestion here of any link with glass production; rather, the similarities are with pottery manufacture.

From Ptolemaic times, much Lower Egyptian faience seems to have used natron as an alkali source, although Memphite faience is high in potassium, suggesting a plant ash source of alkali. Plant ash alkali was traditionally used in Egyptian glassmaking, whereas natron is the source used from Roman times. The reasons for the change are not clear, but it may reflect shifting links between crafts. This Memphis material deserves to be better known, and the writer hopes to examine it in more detail in the near future.

Complicated sculptural pieces were also produced in Graeco-Roman times, including a head believed to be of the Emperor Augustus (30 BC–AD 14), made of a particularly dense turquoise faience with a matte finish ([63], p. 101). The workmanship of this piece suggests that it was hand-modeled, perhaps after the approximate shape had been molded. Relief decoration on bowls and vases was molded, probably in the manner of the relief on *terra sigillata* ("Samian ware") pottery. In this method the paste (or clay for the pottery) is impressed into a mold of the shape of the bowl or vase, and the piece is then revolved on the potter's wheel to smooth the inside. Decorations on the interiors of faience bowls must have been separately molded or incised.[108]

1 Noble 1969, p. 435; and H. Patterson pers. comm. Since the tin glazed pottery is unlikely to occur in the same archaeological contexts as Egyptian faience, and since specialists are usually well aware of which "faience" is meant, as well as the fact the pottery faience has now been renamed majolica, it is usual to drop the "Egyptian" element of the term. Faience is widespread in the ancient world, and is well known from Mesopotamia (Moorey 1994, pp. 166–86), the Mediterranean and as far away as Scotland. Most of this material is locally made, including that from the Scottish Bronze Age (Newton 1980), pp. 173–74; cf. Stone and Thomas 1956; Doran and Hodson 1975; Newton and Renfrew, 1970. The "Egyptian" element is therefore somewhat inappropriate, though it remains a simple way to differentiate this material from the more modern pottery.

2 Vandiver and Kingery 1987, p. 9.

3 Vandiver in Olin and Franklin 1982, p. 167 has determined the typical faience body comprises 92–99% SiO_2; 1–5% CaO_2; 0.5–3% Na_2O with minor quantities of CuO, Al_2O_3, TiO_2, MgO and K_2O.

4 Allan 1973.

5 Wulff et al. 1968, p. 107.

6 Oppenheim et al. 1970, pp. 32ff; Henein and Gout 1974, p. 1.

7 Vandiver in Olin and Franklin 1982.

8 Petrie 1894, p. 26.

9 For example: UC.40568.

10 Kiefer and Allibert 1971, p. 113 claim that between 2 and 6% of the Egyptian sand they analyzed comprised calcareous material. Lime is also one ingredient of ancient glass, but does not seem to be specifically mentioned in the Assyrian texts of the seventh century BC, perhaps implying that it was added unconsciously.

11 This distinction between crystalline and non-crystalline is important when considering the similarity of the raw materials and any possible interrelatedness between crafts (below).

12 Cooper 1972, p. 13.

13 Lucas's work (Lucas and Harris 1962 (1989) p. 175) however, suggested that the alkali was the most effective binder, although its binding effect occurs primarily during firing when the sodium carbonate combines with the silica.

14 Noble 1969.

15 In passing it should be noted that where a layer of fine ground quartz particles was applied over a coarser core this was probably added once the core had partially dried. This would have the advantage of allowing the coarse material to be handled before it became too friable and would also prevent it from taking moisture from the finer layer so that it dried too rapidly causing cracking. It must be stressed that these are assumptions on the part of the writer and need to be tested experimentally.

16 Recent experimental work has shown that, as might be expected, applied glaze works well on pre-fired cores; see Stocks 1997.

17 Peltenburg in Bimson and Freestone 1987, p. 20.

18 Kühne 1969, Boyce in Kemp 1989, p. 161.

19 Boyce in Kemp 1989.

20 Vandiver in Olin and Franklin 1982.

21 The possibility of such a method was first noted by Binns et al. 1932 and developed by Noble 1969.

22 Vandiver in Kaczmarczyk and Hedges 1983, p. A31 notes its formation within 30 minutes of shaping the object.

23 Vandiver in Kaczmarczyk and Hedges 1983, p. A31.

24 Peltenburg in Bimson and Freestone 1987, p. 10 notes that this is most effective for fine grained bodies.

25 Vandiver in Kaczmarczyk and Hedges 1983, p. A33.

26 Sintering, the process by which particles soften at their edges and become fused together marks the transition from the plastic to the ceramic state.

27 A flux is any substance added to assist fusion, in this case the alkalis which serve to reduce melting temperatures (above).

28 I.e. glass developing in the interstices between the quartz grains as a result of incomplete migration of the salts.

29 Wulff et al. 1968. The technique was also studied by Kiefer 1968; also Kiefer and Allibert 1971.

30 Vandiver in Kaczmarczyk and Hedges 1983, pp. A33–34 states that the "low melting alkalies presumably draw away from the mixture of calcium oxide and charcoal and wet the quartz. After firing, the friable, unreacted powder is removed from the object to reveal an even coating of glaze…"
A range of compositions for the glazing powder yield satisfactory results. However, the following compositions have been documented:

SiO_2	40%	$CaCO_3$	50–75%
Na_2O	20%	Bauxite	0–20%
K_2O	3%	Nitre	15–25%
CaO	20%	(mostly potassium nitrate)	
MgO	2%	CuO frit	0–12%
CuO	1%	*or*	
Al_2O_3	6%	$CaCO_3$	5–28%
Fe_2O_3	1.5%	SiO_2	20–36%
PO_4	2%	Na_2CO_3	12–23%
Total:	**98.5%**	(Kiefer 1968, in Vandiver in Kaczmarczyk	
(Wulff et al. 1968, p. 100)		and Hedges 1983 p. A34)	

31 Vandiver in Kaczmarczyk and Hedges 1983, p. A39.

32 Petrie 1894, p. 28; Lucas and Harris 1962 (1989), pp. 172–74.

33 This erroneous assumption derived from European practices. The ancient Egyptians did not produce glazed pottery until Roman times.

34 This was, however, the method used to glaze the solid stone artifacts that predate and co-exist with faience.

35 Vandiver in Olin and Franklin 1982, p. 168.

36 Vandiver and Kingery in Bimson and Freestone 1987b.
37 Tite et al. 1983, p. 26.
38 Cf. Kaczmarczyk and Hedges 1983.
39 Lucas Variant E, Lucas and Harris 1962 (1989), pp. 164–65.
40 Kaczmarczyk and Hedges 1983, pp. 212–13.
41 Lucas and Harris 1962 (1989), p. 165.
42 Lilyquist et al. in Lilyquist and Brill 1993, p. 8.
43 Tite et al. forthcoming. This is a version of Lucas Variant D.
44 Tite 1986; Tite and Bimson in Black 1987.
45 Cooney 1976, p. 37.
46 Vitruvius 1914, VII, 11.
47 Vergès 1992.
48 This analysis was undertaken by Mary Anne Murray of the Institute of Archaeology, London, to whom I am indebted.
49 Petrie 1894, p. 26 records the discovery at Amarna of what he considered a charcoal-burning furnace with large quantities of charcoal inside it. However, whether this was correctly identified, and whether it produced fuel for faience or glass production or both (or indeed some other purpose), is not known and no analyses were carried out on it. I am grateful to Drs. Caroline Vermeeren of BIAX, Netherlands, for informing me that sizable pieces of charcoal such as those from the recently excavated Amarna furnaces are likely to have been produced by incomplete combustion, rather than deliberate production.
50 Petrie 1911, p. 35.
51 Papyrus Vatican 64. Bellion 1987 pp. 320, 397; Marucchi 1891.
52 Aufrère 1991, p. 465 and footnote.
53 Edinburgh 449, Accession No. 1956.153.
54 For discussion see Gaballa 1979 pp. 45 and 51. Note, however, that his statement that the Edinburgh Stela is glass is incorrect, see Nolte 1968, pp. 7–8.
55 Nolte 1977, pp. 138–42. This is contrary to the statement by Drenkahn in Sasson et al. 1995, p. 336 that the stages of all crafts are known.
56 Davies 1902.
57 Vandiver in Olin and Franklin 1982, p. 172.
58 Kaczmarczyk and Hedges 1983.
59 This work is not yet published and I am grateful to Dr. Adams for allowing me to mention it here.
60 One badly damaged brick structure was also unearthed that may possibly be a kiln.
61 Lauer 1938; Lauer 1976.
62 Vandiver in Olin and Franklin 1982, p. 174.
63 Verner 1984; Verner 1986; Nicholson 1993, pp. 21–22.
64 Vandiver in Kaczmarczyk and Hedges 1983.
65 Dorothea Arnold, pers. comm.
66 McGovern et al. 1994. Note that both the jar and the coffin are of the Thirteenth Dynasty, contemporary with the house and kiln.
67 A faience worker is mentioned on the stela of Rekhamun now in Edinburgh (Royal Museum of Scotland 1956.153), see above n. 53. I am indebted to Dr. Florence Friedman for bringing this piece to my attention.
68 This tomb and the material from it are being studied by J.D. Bourriau and J. Allen, and I am grateful to them for allowing them to be mentioned here.
69 The scale is shown on photograph 321 taken at the time. There are plans to re-excavate this structure, in which case a good deal more information could certainly be discovered.
70 Reisner 1923b, pp. 134–75.
71 Reisner 1923b, p.135.
72 MMA 11.215.666, MMA 11.215.668 and MMA 11.215.667.
73 Petrie 1894, pp. 27–30.
74 Petrie 1894, p. 25.
75 Petrie 1894, pl. XXXV.
76 Petrie 1894, p. 30.
77 Petrie 1894, p. 28.
78 There has, however, been some confusion over this aspect of the work. Vandiver in Kaczmarczyk and Hedges 1983, p. A30. Similarly, although Petrie discusses the technological evidence, the remains of actual workshop buildings are not recorded. The remains were probably located in dumps outside the actual working area, or possibly in some part of the courtyard of the workshop. It should be remembered that much of the work probably took place out of doors, much as potting does in the simple Egyptian workshops today (cf. Nicholson 1995b).
79 Nicholson 1995c; Nicholson 1995a.
80 Boyce in Kemp 1989, p. 161.
81 Kaczmarczyk and Hedges 1983.
82 Lilyquist and Brill 1993, p. 4.
83 Petrie also found these, and examples are in the Petrie Museum (UC.40569A, UC.40570), though they are not mentioned in his publications.
84 Victoria and Albert Museum (London) 437-1895.
85 Vandiver and Kingery in Bimson and Freestone 1987b.
86 Vandiver in Kaczmarczyk and Hedges 1983, p. A120.
87 Hamza 1930, p. 51.
88 Hamza 1930.
89 Hamza 1930, p. 42.
90 Hamza 1930, p. 42.
91 Hamza 1930, p. 45.
92 Under the directorship of Dr. Edgar Pusch.
93 These are known as tuyères. Examples are Cairo JdE6421-6423.
94 Hamza 1930, p. 62.
95 Peltenburg 1986.
96 Cooney 1976, p. 153.
97 Lilyquist et al. in Lilyquist and Brill 1993, p. 8.
98 Bianchi 1996c, p. 48 notes that the characteristic brown spots found on some Twenty-Second Dynasty faience may be a deliberate decorative element not widely known in other periods.
99 Petrie and Gardner 1886–1888.
100 Coulson and Leonard 1981.
101 Kaczmarczyk and Hedges 1983.
102 Kaczmarczyk and Hedges 1983.
103 Nenna and Seif el-Din 1993; Nenna and Seif el-Din 1994.
104 Do. Arnold 1988, pp. 6–7.
105 Petrie 1909b; Petrie 1911.
106 Petrie 1909b, p. 14.
107 Petrie 1911, p. 35.
108 The writer would like to thank Dr. Dorothea Arnold and her colleagues at the Metropolitan Museum of Art, New York, for their invitation to examine the faience in their care, and for their help and hospitality during his work there. Dorothea Arnold kindly commented on an earlier version of this text, as did Leonard Lesko.

Work at Amarna has been carried out by the writer under the auspices of the Egypt Exploration Society's Amarna Project directed by Mr. Barry J. Kemp and to both of these he is indebted. The work has been funded by the Wainwright Fund for Near Eastern Archaeology, without whose support the project would have been impossible.

Thanks also go to numerous colleagues, some acknowledged in the text, who have provided specific points of information or references. These include Ms. Barbara Adams, Dr. Matthew Adams, Ms. Janine Bourriau, Ms. Mimi Leveque, Mr. Ian Mathieson, Ms. Mary Anne Murray, Professor Edgar Peltenburg, Dr. John Taylor, and Professor Michael Tite. Finally I am indebted to Dr. Florence Friedman for her invitation to take part in the "Gifts of the Nile" project and for her continual help and encouragement throughout.

THE PLATES

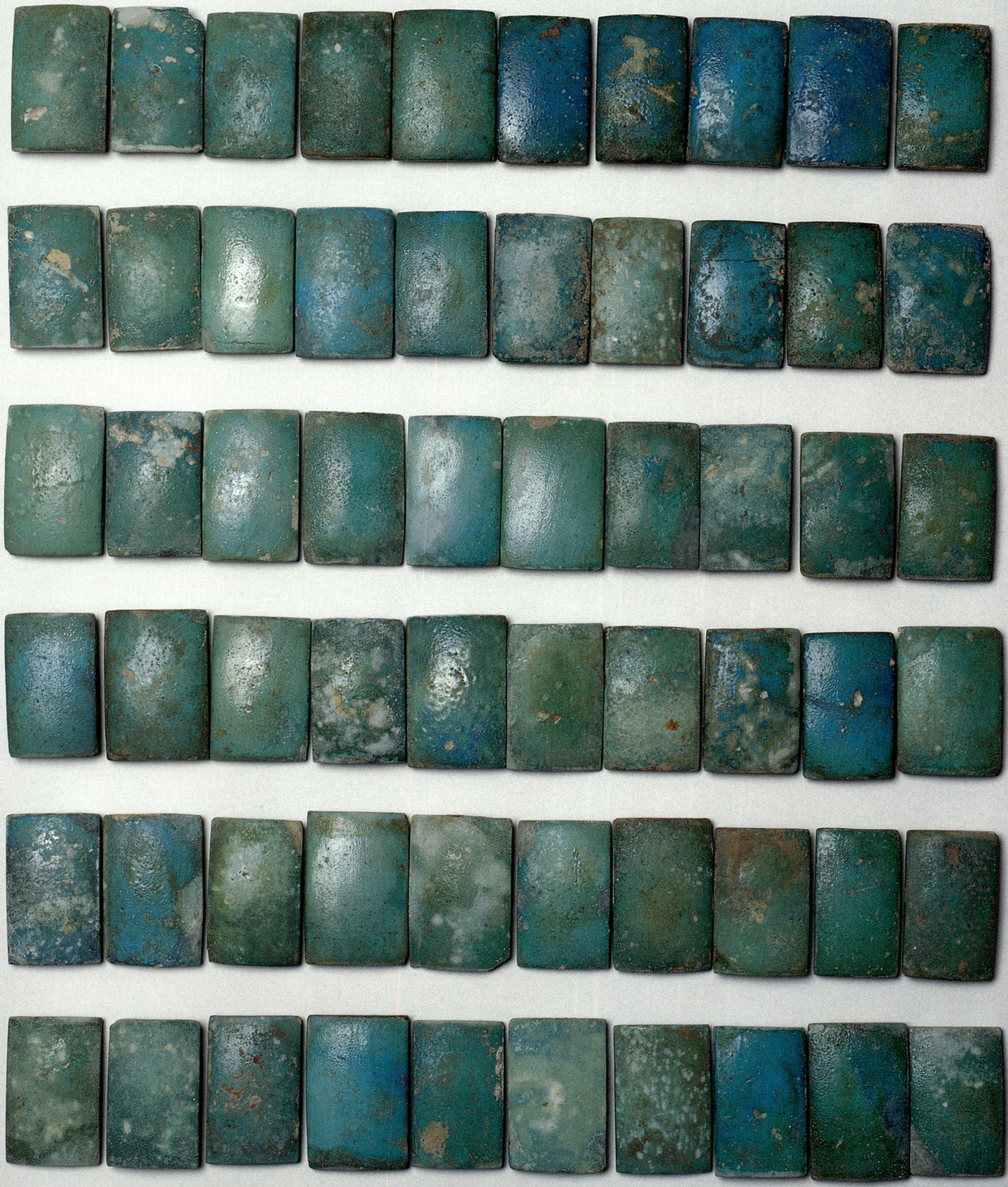

EARLY FAIENCE

Beads were among the earliest objects made of faience in ancient Egypt, soon followed by hand-modeled figures of human, animal, and other forms that served as dedications in sanctuaries throughout the country. At the same time, small faience plaques for furniture inlay were produced as grave gifts, while larger wall tiles were made for temple and tomb decoration, the most dramatic example being the 36,000 faience tiles that lined several underground rooms at King Djoser's Third Dynasty Step Pyramid complex.

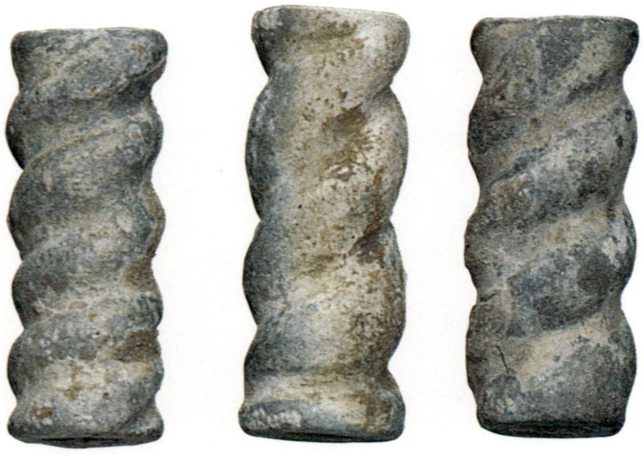

Opposite
DJOSER TILE PANEL [20]
Old Kingdom, Dynasty 3
H. of each tile approx. 6.0 cm; W. 3.5 cm

Above
CURLS FROM A COMPOSITE STATUE (DETAIL) [11]
See p. 70

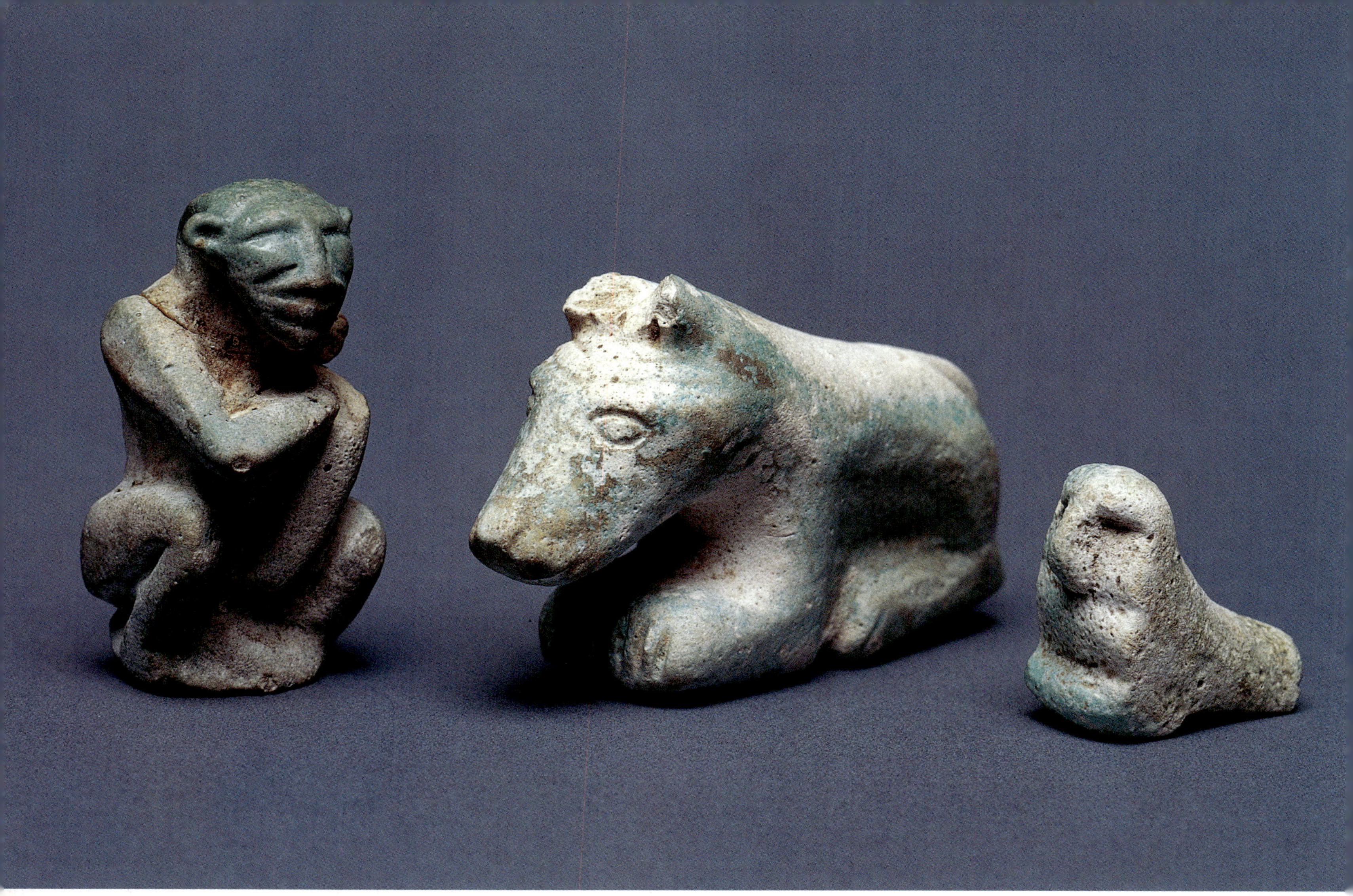

Above, left
SEATED FIGURE [5]
Early Dynastic Period, Dynasty 1–2
H. 8.0 cm; W. 4.0 cm; L. 3.5 cm
Above, center
MODEL DOG [6]
Early Dynastic Period, Dynasty 1–2
H. 7.0 cm; W. 3.2 cm; L. 11.7 cm
Above, right
MODEL BIRD [7]
Early Dynastic Period, Dynasty 1–2
H. 4.0 cm; W. 2.2 cm; L. 4.9 cm

Right
SCORPION [8]
Early Dynastic Period, Dynasty 1–2
L. 10.5 cm
Far right
SCORPION [9]
Early Dynastic Period, Dynasty 1–2
L. 7.0 cm; W. 4.7 cm

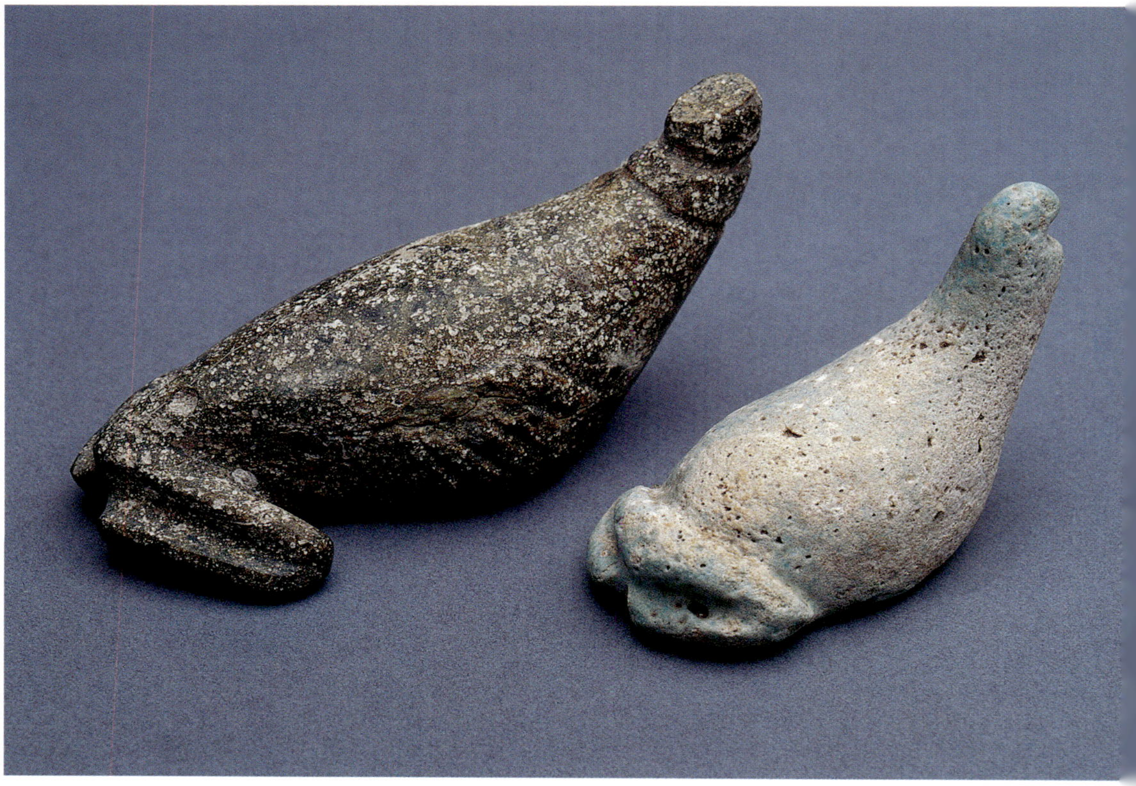

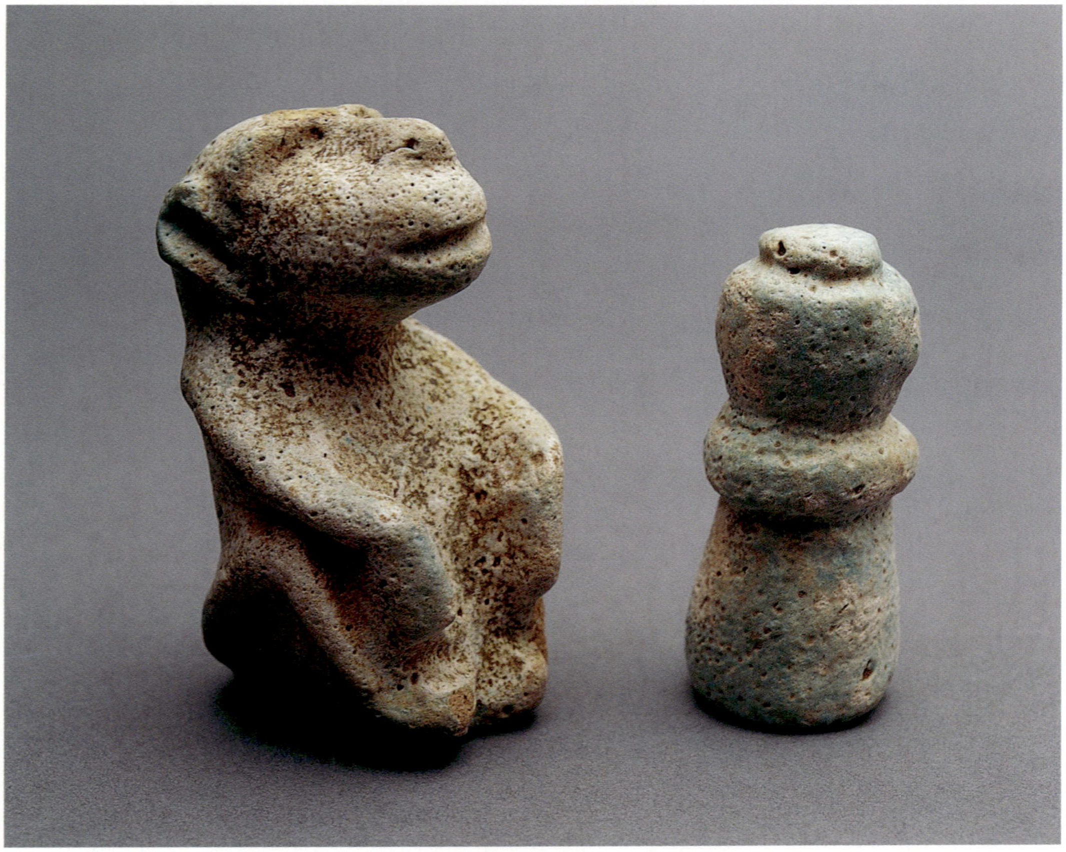

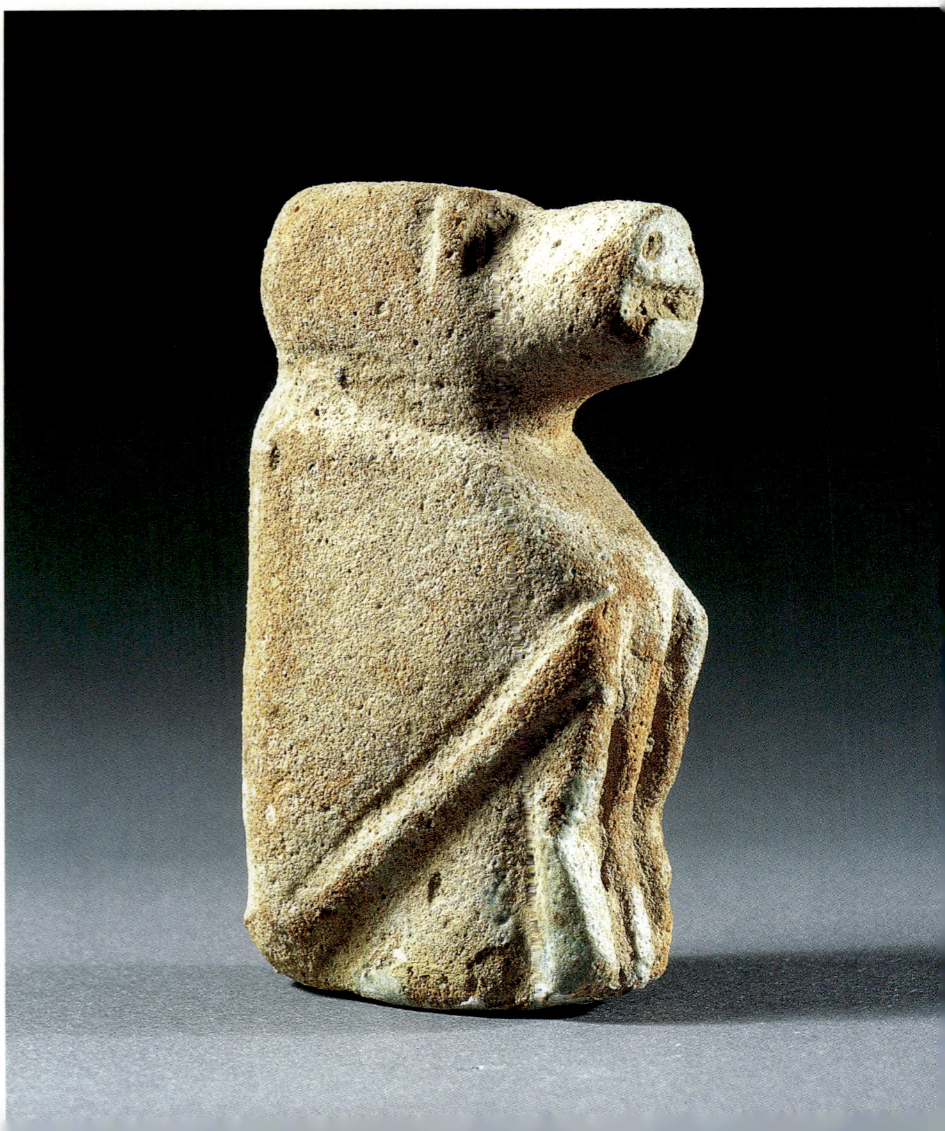

Above, left

BABOON STATUETTE [3]

Early Dynastic Period, probably Dynasty 1–2

H. 8.0 cm

Above, right

MODEL VESSEL [10]

Early Dynastic Period, Dynasty 1–2

H. 6.5 cm

Right

BABOON STATUETTE [4]

Early Dynastic Period, probably Dynasty 1–2

H. 4.8 cm

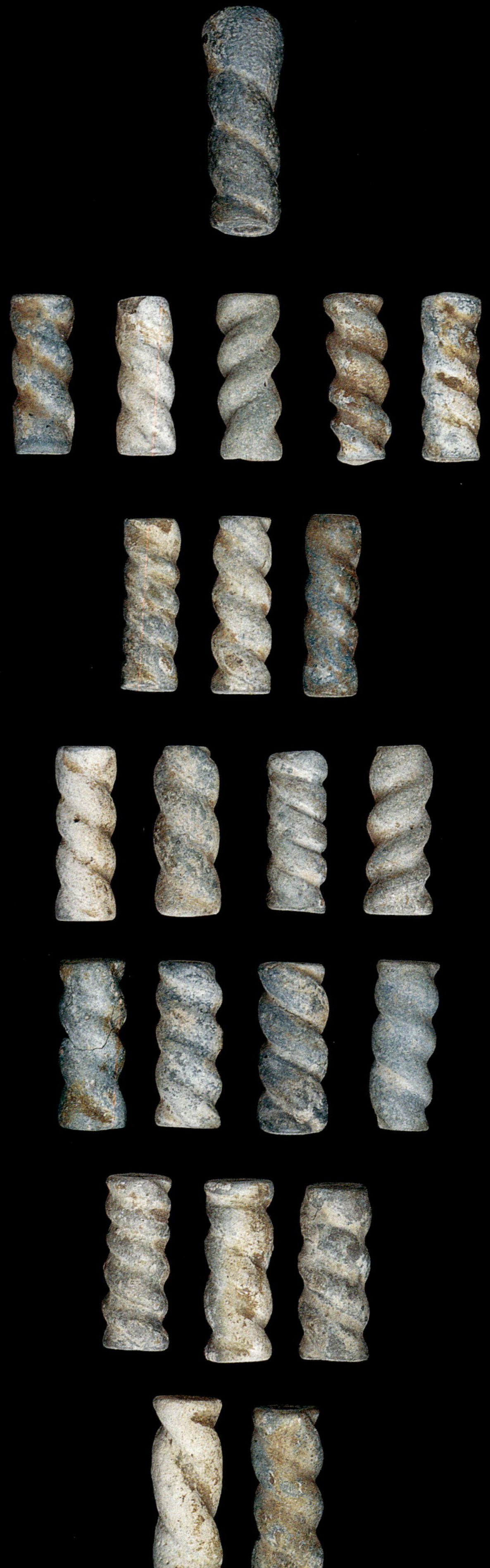

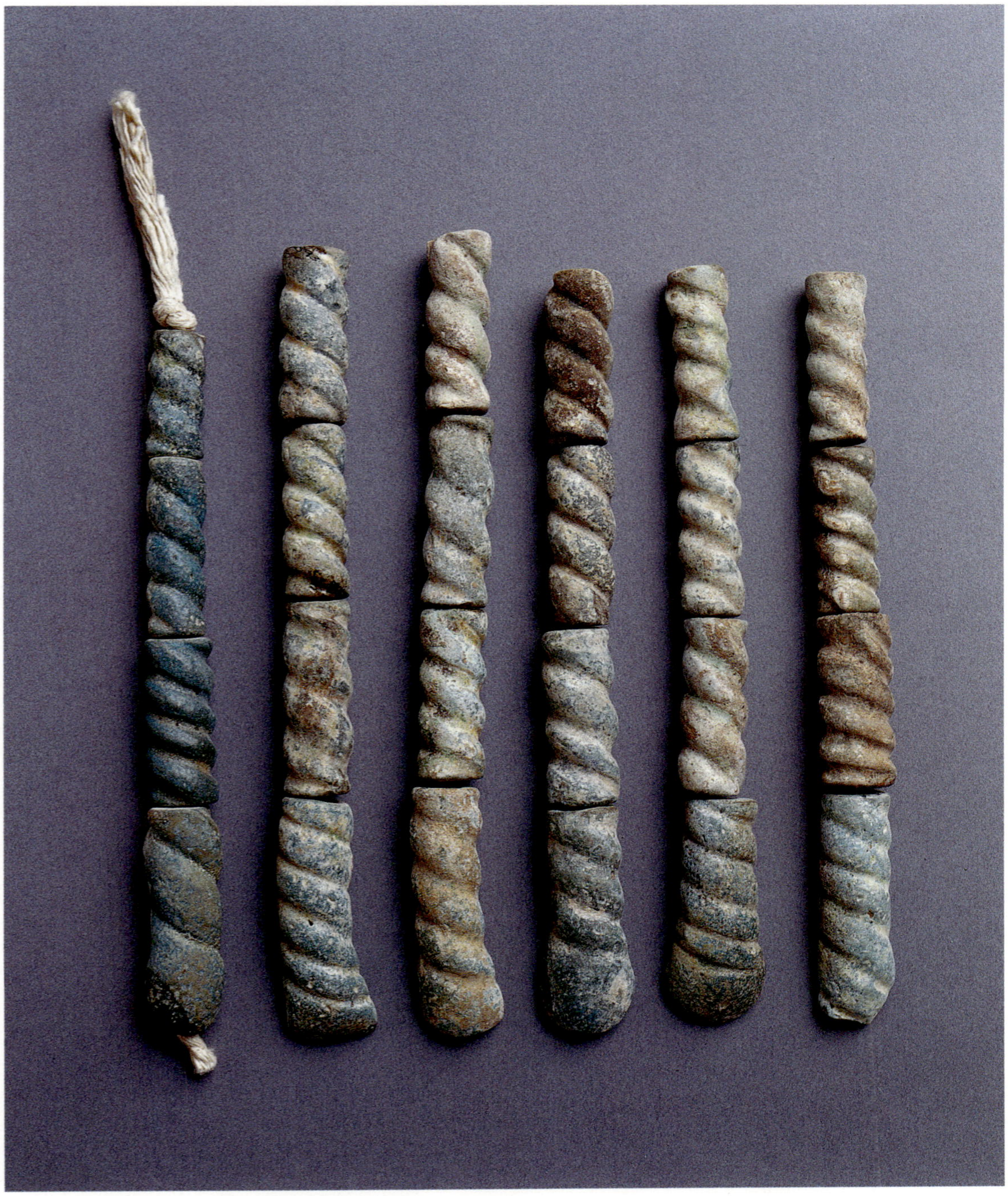

Opposite

CURLS FROM A COMPOSITE STATUE [11]
Early Dynastic Period, Dynasty 1–2
H. 4.0–5.0 cm; W. 0.4–0.6 cm

Above

SPIRAL BEADS [12]
Early Dynastic Period, Dynasty 1–2
Average L. 4.0–5.0 cm

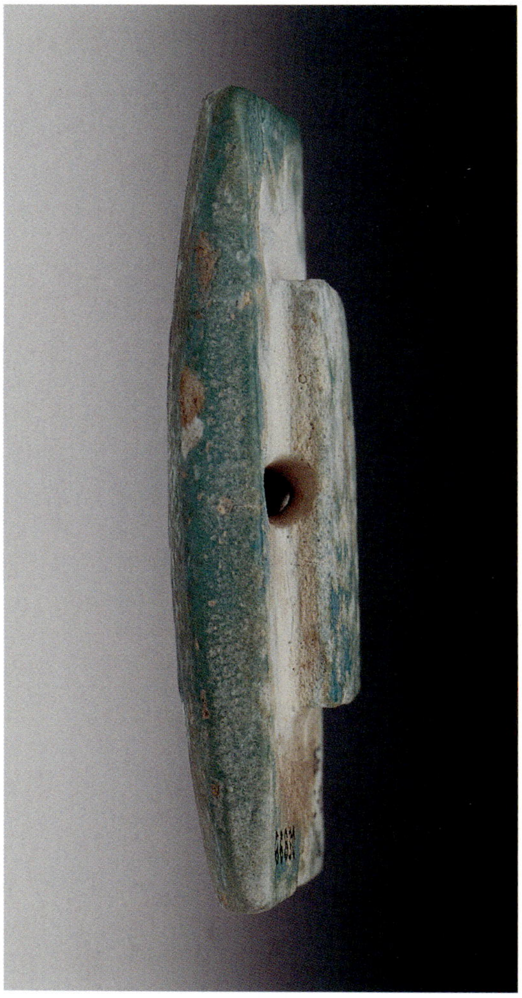

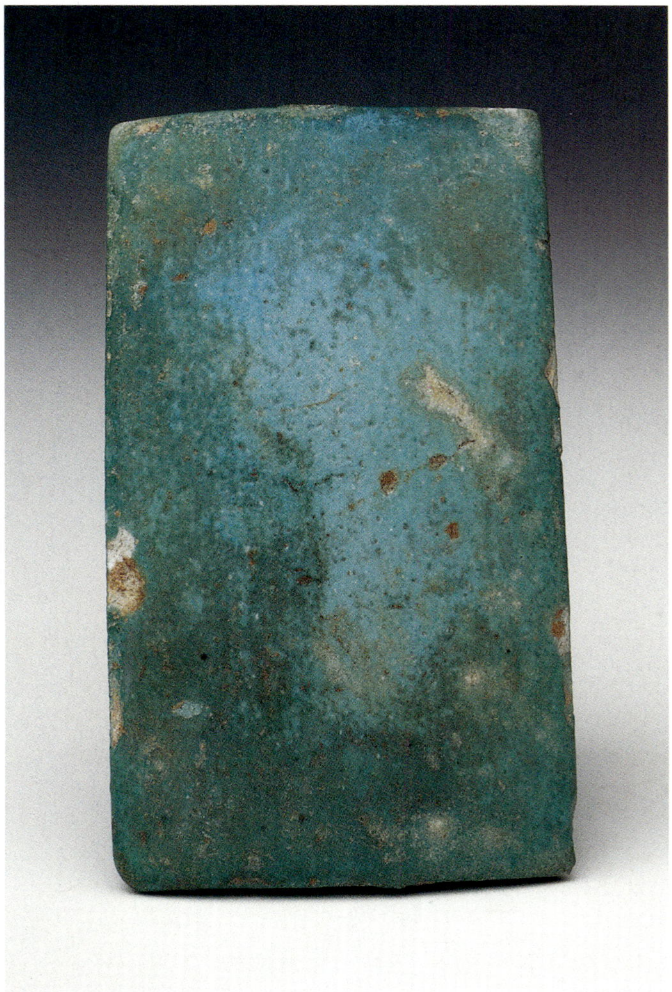

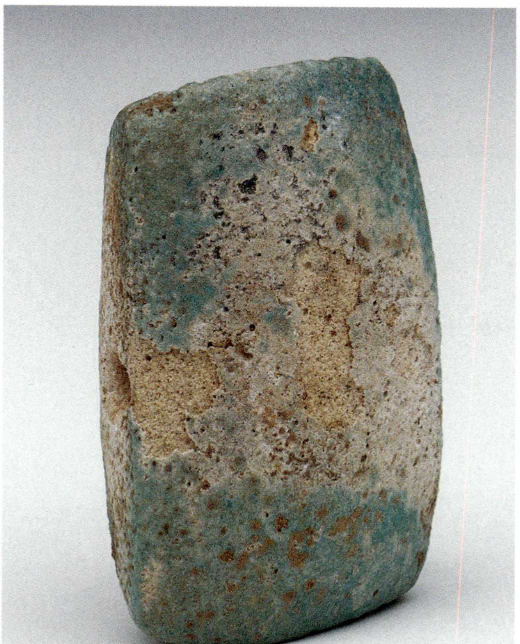

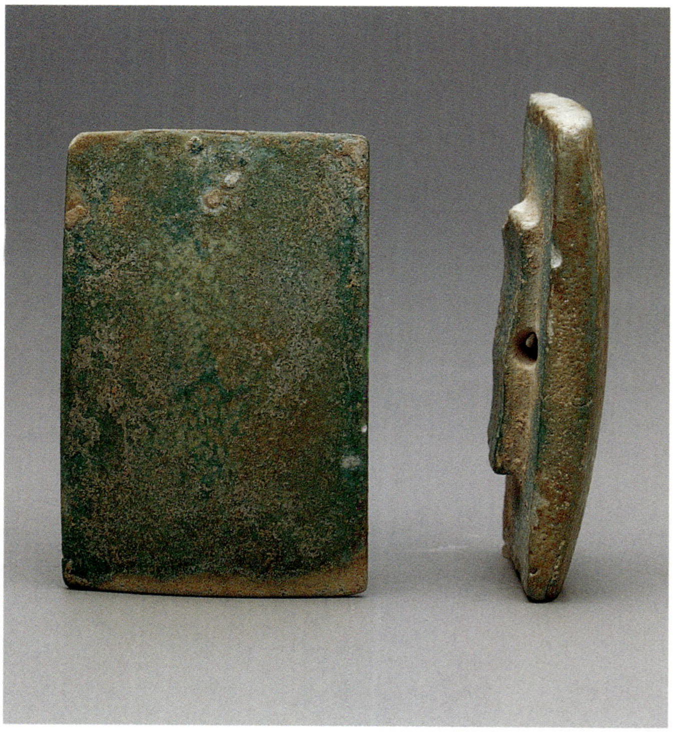

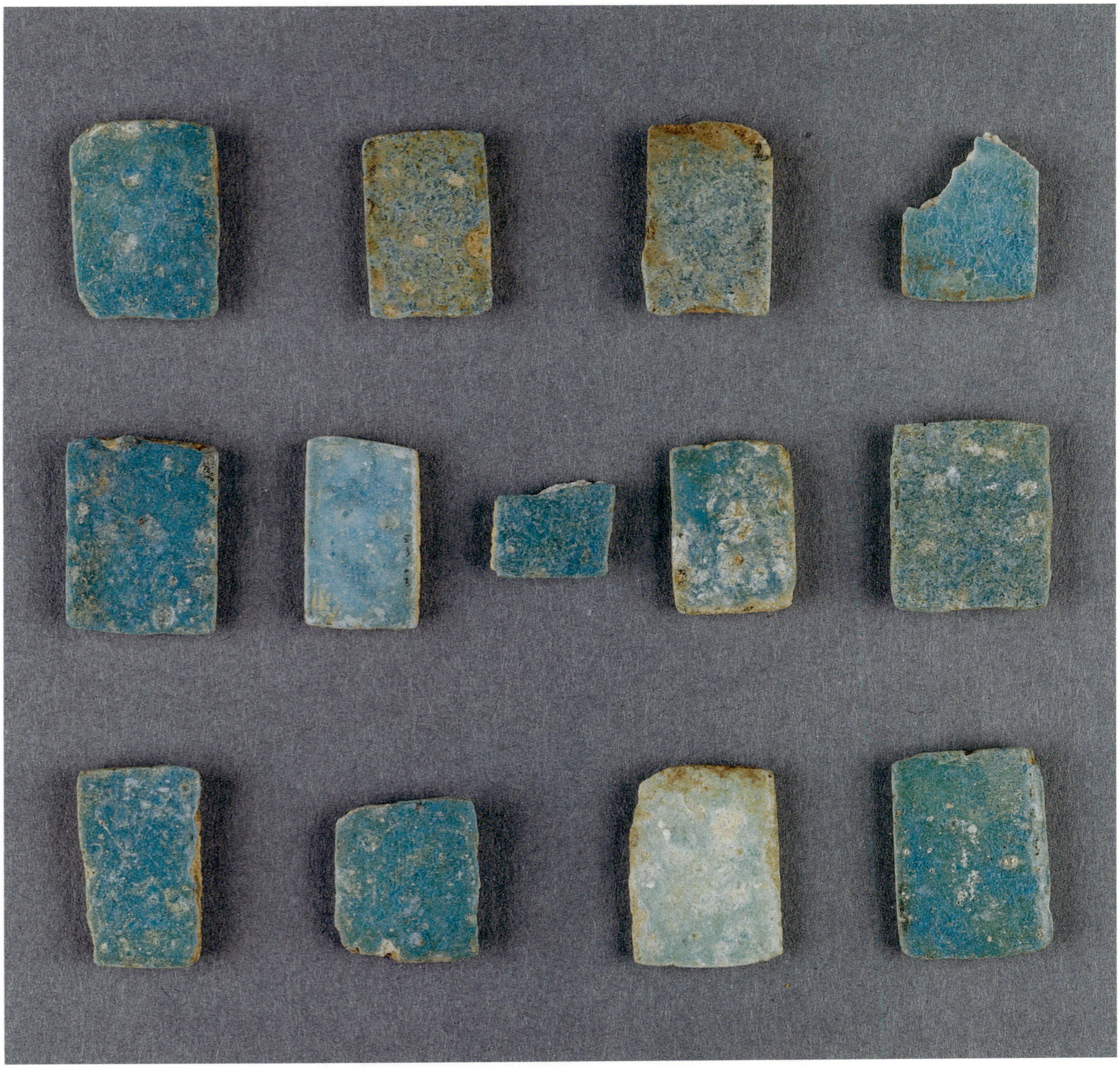

Opposite above, left and right
DJOSER TILE [19]
Old Kingdom, Dynasty 3
H. 6.0 cm; W. 3.6 cm

Opposite below, left
TILE [15]
Early Dynastic Period to Old Kingdom, Dynasty 2 or early Dynasty 3
H. 4.2 cm; W. 2.7 cm; TH. 1.5 cm

Opposite below, right (left)
DJOSER TILE [17]
Old Kingdom, Dynasty 3
H. 6.2 cm; W. 3.8 cm

Opposite below, right (right)
DJOSER TILE [18]
Old Kingdom, Dynasty 3
H. 5.9 cm; W. 3.8 cm;
TH. 0.15–0.25 cm

Above
INLAYS [14]
Early Dynastic Period, Dynasty 1
L. 1.4–1.6 cm; W. 0.9–1.2 cm;
TH. 0.15–0.25 cm

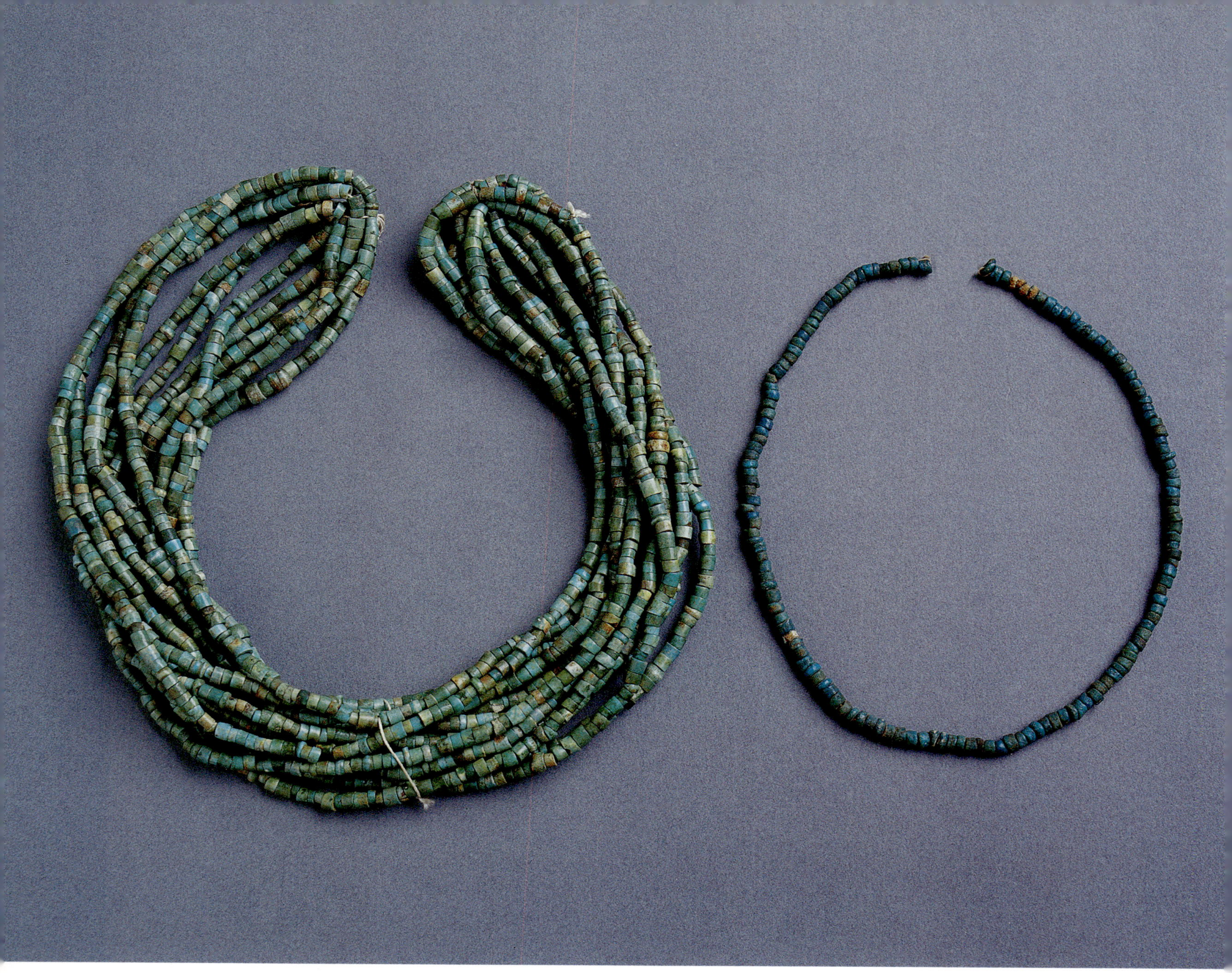

Above, left

BELT (?) [1]

Predynastic Period, Badarian

L. 35.0 cm (bundled)

Above, right

NECKLACE [2]

Late Predynastic Period, Naqada III

L. approx. 30.5 cm

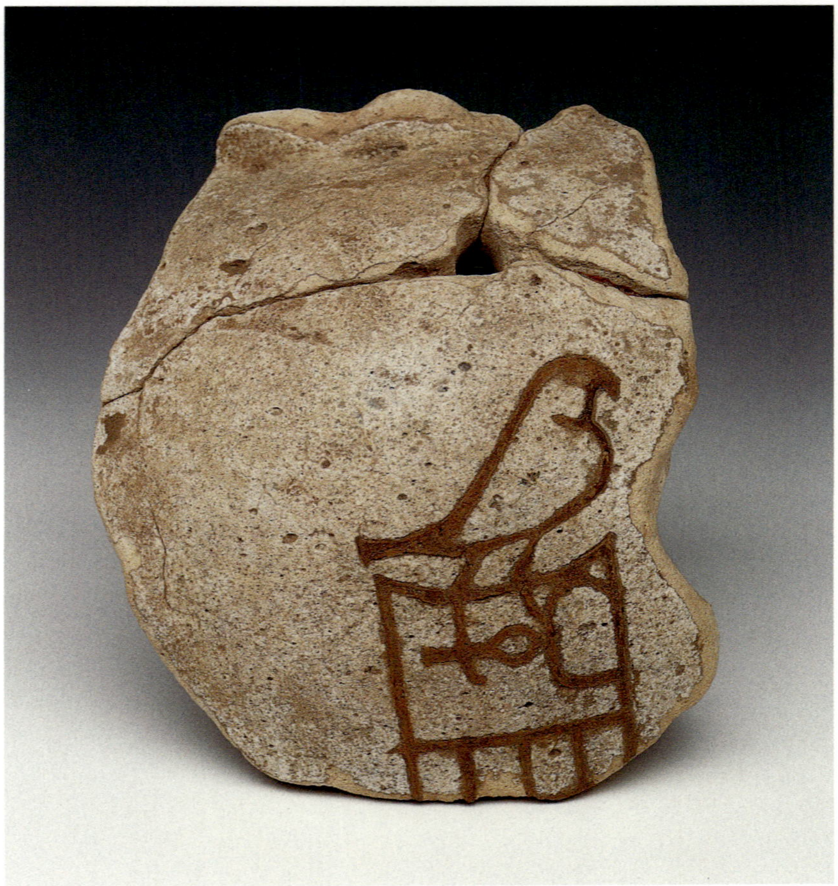

Left

VASE FRAGMENT BEARING A ROYAL SEREKH [13]
Early Dynastic Period, Dynasty 1
H. 14.0 cm; W. 11.4 cm

Below

FRAGMENT OF A TILE [16]
Early Dynastic Period, probably Dynasty 1
H. 6.0 cm; W. 6.2 cm; TH. 1.8 cm

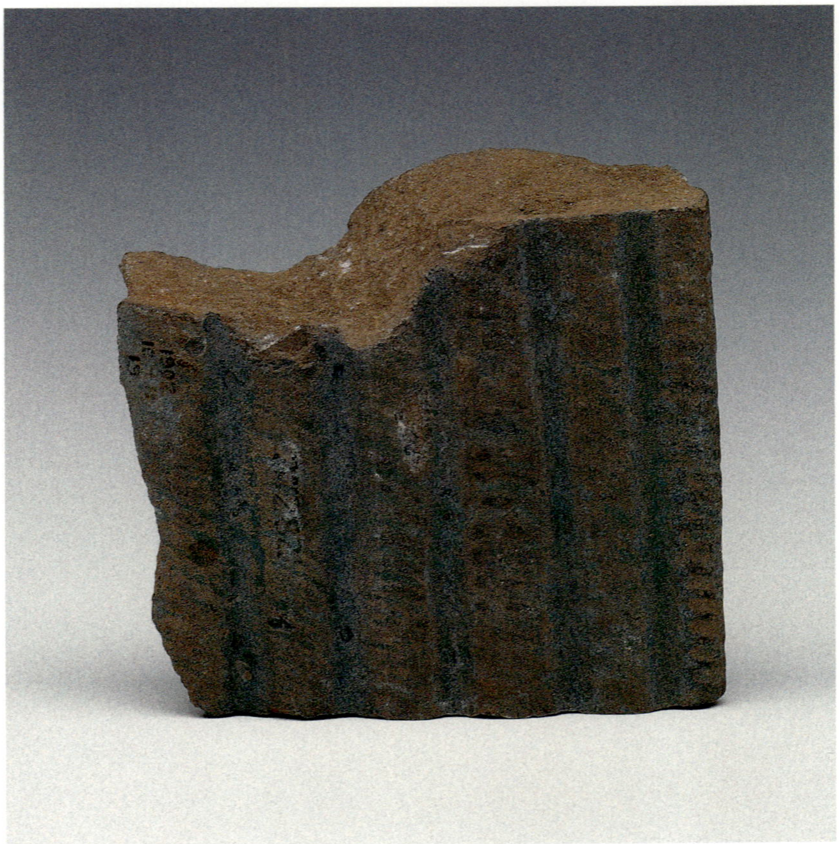

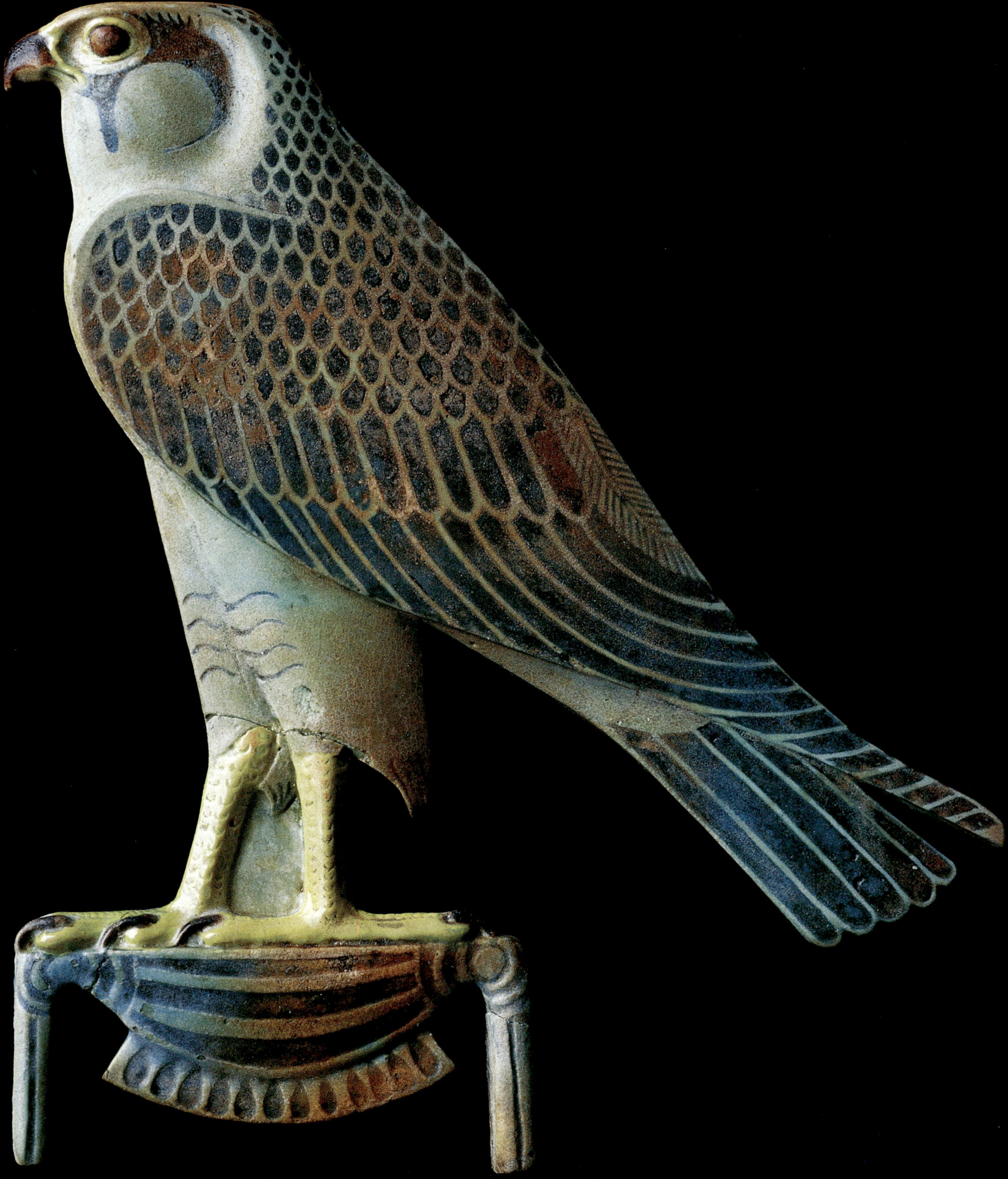

FAIENCE AND ROYAL LIFE

Throughout Egyptian history royalty used faience for objects ranging from furniture inlays and jewelry to small-scale statuary and detailed wall decorations that advertised the cosmic and political power of the king. The inlaid polychrome faience of the New Kingdom, probably Egypt's most accomplished faience form, is but one illustration that this non-clay ceramic was often used not simply as an inexpensive substitute for more costly materials but for its intrinsic properties associated with light and rebirth.

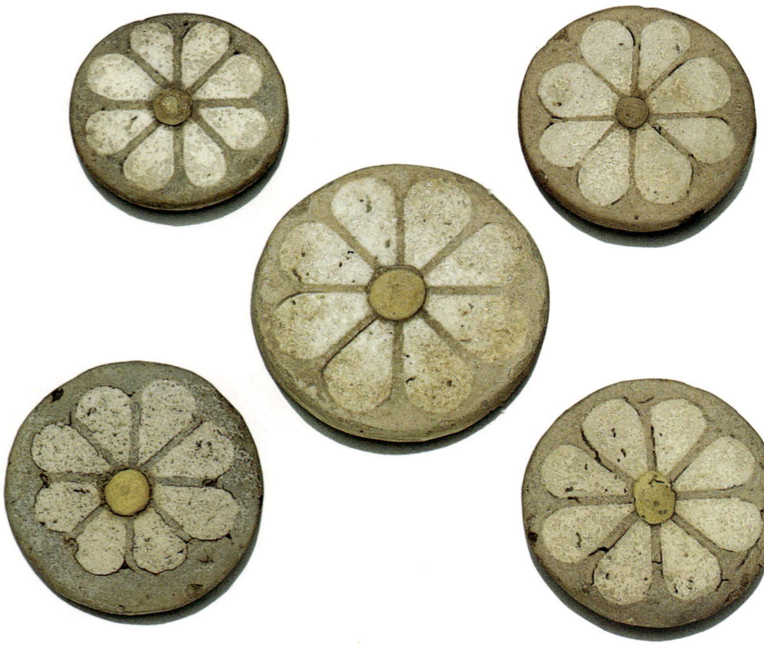

Opposite
INLAY IN THE FORM OF THE COMPOSITE HIEROGLYPH, "THE HORUS (OR FALCON?) OF GOLD" [61]
Late Period, Dynasty 30 to Ptolemaic Period, 380–30 BC
H. 15.4 cm; W. 12.9 cm; TH. 1.2 cm

Right
ROSETTES [55]
See p. 87

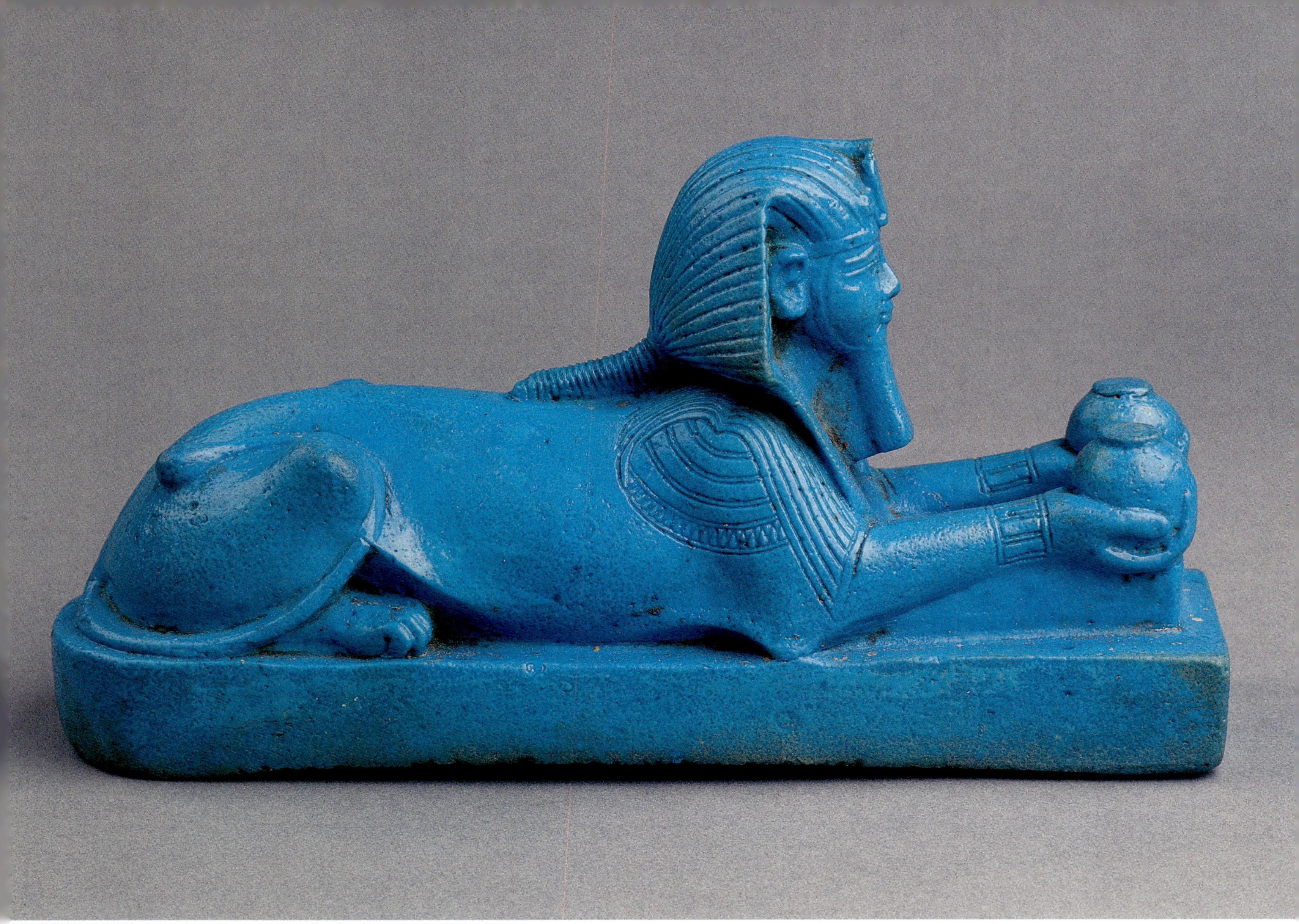

Opposite and above
AMENHOTEP III AS A SPHINX [22]
New Kingdom, Dynasty 18
H. 14.0 cm; W. 7.0 cm; L. 25.0 cm

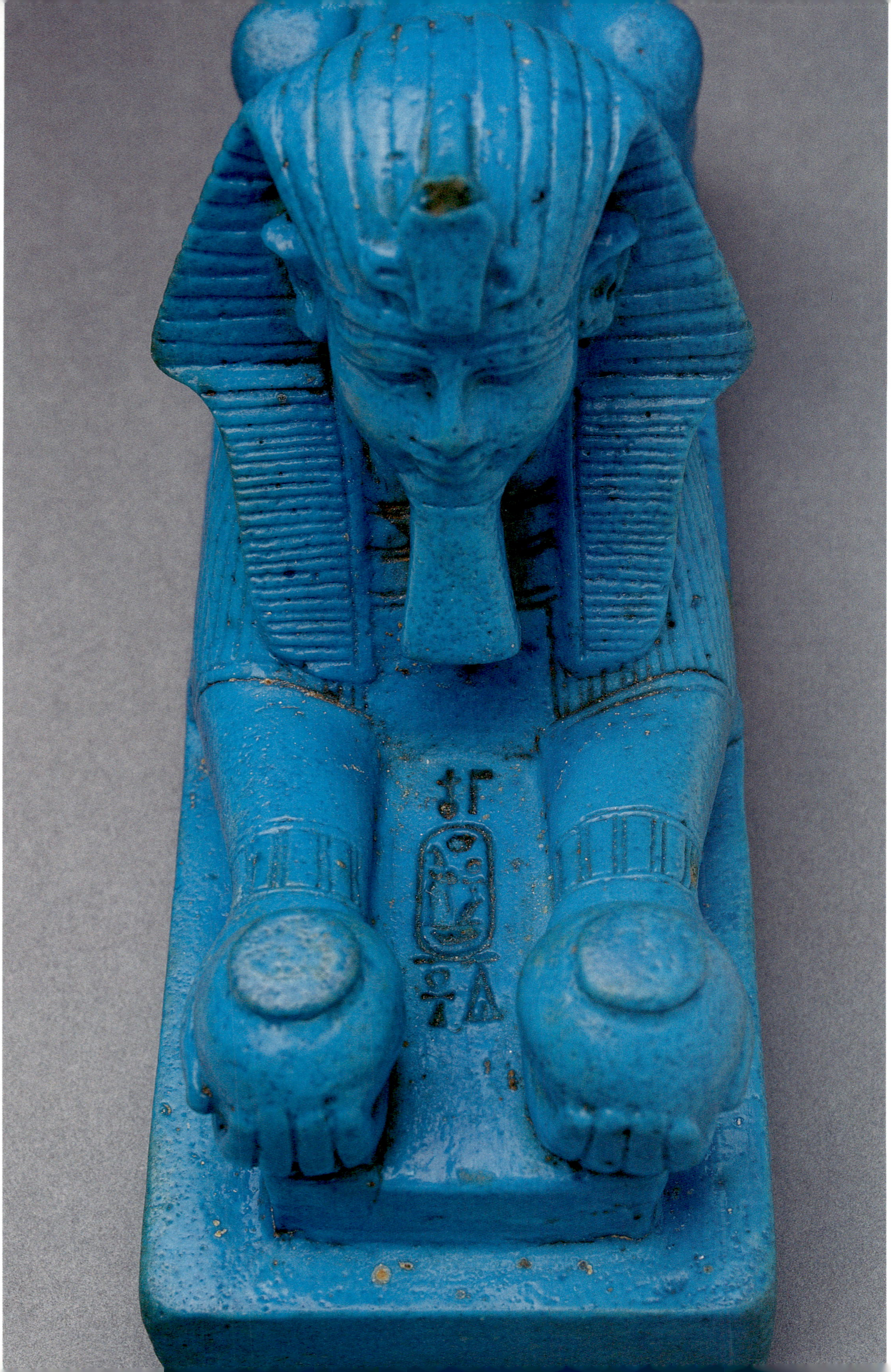

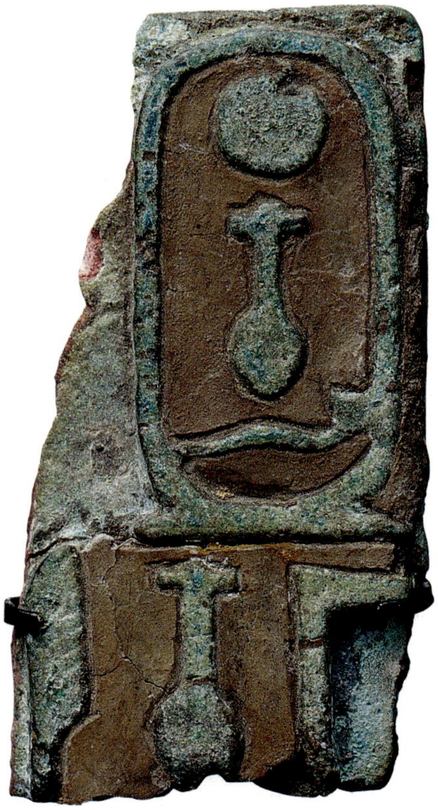

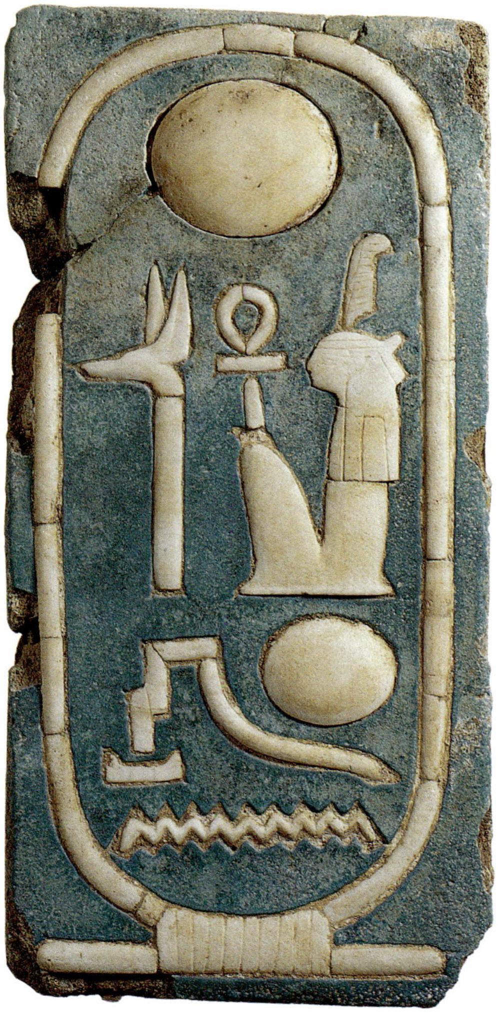

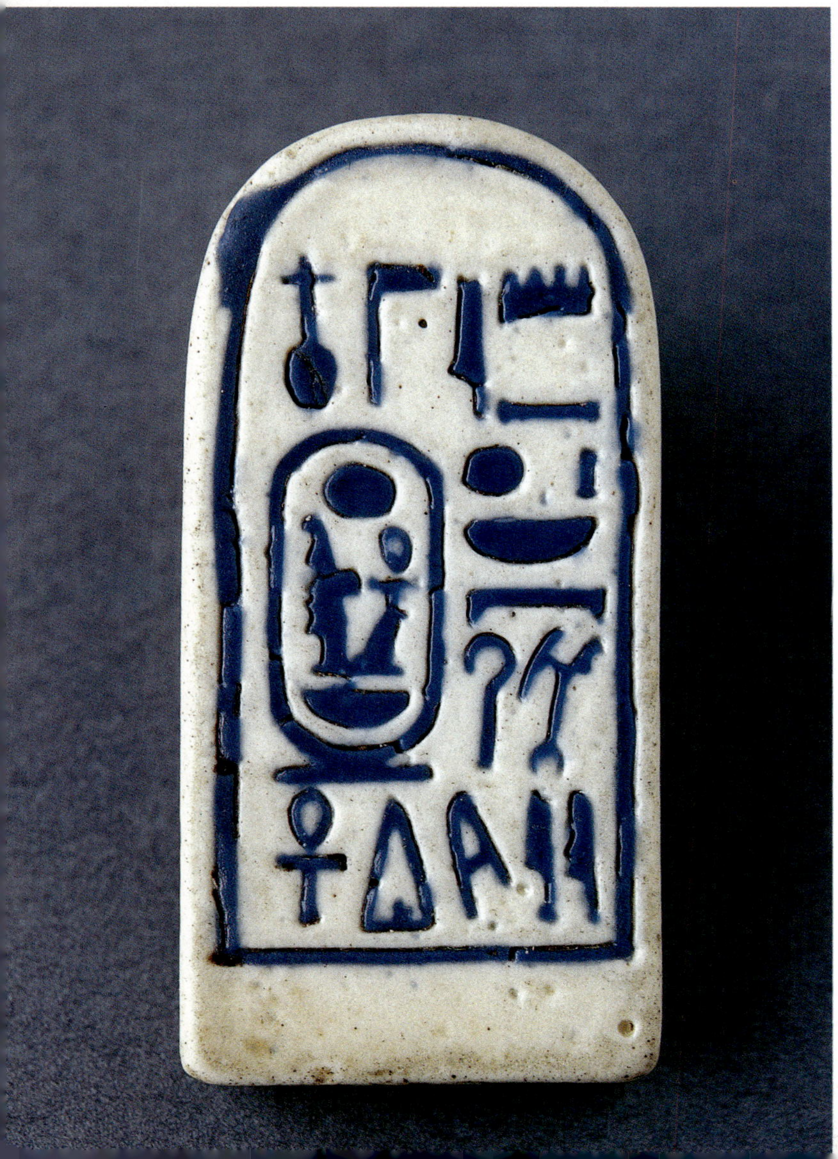

Above left
INLAY WITH CARTOUCHE OF KING RANEFEREF [21]
Old Kingdom, Dynasty 5, reign of Raneferef
H. 6.5 cm; W. 3.2 cm; TH. 0.6 cm

Above
TILE WITH CARTOUCHE WITH CALCITE INLAYS [50]
New Kingdom, Dynasty 19, reign of Ramesses II
H. 26.5 cm; W. 12.6 cm

Left
AMENHOTEP III BOOKPLATE [24]
New Kingdom, Dynasty 18, reign of Amenhotep III
H. 4.3 cm; W. 2.04 cm; TH. 0.6 cm

Opposite
COSMETIC JAR INSCRIBED FOR KING AMENHOTEP III AND QUEEN TIYE [23]
New Kingdom, Dynasty 18, reign of Amenhotep III
H. 8.6 cm; DIAM. at mouth 6.15 cm

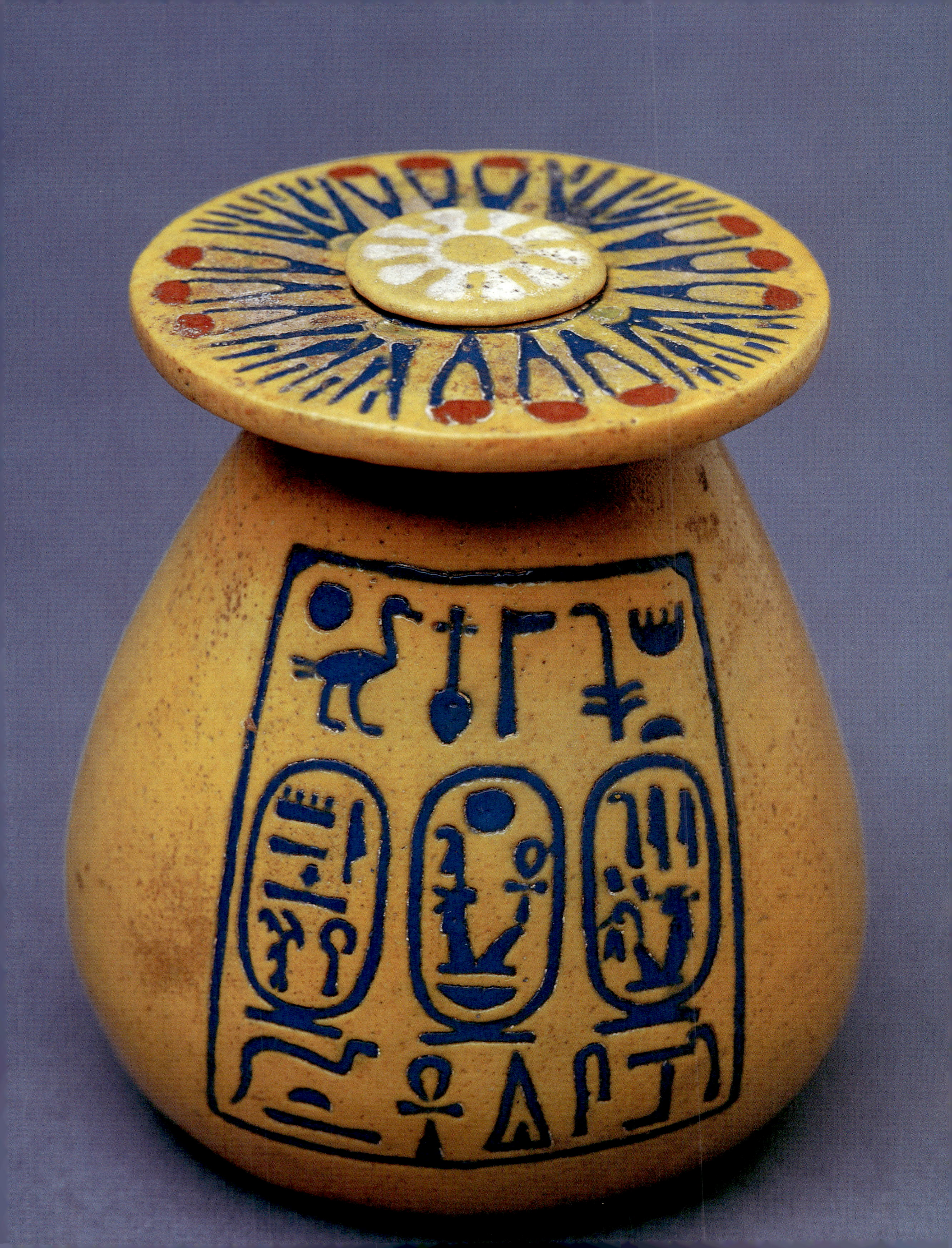

Right, above and below
DIVINE WIG [27]
Probably Third Intermediate Period, *c.* 1000–800 BC
H. 18.5 cm; W. 14.4 cm; D. 10.7 cm

Below
"BLUE CROWN" FROM A COMPOSITE STATUE [29]
New Kingdom, end of Dynasty 18
H. 9.6 cm; W. 8.9 cm; D. 8.6 cm
Interior mortise H. 4.5 cm; W. 3.6 cm; D. 4.0 cm

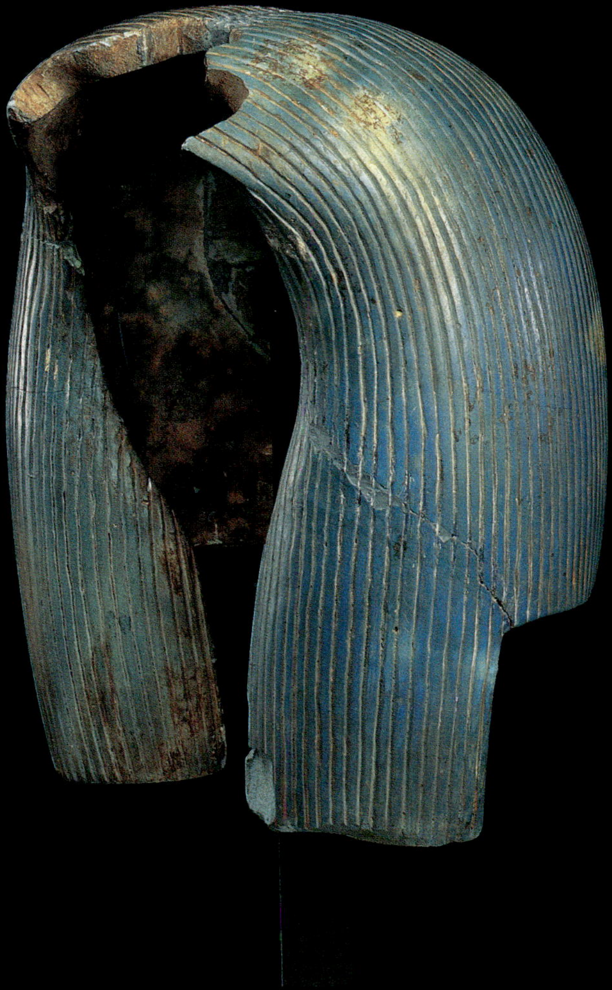

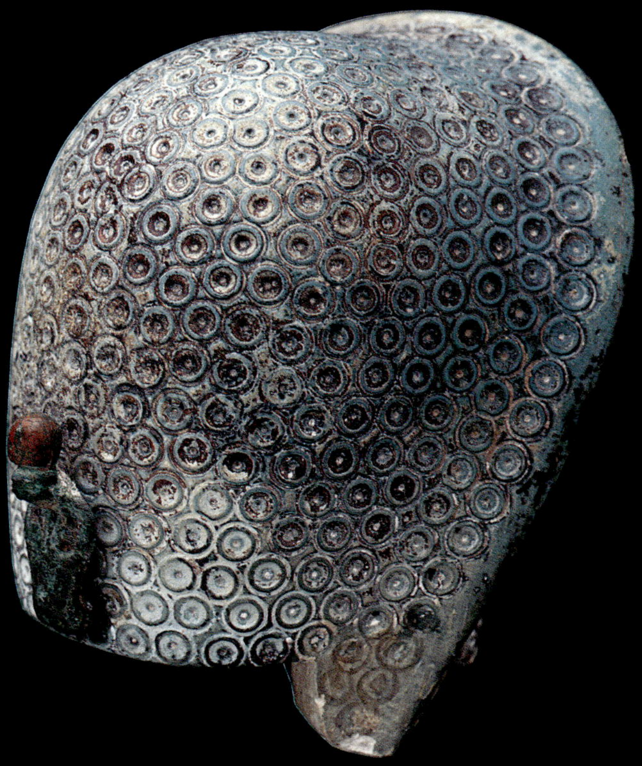

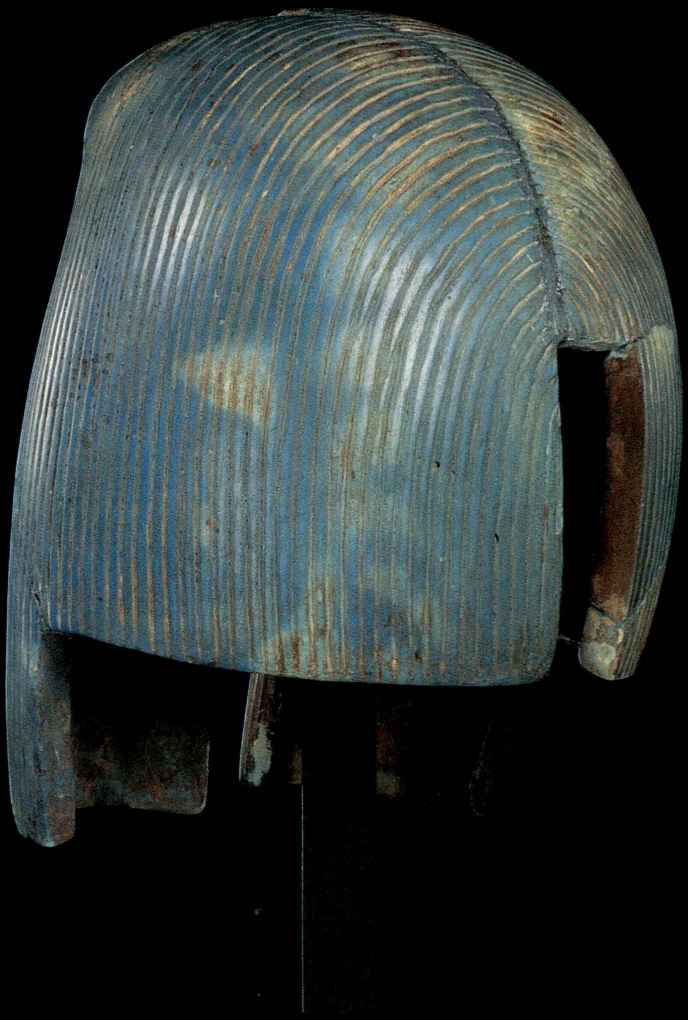

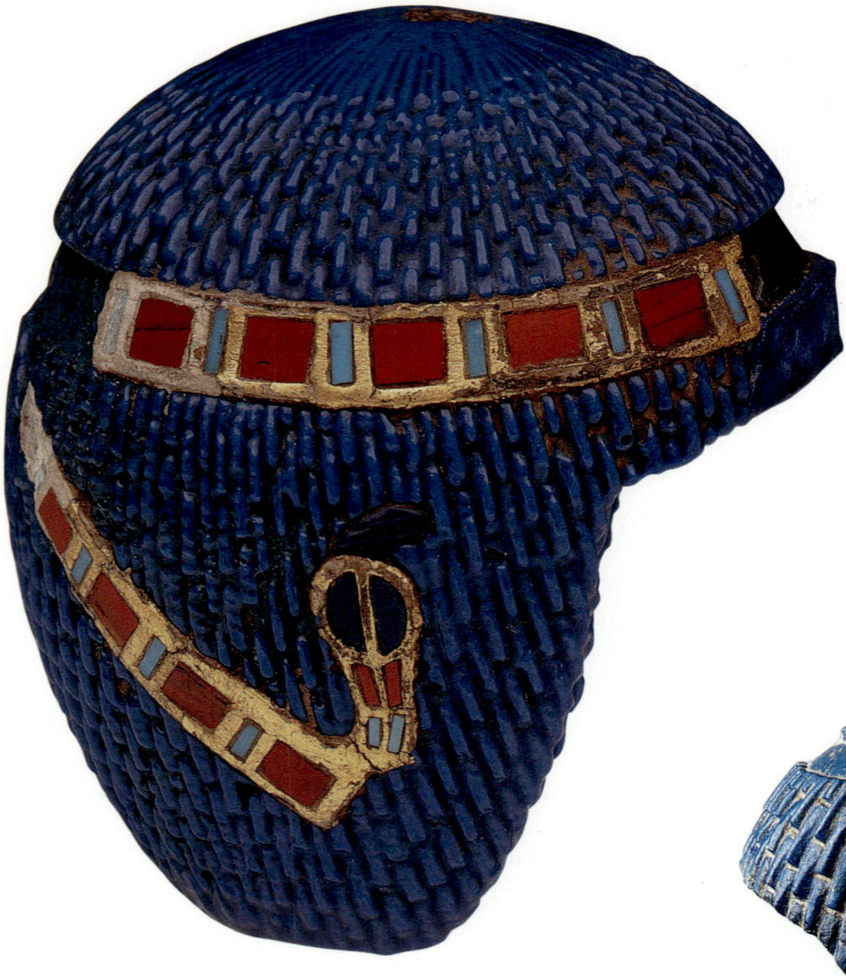

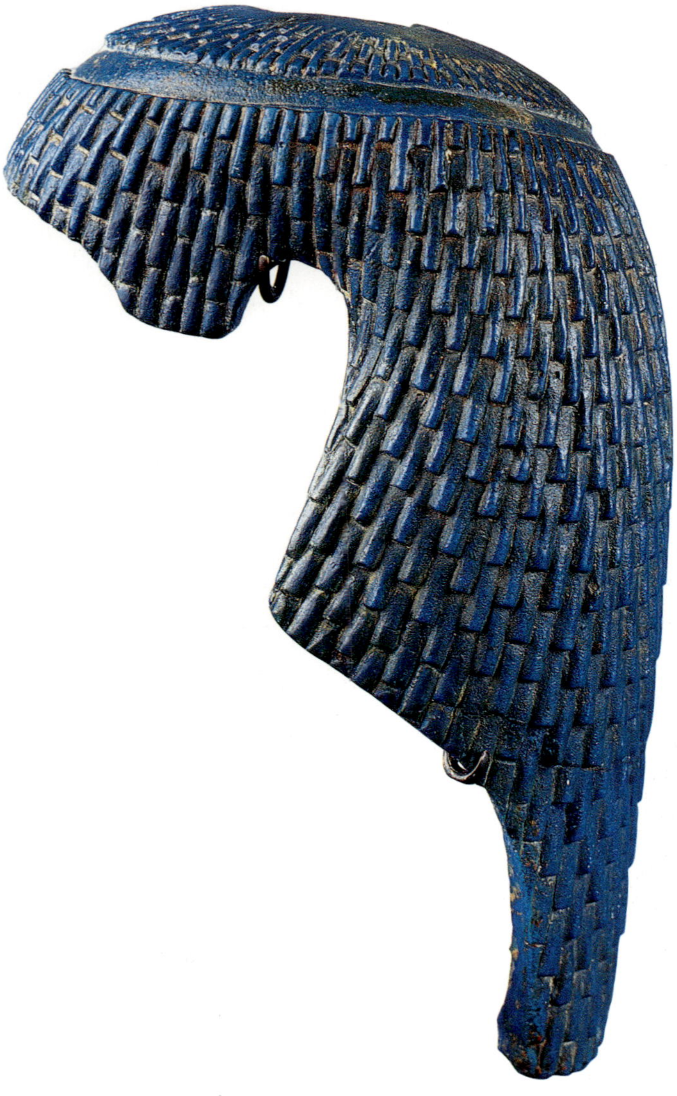

Above

ROUND WIG [28]
New Kingdom, Dynasty 18–19
H. 9.5 cm

Right

FEMALE WIG [26]
New Kingdom, probably Dynasty 18
H. 19.8 cm; W. 13.3 cm; D. 6.0 cm

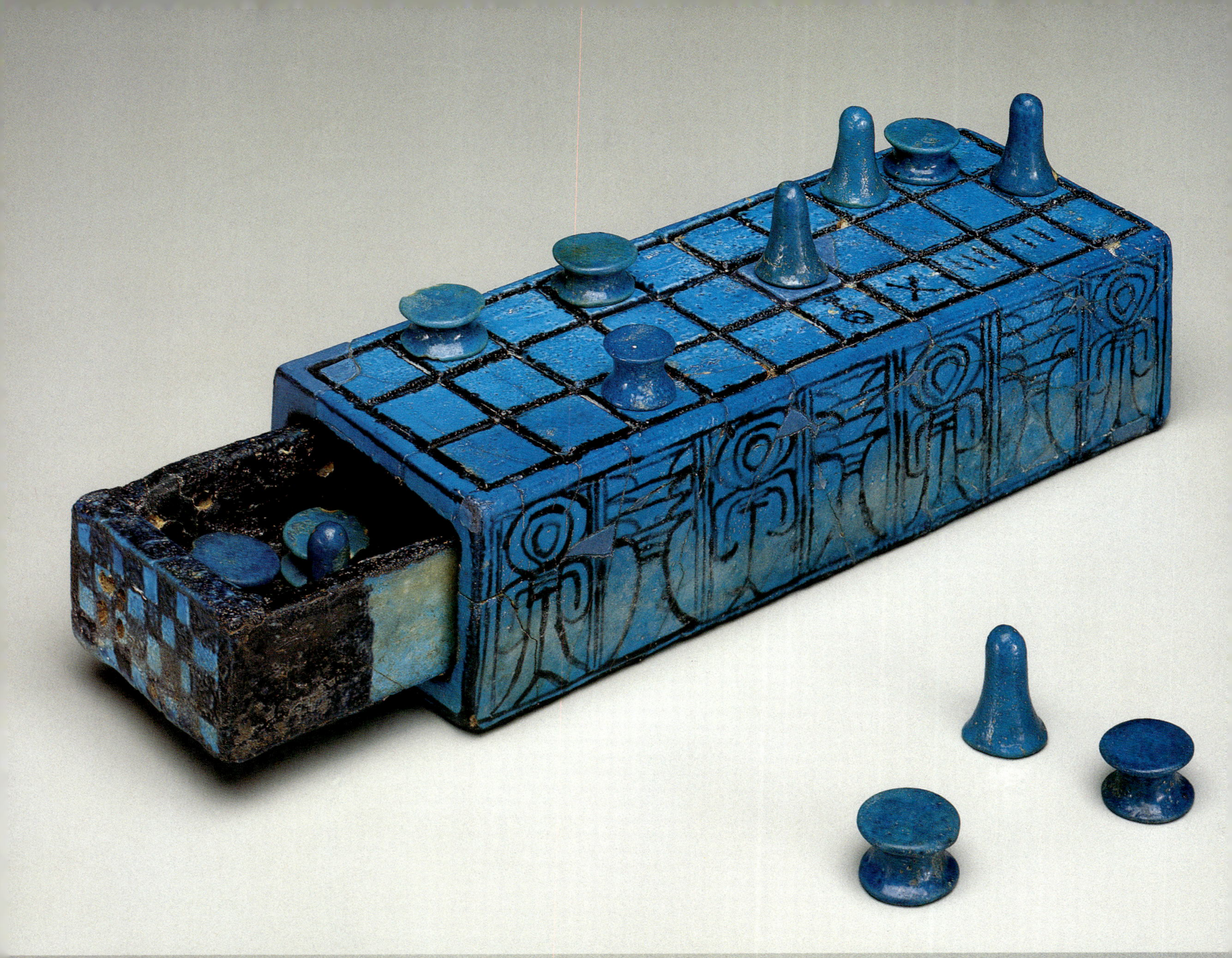

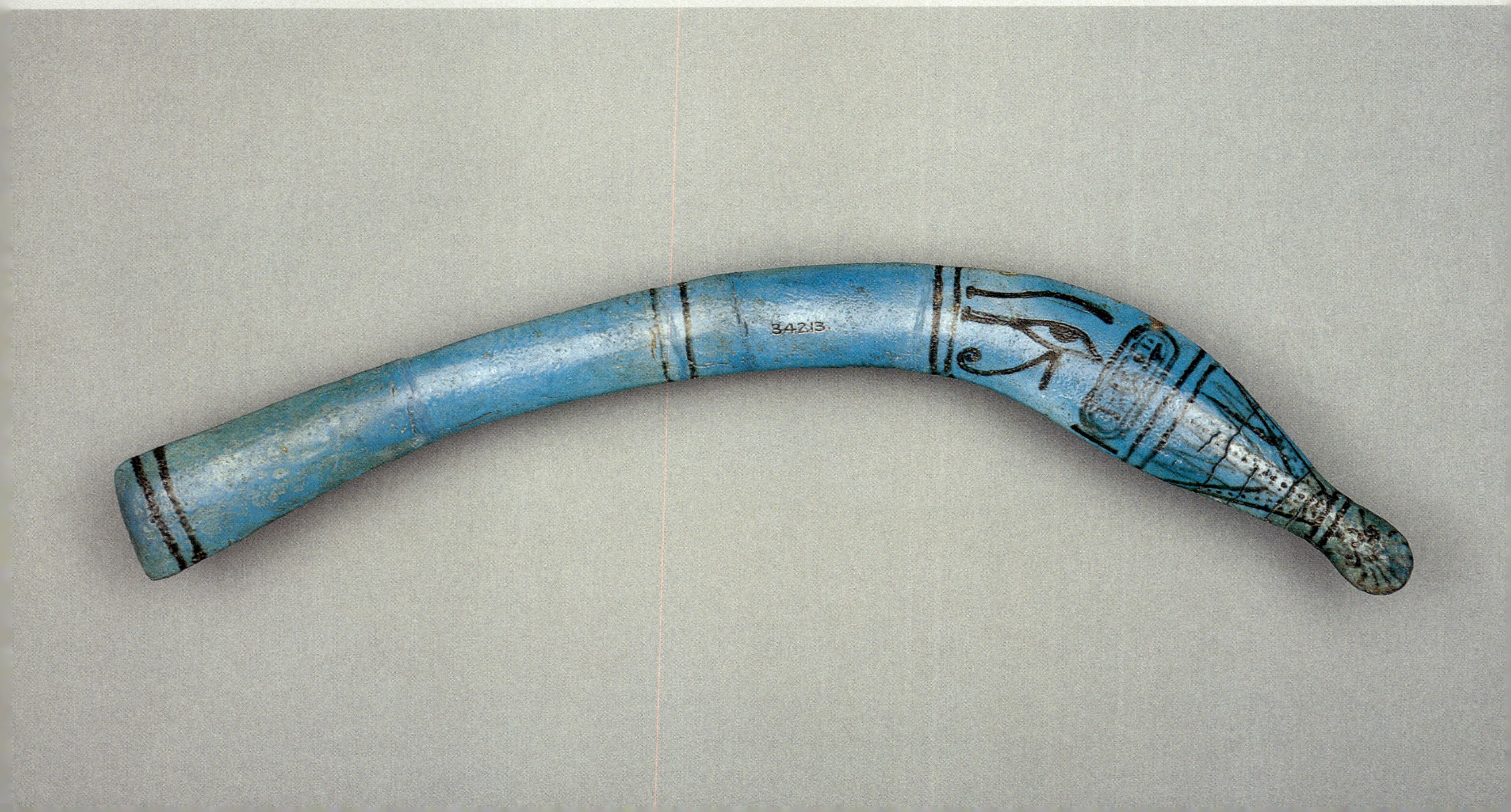
34213

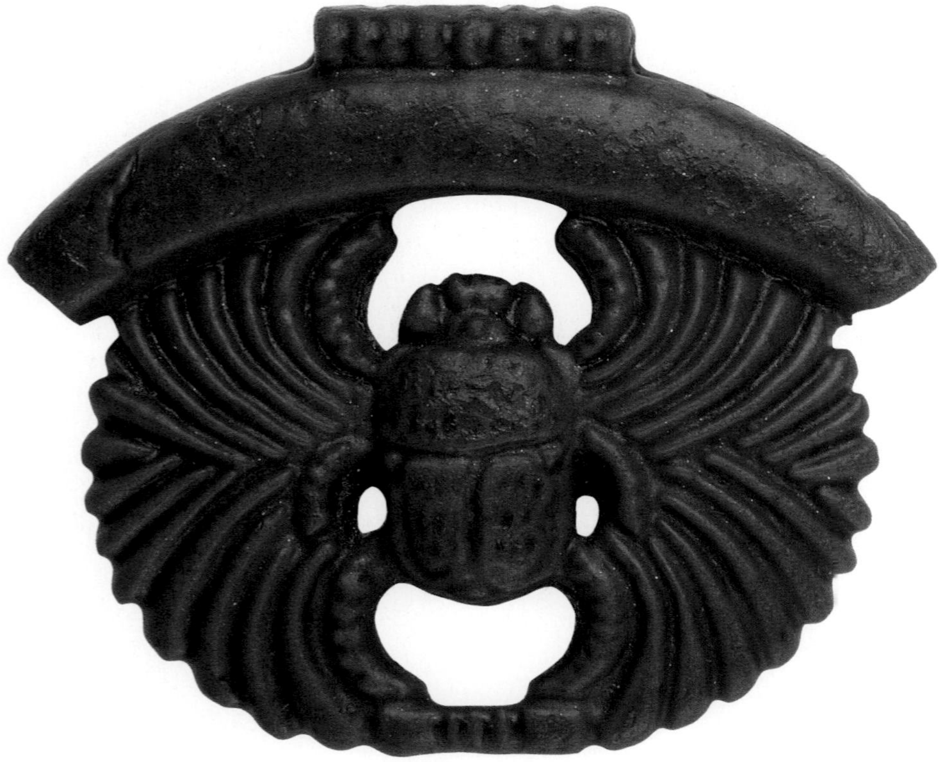

Above

WINGED SCARAB [44]
New Kingdom, Dynasty 18
Max. H. 3.6 cm; max. W. 3.0 cm

Opposite above

SENET GAME BOARD WITH COUNTERS [30]
New Kingdom, Dynasty 18, reign of Amenhotep III
H. 5.5 cm; W. 7.7 cm; L. 21.5 cm

Opposite below

MODEL THROWSTICK OF AKHENATEN [32]
New Kingdom, Dynasty 18, reign of Akhenaten
L. 38.5 cm; max. W. 4.4 cm; max. TH. 1.7 cm

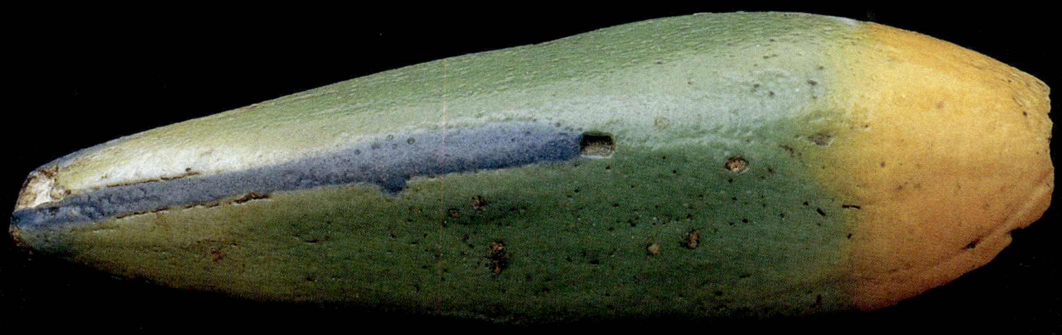

Above
LOTUS BUD [41]
New Kingdom, Dynasty 18
H. 5.5 cm; W. 1.5 cm

Right
BLUE LOTUS A [39]
New Kingdom, Dynasty 18
H. 3.8 cm; W. 3.7 cm; D. 0.5 cm

Far right
BLUE LOTUS B [40]
New Kingdom, Dynasty 18
H. 2.6 cm; W. 2.7 cm; D. 0.4 cm

Below
STYLIZED FLORAL FRIEZE [51]
New Kingdom, Dynasty 20, reign of Ramesses III
H. 7.1 cm; L. 29.1 cm

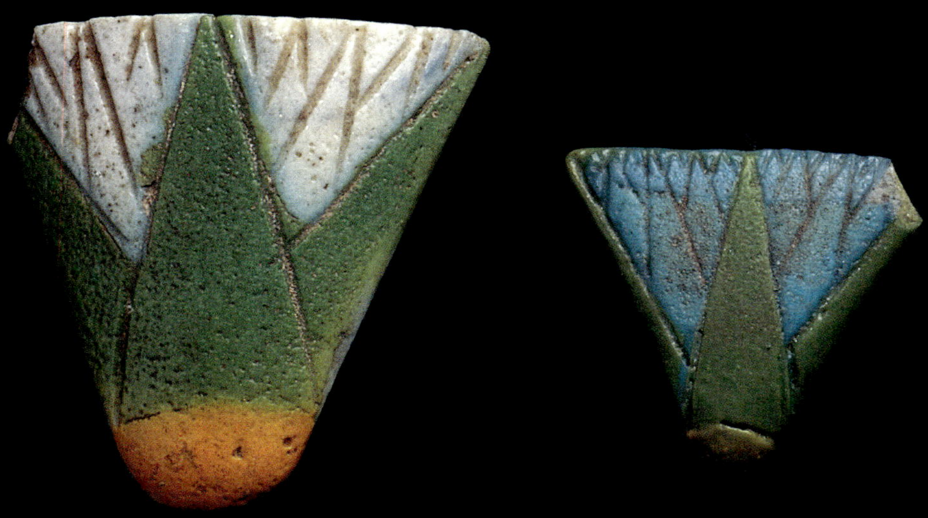

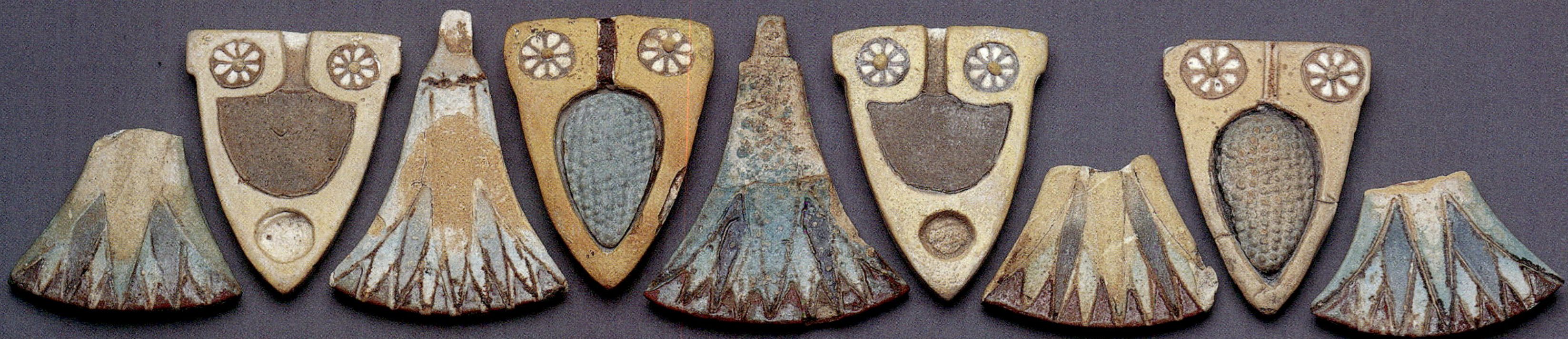

Right

ROSETTES [56]

New Kingdom, probably Dynasty 20

DIAM. 6.1 cm; 3.8 cm; 3.8 cm; TH. 0.9 cm

Center

ROSETTES [55]

New Kingdom, probably Dynasty 20

DIAM. 3.2 cm; 4.3 cm; 3.5 cm; 3.8 cm; 3.7 cm

Below

LOTUS BLOSSOM NECKLACE TERMINAL [31]

New Kingdom, Dynasty 18, reign of Amenhotep III

H. 5.65 cm; W. 10.0 cm; D. 0.8 cm

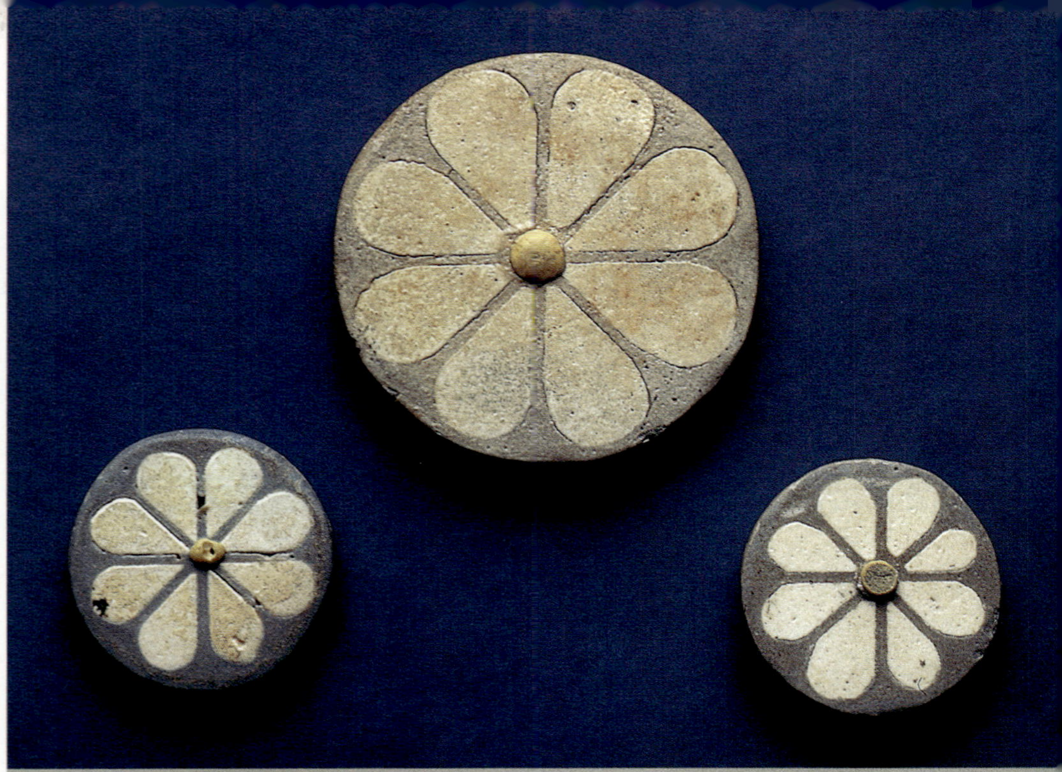

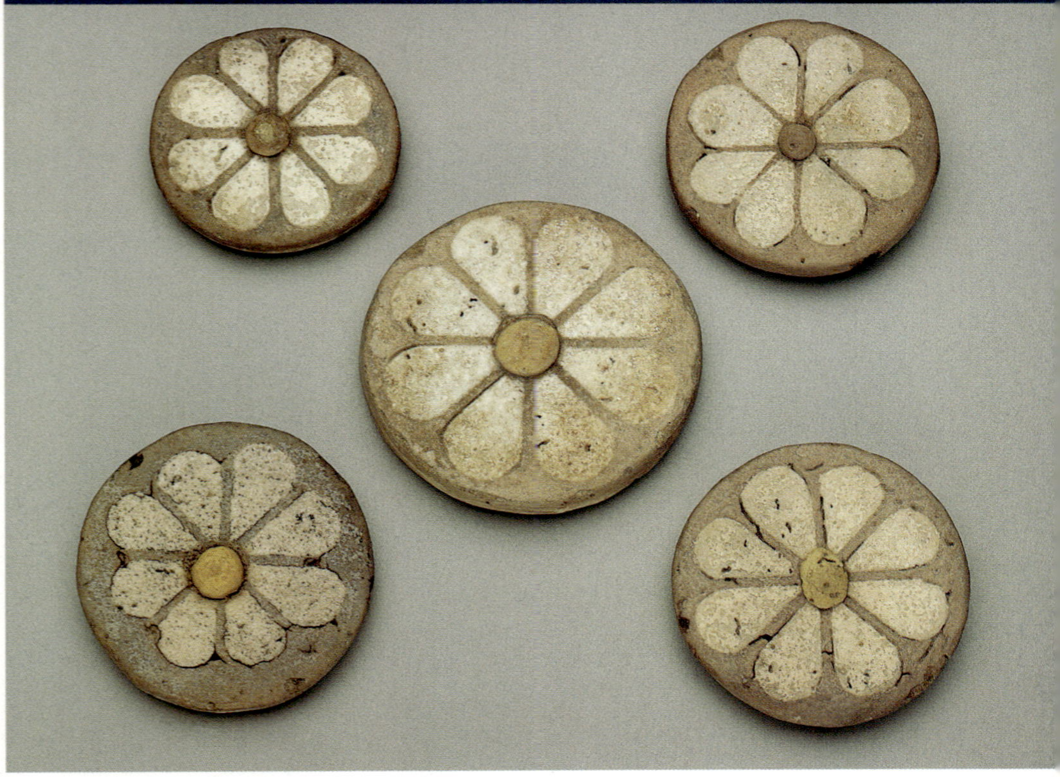

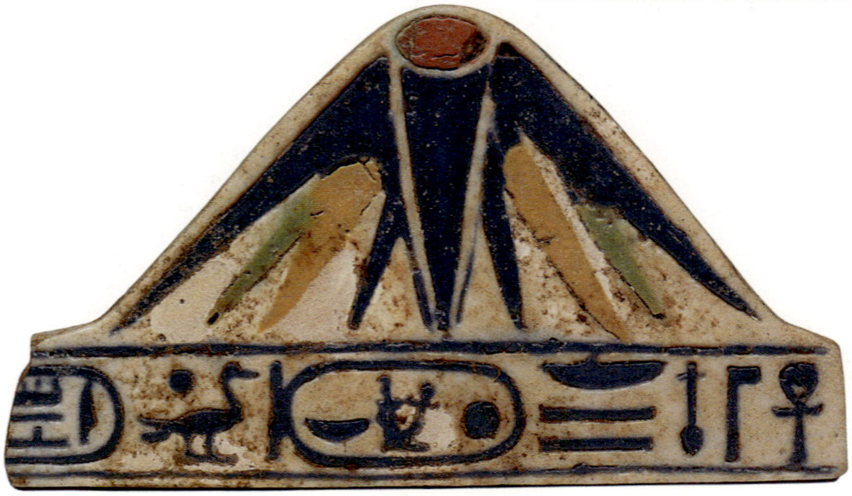

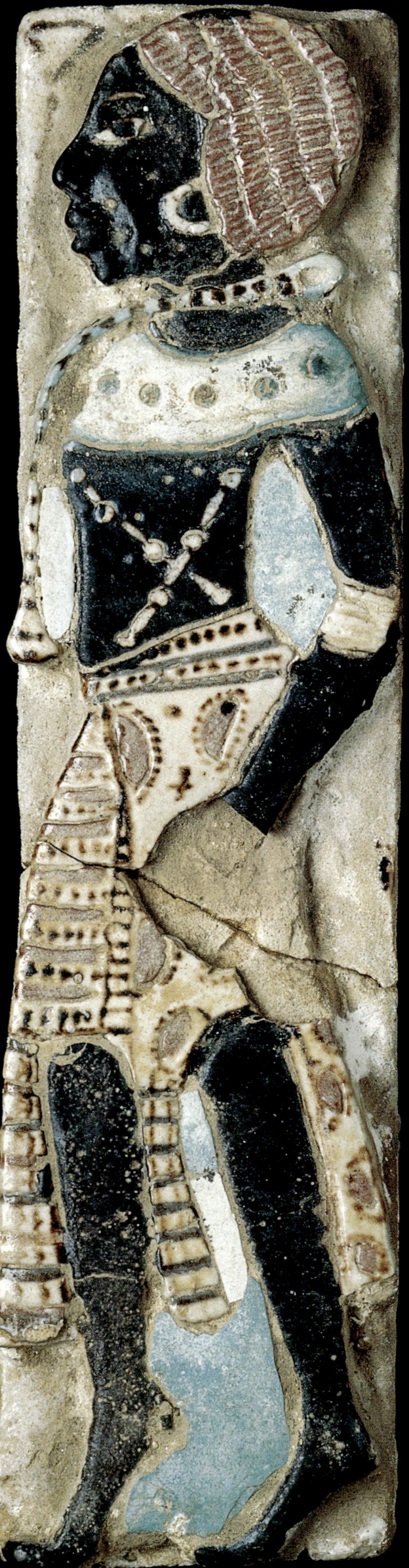
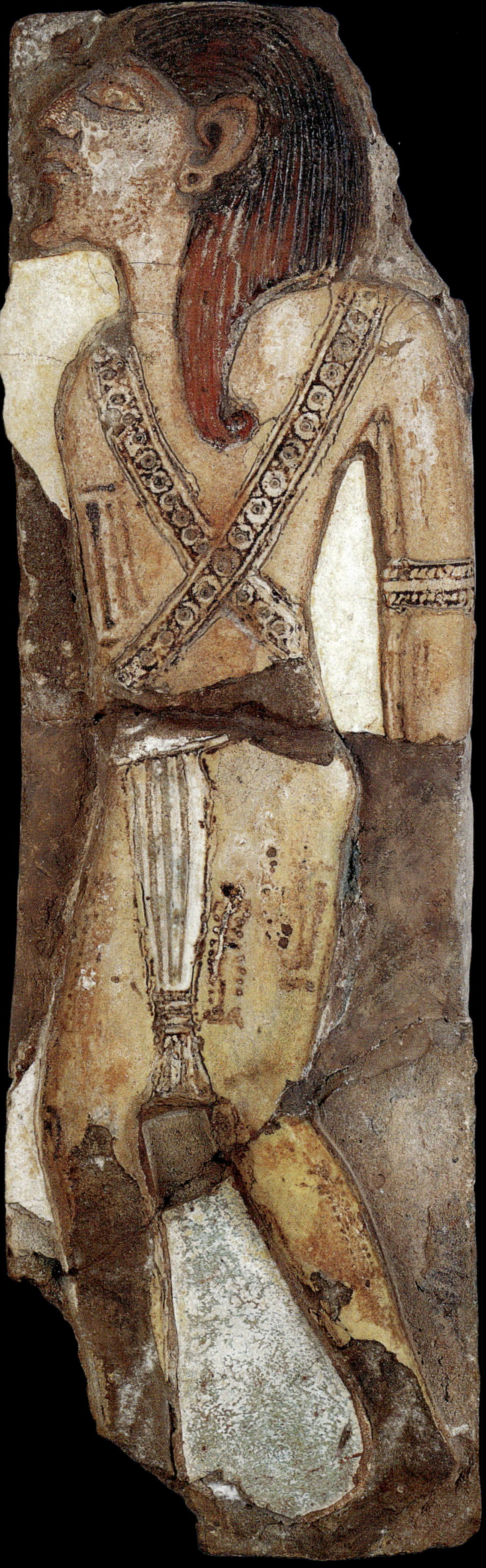

Right

TILE WITH "HITTITE" OR ASIATIC CHIEF [52]
New Kingdom, Dynasty 20, reign of Ramesses III
H. 16.8 cm; W. 5.5 cm

Opposite left

TILE WITH NUBIAN CHIEF [53]
New Kingdom, Dynasty 20, reign of Ramesses III
H. 25.0 cm; W. 6.0 cm

Opposite right

TILE WITH LIBYAN CHIEF [54]
New Kingdom, Dynasty 20, reign of Ramesses III
H. 31.0 cm; W. 9.0 cm

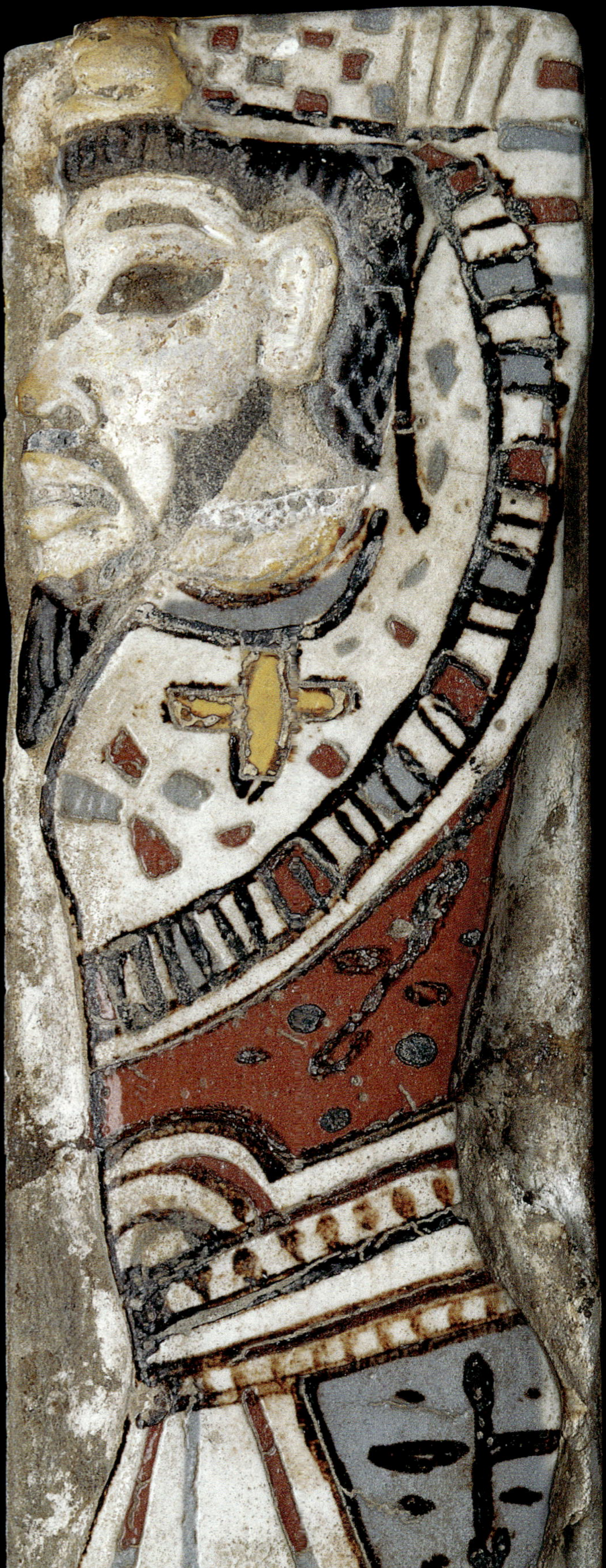

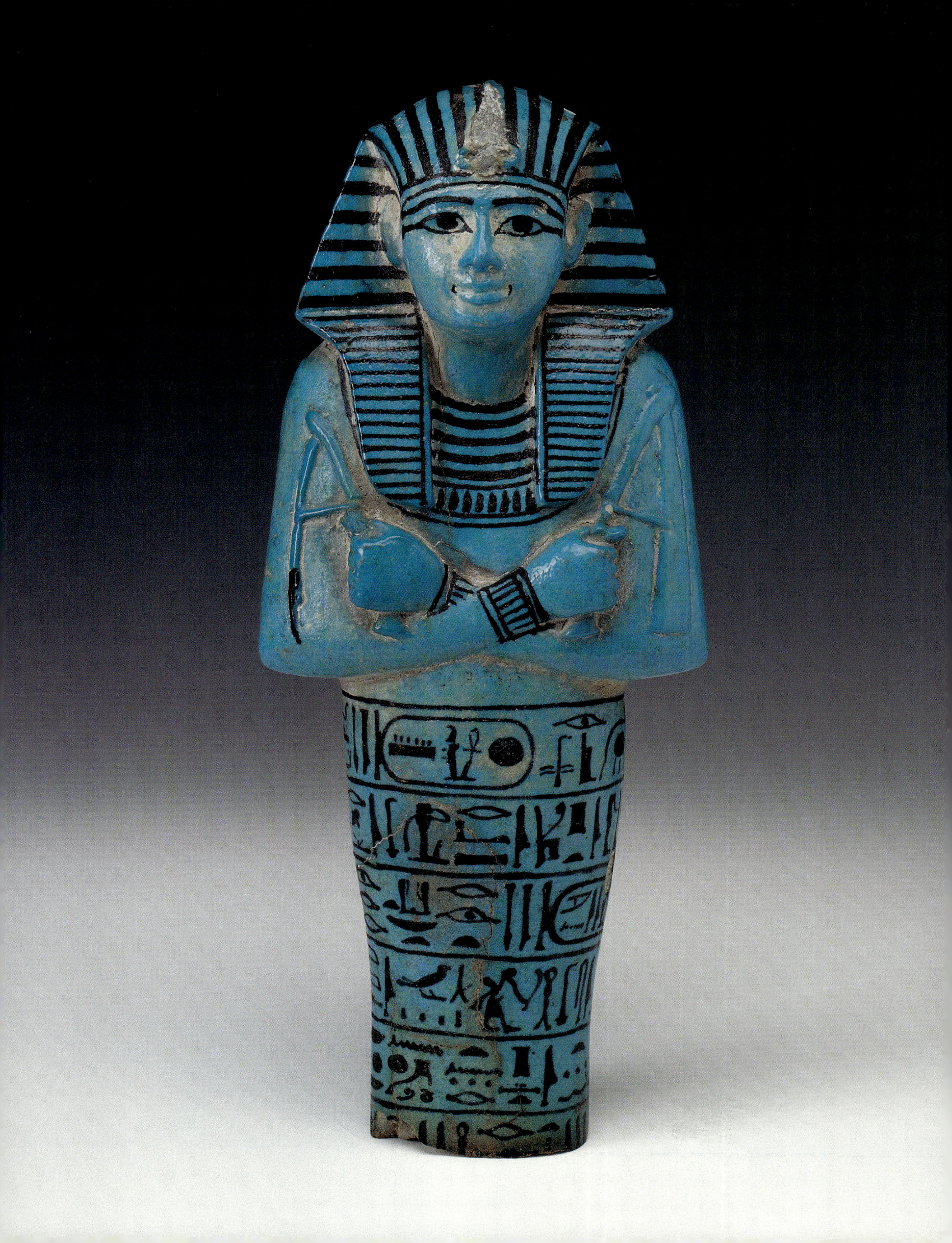

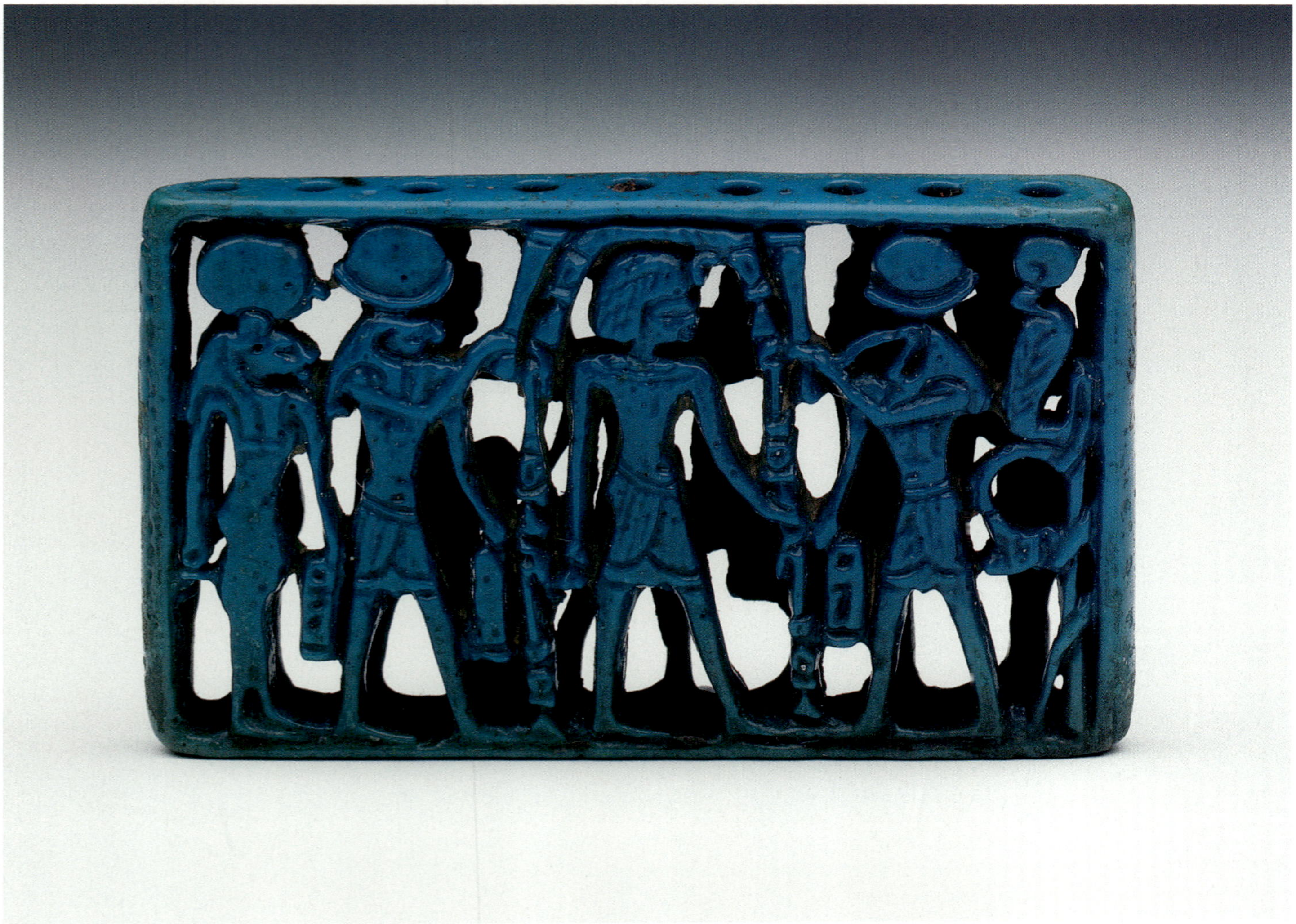

Above

SPACER BEAD FOR A NECKLACE [46]

Third Intermediate Period, 9th to 8th century BC

L. 5.4 cm; H. 3.2 cm; TH. 0.6 cm

Opposite

SHABTI OF KING SETI I [48]

New Kingdom, Dynasty 19, reign of Seti I

H. 22.4 cm; max. W. 9.6 cm

Right

COLUMNAR OBJECT INSCRIBED WITH THE NAME OF RAMESSES II [49]
New Kingdom, Dynasty 19
H. 8.7 cm

Below

BEAKER INSCRIBED FOR NESIKHONS [57]
Third Intermediate Period, Dynasty 21, *c.* 973 BC
H. 6.0 cm

Opposite

AMULET IN THE FORM OF A COUNTERWEIGHT [60]
Late Period, Dynasty 26, reign of Psametik I
H. 12.4 cm; W. 5.8 cm

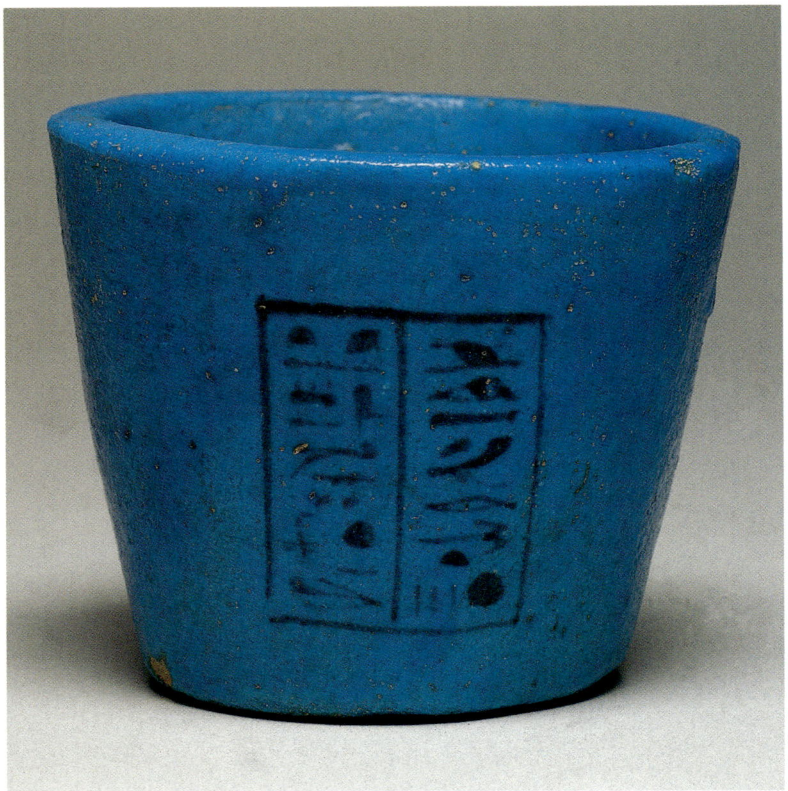

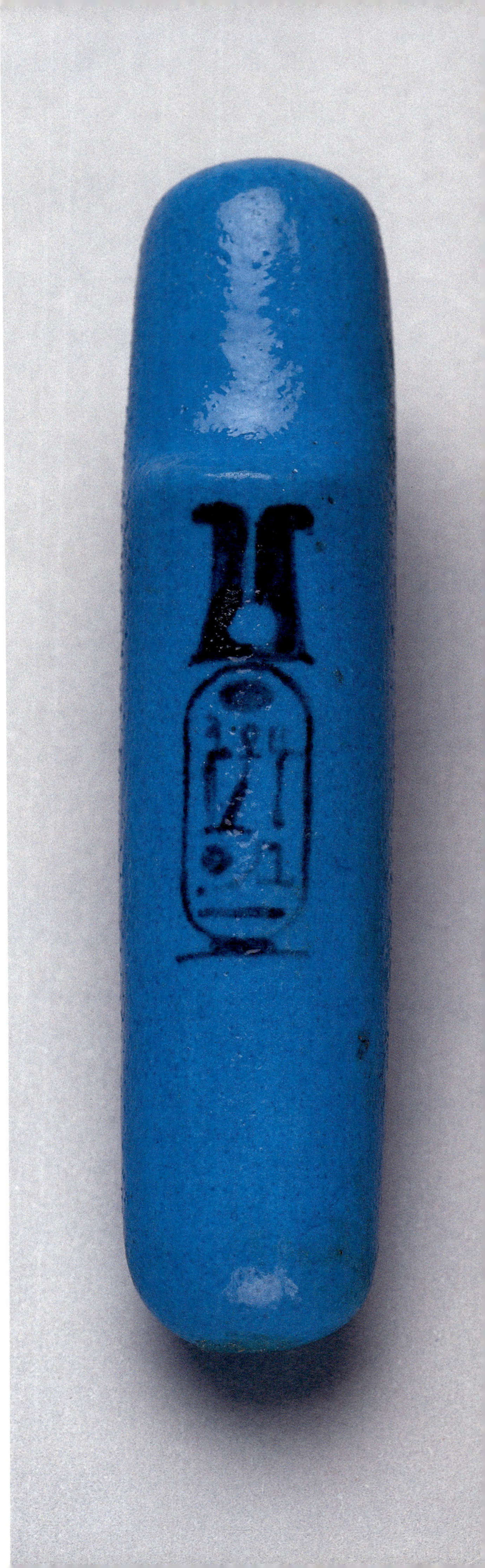

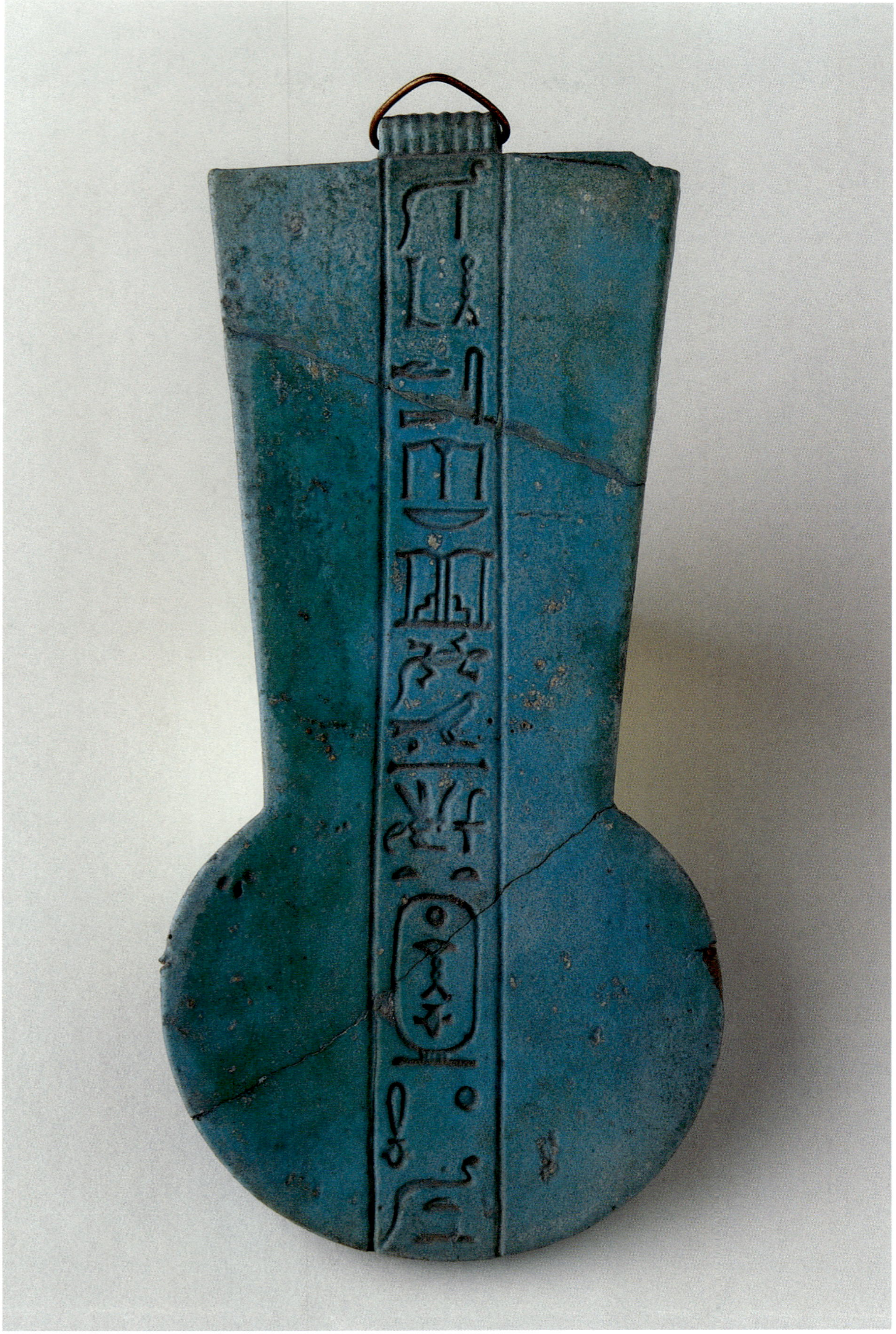

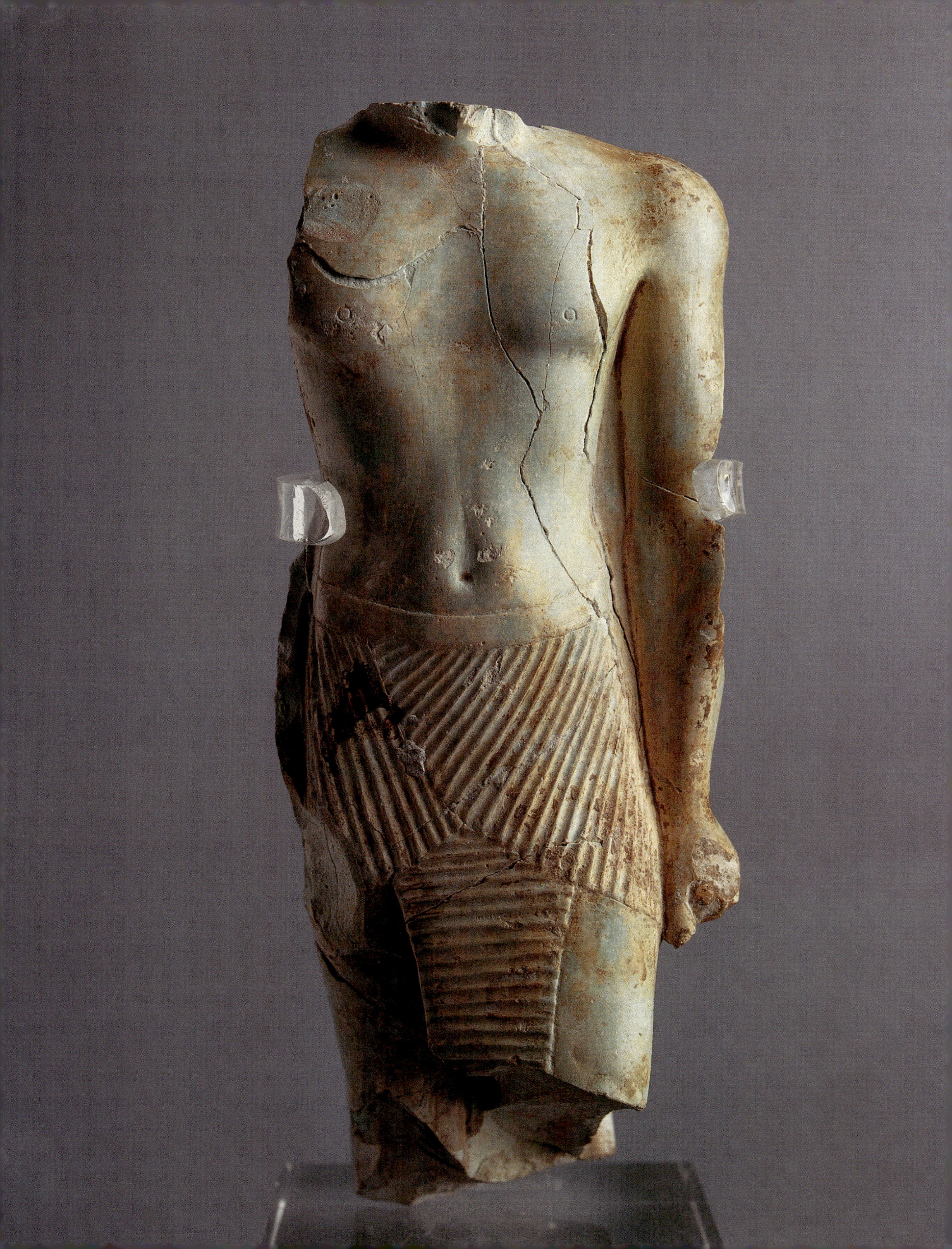

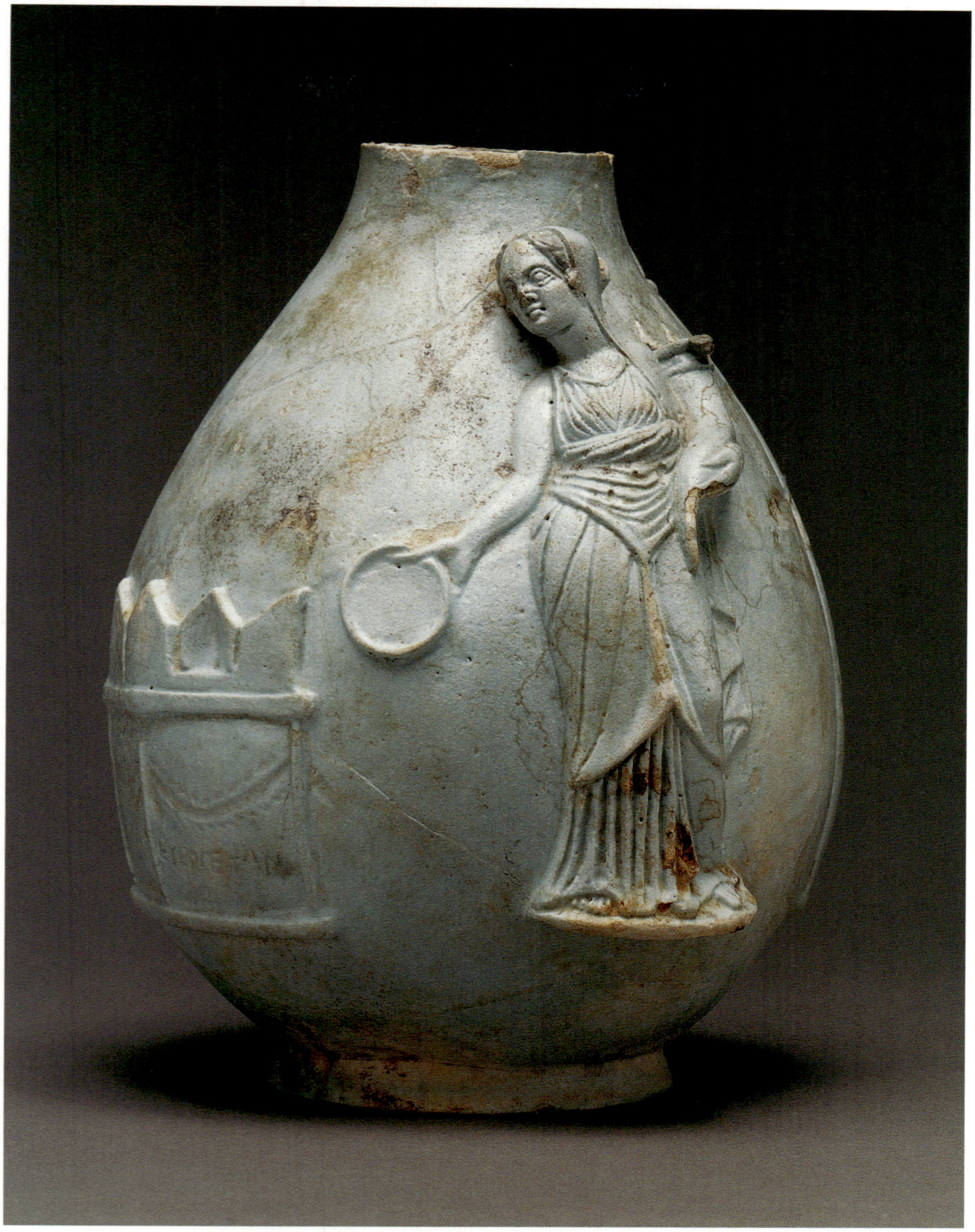

Opposite

TORSO OF A PHARAOH NAMED SHESHONQ [58]
Third Intermediate Period, Dynasty 22
H. 15.0 cm

Above

QUEEN'S VASE [62]
Ptolemaic Period, 240–230 BC
H. 22.2 cm

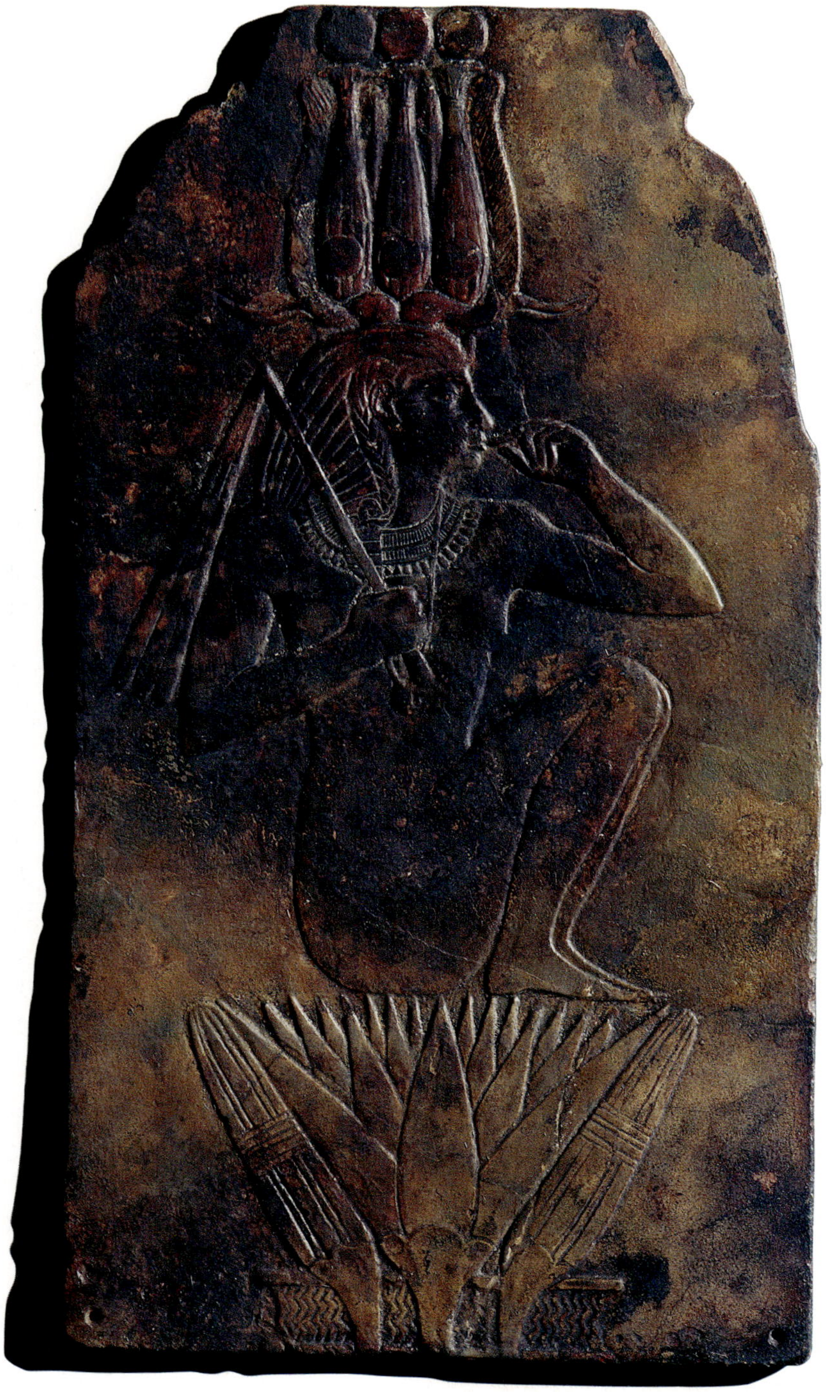

Above

PLAQUE OF IUPUT II [59]
Third Intermediate Period, Dynasty 23
H. 29.5 cm; W. 16.0 cm; D. 0.7 cm

Opposite

HEAD OF THE ROMAN EMPEROR AUGUSTUS [63]
Roman Period, 27–20 BC
H. 6.8 cm

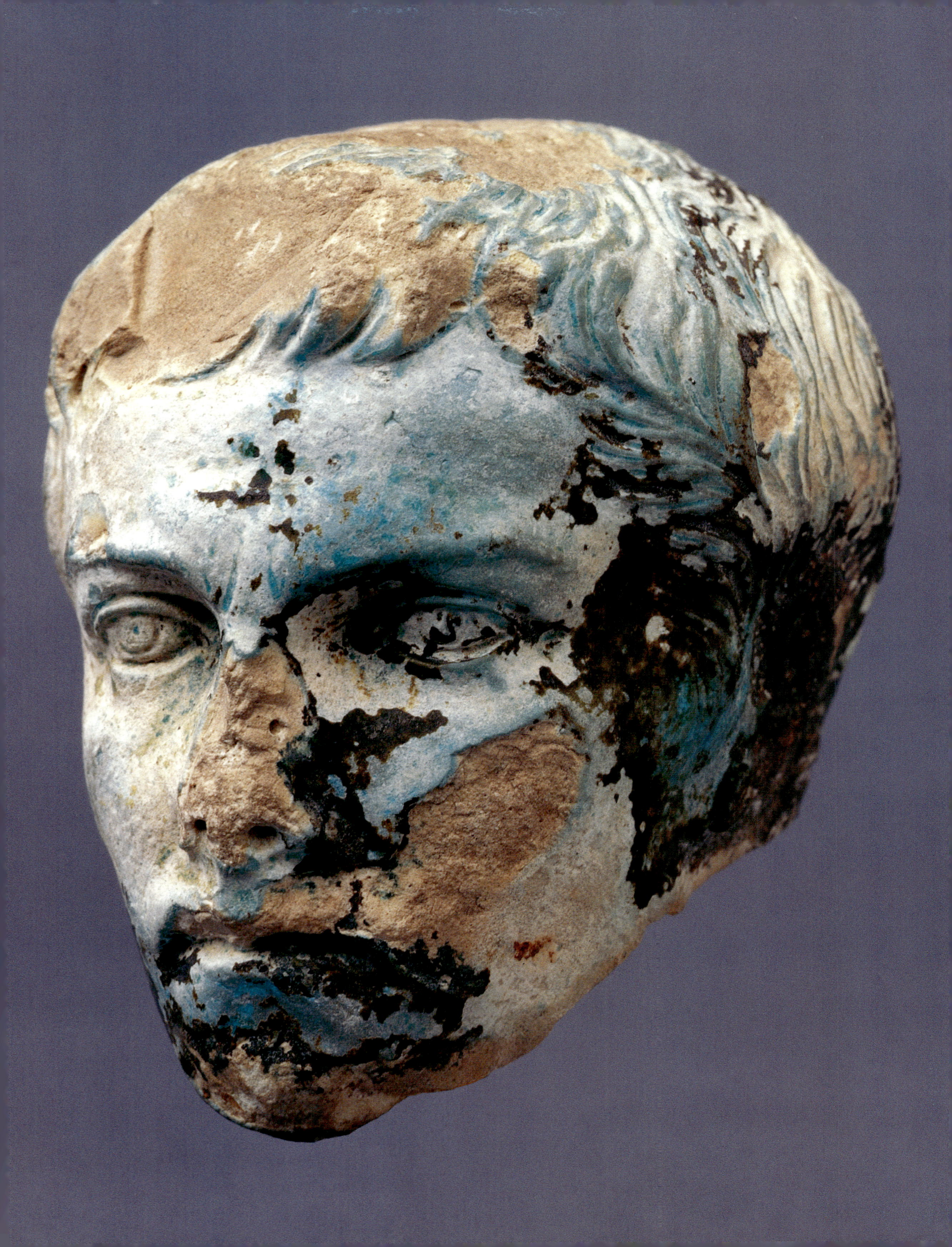

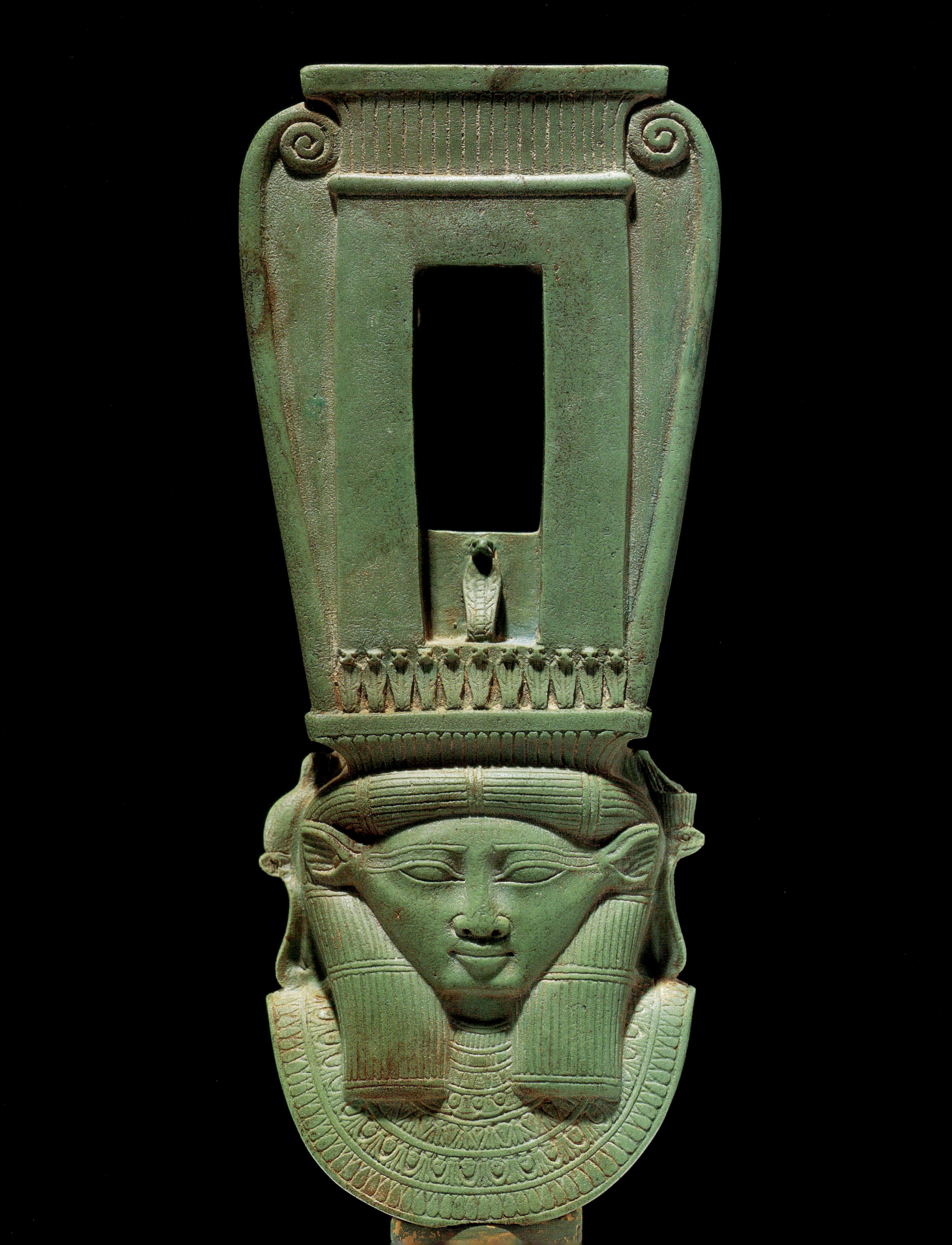

WOMEN'S USE AND FEMALE-RELATED THEMES

Many faience and related glazed steatite and Egyptian blue objects are associated with female fertility, including pregnancy, birth, and childrearing. Objects like the baby feeder and magic wand are decorated with figures that magically protected new mothers and infants. Iconography of the goddess Hathor and the god Bes, two deities associated with fertility and female life, is found on many faience objects, like New Kingdom faience bowls or cosmetic vessels of many periods. Jewelry is included in this section, some of which was worn exclusively by women while other examples could be worn by both genders—indeed, various objects here could also be used by men.

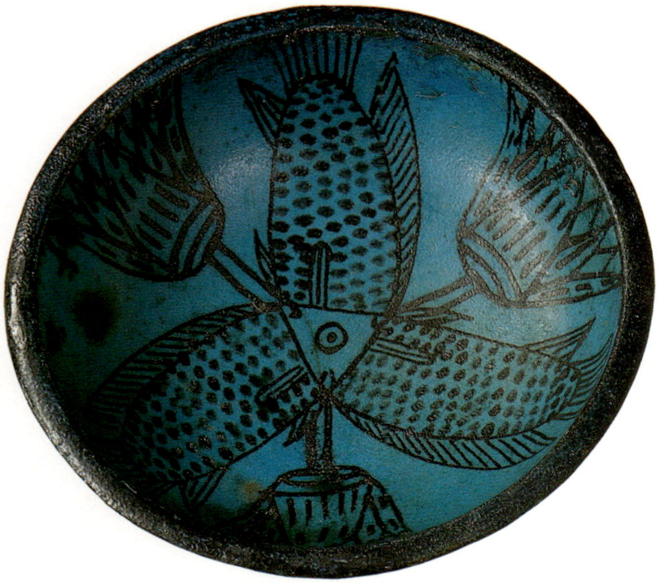

Opposite
SISTRUM (RITUAL RATTLE) [91]
Late Period, Dynasty 26
H. 19.0 cm; W. 7.8 cm; D. 3.5 cm

Right
BOWL WITH FISH AND LOTUS MOTIFS [78]
See p. 113

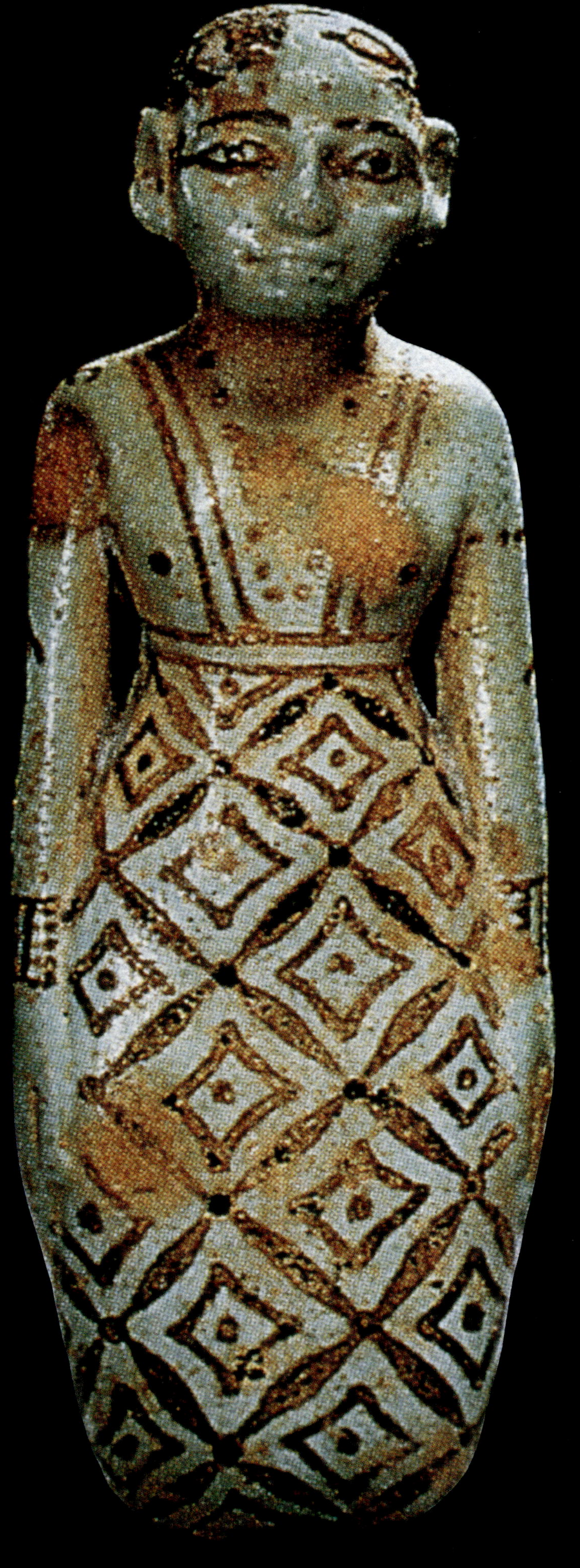

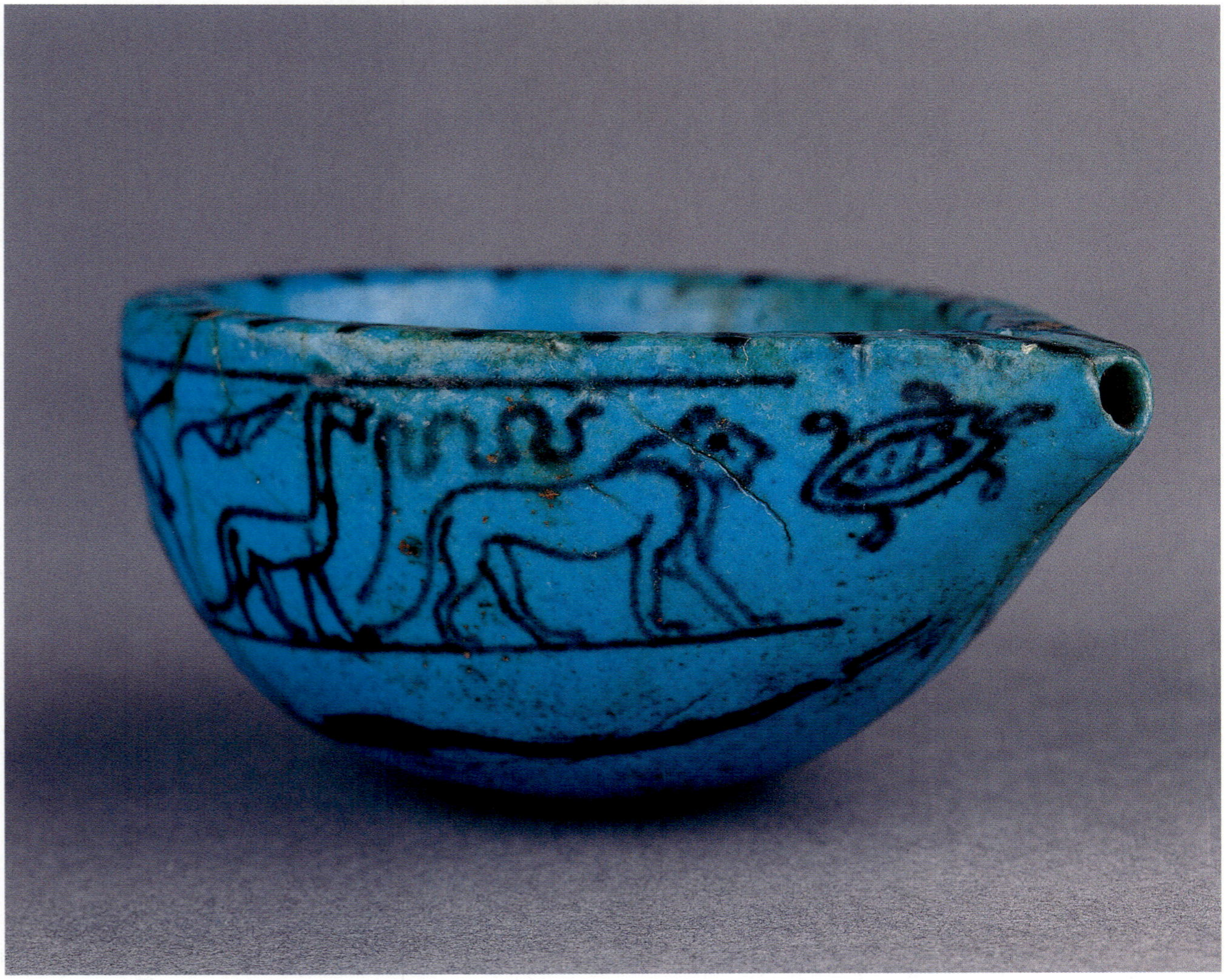

Opposite
FEMALE FECUNDITY FIGURE [64]
Middle Kingdom, Dynasty 12
H. 12.7 cm

Above
BABY'S FEEDING CUP [67]
Middle Kingdom, late Dynasty 12 to Dynasty 13
H. 3.5 cm; max. D. 8.0 cm

Opposite
DOLL [65]
Middle Kingdom, Dynasty 12
H. 7.8 cm

Right
PADDLE DOLL [66]
Middle Kingdom, Dynasty 11
H. 35.0 cm, with wig fully extended

Below
FEMALE STATUETTE [69]
Late Period, Dynasty 25
H. 14.2 cm; W. 4.0 cm. Base front to back 4.5 cm

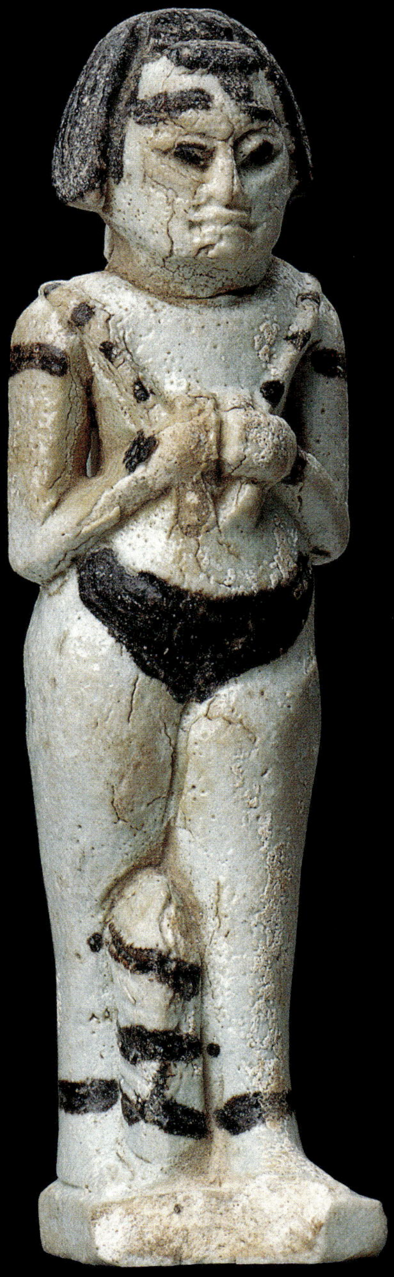

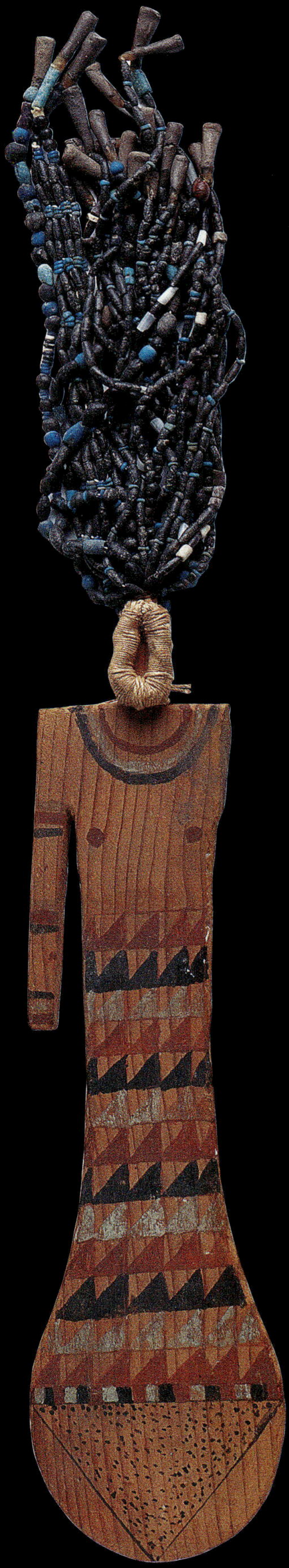

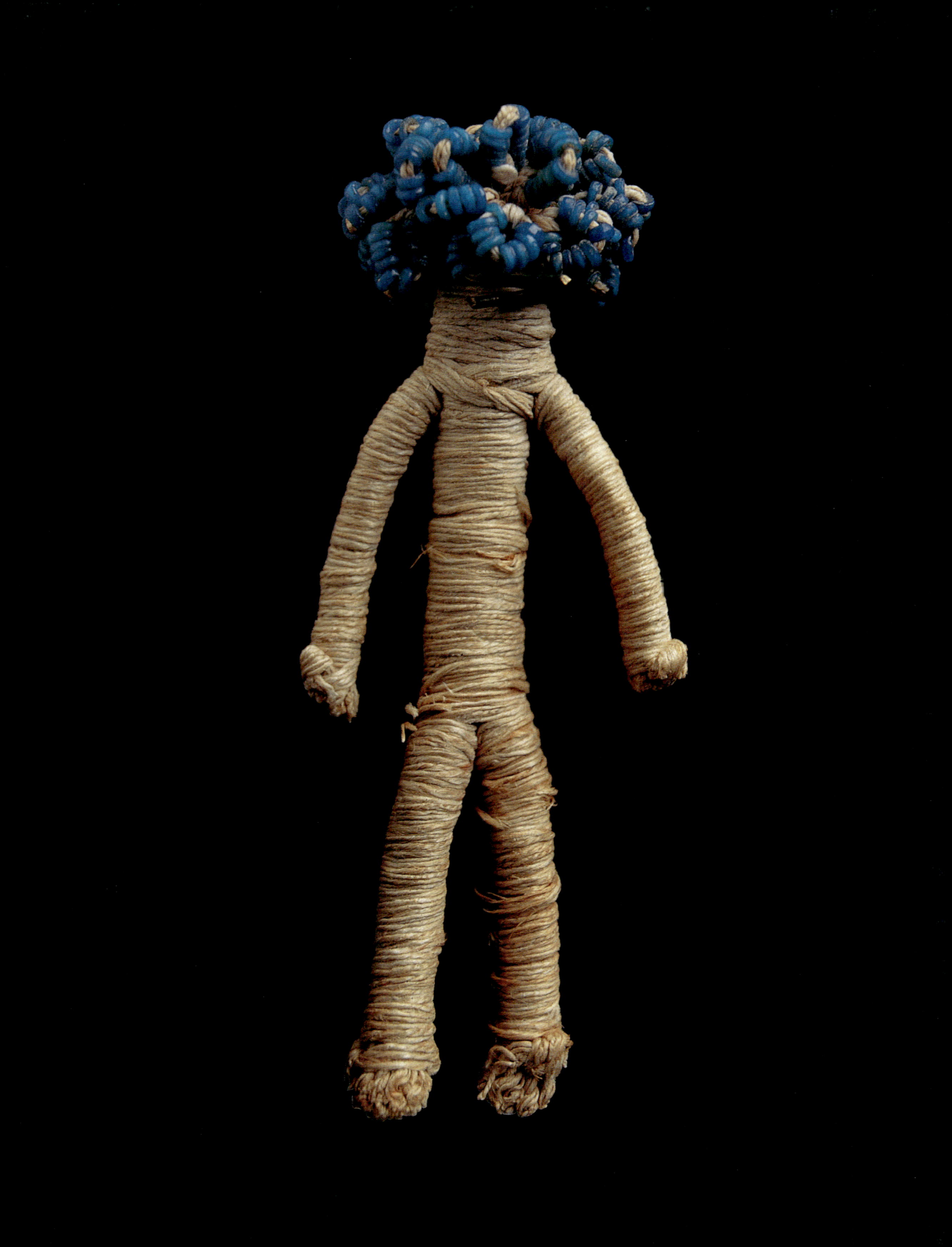

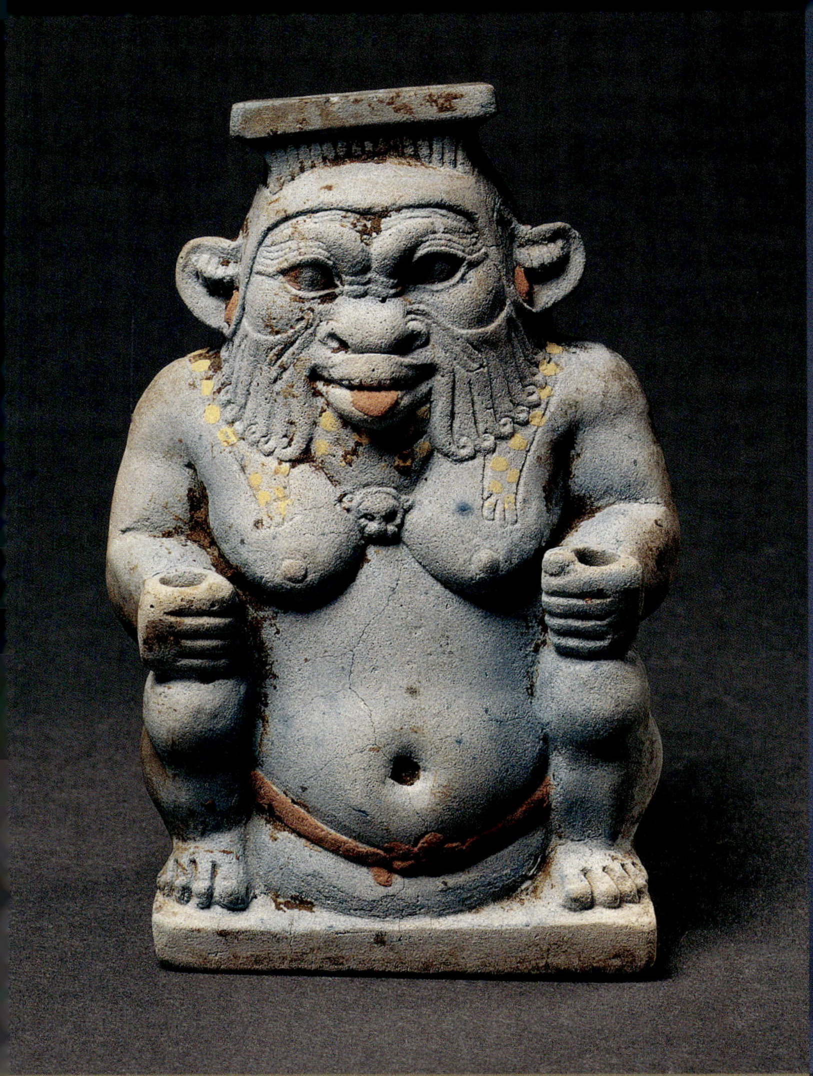

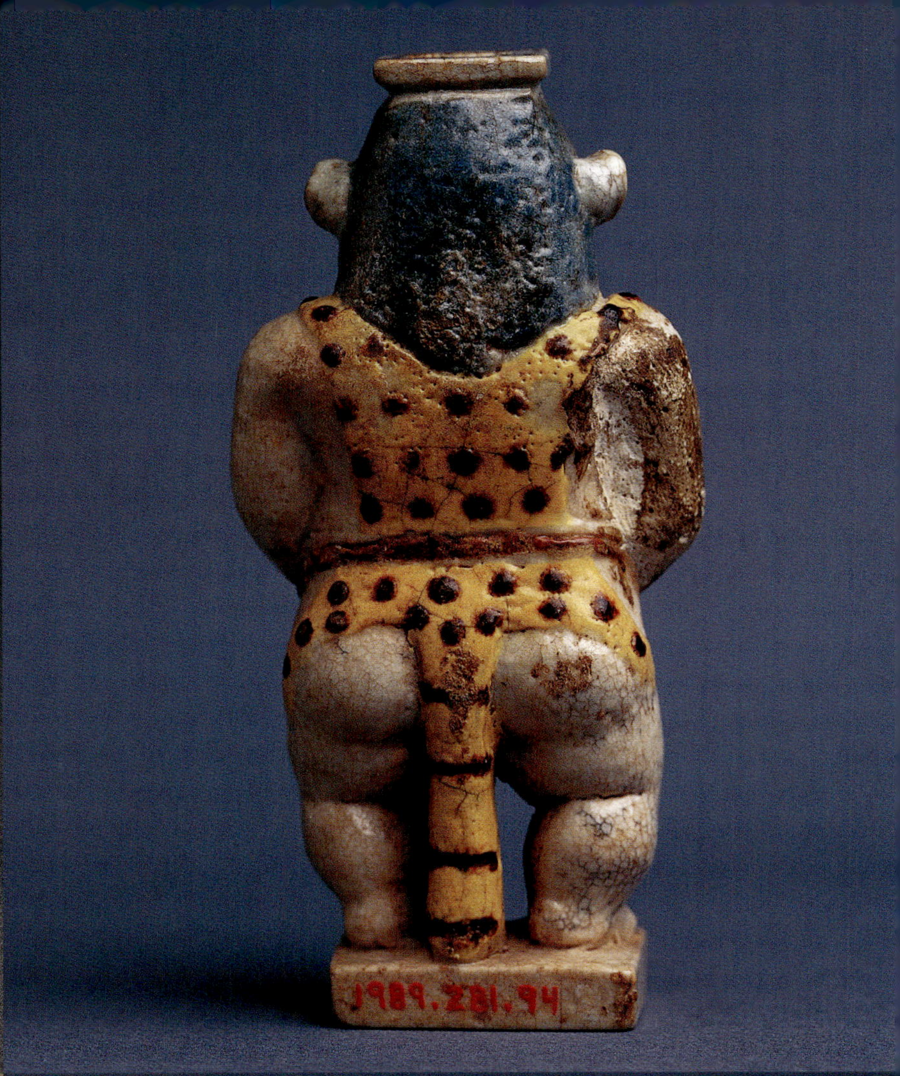
1989.281.94

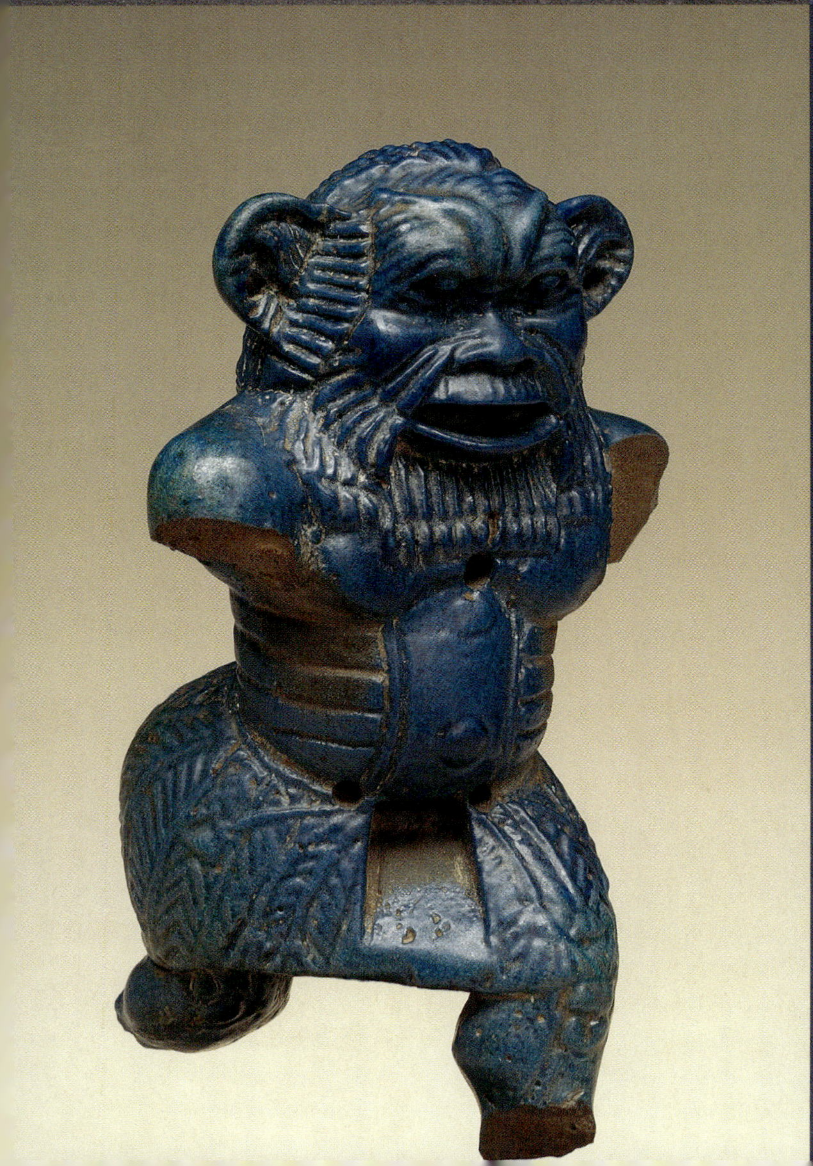

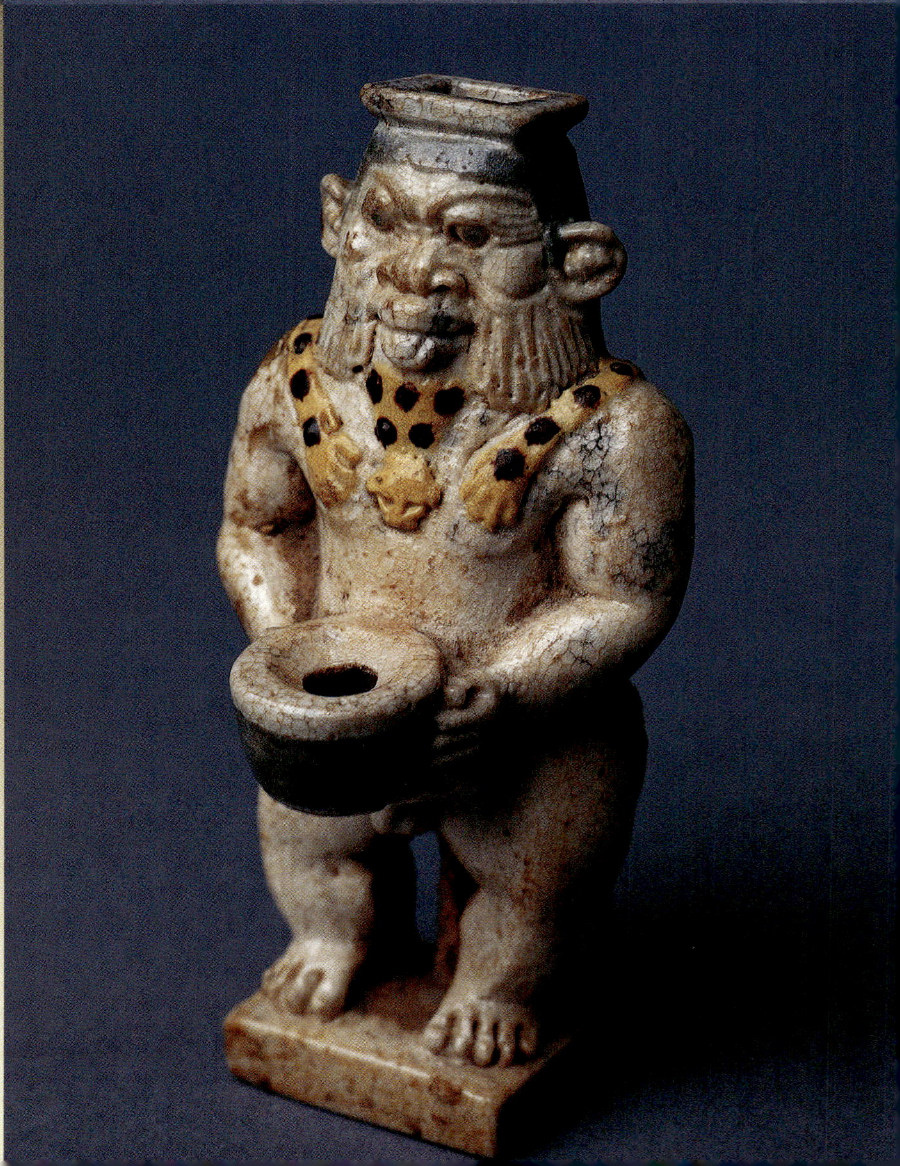

Opposite left, above

PERFUME JAR IN THE IMAGE OF THE GOD BES [73]

Late Period, early to mid-Dynasty 26, *c.* 664–550 BC

H. 9.3 cm

Opposite left, below

STATUETTE OF A BES-IMAGE [72]

New Kingdom, Dynasty 18, reign of Akhenaten

H. 8.7 cm

Opposite right (above and below)

BES-IMAGE HOLDING A RING [74]

Late Period, Dynasty 27

H. 9.2 cm; W. 4.4 cm

Right

THE GOD BES AS A PROPHYLACTIC CHARM [75]

Third Intermediate Period to Late Period, Dynasty 21–25

H. 21.6 cm

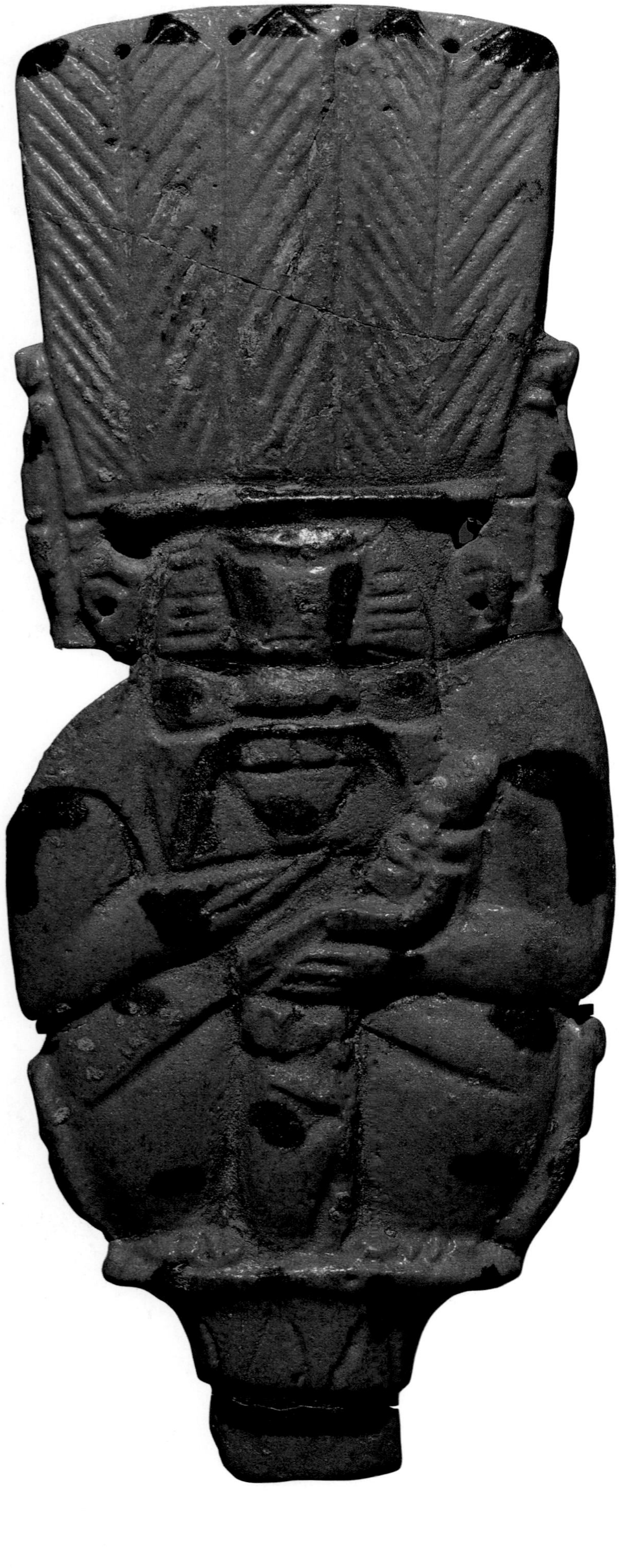

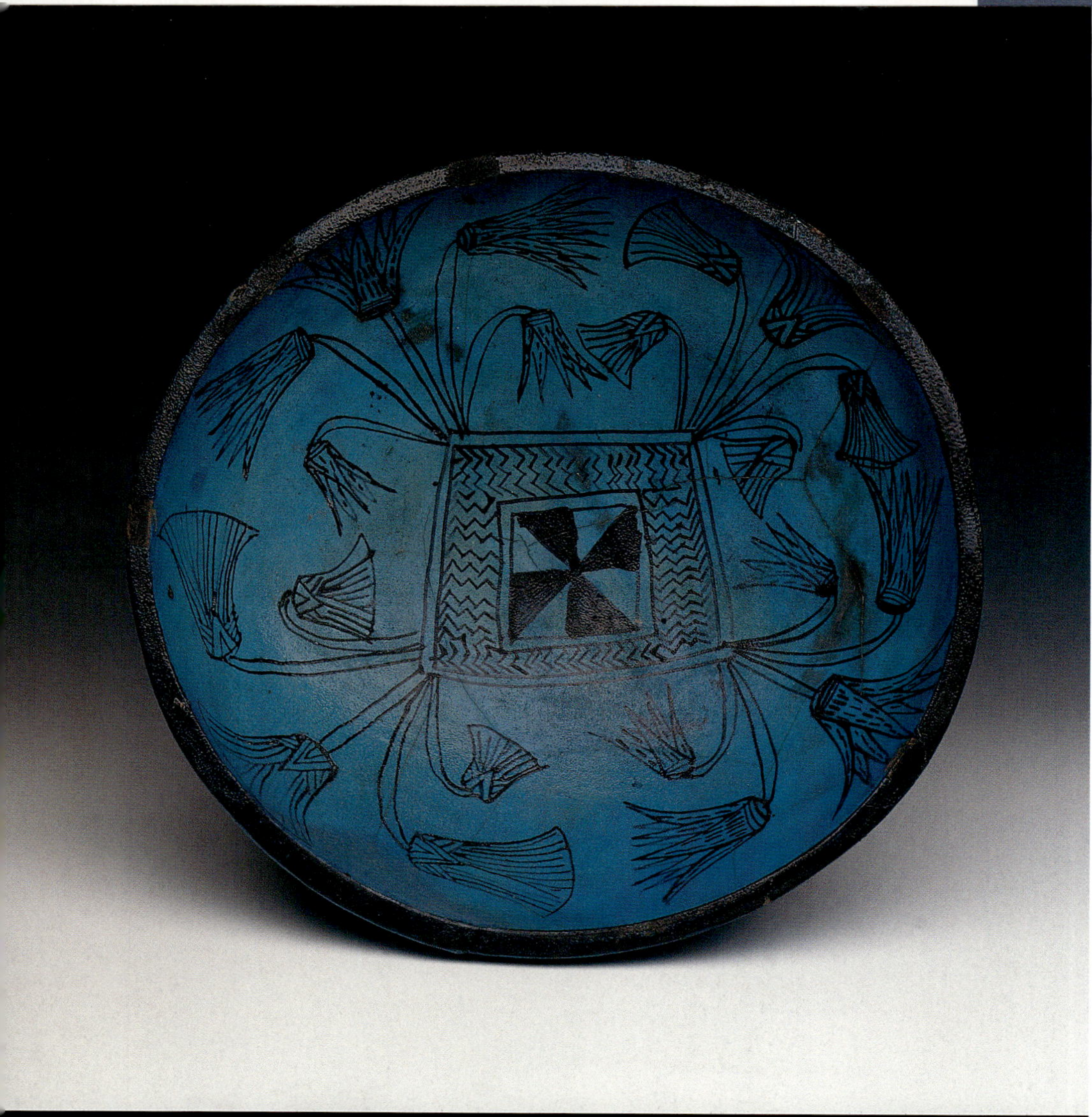

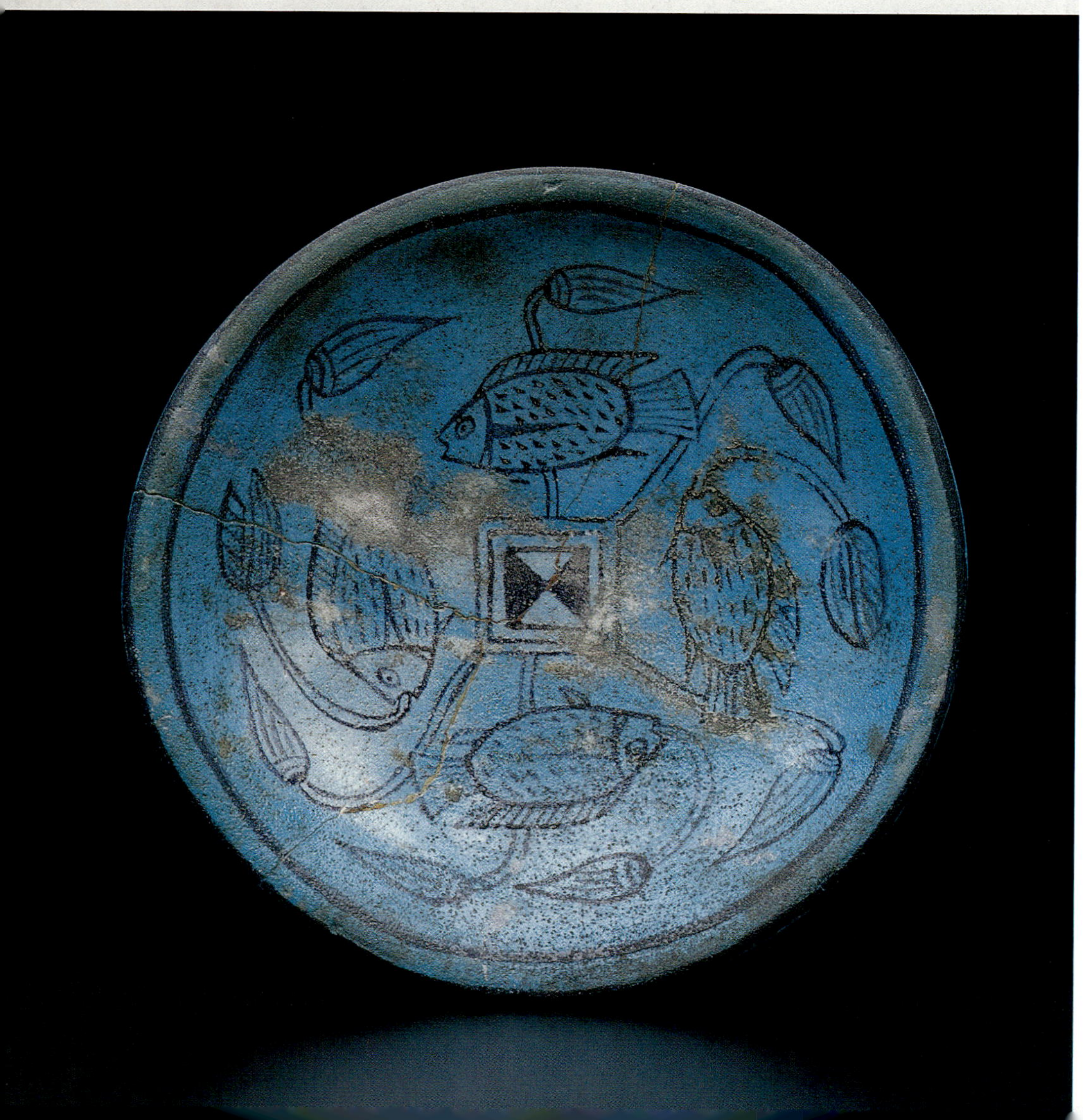

Left above
BOWL WITH POOL AND LOTUS MOTIFS [76]
New Kingdom, early Dynasty 18
DIAM. 25.8 cm

Left below
BOWL WITH POOL AND FISH [77]
New Kingdom, Dynasty 18
DIAM. 15.7 cm; H. 3.8 cm

Opposite above
BOWL WITH FISH AND LOTUS MOTIFS [78]
New Kingdom, Dynasty 18
DIAM. 9.0 cm

Opposite below
BOWL [79]
New Kingdom, Dynasty 19–20
DIAM. 14.0 cm

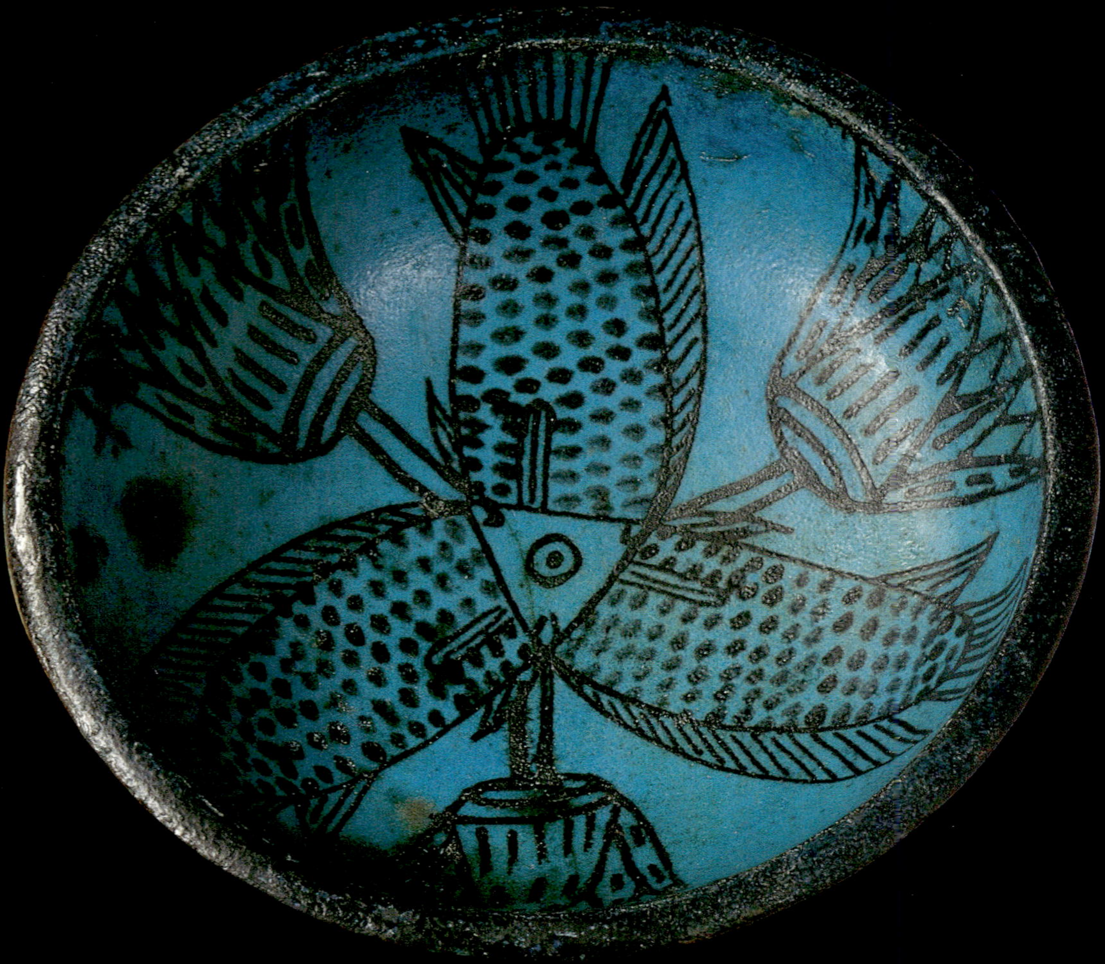
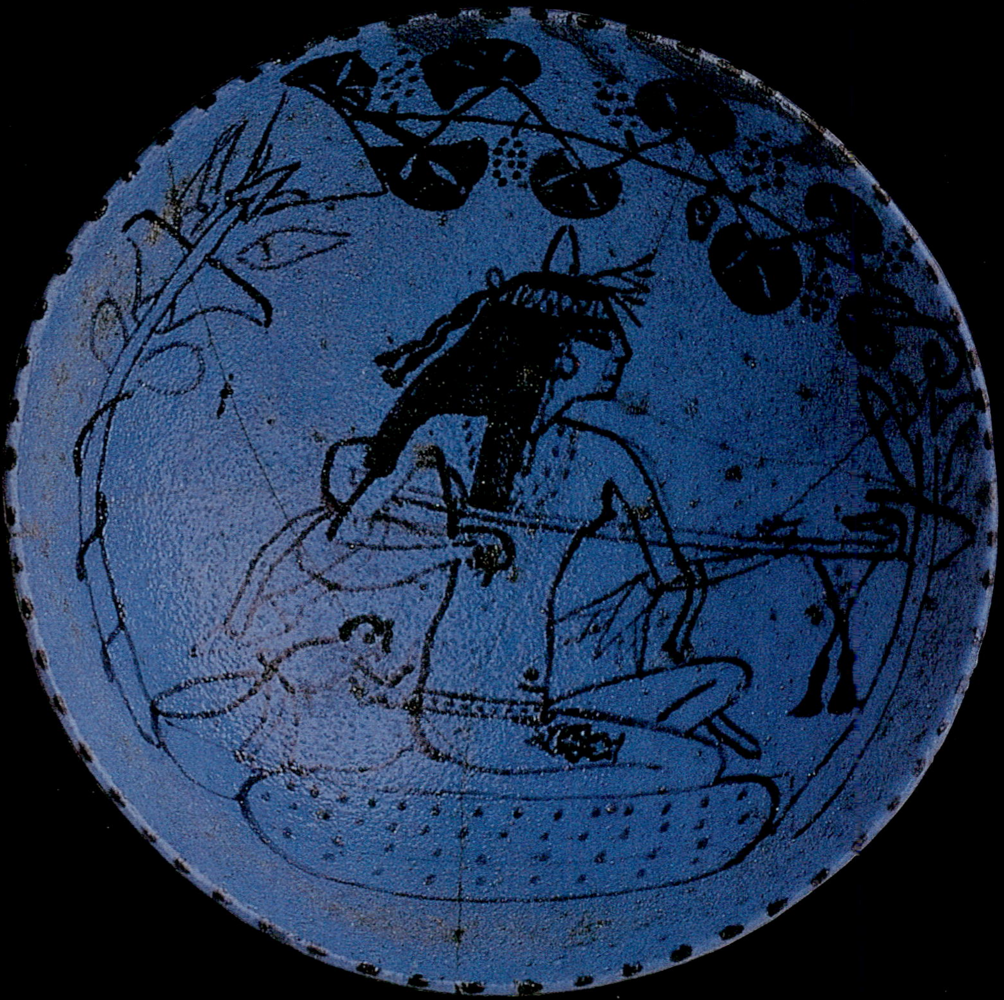

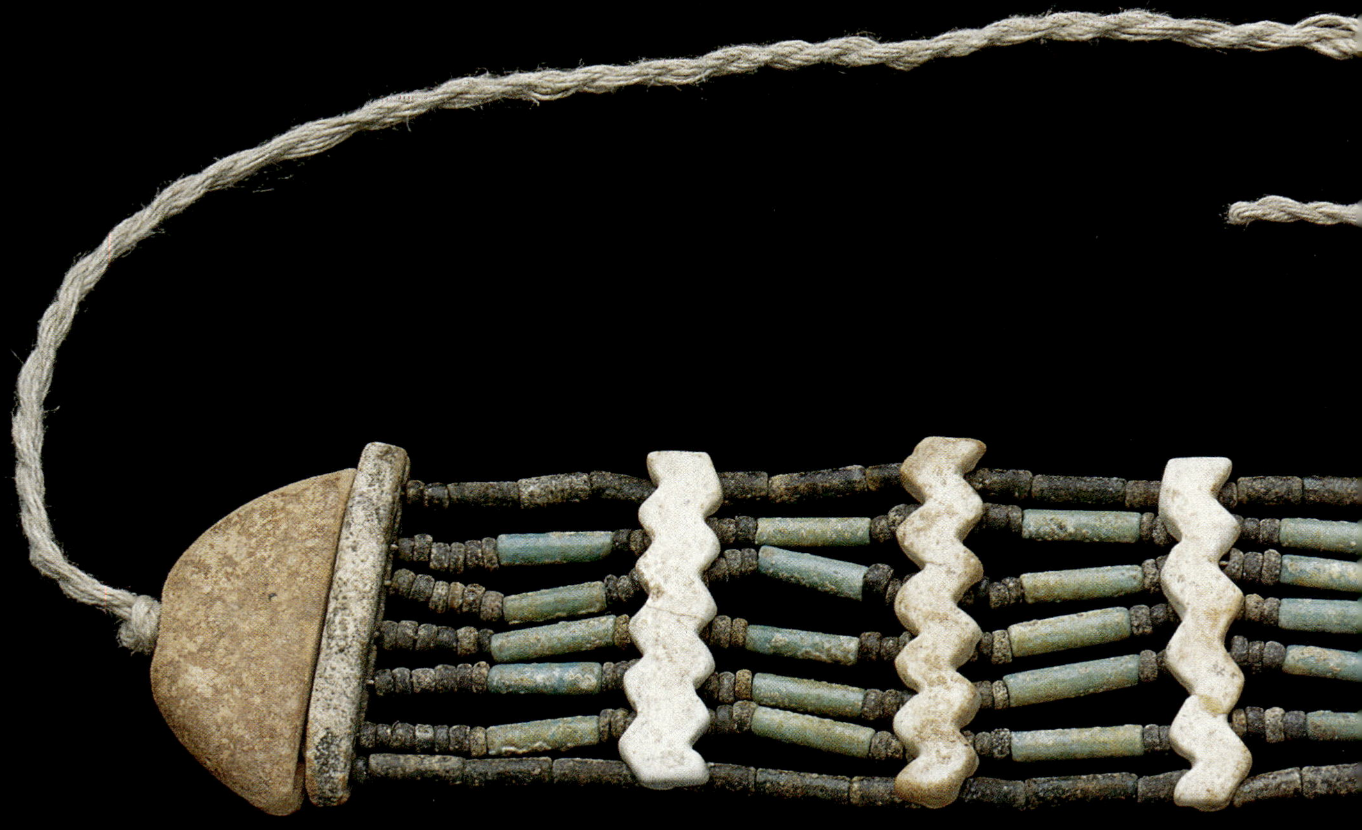

Above

CHOKER [80]

Old Kingdom, Dynasty 4, *c.* 2500 BC

L. 25.0 cm; H. 3.8 cm

Opposite

BALL BEADS [81]

Middle Kingdom to New Kingdom, early Dynasty 18

Max. DIAM. 5.1 cm

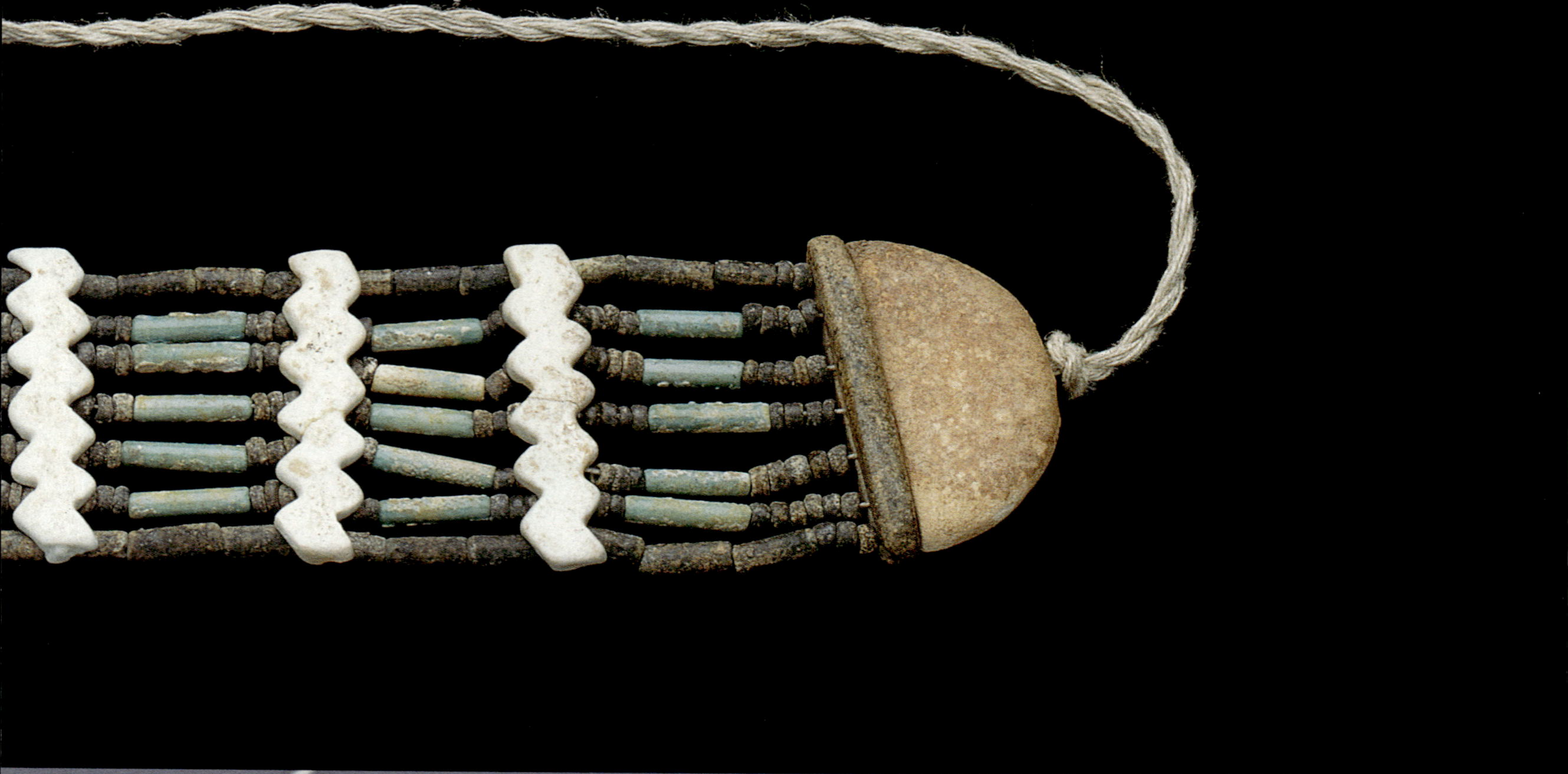

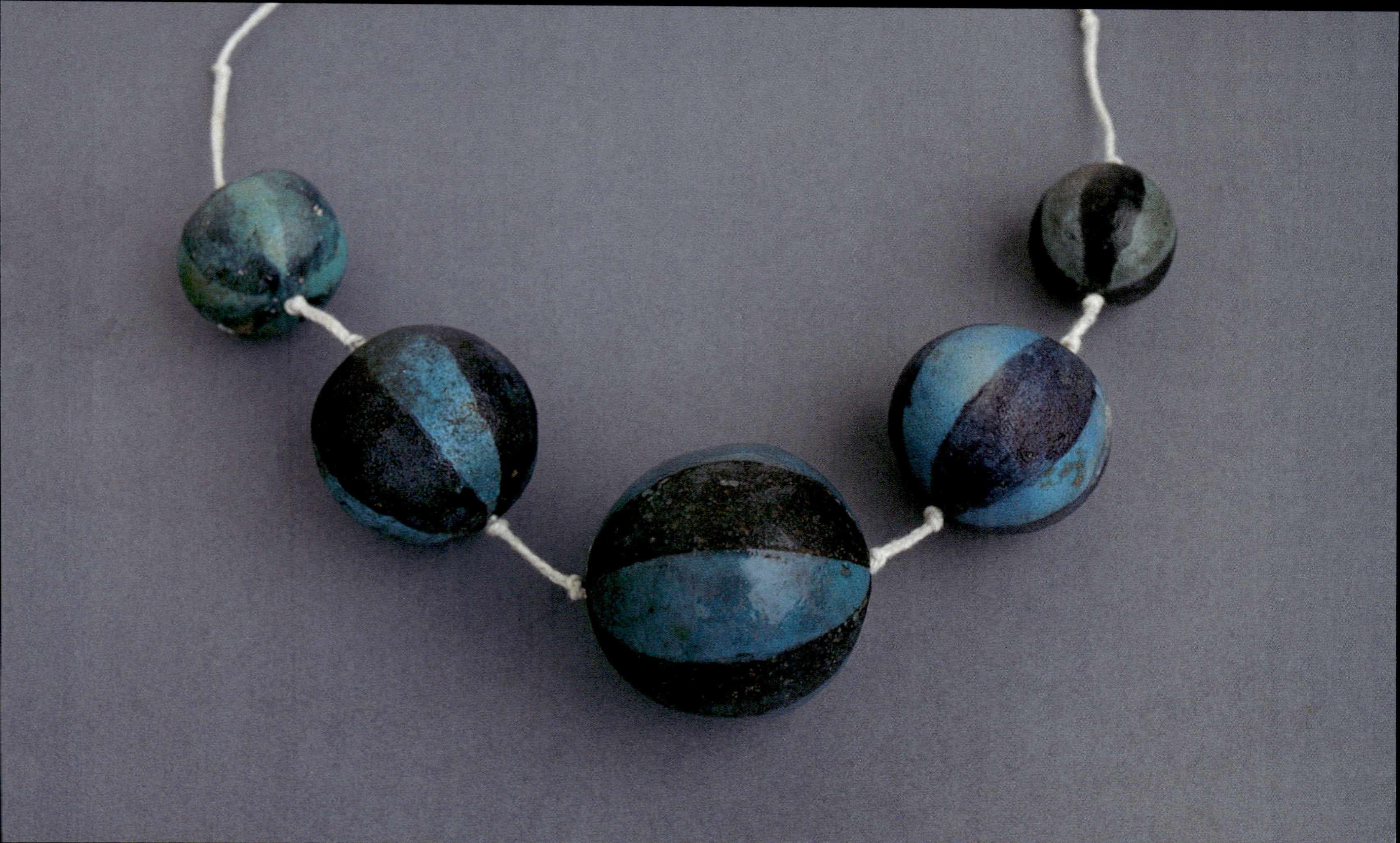

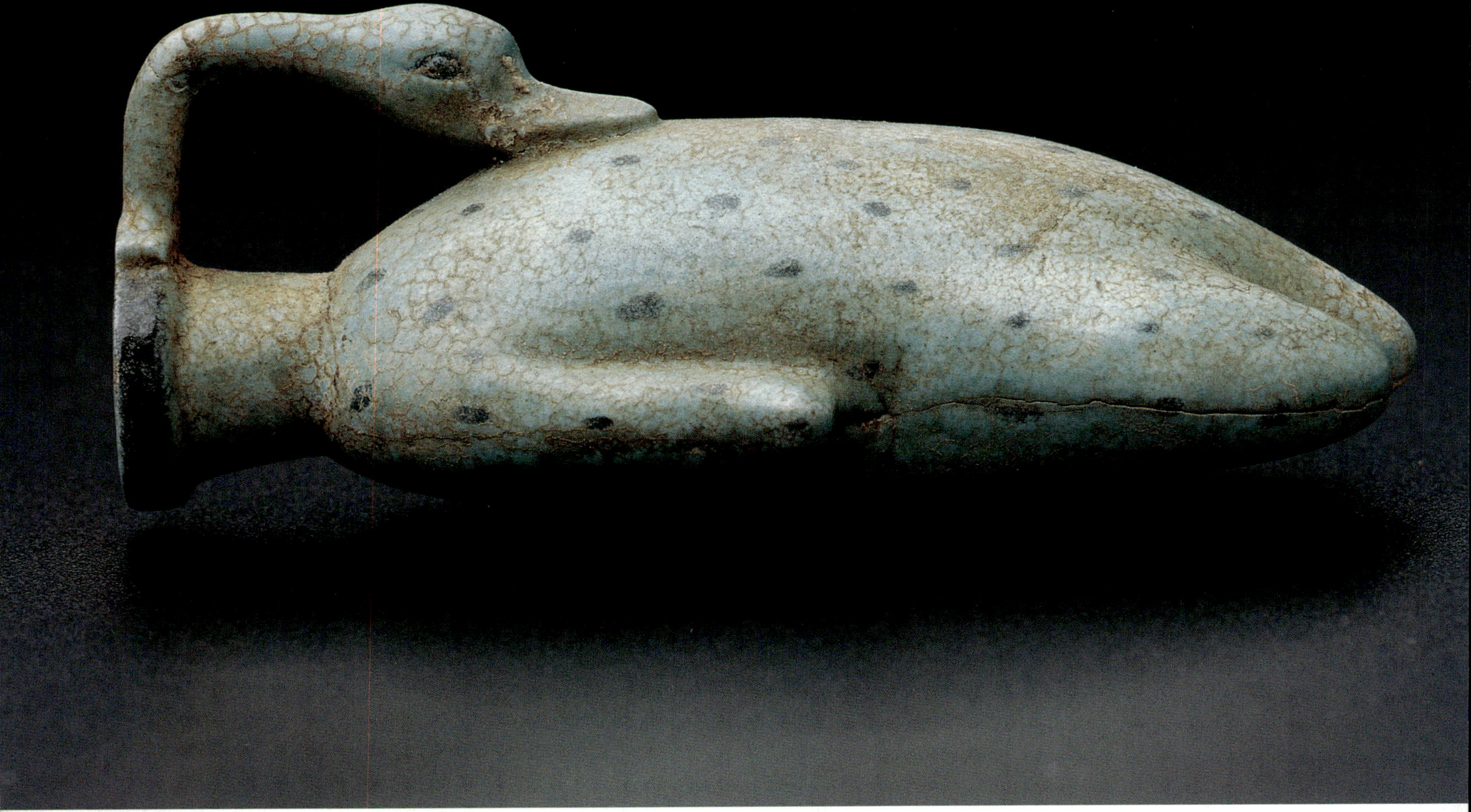

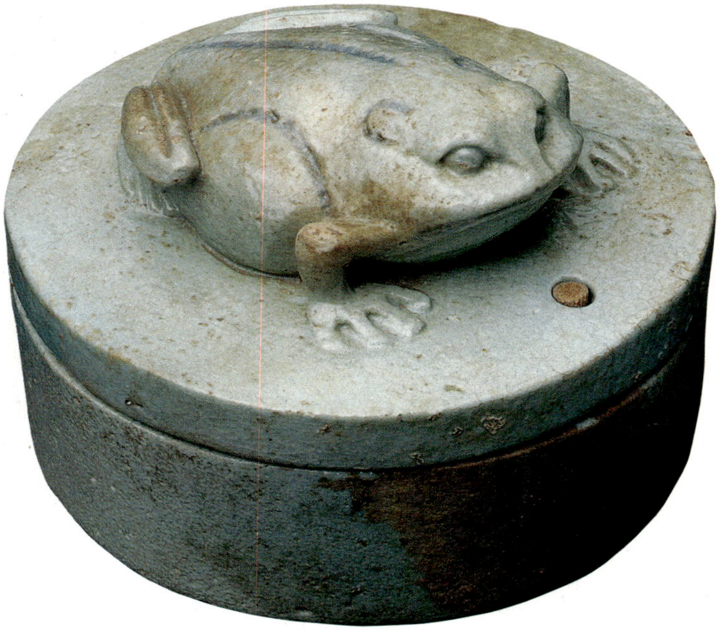

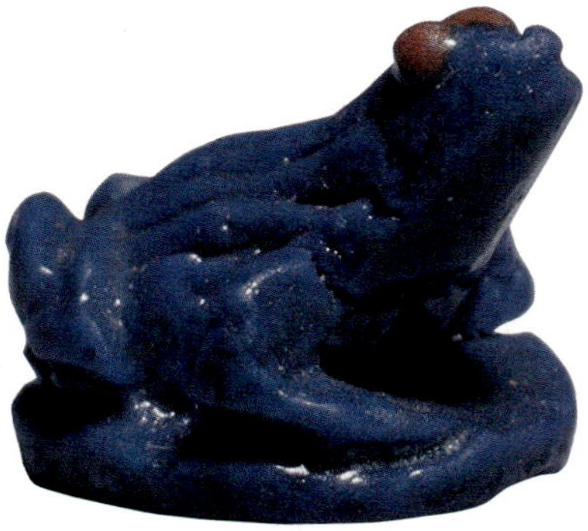

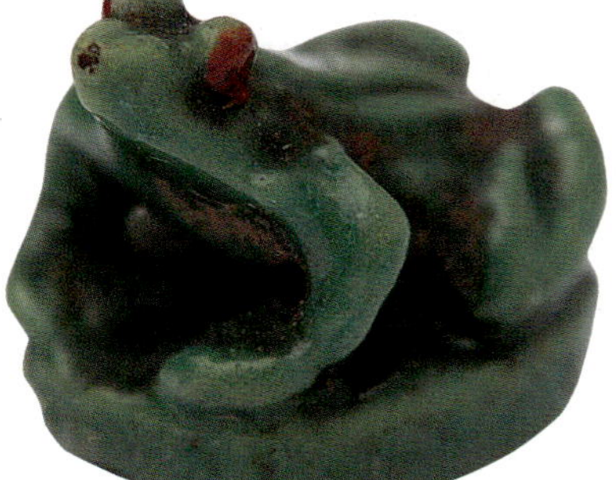

Right
VESSEL IN THE SHAPE OF A MONKEY [88]
Late Period, Dynasty 27 to Second Persian Period, 525–332 BC
H. 6.0 cm

Opposite above
VASE IN THE SHAPE OF A TRUSSED DUCK OR GOOSE [89]
Late Third Intermediate Period to Late Period
H. 2.7 cm; W. 3.6 cm; L. 7.8 cm

Opposite below, left
COSMETIC BOX WITH FROG [86]
East Greek, 6th century BC
H. 5.4 cm; DIAM. 6.6 cm

Opposite below, right (above)
FROG-SHAPED BEAD [70]
New Kingdom, late Dynasty 18, *c.* 1380–1330 BC
L. 1.1 cm

Opposite below, right (below)
FROG-SHAPED BEAD [71]
New Kingdom, late Dynasty 18, *c.* 1380–1330 BC
L. 0.8 cm

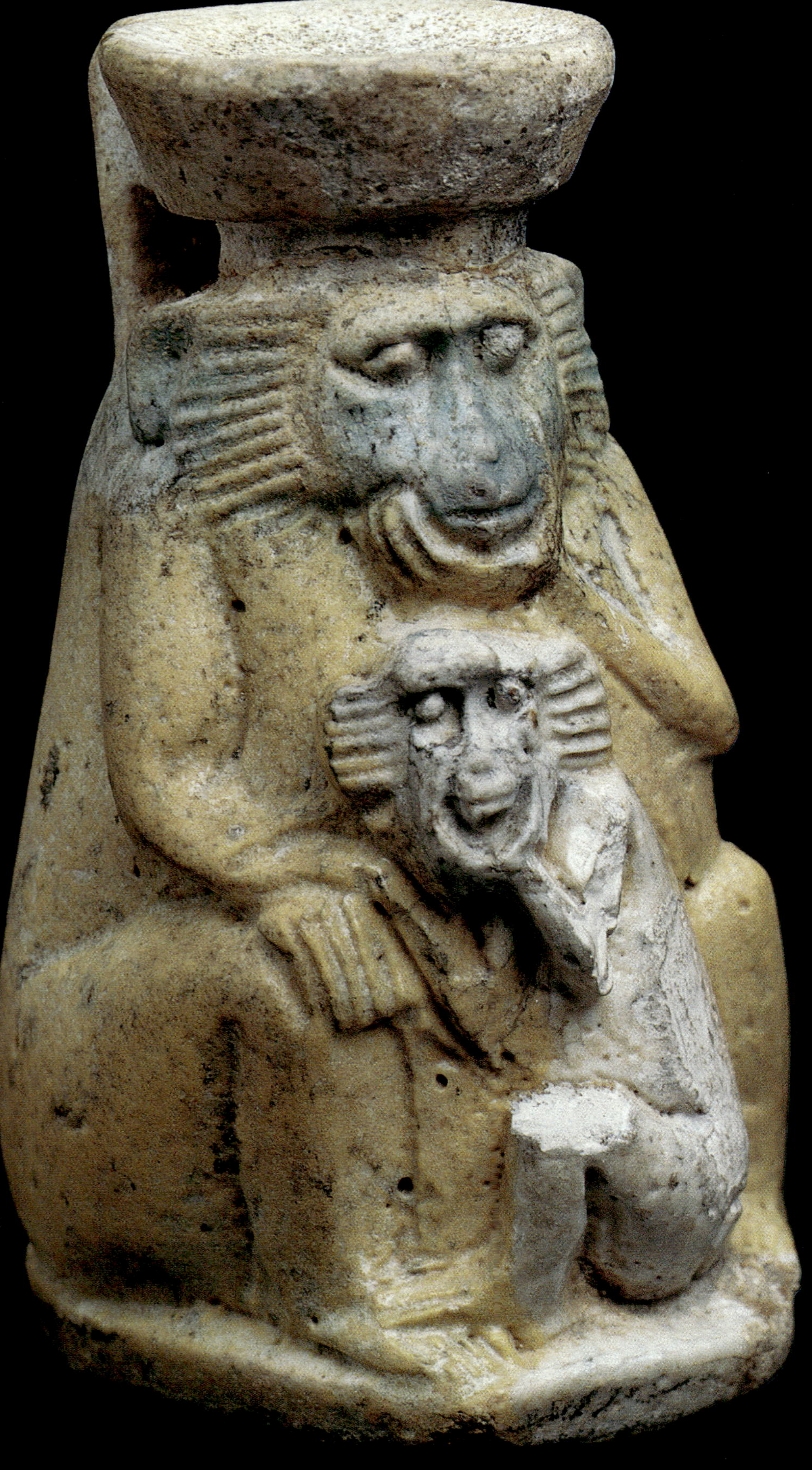

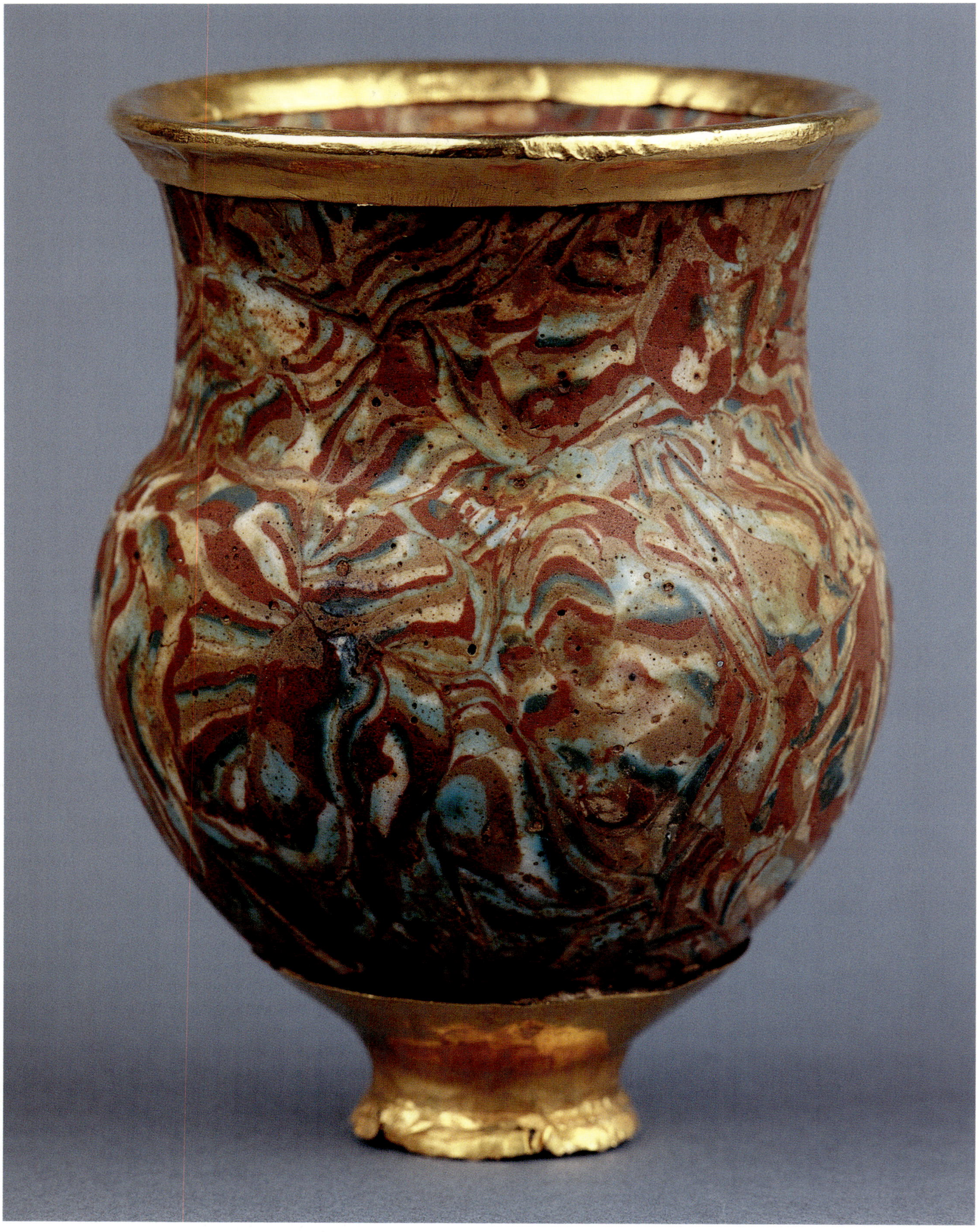

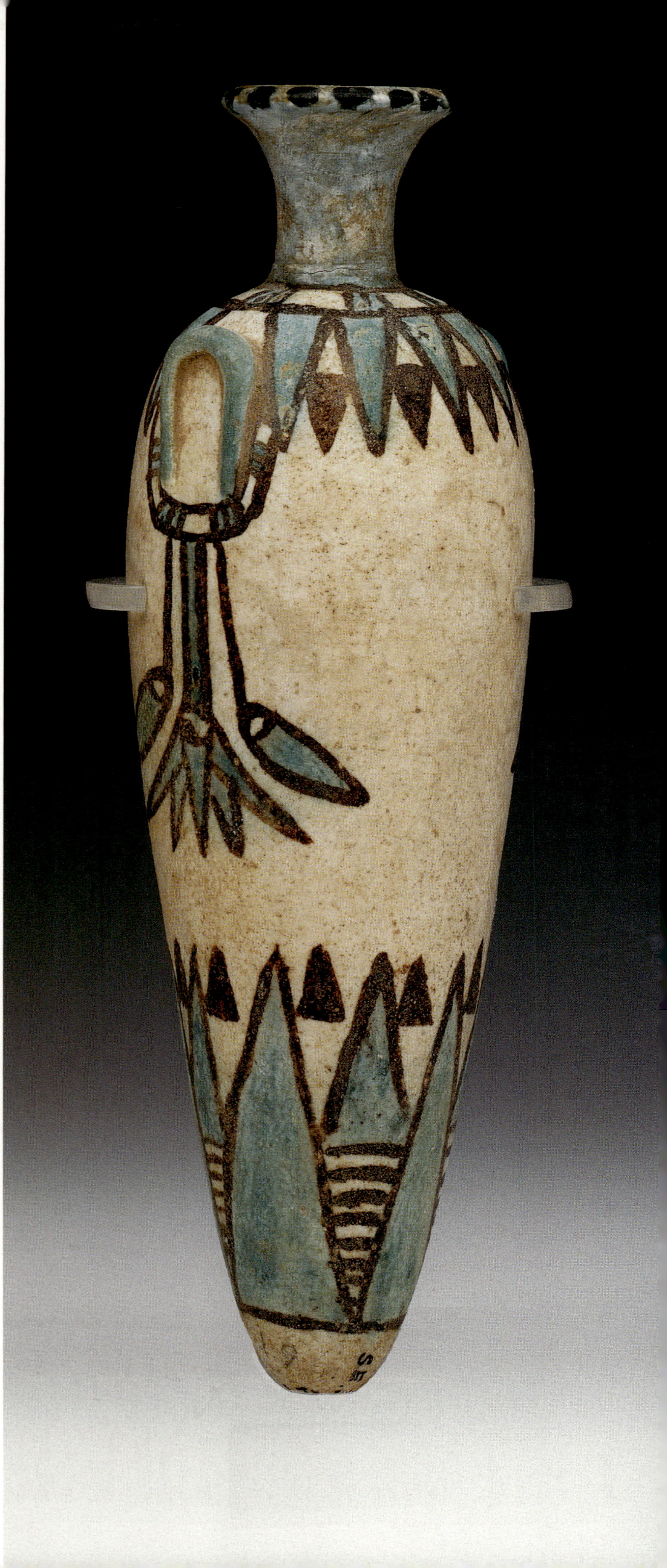

Right

PERFUME VASE [82]
New Kingdom, late Dynasty 18
H. 14.5 cm

Opposite

GOBLET [90]
New Kingdom, Dynasty 18, reign of Thutmose III
H. 10.2 cm; DIAM. 6.9 cm; DIAM. of foot with gold foil 2.7 cm

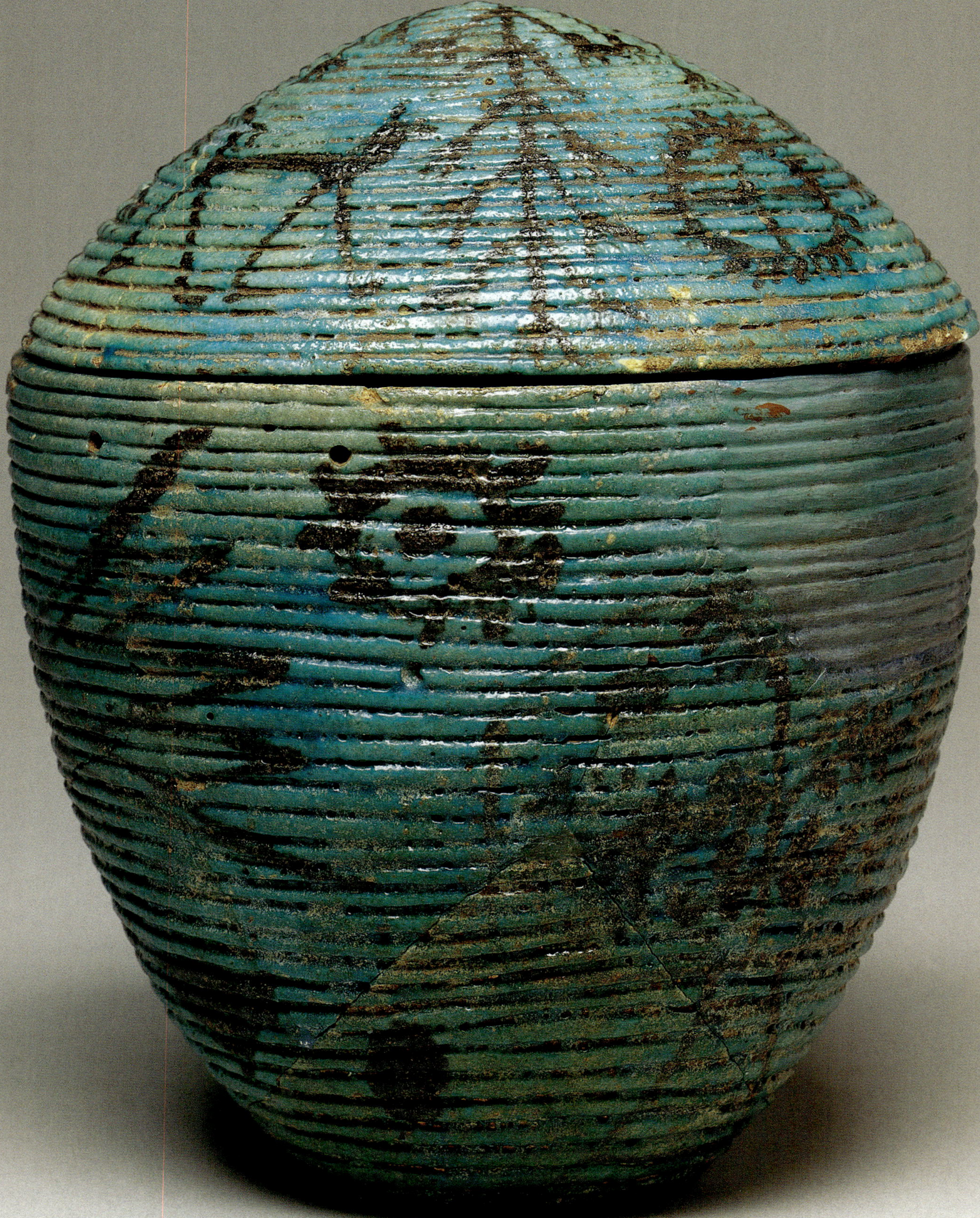

FAIENCE IN DAILY LIFE AND DEVOTION

Objects ranging from small baskets, jars, and chalices to compartmented boxes and perfume containers were made in faience, often in imitation of larger clay, metal, and stone prototypes. Some objects were functional, like the necklaces and rings and possibly the little faience inkwells, though others may have been model tomb gifts, like the dog and pony, mementos perhaps of treasured lifetime friends. Part of daily life also involved religious devotion, represented by some of Egypt's most beautiful small-scale figurines of human and animal deities and a tiny votive shrine.

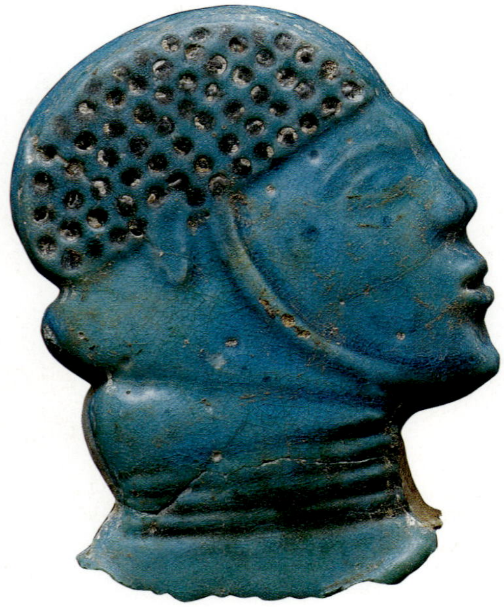

Opposite
BASKET WITH LID [92]
New Kingdom, probably Dynasty 18
H. 14.5 cm; DIAM. 11.07 cm

Right
INLAY HEAD OF A NUBIAN [137]
See p. 130

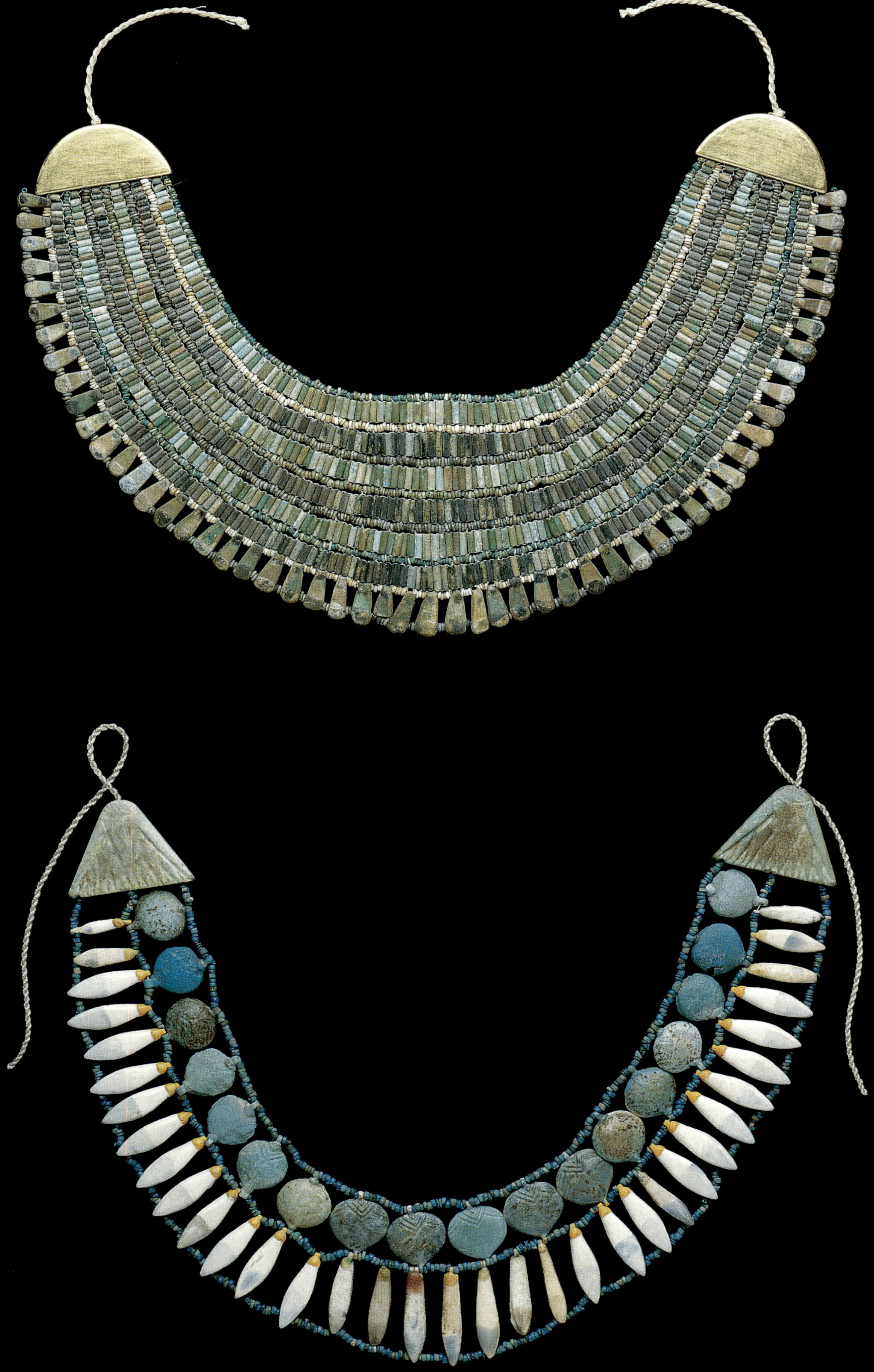

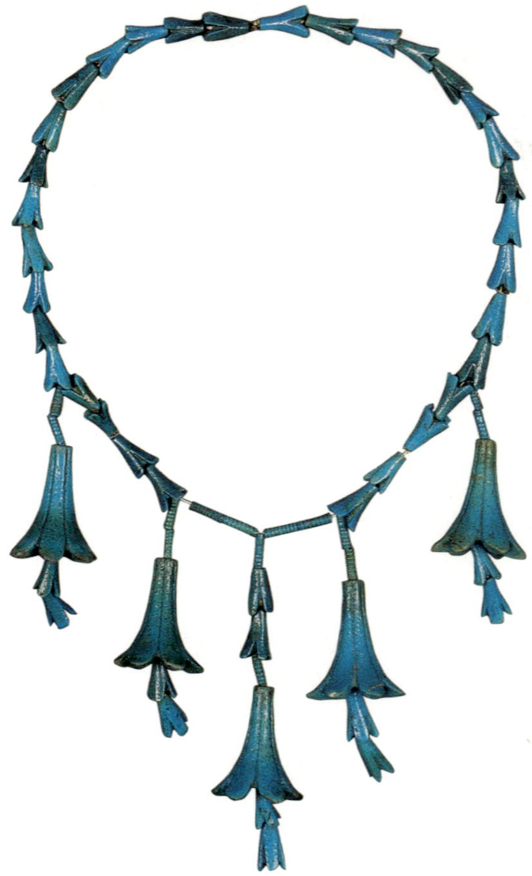

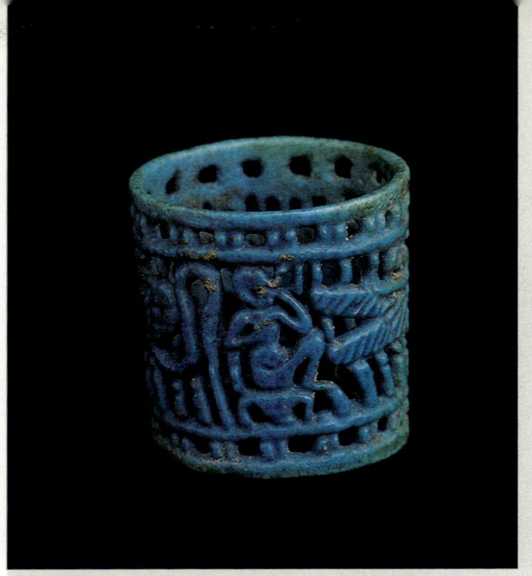

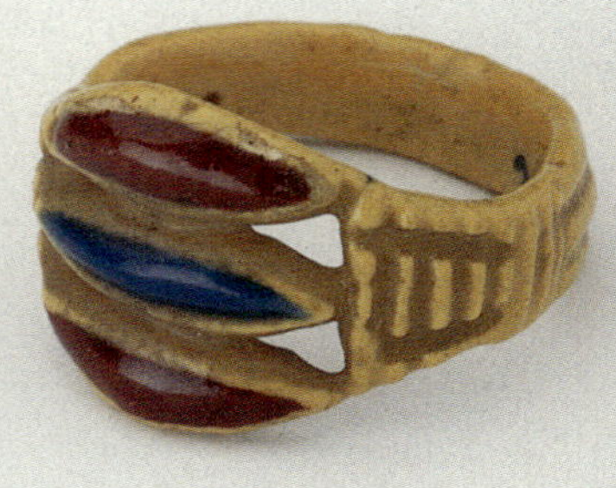

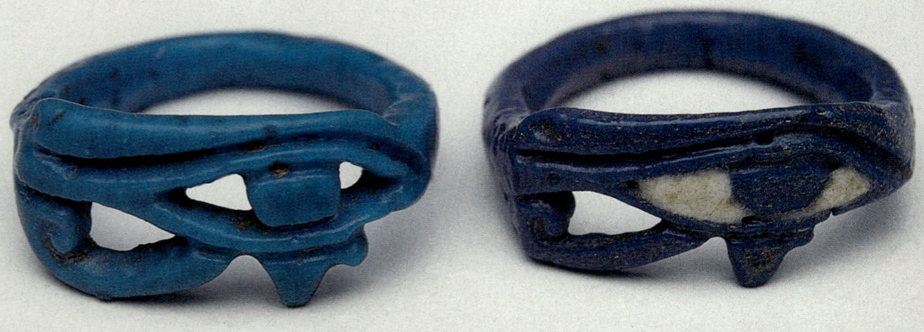

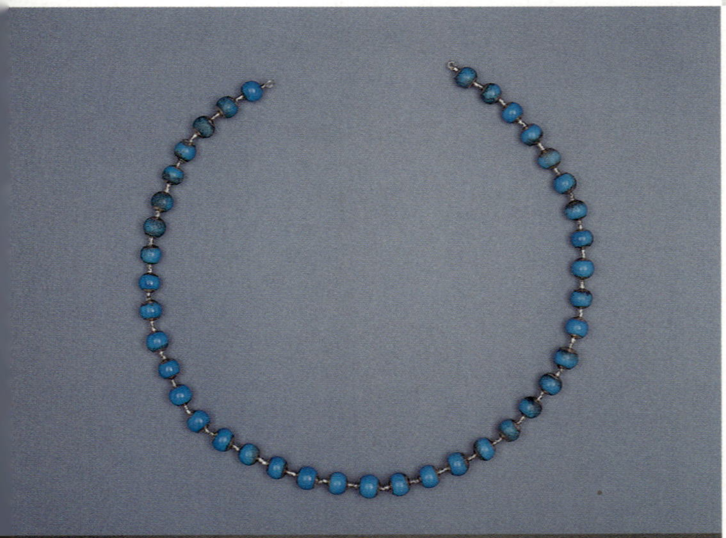

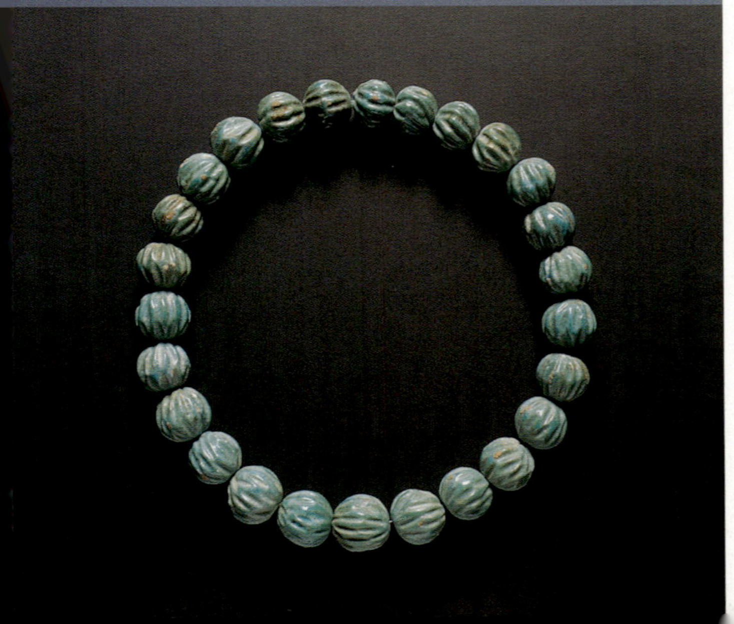

Opposite above
BROAD COLLAR [100]
Old Kingdom, late Dynasty 5,
c. 2150 BC
H. 10.5 cm; W. 33.0 cm

Opposite below
BROAD COLLAR [103]
New Kingdom, Dynasty 18
L. 27.0 cm

Left above
NECKLACE OF JASMINE BLOSSOMS [104]
New Kingdom, Dynasty 18
L. 38.0 cm

Left center
CAPPED BEADS WITH A REEF-KNOT CLASP [101]
Middle Kingdom
L. 72.8 cm; DIAM. of beads 15 mm

Left below
STRING OF RIBBED BALL BEADS [102]
Middle Kingdom
L. 30.0 cm; DIAM. of beads 10–15 mm

Top center
OPENWORK FINGER RING [108]
Third Intermediate Period, Dynasty 21–22
H. 3.2 cm; DIAM. 2.4 cm

Top right
FINGER RING [105]
New Kingdom, Dynasty 18
H. (bezel) 1.3 cm;
H. (shank) 0.5 cm; DIAM. 2.0 cm

Above, left
WADJET-EYE RING [106]
New Kingdom, late Dynasty 18
DIAM. 2.3 cm

Above, right
WADJET-EYE RING [107]
New Kingdom, late Dynasty 18
DIAM. 2.3 cm

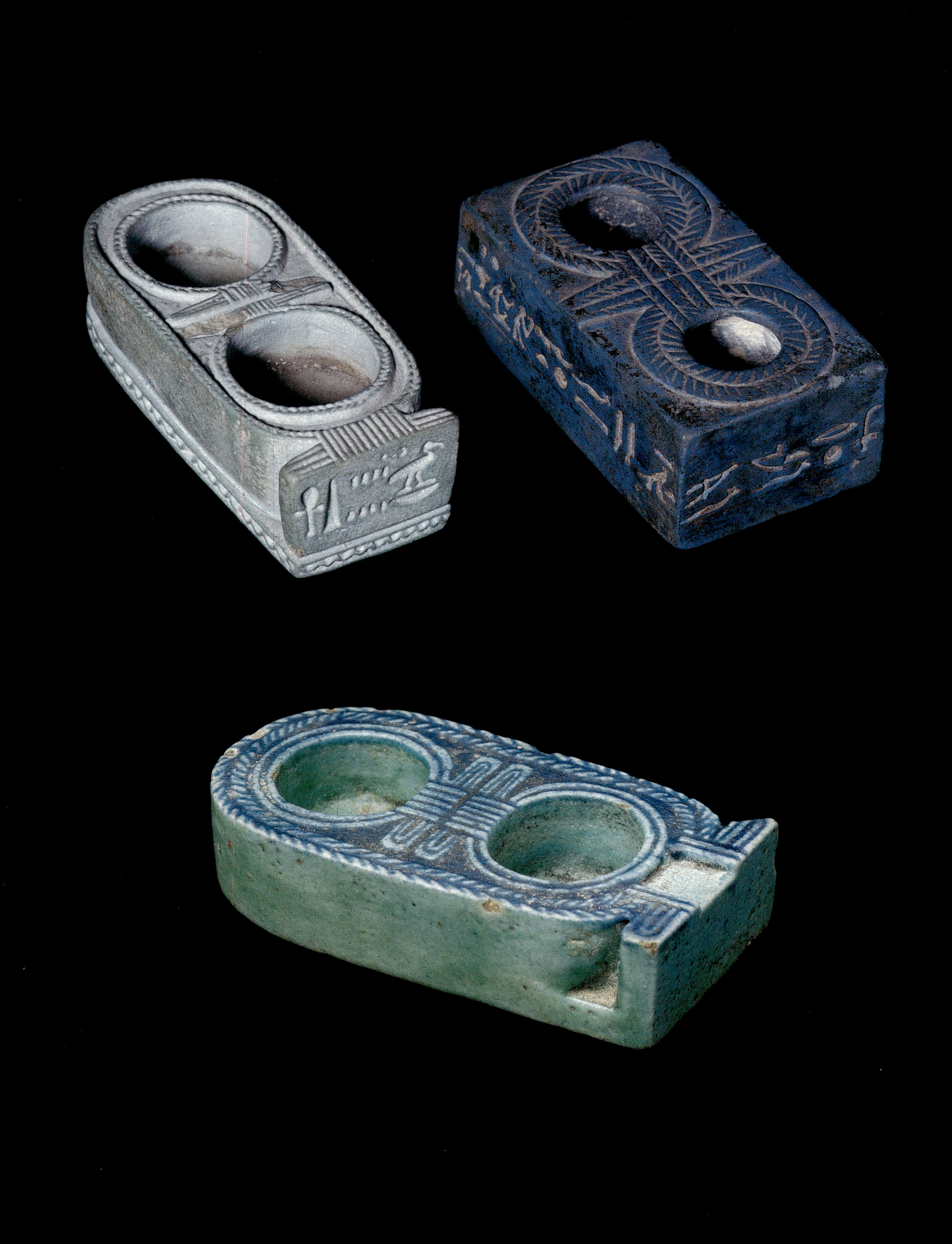

Right and below

COMPARTMENTALIZED BOX [94]
New Kingdom, Dynasty 18
Total H. 2.8 cm; W. 8.5 cm; L. 11.8 cm

Opposite above, left

INKWELL [111]
Late Period, Dynasty 26 or later
H. 2.1 cm; W. 3.0 cm; L. 6.8 cm

Opposite above, right

INKWELL [112]
Third Intermediate Period
H. 2.3 cm; W. 3.4 cm; L. 6.0 cm

Opposite below

INKWELL [113]
Late Period, Dynasty 26
W. 3.4 cm; L. 6.8 cm

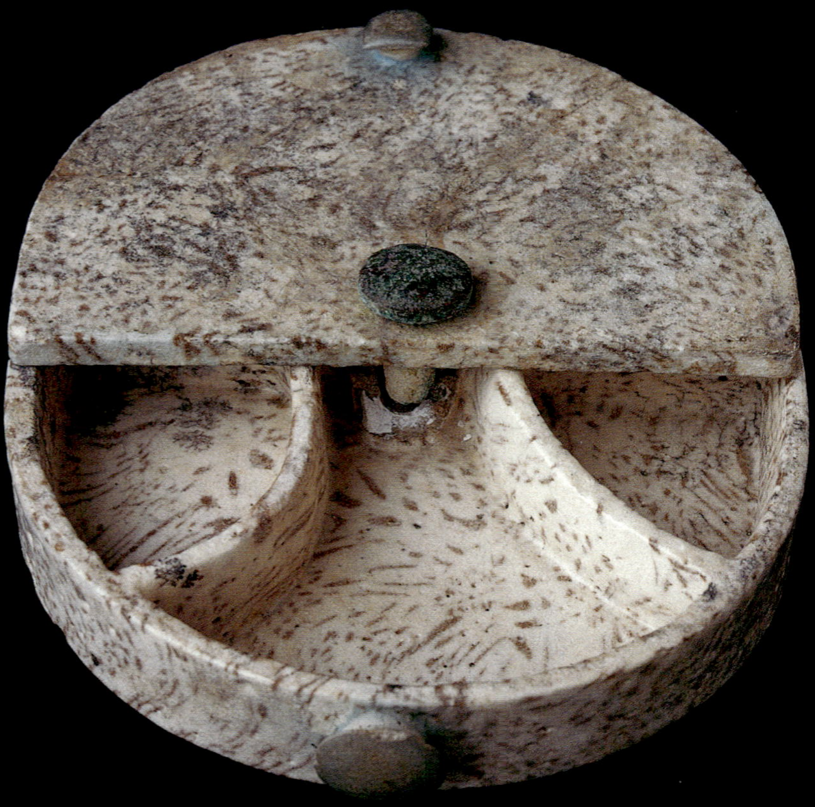

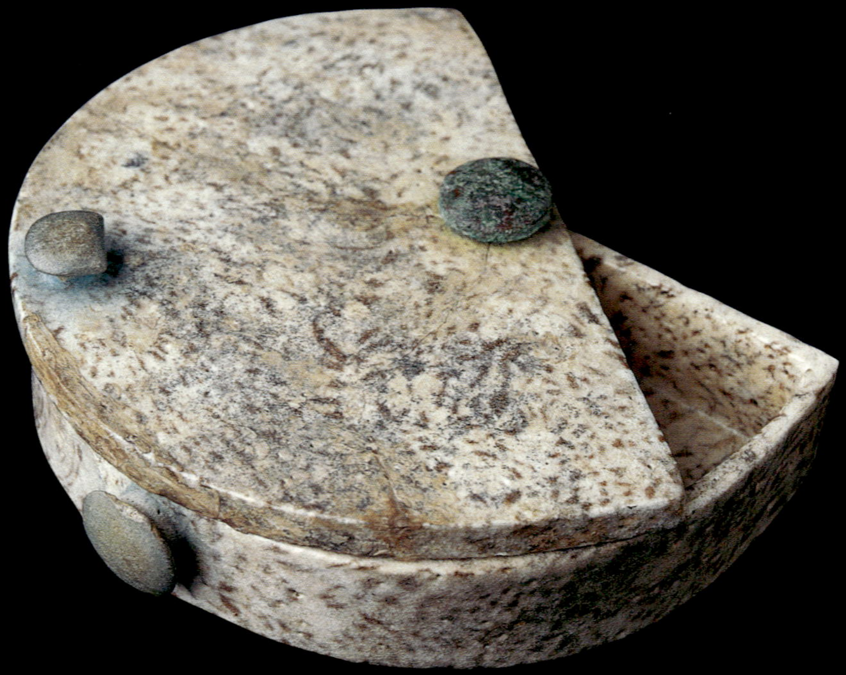

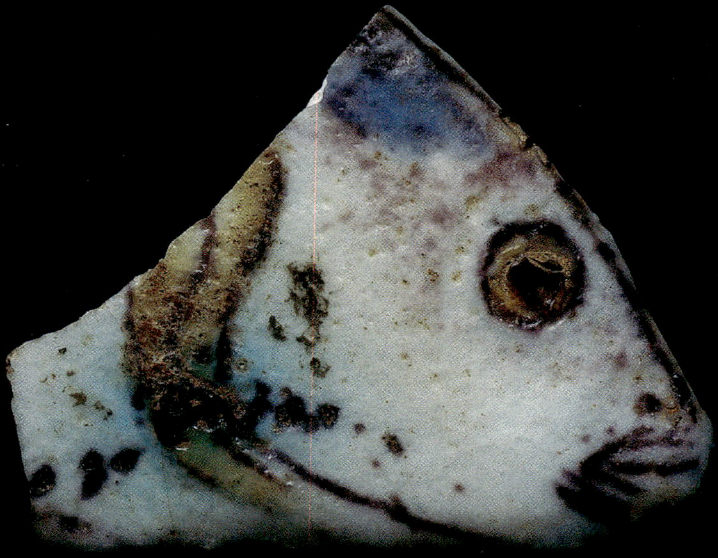

Left

FRAGMENT OF A FISH PLAQUE [110]
New Kingdom, possibly Dynasty 18
H. 3.8 cm; W. 4.2 cm; TH. 0.6 cm

Center left

INLAY IN THE FORM OF AN OWL [128]
Late Period or early Ptolemaic Period,
c. 525–305 BC
H. 2.7 cm; W. 2.0 cm

Center right

FISH AMULET [118]
New Kingdom, Dynasty 18, reign of
Amenhotep III or Akhenaten
H. 2.1 cm; L. 3.9 cm; D. 0.5 cm

Bottom

DUCK [95]
Probably New Kingdom
H. 4.4 cm; L. 7.0 cm

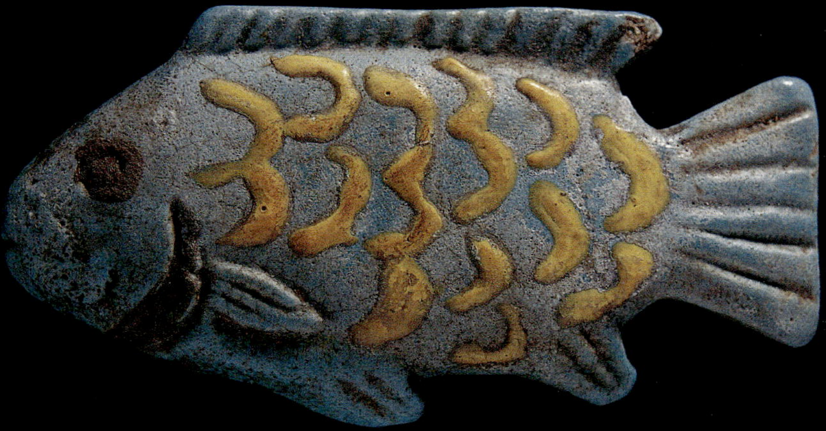

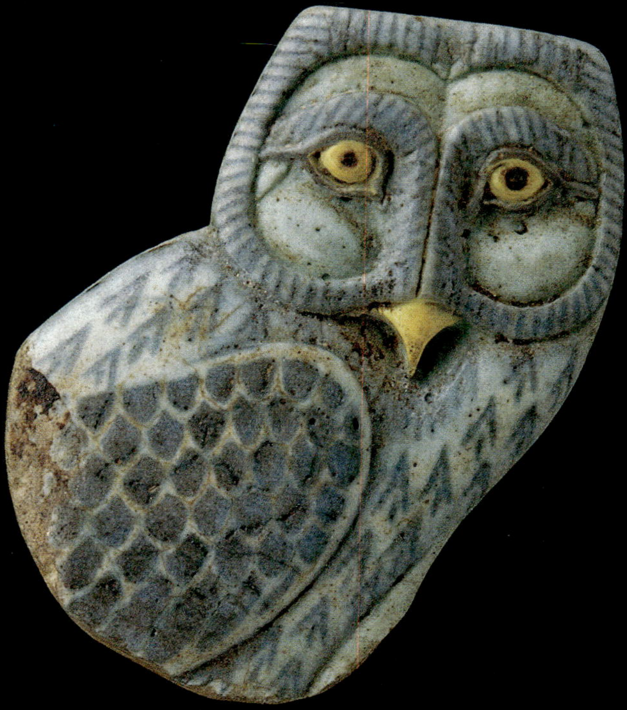

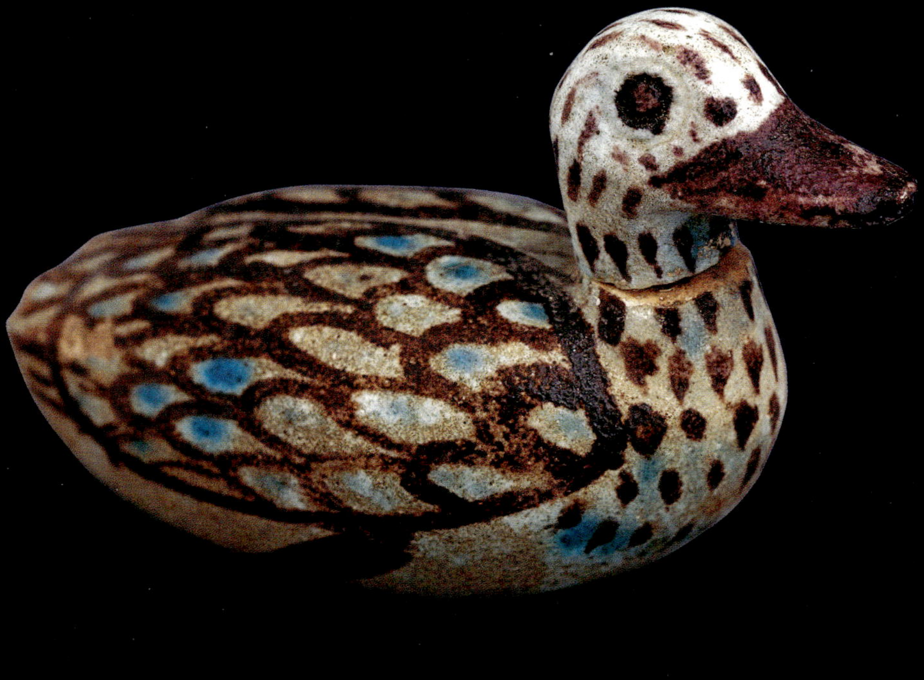

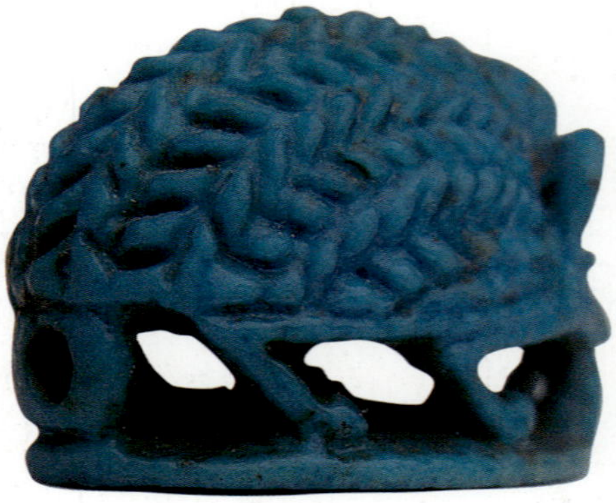

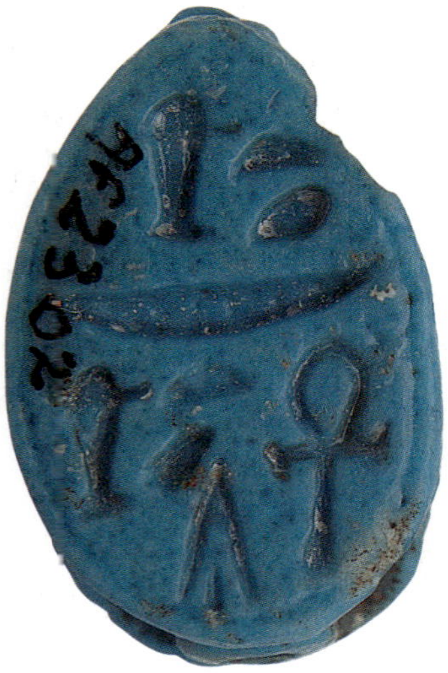

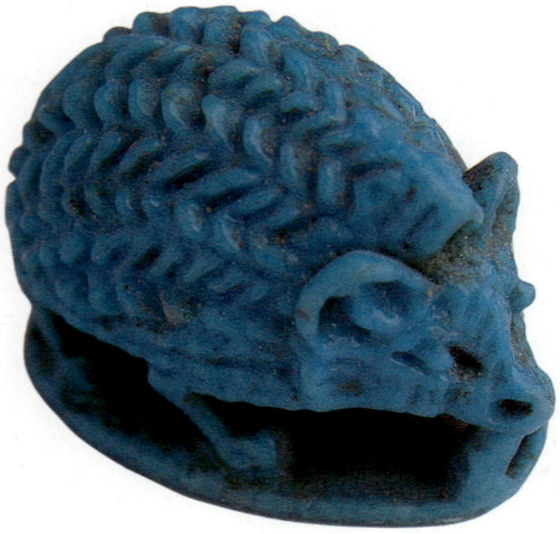

Left and above (3 views)
HEDGEHOG [99]
Third Intermediate Period
H. 1.5 cm

Left below
HEDGEHOG [98]
Middle Kingdom
DIAM. 6.0 cm

Below
DOG [97]
Middle Kingdom, late Dynasty 12
to early Dynasty 13
L. 5.2 cm

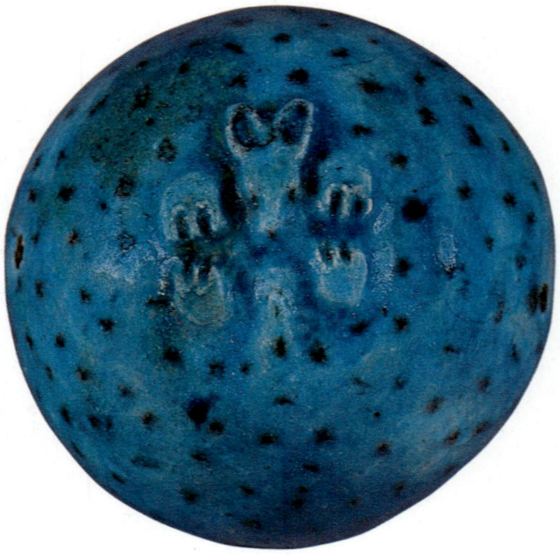

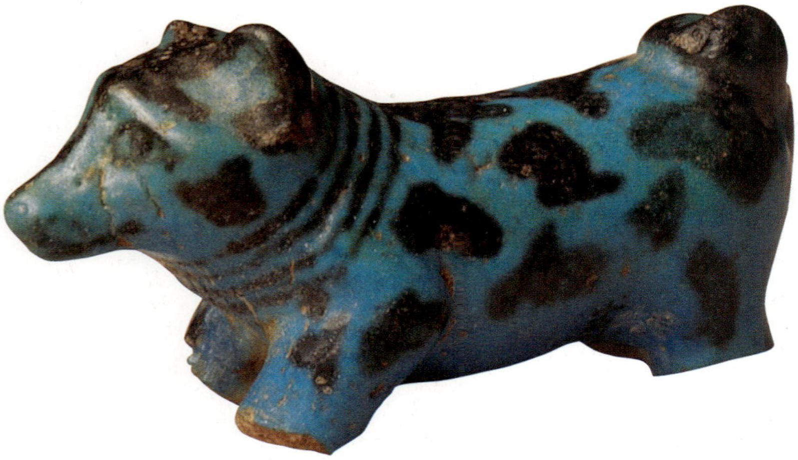

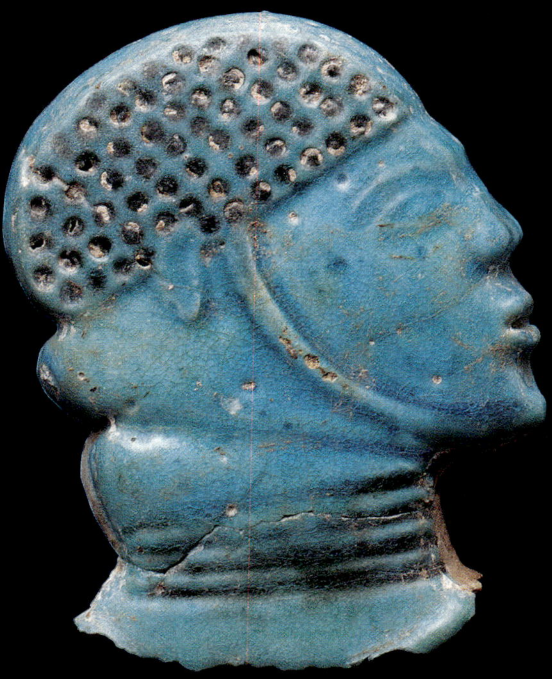

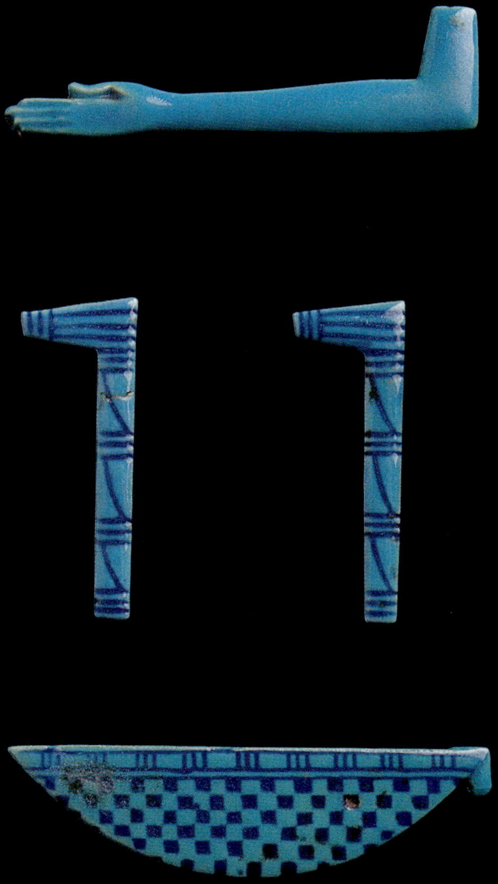

Above

INLAY HEAD OF A NUBIAN [137]
Nubian, Classic Kerma Period, *c.* 1600–1500 BC
H. 7.5 cm; W. 2.3 cm

Above right

HIEROGLYPHS [129]
Late Period, Dynasty 30 to Ptolemaic Period
Outstretched hand:
L. 5.5 cm; W. 1.5 cm; TH. 0.6 cm
Flagpoles–signs for deity:
H. 3.8 cm; W. 1.2 cm; TH. 0.6 cm
H. 3.9 cm; W. 1.2 cm; TH. 0.6 cm
Basket:
H. 1.55 cm; W. 5.45 cm; TH. 0.65 cm

Right

STRIDING FOUR-HEADED RAM [133]
Late Period, Dynasty 30 to Ptolemaic Period
H. 4.9 cm; L. 6.5 cm; D. 2.3 cm

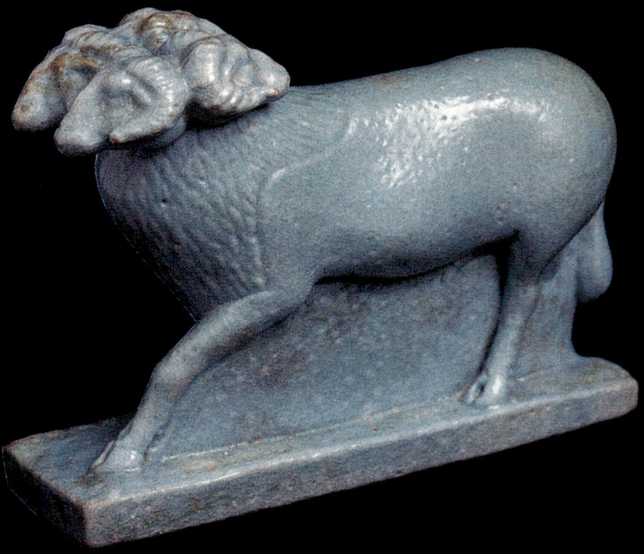

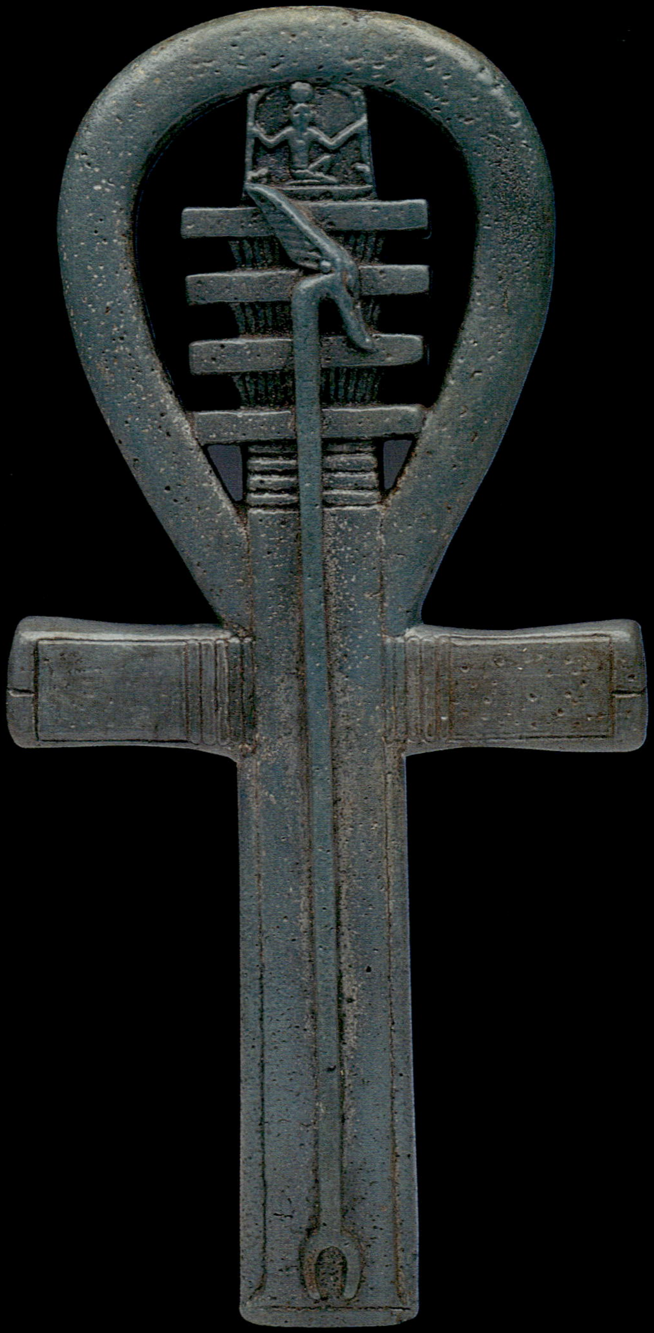

Left

AMULET COMBINING ANKH, DJED, HEH, AND WAS-SCEPTER SIGNS [119]
Dynasty 25 to Late Period,
c. 700–500 BC
H. 23.5 cm

Below

GAME BOARD IN THE SHAPE OF A HIPPOPOTAMUS AND THREE GAMING PIECES FOR THE GAME OF 58 HOLES [96]
Late Period, Dynasty 27–30
H. 7.4 cm; W. 18.0 cm; L. 21.5 cm
Gaming pieces: H. 16.7 cm; W. 3.3 cm

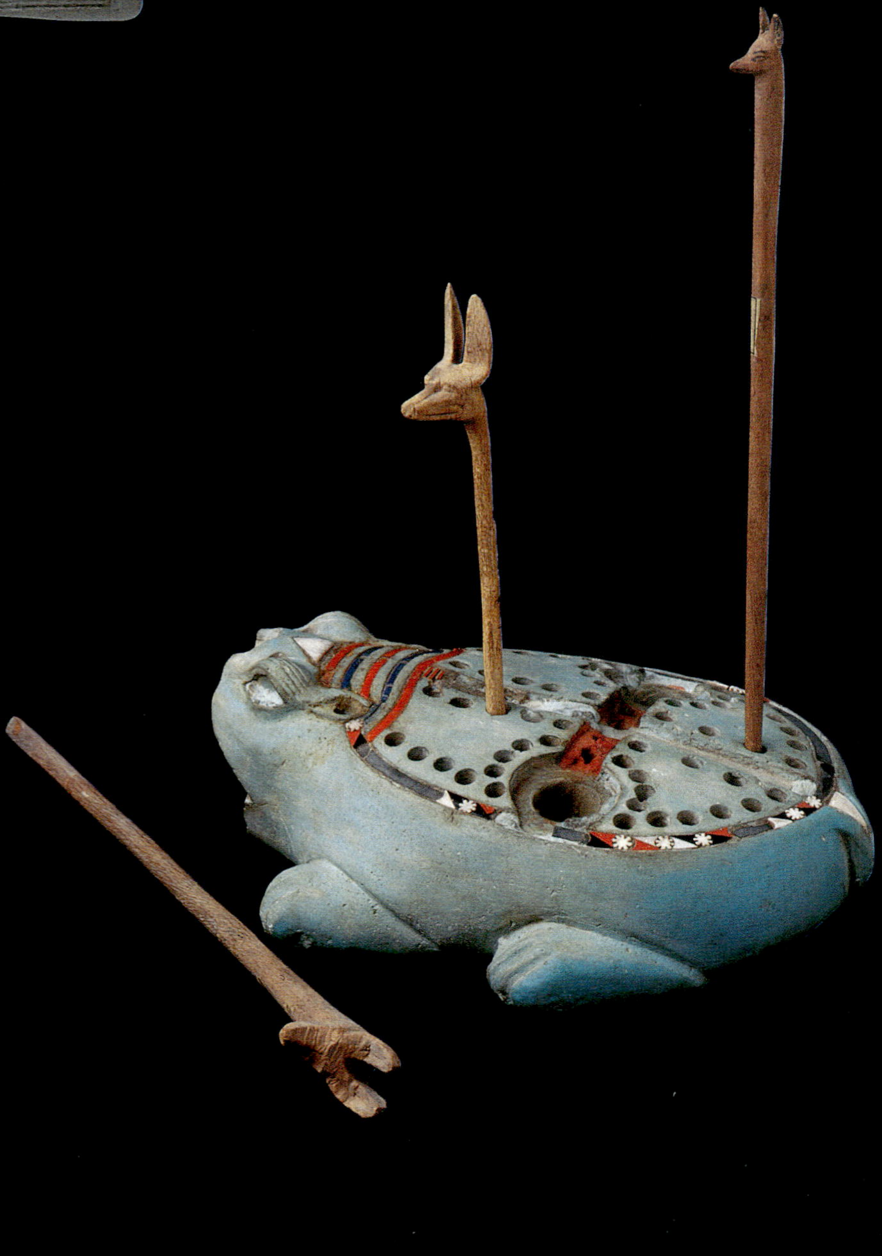

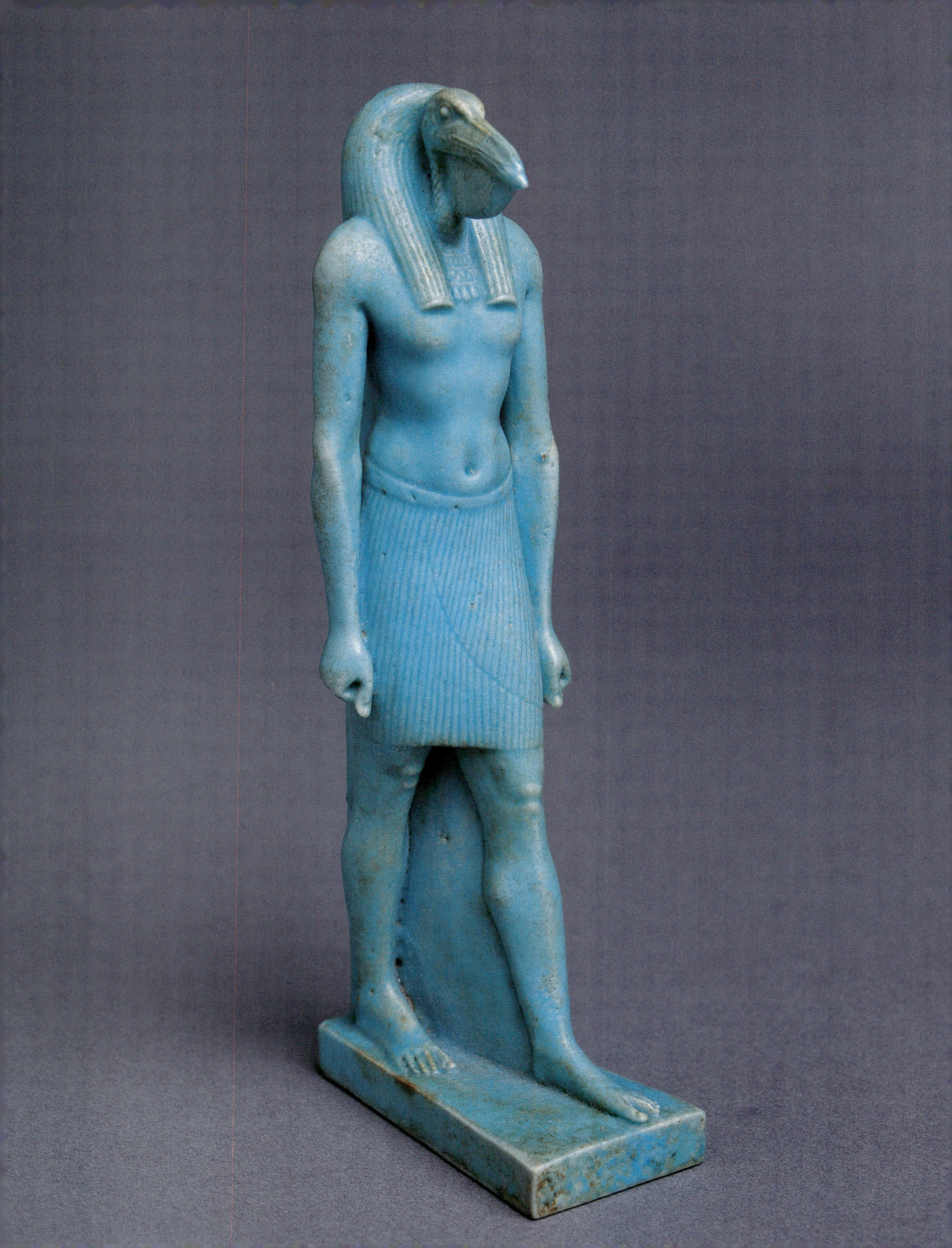

Opposite

STATUETTE OF THOTH AS AN IBIS-HEADED STRIDING MALE FIGURE [130]
Ptolemaic Period
H. 14.0 cm; W. 3.2 cm; D. 5.4 cm

Right

NEFERTUM ON A LION AMULET [120]
Late Saite to Persian Period,
c. 575–400 BC
H. 7.0 cm

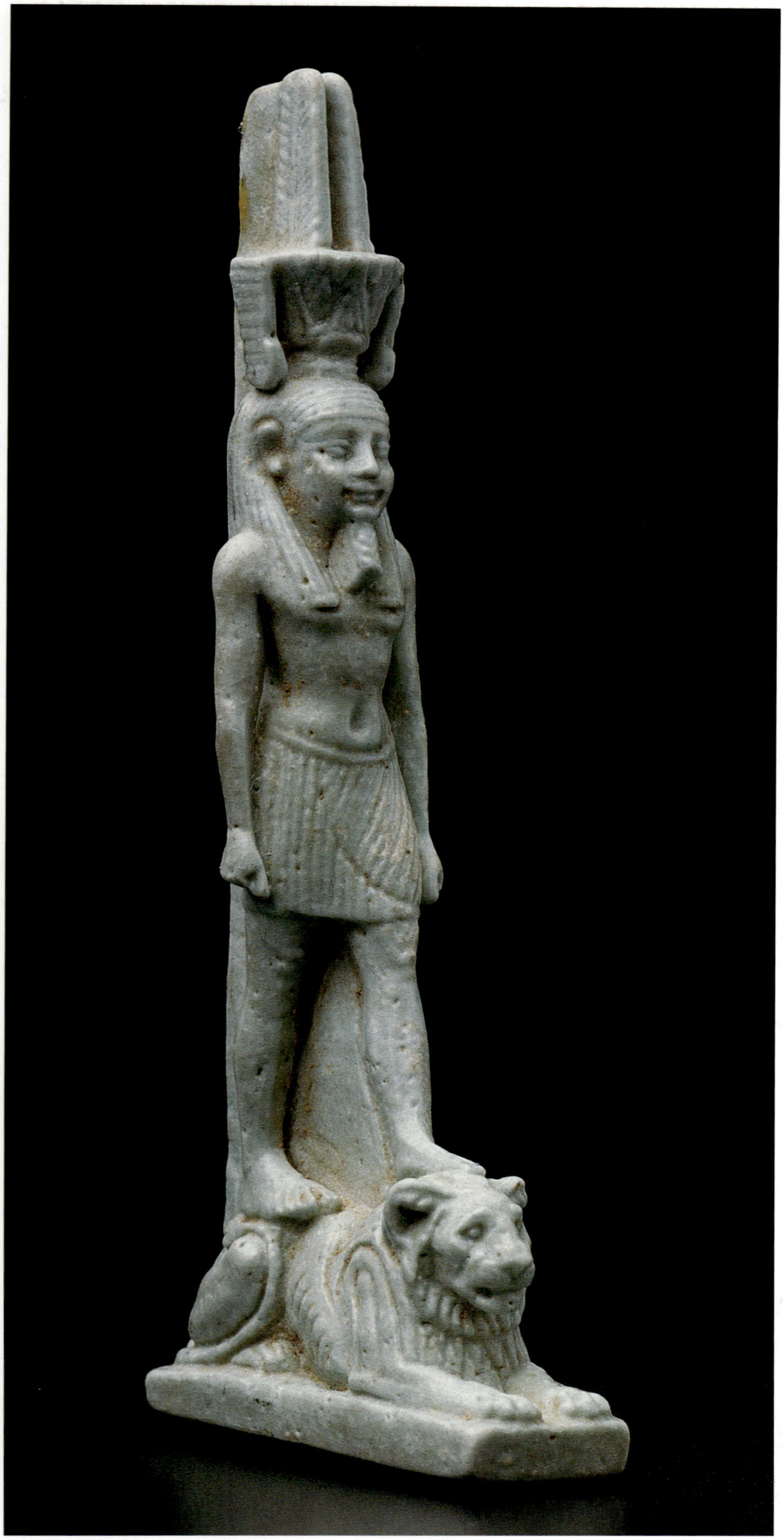

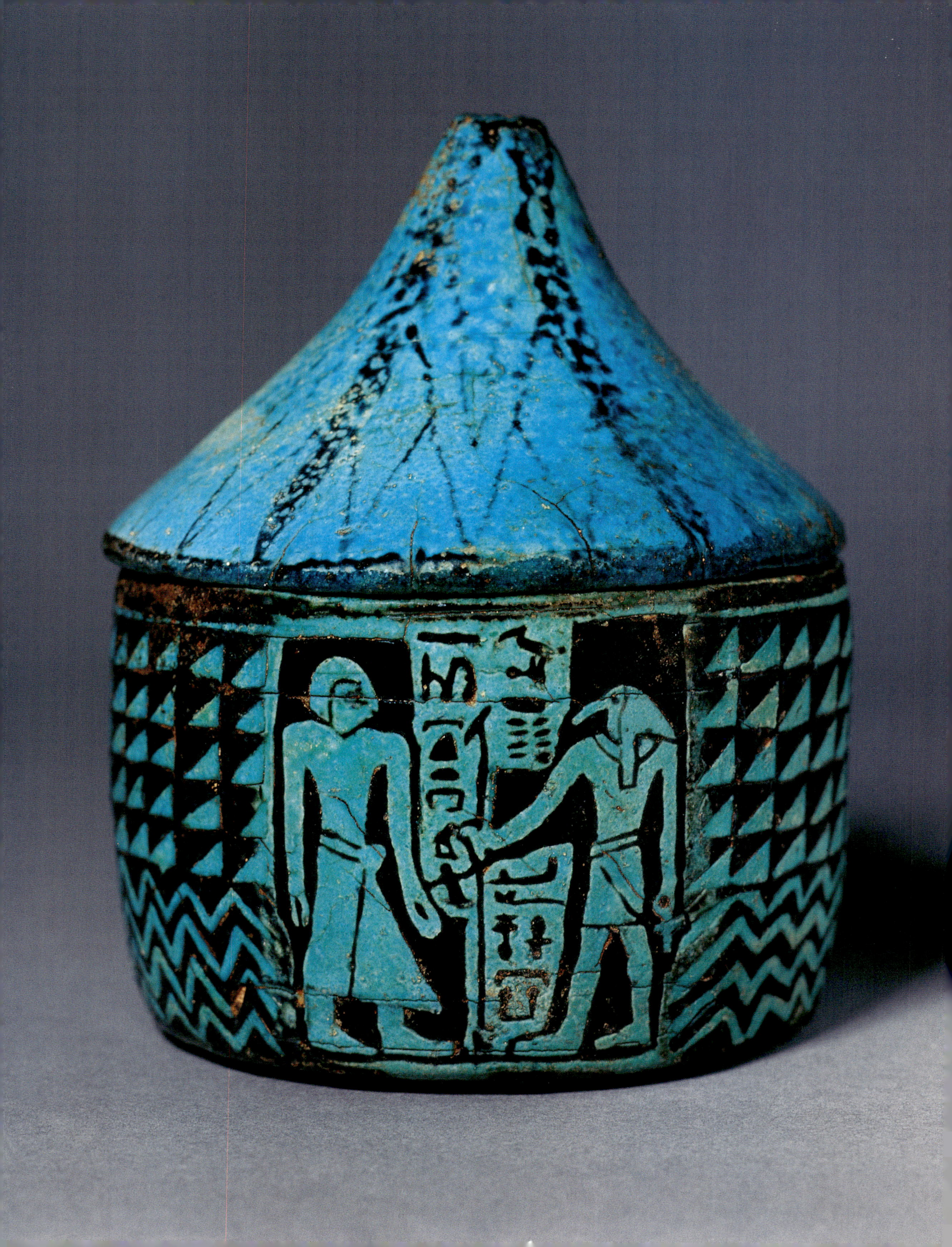

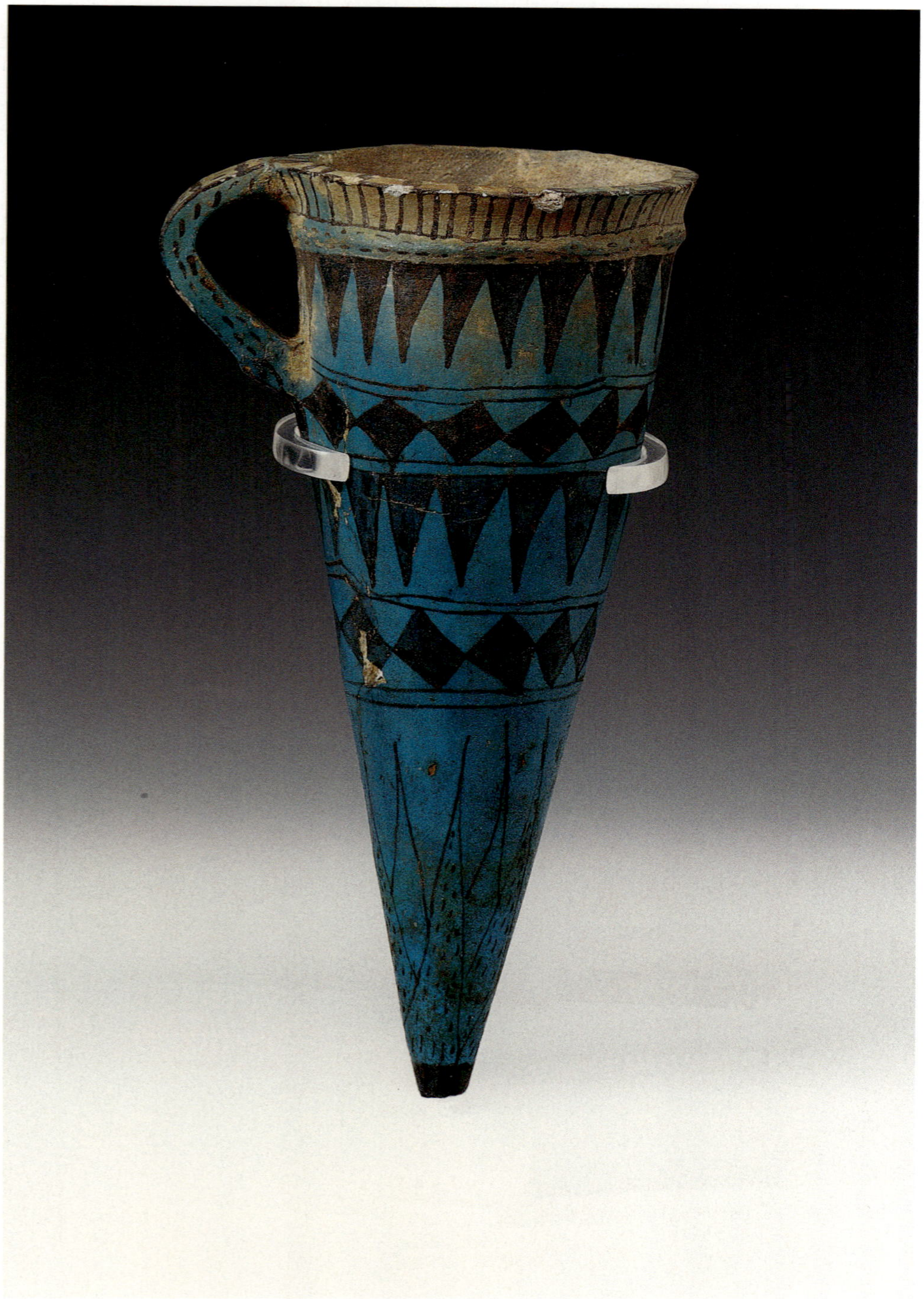

Above

CONICAL RHYTON OR DRINKING CUP [124]
New Kingdom, Dynasty 18
H. 23.0 cm

Opposite

VESSEL IN THE SHAPE OF A BASKET
WITH A CONICAL LID [135]
Late Second Intermediate Period
to New Kingdom, early Dynasty 18
H. 15.0 cm; DIAM. 11.9 cm

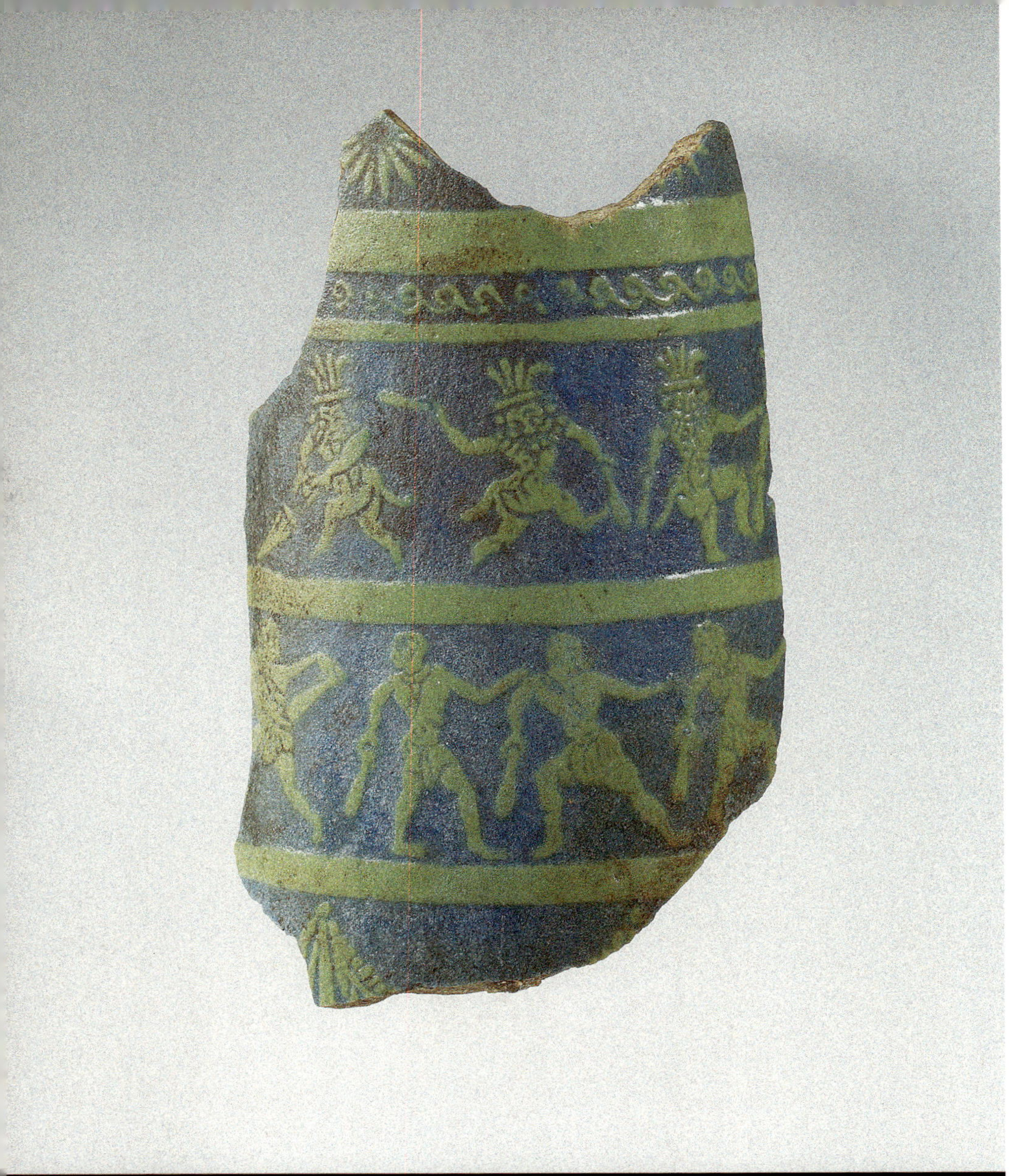

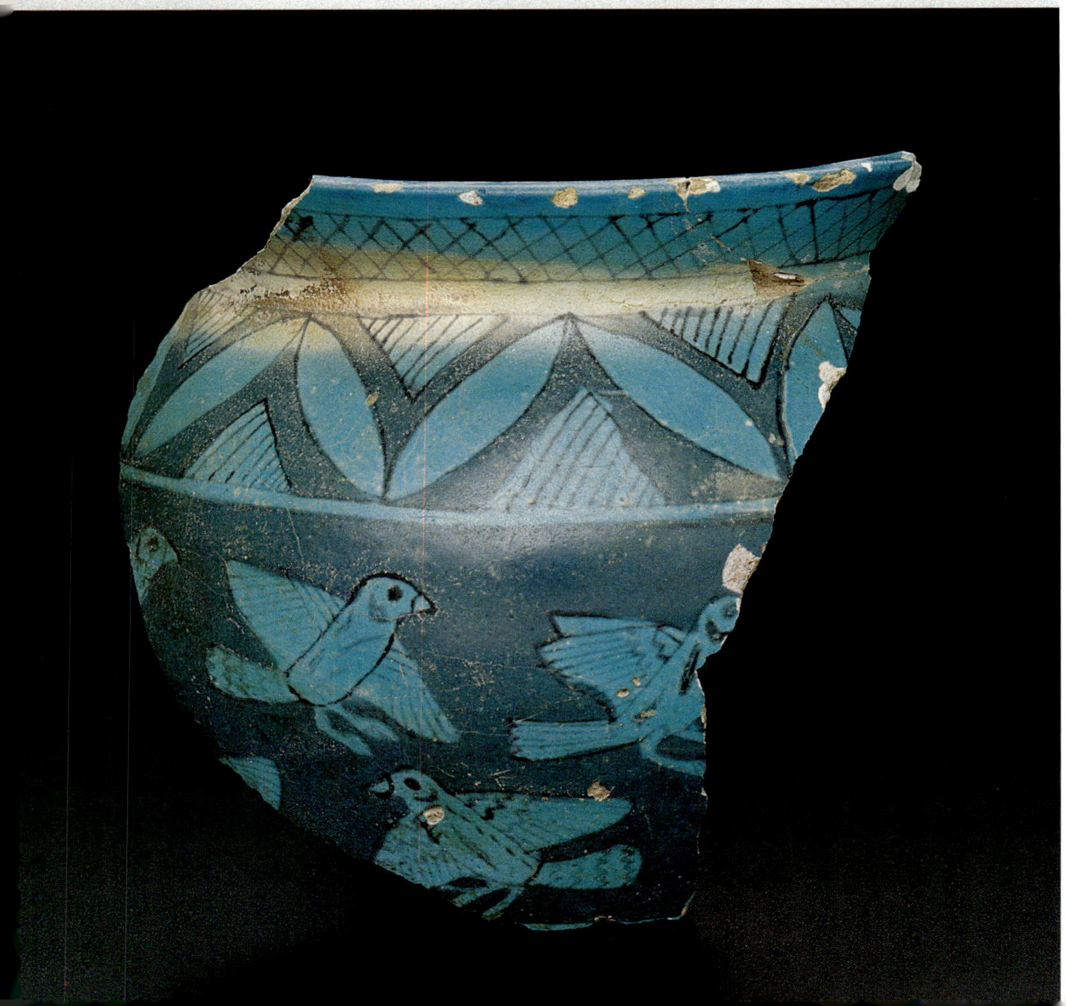

Left above

SHERD FROM A RHYTON OR DRINKING CUP WITH BES IMAGES [139]

Ptolemaic Period, 3rd to 2nd century BC

H. 8.8 cm

Left below

VESSEL FRAGMENT WITH FLYING BIRDS [136]

Late Middle Kingdom

H. 10.3 cm

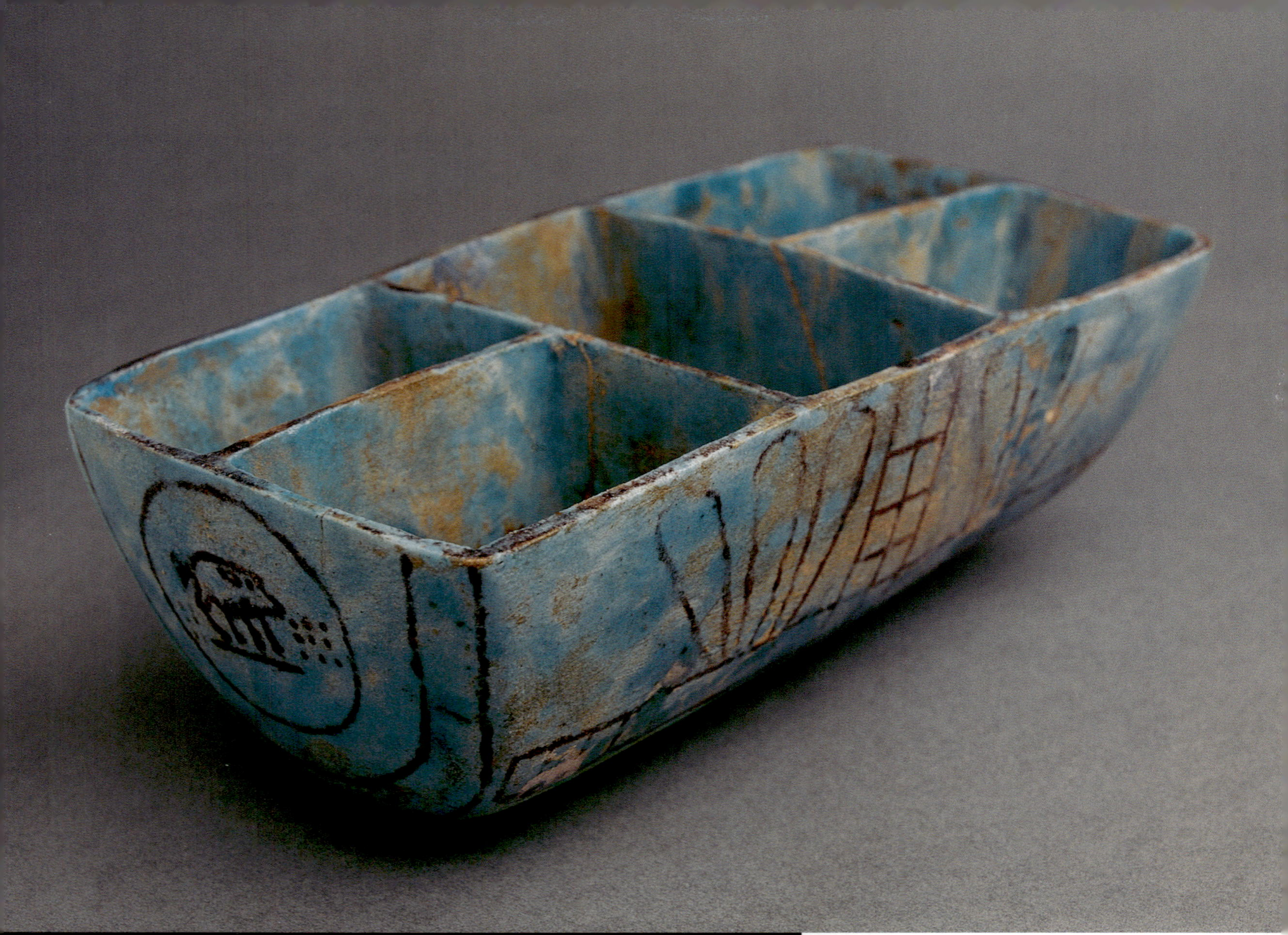

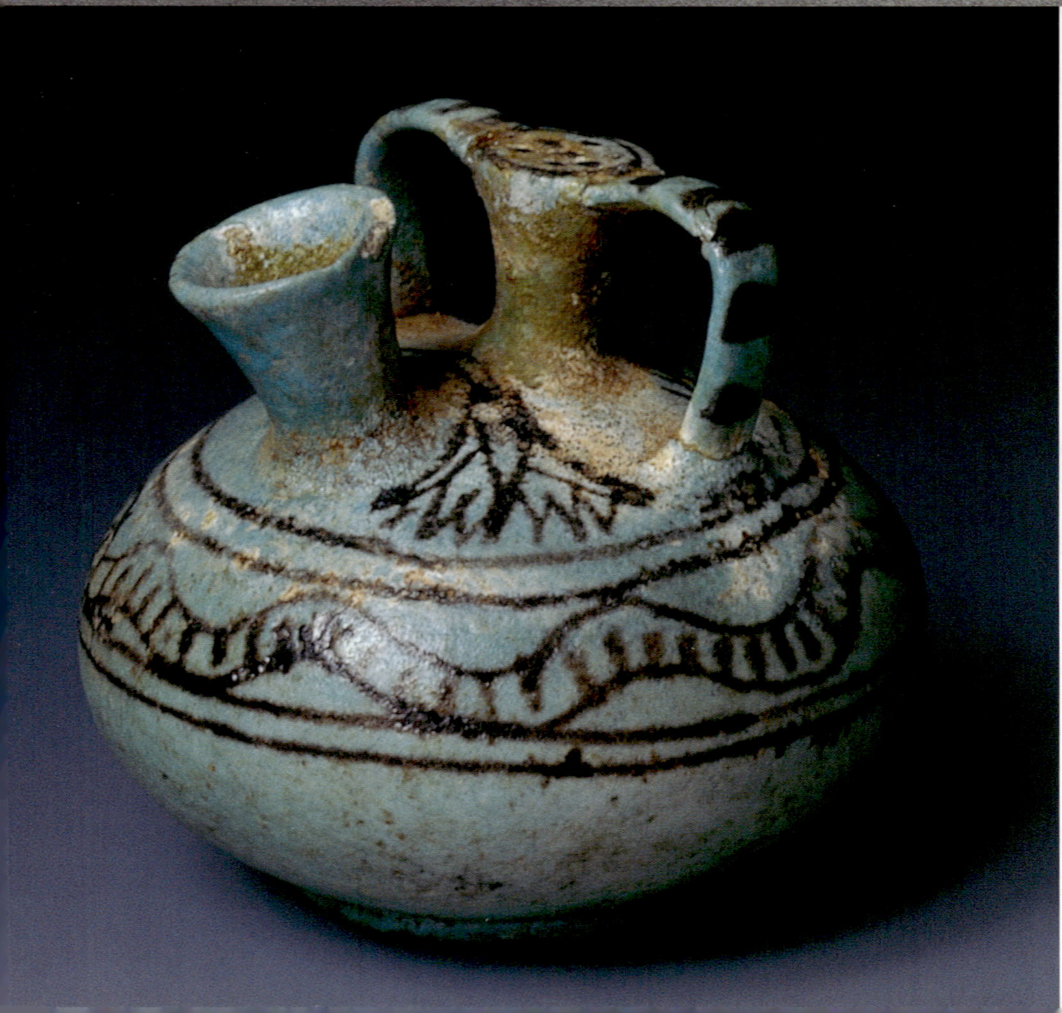

Above

DISH WITH COMPARTMENTS [93]
Middle Kingdom, Dynasty 12–13
H. 6.7 cm; W. 7.6 cm; L. 16.5 cm

Left

STIRRUP JAR [123]
New Kingdom, Dynasty 18
H. 6.5 cm

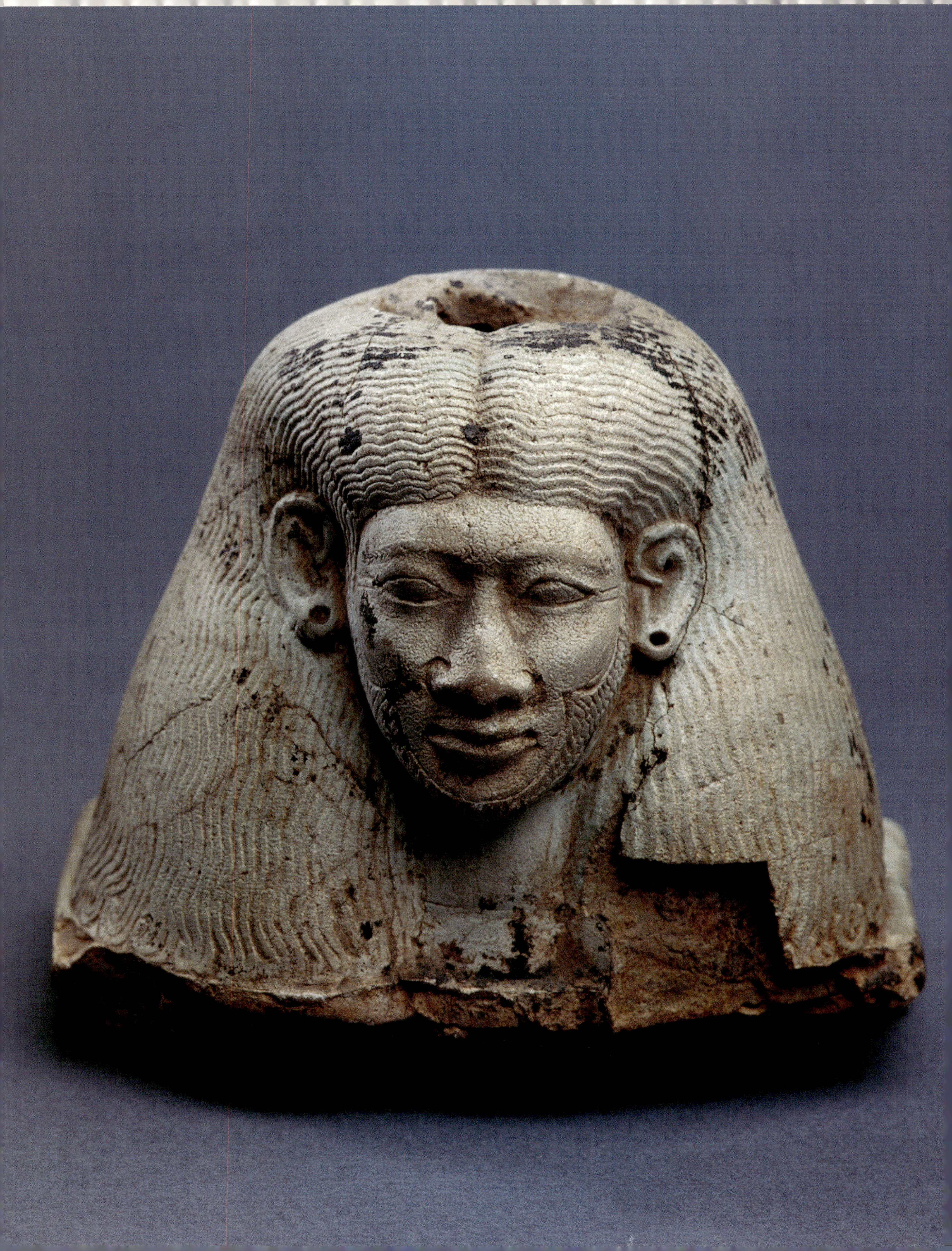

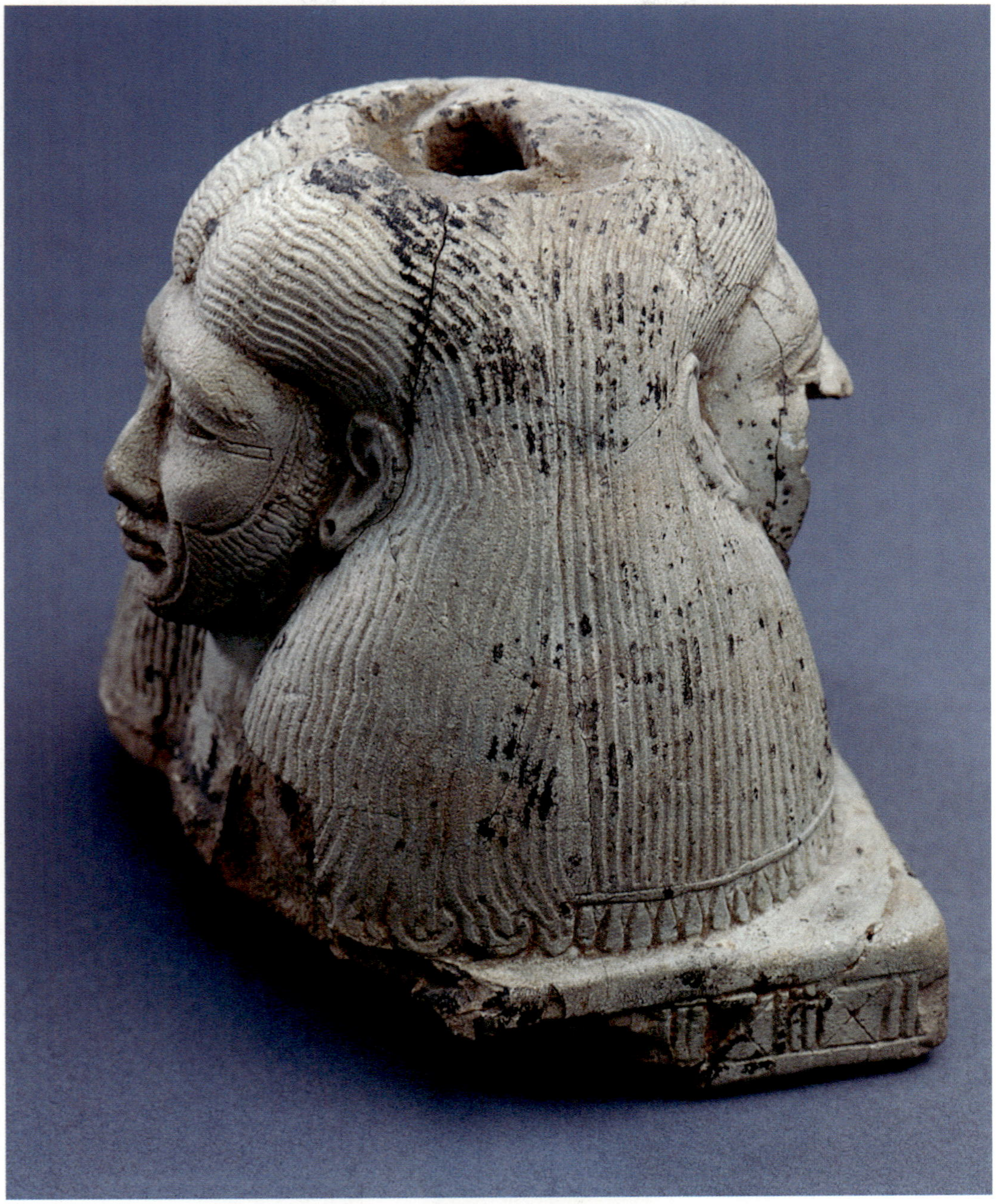

Opposite and above

NECK FROM A PERFUME VASE [125]

Late Period, Dynasty 26

H. 10.0 cm

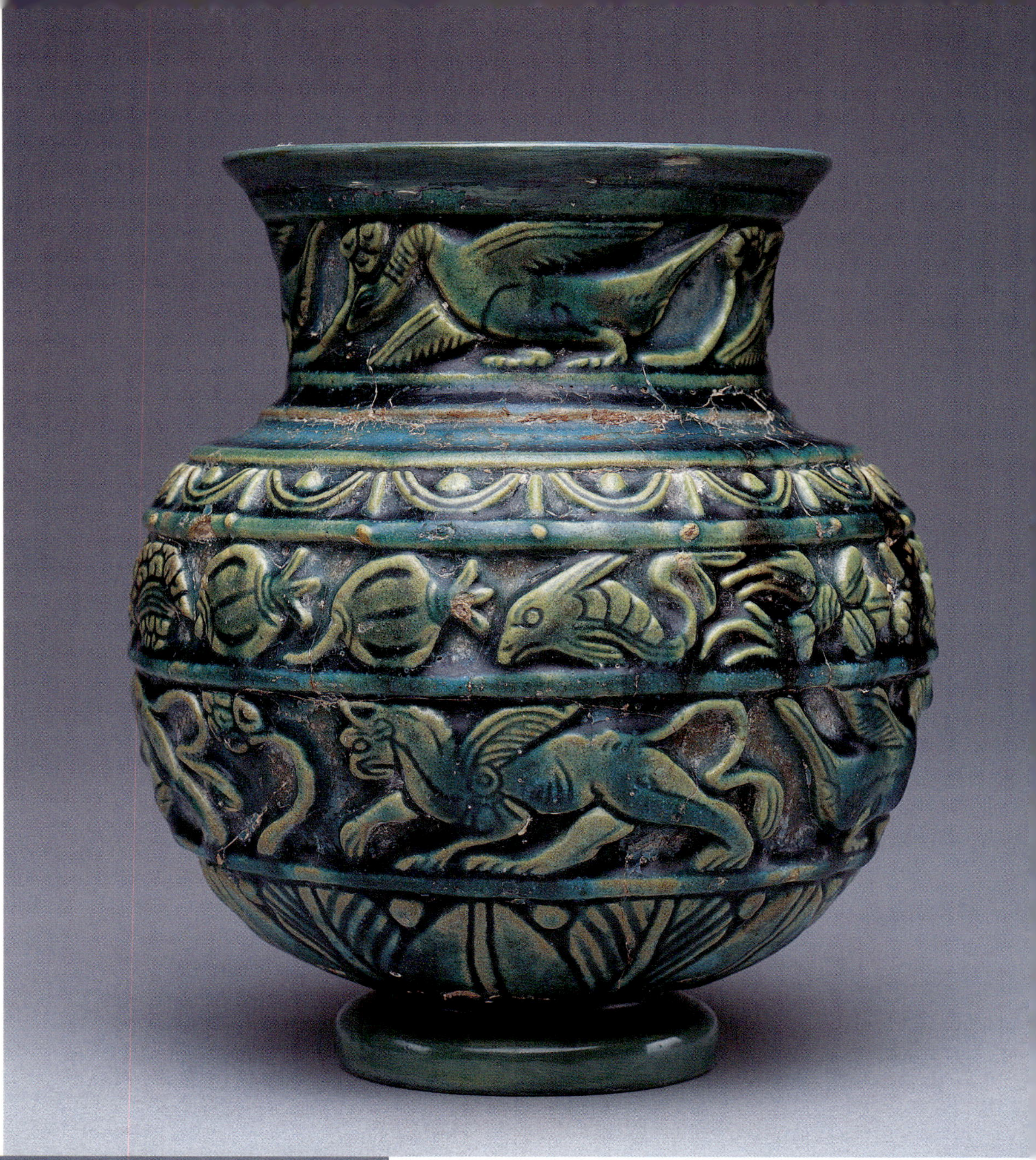

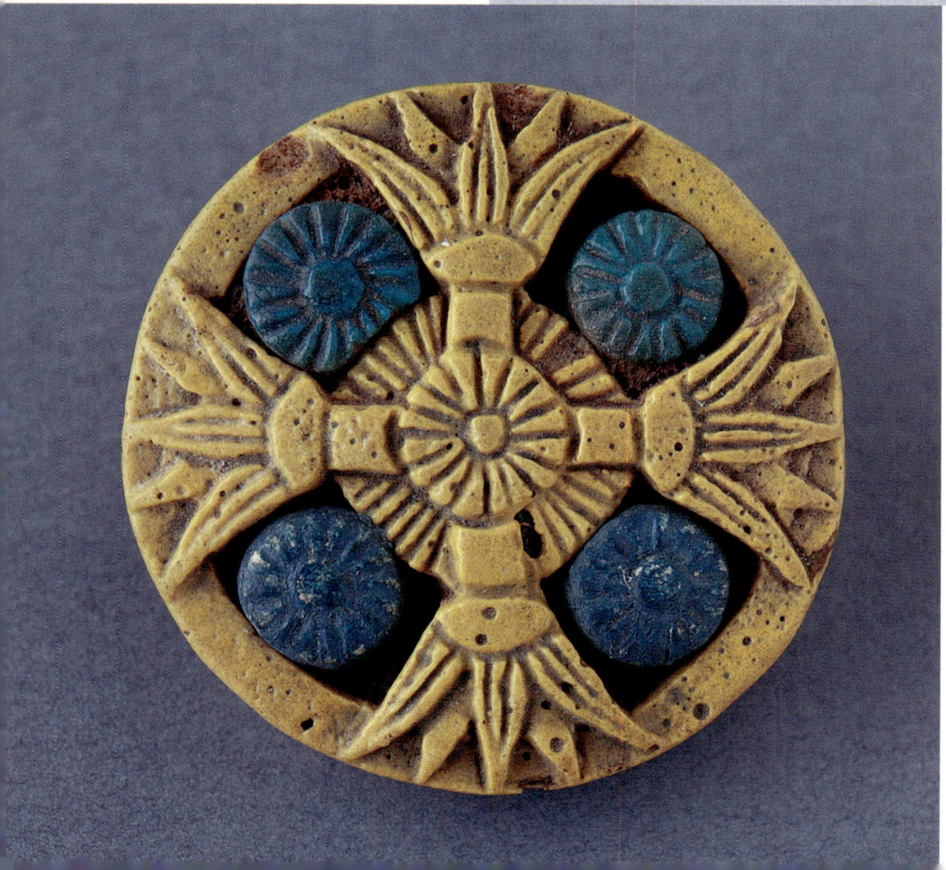

Above

VESSEL WITH RELIEF DECORATION [141]
Roman Period, early 1st century AD
H. 17.0 cm

Left

ROUNDEL, PERHAPS FROM A HEADBAND [109]
Late Period, Dynasty 25–26
DIAM. 4.0 cm

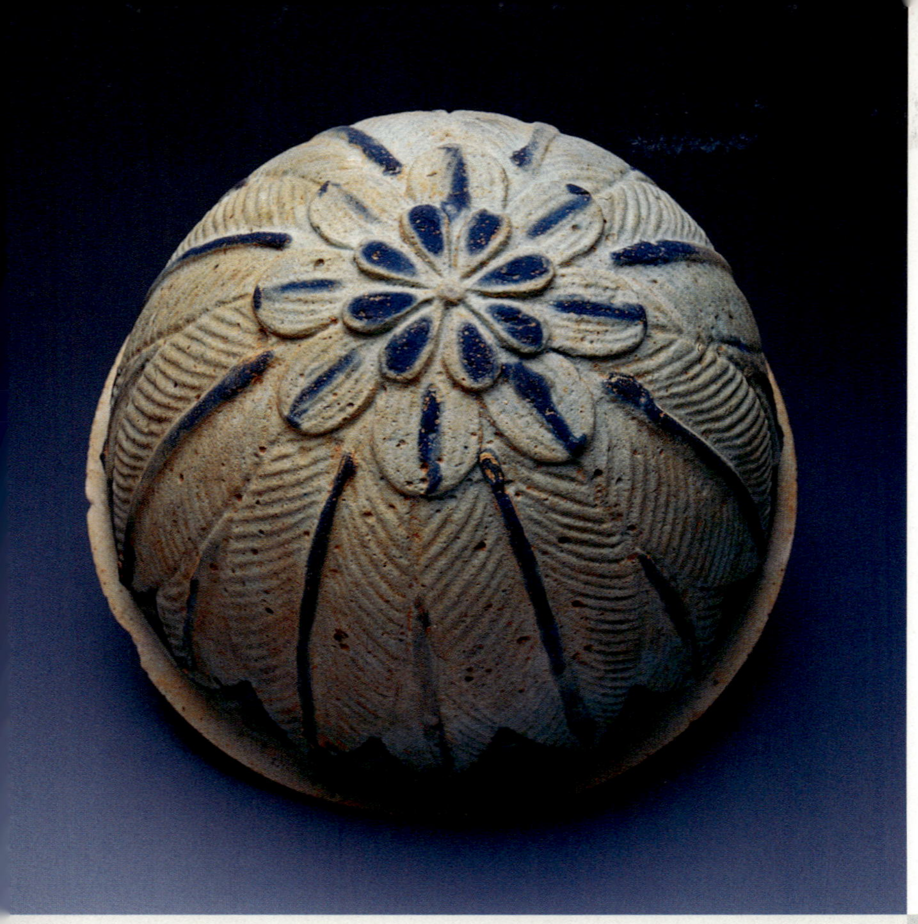

Below, left and right

MINIATURE NAOS,
OR SHRINE [131]
Third Intermediate Period, Dynasty 21–25
H. 2.5 cm

Left

MOLDED BOWL [140]
Ptolemaic Period
H. 15.2 cm; DIAM. 10.3 cm

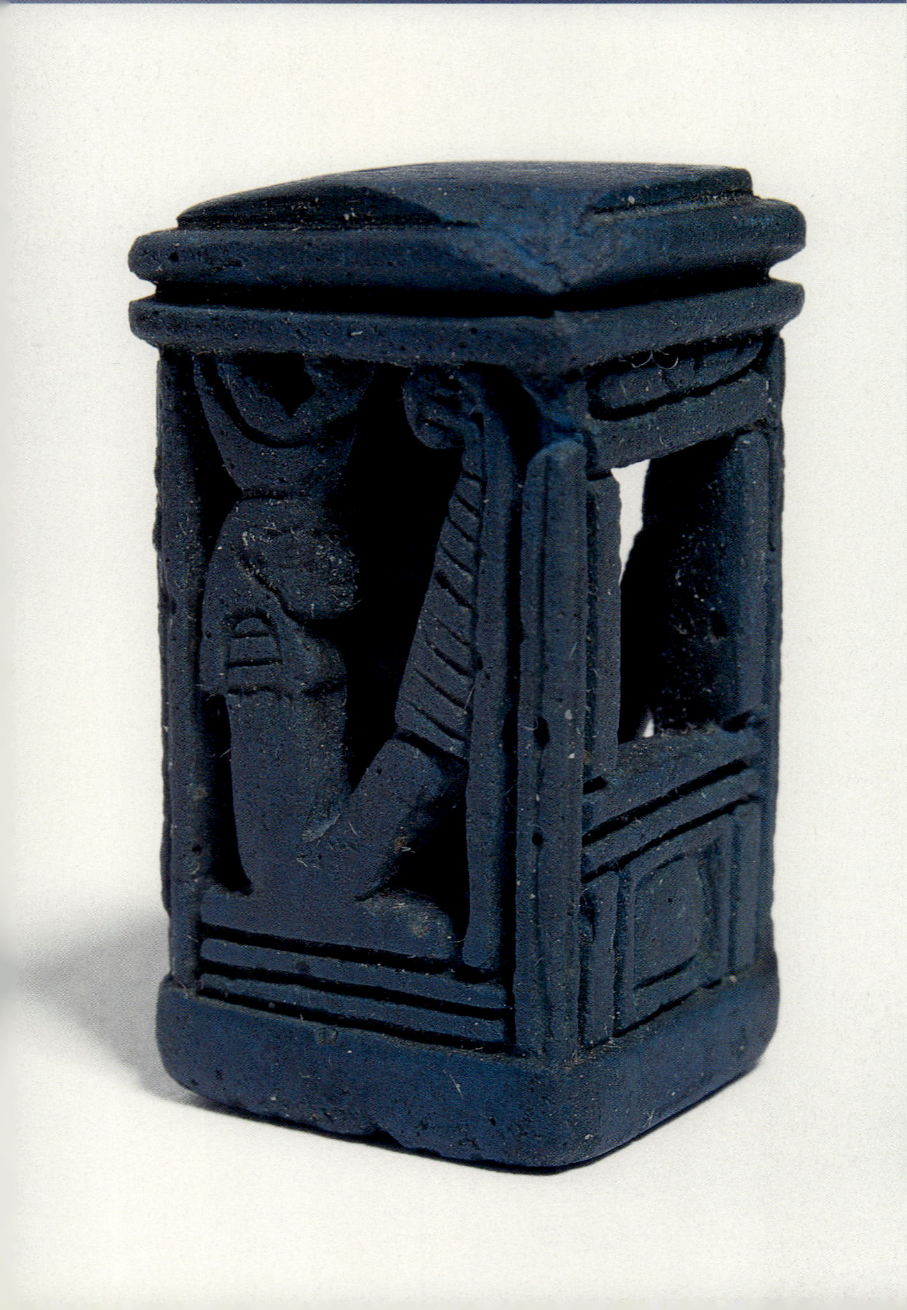

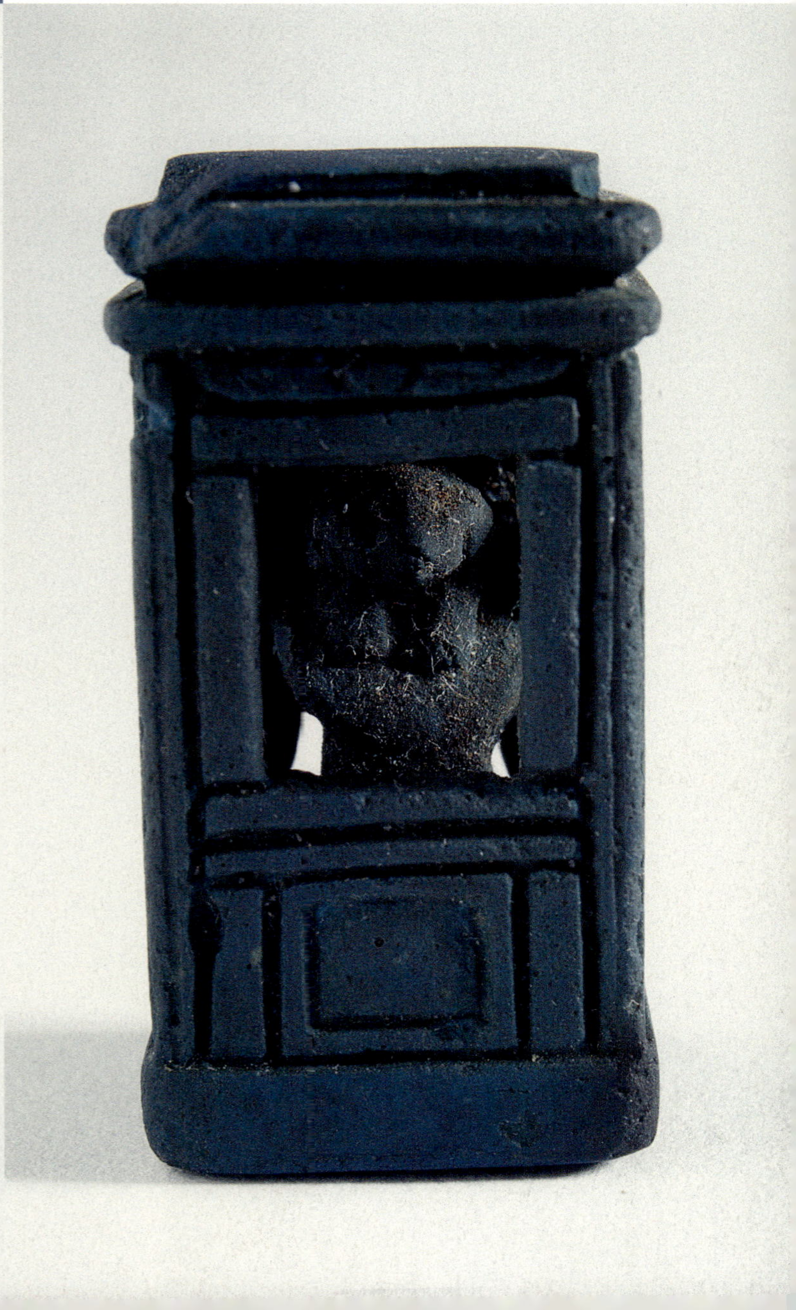

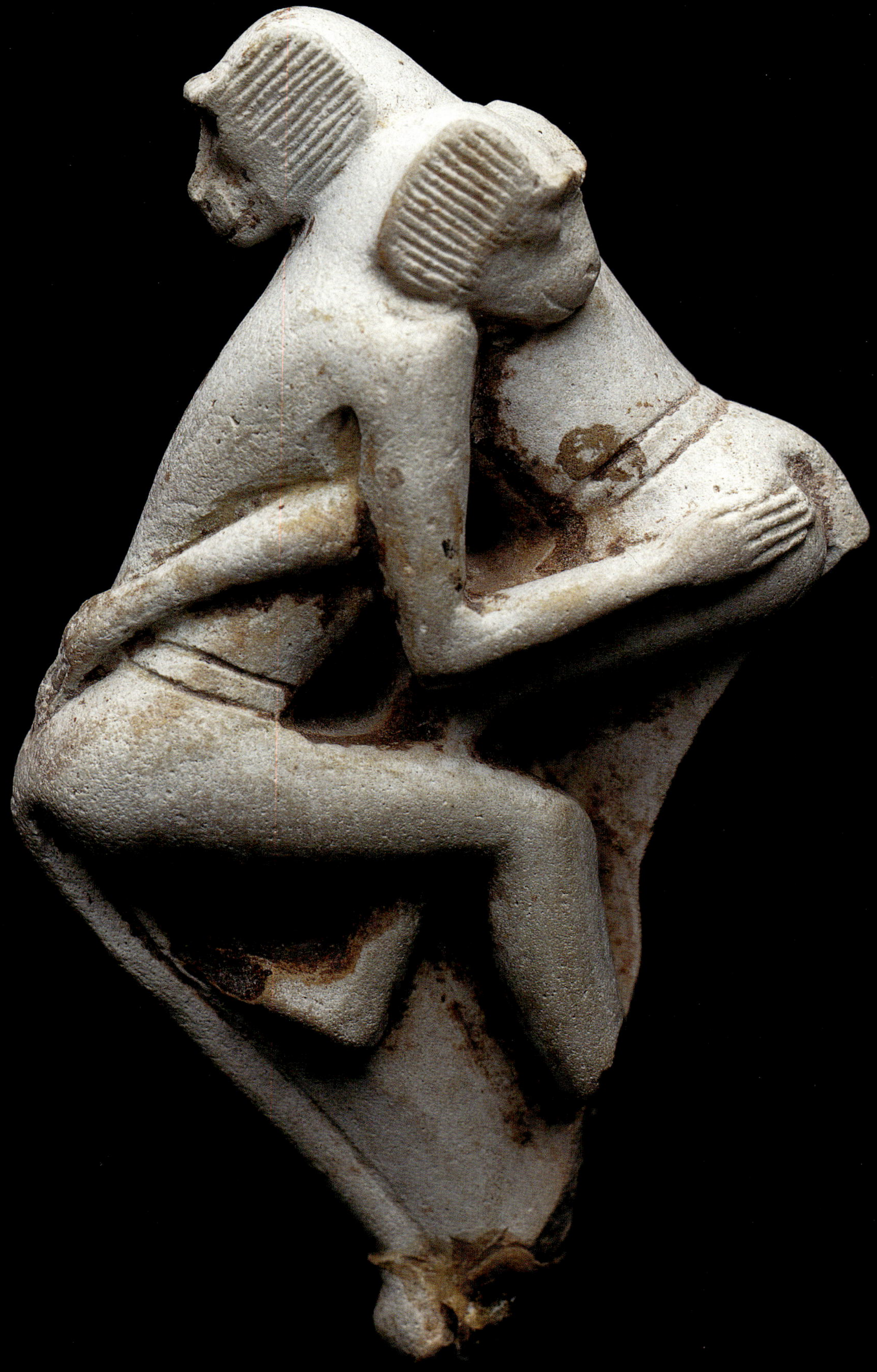

Below

MODEL CLEPSYDRA,
OR WATER CLOCK [132]
Late Period, Dynasty 25 to Ptolemaic
Period
H. 10.0 cm

Opposite

MONKEYS WRESTLING [134]
Ptolemaic Period
H. 9.0 cm

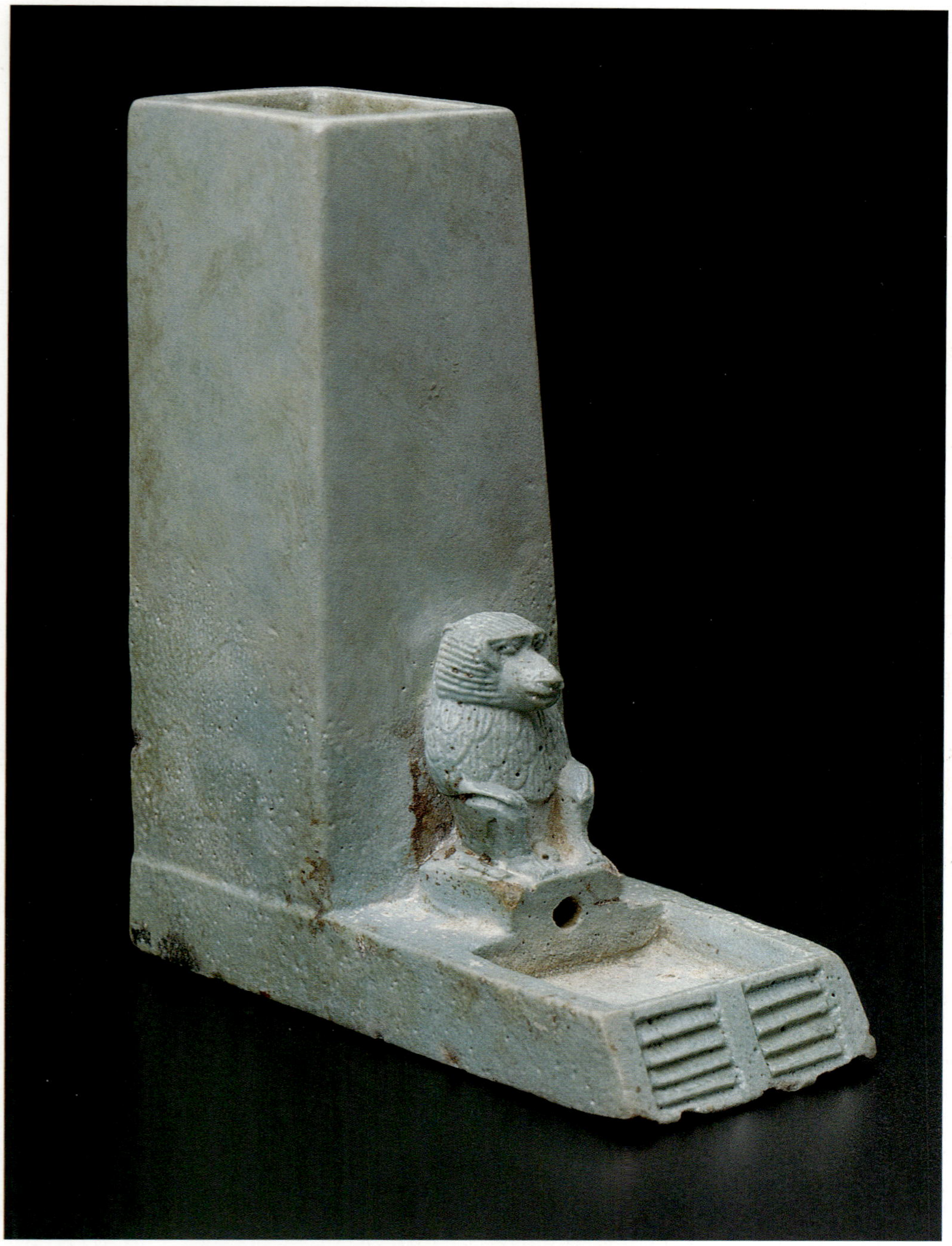

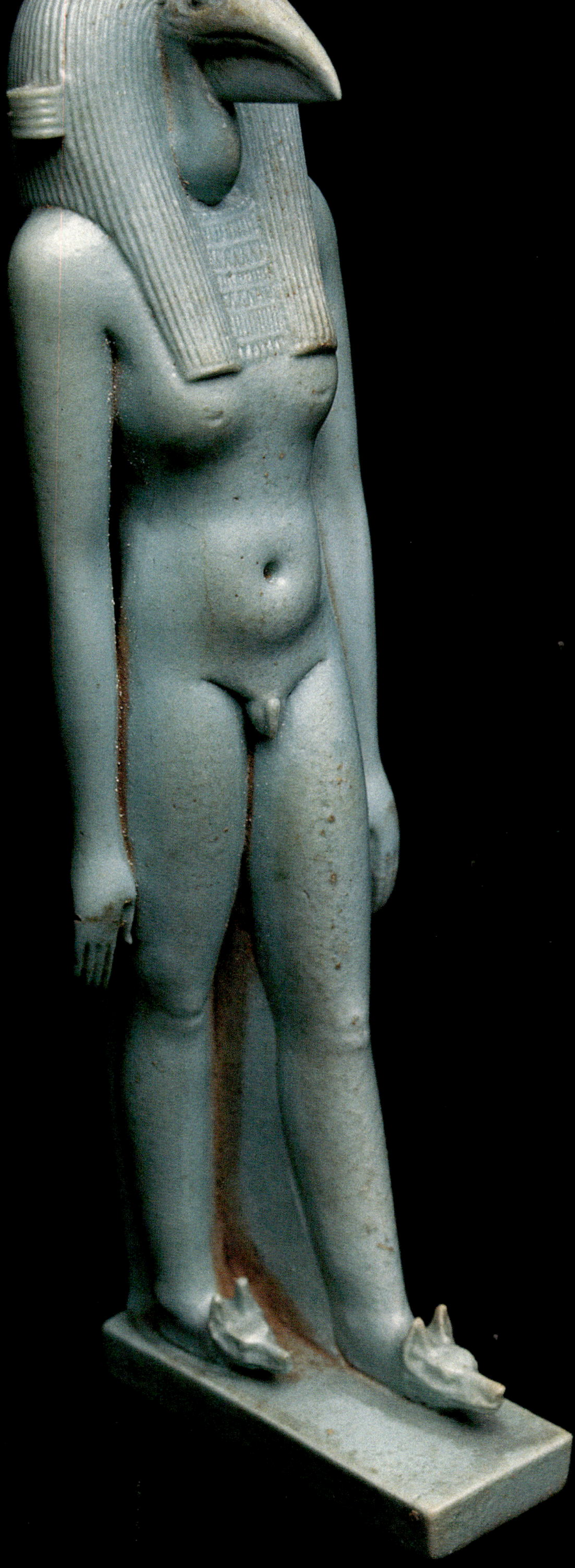

FUNERARY USES OF FAIENCE

Faience, or *tjehnet*, meaning "what is gleaming" like the light of the sun, moon, and stars, was a light-filled material that promoted the deceased's rebirth. The faience shabtis (funerary figurines), stelae (funerary markers), mummy netting, amulets, and other grave goods thus helped to impart life to the dead. A winged faience pectoral of the mother goddess Isis, for example, scintillated with eternal celestial light that immortalized the mummy.

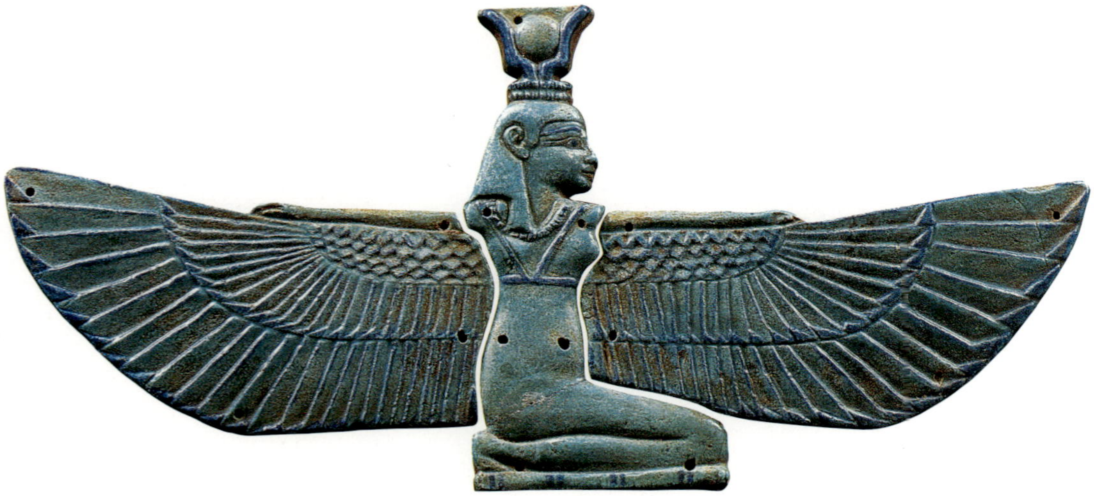

Opposite

STATUETTE OF THE GOD THOTH [169]
Late Period, Dynasty 26 to Ptolemaic Period
H. 13.0 cm

Above

WINGED ISIS PECTORAL [159]
See p. 158

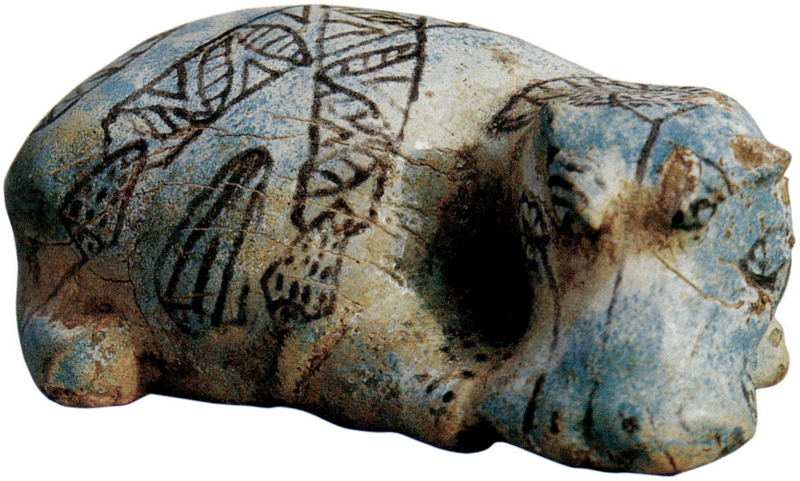

Above
HIPPOPOTAMUS [144]
Middle Kingdom, Dynasty 11–12
H. 5.3 cm; max. W. 6.2 cm; L. 11.7 cm

Right
HIPPOPOTAMUS [143]
Middle Kingdom, Dynasty 11–12
L. 13.5 cm

Below
HIPPOPOTAMUS [145]
Middle Kingdom, Dynasty 11–12
H. 9.7 cm; W. 7.4 cm; L. 20.3 cm

Opposite above
HIPPOPOTAMUS [142]
Middle Kingdom, Dynasty 11–12
L. 12.8 cm

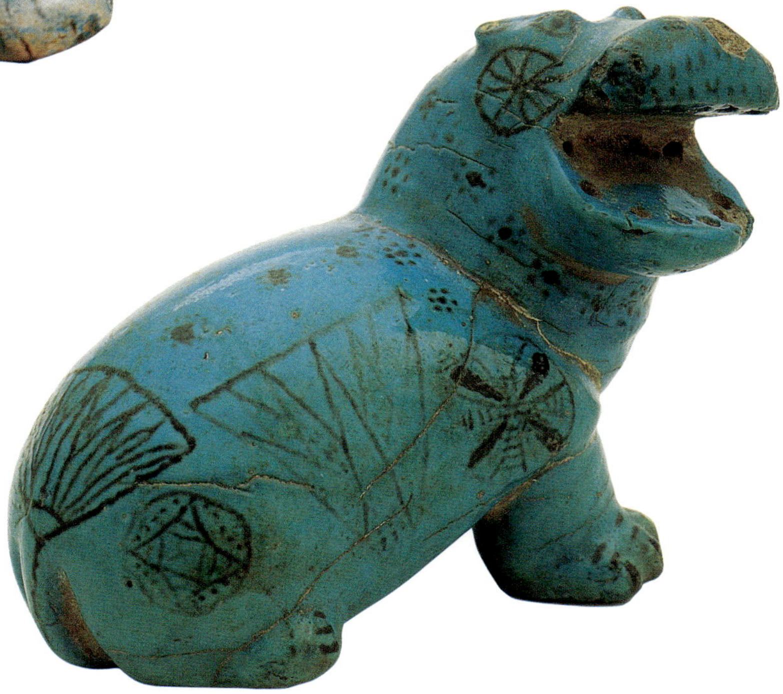

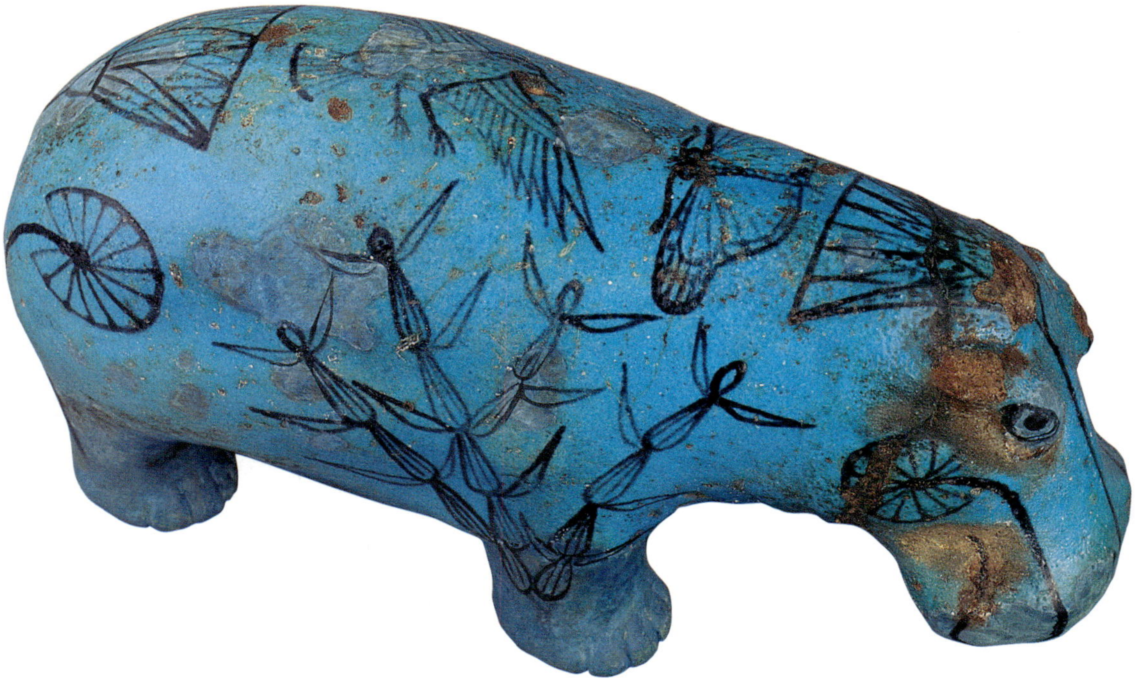

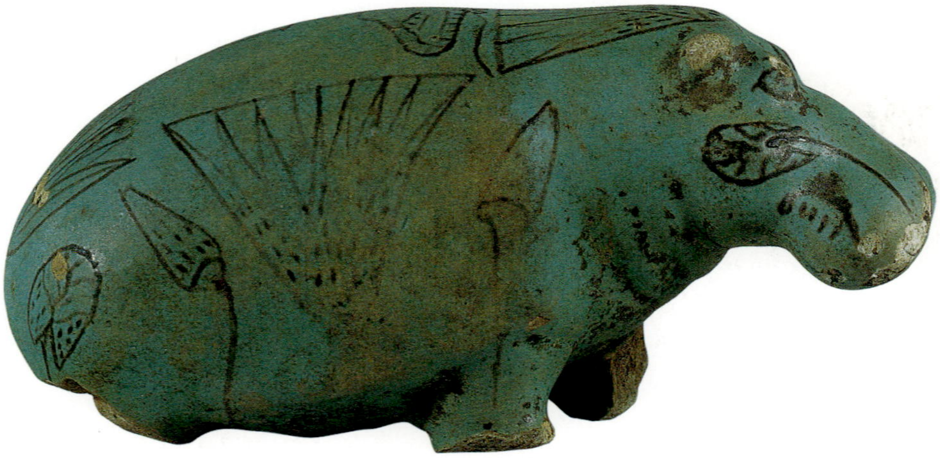

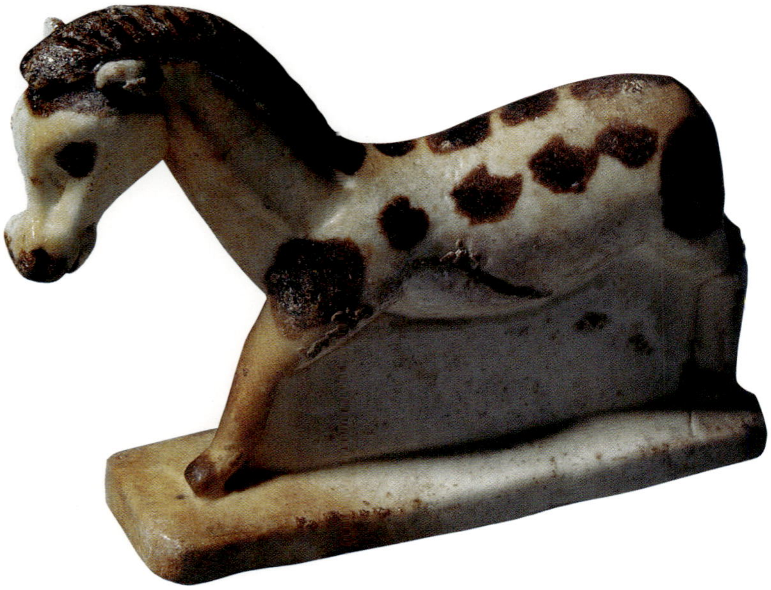

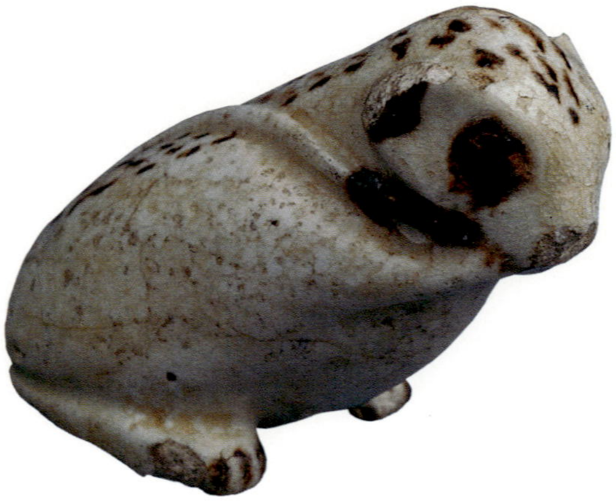

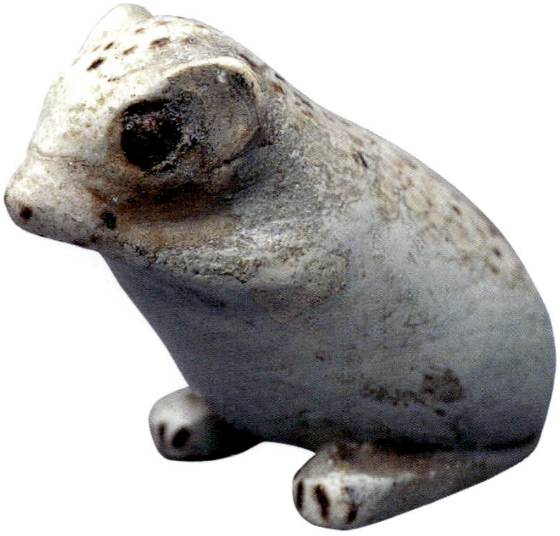

Above right

STRIDING HORSE OR PONY [148]
New Kingdom, Dynasty 18
H. 6.6 cm; W. 9.3 cm; D. 2.6 cm

Above

JERBOA MOUSE [146]
Middle Kingdom, late Dynasty 12 or Dynasty 13
H. 3.7 cm; W. 2.1 cm; L. 5.0 cm

Right

JERBOA MOUSE [147]
Middle Kingdom, late Dynasty 12 or Dynasty 13
W. 2.7 cm; L. 4.1 cm

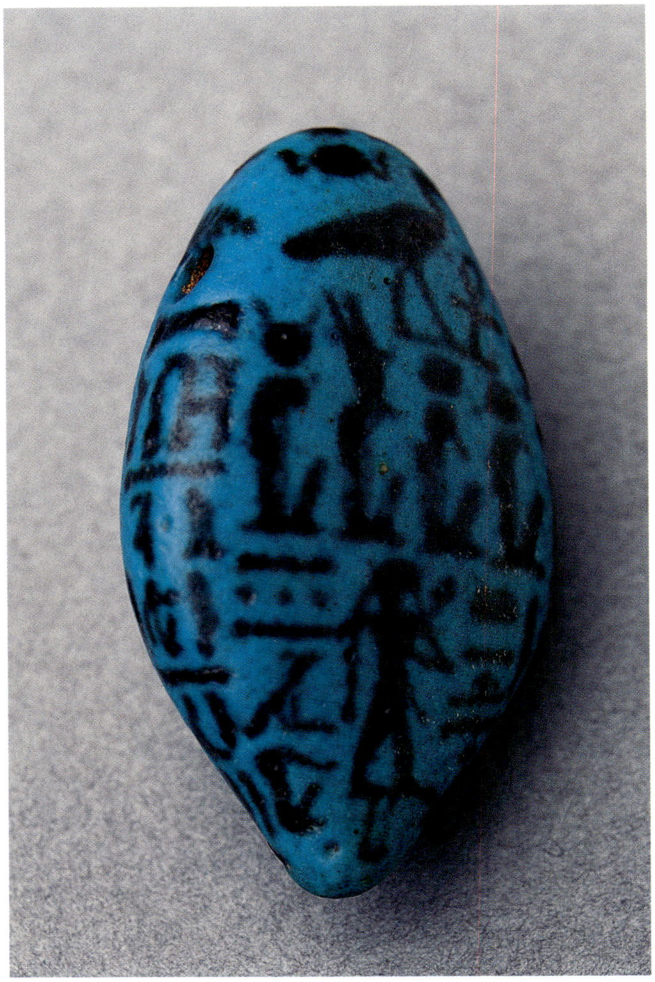

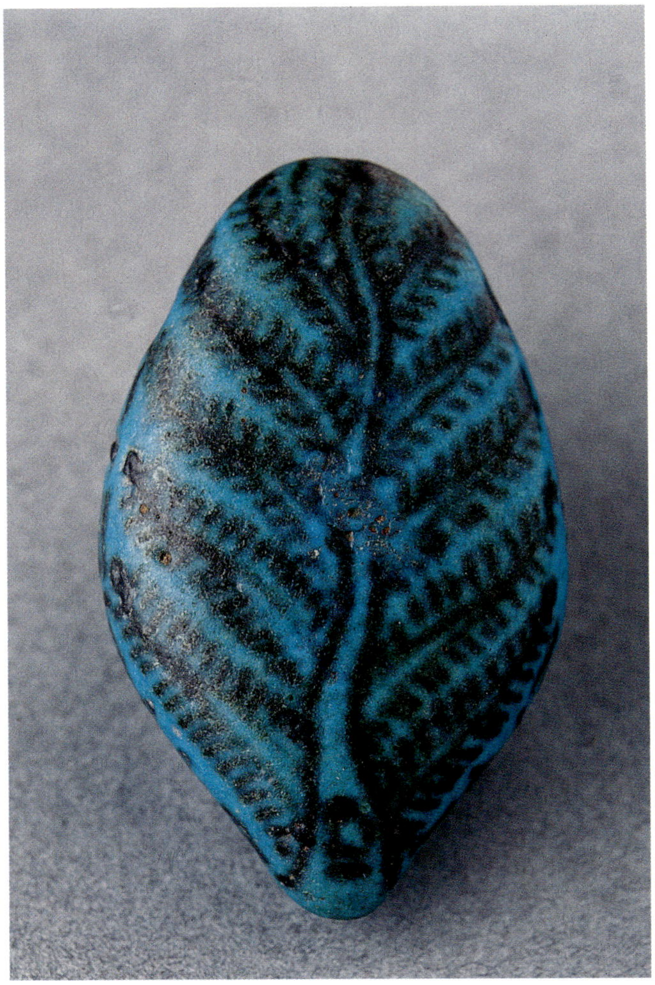

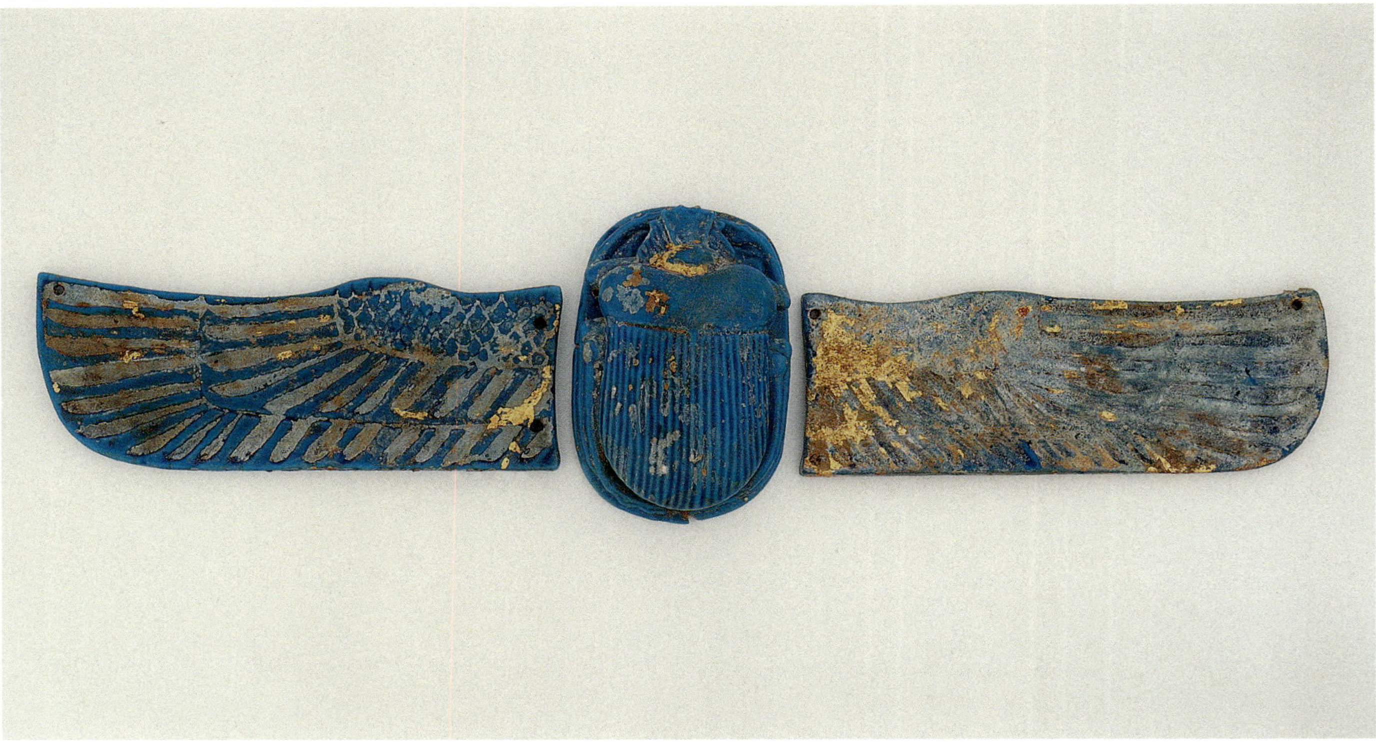

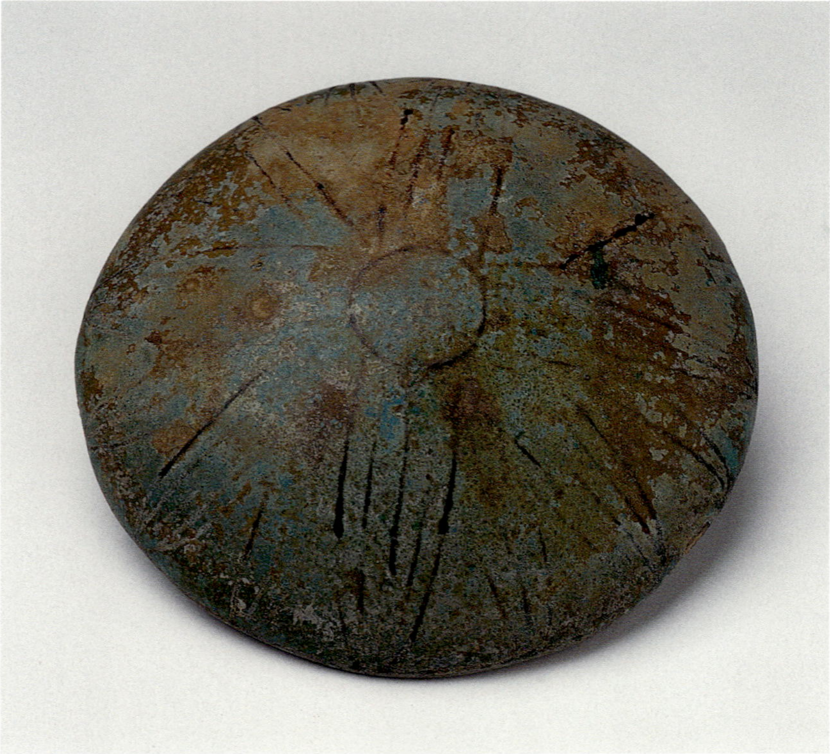

Left and below

DISH WITH MODEL FOOD [149]

New Kingdom, probably late Dynasty 12 to Dynasty 13

Peas: DIAM. 0.8–0.9 cm

Melon or cucumber: L. 12.8 cm; D. 2.9 cm

Melon or cucumber: L. 11.0 cm; D. 2.35 cm

Melon or cucumber: L. 7.44 cm; D. 1.7 cm

Bunch of grapes: H. 7.3 cm; D. 3.0 cm

Figs (green): H. 2.1–2.4 cm; W. 1.2–1.6 cm

Figs (brown): H. 2.1–2.4 cm; W. 1.2–1.6 cm

Dish: H. 3.0 cm; DIAM. 12.8 cm

Opposite above, left and right

PENDANT IN THE FORM OF AN ISHED-TREE [154]

New Kingdom, Dynasty 19–20

H. 4.1 cm; W. 2.3 cm

Opposite below

WINGED SCARAB [158]

Late Period, Dynasty 26

L. 26.0 cm

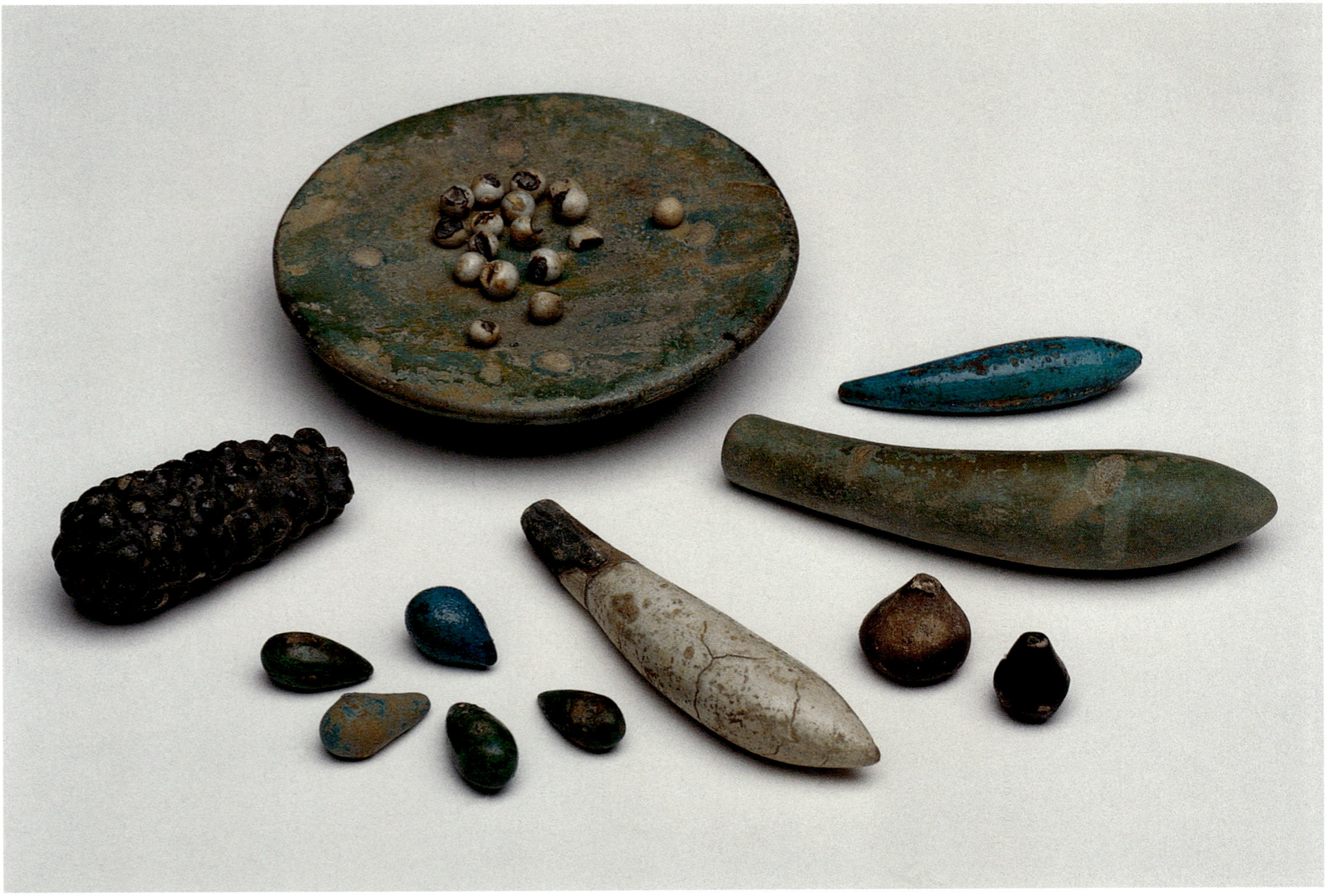

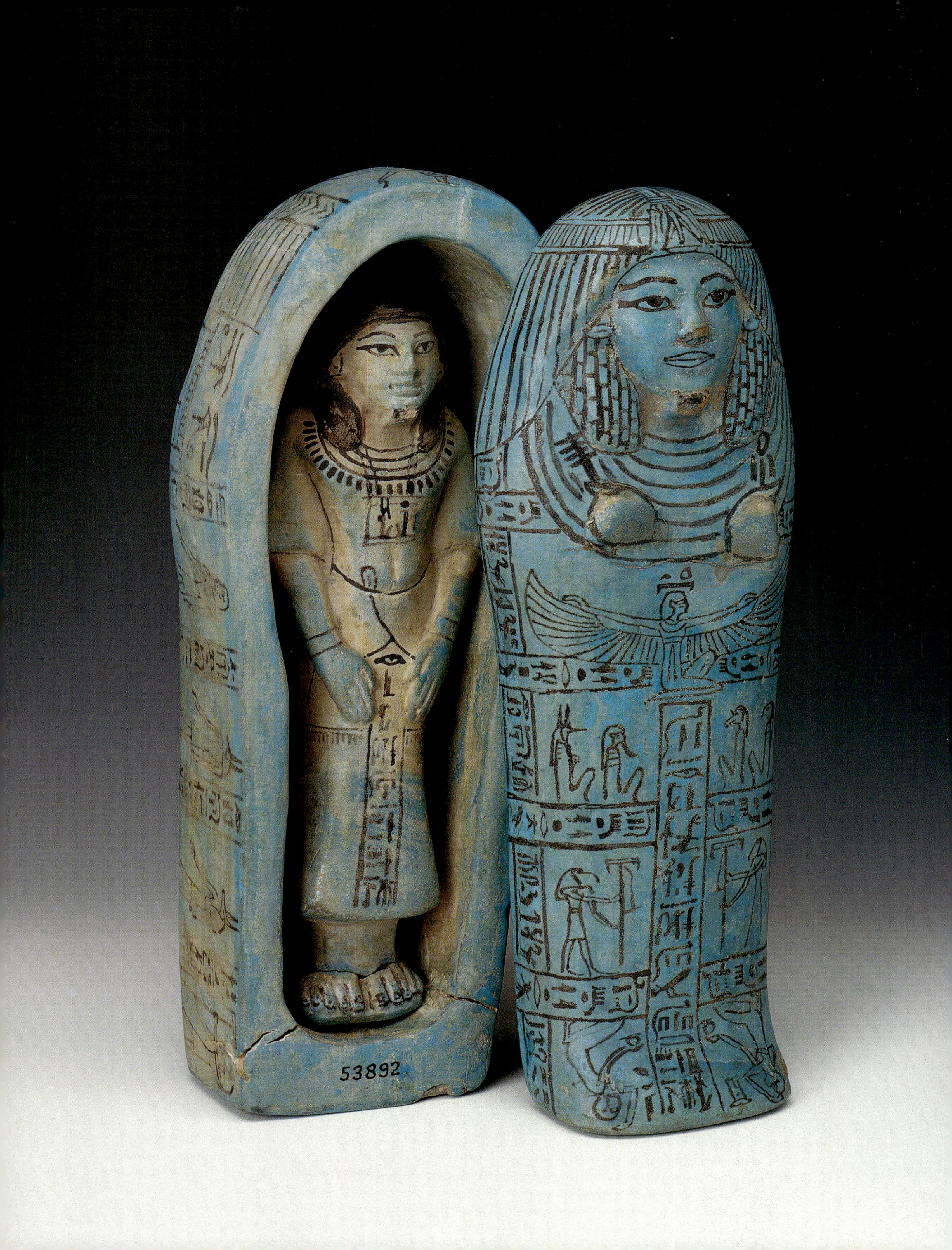
53892

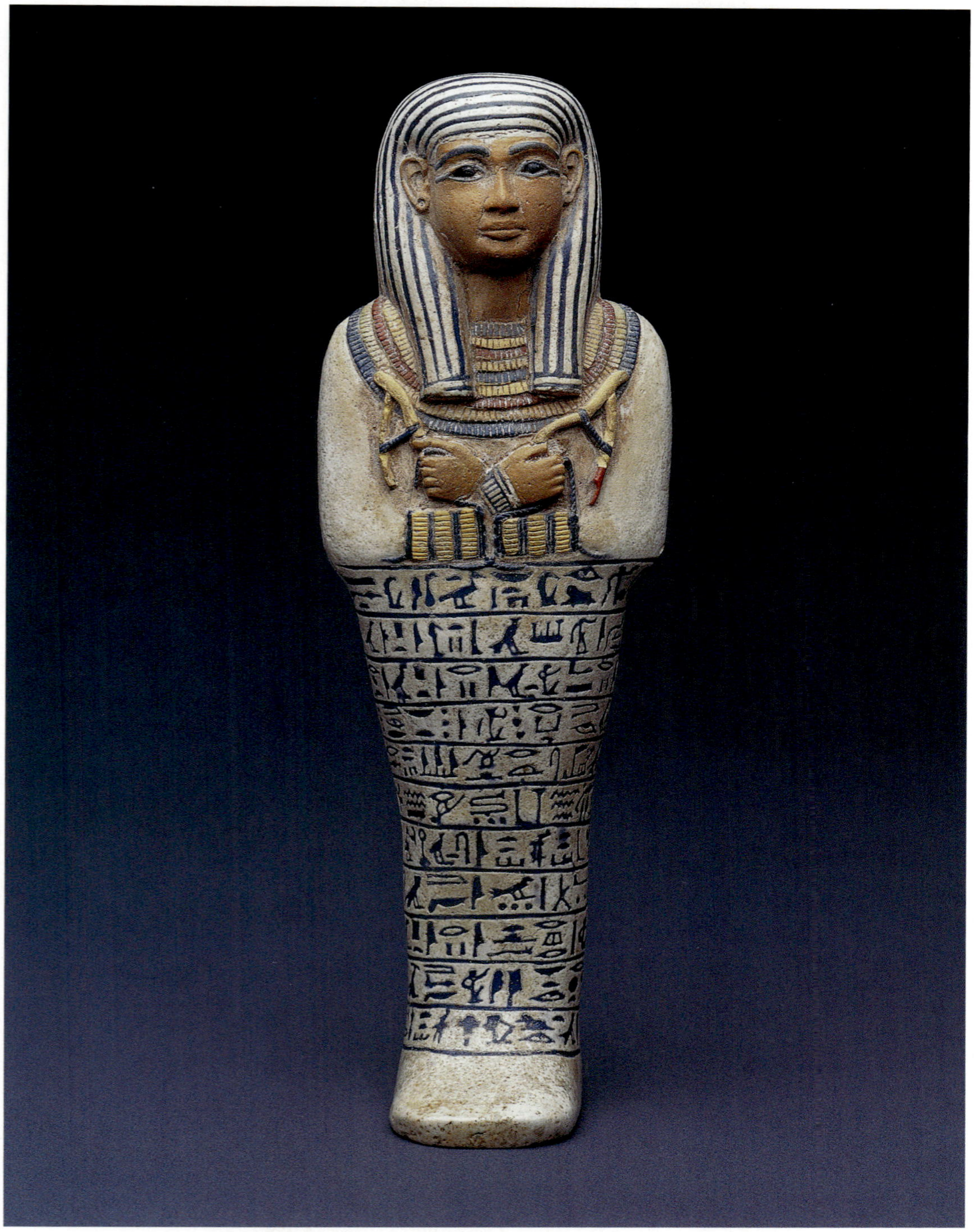

Above

SHABTI OF LADY SATI [150]

New Kingdom, Dynasty 18

H. 25.0 cm

Opposite

SHABTI WITH COFFIN INSCRIBED FOR AMENMES [151]

New Kingdom, Dynasty 19 or 20

Coffin: H. 7.0 cm; max. W. 11.2 cm; L. 28.8 cm

Lid: H. 4.5 cm; L. 28.5 cm

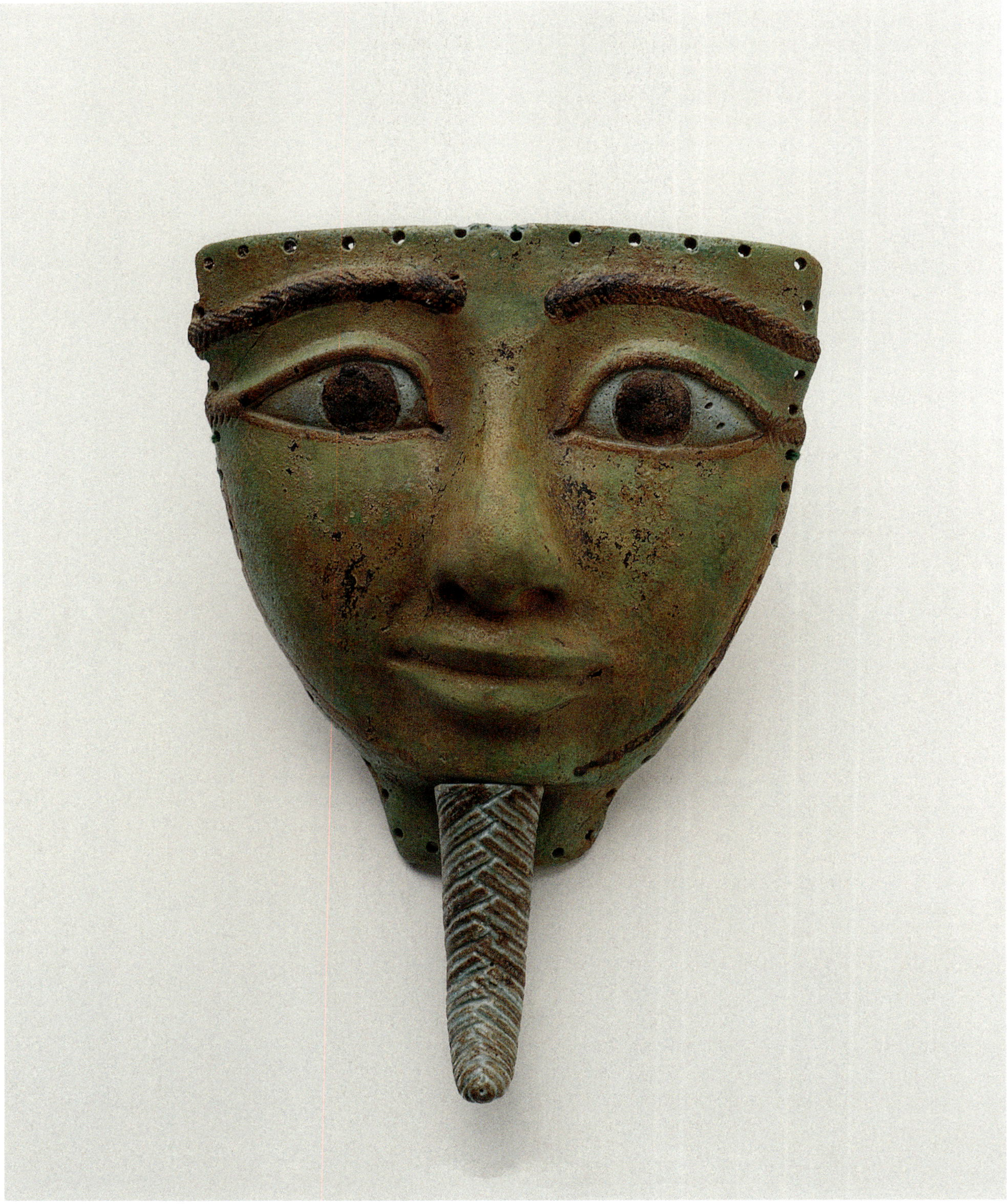

Above

MASK FROM A MUMMY (?) [165]
Middle Kingdom, Dynasty 12 to Second Intermediate Period
H. 16.5 cm; max. W. 11.8 cm

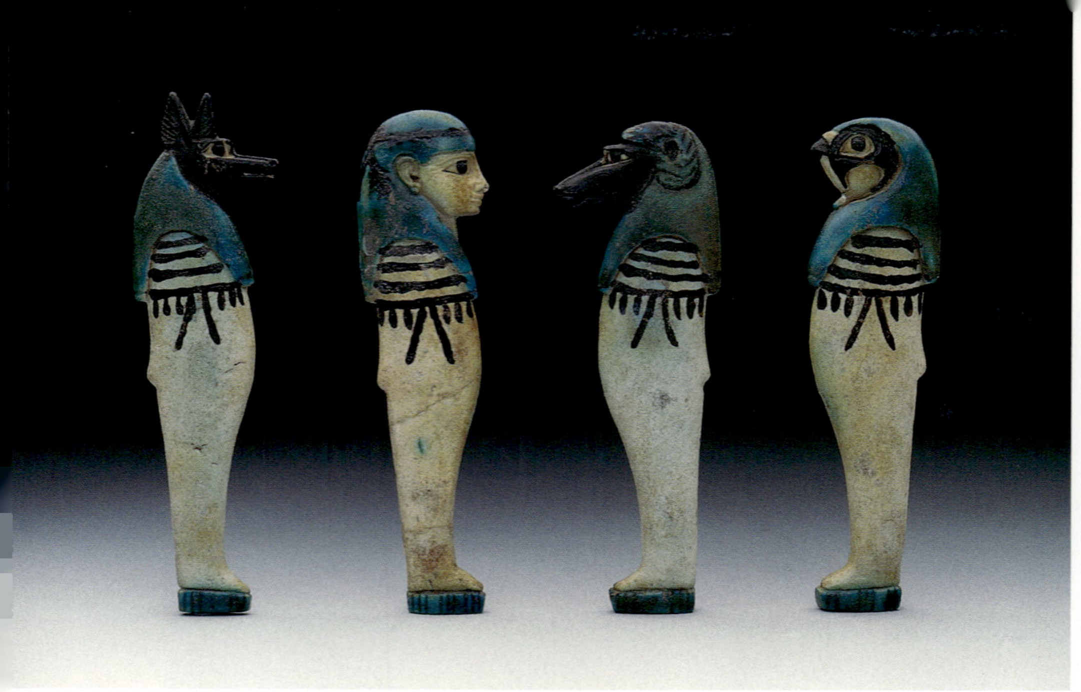

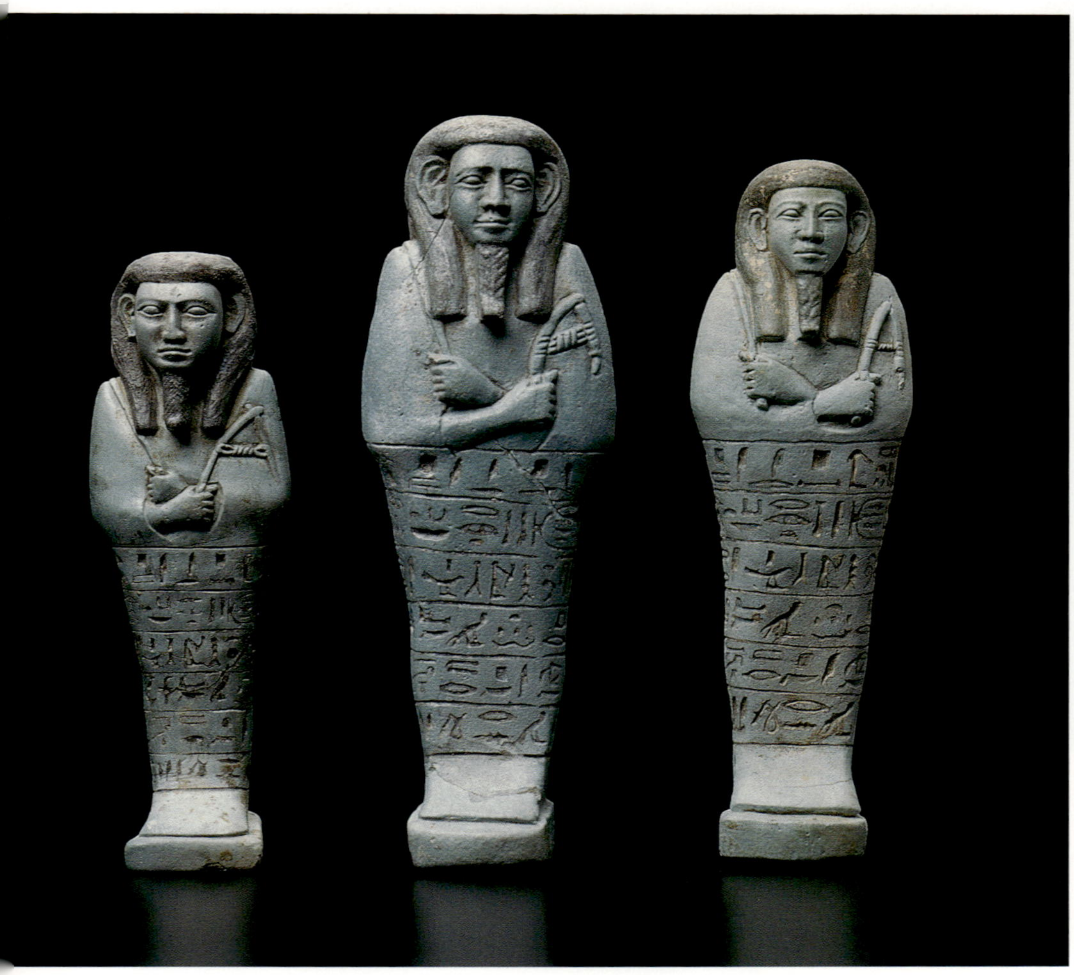

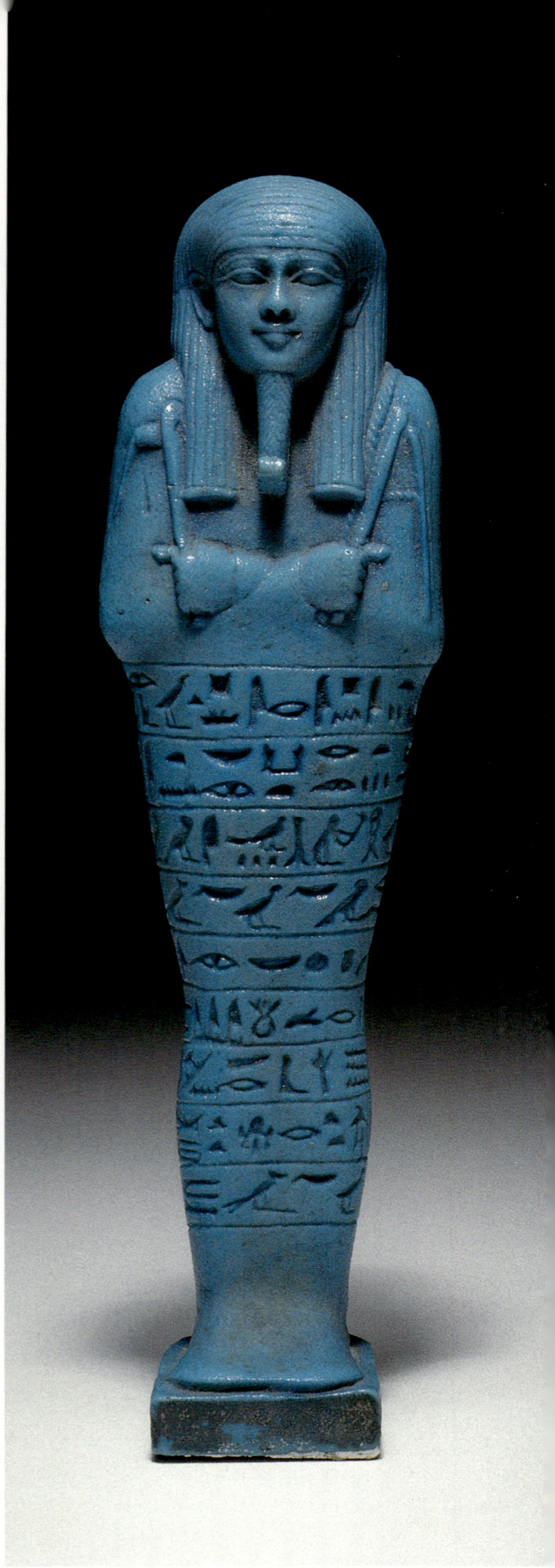

Top

AMULETS: THE FOUR SONS OF HORUS [157]
Late New Kingdom to early Third Intermediate Period (probably Dynasty 21)
(left to right) Duamutef: H. 15.0 cm; Imsety: H. 14.4 cm; Hapy: H. 13.9 cm; Qebehsenuef: H. 14.1 cm

Above left

SHABTIS OF SENKAMENISKEN [153]
Kushite, Dynasty 25
H. 15.8 cm; W. 5.2 cm; D. of foot 3.9 cm
H. 19.1 cm; W. 6.5 cm; D. of foot 4.1 cm
H. 17.8 cm; W. 5.6 cm; D. of foot 3.6 cm

Above

SHABTI OF A NOBLEMAN NAMED PSAMETIK [152]
Late Period, Dynasty 26
H. 18 4 cm; W. 7.1 cm; D. 3.8 cm

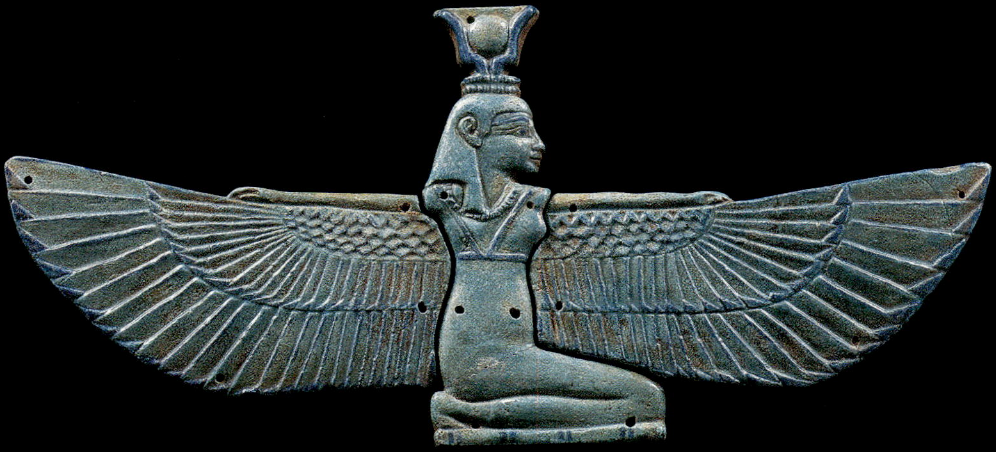

Left

WINGED ISIS PECTORAL [159]
Third Intermediate Period, Dynasty 21–22
L. 22.6 cm; W. 10.5 cm; D. 0.7 cm

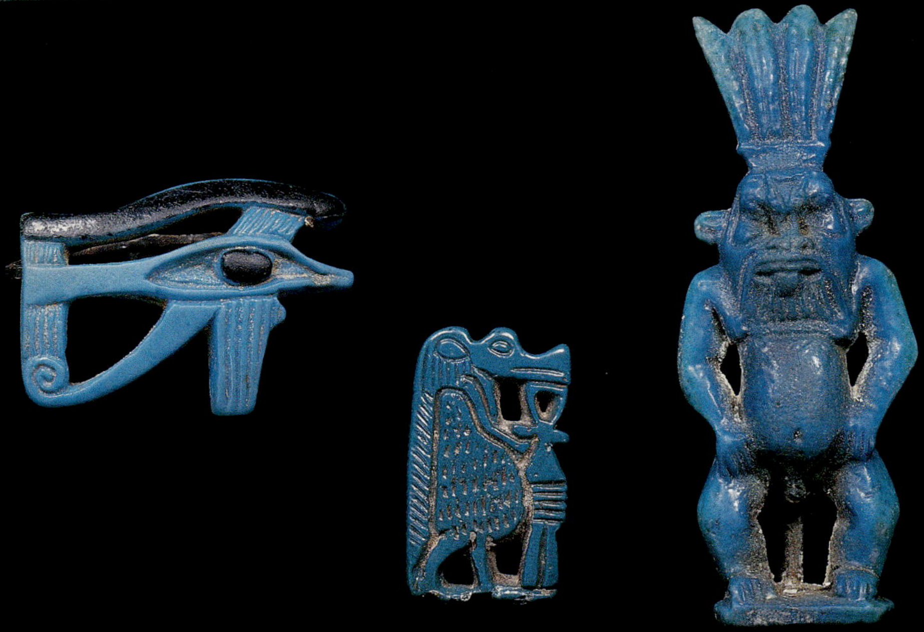

Right

AMULETS [155]
New Kingdom to Late Period
Wadjet H. 3.8 cm
Taweret (Thoeris) H. 3.2 cm
Bes H. 11.75 cm

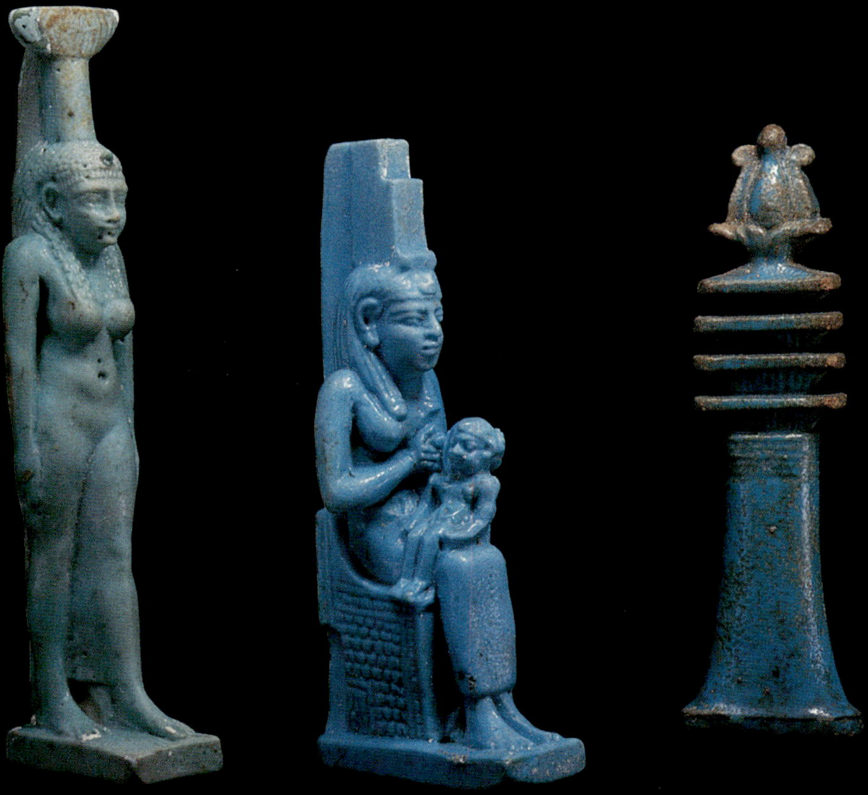

Left

AMULETS [155]
New Kingdom to Late Period
Nephthys H. 14.3 cm
Isis and Horus H. 12.0 cm
Djed-pillar H. 11.8 cm

Opposite

AMULETIC INLAYS [156]
Late Period, Dynasty 27–31
H. of central Osiris 5.4 cm

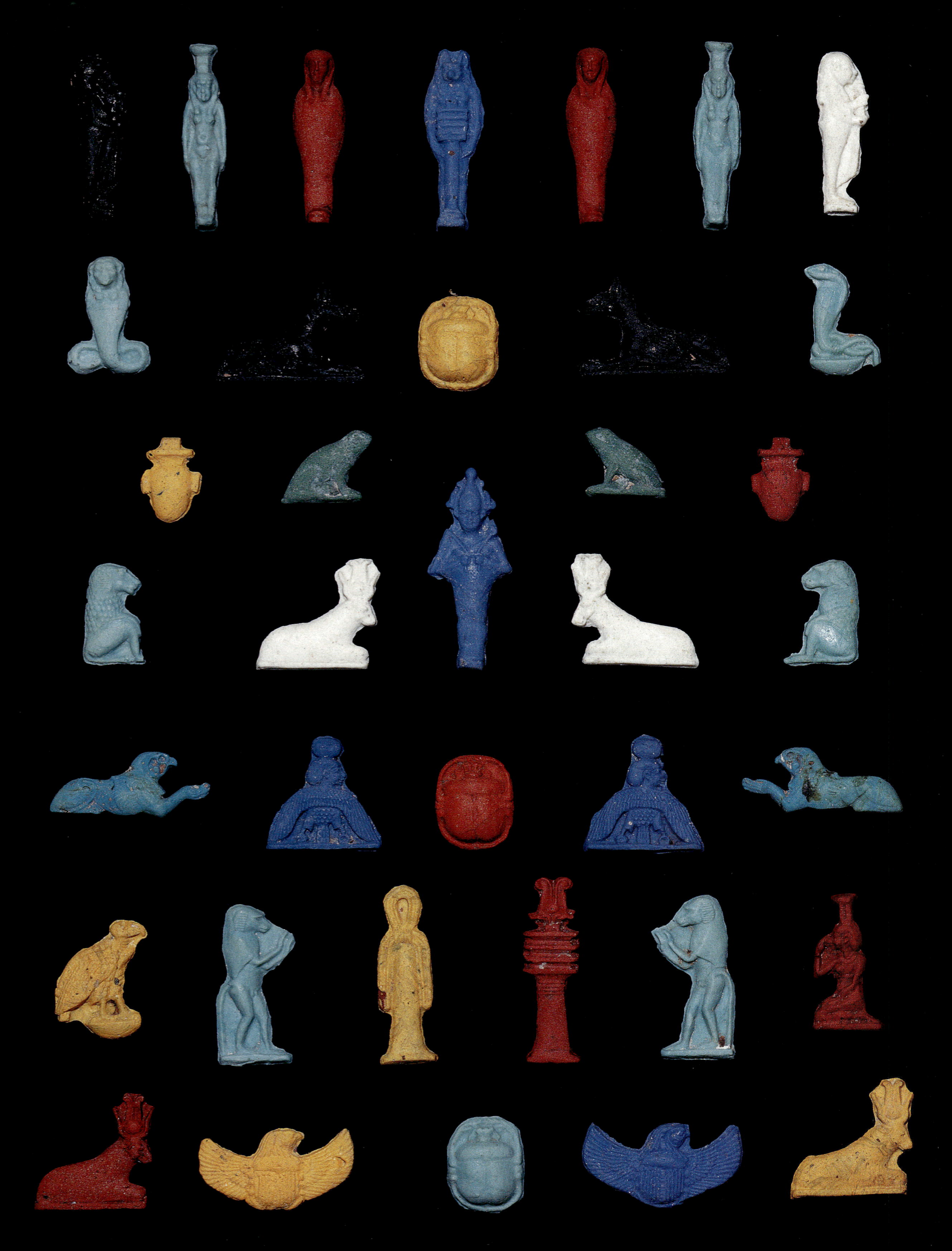

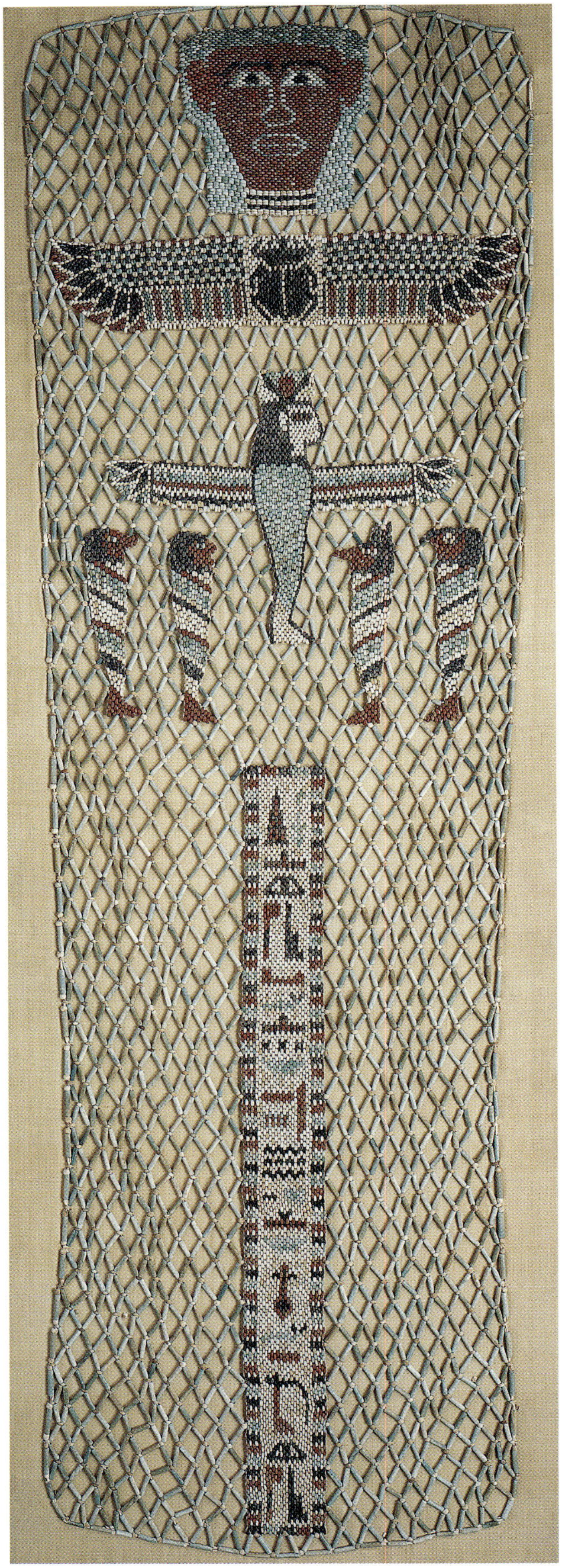

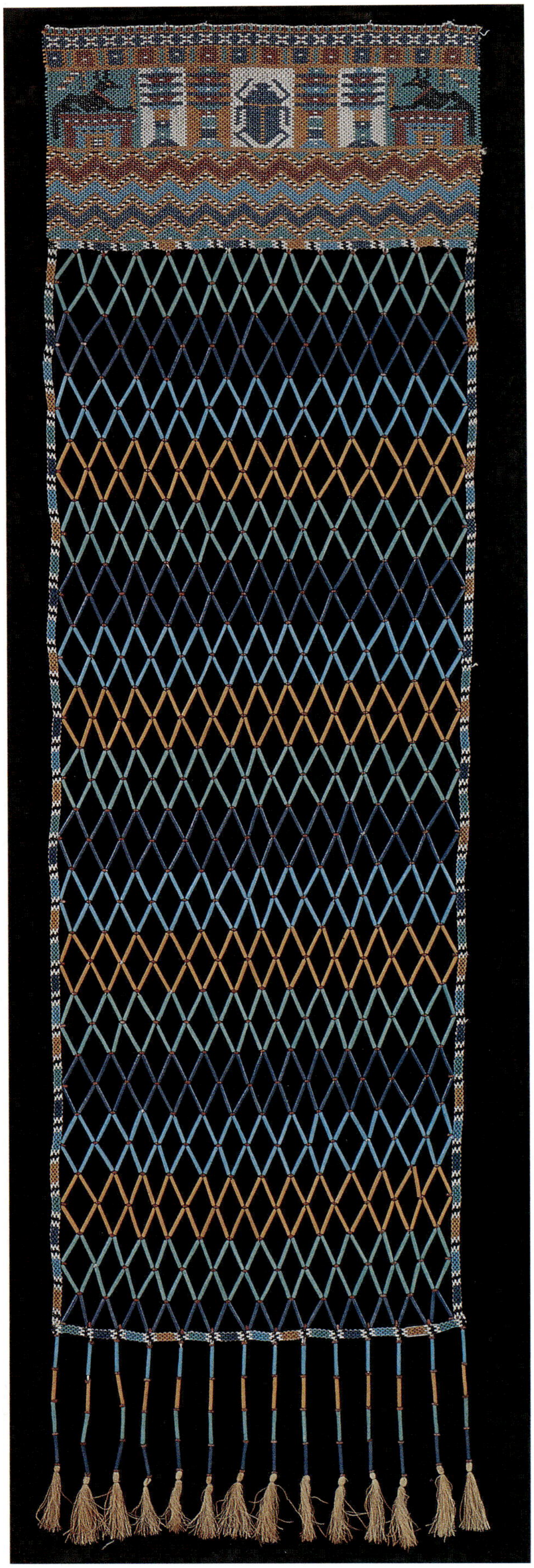

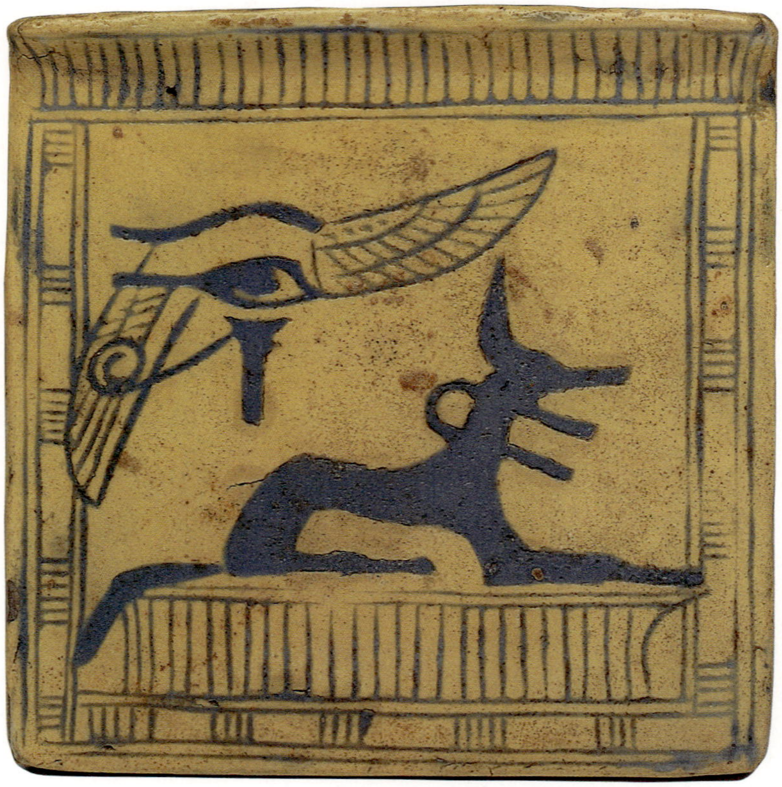

Left
PECTORAL WITH ANUBIS [161]
New Kingdom, Dynasty 19, reign of Ramesses II,
c. 1250 BC
H. 10.7 cm; W. 10.6 cm

Below
PECTORAL INSCRIBED FOR PANHESI [160]
Late Period
H. 10.5 cm; W. 9.0 cm

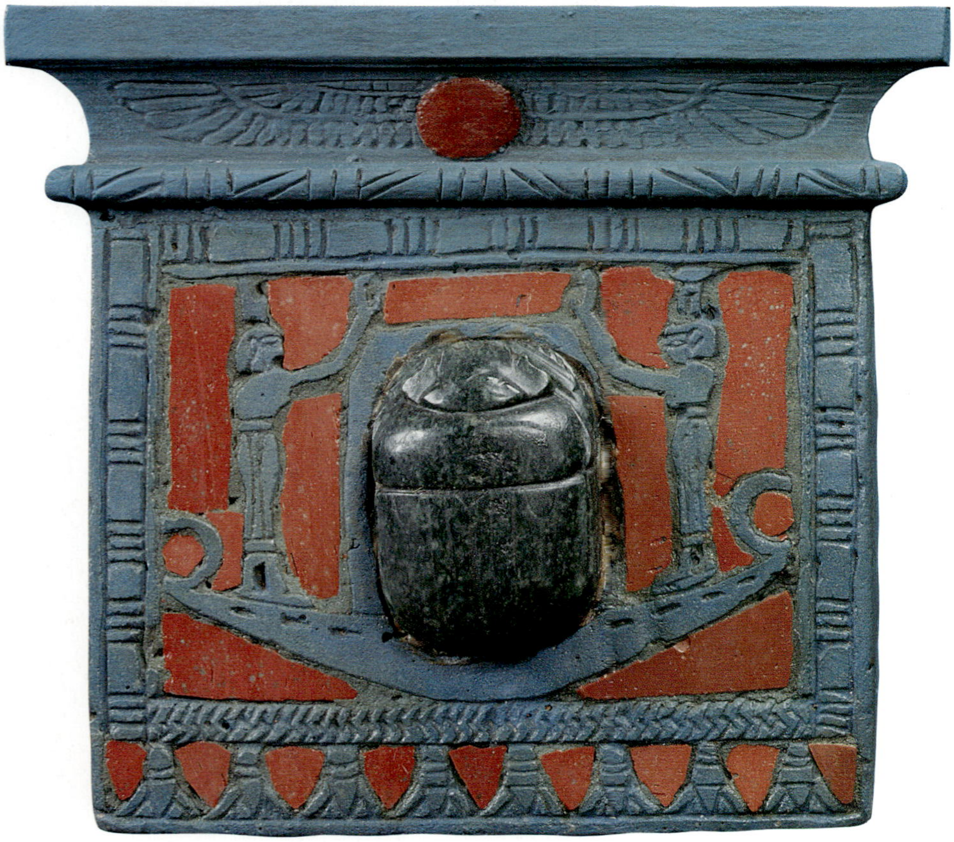

Opposite left
MUMMY BEAD NETTING [164]
Nubian, Napatan Period,
7th to 6th century BC
H. 129.0 cm; W. 39.0 cm

Opposite right
BEAD-NET SHROUD [163]
Third Intermediate Period to Dynasty 30
H. 105.0 cm; W. 29.0

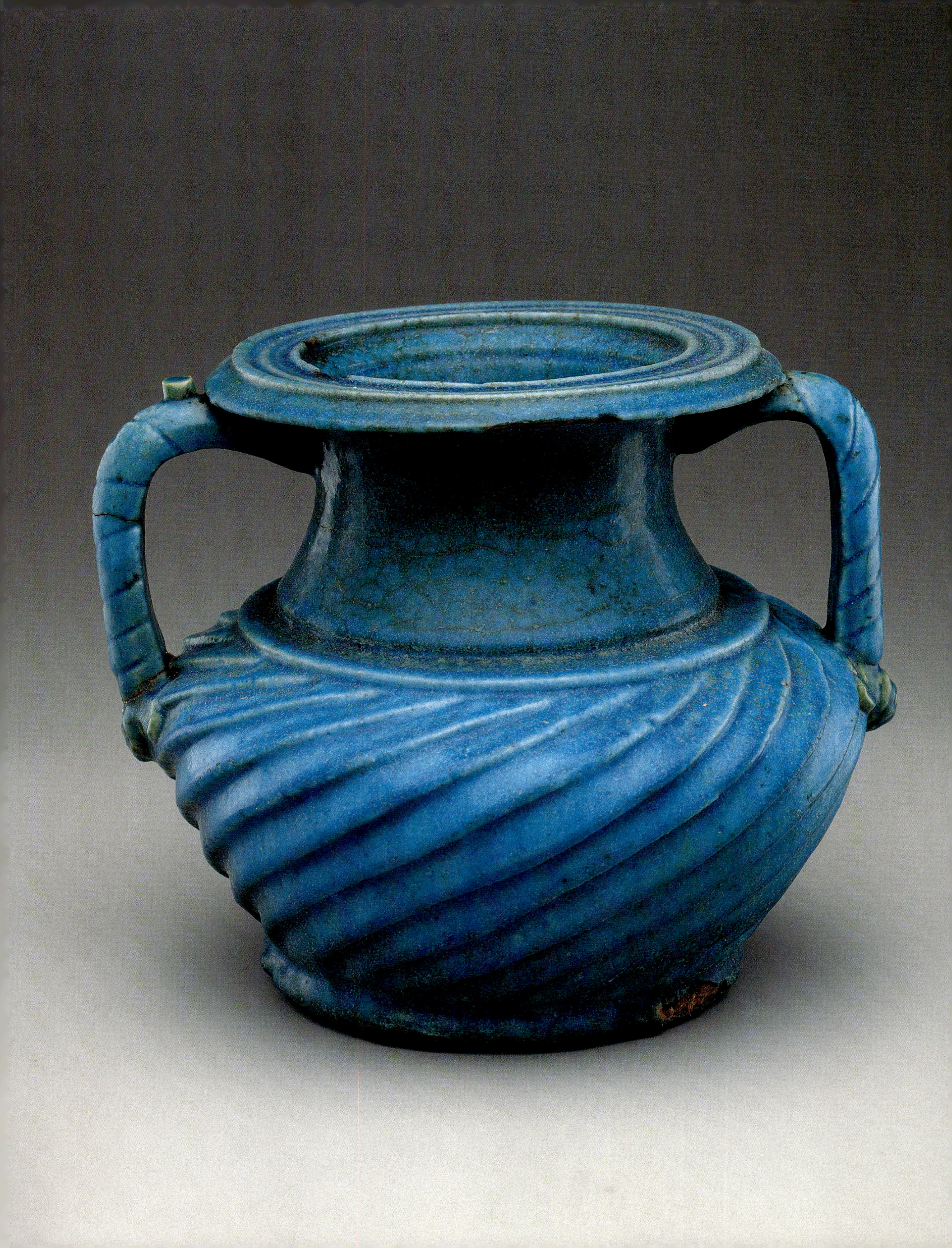

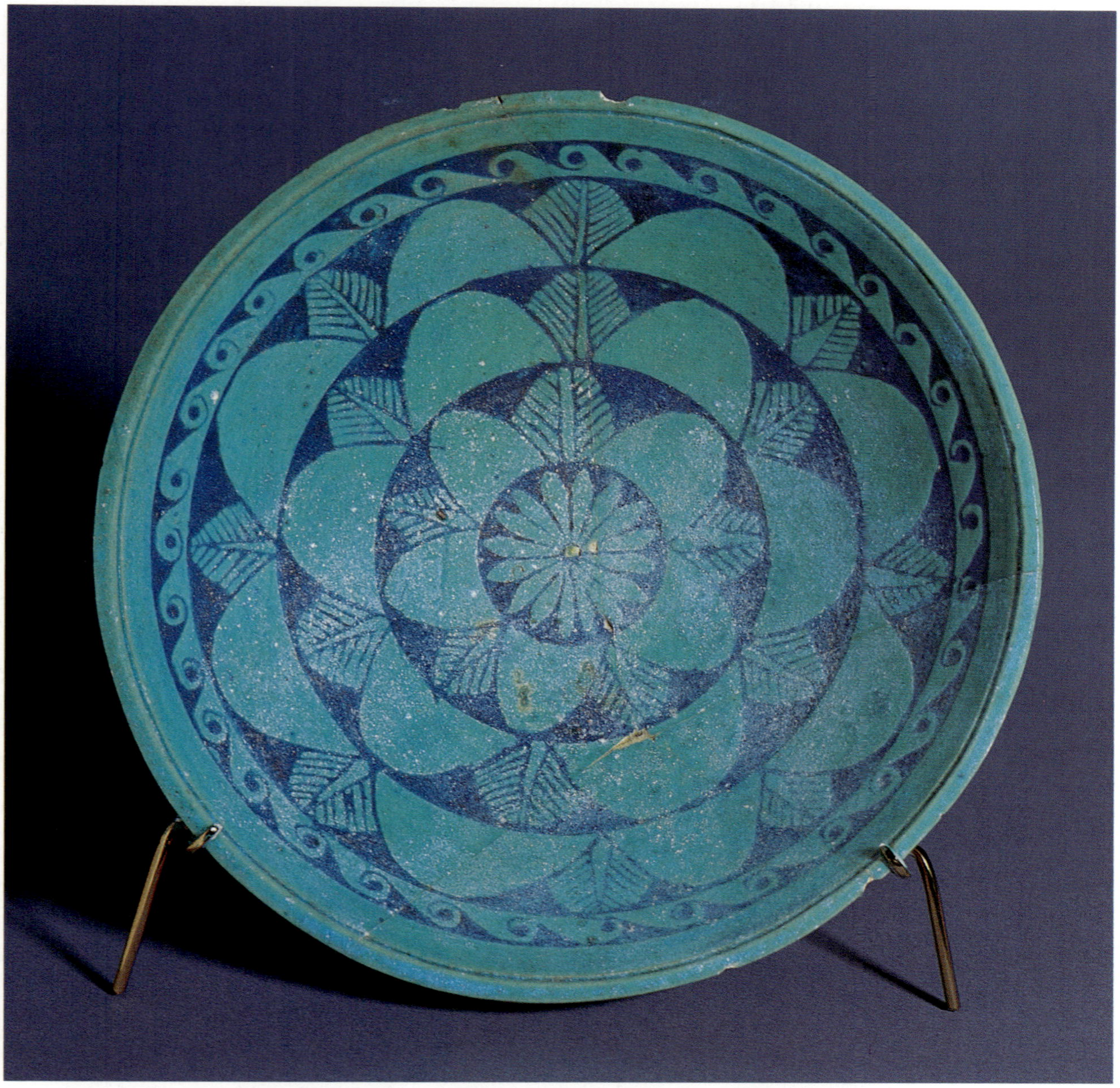

Above

HEMISPHERICAL BOWL
WITH FLORAL MOTIFS [170]
Ptolemaic Period, 3rd to 2nd century BC
DIAM. 16.9 cm

Opposite

TWO-HANDLED URN [171]
Roman Imperial Period, 1st to 2nd century BC
H. 23.1 cm; DIAM. of mouth 19.0 cm;
DIAM. of base 16.0 cm

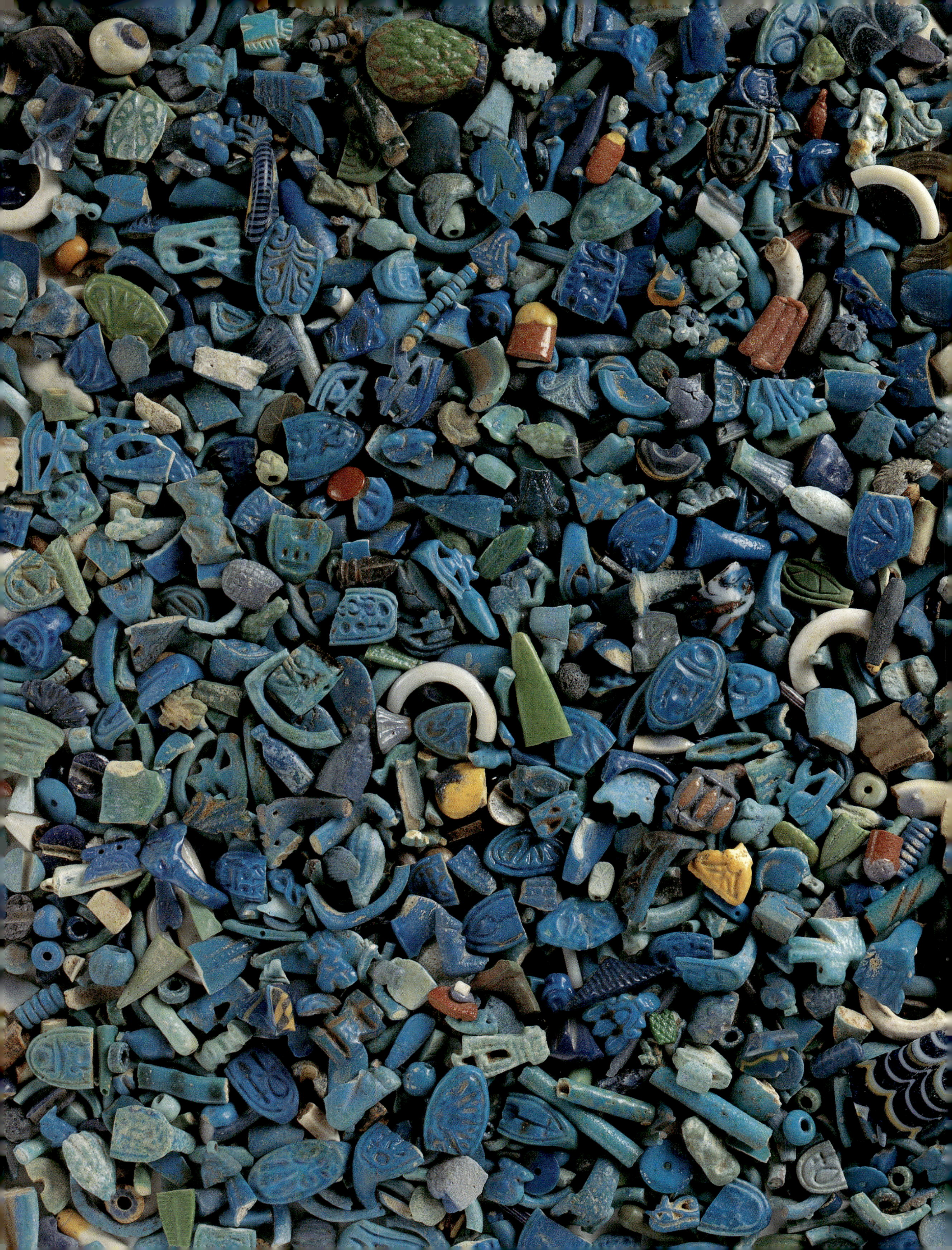

MATERIALS AND TECHNOLOGY

Without detailed ancient Egyptian texts on the manufacture of faience, scholars have had to learn directly from the objects. Although most of our understanding of faience has come from decades of patient scientific analysis, these examples have been chosen because of what they can reveal about aspects of technical and workshop procedures, even to the naked eye.

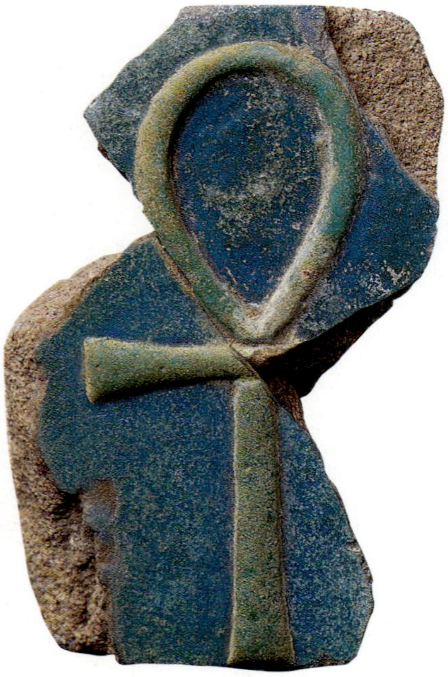

Opposite
MISCELLANEOUS FAIENCE AND GLASS OBJECTS [184]
New Kingdom, Dynasty 18, reign of Akhenaten

Right
WALL TILE WITH FRAGMENT OF ANKH [197]
See p. 173

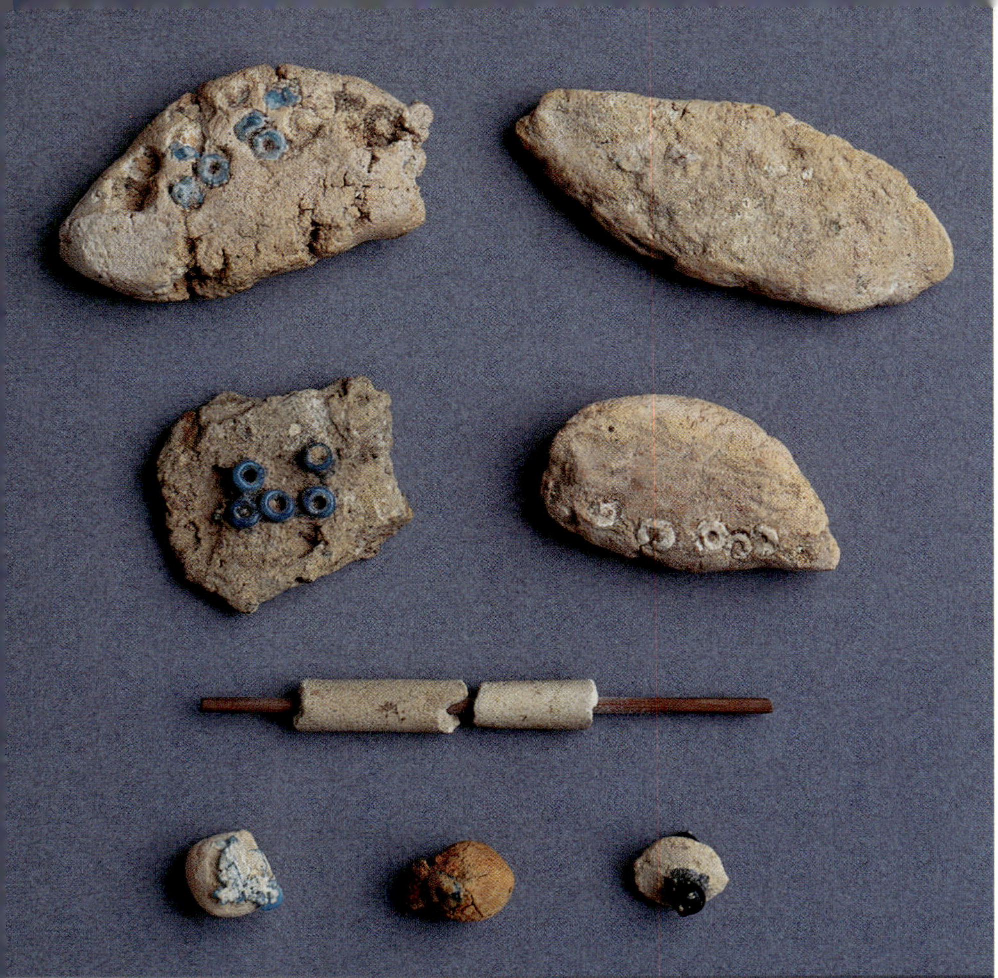

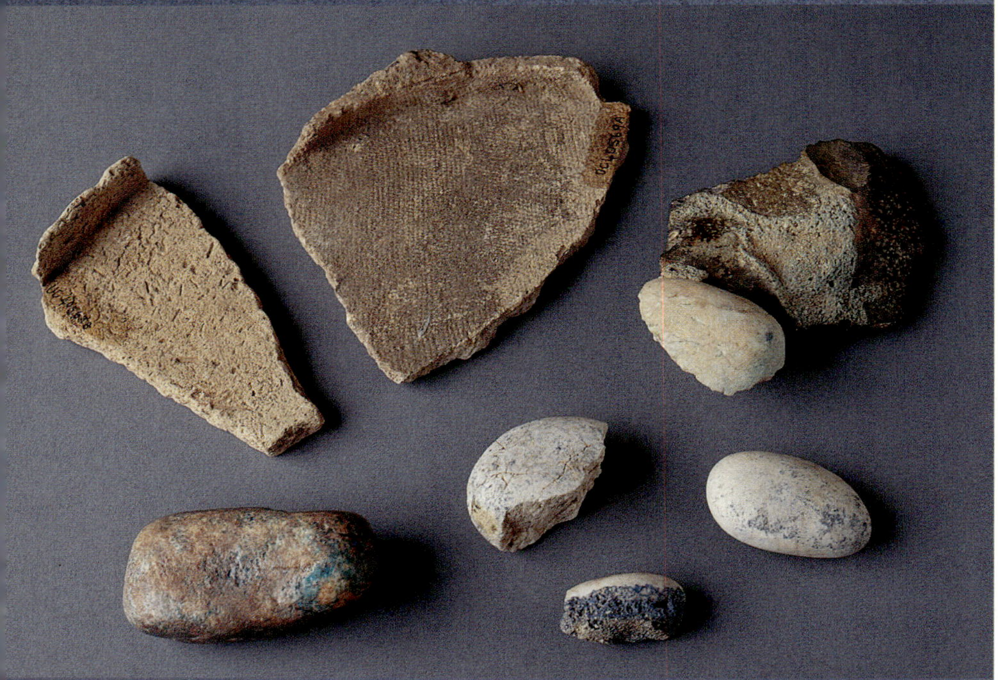

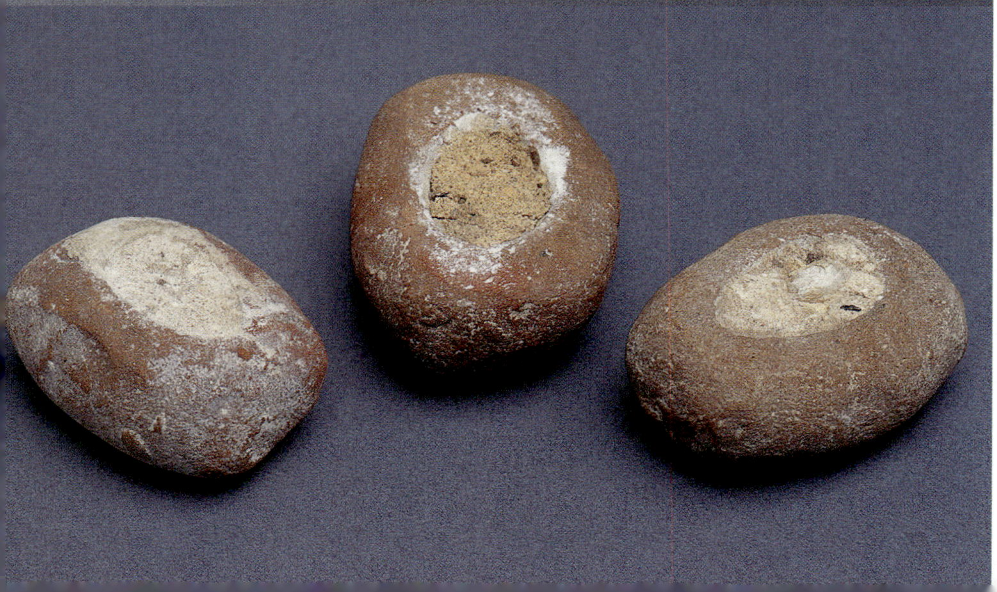

Left above

MATERIALS USED IN THE MANUFACTURE OF BEADS [172]
Middle Kingdom, Dynasty 12
L. 3.0 cm; 3.6 cm; 2.0 cm; 2.4 cm; L. (of beads) 2.3 cm; DIAM. (of balls) 0.5–0.7 cm

Left center

QUARTZ PEBBLES [173]
(center and center right)
New Kingdom, Dynasty 18
A: L. 4.6 cm
B: L. 4.7 cm

QUARTZ PEBBLE WITH GLAZE [174] (below, left)
New Kingdom, Dynasty 18
L. 6.7 cm; W. 3.8 cm

QUARTZ PEBBLE WITH ADHERING FRIT [175] (below, center)
New Kingdom, Dynasty 18
L. 3.4 cm; W. 1.7 cm

"PLASTER TRAYS" [176] (above, left and center)
New Kingdom, Dynasty 18
A: L. 11.2 cm; W. 9.4 cm
B: L. 10.4 cm; W. 4.5 cm

FRAGMENT OF FRITTING PAN WITH ADHERING QUARTZ PEBBLE [177] (above, right)
New Kingdom, Dynasty 18
L. 10.4 cm; W. 3.3 cm

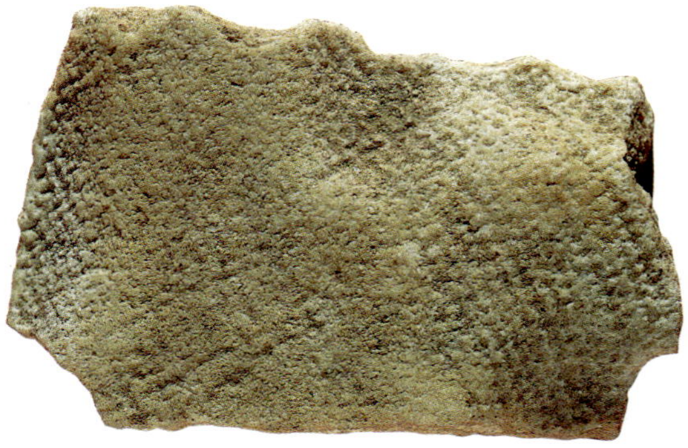

Right (top 4 rows)
MOLDS FOR FAIENCE [185]
New Kingdom, Dynasty 18
H. 2.5–8.0 cm; W. 2.2–6.5 cm;
TH. 0.3–2.0 cm

Right (bottom row)
LUMP OF EGYPTIAN BLUE [181]
New Kingdom, Dynasty 18
H. 8.9 cm; W. 8.3 cm; TH. 2.8 cm

Opposite left, below
THREE MOLDS FOR FAIENCE OBJECTS FILLED WITH PASTE [186]
New Kingdom, Dynasty 18
H. 2.0 cm; W. 4.0 cm; D. 3.0 cm
H. 1.8 cm; W. 3.6 cm; D. 2.7 cm
H. 1.8 cm; W. 3.8 cm; D. 3.0 cm

Opposite right (front and back views)
TILE FRAGMENT [183]
New Kingdom, Dynasty 18
L. 3.5 cm; W. 2.2 cm; TH. 0.6 cm

Below
LUMP OF FUSED BEADS [187]
Roman Period
H. 3.5 cm; L. 5.5 cm

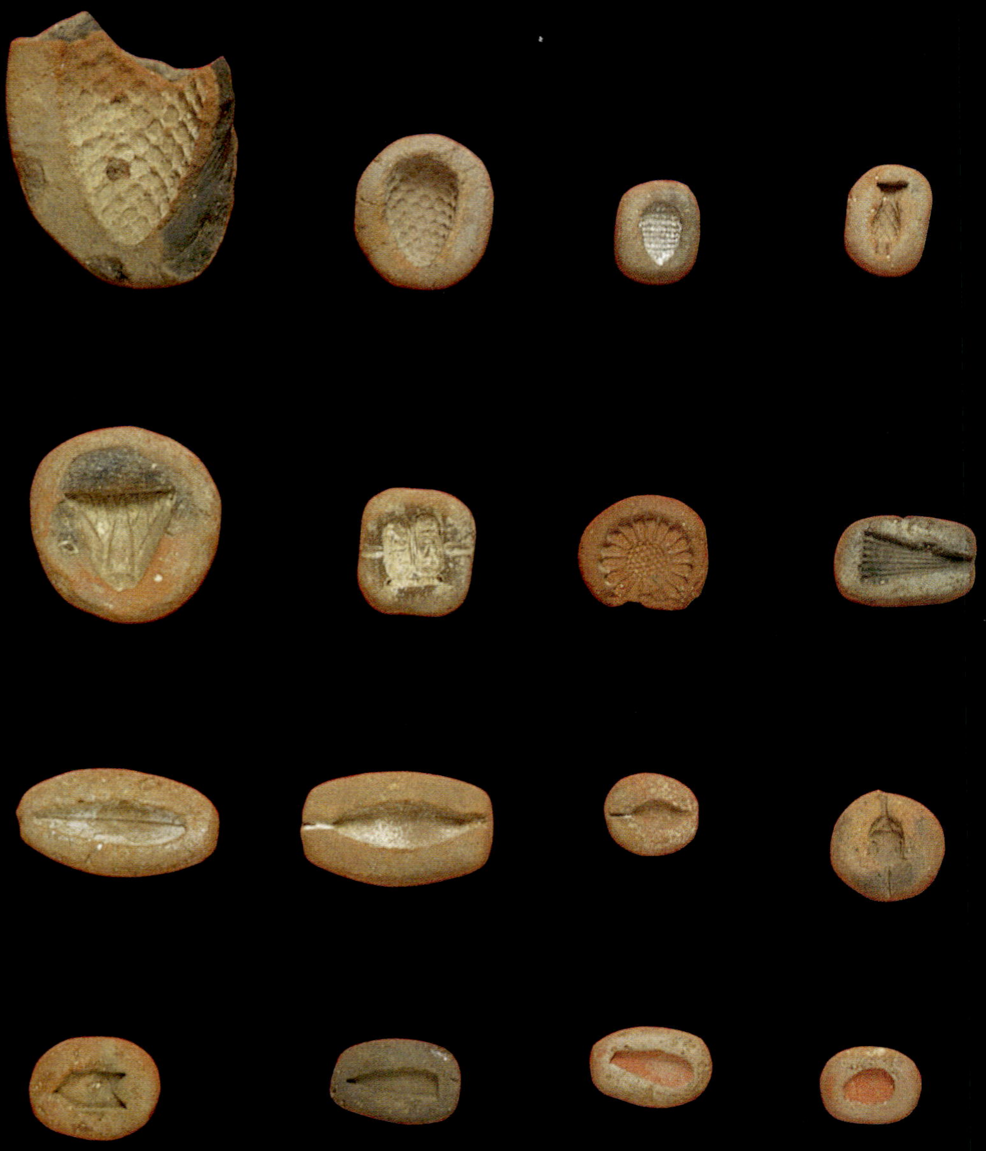

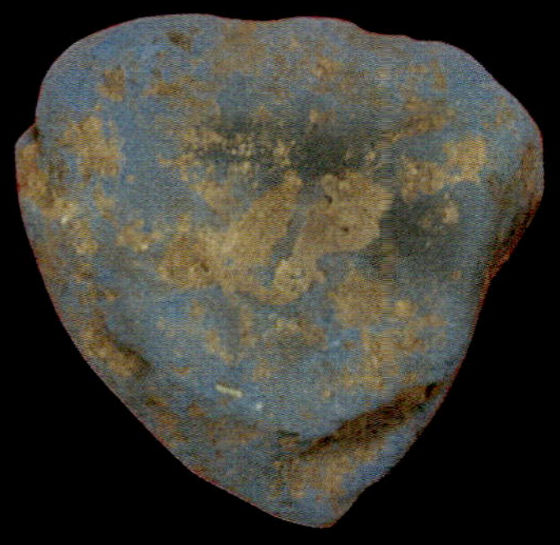

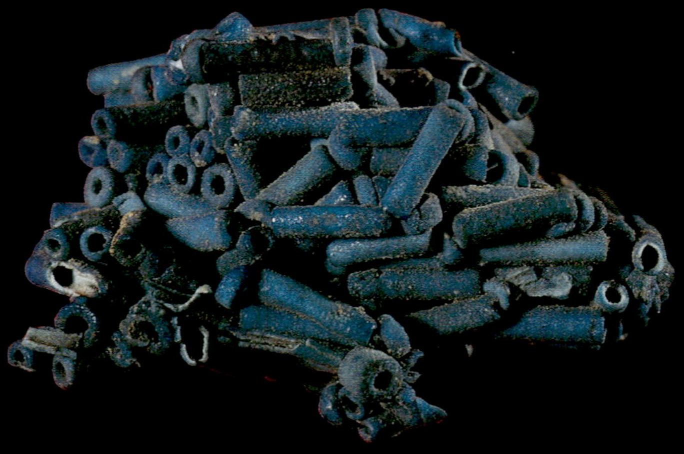

Right
SISTRUM [189]
Late Period, Dynasty 26
H. 16.5 cm; W. 6.2 cm; TH. 3.6 cm

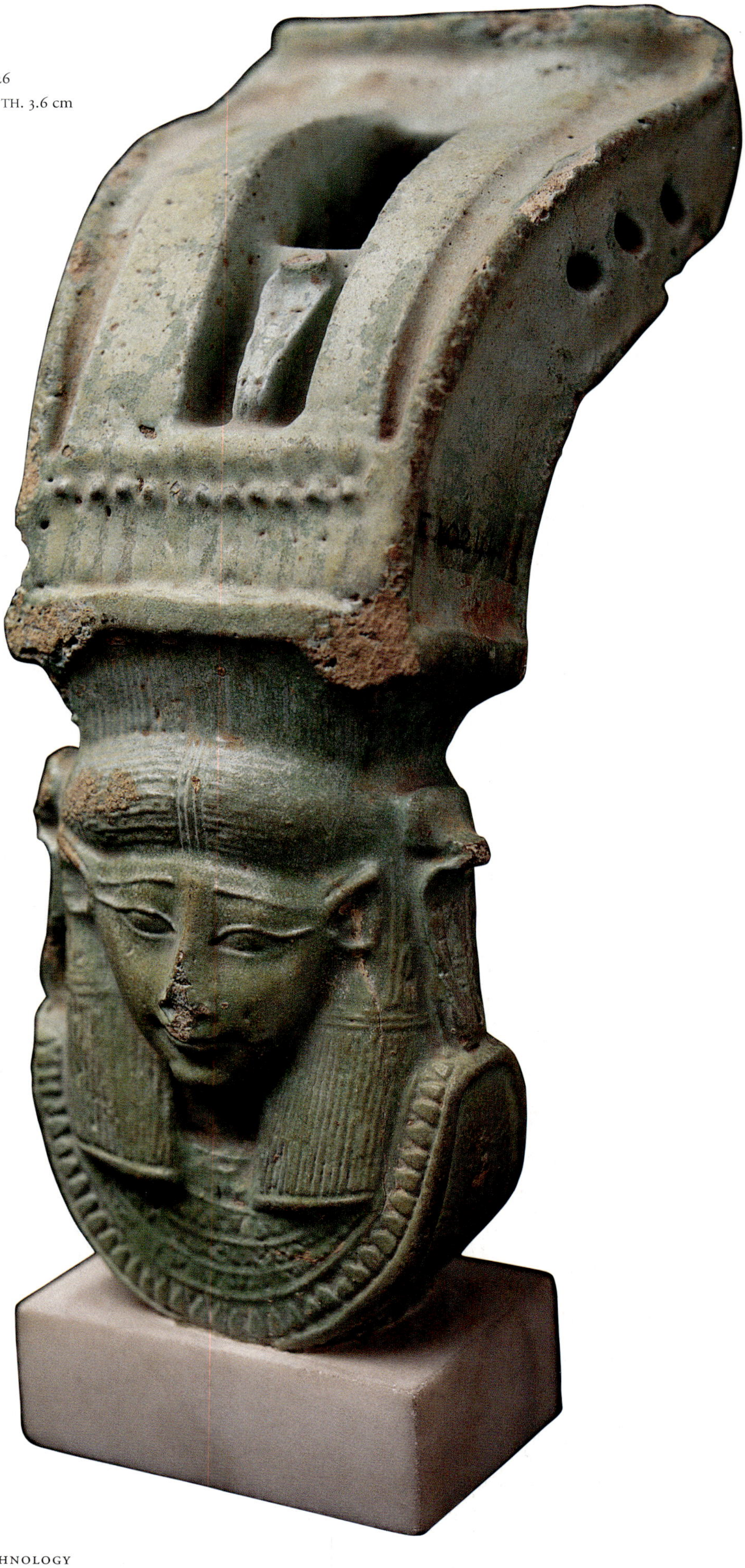

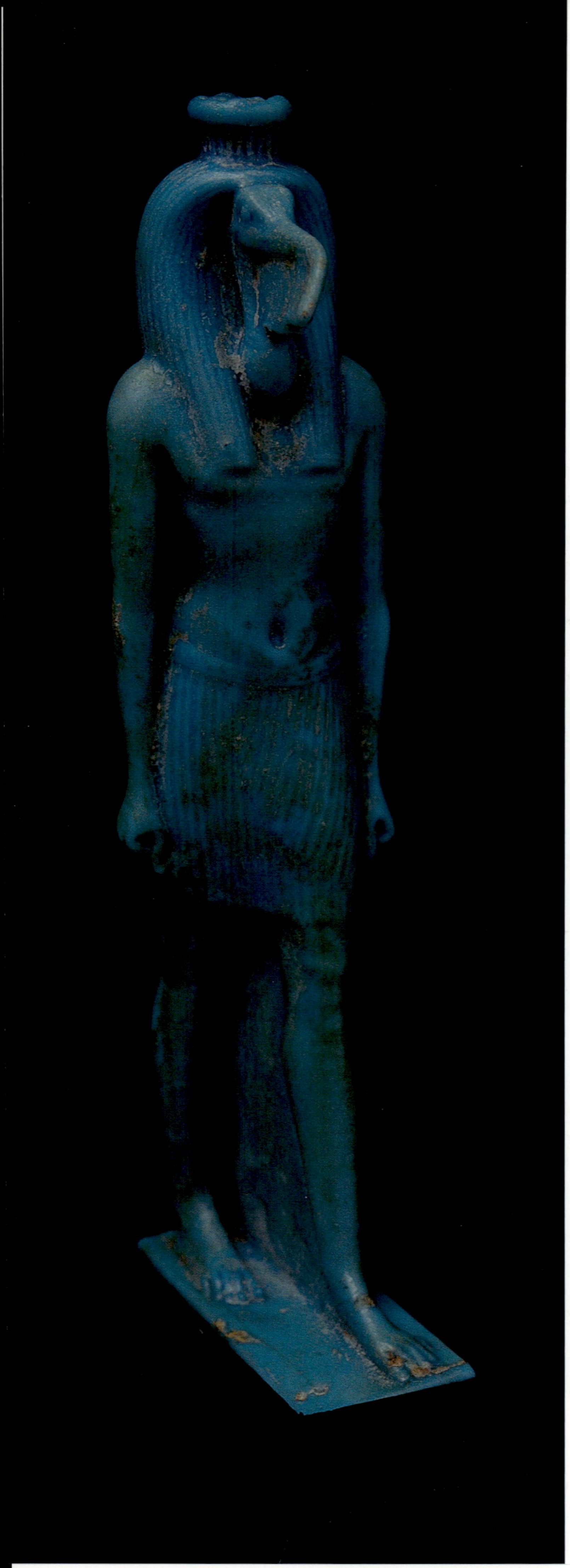

Left

FIGURINE OF THCTH [188]
Late Period to Ptolemaic Period
H. 10.4 cm; W. 2.4 cm; D. 3.7 cm

Below

LION [182]
Nubian, Classic Kerma Period, *c.* 1600–1500 BC
L. 12.0 cm

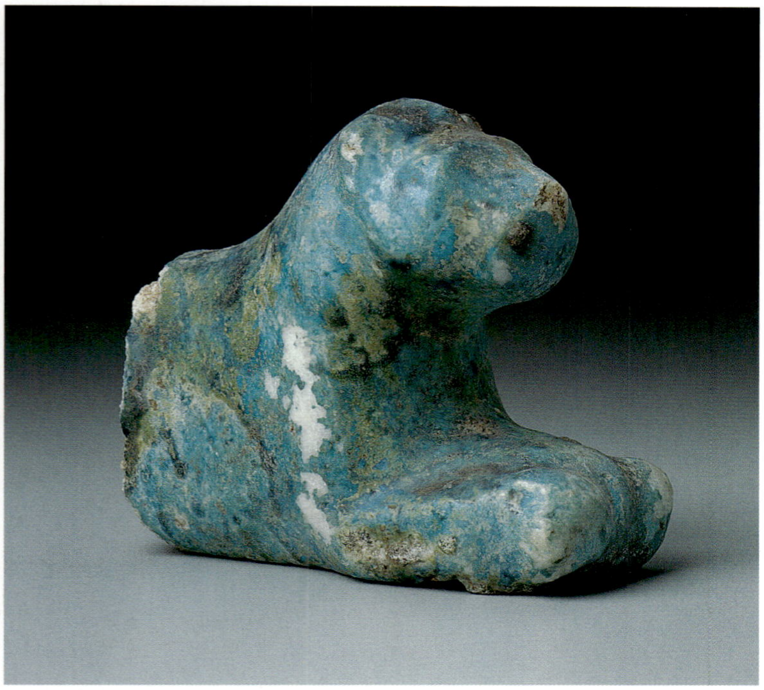

Right

STRIPED BALL BEAD [190]
Middle Kingdom to early New Kingdom
DIAM. *c.* 4.0 cm

Center

INLAY IN THE SHAPE OF A WING [199]
Late Period to Ptolemaic Period
H. 2.5 cm; W. 7.5 cm; D. 0.6 cm

Below

CORNER OF AN UNIDENTIFIED
INLAID OBJECT [196]
New Kingdom, Dynasty 18
Max. H. 2.2 cm; W. 4.8 cm; D. 1.2 cm

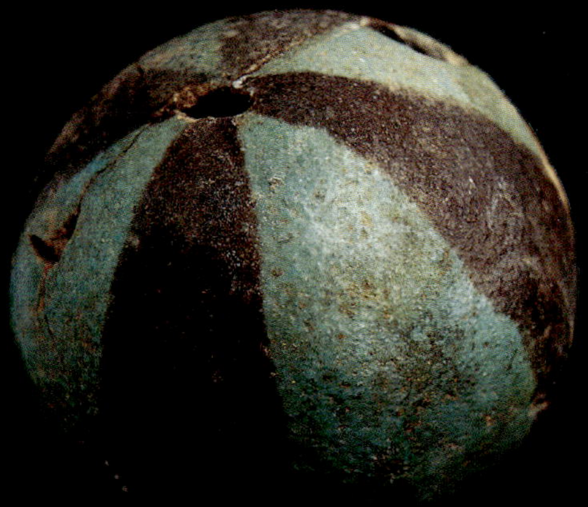

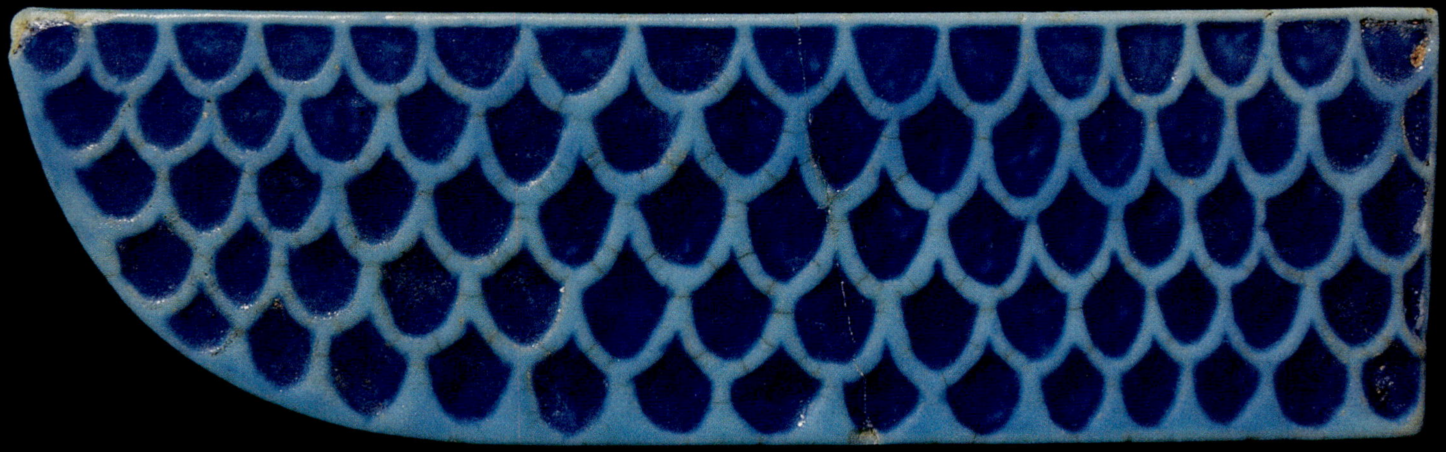

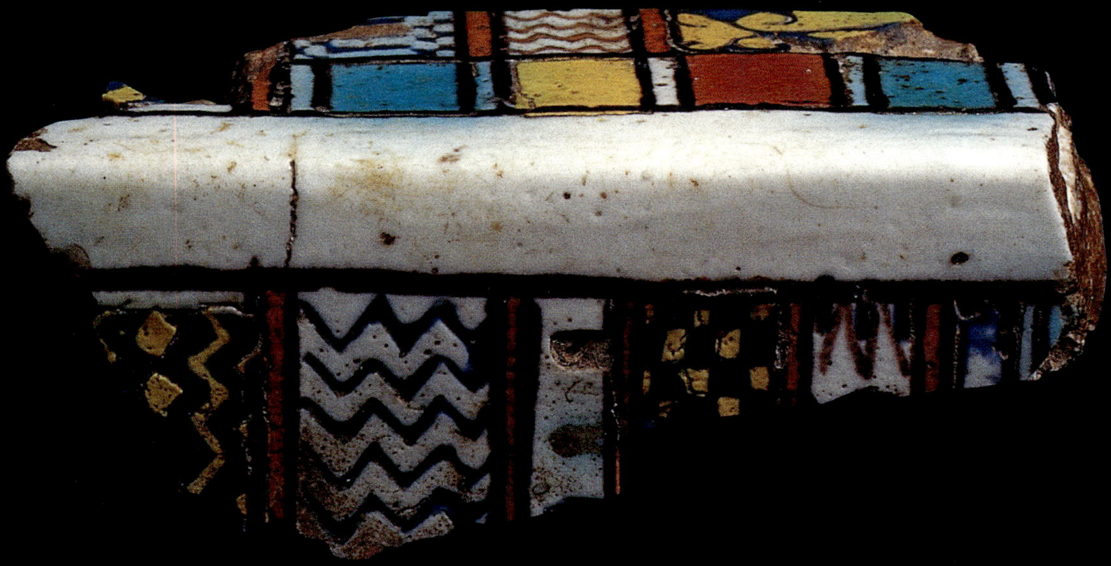

Right

WALL TILE WITH FRAGMENT OF ANKH [197]
New Kingdom, reign of Seti I
H. 9.9 cm; W. 5.0 cm; D. 2.0 cm

Below

CARTOUCHE FRAGMENT [198]
New Kingdom
H. 9.1 cm; W. 14.2 cm; D. 2.2 cm

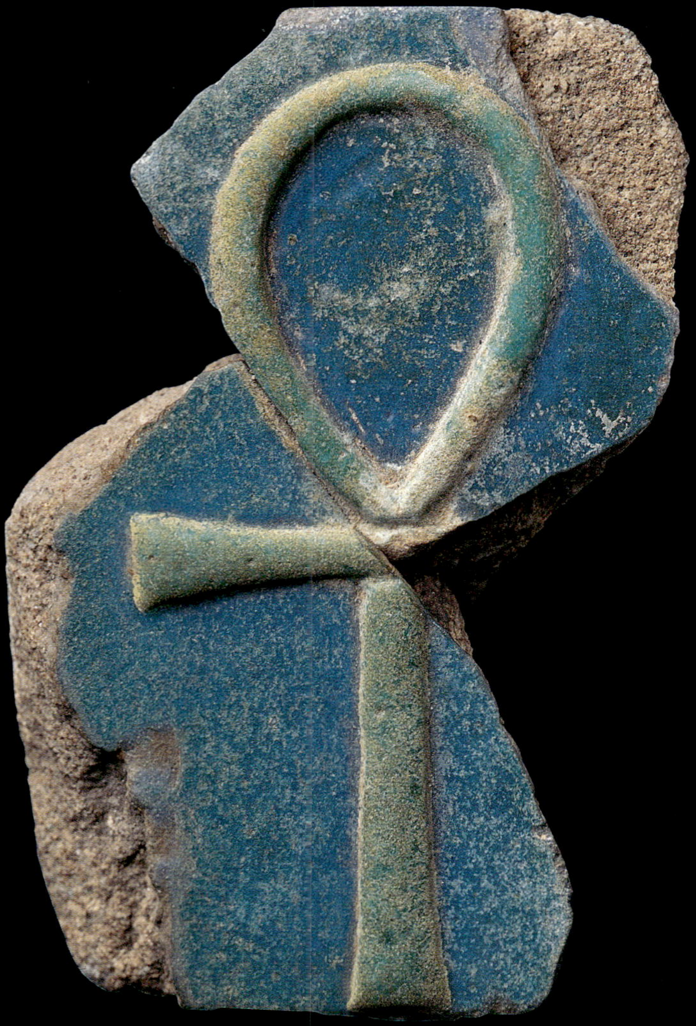

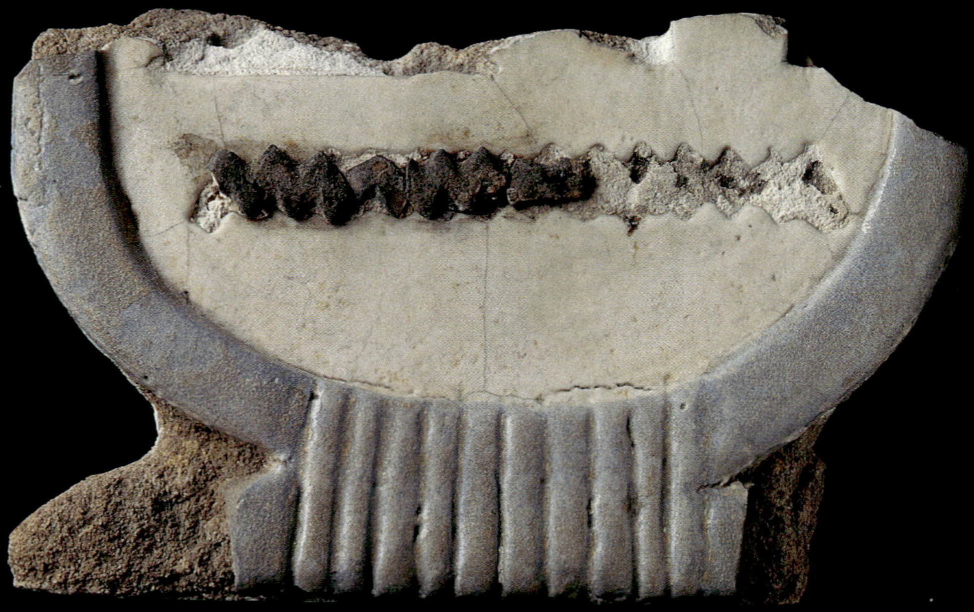

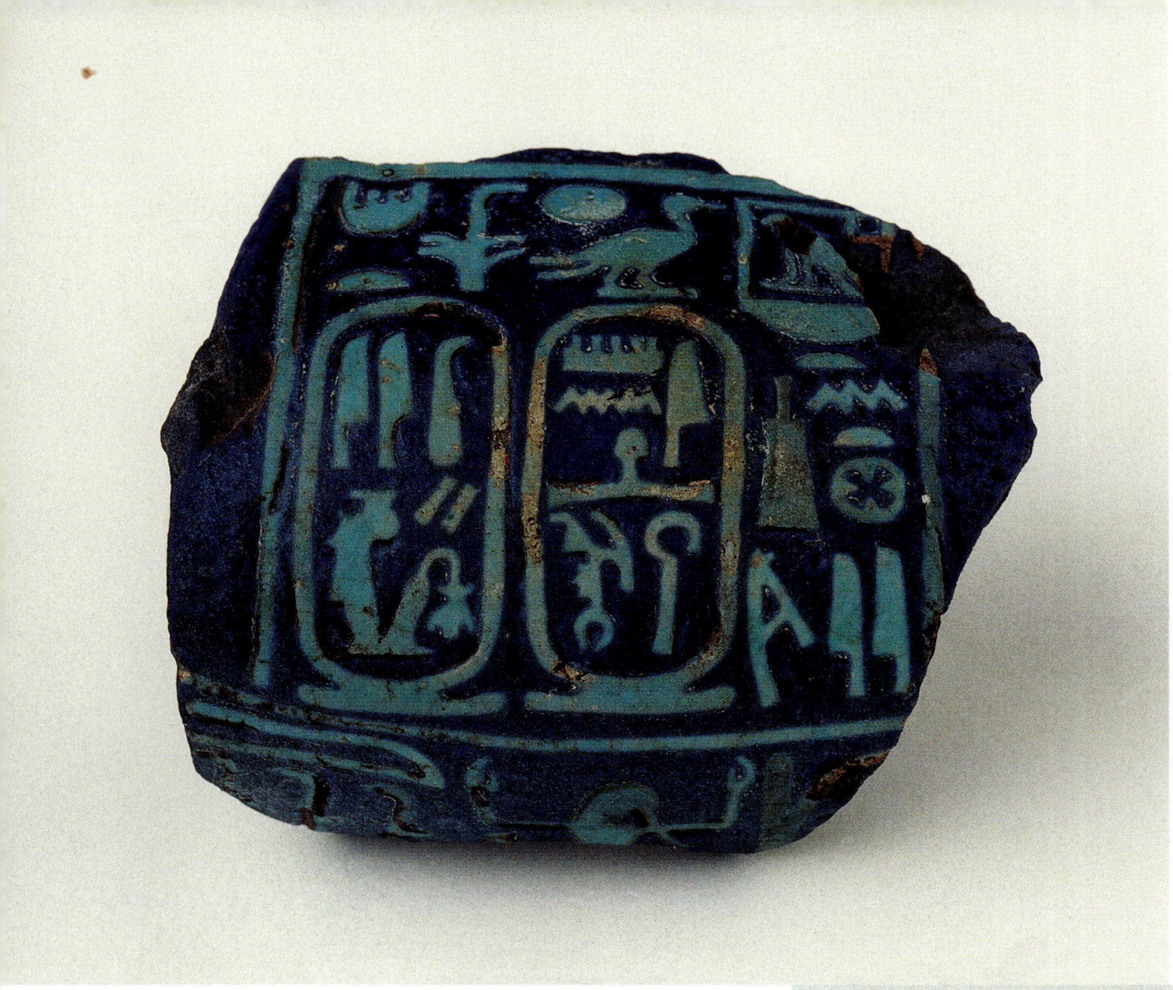

Left

FRAGMENT OF A VASE WITH HANDLE [195]
New Kingdom, Dynasty 18, reign of Amenhotep III
Original dimensions of handle: L. 7.0 cm; TH. 1.1 cm
Preserved dimensions: H. 5.7 cm; W. 6.8 cm

Below

FRAGMENT OF A BOTTLE WITH POLYCHROMATIC GEOMETRIC DESIGN [194]
New Kingdom, end of Dynasty 18
H. 8.8 cm; W. 5.6 cm;
max. orig. DIAM. *c.* 7.0 cm

Opposite above, left

RING BEZEL WITH THE CARTOUCHE OF AMENHOTEP III [191]
New Kingdom, Dynasty 18, reign of Amenhotep III
DIAM. 2.1 cm

Opposite above, right

FRAGMENT OF A RELIEF CHALICE [193]
Third Intermediate Period
Max. H. 5.4 cm; max. W. 4.9 cm; TH. 0.4 cm

Opposite below

TWO FRAGMENTS OF RELIEF DECORATED VESSEL(S) [200]
Roman Period
A: L. 15.7 cm; W. 5.0 cm
B: L. 13.5 cm; W. 5.0 cm

Overleaf

SIDELOCK FROM THE WIG OF A PRINCESS [192]
New Kingdom, end of Dynasty 18
H. 13.0 cm; W. 10.5 cm; D. 2.6 cm;
TH. of faience 1.6 cm

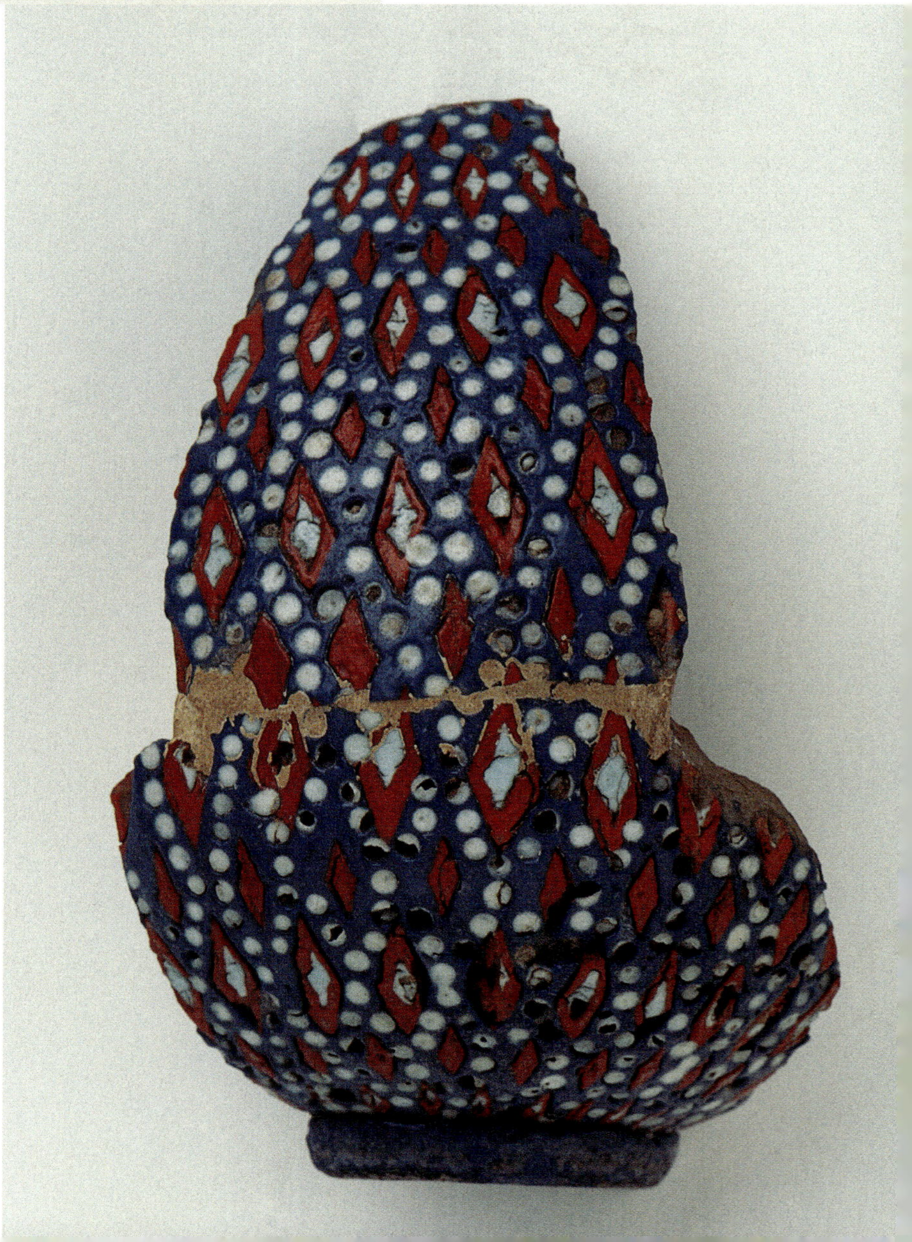

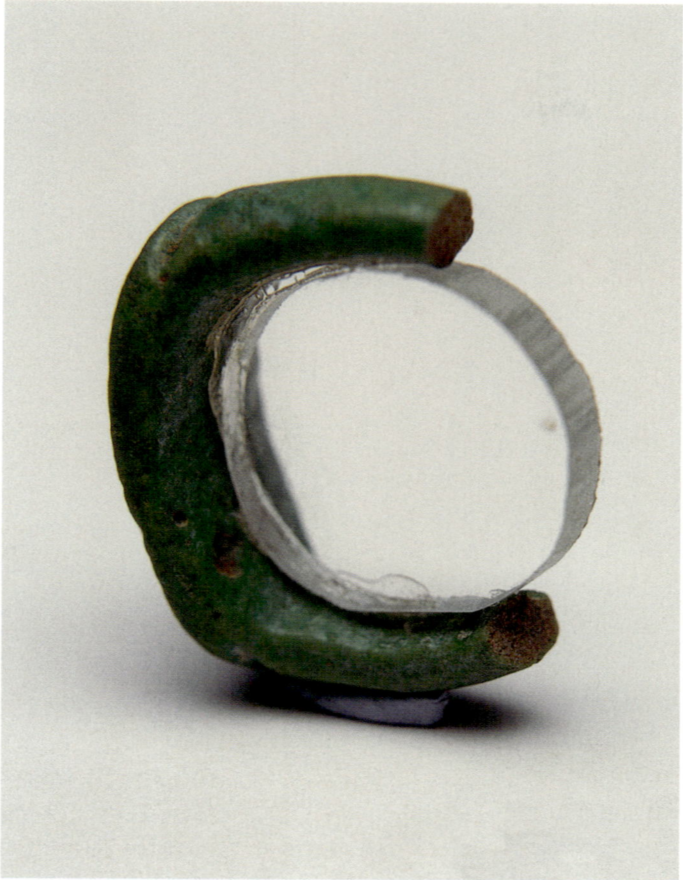

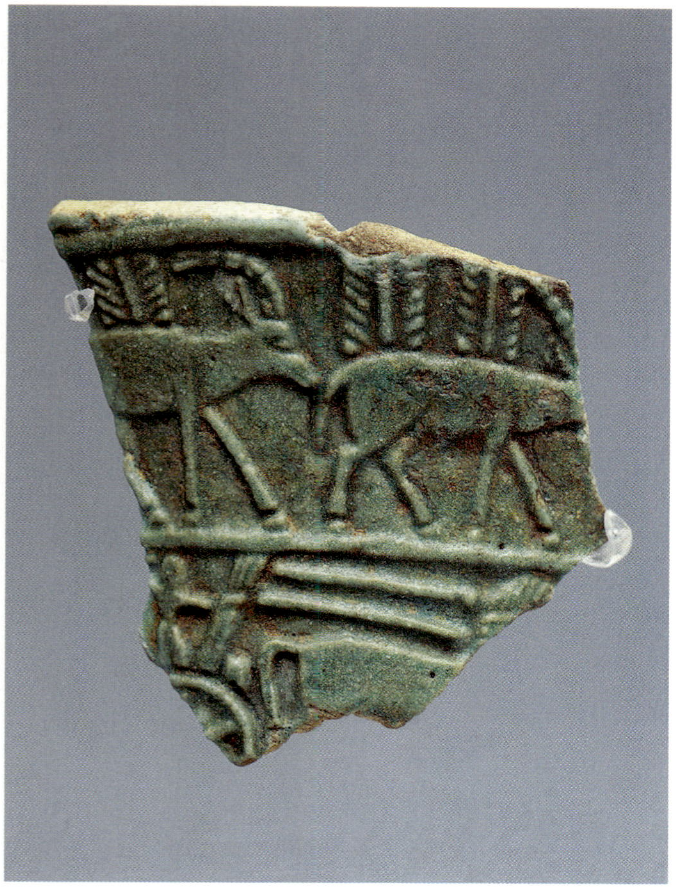

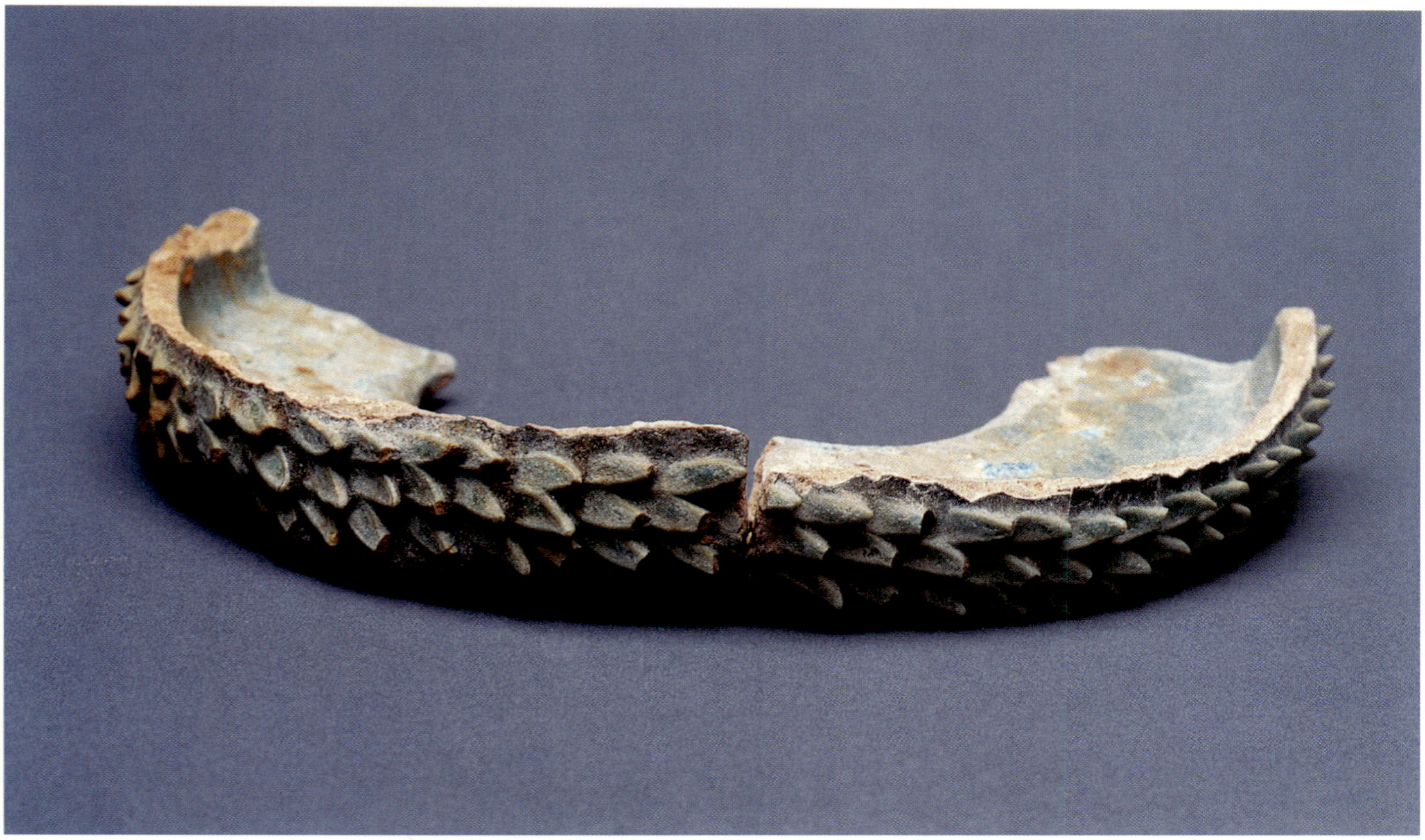

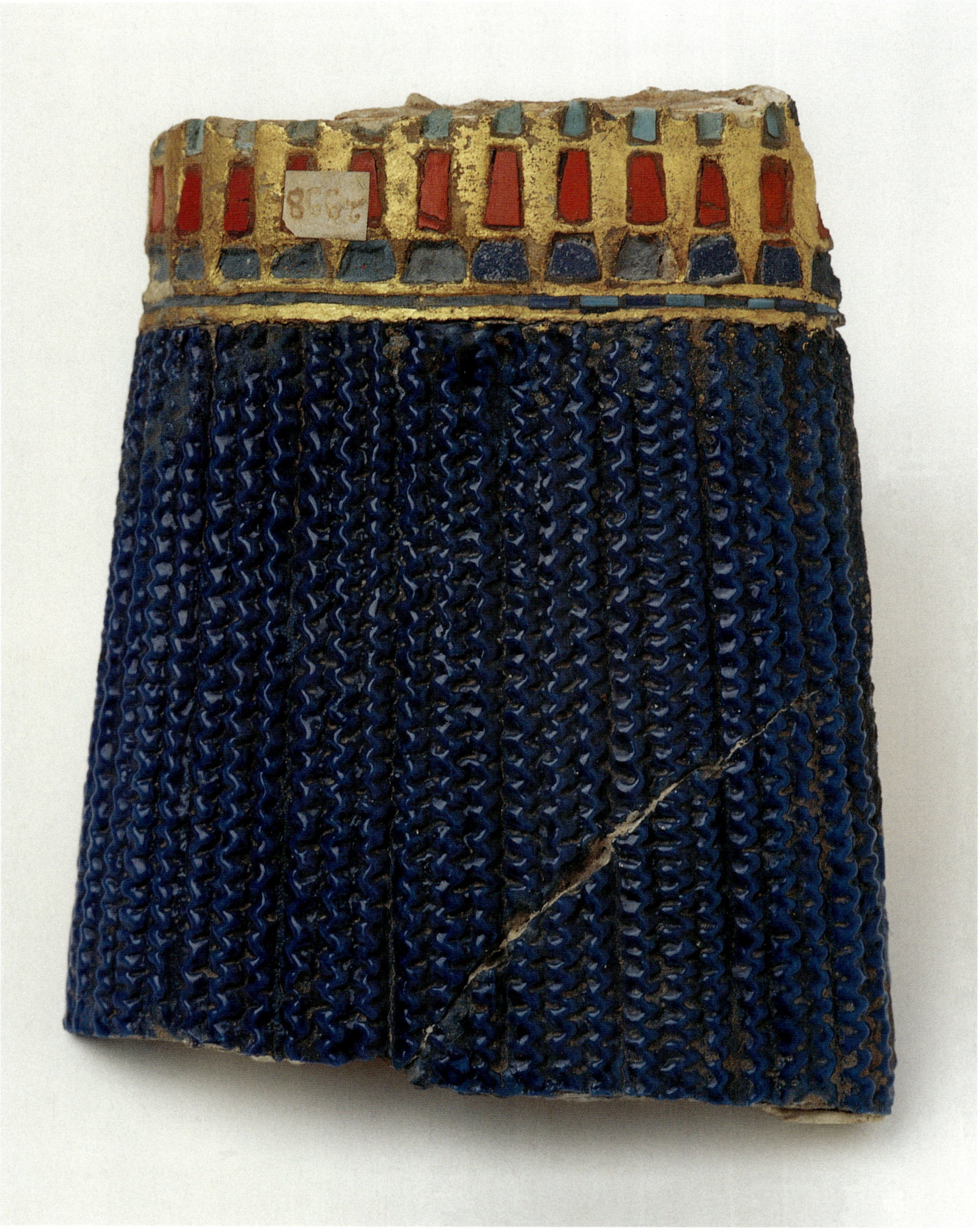

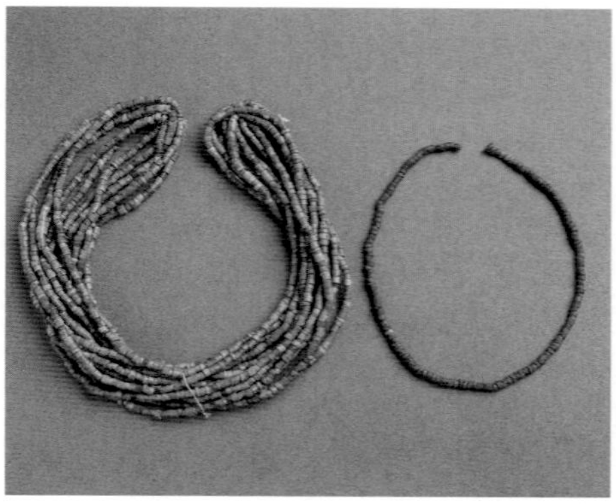

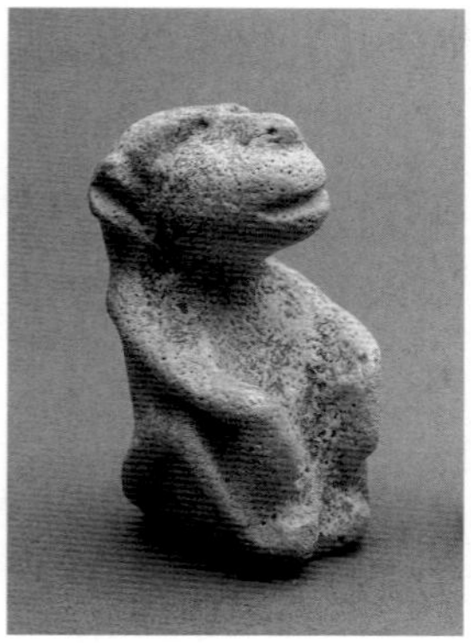

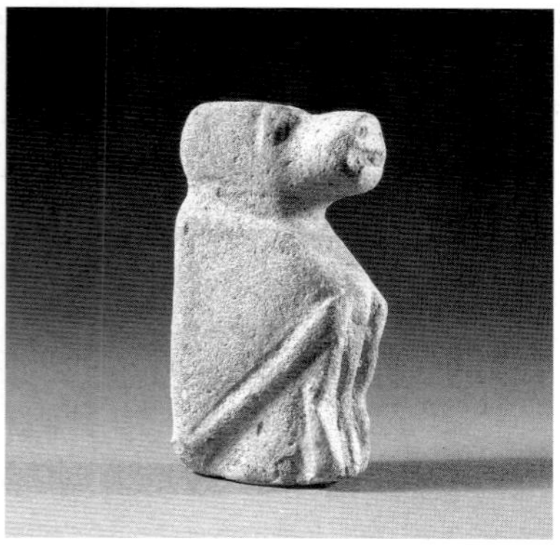

1 BELT (?) PAGE 74

Badarian, Predynastic Period; Badari, Tomb 5735
Glazed steatite, green glaze; L. 35.0 cm (bundled)
Petrie Museum of Egyptian Archaeology, University College London. UC.9250

2 NECKLACE PAGE 74

Late Predynastic Period, Naqada III; Ballas, Tomb Q24
Blue faience and malachite; L. approximately 30.5 cm
Petrie Museum of Egyptian Archaeology, University College London. UC.35976

One of the earliest materials to be glazed was a soft, easily carved stone known as steatite. The first forms were simple disk beads, glazed green or blue-green and strung to form single-strand necklaces. In at least four male burials from the Qau-Badari region of Middle Egypt, dating to the Badarian era in the Predynastic Period, large piles of such beads were found lying on the bodies somewhere between the chest and knees, suggesting use as a belt or girdle. Although the beads were no longer *in situ*, one example, now in the British Museum and consisting of over 5,000 beads, was better preserved and had eight bone spacers that gave more form to the piece.[1] The belt illustrated here was formed from a single long strand of beads that the excavator reported was found wrapped several times around the waist, over a piece of fur.

Several colossal statues of the god Min recovered from the site of Coptos, generally believed to be of late Predynastic date, have belts made from six or eight layers of material wrapped around the god's waist.[2] The Badarian beaded belts seem to represent a different version of the same item.

Shortly after the Badarian Period, the use of faience developed and beads were regularly made from it, although stone still remained the most common medium for bead manufacture. It is only at the end of the Predynastic Period that entire necklaces of faience are known. This example of a short, single strand of faience beads and a single malachite bead was recovered from a tomb in the Upper Egyptian site of Ballas, near Naqada. Such strands most commonly took the form of choker-like necklaces, but occasionally they have been found lying across an individual's forehead suggestive of a diadem. Small groups of beads have also been recovered near ankles and wrists. It therefore seems that small disk beads were used to construct a variety of jewelry types during the Predynastic Period. DCP

Bibliography. [1]: Brunton and Caton-Thompson 1928, p. 15, pl. 27 no. 3. [2]: Petrie n.d.; Bourriau 1984, p. 130.

3 BABOON STATUETTE PAGE 69

Early Dynastic Period, probably Dynasty 1–2; Hierakonpolis Temple, Main Deposit
Faience, pale blue-green glaze; H. 8.0 cm
The Syndics of the Fitzwilliam Museum, Cambridge. E.91.1898

4 BABOON STATUETTE PAGE 69

Early Dynastic, probably Dynasty 1–2; Abydos, Osiris Temple
Faience, green glaze; H. 4.8 cm
Staatliche Sammlung Ägyptischer Kunst, Munich. ÄS 1511

Many small animal sculptures of various materials have been found in deposits of mixed votive offerings at the important early temple sites of Abydos, Elephantine, and Hierakonpolis.[3] Because the deposits clearly contain material from different periods, precise dating of individual finds has been difficult.[4] Nevertheless, most scholars attribute the animal figurines to the Early Dynastic Period.

A variety of animals, including lions, several species of monkeys, boars, gazelles, pelicans, falcons, crocodiles, frogs, and scorpions, are represented, many made of faience. Among the fairly consistent repertoire of finds at all three sites, statuettes of baboons are one of the most common forms. Represented here by pieces from Cambridge and Munich are two very different depictions of a large and aggressive species of monkey, the *Hamadryas* baboon, a primate that had a sacred status throughout the Pharaonic Period.[5]

A baboon deity known as "The Great White One" was worshiped by the Early Dynastic Period, if not earlier,[6] its cult originating in the Upper Egyptian region. This deity had strong ties with the Khentiamentiu temple at Abydos as a component in the royal ancestor cult and many baboon statuettes have been recovered from the temple deposits there. "The Great White One" eventually seems to have been conflated with Thoth, the god of wisdom and writing, whose representation as a large baboon is well documented in later Egyptian history.

The Munich baboon [4] appears to have been made from a cube of faience, modeled with a few strokes to form the primate's image. The result is a blockish representation of a baboon, most clearly identifiable in profile. By contrast, the sculptor of the Cambridge piece [3] has paid close attention to rendering detail, and produced an animated likeness that was intended to be viewed from any angle.

Given the lack of examples from stratified contexts, the reason for two such distinct types is not known, but several suggestions can made. The differences may indicate that the two types represented by the Munich and Cambridge baboons were manufactured decades or even centuries apart (the Early Dynastic Period lasted at least 300 years). Alternatively, their dissimilarity may have been the result of quality in production, perhaps in response to the amount various temple patrons were willing to pay. It is also possible that each baboon type had an independent function in the cult. On the other hand the marked dissimilarity cannot be explained as a result of production in different workshops, because both types are found at temple sites hundreds of miles apart.

It should be noted that [4] represents an adult baboon, with large muzzle and heavy mane, while [3], with its oversized ears, small brow ridges, and lack of ruff, most assuredly represents a juvenile.[7] Both stages of a baboon's life seem to have been acceptable as offerings. DCP

Bibliography. [3]: Quibell and Green 1902, pl. 48b. [4]: Staatliche Sammlung Ägyptisches Kunst 1976, 34; Schoske and Wildung 1976, p. 10, pl. 5.

EARLY FAIENCE

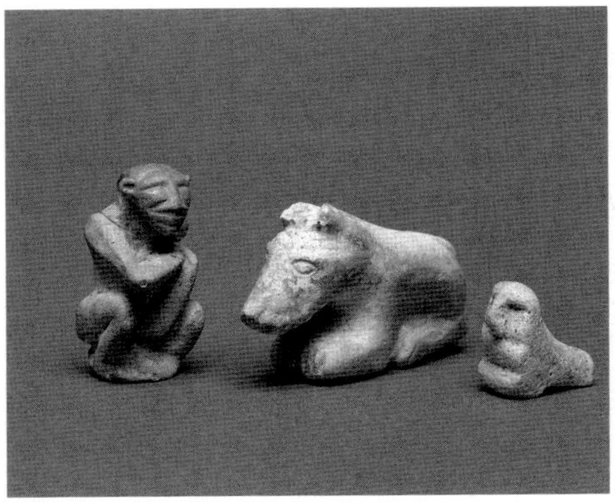

5 SEATED FIGURE PAGE 68

Early Dynastic Period, Dynasty 1–2; Hierakonpolis Temple, Main Deposit

Faience; H. 8.0 cm; W. 4.0 cm; L. 3.5 cm

Petrie Museum of Egyptian Archaeology, University College London. UC.15012

6 MODEL DOG PAGE 68

Early Dynastic Period, Dynasty 1–2; Hierakonpolis Temple, Main Deposit

Faience; H. 7.0 cm; W. 3.2 cm; L. 11.7 cm

Petrie Museum of Egyptian Archaeology, University College London. UC.11001

7 MODEL BIRD PAGE 68

Early Dynastic Period, Dynasty 1–2; Hierakonpolis Temple, Main Deposit

Faience; H. 4.0 cm; W. 2.2 cm; L. 4.9 cm

Petrie Museum of Egyptian Archaeology, University College London. UC.11005

Like the baboon [3] and the scorpions [8], [9], these faience pieces are from the Main Deposit, the modern term for a pile of objects found at Hierakonpolis.[8] In addition to famous royal monuments such as the Narmer Palette, it contained hundreds of figurines, often crude and many made of faience. Similar objects come from temples at Abydos, Elephantine, and Tell Ibrahim Awad, though we do not know which god or gods were the recipient.[9]

The precise meaning of these figures is not clear, though there are parallels with later religious images: the recumbent dog became Wepwawet or Anubis; the bird, with a hole on its underside for attachment, looks like a falcon, which assumed many religious identities, including Horus of Nekhen, who later resided at Hierakonpolis.[10] During the first two dynasties, however, these animals had no sure connection to such deities. Nor can the human figure be associated with a god—its identification is made more difficult as it seems to have a tail, while his prominent ears and headdress, or wig, that hangs at the back mark him as human.

The objects were hand-modeled and reveal the use of surface abrasion on the pre-fired, dry object, as though the craftsmen applied stone carving techniques to faience. The same cold-worked abrasion is seen on the backs of the Third Dynasty Djoser tiles. Weathering has obscured most of the original blue-green surface glaze. FDF

Bibliography. [5]: Adams 1974, p. 28, no. 139/21; pl. 21, no. 139. [6]: Adams 1974, p. 22, no. 108/15 and 17; pl. 15, no. 108, pl. 17, no. 108. [7]: Quibell 1900, pl. XXI, 14; pl. XXII, 14; p. 8; Quibell and Green 1902, p. 9 (12–16); Adams 1974, p. 21, no. 106/14; pl. 14, no. 106.

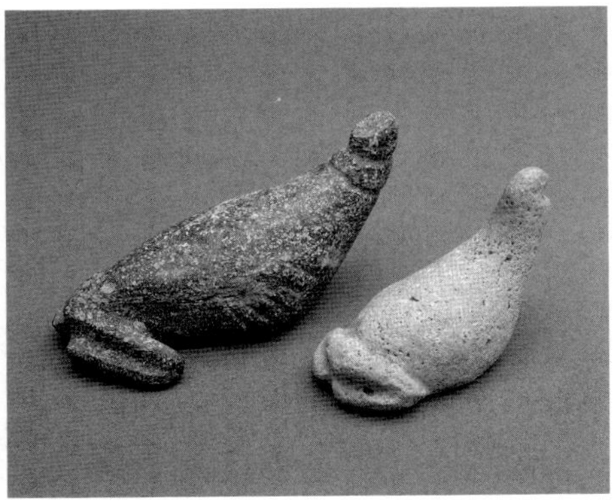

8 SCORPION PAGE 68

Early Dynastic Period, Dynasty 1–2; Hierakonpolis Temple, Main Deposit

Serpentine; L. 10.5 cm

The Syndics of the Fitzwilliam Museum, Cambridge. Gift of Egyptian Research Account. E.11.1898

9 SCORPION PAGE 68

Early Dynastic, Dynasty 1–2; Hierakonpolis Temple, Main Deposit

Faience; H. 4.7 cm; L. 7.0 cm

The Syndics of the Fitzwilliam Museum, Cambridge. Gift of Egyptian Research Account. E.18.1898

10 MODEL VESSEL PAGE 69

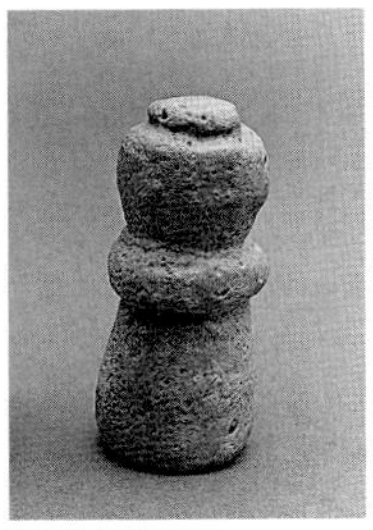

Early Dynastic Period, Dynasty 1–2; Hierakonpolis Temple, Main Deposit

Faience; H. 6.5 cm

The Syndics of the Fitzwilliam Museum. Gift of Egyptian Research Account. E.21.1898

Scorpions, like baboons, were a favorite offering in the early shrine at Hierakonpolis.[11] Fearsome creatures—the tips of their upright tails are equipped with a poisonous sting that can inflict mortal wounds—they may have been left at this and other shrines throughout Egypt in hopes of divine protection against this venom. In similar expectation, they may allude to the protective scorpion-goddess, Selket, whose cult was already known from the First Dynasty.[12]

Most Early Dynastic Period votive animals from Hierakonpolis are made of faience, but a number are also of harder natural materials. The larger scorpion here is carved from serpentine. In an interesting juxtaposition, the serpentine's natural green surface was probably the reason this mineral was chosen, while a blue-green glaze (now largely gone) was sought for the hand-modeled faience example.

Numbers of non-functional faience model pots on stands like that shown here were also left for the gods. They probably imitate on a small scale the full-size examples that held real food for the deity. FDF

Bibliography. [8]: Quibell and Green 1902, pl. XLVIII b. [9]: Quibell and Green 1902, pl. XLVIII a, col. 3 (but L. is given there as 10.0 cm); Adams 1974, p. 129. [10]: Quibell and Green 1902, pl. XLVIII b, col. 2.

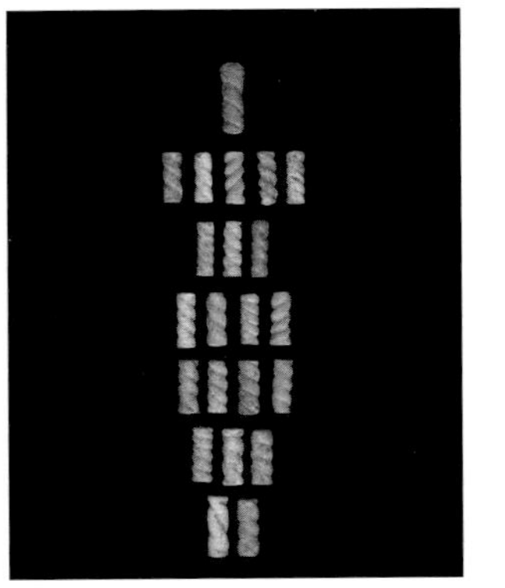

11 CURLS FROM A COMPOSITE STATUE PAGE 70

Early Dynastic Period, Dynasty 1–2; Hierakonpolis Temple, Main Deposit

Faience; H. 4.0–5.0 cm; W. 0.4–0.6 cm

Museum of Fine Arts, Boston. Gift of Egyptian Research Account 1898. 1832a-v

Formed in the shape of large, tubular, twisted beads, these 22 faience cylinders come from the excavations of the Egyptian Research Account at the Main Deposit in the Temple at Hierakonpolis.[13] They vary in color from blue-green to gray, with extensive surface pitting, a characteristic of Archaic Period faiences. There is a central boring through each bead of about 0.5 cm in diameter. No copper staining or traces of wood remain on the inside, suggesting that rope or thread was the means used to secure them together.[14] A large number of these faience cylinders were found and distributed throughout collections in Europe and America. They have been variously described as "beads for a necklace" or "curtain ties," however there are obvious top and end pieces which indicate that long braids of hair are being imitated. A top element in the collection of the Museum of Fine Arts (fig. 37) has a round, flattened end that would have been attached to the head. An end piece in the Royal Museum of Scotland in Edinburgh (fig. 38) has a diagonal, finished edge that would simulate the staggered, cut ends of the braids.[15]

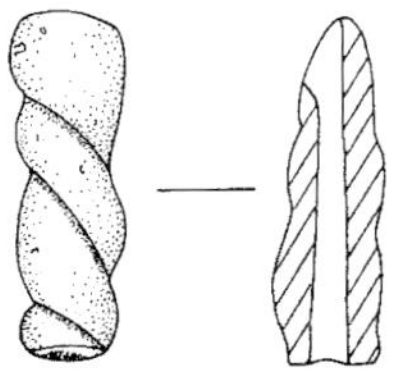

Fig. 37 A faience top curl with attachment for stringing. Hierakonpolis. Museum of Fine Arts 1898.1832a, drawing by Yvonne Markowitz.

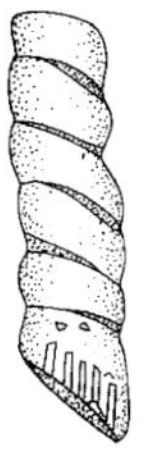

Fig. 38 A faience bottom curl. Hierakonpolis. Trustees of the National Museums of Scotland A.1956.329, drawing by Yvonne Markowitz.

Archaic Period sculptures in wood and stone depict both men and women with long, braided hair (fig. 39).[16] Coming from the Main Deposit, a *favissa* or burial place for sacred objects, the curls must have been part of a figure of a god or goddess. The faience would have represented the divine hair of lapis lazuli in Egyptian mythology and is one of the earliest examples we have of the use of faience in composite sculpture.[17] PL

Bibliography. Adams 1974, p. 129.

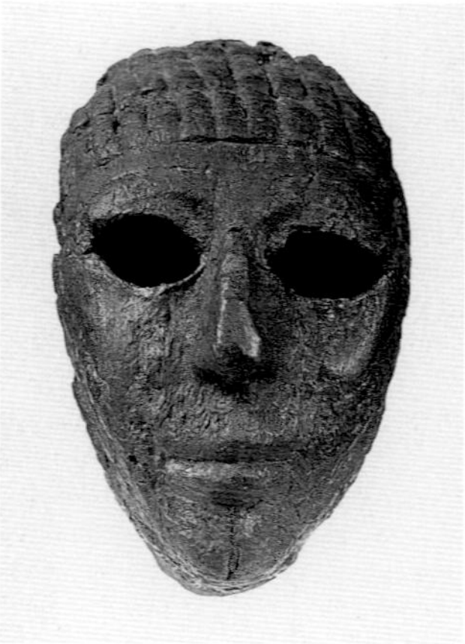

Fig. 39 A wooden face from a composite statue with curled hair. Dynasty 1. From Abydos. Museum of Fine Arts, Boston. 1960.1181

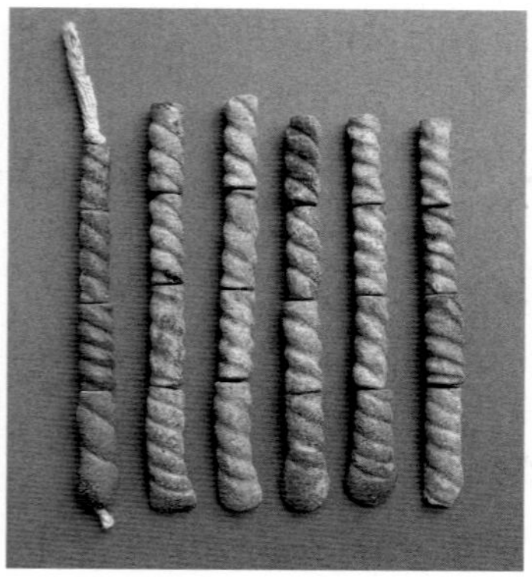

12 SPIRAL BEADS

PAGE 71

Early Dynastic Period, Dynasty 1–2; Hierakonpolis Temple, Main Deposit

Faience, average L. of beads 4.0 to 5.0 cm

Petrie Museum of Egyptian Archaeology, University College London. UC.14893

Over a thousand of these spiral faience beads were excavated in the so-called Main Deposit at the Temple at Hierakonpolis,[18] but exactly what they were used for eludes us. Two theories can be proposed. The first, discussed in [11], is that they served as curled ringlets attached to the heads of statues made of wood or other material,[19] though if so, one would expect numbers of such heads with attachment holes to have survived, which is not the case. The second theory is that they were threaded to form a beaded curtain, in which case the shape of the beads is interpreted not as curls but as twisted rope. Since each bead has a longitudinal hole they could have been strung on vertical cords to make ropelike curtains for the temple's doorways.[20] The abundant faience wall tiles with reed designs found at the site might have flanked such doorways.[21] Such a scenario recalls the Third Dynasty doorways of Djoser's Step Pyramid, where a reed curtain simulated in faience tiles is shown "rolled up" like a Venetian blind, with flanking faience tiles also simulating reeds (fig. 40).

It has to be admitted, however, that beaded curtains are not known elsewhere nor is any represented in Egyptian art. It is possible, though pure speculation, that they were used only at this temple and then abandoned for the rolled curtain type seen in Djoser's doorways. The spiral perforated beads, though durable and not easily broken,[22] are not found at later sites. Flat-backed faience curl inlays for coffins, however, do appear from the New Kingdom, possibly recalling the use of such beads as three-dimensional curls.[23]

To make the beads, one might suggest that the faience paste, while still damp, was twisted by hand around a core that was later pulled or fired out,[24] then dried and fired. In replication experiments, however, we found that twisting the faience paste was difficult, since it lost its shape or cracked. What worked better was turning the paste on a reed by hand while guiding a tool against it to create spiral incisions similar to those seen on the beads. The beads were assuredly made in the same workshops as faience wall tiles and inlay elements. FDF

Bibliography. Quibell 1900, p. 8; pl. XXIV, 1,3; Quibell and Green 1902, p. 30, section 73; Adams 1974, pls. 22, 31, no. 150; Adams 1987, p. 239, p. 130; Hoffman 1988, p. 86, cat. no. 78.

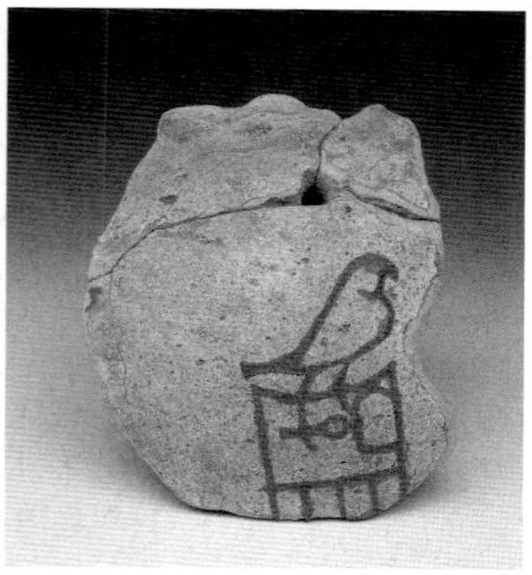

13 VASE FRAGMENT BEARING A ROYAL SEREKH

PAGE 75

Early Dynastic Period, Dynasty 1; Abydos, Osiris Temple, near M.69

Faience, H. 14.0 cm; W. 11.4 cm

The Trustees of the British Museum, London. EA 38010

In order to keep the gods happy and ensure the state of *maat* (roughly speaking, universal order), Egypt's ancient kings gave gifts to deities at their temples or shrines. On the walls of every temple are depictions of pharaohs before the gods offering wine, cloth, or small statues. This fragment from a large faience jar, possibly the earliest example of inlaying one faience colored paste into a faience body of another color,[25] displays in its inlay the name of Aha, the first king of the First Dynasty. The vase's find spot in a deposit of votive offerings indicates that its original purpose was as a gift to the temple at Abydos.

From the shape of the fragment we can tell that it was originally part of a large globular vase with a neck.[26] Unfortunately no portion of its rim survived. At this early date virtually all objects made from faience were small—such as beads, tiles, and statuettes—so that a faience piece of this scale is unexpected and must have been rare. It is thus not surprising to find that the jar bears a king's name, making it a royal donation, probably to Khentiamentiu, the local deity.[27] Once green with the inlaid inscription dark brown or black, it is now white with a dull brownish yellow inscription.

Aha's name is enclosed in a *serekh*,[28] and is written with a falcon's talons holding a mace and a shield. The rest of the bird sits atop the *serekh* structure—a symbol of the king. The lower portion of the *serekh* is only partially preserved, but formed a pattern derived from the niched mud-brick paneling of contemporary palace walls. This combination of royal name and architectural element indicates the intimacy of the relationship between king and palace.

Aha is generally accepted as being the first king of a unified Egypt and is therefore often equated with the legendary Menes, the founder of Memphis and ruler of all Egypt.[29] Fragments of historical inscriptions pertaining to Aha suggest that he had a long and prosperous reign.[30] DCP

Bibliography. Petrie 1903, pls. 4–5; Spencer 1980, p. 73 (no. 532), pl. 58; Spencer 1993, fig. 39.

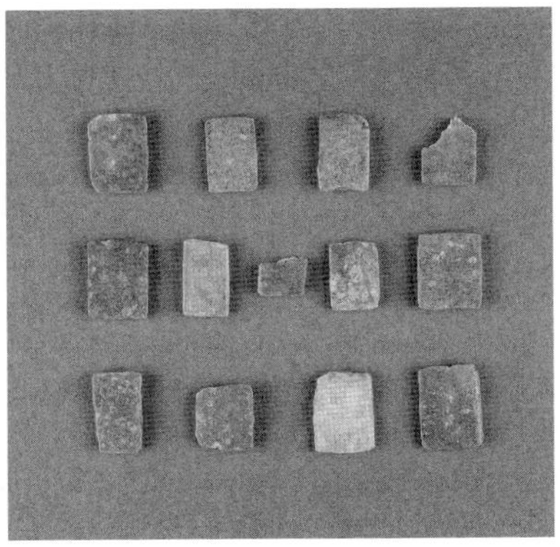

14 INLAYS PAGE 73

Early Dynastic Period, Dynasty 1; Saqqara, Tomb 3504, Magazine R

Faience, blue glaze; L. 1.4–1.6 cm; W. 0.9–1.2 cm; TH. 0.15–0.25 cm

The Trustees of the British Museum, London. EA 68151

Many people are familiar with the impressive inlaid furniture of ancient Egypt's New Kingdom, especially the exquisitely detailed pieces among Tutankhamun's furnishings. Few realize, however, how far back the tradition of inlaying precious materials into wood extends into Egyptian history.[31] Inlaying tiles and strips to form patterns was a well established craft by the Early Dynastic Period, although usually incised ivory or a variety of woods were used.[32]

The thirteen small tiles displayed here were recovered from a storage chamber of a large elite tomb of the First Dynasty.[33] Little survived the tomb's destruction, but fragments of wooden furniture were found in the same magazine.[34] The rectangular shape, small size, and thin profile of each faience piece suggest that they once embellished a box or piece of furniture as inlay.[35] DCP

Bibliography. Emery 1954, p. 44, no. 160 and pl. 27; Spencer 1980, p. 72 (no. 508), pl. 59.

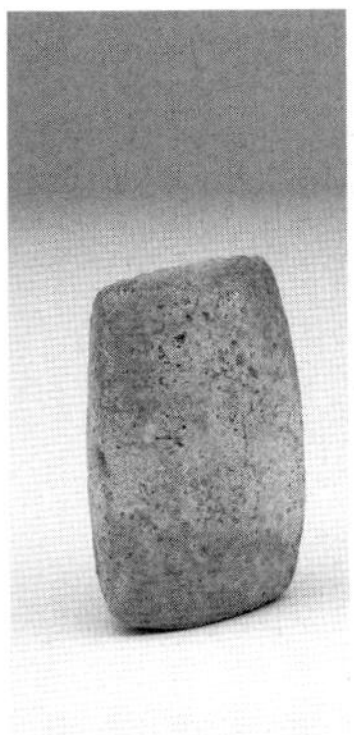

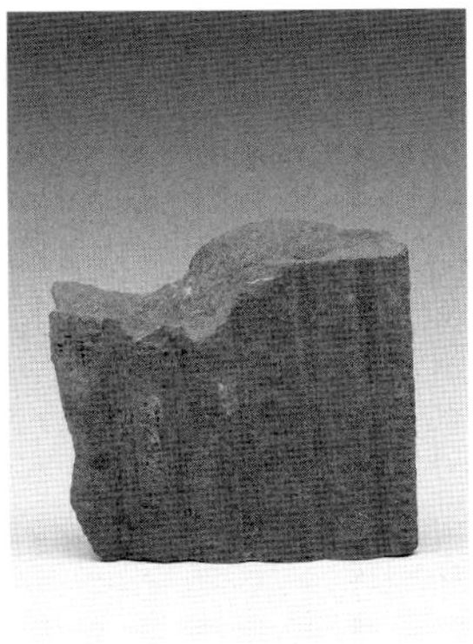

15 TILE PAGE 72

Early Dynastic Period to Old Kingdom, Dynasty 2 or early Dynasty 3; Abydos, Osiris Temple, deposited in M.69

Faience, pale blue glaze; H. 4.2 cm; W. 2.7 cm; TH. 1.5 cm

The Trustees of the British Museum, London. EA 38025

16 FRAGMENT OF TILE PAGE 75

Early Dynastic Period, probably Dynasty 1; Abydos, Osiris Temple

Faience, blue and green glazes; H. 6 cm; W. 6.2 cm; TH. 1.8 cm

The Trustees of the British Museum, London. EA 37282

An earlier and smaller version of the Djoser tiles [17–20] this tile [15] was found in a deposit of sacred objects from the Osiris Temple at Abydos. Although the tile's upper side is convex, the back lacks the distinctive tenon of the Djoser tiles, but is instead pierced to facilitate its attachment to a wall.[36] Precisely what this tile decorated at Abydos is unknown because no tiles have been found *in situ*, but it is quite likely that the walls of the sanctuary and nearby shrines were decorated in the same manner as the niches of Djoser's funerary complex (see fig. 40).

A fragment of a much larger rectangular faience tile [16] was incised lengthwise during manufacture, probably in imitation of the stems of bound plants. There is no indication of how this piece would have been mounted, but several superb parallels were recovered from the following season's excavation at Abydos.[37] At the back, these tiles have a wide tenon that was pierced twice for threading with wire in order to mount them in place on a wall. Several were inscribed, with either the craftsman's name or perhaps the destination of the decoration. The tile illustrated here was found in debris associated with the early Osiris Temple at Abydos, but has no specific context. It too probably decorated a wall in the temple of Khentiamentiu sometime in the late Early Dynastic or Old Kingdom period.[38] It is interesting to note that, while the tile is green, the unbroken edge displays a light blue color. DCP

Bibliography. [15]: Spencer 1980, p. 72 (no. 512), pl. 59. [16]: Petrie 1902, pl. 53, no. 19; Spencer 1980, p. 72 (no. 509), pl. 59.

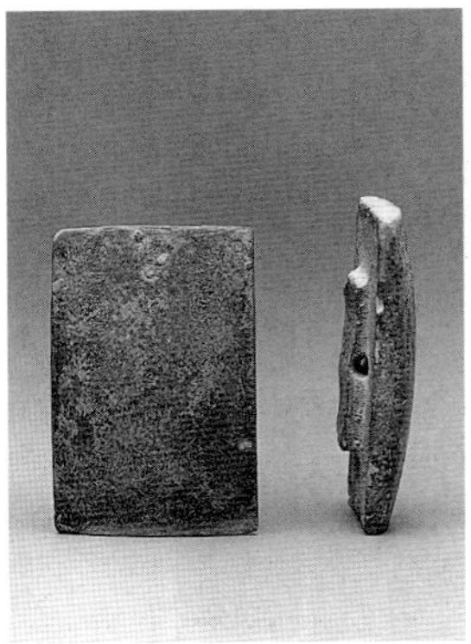

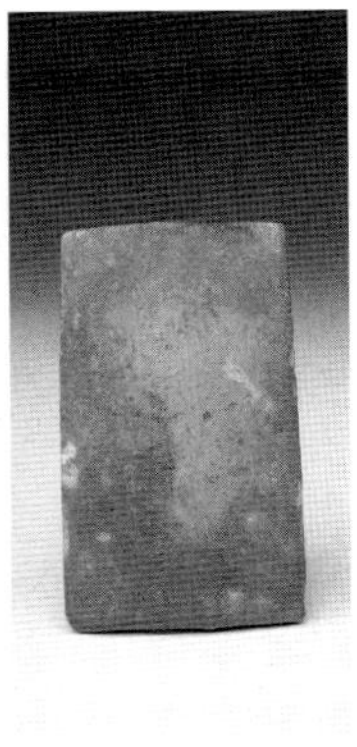

17 DJOSER TILE PAGE 72

Old Kingdom, Dynasty 3, reign of Djoser; Saqqara, Step Pyramid complex

Faience; H. 6.2 cm; W. 3.8 cm

Collection of William H. Peck.

18 DJOSER TILE PAGE 72

Old Kingdom, Dynasty 3, reign of Djoser; Saqqara, Step Pyramid complex

Faience; H. 5.9 cm; W. 3.8 cm

Collection of Dr. Irving F. Burton.

19 DJOSER TILE PAGE 72

Old Kingdom, Dynasty 3, reign of Djoser; Saqqara, Step Pyramid complex

Faience; H. 6.0 cm; W. 3.6 cm

The Trustees of the British Museum, London. EA 66830

20 DJOSER TILE PANEL PAGE 66

Old Kingdom, Dynasty 3, reign of Djoser; Saqqara, Step Pyramid complex

Faience; H. of each tile *c.* 6.0 cm; W. 3.5 cm

The Syndics of the Fitzwilliam Museum, Cambridge. EGA.xxxx.1943: 4414; 4417; 4421; 4425; 4426; 4431; 4434; 4449; 4453; E.57.1935 (three perfect tiles), etc.

Some 36,000 of these little blue-green tiles with convex upper surfaces once covered underground chambers of Djoser's Step Pyramid and his South Tomb, most notably surrounding six limestone reliefs forming false door stelae showing the king performing a ritual run and other acts (fig. 40).[39]

In their arrangement the tiles imitate reed matting,[40] a common Egyptian motif. The reeds that grew in the Nile waters, a mythological site of primeval creation in Egyptian thinking, were used for the actual reed matting of the king's palace. They are also known from the Pyramid Texts where they are connected with the afterlife abode called the Field of Reeds (*sekhet yaru*).[41] The blue-green color of the tiles is also associated with water and regeneration.[42] Thus the tiles evoke not only the earthly and afterlife home of the king, but also the Egyptian notion of the primeval waters, a place where creation arose at the beginning of time and from which the deceased king could arise reborn.[43]

The tiles are an early example of mold-making, and slight differences in their lengths suggest the use of multiple molds (see the essay by Nicholson, p. 57) as faience paste exhibits virtually no shrinkage in drying and firing.[44] At the rear of the tiles, undercut projections with longitudinal holes were produced

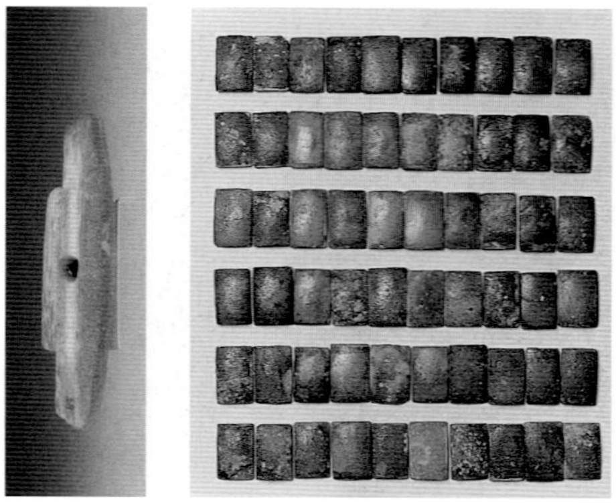

by grinding the dry faience prior to firing, thus removing the salts that would become the glaze in those areas (in the efflorescence process).[45] The holes were strung through with cords of some vegetal matter, probably papyrus.[46] Using the cords for alignment, the tiles were embedded in plaster on the limestone chamber walls. Markings at the top of some of the tile backs are probably workshop batch markings or designations for wall placement.

Similar tiles have recently been found in the now-lost complex to the west of Djoser's monument, as well as the Temple at Elephantine.[47] Others appear to have been used in non-royal mastaba tombs of the Third Dynasty.[48] Manufacturing faience wall tiles was clearly a flourishing industry, though no workshop locations are known. FDF

Bibliography. [19]: Spencer 1980, p. 72, no. 520, p. 59.

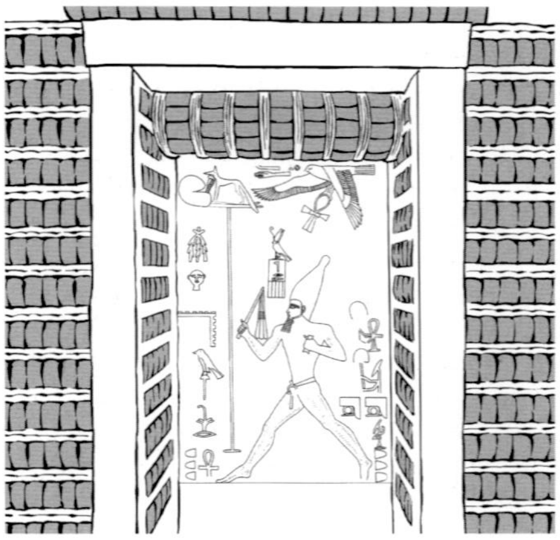

Fig. 40 A relief showing the running king from a chamber below his Step Pyramid complex at Saqqara. The panel is surrounded by blue faience tiles in imitation of reed mats, including one "rolled up" above the doorway.

1 BM EA 62150. Brunton 1937, 37, pl. 8; Andrews 1990, 50, no. 37.
2 The strips have an end that hangs down and are not subdivided to indicate beads. Payne 1993, 12–13, pls. 2–3.
3 Adams 1974, pp. 20–30, pls. 13–23; Dreyer 1986, pp. 68–76, pls. 24–35; Quibell and Petrie 1902, pls. 18–22; Quibell and Green, 1902; Petrie 1902, pp.23–28, pls. 2–11.
4 Because faience figures were found in non-stratified contexts at all three temples, the small figures cannot be dated more specifically than the latest date of the associated objects or the stratum sealing the deposit. At Abydos, for example, this date cannot be any earlier than the Eighteenth Dynasty (Kemp 1968, pp. 153–55).
5 Störk 1982a, cols. 915–20.
6 Kaplony 1977, cols. 1078–80.
7 Altmann 1980, figs. 42–43 and 46.
8 Adams 1995b, p. 72 suggests that rather than being "'holy rubbish,' come upon and reburied by later builders," they could have been "contemporary with the use of the Early Dynastic temple, and ... buried shortly after their dedication..."
9 Kemp 1989b, p. 75.
10 Sandstone birds with holes in the bases were found beside Tomb II at Hierakonpolis (Adams 1995b, p. 13).
11 Scorpions and baboons may be early cult images (Kemp 1989b, p. 74).
12 Mentioned on the Merka Stela, Tomb 3505, Saqqara, etc. (Shaw and Nicholson 1995, p. 262).
13 Adams 1974, pp. 129.
14 A similar method of securing the tiles from the Step Pyramid complex at Saqqara points to this being a general method in use in the Archaic Period.
15 RSM 1956.329.
16 Cf. Smith 1967, pp. 70–78; Capart 1905, 247–66.
17 Examples exist particularly from the New Kingdom, cf. Phillips 1994, pp. 58–71. Both faience and glass inlays are also used for inlaid hair on coffins, cf. Partridge 1994, pp. 47–49; also N. Reeves pers. comm.
18 Quibell found 1,400 (Quibell and Green 1902, p. 30, section 73). There are 755 now in the Petrie Museum of Egyptian Archaeology, University College London (Adams 1974, p. 31, no. 150 notes 754, and another, UC.14893A, was recently located, pers. comm. Barbara Adams). The total found in other museums is 123: Egyptian Museum, Cairo, has 13 (JE 46498); Fitzwilliam Museum, Cambridge, 17 (E.15.1898); Ashmolean Museum, Oxford, 54 (E.E.26); Oriental Institute, Chicago, 17 (4754.477i); and Museum of Fine Arts, Boston, 22 (98.1010), according to a personal communication from Barbara Adams. See also Adams 1974, p. 31, no. 150; and Adams 1987, p. 239, p. 130.
19 First suggested by Quibell 1900, p. 8.
20 Adams 1974, p. 31, cat. no. 150. A small proportion of the total beads found so far in museums have flattened ends and some a single rounded tip; these were possibly the end pieces of the curtain cords.
21 Pers. comm., Barbara Adams.
22 Faience is often more durable and may have experienced more wear than generally thought.
23 New examples, mostly in faience, a few in Egyptian blue, in Schaden 1997, pp. 10–11. I thank Janice W. Yellin for drawing my attention to this recent find, and Otto Schaden for sharing his latest research with me.
24 I thank Peter Lacovara for this description.
25 Petrie 1903, p. 25.
26 Petrie 1903, pl. 4: his drawing of the reconstructed jar indicating a greatest diameter of 21 cm (8¼ in), a sizeable piece for any medium except perhaps pottery.
27 Khentiamentiu was conflated with Osiris by the time of the Old Kingdom.
28 Meaning "to make known." See Spencer 1993, p. 59.
29 New data is coming from the German excavations at Abydos on the earliest kings, including Narmer, and this interpretation may well change.
30 For a summary, see Kaplony 1975, cols 94–96; Grimal 1992, pp. 49–50.
31 Emery 1961, pp. 216 and 220. The sophisticated use of inlay during the Early Dynastic Period is perhaps best exemplified by the exquisite inlaid gaming disks from Saqqara (Emery 1938, pp. 28–32, pl. 12).
32 Ebony box (Emery 1938, p. 41, pl. 23); ivory inlay from the royal tombs (Petrie 1900, for example, pl. 40, nos. 40–68, pl. 41, nos. 1–22, pl. 42, nos. 38–65).
33 Originally 16 were recovered but the British Museum received only the thirteen illustrated here.
34 This assumption is supported by finds of furniture pieces in nearby storage units.
35 Reconstruction of a fragmentary box from Semerkhet's tomb at Abydos shows that triangular pieces of wood and molded faience formed a pattern on one portion of it (see fig. 5).
36 For a parallel from Hierakonpolis, see Adams 1974, p. 35, no. 165, pl. 25.
37 Petrie 1903, p. 26, pl. 8, nos. 181–83, while Dreyer 1986, pl. 60a provides good close-up photographs of another now in the collection of the Ashmolean Museum, Oxford (E49+58+59+60).
38 Tiles of similar size, shape, and design have been recovered from temple debris at Elephantine (Dreyer 1986, p. 138, nos. 378–81, pl. 49).
39 On the reliefs, see Friedman 1995, with biblio.
40 Lauer 1936, vol. I, pp. 34–38; Lauer 1962, pp. 76–79. On the tiles, see Schliegl 1988, pp. 242–43; Vandiver in Kaczmarczyk and Hedges 1983, esp. A 83–85; Vandier 1952, pp. 883–87, fig. 584.
41 The Pyramid Texts, Egypt's oldest body of religious literature, were written down in the Fifth Dynasty, but their ideas were probably operative in Djoser's day.
42 For the multiple meanings of *w3ḏ*, see most recently Vergès 1992, pp. 17–18. The author asks whether the blue was intended to insure the protection of the king or merely arose from the manufacturing technique. But examples of Djoser faience tiles with originally reddish brown glaze (Spencer 1980, cat. no. 524, EA 2444; cat. no. 525, EA 2445), presumably furniture inlays, show that other colorants could have been used and thus suggest that the blue-green glaze of the Djoser tiles was deliberate.
43 Friedman in Der Manuelian 1996, pp. 342–43. Such regenerative notions may also have been relevant for the dwelling of the gods, as illustrated by palm tree and vegetal inlays or tiles from the Archaic Osiris Temple at Abydos, the Archaic temple at Hierakonpolis, and earlier as well as contemporary temple tiles at Elephantine. Djoser was thus drawing on an already established faience tradition and the regenerative meaning it probably carried in early tomb (e.g., Khasekhemwy's Abydos faience inlays) and temple contexts (Friedman in Der Manuelian 1996, p. 343).
44 Nicholson 1993, p. 21. But see also Vandiver in Kaczmarczyk and Hedges 1983, A-83 for more details.
45 Vandiver in Kaczmarczyk and Hedges 1983, A-84.
46 Lauer 1962, p. 78. Lauer also states that Firth found fragments of what looked like papyrus within some tile holes. Thus Borchardt's assertion that metal filament was used (p. 78, n. 1), an assertion still restated today, is probably incorrect. The lack of copper corrosion in the tiles' holes makes the use of copper doubly unlikely. Also, there is no evidence that the Egyptians knew how to make wire (Andrews 1990, p. 96).
47 Dreyer 1986, pp. 91–92.
48 E.g., Petrie Museum of Archaeology, University College London, UC.14891, a convex tile from East Mastaba at Hierakonpolis (Adams 1974, p. 35, cat. no. 165; parallels pl. 25, no. 165). Tile dimensions—H. 6.0 cm; W. 3.7 cm; TH. 1.1 cm—are similar to Djoser's.

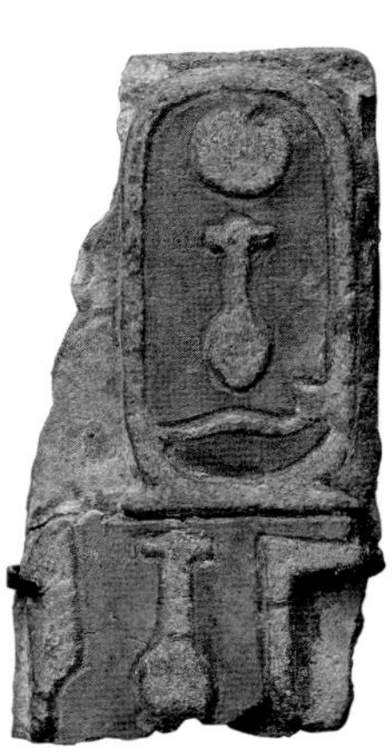

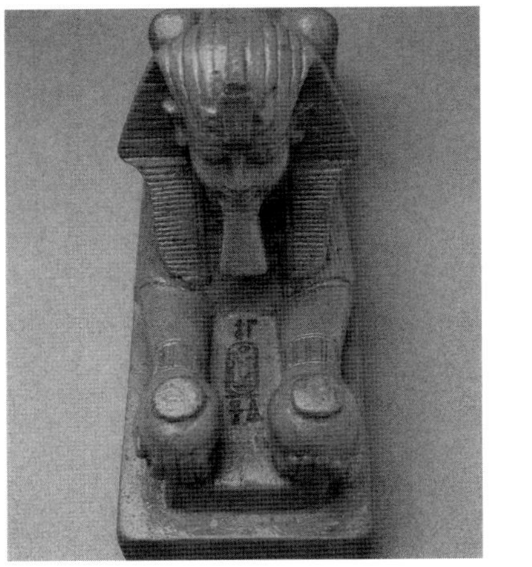

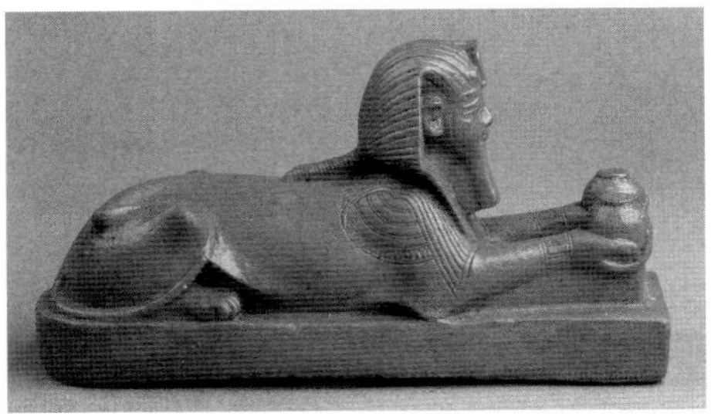

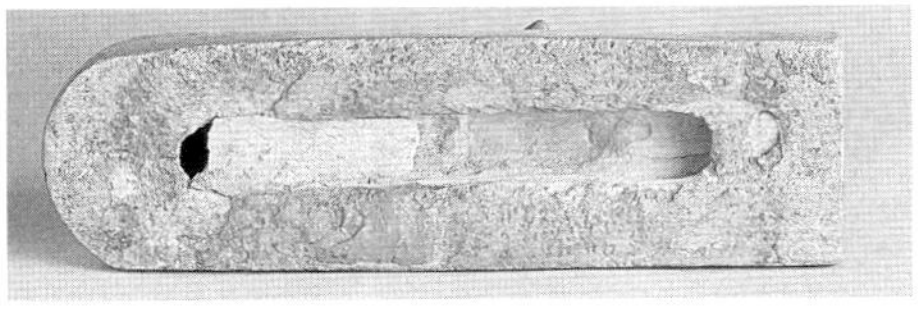

Fig. 41 Underside of the sphinx.

21 INLAY WITH CARTOUCHE OF KING RANEFEREF PAGE 80

Old Kingdom, Dynasty 5, reign of Raneferef; mortuary temple of Raneferef, Abusir

Faience with gilded gesso inlay; H. 6.5cm; W. 3.2 cm; TH. 0.6 cm

Private Collection

Until recently the Pyramid Age of the Fourth through the Sixth Dynasties was thought to have produced little faience. But recent Czech excavations at Abusir have revealed a number of faience inlays. Some, like that shown here, had already left the site in the nineteenth century.

This small inlay, along with its companion pieces, once held bright blue glyphs set against a gilded background, part of the brilliant decoration for what was most likely a royal wooden box.[1] The inlay is from the Fifth Dynasty mortuary temple of King Raneferef at Abusir and presents the pharaoh's cartouche with, below, the glyphs *nṯr nfr*, meaning "the Good God," a standard royal epithet. A reed leaf, part of a missing word, appears at the left. A virtually identical piece was recently excavated at Abusir,[2] probably from the same object as this one.

The faience portion of the object probably did not start from a mold but from a slab of faience paste from which sections were cut using sharp tools that have left their mark in the final product.[3] After the excess paste was removed, the cartouche and glyphs were left in relief with recesses between. When originally fired, the upper surface of the faience was a bright blue produced by the selfglazing (or efflorescence) process, though it has now weathered to a patchy green.[4] What is unusual is the core of the faience (below the green), which is red, due to exposure to a reducing environment in the kiln,[5] probably a result of a firing accident. Interesting also is the soft brown inlay in the recesses around the cartouche and glyphs. It is made not of gypsum plaster, as seen on at least one other faience object from Abusir,[6] but an unfired material which is a calcareous (calcium-rich) gesso[7] used as a support for gilding, tiny traces of which remain.[8] Although using gesso as a ground for gilding is common in later periods,[9] this appears to be an early application of the technique to faience. The complexity of the piece illustrates the experimental nature of inlay production in the Old Kingdom. Compare the Fourth Dynasty reliefs in the tomb of Atet and Nefermaat in which colored pastes were let into the limestone walls (see fig. 6), a practice abandoned soon after. FDF & ML

22 AMENHOTEP III AS SPHINX PAGE 78

New Kingdom, Dynasty 18

Faience; H. 14.0 cm; W. 7.0 cm; L. 25.0 cm

Hole on underside: L. 16.6 cm; W. 2.3 cm

The Metropolitan Museum of Art, New York. Purchase, Lila Acheson Wallace Gift, 1972. 1972.125

Ex-Collections: Howard Carter; Cranbrook Academy, Bloomfield Hills, Michigan

This unique blue sphinx of Amenhotep III is one of the great masterpieces of royal faience workshop production. It is also one of the clearest illustrations that faience was not merely a substitute for more costly materials: Amenhotep III could surely have commissioned such a work out of stone, including lapis, which occurs naturally in large sizes. The symbolism of the color was apparently the significant feature, since this king also produced sphinxes in Egyptian blue and glazed steatite.[10]

Amenhotep III is depicted here as a sphinx, with the powerfully modeled body of a lion and the head of the king. He wears the striped royal headcloth (*nemes*) surmounted by the royal uraeus cobra,[11] false royal beard and a broad collar, possibly itself imitating faience beads. While sphinxes normally have lion paws, in the Eighteenth Dynasty they were often shown with human arms and hands,[12] and parallels can be found, though less frequently, stretching back to the Old Kingdom.[13] A human-handed sphinx of Merenre from the Sixth Dynasty, the earliest parallel to the Metropolitan example, holds *nw*-jars, offerings of wine or milk intended to propitiate a solar deity.[14] Here, Amenhotep III appears in the same form, with braceleted arms and hands supporting *nw*-jars, which rest on a slab inscribed with: "the Good God, Neb-Maat-Re [the King's Throne Name], given life."

The original purpose of this Eighteenth Dynasty Metropolitan sphinx is unknown, though it may have been a New Year's, temple, or tomb gift.[15] One significant feature is the long oval hole on its underside, which may have enabled the sphinx to be fitted onto an attachment, suggesting it was part of a larger work (fig. 41).[16] Examination of the underside supports this interpretation. An X-radiograph performed by Ann Heywood of the Sherman Fairchild Center for Objects Conservation at the Metropolitan Museum of Art reveals a large hollow area within the sphinx, a portion of which retains a fragment of alabaster wedged in with an adhesive[17] (fig. 42). Heywood notes that "the top and side edges of the fragment are finished, suggesting that the fragment may be the remains of a tenon used to attach the sphinx to an alabaster base," presumably in some larger stone unit (fig. 43). Sphinxes often appear in architectural settings, typically in flanking pairs as protective sentinels. It is therefore not unreasonable to assume that a companion tenoned sphinx—a mirror opposite to this one, with its tail wound about the left flank—once existed. Such offering fig-

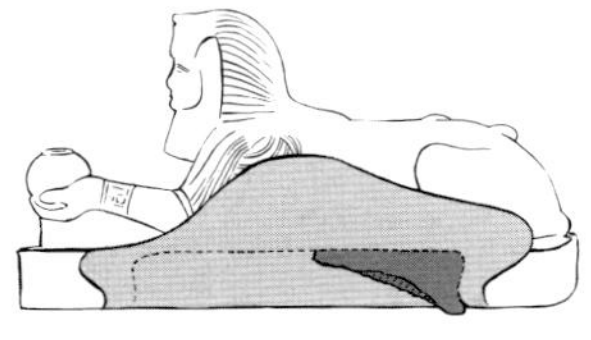

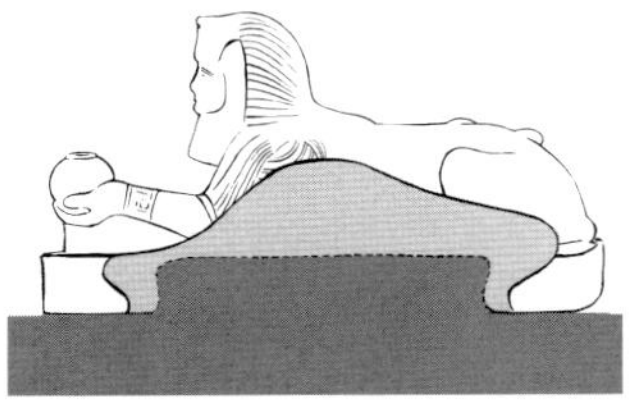

Figs. 42–43 Cross-section drawing of the sphinx, showing the piece of alabaster (darkest area) wedged inside, the possible remains of a tenon and how the sphinx may have been attached to a larger stone unit.

ures of Amenhotep III would have been more propitiatory than protective in function.

One possible architectural setting for such small-scale offering sphinxes is a temple model. From the Archaic Period on kings are noted in inscriptions of temple foundation ceremonies as "Presenting the House to its Lord."[18] Though the kings are not shown presenting actual models, fragments of two votive examples do exist from the reign of Seti I at the beginning of the Nineteenth Dynasty. The more complete consists of a quartzite base depicting a solar temple's gateway[19] with sockets for now-lost emplacements, including pylons, doors, obelisks, statuary, and four sphinxes, the last distinguished by typically curved backs and straight fronts as in the Metropolitan example (fig. 44). The Metropolitan sphinx could, with its pair, have served as symmetrically placed elements across two sides of such a model.[20] The larger of Seti I's now-lost sphinxes measured 22.6 cm (9 in) long[21] and 6.5 cm (2½ in)

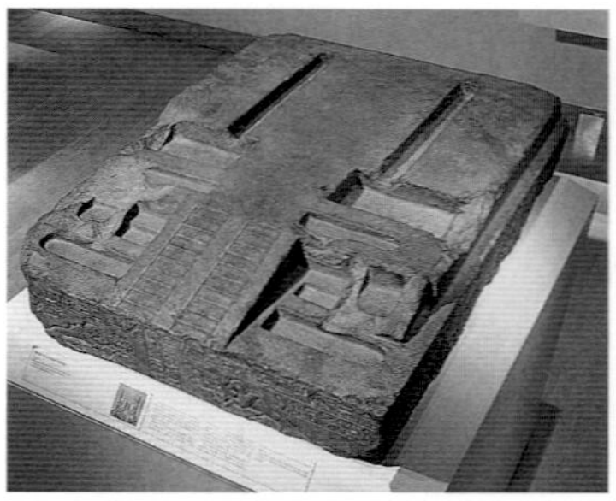

Fig. 44 A quartzite base from Tell el-Yahudiya, of the reign of Seti I, for a model of a temple's gateway with sockets for emplacements, including pylons, doors, obelisks, statuary, and sphinxes. (28.0 x 87.5 x 112.0 cm; the Brooklyn Museum of Art, Charles Edwin Wilbour Fund. 49.183.)

wide, dimensions very close to those of the Metropolitan sphinx, while the sockets for the smaller, slimmer sphinxes on the upper terrace were 20.0 cm (8 in) long and 4.5 cm (1¾ in) wide. Badawy has proposed that these would have been human-handed versions holding offering jars,[22] like the Amenhotep III example.

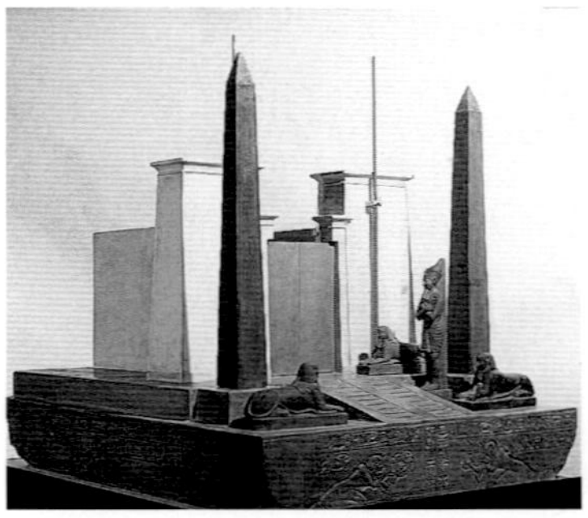

Fig. 45 Model of a gateway at Heliopolis. Reconstruction by Albert Fehrenbacher, from drawings by Alexander Badawy. Charles Edwin Wilbour Fund. 66.228. *Courtesy of the Brooklyn Museum of Art.*

Taking the Seti I base as a dimensional standard, such a model could easily have accommodated two Metropolitan sphinxes plus other architectural features,[23] some of which are said in the accompanying inscriptions around the Seti base to be made from stone and bronze.[24] Oddly, there is no mention on the Seti examples of the sphinxes and the royal statuary or their materials; nonetheless, the addition of faience elements would not be out of place.[25]

The sphinx's bright blue glaze and the inherent solar associations of its faience material would be appropriate aesthetically and symbolically for a temple model—albeit unknown—of Amenhotep III, a pharaoh who favored cobalt and copper blues in his faience and glass production,[26] who called himself the Dazzling Sun-King, and who produced an especially large number of sphinxes of varied sizes during his reign.[27] FDF

Bibliography. Hornemann 1951–69, vol. 6, pl. 1531; Sotheby's, New York, May 4, 1972, no. 344; *Burlington Magazine* 114, No. 829 (Apr. 1972), xlviii; *Art Quarterly* 36, Nos. 1–2 (1973), 112, 122; Vandersleyen 1975, pl. LIII; Lilyquist in Hoving 1975, pp. 107–10; Hibbard 1980, fig. 63, p.38; Baines and Málek 1980, p. 225; The Metropolitan Museum of Art Guide 1984, p. 100, fig. 31; Gold 1983 (plate); Dorman et al. 1987, p. 56; Kozloff and Bryan, 1992, cat. no. 32, pp. 223–24, also pl. 19, p. 230; Kozloff in Goring et al. 1997, p. 179, fig. 1, p. 192.

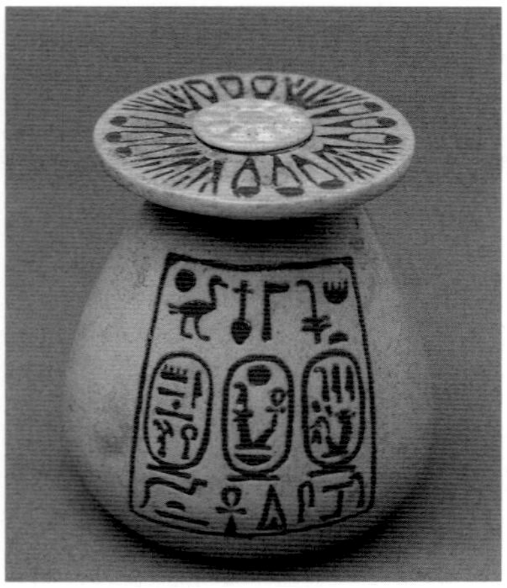

23 COSMETIC JAR INSCRIBED FOR KING AMENHOTEP III AND QUEEN TIYE

PAGE 81

New Kingdom, Dynasty 18, reign of Amenhotep III
Faience; H. 8.6 cm; DIAM. at mouth 6.15 cm
Musée du Louvre, Paris. E 4877
Ex-Collection: Alphonse Raifé (1867)

The reign of Amenhotep III, the father of Akhenaten, saw the manufacture of some of the most colorful and technically accomplished faience in Egyptian history. The craftsmen who worked for this king produced especially ambitious polychrome inlaid pieces, of which this cosmetic jar is a superb example. Its top is inlaid with four open lotuses interspersed with four groups of three closed lotus buds. Its button stopper, which fits well but not tightly, is decorated with a white daisy, a motif common on stone vessels and copied in faience. In shape the jar imitates the contemporary baggy flask, a vessel found in painted clay and its prototype, stone,[28] as well as examples in painted wood known from the tomb of Yuya and Thuya, Amenhotep III's in-laws.[29]

Instead of the more common blue-green *w3ḏ*-colors of freshness and new life, this jar is predominantly a rich yellow, more like that of egg-yolk than lemon. Blue glyphs are inlaid within a trapezoidal panel outlined in blue inlay across the front. In the panel are the names and titles of the king and his wife, Queen Tiye. The central column reads: "the Good God, Neb-Maat-Re" (the King's throne name) and the left column: "Son of Re, Amenhotep, ruler of Thebes." The standard royal phrase, "given life forever," extends beneath both these columns of the king's titles. The right column is for the queen and reads: "the King's wife, Tiye," with "may she be healthy" at the base of the column. Since Egyptian hieroglyphs can be written both right to left and left to right, the words and seated figure in the cartouches of the king face right, toward those of his queen, while hers, in turn, face those of the king.[30]

To the palette of yellow and blue, the lid adds inlaid red (in the 12 dots at the outer tips of the closed lotus buds) and apple green (four dots at the interior tips of the open lotus flowers), while the stopper[31] adds white (in the daisy), making this jar a five-tone faience masterwork. Though parallels with three colors exist, this is the only extant work that attempted the use of five colors.[32] Each color melted at a slightly different temperature, though not so different as to disrupt fusion with the body; nonetheless, achieving such color variation is a technological challenge (compare also [150]). As in so many faience works of Amenhotep III, the inlays remain today in almost perfect condition.[33]

Though royalty had at their disposal gold and semiprecious stones such as lapis, turquoise, or carnelian, the technological feat of producing a five-color faience work may have made it more valuable than gold, the very material alluded to by the yellow body. Yellow and red were also colors associated with the sun in Egyptian thinking[34] and thus reminiscent of King Amenhotep III's epithet as the Dazzling Sun-Disk (*'Itn ṯḥn*).[35]

This jar appears to be a container for eye paint (kohl), though there is no evidence that it was actually used since no residue is present.[36] Probably a tomb gift in imitation of utilitarian examples, this beautiful object reveals the luxurious aspect of royal cosmetic accouterments.[37] FDF

Bibliography. Pierret 1873, p. 88, no. 362; Wallis 1898, p. 9, fig. 16; Morant 1939; Goto 1968, p. 116, fig. 89; Vandier d'Abbadie 1972, p. 73, OT 240; Kozloff in Kozloff and Bryan 1992h, p. 398, cat. no. 100.

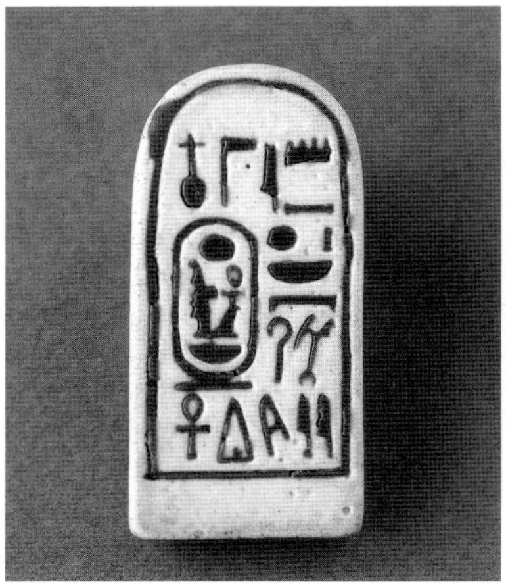

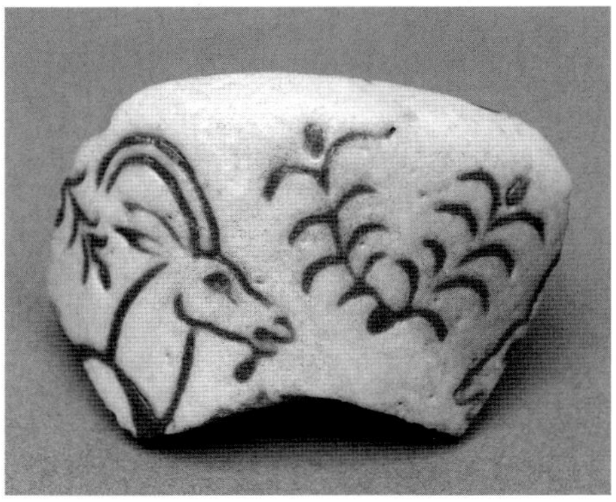

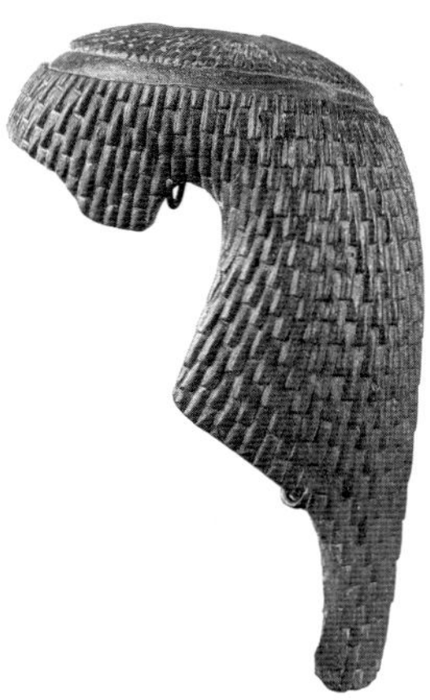

24 AMENHOTEP III BOOKPLATE PAGE 80

New Kingdom, Dynasty 18, reign of Amenhotep III
Polychrome faience; H. 4.3 cm; W. 2.04 cm; TH. 0.6 cm
Musée du Louvre, Paris. E 3043

Some people today claim ownership of a book with an "ex-libris" ("from the books of") bookplate inside the front cover, and some ancient Egyptian kings did likewise. Their books in the palace library took the form of papyrus rolls, stored for safe-keeping in boxes with the owner's name and sometimes that of the book written on the surface. Three faience examples of bookplates, including this one, are known for Amenhotep III,[38] and there is also one possible calcite example for Akhenaten, his successor.[39]

This faience bookplate, the finest of the group, bears the names and titles of Amenhotep III and his wife, Queen Tiye. The delicacy of the workmanship on this tiny object is extraordinary and the condition is excellent: the colors are as fresh as the day the object was made. Deep blue glyphs, some as small as 0.2 cm across (the sun-disk), have been sunk into a white body—blue and white being a favorite color scheme of this king[40]—with a white glaze thick and bubbly in places from the firing. The only slip by the craftsman occurred in the drawing of the upper left corner of the framing arch, where the blue has run beyond its intended border.[41]

This tiny round-topped object is inscribed with two vertical columns of glyphs. The left column is to be read first: "The good God, Neb-Maat-Re [the throne name of King Amenhotep III in the oval cartouche] given life." And the column to the right, which faces inward toward the left one, reads: "Beloved of [the god] Amun-Re, Lord of Heaven, Ruler of Thebes." The section for the book's name, which would have been at the bottom, is blank, and there are no holes for attaching the plate to a papyrus box.[42] It is therefore possible that this bookplate was meant for insertion into the wooden[43] lid of a storage box for an unnamed papyrus. FDF

Bibliography. Berman in Kozloff and Bryan 1992b, p. 399, no. 101.

25 VESSEL FRAGMENT WITH GAZELLES PAGE 90

New Kingdom, Dynasty 18, reign of Amenhotep III
Polychrome faience; max H. 3.9 cm; max W. 5.6 cm
The Metropolitan Museum of Art, New York. Purchase, Edward S. Harkness Gift, 1926. 26.7.954

Spirited images of desert gazelle and vegetation decorate this curved fragment from a faience vessel from the court of Amenhotep III. The work illustrates the king's preference for white with cobalt blue, a combination he used for objects jointly inscribed for himself and related court women, and less commonly for himself alone (see also [24]).[44] The vessel from which this fragment comes may thus once have been inscribed.

Breaks are often illuminating in revealing methods of faience manufacture; we see here how the cobalt blue is a separately colored faience paste let into the surface (fig. 46). Blue is the dominant inlay color with touches of red accenting the floral sprays, which are the focus of the grazing beasts on either side, though only a fragment of one beast can be seen to the right. The curving lines of the main gazelle's arched neck, horns, and ears are characteristic of the art of the period,[45] while the interest shown in capturing the gazelle's sensitive expression is well known in earlier Eighteenth Dynasty tomb paintings such as those of Userhet.[46] FDF

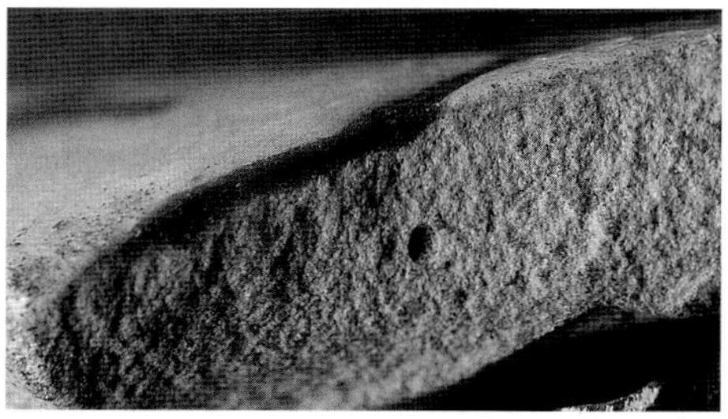

Fig. 46 Magnified detail of the section of a break in the vessel fragment, showing the insertion of blue inlay.

26 FEMALE WIG PAGE 83

New Kingdom, probably Dynasty 18
Egyptian blue; H. 19.8 cm; W. 13.3 cm; D. 6.0 cm
Private Collection

27 DIVINE WIG PAGE 82

Probably Third Intermediate Period, *c.* 1000–800 BC
Egyptian blue; H. 18.5 cm; W. 14.4 cm; D. 10.7 cm
Staatliche Museen zu Berlin - Preussischer Kulturbesitz Ägyptisches Museum und Papyrussammlung. 22726

Whatever the actual age of individuals, they were usually represented in art with taut young bodies, unlined faces and thick, black hair[47] in the form of a wig. In sculptural representations, a bit of natural hair sometimes peeps out under the wig at the forehead. Hair could be added as a separate element in composite statues, however, in which case it might be of another material and color, as with these two wigs in Egyptian blue. This is a material related to faience that, to the eye, is homogeneous throughout as opposed to faience with its thin glaze layer over a quartz body (see p. 55).

Stone votive statuettes from Amarna private homes and garden shrines illustrate the practice of adding the wigs and crowns of Akhenaten and Nefertiti in blue faience.[48] Compare the New Kingdom royal round wig also for a composite statue [28]. That blue faience and Egyptian blue were chosen for these wigs for the same symbolic reasons is illustrated by the fact that the Egyptian blue wig [26] has an identical mold-made counterpart in blue faience in a New York collection; the latter is a right profile while the one shown here is a left. It is probable that the faience and Egyptian blue wigs were made in the same royal workshop, the color being the key symbolic feature.

Belonging to an under-lifesize composite statue, [26] seems to have been intended for a relief figure, not a statuette in the round. From its resemblance to the wig of echeloned curls with fillet worn by Nefertiti in relief sculpture, it might date to the Amarna Period. Yet Nefertiti's wig is clearly a tripartite form with lappets falling over the breast. The wig here [26] has a lappet down the back but none over the breast, nor is there any indication that the piece ever had such an attachment.[49] A rectangular hole at the top, however, may possibly have been for a crown attachment, as on an Amarna queen's wig,[50] and there is a recess for a fillet around the top of the head.

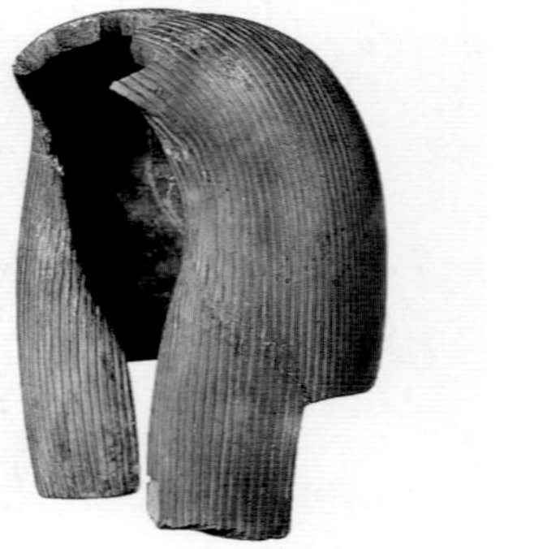

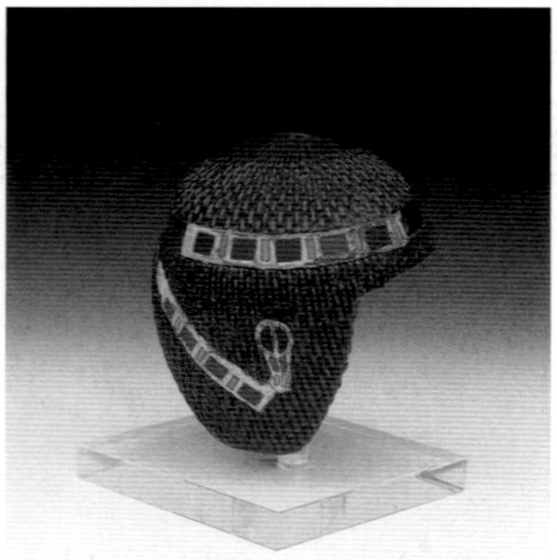

The Berlin wig [27], also from a composite statue, might at first be mistaken for a tripartite female wig. The shape of the opening at the forehead (as distinct from the minor damage in that area, where the Egyptian blue fabric is clearly discernible) shows, however, that the wig had attached to it a uraeus cobra, crown, and horns. That the wig was for a falcon-headed deity is suggested by the contour of the face and narrow neck areas.[51] The hair fitted closely the shape of the bird's face down to the chin area where it then gently swelled into cylindrical lappets over the god's human chest.

The statue to which [27] belonged was probably a metal figure of a bare-chested god commissioned by the king for a temple. It was probably clothed in a kilt, such as the silver seated cult statue of the falcon-headed deity in the Shumei Family Collection. On this figure the god's divine hair was of lapis lazuli with gilded striations.[52] On the Berlin example, the striations have been tooled into the ceramic before firing. At the back of the wig is a hole for fitting the piece to a backpillar, evidence that it was attached to a standing statue. Standing bronze statues of deities, about a meter high, do survive from the Third Intermediate Period, the suggested date for this wig.[53]

The two halves of the wig were made separately and are not perfectly symmetrical; the (viewer's) right side is slightly longer, and the parting at the top of the head is not centered—features that reveal the imperfect hands of the craftsmen in these temple workshop products. FDF

Bibliography. [26]: Christie's London 1994, Lot 52, p. 27. [27]: Schoske et al. 1990, p. 113, cat. no. 88.

28 ROUND WIG PAGE 83

New Kingdom, Dynasty 18–19; said to be from Thebes

Polychrome faience, glass and gilding; H. 9.5 cm

The Trustees of the British Museum, London. EA 2280

The round wig with ringlet curls was a common Nubian-influenced hairstyle worn by both men and women in the New Kingdom.[54] Among kings and queens it was found with or without a diadem and a surmounting crown, as illustrated on numerous stone reliefs and statues of royalty from the New Kingdom[55] through Ptolemaic times.[56] Fragments of such wigs also exist in faience,[57] though complete examples in the round such as this extraordinary example are rare, much less one with such well preserved glaze.

The wig's glossy blue—the color of the gods' hair—is consistently found in fragments of faience crowns and wigs from the Amarna Period,[58] thus suggesting a possible date for the piece. In its original context it must have been part of a dazzling multicolored composite statue of a king or queen (or possibly a prince or princess). The statue it belonged to, probably of wood, would have been emblazoned with color through the use of multimedia additions, including inlays of faience[59] and other materials such as glass or jasper. Ancient plaster covers the interior of the wig, revealing how it was attached to the statue's head; a hole, which seems original, is in the interior top of the wig, an expected feature for a tenon for a crown,[60] especially since a crown was probably intended to surmount the wig.[61] Yet the hole does not extend through to the exterior. There is, however, a small square area on the top bare of glaze on which some attachment may have been fixed, such as a horned *atef* crown. Such a crowned wig may also have been for a figure of a god.

The inlaid gilded plaster diadem with streamers, set in a channel above the brow of the wig, mimics a golden ribbon. Polychrome rectangular glass inlays are in red, to imitate carnelian, alternating with robin's egg blue, to imitate turquoise. Their colorful pattern of broad and narrow inlays against the gold is repeated on the diadem worn by Tutankhamun on the back of his throne.[62] A uraeus (cobra), symbol of royalty, originally reared up at the front.[63] The inlaid headband and streamers were once "tied" in a bow of lotus blossoms at the back[64] in a pattern already a thousand years old, deriving from Old Kingdom boatmen's headgear and in turn based on plant forms.[65] The pendant streamers ended in inlaid blue glass uraei (cobras), though only that on the proper right is preserved.[66]

The round wig was especially popular in the Ramesside Period,[67] both in relief and in the round. When it occurs in the round on statues of Ramesses II and Seti II, however, it is heavily undercut at the brow,[68] a contour differing from that of this wig.[69] Round wigs on examples of statues of Ramesses II could also be surmounted by the double crown, *atef*, or solar disk.[70] This wig, which most probably had a crown attachment, lacks the deep undercutting of Ramesside examples but nonetheless finds one of its best parallels in a figure of Ramesses II from Abu Simbel, which shows him wearing the round wig surmounted by the double crown in a coronation (sed?) festival.[71]

Probably produced in a Theban palace workshop, the wig was small enough to be mold-made in one piece. Given the lack of glaze in many crevices between the curls it was probably glazed by efflorescence.[72] The wig's interior, which seems to have been strengthened by extra application glaze, was covered by plaster, with the bright blue showing through only along the curved, interior edges that remained visible when the wig was set on the head of its statue. FDF

Bibliography. McNaught 1978, p. 231, fig. 14.

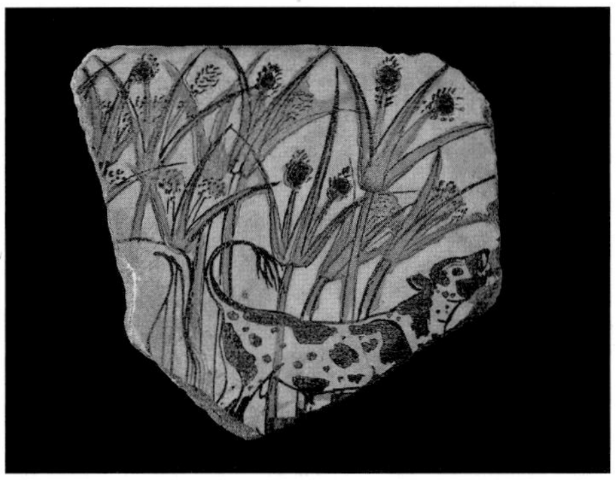

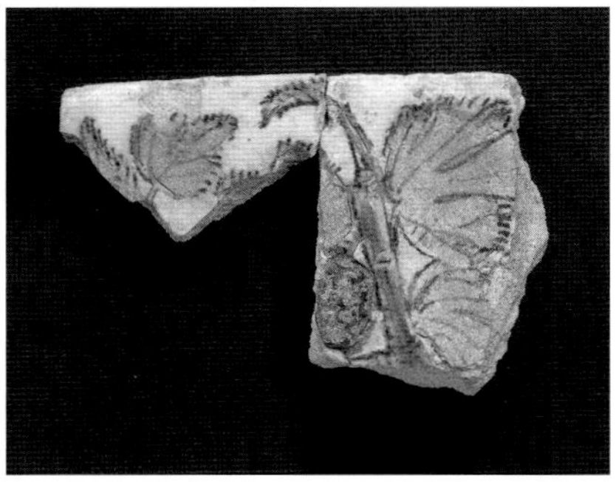

33 CATTLE AMONG REEDS PAGE 88

New Kingdom, Dynasty 18, reign of Akhenaten; Amarna

Polychrome faience; H 10.8 cm; W. 11.4 cm; TH. 2.0 cm

Musée du Louvre, Paris. Alphonse Kahn Bequest 1949. E 17357

This fragment of a rectangular tile with its charming vignette of two bovines grazing in a marshy landscape uses a white faience background to set off colorful inlays. The artist has created a figurative scene, capturing a single peaceful moment infused with life.[99]

A mild breeze blows the reeds to the right; a bullock, with legs stretched backward, lifts his head to nibble a stalk and flicks his tail; a companion faces in the opposite direction. A single green stalk placed in front of the calf's body sets the animals in the midst of the plants. The larger animal with hanging tail is portrayed in a brown manganese outline and wash and the calf is depicted with a single fluid brown outline and black dapples.

Rarely in Egyptian art are living creatures represented with such candor or so well integrated into an environment. Earlier scenes of freely moving animals treat the plants as an isolated motif.[100] But at Amarna, many murals show calves in a landscape portrayed in realistic perspective.[101]

Faience inlays and bright colors had previously been used only on vessels and other objects. Here the marsh grasses are formed of green inlay for stalks and leaves and red accents for the blossoms. The plant shown so naturalistically with curling leaves and central tufted blossom appears frequently in Amarna mural paintings.[102] Recent technological advances had made it possible to recreate in faience such scenes using new pigments produced with lead compounds for the soft natural greens and brilliant red hues.[103]

Other rectangular tiles, such as a fragment now in Cairo showing the back of another black dappled calf in an identical setting,[104] suggest the original context and purpose of this one. It is possible a series of such tiles may have been used to form a dado for one or more rooms.

A third tile with its base preserved shows a dappled calf with golden markings standing on a thick black ground line from which similar reeds grow.[105] This ground line, a standard convention in Egyptian art for the embankment of a pond, thus places the tile in the same milieu as the mural paintings of calves in marshes bordering a pool. The faience tiles, like the mural paintings,[106] may have symbolic content with themes suitable for rooms of state and they may have adorned rooms used in state functions.[107] Scenes of pools surrounded by animals in the marshes appear to have had special value, emphasizing the teeming life within the cosmic order provided by Pharaoh[108] — a natural world given life through his auspices. BC

Bibliography. Vandier 1950, p. 25, fig. 1; Desroches-Noblecourt 1963, p. 165, fig. 97; Musée du Louvre 1967, p. 23, no. 107 with ill on p. 34; Vandier 1967, p. 308, fig. 11; Aldred 1973, no. 86, p. 158; Leclant 1980, fig. 97, p. 113; Vermeule 1981, p. 193, fig. 4; Musée du Louvre 1987, no. 73; Ziegler 1990, p. 50 top, right.

34 TILE WITH GRAPE VINE PAGE 88

New Kingdom, Dynasty 18, reign of Akhenaten; Amarna

Polychrome faience; H. 5.6 cm; W. 8.5 cm

Staatliche Museen zu Berlin - Preussischer Kulturbesitz Ägyptisches Museum und Papyrussammlung. 30552

35 TILE WITH WILD CAPER LEAVES PAGE 88

New Kingdom, Dynasty 18, reign of Akhenaten; Amarna

Polychrome faience; H. 4.1 cm; W. 8.0 cm

Staatliche Museen zu Berlin - Preussischer Kulturbesitz Ägyptisches Museum und Papyrussammlung. 30541

These two semicircular faience tiles[109] with botanically accurate plant depictions were found in houses at Amarna[110] and illustrate that site's innovations in skillfully painted designs in bright, naturalistic colors inlaid on white backgrounds.

The first tile depicts the Egyptian domesticated grape vine[111] and combines green inlay for the leaves and woody stalk and a bright blue for the grape cluster with warm brown glaze overpainting. The artist depicts a growing vine with the top leaf beginning to unfurl, while other leaves appear at different angles in natural perspective. To create this composition, the technician who set the inlay into the tile worked closely with the draftsman who planned the design and added details with freehand painting in glaze around the areas of inlay.

Naturalistic depictions of grape vines occur in other media at this site, but in those examples the plant is not the exclusive focus as here, where it is free of context or symbolic content.[112]

The second tile shows the wild caper (*Capparis aegyptia*),[113] a plant indigenous to Egypt that produces an edible ovoid fruit. Green inlay with brown outlines and details portrays the moment when the fruit is forming. The depiction is true to nature, showing the precise form of the heart-shaped leaves and the green fruit with vertical striations, all in perspective. Indeed, in the center it captures a precise moment of growth, with a new fruit swelling from the flower at its end.[114] This shrub is suited to a rocky environment and must have grown in the vicinity of Amarna.

These faience tiles are part of a group of semicircular polychrome examples that portrayed a range of Egyptian plants, including reeds, lupin, and the

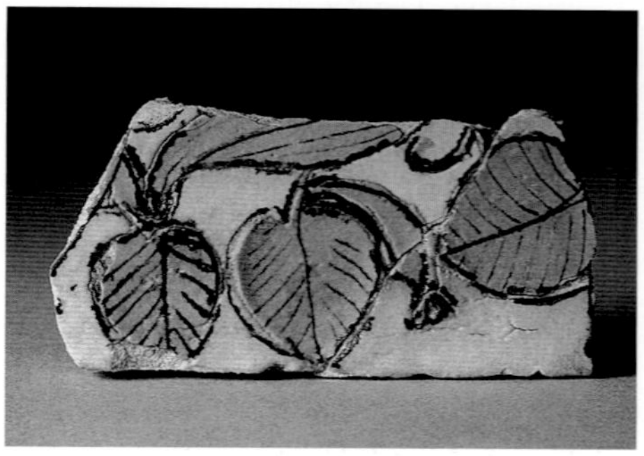

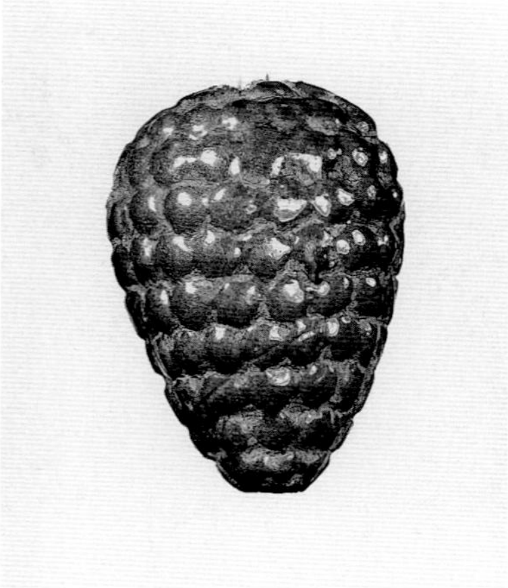

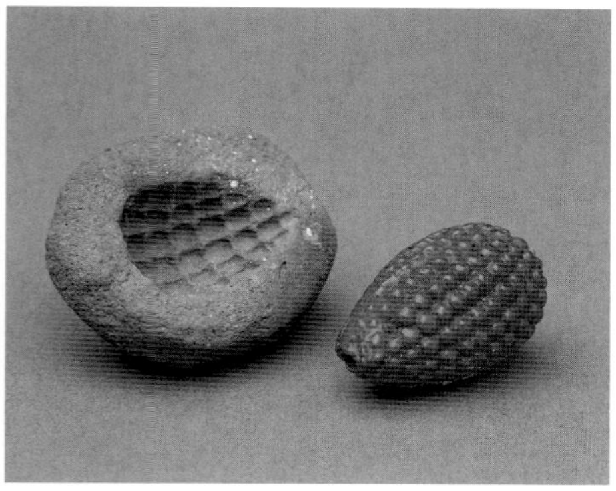

dom-palm.[115] Many such tiles were found scattered among poor houses in the northern Amarna suburb. But since most scholars believe the tiles were intended for important buildings, it is thought that later looters probably brought them to this secondary location.[116] Given the variations in size and thickness of these tiles, they could have served as decoration in several buildings, possibly inlaid into stone.[117] BC

Bibliography. [34]: Berlin 1991, no. 77, p. 126; Schoske et al. 1992, no. 14f, p. 83; Freeman 1997, p. 59. [35]: Schoske et al. 1992, no. 14g, p. 83.

36 GRAPE CLUSTER PAGE 89

New Kingdom

Blue faience; H. 5.9 cm; W. 4.1 cm

Staatliche Museen zu Berlin – Preussischer Kulturbesitz Ägyptisches Museum und Papyrussammlung. 21971

37 GRAPE CLUSTER PAGE 89

New Kingdom, Dynasty 18, reign of Akhenaten; Amarna

Blue faience; L. 3.7 cm; W. 2.3 cm

Petrie Museum of Egyptian Archaeology, University College London. UC.23267

38 MOLD FOR GRAPE CLUSTER PAGE 89

New Kingdom, Dynasty 18, reign of Akhenaten; Amarna

Terra-cotta: fired alluvial clay; H. 0.9 cm; W. 4.0 cm; L. 5.0 cm

Petrie Museum of Egyptian Archaeology, University College London. UC.1703

The three-dimensional bunch of ripe grapes in deep blue faience was a highly symbolic architectural ornament. Its typical stylized form has symmetrical contours and a uniform pattern of grapes in relief. This convention can be seen in New Kingdom art in the schematic rendering of the grape cluster as an oval with a series of blue dots in grape-harvesting scenes in tomb paintings and in the depictions of trellised and pendant grapes in scenes associated with regeneration, kingship, and divinity. Faience grape bunches of the type shown here have been found at a number of New Kingdom sites, often in association with palaces.

The grape cluster's standardized form was made possible by the New Kingdom use of the mold, which permitted mass production. The only variables are size and post-molding modifications. It was made of two identical parts which were removed from the mold, partly dried, and joined with slurry before firing. The join line is almost always visible:[118] no effort was made to disguise it because these items were meant to be viewed from a distance. Richer blues[119] developed at Amarna and other sites enhanced the distinctive appearance of the grape cluster in the New Kingdom.

Unless grape clusters are found through excavation, like the example from Amarna [37] here, establishing provenance can be difficult because this classic type is not site-specific. At Amarna, where many grape clusters were manufactured, they were probably intended for important buildings or shrines, although they are found in scattered locations throughout the site.[120] Additional examples have been excavated at the New Kingdom palace or temple palace sites of Malkata, Gurob, Qantir, the Palace of Merneptah at Memphis, and Medinet Habu, where they probably served the same functions.[121]

Faience examples specifically adapted for attachment establish their architectural use. Some have a suspension ring inserted at the top,[122] while others were modified after molding—the upper half of one side was cut off and holes were pierced in the other for attachment to a beam.[123] This type was used frequently at later palace sites.[124]

Pendant grapes occur as a decorative motif in Amarna temple reliefs.[125] The special significance of faience grapes in an architectural context may be seen in their use in scenes connected with royalty. A row of pendant grapes is first found in the reign of Amenhotep II, with very clearly depicted grape clusters hanging from the baldachin of the royal kiosk.[126] After this time, important scenes of kings and gods in tomb paintings and papyri, and on temple walls are framed at the top by a line of pendant grape clusters portrayed in colorful detail or reduced to an oval outline.

The pendant grape creates an arbor-like setting, and ripe grapes on the royal kiosk could signify fertility and well-being. But the grape cluster may have become an emblem of royal and divine superiority as a symbol of the higher status and good fortune of one who sits within the framing arbor reviewing the toil of others.[127]

Petrie collected this mold, along with its faience grape cluster, at Amarna in order to create a type series, reflecting his interest in faience technology. This site was ideal for creating his typology of 500 forms (from a total of 5,000 molds and 200 positives), for duplicates of each form were preserved in abundance, by contrast with the meager numbers found at other sites. After distributing sets of each type to museums he kept in reserve additional examples like this mold and grape cluster.[128] Similar molds are known from other New Kingdom sites.[129]

Since each grape cluster was formed of two halves created in open molds, it is probable that many sets of identical molds were in use at the same time. Any alterations to the basic form were always made after the molding stage. For the New Kingdom faience

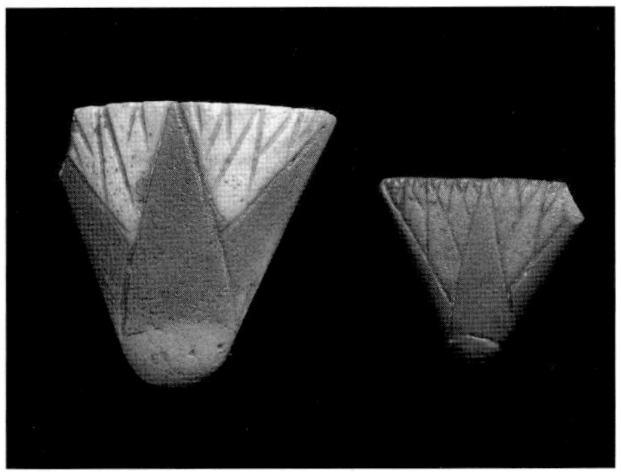

grape cluster, the mold was an essential tool, permitting both production in quantity and a standardized appearance suited to specific royal contexts. BC

Bibliography. [36]: Schoske et al. 1992, no. 22.b, p. 91. [37]: Nicholson 1993, p. 33, fig. 25.

39 BLUE LOTUS A PAGE 86

New Kingdom, Dynasty 18; probably from Amarna
Polychrome faience; H. 3.8 cm; W. 3.7 cm; D 0.5 cm
Private Collection

40 BLUE LOTUS B PAGE 86

New Kingdom; probably from Amarna
Polychrome faience; H. 2.6 cm; W. 2.7 cm; D. 0.4 cm
Private Collection

These two small Amarna plaques both take the form of the blue lotus, a flower with sharply pointed petals that opened each day with the rising sun. For the Egyptians this flower had magical associations with renewal and in Egyptian art and literature it is commonly represented growing in shallow waters and ponds that "shine with flowers."[130] The plaques here portray the flower with three green sepals rising from a yellow calyx to frame a cluster of petals. In fact the petals on the larger lotus are too white and those of the smaller too blue to match the lotus's canonical representation. In the New Kingdom faience industry, however, a wide range of sizes, styles, and technical variations were used to produce this popular motif.

Both were made in molds from a white-bodied faience paste (see [185]).[131] The details of the lotus blossom were added by incision alone on the larger lotus, as shown by the crossing of lines. On the smaller lotus it is unclear whether the details derived primarily from the mold or incision with a sure hand. The calyxes of both were inlaid with a yellow paste, probably colored by lead antimonate, and the sepals brushed with a glaze slurry probably derived from a mixture of lead antimonate and copper, as seen by the diffusion of an aura of copper blue onto the white.[132] The smaller lotus had an additional copper blue glaze added to the petals. The artist of this lotus seems to have been heavy handed with the glazes—the green extends across the edge of the calyx and entirely across the back and a drip of blue glaze crosses over the sepals on the left side. The larger plaque is convex, whether intentionally or accidentally, giving it a three-dimensional appearance.

The more standard type of lotus plaque, like Blue Lotus A, was used for several different purposes. It was adapted for jewelry by the addition of holes along the edge for stringing, or could be inlaid into larger faience compositions on tiles.[133] Some examples were directly inlaid into another surface.[134] At Amarna the use of this type of plaque in architecture is suggested by the popularity there of the pendant lotus as a decorative form,[135] alternating with other plants suspended above the head of the king.[136] Some of the plaques were created for use in a particular type of polychrome frieze, noted by Petrie at Amarna, which was composed of the pendant faience lotus alternating with a plaque of red faience with centered polychrome buds.[137] Such friezes were made in a range of sizes.[138] An identical painted frieze composed of these two elements appears in the tomb of Huy, dating to just after the Amarna Period, and illustrates how such faience plaques would have looked. BC & ML

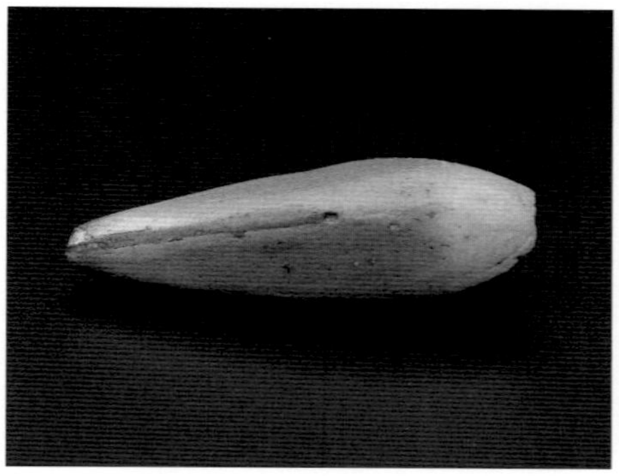

41 LOTUS BUD PAGE 86

New Kingdom, Dynasty 18; probably from Amarna

Polychrome faience; H. 5.5 cm W. 1.5 cm

Museum of Fine Arts, Boston. Gift in Memory of Dows Dunham. 1988.339

This three-dimensional blue lotus bud in polychrome faience is a rare, well-preserved architectural ornament. The sepals, with slightly flattened sides, are a deep, naturalistic green, defined by four lines of cobalt blue faience inlaid flush with the surface. These lines give a hint of the blue petals that lie beneath.[139] The calyx is made of bright yellow faience set into the base, with a deep hole for attachment.[140]

A similar three-dimensional faience bud from Amarna also has a hole in the base and probably served the same purpose.[141] At that site a variety of buds of this design and exact color combination were created in a range of sizes, not only in three dimensions but also in convex and flat forms.[142] Buds were also set into the center of flat red plaques.[143] While other three-dimensional faience architectural ornaments, such as the blue uraeus and grape cluster [37], appear at many sites, buds of this type seem to be associated primarily with Amarna.

The new shades of yellow and green faience that derived from lead antimonate were used at Amarna for many types of objects.[144] These pigments made it possible to reproduce the color conventions used in mural paintings. In pond and canal scenes at Amarna and in Theban tombs, buds flank the lotus symmetrically or float nearby. In some cases they have closed sepals indicated by deep blue lines, in others the buds are beginning to open, with the blue petals emerging at the top.[145]

The design of buds flanking a lotus appears frequently in Egyptian art.[146] It is the natural accompaniment to the lotus and on a symbolic level it reinforces the regenerative meaning of the lotus, with its element of anticipation.[147]

It is likely that this bud was an ornament on a shrine or in an architectural setting designed for royalty. One suggestion is that such buds would have been suspended in a row from a baldachin above the throne[148] in a pattern of pendant buds and lotus flowers well known at Amarna.[149] However, these buds have not been found in sufficient quantity to support that theory, and it is more likely that they were used in pairs on the lotus columns of the throne dais. At the palace of Malkata wooden buds were inlaid on either side of a doorway.[150]

Depictions of the columns of the royal kiosk often have lotiform capitals, frequently with two buds that are sometimes shown with long stems tied to the capital.[151] While lotiform capitals are depicted more rarely in the Amarna Period, two examples clearly show such a column with flanking buds, in one case with the vertical line indicating the sepal explicitly marked.[152] BC

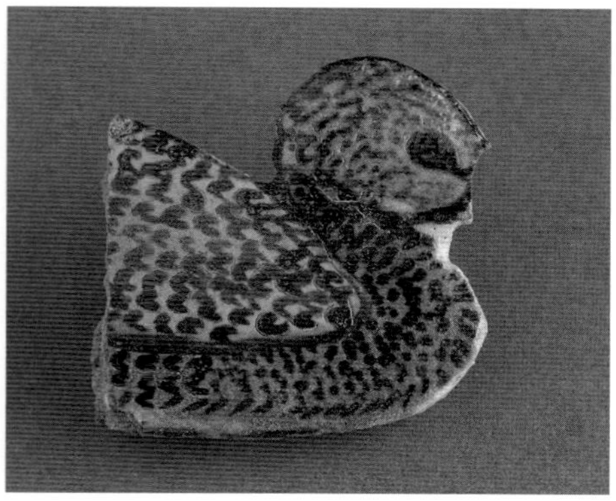

42 DUCK INLAY FRAGMENT PAGE 90

New Kingdom, Dynasty 18, reign of Akhenaten; Amarna

Polychrome faience; H. 4.5 cm; W. 4.6 cm; TH. 0.75 cm

Petrie Museum of Egyptian Archaeology, University College London. UC.509

This fragmentary duck inlay is an artistic tour-de-force.[153] For such inlays master artists must have worked in cooperation with technical assistants to create fluid lines and patterns reminiscent of Amarna mural paintings. Yet the choice of colors and washes owes much to the painting style perfected earlier at Thebes, for instance in the marsh scene in the tomb of Menna (TT 69).[154] It is as if artists trained at Thebes had turned their hands to creating the faience inlays at Amarna.[155]

The duck's shape was probably formed in a mold,[156] and the piece was then laid on a textile, as indicated by impressions of cloth on the back.[157] Additional glazes were applied to the surface before firing. The grey-blue glaze on the breast contrasts effectively with the yellow of the wings and head.[158] Warm brown glaze was used to paint the eye, the bird's outline and the feather pattern, with its three-dimensional appearance. Incision emphasized the separation between the body and the wing, which is built up in a thicker glaze.[159] A further combing of the glaze in selected areas has produced a rippled effect.[160]

It is not known exactly how this inlay was used, although the mortar that attached it to its support is still preserved on the underside. Some inlays were intended as architectural decoration,[161] while others, generally thinner, were used on furniture and other wooden objects. Similar inlays were incorporated into larger faience compositions.[162] Ducks were a popular motif in the Eighteenth Dynasty and were found in a number of contexts such as in the form of cosmetic spoons[163] as well as depicted in pond[164] and marsh scenes.[165] BC

Bibliography: Burlington Fine Arts Club 1922, p. 32, pl. XL (g); Samson 1972, pp. 69, 91, pl. VII; Nicholson 1993, p. 32, fig. 23.

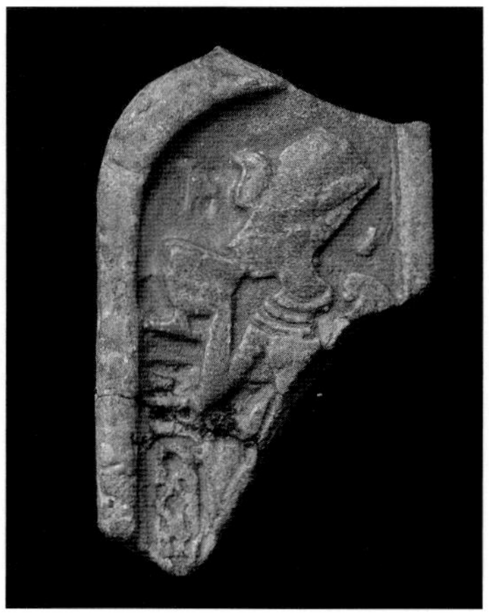

43 COLLAR TERMINAL PAGE 91

New Kingdom, Dynasty 18, reign of Tutankhamun
Faience; H. 3.9 cm; W. 2.5 cm; D. 0.4 cm
Myers Museum, Eton College, with Permission of the Provost and Fellows. Bequest of Major W.J. Myers, 1899. ECM 1887

Terminals for broad, multi-stringed, beaded collars are found in a number of different forms—most commonly semicircular or falcon-headed. They are made in a variety of materials, most frequently in easily produced faience for presentation as gifts by pharaoh to his subjects on festal occasions.

The form of this particular collar terminal seems originally to have been asymmetrical, and is unusual both in subject matter and in technique. It shows, in high raised relief, a (seated?) king wearing the *khepresh* crown in the act of drinking from a white-lotus chalice (easily recognizable by its relatively shallow form).[166] The subject is identified by a single column of hieroglyphs incised, somewhat crudely, into the recessed background before firing: "The good god, lord of the Two Lands, Nebkheprure [...]." NR

Bibliography. Tait 1963, p. 97, fig. 1; Reeves 1990a, p. 29.

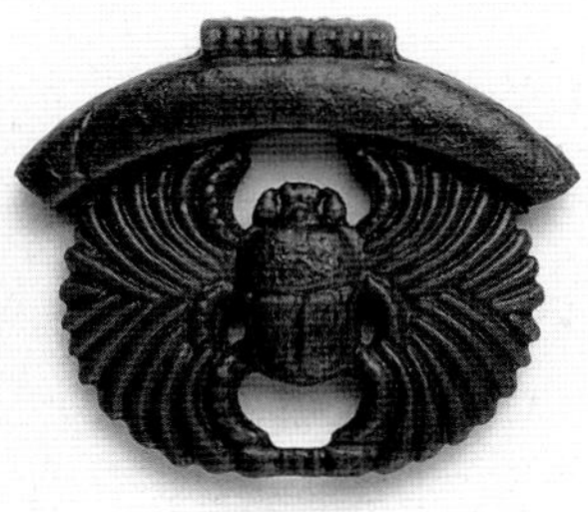

44 WINGED SCARAB PAGE 85

New Kingdom, Dynasty 18
Faience; max. H. 3.6 cm; max. W. 3.0 cm
Julia Schottlander, London
Ex-Collection: J.J. Acworth

This beautiful dark blue faience amulet, molded on both faces, represents the common solar symbol of the winged scarab. A ribbed suspension tube lies along the top of a downward-facing crescent moon (its ends broken), from which is suspended a scarab. Its elaborate spreading wings formed from radiating ridged sections reflect the curves of the legs; its head and the divisions of its back are well defined, and both the body and legs have markings indicating hairs. The back legs stand on a flat mat with vertical grooves.

A parallel amulet with similar wing configurations but lacking the crescent is firmly dated to the Amarna Period[167] and it can also be compared with collar elements in the Metropolitan Museum of Art, New York, dated to the reign of Tutankhamun. In a number of pieces of Tutankhamun's jewelry, the sun disk that forms part of the writing of his prenomen, or throne name, is replaced by a moon disc and crescent; perhaps a similar cryptography is at play here. CA

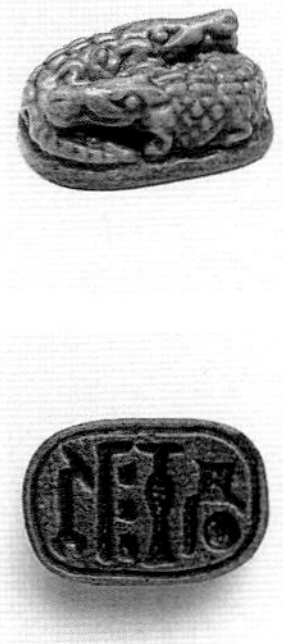

45 CROCODILE SCARAB PAGE 90

New Kingdom
Faience; H. 1.0 cm; W. 1.7 cm; L. 2.5 cm
Julia Schottlander, London

This scaraboid of rich bluish-green faience has two crocodiles lying head-to-tail and carved in high relief forming the back. The oval base on which they recline is pierced through its length for suspension. On the underside incised hieroglyphs read *ìmȝḫ ḥs nṯrw Wȝst*, which can be interpreted as "revered and praised [before] the gods of Thebes" referring to the scaraboid's wearer, or "the gods of Thebes are revered and praised," a statement of religious content typical on scarabs and scaraboids of the period.

As an amulet, the crocodile might either represent the god Sobek, be symbolic of regeneration or, acting apotropaically, ward off evil. However, since the Twelfth Dynasty two crocodiles could be used as a playful rendering of the word for "sovereign," and it might well be the royal interpretation that is to be understood in this case. CA

Bibliography. Ruffle 1988, no. 29.

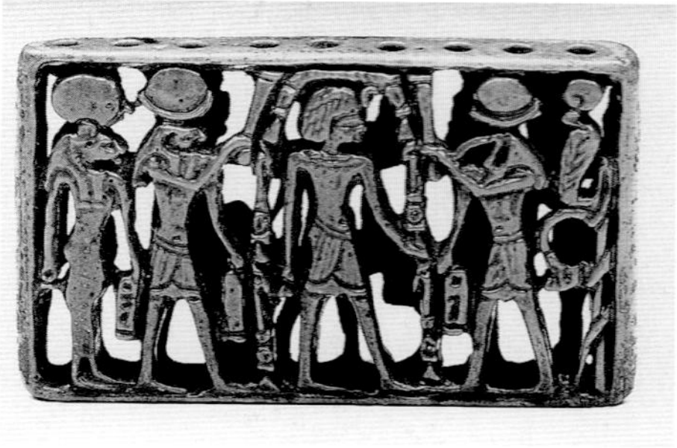

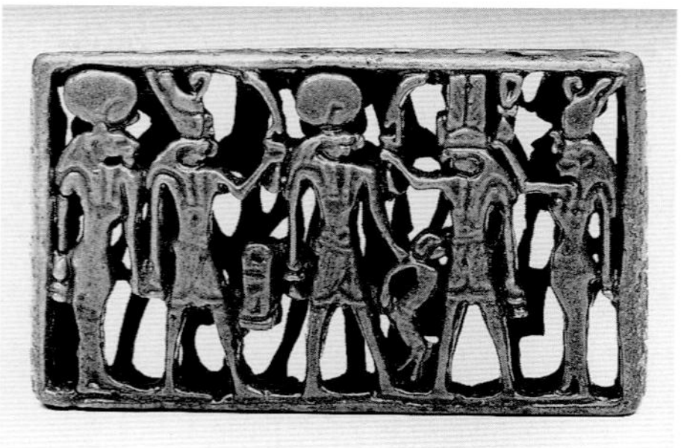

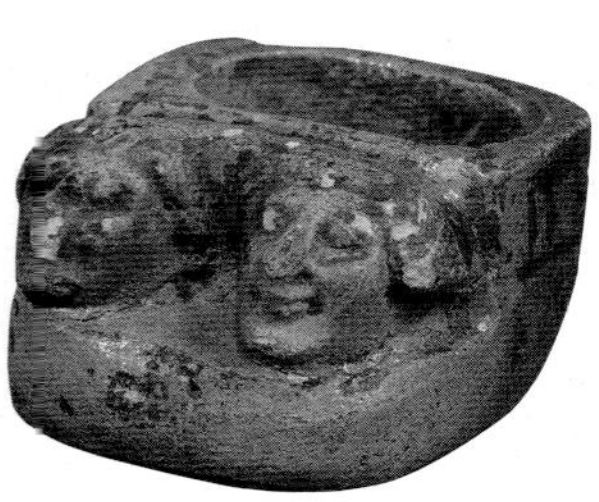

46 SPACER BEAD FOR A NECKLACE

PAGE 95

Third Intermediate Period, 9th to 8th century BC; possibly from Tuna el-Gebel

Faience; L. 5.4 cm; H. 3.2 cm; TH. 0.6 cm

The Trustees of the British Museum, London. EA 14556

Spacer beads, common in Egyptian jewelry since the Old Kingdom (see [100]), were not merely decorative but also served a function: as bars or plaques they were strung at intervals along the length of a necklace, choker, or anklet, or at the terminal points, to keep the strings from sagging and tangling.[168]

The beads often had as subjects[169] either the youthful or rejuvenated king or the subjugation of foreign enemies. In the politically fragmented times of the Third Intermediate Period, royal themes that had traditionally been depicted on temple and palace walls or inscribed in funerary texts now found new and smaller fields for expression, such as these spacer beads.[170] With images of the ever-youthful, powerful king who ruled under the eternal protection of the gods, the beads may allude more specifically to a coronation theme.[171] This interpretation is in keeping with the suggestion that some or all such openwork spacers were made to celebrate the New Year at Hermopolis (Tuna el-Gebel), the possible production site of openwork faience spacers and related relief chalices of the Third Intermediate Period.[172]

Two scenes, essentially amuletic in purpose, are presented on this spacer bead. On the obverse is a figure of a king in the center, facing right, wearing a broad collar and kilt, with a uraeus at the brow of his wig; he is flanked by the gods Horus on the left and Thoth on the right, who pour streams of purifying, vivifying waters over him in a reference to his coronation. A lioness goddess (Sekhmet) stands to the far left, with a cobra on a papyrus to the right.

On the reverse is a central figure of Horus, a falcon-deity with sun-disk, holding in his left hand a bound and cowering prisoner. Flanking deities that aid in this typically royal triumph are, on the right, Montu in double plumes and Mut in double crown, waving a sistrum; and on the left, Horus in a double crown, and a lion-headed goddess,[173] possibly again Sekhmet, wearing the sun-disk.

Technically, the spacer is a miniature marvel that illustrates an extraordinary ability to produce small-scale, openwork figural pieces through free-hand carving.[174] Although the actual method of manufacture is unknown, we can make conjectures based on RISD replication experiments. The two faces of the bead's design were cut separately from a thin, flat slab of faience paste.[175] Additional details could have been made with fine modeling tools. When nearly dry, the two sides were held together by the faience frame. Seam lines at two diagonal corners of the frame suggest that it is made from two L-shaped sections that were joined. To facilitate assembly of the panels and frame, a thin rectangle of organic material like wood, papyrus, or cartonnage could have been used as a rigid support between the panels that would later fire out. Such a support would also have prevented shifting or slumping of the tiny figures during firing. A slurry of faience paste with the addition of gum or glue could have served to adhere the cut-out panels to the frame. The stringing holes, nine at the top but oddly ten at the bottom, would have been pierced with a sharp tool before firing.

When dry, the bead would have been painted with a glaze slurry with a copper colorant that fired to bright blue. The artisan also sharpened some contours before firing for carved areas are visible on the interior of some of the figures. FDF & ML

Bibliography. Tait 1963, p. 130, iv, pl. XXIV, 4; Andrews 1994, p. 101, fig. 101 c.

47 INKWELL INSCRIBED WITH THE NAME OF HOREMHEB

PAGE 91

New Kingdom, end of Dynasty 18 to early Dynasty 19

Faience; H. 3.0 cm; W. 5.1 cm; D. 5.3 cm

Staatliche Sammlung Ägyptischer Kunst, Munich. ÄS 7121

The image of prisoners suppressed beneath the literal or metaphorical weight of the king is a common motif in royal art and architecture throughout Egyptian history. Already present in late Predynastic art, this propagandistic declaration of royal power appears at Hierakonpolis in a Second Dynasty stone door socket in the form of a bound prisoner,[176] and in expanded form in the Third Dynasty stone corbel with prisoner heads from Djoser's Step Pyramid complex.[177] The motif is popular on New Kingdom objects ranging from the innersoles of Tutankhamun's sandals, which allowed the king to trample his enemies at every step,[178] to the faience tiles of bound prisoners from the later Ramesside palace and mortuary temple at Tell el-Yahudiya and at Medinet Habu [52–54].

This little inkwell's curved base is decorated with the heads of two prisoners,[179] a miniature version of the ancient door socket motif but also reminiscent, when viewed frontally, of yet another, and later, prisoner motif: the row of stone prisoner heads beneath the Window of Appearances at Medinet Habu of the reign of Ramesses III.[180] The shape of the inkwell's opening is a cartouche, the oval form used in inscriptions to hold the king's name. Thus the king's presence is implied, as though he stands above and suppresses the prisoners below. The inscription on the bowl names the owner as Horemheb, a remarkable man of non-royal blood who, after being Great Commander of the Army, became the Eighteenth Dynasty's last king. The greenish-yellow color of the faience is in keeping with such a post-Amarna to early Ramesside date.[181]

Horemheb himself may have used this inkwell, which through sympathetic magic guaranteed his ritualistic if not actual victory over foreigners, Egypt's eternal symbols of chaos.[182] FDF

Bibliography. Munich 1995, pp. 193; 198 (notes).

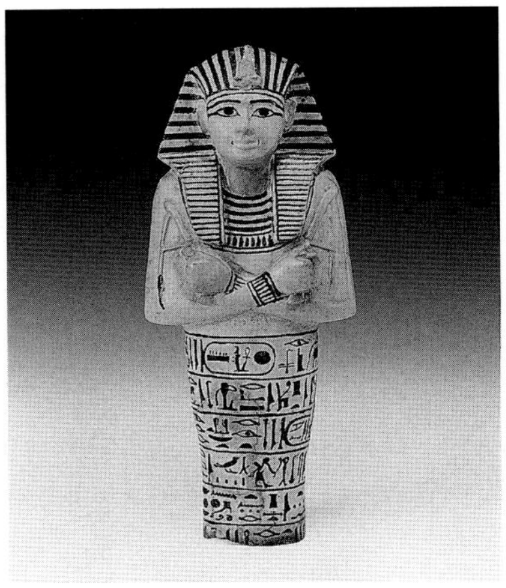

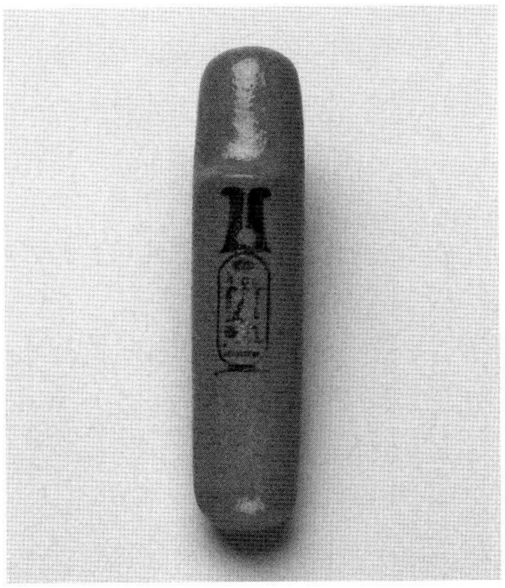

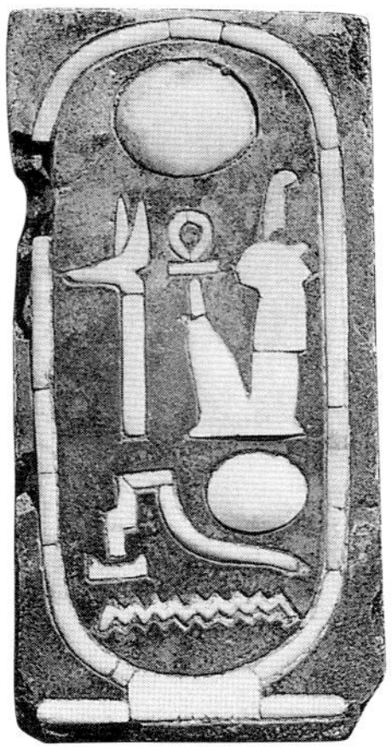

48 SHABTI OF KING SETI I — PAGE 94

New Kingdom, Dynasty 19, reign of Seti I; Valley of the Kings (KV 17), Western Thebes

Faience; H. 22.4 cm; max W. 9.6 cm

The Trustees of the British Museum, London. EA 22818

Given the simplicity of molding faience figurines and the symbolic properties of faience connected with rebirth, we would expect to see numerous faience shabtis in most periods. Yet kings from Ay, at the end of the Eighteenth Dynasty, to Ramesses I, at the beginning of the Nineteenth, seem to have produced none.[183] Seti I, however, resumes the use of shabtis on an unprecedented scale.[184] Scattered throughout his tomb in the Valley of the Kings were hundreds of wooden or glossy blue faience shabtis, possibly the largest gang of substitute workmen ever made.[185] Only a few surviving faience examples are as fine as this one, however, despite the loss of the lower legs.[186]

With details painted in black (probably manganese dioxide), Seti I is shown wearing the striped royal *nemes* headcloth, once equipped with a rearing cobra above his brow, a broad collar that imitates faience beads (see [100] and [103] for actual faience examples), and bracelets that also would have been of faience. In each hand he holds a hoe,[187] and from over his proper left shoulder hangs a rectangular grain bag[188] —agricultural instruments recalling the function of such shabtis as servants for manual labor in the Beyond (compare [152]). The tasks are enumerated in the carefully drawn bands of text drawn from Chapter 6 of the Book of the Dead. As pharaoh, Seti would surely not have been required to do such tasks as hauling sand or digging ditches, however, and this shabti must be viewed as the servant of the king who wears the name and emblems of his master.[189]

Though mold-made, details of the facial features, hoes, and grain bag were probably added with a sharp tool before firing, a general practice that accounts for the variation of features in mold-made shabtis.[190] The lack of glaze in the crevices suggests the piece was self-glazed.[191] FDF

Bibliography. Whyte 1896, pp. 144–45, pl. V; British Museum 1922, p. 142.

49 COLUMNAR OBJECT INSCRIBED WITH THE NAME OF RAMESSES II — PAGE 96

New Kingdom, Dynasty 19; Western Thebes

Faience; H. 8.7 cm

Brooklyn Museum of Art. Charles Edwin Wilbour Fund. 52.54

This small, enigmatic object, in shape apparently without parallel, is said to have been discovered in "a deposit under the tomb of a Ramesside noble in the Theban necropolis."[192] Nothing more is known about its context and as a result its significance is also unknown. Whereas some scholars interpret its shape as a stylized version of a palm branch stripped of leaves and notched, which served as the hieroglyph for the word "year" (*rnpt*),[193] others, perhaps more correctly, regard the form as an abstraction of an as yet unidentified instrument used by bricklayers(?),[194] employed as a hieroglyph for the word "builder" (*ḳd*).[195] This latter interpretation would be consistent with the object's alleged findspot as well as with the observation that Ramesses II was himself a prolific sponsor of architectural projects throughout his realm.

The cartouche, surmounted by two plumes and a sun disk and containing the hieroglyphs of the prenomen of Ramesses II, User-Maat-Re Setep-en Re, was neatly painted in black before the object was fired. RSB

Bibliography. Riefstahl 1968, no. 41.

50 TILE WITH CARTOUCHE WITH CALCITE INLAYS — PAGE 80

New Kingdom, Dynasty 19, reign of Ramesses II; Qantir

Blue faience with calcite inlay; H. 26.5 cm; W. 12.6 cm

Staatliche Sammlung Ägyptischer Kunst, Munich. ÄS 5535

Ex-Collection: William Esch

This brilliant blue faience tile with pure white Egyptian alabaster (calcite) inlay comes from the palace of the pharaoh Ramesses II at Qantir in the Eastern Delta. Encircled by a cartouche, the king's throne name, User-Maat-Re Setep-en Re is spelled out in stone hieroglyphs carefully carved in relief with incised detail. With its vertical format and glyphs facing left, it was set into the right-hand jamb of a doorway in a throne room or nearby, perhaps within view of the great pharaoh himself. A number of similar vertical and horizontal tiles with the king's titles come from a single door or set of doors.[196] These elaborate tiles, unique to this site, were architectural embellishments in rooms of state.[197]

The chance discovery of tiles of this type led to the systematic excavation of the site of Qantir,[198] where tiles with the name of Seti I, Ramesses II's predecessor, had previously been found. Many additional tile fragments with calcite inlay were uncovered—obviously from a palace[199]—as well as the workshop that produced them. Both finds were essential in establishing that Qantir was indeed the site of Pi-Ramesse, Ramesses II's legendary palace city.[200] It was proclaimed in ancient times as "beauteous of balconies, dazzling with halls of lapis lazuli and turquoise,"[201] epithets undoubtedly inspired by tiles like this.

With so little of the palace preserved, the tiles provide an important clue to the original architecture.[202] They were probably attached to limestone or mud-brick doorways using two small holes cut in the back, carefully concealed by the stone inlay.[203] A limestone doorway from the palace, now in the Cairo Museum, shows that the inscription should run horizontally in two directions from the center of the lintel, then vertically in continuous bands down the jambs with the glyphs facing the center.[204]

The tiles vary in height up to approximately 26 cm (10½ in). The narrower examples, with a width of 10 cm and 12.5 cm (4 in and 5 in) were designed for the jambs, while the wider examples, averaging 16.8 cm (6¾ in) appear suited to the broader format

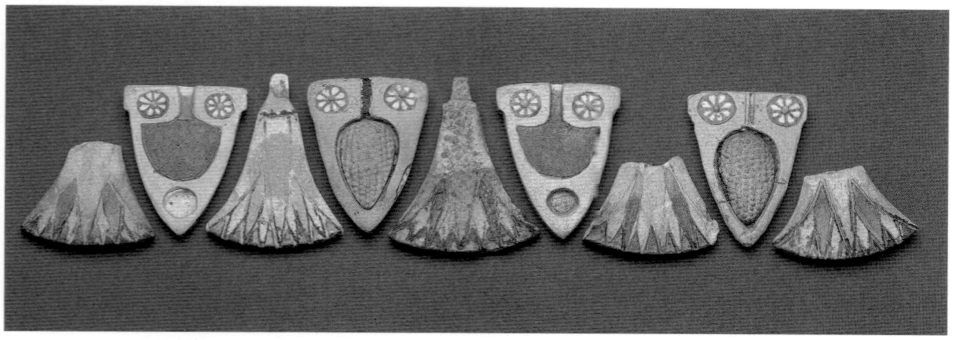

of inscriptions on lintels in New Kingdom palaces.[205]

The glaze works where the tiles were made was close to the palace.[206] Alabaster glyphs were cut in a workshop at the site of the factory, proving that the craftsmen worked in close cooperation.[207] Tools and materials used by the stone cutters and stone glyphs in various stages of preparation were found in excavations.

For the clear turquoise glaze of these tiles, a fine layer of white sand or crushed quartz was placed over the surface of the local iron-bearing sand in order to disguise the coarse gray-brown core typical of all Qantir faience.[208] Using a technique also used for stone jewelry, stone cutters traced on the glyphs fine patterns similar to the designs on the blue molded relief tiles produced here earlier for Seti I.[209] Curved elements and complex glyphs were made in two or more pieces. Mortar was used to secure the stone inlays in specially formed recesses. In view of the labor-intensive production of these tiles, it is not surprising that they are unique to this site and period. BC

Bibliography. Villa Hügel 1961, p. 118, nr. 159, pl. II; Müller 1961, pp. 22–24 and pl. II, lower right; Munich 1966, Cover and cat. no. 62; Kayser 1969, p. 120, no. 108; Munich 1976, p. 118, No. 79; Arnold et al. 1978, p. 175, no. 289, frontispiece; Clayton 1994, p. 194.

51 STYLIZED FLORAL FRIEZE PAGE 86

New Kingdom, Dynasty 20, reign of Ramesses III; Tell el-Yahudiya

Polychrome faience; H. 7.1 cm; L. 29.1 cm

Brooklyn Museum of Art. Charles Edwin Wilbour Fund. 55.182 a–i

This polychrome faience frieze, portraying a colorful garland of grape clusters and lotus flowers, reinterprets a popular design in polychrome faience. The frieze was used as an architectural inlay in the palace of Ramesses III at Tell el-Yahudiya in the Delta.[210] It evolved from a pattern of alternating lotus and grapes, frequently used as a wall border in Eighteenth Dynasty tombs.[211] In the Ramesside Period, this more geometric version adorned a variety of objects, including a gold vessel from the site of Bubastis.[212] It was favored well into the Twenty-First Dynasty, when it was especially popular in the funerary arts, and appears in floral garlands decorating coffins.[213]

In this Brooklyn frieze stylized pendant lotus flowers alternate with shield-shaped plaques inlaid with greenish-brown flowers or with molded grape clusters in relief. Miniature rosettes are inlaid along the top of the plaques on either side of the stems, some of which have fallen out. To ensure a good fit, the edges of the pieces are bevelled. Now weathered from Delta humidity, the individual pieces were created by molding, inlay, and glazing.[214]

The plaques with the grapes have a thick mustard yellow glaze[215] used in this period for faience cartouche plaques and also favored in royal tomb painting.[216] The tiny inlaid rosettes were made in same way as larger versions also at this site [55], [56]: molded white petals were surrounded with warm beige glaze, then topped with a yellow boss.

The combination of sophisticated inlay techniques and occasional sloppy workmanship is not surprising, as artistic parallels suggest that the frieze would have been set at a considerable height and therefore poorly handled details would not have been visible to the viewer at ground level.

While the special significance of the design is not known, elements of it were used in royal and divine contexts in the period of Ramesses III.[217] At Medinet Habu,[218] in rooms intimately associated with the king, friezes of carved stone borders almost exactly like this faience example here are used at the top of every scene—giving an architectural counterpart for the pieces without context at Tell el-Yahudiya.

Marks incised in the backs of some elements of this frieze may have indicated their placement on the walls at Tell el-Yahudiya or perhaps the pattern of assemblage of the individual pieces (see [20]).[219] BC

Bibliography. Brooklyn Museum 1956, p. 37, no. 41, pl. 62; Riefstahl 1968, no. 48, p.49, p. 103; Baines and Málek 1980, p. 174, top right.

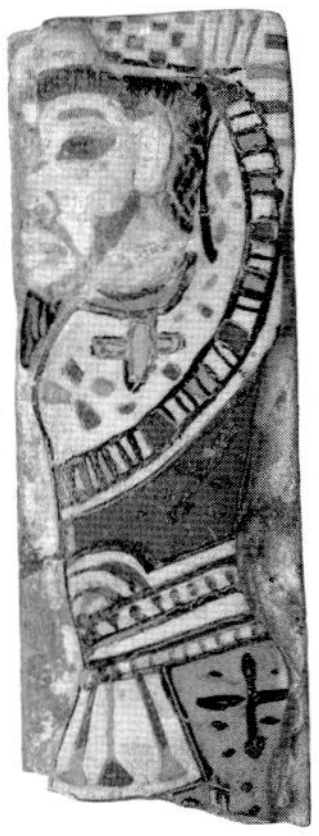

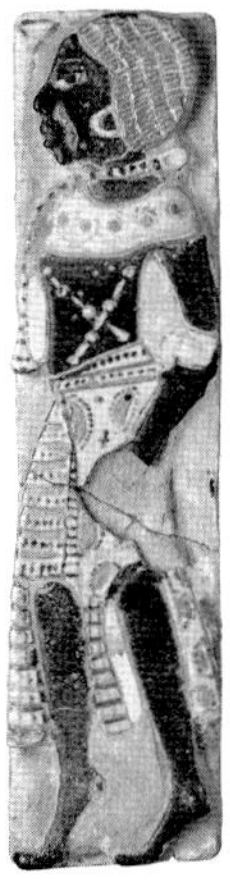

52 TILE WITH "HITTITE" OR ASIATIC CHIEF PAGE 93

New Kingdom, Dynasty 20, reign of Ramesses III; Medinet Habu

Polychrome faience; H. 16.8 cm; W. 5.5 cm

Museum of Fine Arts, Boston. Emily Esther Sears Fund 1903.1569

53 TILE WITH NUBIAN CHIEF PAGE 92

New Kingdom, Dynasty 20, reign of Ramesses III; Medinet Habu

Polychrome faience; H. 25.0 cm; W. 6.0 cm

Museum of Fine Arts, Boston. Emily Esther Sears Fund 1903.1570

Bold portraits of captive foreign chiefs adorn polychrome relief tiles from Medinet Habu, the mortuary temple of Ramesses III in western Thebes.[220] This is a well-preserved monument providing a clear context for the tiles. Their elaborate details show an interest in and knowledge of foreign costumes and features.[221]

While the tiles would have impressed and awed spectators, they were probably not intended as literal depictions of specific groups, but rather served to emphasize the extent and diversity of the subjects over which Pharaoh ruled. Placed in the vicinity of the "window of appearance," where the king appeared before the populace, they were emblems that showed all mankind physically beneath the feet of pharaoh, magically reinforcing his supreme power and his ability to honor and serve the gods in his cosmic role as Horus above the people.[222]

The first tile [52] depicts a foreign chief, often called a Hittite. His wool garments, a modified Syrian fashion,[223] are a rich jewel-like tapestry of contrasting colors skillfully created using only two shades of inlay. His undergarment has sleeves with red and gray bands and checks. Over this he wears a fringed cape with woven patterns also in red and gray. His red garment is covered with a gray cloth wound around it like a skirt, both fabrics embroidered with a pattern of black crosses and dots.[224] A woven belt, tied in a wide loop and with three tassels in alternating colors, completes the outfit. This type of belt is shown as an Asiatic product in tribute scenes and was imitated in the period of Ramesses III.[225] The chieftain's amulet, suspended from his neckband, is a four-pronged cross with yellow inlay representing gold. Worn by many types of Asiatic chiefs, the amulet cannot be used to identify nationality, though he has frequently been called Hittite.[226]

Prisoner tiles like this were inlaid into the niches at the base of walls ritually to maintain the authority of pharaoh. Indeed, there is a direct progression of the prisoner motif in New Kingdom art: Eighteenth Dynasty depictions show, at the base of the throne dais, foreign chiefs above foreign place names in the presence of the pharaoh; these evolve into depictions of kneeling chiefs or suppliants in the same position; and then to standing captives shown on the front of the "window of appearance," with the series culminating in these prisoner tiles, which occur only in this period of the Twentieth Dynasty.

A second well-preserved tile from the mortuary temple at Medinet Habu portrays a chief of Nubia [53], at the opposite end of the Egypt's empire. Also facing left, he is attired in full native dress. This ethnic type is well represented on the prisoner tiles and in temple scenes; it contrasts with other tiles showing assimilated Nubian chiefs who wear Egyptian dress of starched white linen beneath their native garb.[227] Both reflect the special status of Nubia within the Egyptian empire as a colonized area under full Egyptian control.[228]

The Nubian chief's features and costume are formed in molded relief and inlay in brilliant colors.[229] His dark skin, molded orange-red wig, and hoop earrings are typical for all Nubian chiefs on these tiles.[230] His face has high cheek bones and a vertical crease or scar by his nose. The looped cord around his neck, in white faience with painted black dots, is standard for all prisoner chiefs.

Two strands of white beads cross his chest.[231] His traditional Nubian costume consists of a short kilt combined with patterned sashes worn with an animal skin behind his back tied over the kilt.[232] A more prestigious variant here is the leopard skin with long paws hanging down around his legs.[233] On the tiles these garments appear to be imitations of the animal skins in leather or cloth, painted or stitched with geometric designs that resemble the leopard's spots. He wears the broad collar with a row of dots first introduced in the period of Ramesses III as a standard fashion for all Nubians.[234]

The battle scenes at Medinet Habu show only a token skirmish with a Nubian village, with Nubian chiefs of both types portrayed. While there appears to have been little military involvement with Nubia at this time,[235] curiosity and personal observation of Nubian characteristics and costume may have inspired this tile's depiction, for Ramesses III settled a large Nubian contingent in the vicinity of Medinet Habu.[236]

On the back of this tile is an incised face, a code for placement.[237] These tiles would have been set in niches at the base of walls—the temple still has recessed niches in doorways leading from the palace into the temple near the window of appearance. In the Cairo Museum tiles have been reconstructed in a doorway to give an idea of the original appearance.[238] That the tiles from this site occur in different sizes,[239] however, is evidence for their use in several locations, some of which are not preserved.

Depictions of captive chiefs standing below the window of appearance give a good idea of how these tiles might have been arranged. A number of scenes from the period of Akhenaten show a similar convention for bound prisoners, who stand either on flat feet or on their toes,[240] the stance used on this tile. This tile would probably have been paired with a similar one in Boston of the same size, also with raised feet.[241] Facing in opposite directions, they may once have stood on either side of a doorway facing toward the center. BC

Bibliography. Rowe 1908, p. 48 (Hittite), p. 49; (Nubian), p. 50, right (back of tile); Museum of Fine Arts, Boston 1920, fig. on p. 47; 1930, fig. p. 24; Capart 1927, 1931, pl. 77; 1935, ibid.; Smith 1942, p. 131, fig. 86; Riefstahl 1944, p. 19, fig. 25 ([53] Nubian only); 1947, fig. on p. 25; Smith 1942, p. 131, fig. 84; Smith 1942, p. 147, fig. 97 ([53] Nubian only); Terrace 1962, fig. 15; Smith 1965, fig. 70; Terrace 1968a, p. 55, fig. 14; Porter and Moss 1972, p. 524; Kendall 1982, p. 7, fig. 4 ([53] Nubian only).

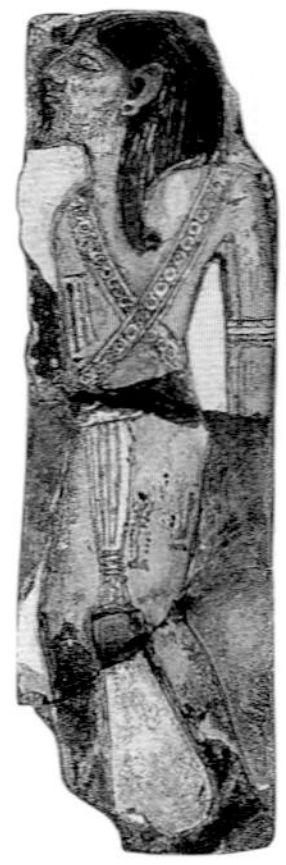

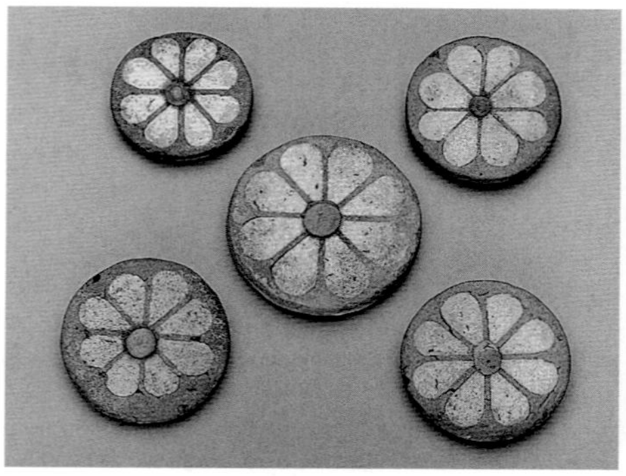

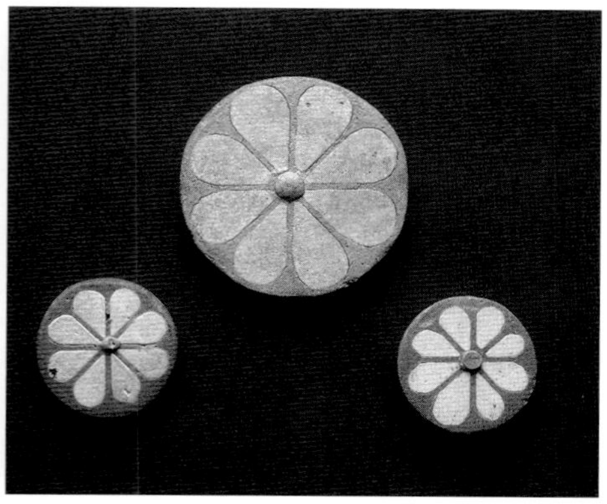

54 TILE WITH LIBYAN CHIEF PAGE 92

New Kingdom, Dynasty 20, reign of Ramesses III; Tell el-Yahudiya

Polychrome faience; H. 31.0 cm; W. 9.0 cm

The Trustees of the British Museum, London. Purchased from Rev. Greville J. Chester; Acquired 1871. EA 12337

This expressive tile of a captive Libyan chief comes from Ramesses III's temple palace at Tell el-Yahudiya in the Delta. Portrayed with uplifted face and one arm bound by a rope, he wears the simple costume of an overlord of the ancient Libyan, or Tjehenu,[242] tribe. His tattoos and pierced ear reflect current Libyan fashion. The surface of his body is modeled in relief, with molded pieces like the face added separately.[243] Such tiles from Tell el-Yahudiya[244] display a greater variety of pose, scale, and detail than their counterparts from Medinet Habu [52], [53], and include some of Egypt's most accomplished works from this final era of polychrome faience.

Another Libyan chief of this type appears on the faience throne dais of Ramesses II[245] with the same pale skin, bright free-flowing hair, bare chest with crossed straps, and phallus sheath,[246] a depiction contrasting sharply with the garb of most of the contemporary Meshwesh/Libu tribes and chiefs. It is possible that Ramesses III chose this image to continue his pattern of imitating works by his famous predecessor.

Unlike some of the other foreigners shown on the tiles, the Libyan tribes were a real threat to the Egyptians in the period of Ramesses III, and much wall space at Ramesses III's temple at Medinet Habu depicts battles involving this group. While prisoner tiles are usually emblematic—lacking specific titles or place names—a chief of this type comes to life at Medinet Habu[247] as a semi-legendary individual named Meshesher, shown with his father Keper.[248]

Representations on the base of the window of appearance where the king appeared before the public often show prisoners in the stance on this tile, with feet raised off the ground. The prisoner tiles from Tell el-Yahudiya were probably positioned in the same way as those at Medinet Habu, where the architectural context is well preserved, that is, set into the wall at the base of an area where the king appeared before the public. BC

Bibliography. Quirke and Spencer 1992, p. 181, fig. 141; Shaw and Nicholson 1995, p. 308; Robins 1997, p. 16, fig. 4.

55 ROSETTES PAGE 87

New Kingdom, probably Dynasty 20; probably from Tell el-Yahudiya

Polychrome faience; DIAM. 3.2 cm; 4.3 cm; 3.5 cm; 3.8 cm; 3.7 cm

The Detroit Institute of Arts. Gift of Frederick K. Stearns.

90.1S12593.1; 90.1S12821.1; 90.1S12821.3; 90.1S12821.4; 90.112821.5

56 ROSETTES PAGE 87

New Kingdom, probably Dynasty 20; probably from Tell el-Yahudiya

Polychrome faience; DIAM. 6.1 cm; 3.8 cm; 3.8 cm; TH. 0.9 cm

Private Collection

Rosettes of this type, with eight white petals on a gray background and with a bright yellow central boss, generally come from Tell el-Yahudiya and date to the reign of Ramesses III. The early discovery at this Delta site of a small palace of Ramesses III[249] with its thousands of rosettes and other tiles formed our earliest modern idea of Egyptian palace decor.[250]

The rosette has a long history in Egyptian decorative borders and ornamental bands and was popular at most palace sites.[251] Rosettes from the period of Ramesses III, however, are distinctive: they are always bichrome, apart from the central boss, and usually combine silver gray or light brown with white.

The colors imitate real precious metals used in architectural inlays. The yellow boss, which may resemble a daisy's center, also imitates the gold of the nails securing rosettes to palace walls. Some rosettes found at this site actually have a central hole and copper alloy nails with broad heads still in place.[252]

The rosettes were mass-produced, probably at a factory near the site,[253] and made by a combination of mold- and hand-forming techniques that produced slight individual differences in size and appearance. First a mold was used to form a disk with eight raised white petals. After partial drying, a purple gray glaze material was inlaid around the edges of the petals to create a flat surface.[254]

A hand-formed boss was added at the center. Always the same bright yellow color, undoubtedly produced by lead antimonate, this element varies from a small dot to a large glob, sometimes carefully rounded but occasionally distorted or accidentally flattened in drying.[255]

While the original context and purpose of most rosettes are still unclear, at the palace at Tell el-Yahudiya some limestone elements with inlaid rosettes were found still in place. A drawing of one of these pieces *in situ* depicts a tiered pedestal, placed against a wall, that appears to have faience rosettes inlaid into the top and in rows on the side.[256] Limestone fragments from this site, now in the British Museum, show how areas of the stone were cut back for inlay—rows of rosettes were set into recessed bands and glued flush with the surface.[257] An ornate pedestal with two semicircular platforms, in the Cairo Museum, has bands of rosettes on its side similar to those shown here.[258] BC

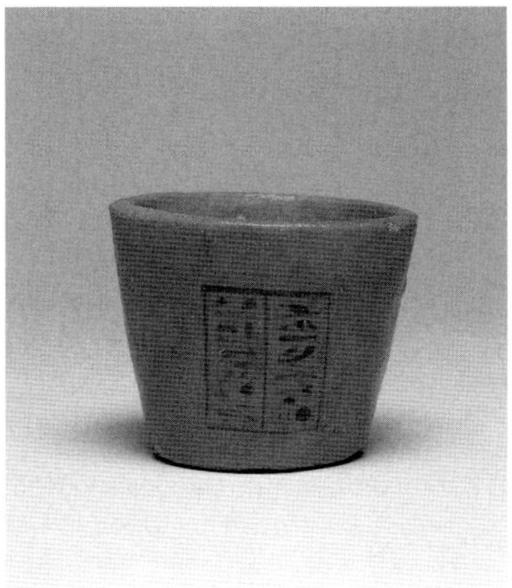

57 BEAKER INSCRIBED FOR NESIKHONS

PAGE 96

Third Intermediate Period, Dynasty 21, *c.* 973 BC; Deir el-Bahri

Blue faience with inscriptions in black glaze; H. 6.0 cm

The Walters Art Gallery, Baltimore, Maryland. Acquired by Henry Walters before 1931. 48.412

In the Twenty-First Dynasty, the High Priests of Amun at Thebes were "lords of the southland."[259] One such ruler was Pinodjem II. This small beaker is inscribed with the name and title of the wife of Pinodjem II, Nesikhons, First Chief of the Harem of Amun. It belongs to the series of some 64 vessels, one of them in Brooklyn,[260] found in the famous cache at Deir el-Bahri. That find, systematically excavated in 1881, can be dated to Regnal Year 5 of Siamun, ruler of the north.[261] The shape of these vessels appears to be a continuation of a type already fashionable in the Eighteenth Dynasty, as comparison with stone[262] and metal examples reveals.[263] The combination of the bright blue color of the vessel's fabric with the inscriptions in black glaze appears to be a hallmark of the faience production of the period and occurs also on contemporary shabtis. It is very possible that blue was chosen for these funerary objects because of its symbolic associations with resurrection and rebirth. RSB

Bibliography. Porter and Moss 1973, p. 665.

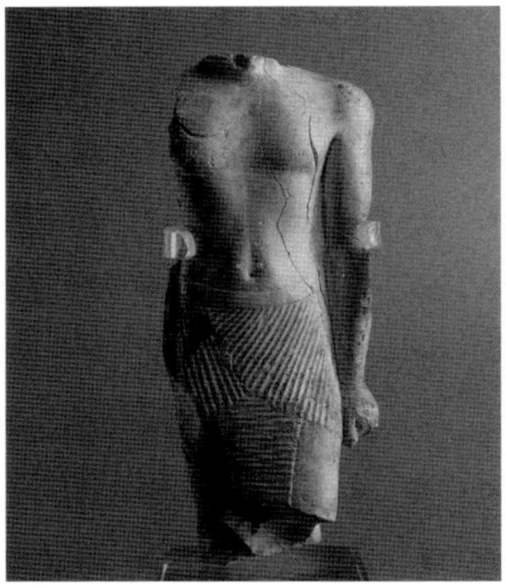

58 TORSO OF A PHARAOH NAMED SHESHONQ

PAGE 98

Third Intermediate Period, Dynasty 22; Saqqara, the Sacred Animal Necropolis, debris in sector I

Frit; H. 15.0 cm

The Syndics of the Fitzwilliam Museum, Cambridge. E.6.1969

This extraordinary torso comes from a striding statuette of a pharaoh, depicted with left leg advanced and arms held along his sides. He is dressed in a kilt, the central flap of which indicated royal status during the Old Kingdom but had lost this significance during the Middle Kingdom when it was appropriated for depictions of non-royals.[264] In keeping with this costume and pose, the pharaoh is bare-chested. The absence of any indications of a *nemes*-headdress on the upper torso suggests that the king was wearing a less full headdress, perhaps either a crown of action or a cap crown.[265]

The material has been identified as frit (see Glossary) that was abraded and engraved by hand.[266] An added detail was the incising on the back pillar of the titulary containing the prenomen Aakheper Re, which applies equally to pharaoh Sheshonq IV or Sheshonq V.[267] The seemingly perfunctory manner in which this inscription was cut is perfectly in accord with the appearance of another inscription, in cursive text, on a relief chalice also associated with a Pharaoh Sheshonq of the Twenty-Second Dynasty.[268]

These two royal examples contrast with the artistic integrity of text and object encountered, for example, on the contemporary glassy faience statuette of Nes-ba-neb-djedet in Brooklyn.[269] Is it possible to deduce from this contrast that non-royal commissions of objects in glazed materials were thoroughly planned from the beginning to include their accompanying inscriptions, whereas the royals were content to acquire stock objects to which their names were added secondarily?

This dichotomy between the apparent quality of royal and non-royal objects is not confined to the production of the Third Intermediate Period, but is encountered in earlier epochs as well: consider the disparity in artistic accomplishment between the two-dimensional representations in the tomb of Pharaoh Amenhotep III and in those of the officials who served under him, such as Khereuef.

Clearly, Western art-historical notions modeled on Renaissance art that link political status with aesthetically accomplished products are inappropriate when discussing the material culture of ancient Egypt. RSB

Bibliography. Vassilika 1995, pp. 96–97, no. 44.

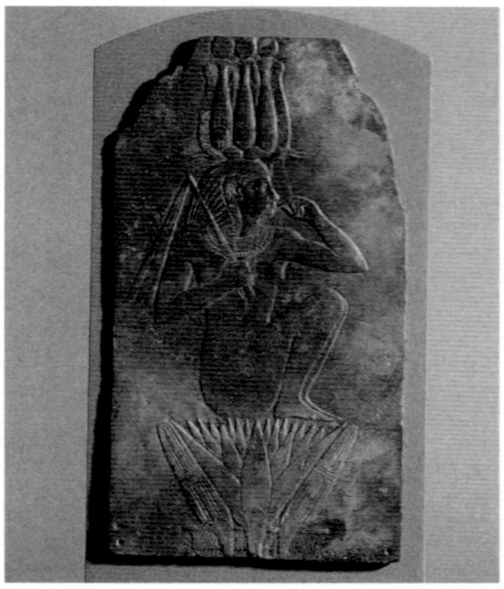

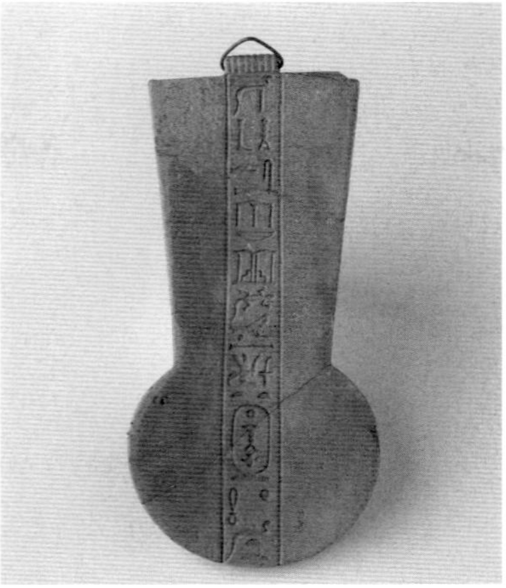

59 PLAQUE OF IUPUT II PAGE 100

Third Intermediate Period, Dynasty 23

Purplish-brown faience, heavily discolored; H. 29.5 cm; W. 16.0 cm; D. 0.7 cm

Trustees of the National Museums of Scotland. 1956.1485

The image of a child god emerging from the blue lotus, succinctly covered by Fazzini[270] following Schlögl, is a motif probably introduced during the Twenty-First Dynasty but belonging to an older tradition that associates the pharaoh with the young sun, visually represented as a child, and susceptible to various interpretations depending on the circumstances of each particular representation.[271]

Schlögl argues convincingly that the image on this plaque is that of Pharaoh Iuput II, 731–720 BC,[272] an ephemeral ruler of the Third Intermediate Period.[273] The king wears a composite crown, *nemes*-headdress with a sidelock, a broad collar, and a necklace from which is suspended an amulet whose identification and meaning are debated.[274] The original function of this plaque is also uncertain, but its similarity in material and dimensions to a second in Brooklyn, perhaps representing this same monarch, seems to indicate that both served the same function—perhaps as elements decorating a shrine.[275]

The style of both this and the Brooklyn plaque has caused a great deal of discussion about the origin and artistic pedigree of Egyptian representations of Kushites in the Third Intermediate Period. While there is no consensus,[276] the markedly Kushite physiognomy of Iuput II is unmistakable. Moreover, the use of overlapping motifs to achieve depth within the very shallow relief rivals in skill the technique employed for the highly acclaimed reliefs on the walls of certain chapels of the Temple of Seti I at Abydos.[277] The number of overlappings is extraordinary in comparison with more traditional ancient Egyptian two-dimensional representations. Here, they include the upper torso covered by the broad collar over which the necklace-with-amulet is placed, which are, in turn, covered by the king's fingers clasping the flail. RSB

Bibliography. Schlögl 1977, pp. 19 and 44–45.

60 AMULET IN THE FORM OF A COUNTERWEIGHT PAGE 97

Late Period, Dynasty 26, reign of Psametik I

Turquoise green faience; H. 12.4 cm; W. 5.8 cm;

Musée du Louvre, Paris. Gift of L., I., and A. Curtis. E 22634

This amulet, in the form of a counterweight called a *menat*, appears to have been molded as one piece, fairly early in the use of its mold, as the sharp clarity of the hieroglyphs suggests.[278] Although subsequently broken, the fragments of the *menat* have been restored, break to break, without appreciable loss. The metal attachment passing through the suspension loop at the top is modern.

In general a *menat* was employed as a counterpoise to balance multiple strands of beads (fig. 47). In its practical form it was utilized not as jewelry but rather as a musical instrument:[279] when held in the hand and shaken, generally by female priestesses, the *menat* produced a swishing sound complementing that made by a sistrum, or rattle, with which it was regularly paired. The numerous examples of *menats* of this type as well as much smaller ones used as amulets[280] were apparently never intended to receive the rows of beads such as those represented with *menats* in paintings. The absence of these strings of beads in no way diminishes the symbolic value of such *menats*, however, since ancient Egyptian art often exploits truncated forms in which a part substitutes for the entire object.[281] This was certainly the intention for the *menats* found in the royal burials at Nuri.[282]

The single line of hieroglyphs may be translated as, "A spell [by X]: many great royal jubilees for the King of Upper and Lower Egypt, Wah-ib-re, [living eternally] like the sun god Re forever." The absence of a name of a deity, which would be expected as the one pronouncing the spell, and the signs for "living eternally" or the like, is noteworthy but not sufficient to condemn the object as a forgery, inasmuch as ellipses of this type are frequent in numerous *menats* dated to the Late Period.[283] The identification of the pharaoh named is assured because only Psametik I of the Twenty-Sixth Dynasty bore the prenomen Wah-ib-re.

The inscription states that this particular *menat* was associated with a royal jubilee[284] of Pharaoh Psametik I. Such celebrations, the exact details of the performance of which remain under debate, were rituals intended to renew and regenerate the pharaoh and were often associated with the spiritual rebirth of the king, as the scene of Pharaoh Taharka nursed by the goddess Bastet on a faience *menat* in New York reveals.[285] During the performance of such rituals it was imperative that the forces of the Egyptian cosmos were brought into equilibrium, and the playing of the sistrum and *menat* were believed to hold inimical forces in check. It can therefore be suggested that such faience *menats* were votive offerings commemorating a royal jubilee in honor of Psametik I. The turquoise green color reinforces the ceremony's themes of renewal, regeneration, and spiritual rebirth. RSB

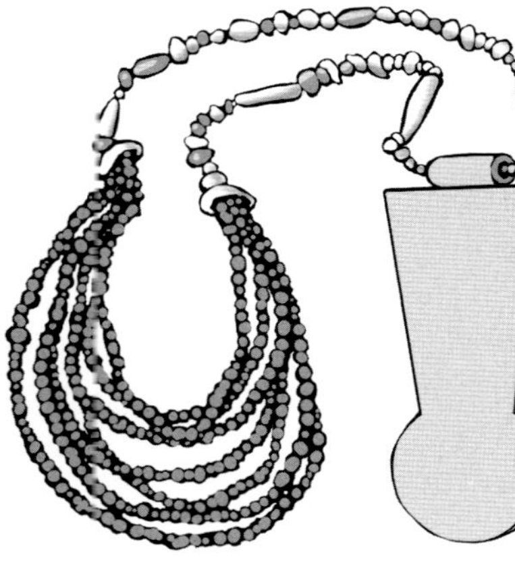

Fig. 47 A *menat* with strung beads.

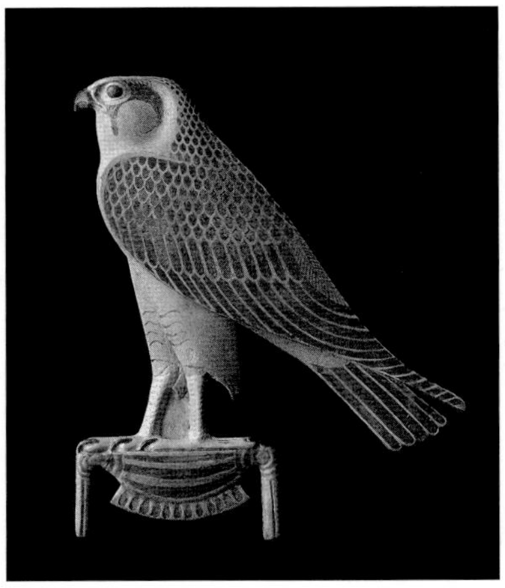

61 INLAY IN THE FORM OF THE COMPOSITE HIEROGLYPH, "THE HORUS [OR FALCON?] OF GOLD"

PAGE 76

Late Period, Dynasty 30–Ptolemaic period, 380–30 BC; said to be from Ashmunein (Hermopolis)

Pale greenish blue, dark blue, yellow, and black-brown faience; H. 15.4 cm; W. 12.9 cm; TH. 1.2 cm

The Metropolitan Museum of Art, New York. Purchase, Edward S. Harkness Gift, 1926. 26.7.996

This strikingly beautiful figure represents the falcon of Horus standing on a collar of beads, together forming a composite hieroglyph for one of the five names of an Egyptian pharaoh, "the Horus [or falcon?] of gold."[286] Although very few objects have been found in which such inlays are still intact, there seems little reason to doubt that this inlay was used in a piece of furniture,[287] perhaps made of wood, that contained the complete titulary and names of one of the kings of the Late Period. Though the body is molded in one piece, the plumage of the bird consists of tiny separate inlays let into the body.

Its dating is suggested by the fact that it was reportedly found with a group of inlays of which one represents the torso and head of a pharaoh[288] whose style is very much in keeping with that current during the Thirtieth Dynasty and the beginning of the Ptolemaic Period. RSB & FDF

Bibliography. Schäfer and Andrae 1925, p. 629 and pl. 447.

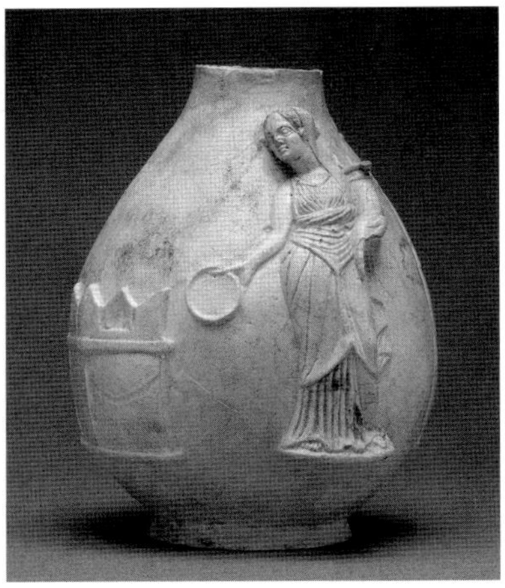

62 QUEEN'S VASE

PAGE 99

Ptolemaic Period, 240–230 BC

Faience; H. 22.2 cm

The J. Paul Getty Museum, Malibu, California. 96.AI.58

Ex-Collection: Barbara and Lawrence Fleischman, New York

This exceptionally fine, robin's-egg blue *oinochoe* belongs to a class of faience wine pitchers, mostly fragmentary, each bearing the high-relief image of a Ptolemaic queen pouring a liquid offering before an altar.[289] In this case it portrays Queen Berenike II, wife of Ptolemy III (*c.* 246–222 BC), with cornucopia. She is identified by her name in Greek (above the altar), followed by her title (indistinct)[290] and the phrase, "Good Fortune."[291] Her full coiffure, large eyes, straight nose, and voluptuous mouth resemble her portraits on coins and in marble.[292] Her hair became legendary when she dedicated a tress to Aphrodite for her husband's safe return from war in Syria. The lock disappeared from the temple and was transformed, according to the court astronomer, into the constellation Coma (the curl of) Berenices.[293]

Remains of these vases are found around the Mediterranean basin, suggesting that they were used not by, but rather in honor of, royalty.[294] Pouring wine offerings from these pitchers may have brought the queen's personal *tyche* or good fortune, to cities distant from yet within the orbit of the Ptolemies.[295]

Several details on the Getty vase point to a date in the middle years of Berenike's reign: her slightly fleshy, but not dumpy figure; the high relief, the swing of her body and the delicate modeling of toes and hands;[296] her *himation* worn like a mantilla;[297] and the broad, flat planes of drapery.[298] Other details confirm the date: the garlanded altar is set at an angle, as on a fragment in the Alexandria Museum[299] and on another excavated at Carthage in a context dated 230 BC;[300] and the altar inscription, "Divine Benefactor," a name Ptolemy III received after his successes in the East in 243 BC.[301]

The Getty vase is one of the best examples of this type. A relatively complete (restored) one is in the British Museum,[302] while one with intact body, but no handle, is in the Bibliothèque Nationale,[303] and another similar in style and condition to the Getty vase is in Antalya.[304] The queen's hair and the cornucopia are dark blue. The vessel's body has been restored from several large pieces. Lost are its trefoil-mouth[305] and handle, though there is the ghost of an attachment in the form of a silen face.[306] APK

Bibliography. Manchester 1994.

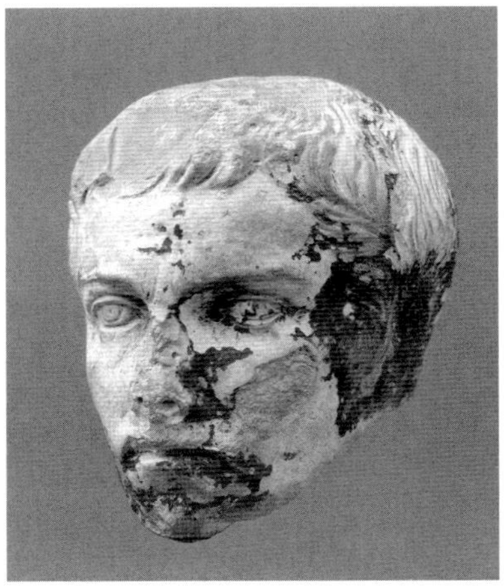

63 HEAD OF THE ROMAN EMPEROR AUGUSTUS

PAGE 101

Roman Period, 27–20 BC; Memphis

Blue green (glassy?) faience; H. 6.8 cm

The Metropolitan Museum of Art, New York. Purchase, Edward S. Harkness Gift, 1926. 26.7.1428

Ex-Collection: Earl of Carnarvon

Although little of the hairline is preserved, enough is left to detect the configuration of several locks in a "crab's claw" pattern to the proper left of the center of the forehead. These locks, together with the distinctive facial features, clearly indicate that this miniature portrait represents Augustus, the first emperor of Rome.[307] Moreover, the proportions of the face suggest that this head is based on the Prima Porta type introduced into the repertoire of the Emperor's images shortly after 30 BC.[308] Because of its small scale, the head may have belonged to a statue dedicated to the cult of the Emperor Augustus[309] erected at Memphis. Its anonymous dedicator may have demonstrated his fealty to Augustus by this shrine, since Augustus (at that time still called Octavian) took punitive measures against the Egyptian priesthood at Memphis[310] immediately after his entry into Egypt after his victory at Actium, off the western coast of the Greek mainland, in 31 BC. Such shrines appear to have been extremely popular, to judge from the number of surviving small-scale images of the Emperor Augustus in a variety of materials.[311]

Whereas Augustus did his utmost to suppress pharaonic Egyptian cultural expressions in Rome, he was not averse to employing those same proscribed expressions for his own benefit in Egypt.[312] It can thus safely be assumed that green faience's already ancient connotations of longevity and prosperity were operative in the choice of material for this image of the Roman emperor, whose Egyptian titulary was likewise indebted to pharaonic traditions.[313] Like the pharaohs of old, Augustus aspired to a lengthy, peaceful reign.

On the faience composition, see Wypyski's analysis in the Appendix. RSB

Bibliography. Stuart 1944; Richter 1948, fig. 21; Cooney 1960, p. 39.

1 Verner 1984, p. 74; cf. Lacovara in Der Manuelian vol. 2, 1996, pp. 487–91. Inlaying wooden boxes with faience begins in the First Dynasty: see Killen 1994a, pp. 21–22, p. 23, fig. 24.
2 Verner 1984, pp.74–75; p. 76, fig. 7; Verner 1994, p. 139, bottom figure.
3 Preliminary molding may have been used though no direct evidence remains.
4 Verner 1994, p. 189 (bottom figure) is of a recently excavated parallel where the faience is still blue. See Weathering in the Glossary.
5 The kiln atmosphere can be either full of oxygen, called an oxidizing atmosphere, in which case the copper colorants in faience develop the traditional turquoise color, or it can be deprived of oxygen, which is a reducing environment that turns the faience copper red.
6 Lacovara in Der Manuelian vol. 2, 1996, p. 487 (analysis by Richard Newman, Museum of Fine Arts, Boston).
7 With an organic binder like a gum or a glue.
8 Eugene Farrell of the Straus Center for Conservation at the Harvard University Art Museums sampled this object and determined, through FT-IR spectra, the presence of calcium carbonate in the form of fine-grained, nicely rounded crystals that are limestone. He notes that "the nature of the binder that held the calcium carbonate grains together and the binder for the gilding to the base is not known." Pers. comm. June 1997.
9 Hatchfield and Newman's analyses show that calcium carbonate, the same material as in this inlay, was the most common support for gold leaf (Hatchfield and Newman in Bigelow et al. 1991, pp. 32–33, Table 1). On early gilding methods, see Lucas and Harris 1962 (1969), pp. 231–33; Hatchfield and Newman in Bigelow et al. 1991, p. 28.
10 Egyptian Museum, Cairo CG 42088; Victoria and Albert Museum C 780-1923 (Kozloff in Kozloff and Bryan 1992, p. 224). Cf. an Egyptian blue sphinx with gilding for Horemheb, Egyptian Museum, Cairo JE 42096. I thank John Ross and May Trad for drawing my attention to the latter and for providing an accession number and photograph.
11 Its earliest antecedent is the Fourth Dynasty Sphinx of Khafre at Giza.
12 Zivie in *LÄ* V, 1141.
13 Fay 1995, pp. 29–30, pls. 4–5 cites a Fifth Dynasty Sahure example from Berlin (19907).
14 Aldred 1988, pp. 41–47, pl. 10 discusses a 5.7-cm (2¼-in) long unprovenanced stone sphinx of Merenre from Edinburgh (NMS 1984.405), which, like MMA 1972.125, bears an inscription between the forearms, but is additionally inscribed on the underside. For a reference to propitiating aspects of the sun god through the libation offerings, see p. 46.
15 Lilyquist in Hoving 1975, p. 108. Kozloff in Kozloff and Bryan 1992, p. 224 emphasizes its votive use in a temple context.
16 That the sphinx did not sink into but was rather attached over an object is also suggested by the lack of wear lines around its base.
17 Concerning the adhesive: "The remains of a reddish brown material that was used to secure the join between the sphinx and the tenon are also visible from the bottom. This material was analyzed by FTIR by Dora Henel, a volunteer research scientist at the Sherman Fairchild Center for Objects Conservation. FTIR was performed using a BIO-RAD FTS-40 spectrometer. The samples were mounted in a Spectra-Tech diamond cell and placed in a BIO-RAD UMA 500 infrared microscope. The spectra were collected at four wavenumber resolution with a total of fifty scans each. The material was found to be a resin mixed with calcium carbonate." Pers. comm. Ann Heywood, the Sherman Fairchild Center for Objects Conservation at the Metropolitan Museum of Art.
18 See Berg 1990, p. 104 for examples from the Hypostyle Hall at Karnak.
19 Badawy 1972, pp. 1–20. Fragments of the other are at McGill University Ethnology Collections (2441), published in Berg 1990, pp. 81–106, pls. 2–4.
20 The Seti I model, however, bears recesses for the elements, while the suggested Amenhotep III model had projections.
21 Badawy 1972 gives the length as 22.4 cm (9 in) in the right-hand table on p. 7, an error, since to arrive at the dimensions (3.766/4.746m) given in the left-hand table on p. 7, the 22.6 cm measurement from p. 3 is required. I thank Stephen Thompson for noting the error.
22 Badawy 1972, p. 3.
23 Berg 1990, p. 105, however, suggests such temple models were a class of object unique to Seti I's reign, a supposition with which I disagree.
24 Badawy 1972, pp. 1; 15.
25 Aldred 1988, pp. 46–47 suggests similarly that the Edinburgh Merenre sphinx (less than a quarter the length of the Metropolitan sphinx) may either have been a part of such a votive temple model or "an article of altar furniture."
26 Kozloff in Goring et al. 1997, pp. 178–92; she refers to the color of this sphinx as sky blue, the result of copper oxide (CuO) (pp. 178–79). Mark T. Wypyski, Associate Research Scientist at the Metropolitan Museum of Art's Sherman Fairchild Center for Objects Conservation, gives a quantitative analysis of the glaze in the Appendix, which also includes his SEM/EDS analysis of the object.
27 Kozloff in Kozloff and Bryan 1992, p. 223, with a listing of the most important examples on pp. 223–24.
28 Holthoer 1977, p. 145, pl. 33. For stone examples, see, e.g., Guidotti 1991, nos. 231–39.
29 Quibell 1908, pl. xx, nos. 51072, 51074, though these shapes are less broad and baggy.
30 This hieroglyphic arrangement also maintains the preferred rightward orientation of two- and three-dimensional figures of the king.
31 Though the yellow ground of the stopper is lighter than that of the vessel's rim, when the stopper is turned over it is clear that the fabrics are the same. However, the stopper's white daisy decoration, which does not appear inlaid, and yellow background are a bit runny and porous, unlike the crisp inlays in the jar.
32 For parallels in different media and colors, see Kozloff in Kozloff and Bryan 1992h, p. 398, cat. no. 100.
33 The colors are probably lead antimonate for yellow, cobalt for blue, iron oxides for red, calcium antimonate for white, and copper and lead antimonate for green, with admixtures of glass or frit; as based on the research of Kaczmarczyk and Hedges 1983.
34 Pinch 1996, p. 6. My thanks to Dr. Pinch for allowing me access to her manuscript before publication.
35 Also applied to his palace, royal barge, and a company in the army: Berman in Kozloff and Bryan 1992a, p. 35.
36 The interior is today clean but it was most likely washed (pers. comm. Geneviève Pierrat-Bonnefois, Louvre).
37 One would have expected the three red dots of the closed buds at the front of the lid to sit symmetrically above the center of the inscribed panel. Such asymmetries are common in Egyptian work of the highest quality, however, and may reflect the work of multiple hands in the design and fabrication of a single object.
38 British Museum, EA 22878, from Amarna and Yale University Art Gallery, YAG 1936.100, both with a pale blue background with dark blue inlaid glyphs.
39 Berlin 2045 (Weber 1969, p. 219, n. 735).
40 See [25]; on this favorite color scheme of the king, see Kozloff in Goring et al. 1997, pp. 184–85.
41 The back, unlike the front and sides, is matte and was probably laid down on a surface during drying and before firing.
42 What appear to be two attachment holes are found on British Museum EA 22878 (Silverman in Brovarski et al. 1982, p. 289, no. 400).
43 Hall 1926, p. 31.
44 Kozloff in Goring et al. 1997, p. 184, who notes, however, that the dominant color choice was cobalt blue with copper blue both for objects inscribed solely for Amenhotep III or for him and a female family member.
45 Cf. an Amarna limestone relief of gazelles (?) before a feeding trough (Houlihan 1996, p. 61, fig. 43); or the earlier, more decorative use of gazelle heads that spring from the forehead of the gold circlet of one of the three wives of Thutmose III, which Winlock suggested referred to the non-reigning women not allowed to wear the Queen's headdress (Hayes 1990 (1959), p. 131; p. 133, fig. 7c); the almost contemporary small tinted ivory and wood gazelle with blue pigment inlay (MMA 26.7.1292; Arnold 1995, p. 11, cat. no. 3); or the contemporary pair of bronze gazelle protomes, possibly for attachment to a chair or vase (Ortiz 1996, no. 40).
46 See e.g., Houlihan 1996, pl. XVIII.
47 Green 1993, p. 35.
48 Johnson 1996, p. 74.
49 The area along much of the interior edge from around the ear almost to the base has, however, been restored. But the parallel, intact New York example in faience also lacks any sign of attachment for another lappet. Since both wig halves seem complete, they were probably not meant for anything other than a relief figure.
50 I thank Dorothea Arnold for this observation. Cf. Arnold in Arnold 1996, p. 19, fig. 11; p. 26, fig. 19 for relief images of Nefertiti with a wig surmounted by a crown attachment, though she also wears the uraeus that does not seem to have been on the Private Collection wig. Cf. also Tiye in related wig with crown attachment in the round (Drenkhahn and Schmitz 1985, p. 81, cat no. 134).
51 Schoske et al. 1990, p. 113.
52 Roehrig 1996, pp. 4–7, cat. no. 2; the bedding material underlying the lapis is Egyptian blue (p. 7, n. 5); cf. also Daressy 1905, vol. 29, t. II, pl. XXXV, 38.621.
53 Schoske et al. 1990, p. 113.
54 Green 1993, p. 36; p. 34, fig. 11 (right).
55 Mysliwiec 1976.
56 Mysliwiec 1988, pp. 89–103, with plates.
57 Other examples of faience round wigs include fragments in University College London (UC.23413; 23406) in Samson 1973, p. 57, pl. XXIX, 1 a–b.
58 E.g., those in the Petrie collection in Samson 1978, p. 117.
59 Cf. the wooden sculpture fragment with a round wig on the head of an Eighteenth Dynasty king or prince, in which there are minute traces of blue in the brows and eyes, suggesting that blue paste was used to enhance these facial features, assuming that a white material would have been used for the irises of the eyes. See Müller 1964, p. 72.
60 A wig fragment in Samson 1973, pl. XXIX, 1, b "has part of a rectangle prepared for such a tenon" (p. 47).

205 Measurements taken from the tiles in Munich, Müller 1981, p. 342.
206 See map for this location in Kitchen 1982, p. 123, fig. 42.
207 Hamza 1930, p. 42. The use of tiles with stone inlay was initiated here in the time of Seti I: see Müller 1981, p. 345, n. 16, and pl. 93a.
208 Müller 1981, p. 341. This is characterized as Faience "Variant A" in the categories established by Lucas and Harris 1962, pp. 161–62.
209 Müller 1981, p. 351, and pl. 94.
210 For other sections of this band, both excavated and unprovenanced, with description, see Schlick-Nolte 1984, no. 53, pp. 104–05. For a description of this piece and bibliography for the general type, see Riefstahl 1968. Unprovenanced pieces come from this site. The faience design frequently mentioned as a close parallel, from the Western Gate of Ramesses' temple palace at Medinet Habu, is not the same: Hölscher 1951, p. 44, pl. 35d, pl. 38c.
211 Mackay 1921, pp. 39–41. A more elaborate version added sets of daisies along the top.
212 JE 38706: Edgar 1907, pl. XLV.
213 For instance Brooklyn 08.480 2 A-C.
214 See Cairo JE 21842, with a large section preserved, illustrated in Freed 1983, no. 39 p, 173. H. 7.7 cm (3 in); L. 60 cm (24 in). Found at the site, it gives a good indication of the standard design and intended colors. For the lotus fine yellow paste was first inlaid into the convex white body to form the sepals. The petals were incised, cut out along the top for the red inlay inserted between the points, and defined with black paint. The entire piece was finally coated in a turquoise glaze which turned the sepals green and the petals blue. The "brick" red inlay used a special compound of iron oxide and lead: see Kaczmarczyk and Hedges 1983, p. 256; and p. 168 (Ashmolean Museum 1871.34C).
215 The other plaques are pale yellow, possibly a technical error or variant, like the unusual brown color of the inlaid flower.
216 For some complex faience pieces, the royal workshop of Ramesses III deliberately reproduced a range of the unusually bright colors found in the murals.
217 E.g., the same complex frieze, also omitting the grapes, decorated the shrine of Ptah in the tomb of Ramesses' son Amenherkhopeshef and appears at the base of a naos on a pectoral commemorating his heb-sed festival: Feucht 1967, no. 15, p. 168, pl. VII.
218 The Epigraphic Survey 1970, pls. 639, 640. It also includes a pomegranate motif.
219 The pendant lotus flower 55.182 G has a cross on the back; a shield-shaped plaque inlaid with a flower, 55.182 D, has an inverted v. (as noted in Schlick-Nolte 1984, no. 53 p. 104).
220 Porter and Moss 1972, p. 524.
221 Daressy 1911, pp. 49-63.
222 The prisoner tiles specifically contribute to this cosmic symbolism: Ritner 1993, p.120, n. 567 and p.127, n.580, 581; p. 131: "the motif of the prisoner... makes concrete the superiority of the victor as 'Horus atop the masses.' Physical elevation produces political, social, and cosmic domination."
223 This Syrian costume consists of a long-sleeved garment with a "robe of woven design...wound around the body and then over the shoulder to form a cape." It appears in Egyptian art by 1425 BC (Pritchard 1958, p. 14, fig. 43; p. 255) and continues into the Nineteenth and Twentieth Dynasties, p. 18, fig. 53, 54. Hayes 1937, p. 36.
224 It is a remarkable feat to replicate the colors of these dyes in faience. Great attention has been paid to reproducing details of the textiles effectively. It is interesting to speculate whether foreign workmen with first-hand knowledge of these costumes might have been employed in the faience industry.
225 Presented as Syrian tribute in Eighteenth Dynasty tombs: e.g. TT 84, Davies 1941, p. 97, n. 7, pl. XIII. The so-called girdle of Ramesses III produced in Egypt in this period shows a contemporary interest in Eastern weaves and garments. See Riefstahl 1944, pp. 26–27, fig. 38; p. 53, ft. 62.
226 Hayes 1937, p. 35, n. 150, pl. VIII, top; Daressy 1911, p. 54, pl. II, 3. The original identification as a Hittite, made soon after the tile was found, was based on Petrie 1887, pp. 246–51: Rowe 1908, p. 49, and then applied to the main chief with similar profile and beard on a faience throne dais of Ramesses II (Hayes 1937, p. 35, ft. 143, pl. III). While the standard Hittite profile showed a prominent nose and receding chin, all representations on Ramesside monuments that are specifically labeled as Hittites portray them without beards (Oosthoek in Obsomer and Oosthoek 1992, pp. 336, 339, ft. 10). In this they followed the Hittites themselves who show only their gods with beards. For depictions of Hittites, see Pritchard 1958, p. 12, figs. 31–33 and p. 4, fig. 9, from Medinet Habu. Long flowing hair is another important characteristic shown on tiles of the period of Ramesses III more likely to be Hittites despite garments borrowed from other nationalities (Berlin Äg 17727 and Cairo JE 36457f: Pritchard 1958, figs. 34, 35 and pp. 253, 254). Facial characteristics and hairstyle seem to be the most constant factors used to determine identity in this period. It has been suggested that in Egyptian art apparent Hittites with beards are more likely to be Syrian allies of the Hittites (Gurney 1990, p. 179).
227 Cairo JE 36457b in Saleh and Sourouzian 1987, no. 226. This is standard garb for the Nubian elite who were acculturated into Egyptian styles and served in the bureaucracy, and is the normal style for their depiction in Egyptian art from the late Eighteenth Dynasty on: T. 40, Davies and Gardiner 1926, pl. XXVII.
228 Trigger 1976, pp. 109ff. While the Egyptians certainly maintain this attitude, the extent of Egyptian domination has been questioned: Morkot in Davies 1991, pp. 294–301, a new analysis, which attributes to Nubia/Kush more autonomy.
229 A second tile, with another Nubian chief in similar garb facing in the opposite direction, is a companion to this tile, with much the same scale and feeling: Museum of Fine Arts, Boston 1903.1574 (Rowe 1908, p. 49).
230 Despite the difference in dress, the tiles show similar features for both groups of Nubians, a standard appearance that is established in the late Eighteenth Dynasty, e.g. Davies and Gardiner 1926, when Egypt's contacts and control reached as far south as the Fourth Cataract. It was at this time that the Egyptians began to portray these Nubian/Kushite groups with darker skin, often with the features shown on the tiles. See Trigger in Hochfield and Riefstahl 1978, p. 33.
231 Described as beads or shells on a tile in Cairo J 36457, which portrays a chief in costume very similar to this tile. See Daressy 1911, p. 62, no. 18. Other fragments illustrate this element: Museum of Fine Arts Boston 1903.1574, see Rowe 1908, p.49; Hölscher 1951, pl. 34l.
232 The elite of this time also wear this combination over their long linen garment: see Cairo JE 36457b, n. 227 above. It replaced the chamois cloth in this position, beginning in the late Eighteenth Dynasty (Drenkhahn 1967, p. 45).
233 This skin is worn by enslaved Nubians given as tribute in the temple of Ramesses II at Beit el-Wali. Here it is worn as an accessory garment by Nubian chiefs. Drenkhahn 1967, p. 46.
234 Drenkhahn 1967 pp. 47–48. Possibly leather, this collar is shown in many brightly colored variants, for instance in a scene of mercenary Nubian soldiers (Nelson 1932, pl. 65E) and on a tile with an Egyptianized Nubian, see Cairo JE 36457b (see n. 227 above), both from this temple.
235 Nelson 1930, pl. 9, 10. Pl. 11 shows chiefs in both styles of dress.
236 Trigger 1976, p. 113.
237 Rowe 1908 p. 50 right. A similar sketch (illustrated in Daressy 1911, no. 18, p. 62) was incised on the back of Cairo JE 36457, which closely resembles this tile (see n. 231 above).
238 JE 36497, Hölscher 1941, pl. 35D. For a plan of this structure and the recessed niches for the tiles, see Hölscher 1951, pl. 39; see pl. 5 for a composite reconstruction of three doorways that once held tiles in the first court of the temple.
239 Most are one of two sizes: 25 cm x 6.5 cm (10 in x 2½ in) like the one here, and a larger size, approximately 30 cm x 7 cm (12 in x 2¾ in). See Daressy 1911, p. 50.
240 E.g., Davies 1905, pl. XXXIV for prisoners on the balcony below the window of appearance on raised feet; for captives shown with flat feet, see Davies 1906, pl. IV.
241 Museum of Fine Arts, Boston, 1903.1574, see n. 229 above.
242 The archaic style of this type of chief at Medinet Habu, in contrast with that of the rest of the Meshwesh peoples whom he leads, has been explained by saying that such leaders were actually descendants of the Tjehenu (Wainwright 1962, p. 92). This group was shown in the Fifth Dynasty (Borchardt et al. 1913, pt. II, pl. I, 5). Two other tiles dating to the reign of Ramesses III and said to be from Medinet Habu have the features shown here. K 9620 is similar, with long strands of brilliant orange hair and trained beard: Müller 1964, p. 101, no. A 139; Schlögl 1978, p. 69, no. 218. Another tile fragment, similar but less well done, shows a stylized version with chalk-white skin and bright red hair and beard: Berlin Museum Nr. 15729, Staatliche Museen zu Berlin 1991, no. 94.
243 The similarity of faces on other tile fragments suggests that some were produced in molds and then altered to fit the type.
244 A variety of tiles, including many fragments of prisoner tiles, was collected at this site by Rev. Greville J. Chester and sold to the British Museum. See Wallis 1900, p. xiv and pl. V, VI; Porter and Moss 1934, p. 57.
245 Hayes 1937, p. 34 and pl. IV.
246 Unlike the more frequent group on New Kingdom monuments, the Tjemehu Libyans with dark bobbed hair, long side-lock and patterned robe tied on one shoulder, as in the Book of Gates in Seti I's and Ramesses III's tombs (O'Connor 1990, pp. 47–48, fig. 1; Hornung 1990, p. 147, fig. 105; p. 148, fig. 109). Tiles from Medinet Habu and battle scenes show this type: Cairo JE 36457a (Saleh and Sourouzian 1987, no. 226).
247 In the second cycle of battle scenes (Wainwright 1962, pp. 89–99).
248 They stand out from the other chiefs of the land of Meshwesh, differentiated in appearance from the rest of the Tjemehu Libyans, including the soldiers under their command. O'Connor 1990, pp. 29–113, and esp. ch. IVa, places this type within the whole program of Libyan battles at Medinet Habu. For the role of these two chiefs, see pp. 66–76 and fig. 4, with discussion of their costume on pp. 68–74.
249 The small palace adjoins a temple there: Zivie 1985, cols. 331–35.

250 Maspero 1914, p. 304, fig. 266. Examples of these rosettes can be found in many museum collections: see Schlick-Nolte 1984, no.52, p. 102.

251 Rosettes from other sites often have ten petals and a greater range of size and thickness, and use several different, sometimes brighter colors: see for example Metropolitan Museum of Art 35.1.127-139; Hayes 1937, p. 41 *kk*, pl. XIII bottom.

252 A number are in the British Museum, e.g., nos. 49156, 49157, 49158, all from Tell el-Yahudiya, acquired from Greville J. Chester in 1871.

253 Along with the larger version, others types made in smaller quantities in the workshops have the colors reversed and more complex patterns, but all use the eight-petal rosette, white combined with gray, gray-blue or beige, and a yellow boss (Hayes 1990 (1959), p. 368, fig. 232).

254 The crack around the edge of the petals is characteristic of inlay. These details of manufacture are described in Kaczmarczyk and Hedges 1983, p. 177. See also Schlick-Nolte 1984, no. 52, pp. 102, 103.

255 Vandiver in Kaczmarczyk and Hedges 1983, p. A-118 for technique of adding the central boss.

256 Lewis 1881, pp. 177ff. pl. IV.1.

257 British Museum 38273: see Lewis 1881, pl. IV.2, with a different type of rosette.

258 A line of the larger rosettes is set along the base with a second row of smaller ones above. On the top, surrounding a lotus flower design, large and small faience rosettes form an attractive all-over decorative pattern. Maspero 1914, p. 305. On display in Room 44. See cases 463 and 464.

259 Kitchen 1973, p. 3.

260 Brooklyn Museum of Art 16.73: Riefstahl 1968, no. 49.

261 Kitchen 1973, p. 65, no. 315.

262 Riefstahl 1968, no. 49.

263 Pelizaeus Museum, Hildesheim 5515: Eggebrecht 1987, p. 267, no. 210.

264 Vassilika 1995, p. 96.

265 For the crown of action, once called the Blue Crown, see Bryan in Kozloff and Bryan 1992c, p. 162; for a convenient summary of the issues involved with the cap crown, consult Török 1987, pp. 5–7.

266 Vassilika 1995.

267 Vassilika 1995.

268 Staatliche Museen zu Berlin - Preussischer Kulturbesitz Ägyptisches Museum und Papyrussammlung. 4563.

269 The Brooklyn Museum 37.344E: Riefstahl 1968, pp. 59 and 106, no. 57.

270 Fazzini 1988, p. 8.

271 Schlögl 1977, pp. 25 and 34.

272 Kitchen 1973, p. 467, table 3, admitting that the reign may have ended as recently as 715 BC.

273 Schlögl 1977, pp. 19 and 44–45.

274 For a convenient summary of the views, see Bothmer 1985, p. 102, notes 21–24, to which should be added the earlier discussion of this amulet by Bissing 1905, pp. 23–26; Delange in Eggebrecht 1987, p. 31; and Brovarski 1991, pp. 32–33.

275 Brooklyn 59.17: Fazzini et al. 1989, no. 69.

276 Fazzini et al. 1989, no. 69.

277 Bianchi 1980, pp. 41–43.

278 Or the glyphs could have been cut by hand.

279 Manniche 1991, pp. 63–65.

280 London, British Museum 7511; Andrews 1994, p. 96, fig. 97g.

281 Fischer 1986, pp. 130–35.

282 Dunham 1950, 1955–65, plate CXIX.

283 *Inter alia*, Frankfurt, Liebieghaus, inv. nr. 2328: Schlick-Nolte and Droste zu Hülshoff 1990, pp. 329–30, no. 327.

284 The long-held opinion that such jubilees were celebrated by pharaohs after reigning for 30 years has been called into question; see both Kees 1958, pp. 194–213, and Berman in Kozloff and Bryan 1992a, pp. 38–41.

285 New York, The Metropolitan Museum of Art, 41.160.104: Fazzini 1988, p. 31 and pl. VI, 3.

286 Gardiner 1957, pp. 468, G8, and 505, S 12.

287 Bianchi 1983a, pp. 29–35; Bianchi 1983b, pp. 9–29.

288 New York, The Metropolitan Museum of Art 26.7.1006: Ricketts 1918a, pp. 70–80.

289 Thompson 1973 is the basic text for this type.

290 Similar reading by Brian Shefton communicated by telephone.

291 Thompson 1973, pp. 19–20.

292 Thompson 1979, p. 252; Bianchi et al. 1988, pp. 160, 162, no. 61 f (gold quarter drachm), pp. 172–73, no. 67 (marble).

293 Burnham 1978, pp. 661–91.

294 Thompson 1973, p. 8; Parlasca 1976, p. 146; Bianchi et al. 1988, pp. 174–75, no. 68; Nenna and Seif el-Din 1993, pp. 586–89, fig. 11; Nenna and Seif el-Din 1994, p. 319.

295 Thompson 1973, p. 83; Smith in Matheson 1994, pp. 88–92; Broucke in Matheson 1994, pp. 34–49; Matheson 1994, pp. 18–33; Metzler in Matheson 1994, pp. 76–85.

296 Thompson 1973, pp. 149–53, pls. XXIX–XXX, nos. 75–86 (figure type IIa).

297 Thompson 1973, p. 132, pl. VIII, no. 22; Besques 1984, pp. 273–76, pl. XLVIII.

298 Thompson 1973, p. 130, pl. VII, no. 17; pp. 149–50, pl. XXVI–XXVII, no. 75; and pp. 151–52, pl. XXIX, no. 8c.

299 Thompson 1973, p. 175, pl. LI, no. 152.

300 Niemeyer and Docter 1993, pp. 239–40, pl. 59, 3.

301 Thompson 1973, p. 150.

302 Thompson 1973, pp. 125–26, pls. I, II, LX, LXII, no. 1.

303 Thompson 1973, pp. 134–35, pls. C, XI, no. 29.

304 Thompson 1973, pp. 149–50, pls. B, XXV–XXVII, no. 75.

305 Thompson 1973, pl. XLIX.

306 Thompson 1973, pp. 41, 44–45.

307 Stuart 1944, pp. 171–75.

308 Schneider 1976, pp. 15–16; Vierneisel and Zanker 1979, pp. 45–46, 50–51, 52, and 55; and Walker and Burnett 1981, pp. 20–21. See also Pollini 1987–88, pp. 103–08.

309 Thompson 1988, pp. 135, and 271–72.

310 Thompson 1988, pp. 135 and 271–72; Reymond 1981, pp. 54–55, and 214–21; and Cheshire 1986, p. 41.

311 Kiss 1984, pp. 105–06, to which one should add the example in Painter and Whitehouse 1990, pp. 160–63.

312 Pollini 1990, pp. 334–63; Becher 1985, pp. 61–64.

313 Grenier 1987, pp. 99, 100, passim.

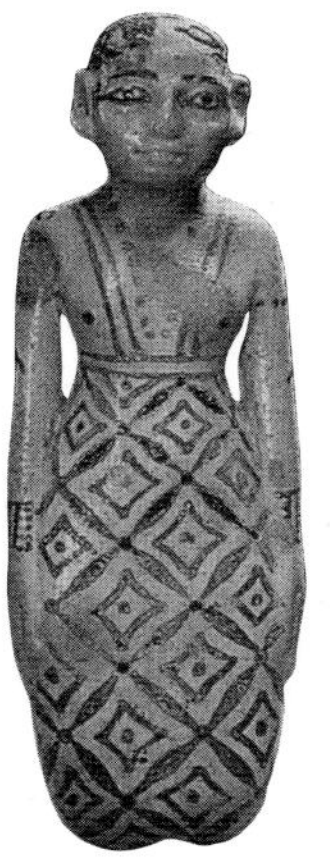

64 FEMALE FECUNDITY FIGURE PAGE 104

Middle Kingdom, Dynasty 12

Turquoise green faience with details in dark brown glaze; H. 12.7 cm

The George Ortiz Collection

Ex-European Private Collection

This female figure, possibly the finest of this class of faience fertility figurines, wears a closely cropped coiffure parted in the center, and a dress with an interlocking four-petalled pattern that is held in place by two straps, one over each shoulder. The pattern may represent a fishnet fashion, attested in ancient Egyptian art from the Old Kingdom[1] to Late Period, traditionally imbued with erotic overtones.[2] In keeping with its salacious character, the garment exposes the breasts, with the nipples rendered in brown. As accessories the figurine has beaded armbands and bracelets, the latter decorated with what may be a bird's talon. Around her neck is a string of beads, tied at the back where its two ribbon-ends fall down. This element represents a necklace rather than a tattoo,[3] as shown by an actual tattoo rendered on her right shoulder. The tattoo contributes to the eroticism inherent in the piece, as does the treatment of the legs and arms: the legs are purposely truncated at the knees and the arms coalesce into the thighs, thereby magically depriving the figure of both mobility and manual dexterity.[4]

Such figures, although never depicted on walls of contemporary tombs, have been excavated not only in male and female burials, where they served as grave goods, but also at town sites.[5] Without a clear archaeological context it is difficult to define with precision the original purpose of this figure because of the polyvalent nature of ancient Egyptian symbols. Nevertheless, its eroticism is undeniable. Furthermore, since the ancient Egyptians did not maintain a distinction between sex and procreation, any of these figurines might in principle have affected any aspect of human sexual experience, from physical sex, including conception and childbirth, to metaphysical regeneration and fecundity in the broadest sense. In life, then, as the finds in town sites suggest, such figurines may have been intended to guarantee the fertility of the home and field or the *abbondanza* of the household in general, whereas in the tomb these statuettes might be beneficial for the deceased's resurrection. RSB

Bibliography. Christie's 1992, pp. 80–81, Lot. 81.

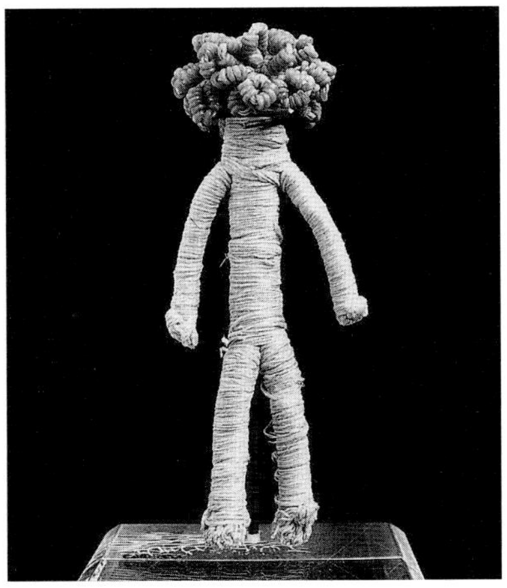

65 DOLL PAGE 107

Middle Kingdom, Dynasty 12; Beni Hasan, tomb 420

Bound flax with blue faience beads; H. 7.8 cm

Myers Museum, Eton College, with Permission of the Provost and Fellows. ECM 1843

Gift of Prof. P.E. Newberry, acquired by him at the sale of the collection of the Rev. William MacGregor, 1922

John Garstang, the excavator of this charming image, believed that both it and a larger and more elaborate companion piece (without beaded embellishment) found in the same plundered tomb (no. 420) at Beni Hasan in Middle Egypt were children's playthings. He did, however, acknowledge that some Egyptologists might be tempted to see in them a "religious significance."[6] Garstang was evidently alluding to other female figurines frequently encountered in tombs of Middle Kingdom date, executed in a variety of materials and generally characterized by an exaggeration of the genital region and a curtailment of the lower limbs [64] and [66].[7] In the past, such figures have tended to be interpreted as concubines for the deceased's afterlife pleasure, though their occurrence in the burials of young girls and the occasional presence of an infant in the model's arms[8] point to broader regenerative associations.[9]

The body of the Eton figure is formed from tightly bound, white linen thread, with hair of clusters of small beads of brilliant blue faience. Neither it nor its companion displays any sexual emphasis to connect it with the "concubine" genre.[10] Equally, however, Garstang's scant published (and unpublished) descriptions of the tomb in which the images were found and its contents—fragments of a coffin with text (evidently not preserving the owner's name or title), a wooden headrest, the remains of granary, brewery, and boat models in wood, a pottery (canopic?) stopper, and two shouldered jars and a dish[11]—offer no firm indication that tomb no. 420 necessarily belonged to a child. NR

Bibliography. Garstang 1907, pp. 152–53, fig. 151 (right); Sotheby, Wilkinson, and Hodge 1922, p. 70, part of lot 561; Eton College 1990, p. 114, no. 172; Reeves and Spur 1995, p. 22, top right.

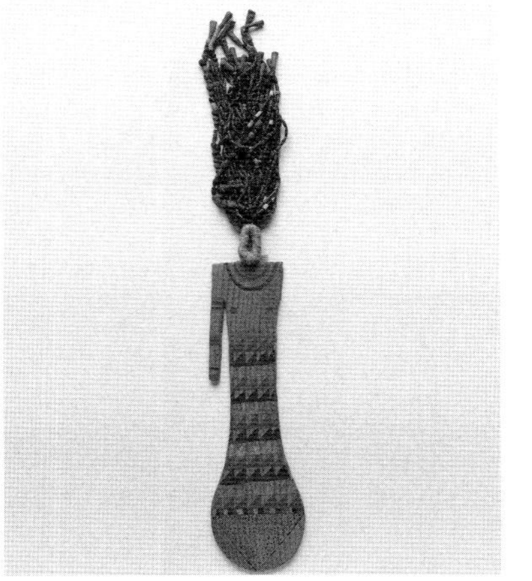

66 PADDLE DOLL PAGE 106

Middle Kingdom, Dynasty 11; Thebes, at the entrance of Tomb H4 at Khokheh

Wood painted black, red, and white with a wig composed of mud and faience beads and elongated blobs of mud on string; H. 35.0 cm, with wig fully extended

The Metropolitan Museum of Art, New York. Rogers Fund, 1915. 15.10.90

Both the dating and interpretation of this object can be precisely identified because of its findspot at the entrance of a Middle Kingdom tomb contemporary with Mentuhotep Nebhepetre. Called a paddle doll because of the general shape of the body, it represents a female figure abstracted in the extreme. The legs and feet are completely missing, and the arms are rendered as if atrophied and without hands. Anatomical interest is focused in the clearly articulated pubic triangle and breasts. The inherent sexuality of the piece is enhanced by the garment, the exact identification of which is elusive, which covers only the midriff.[12] Armbands, bracelets, necklace, and a girdle around the pelvis complete the figure's accessories. The image is deprived of individuality by the absence of a head and the lack of accompanying inscriptions, but the long tresses, made of mud and faience, enhance its erotic overtones.[13]

In discussing the eroticism of such figures[14] it should be remembered that the ancient Egyptians did not maintain the separation between sex and procreation that many moderns do.[15] Within the funerary context in which this figurine was found, its function was to arouse its owner's procreative powers by analogy with those stimulated by Isis in her ministrations over her deceased husband, Osiris. Since human procreation is linked to rebirth and resurrection, such fertility figures play a significant role in the hoped-for resurrection of the deceased.[16] The fact that the hair is composed of both clay and faience beads is not insignificant. Clay is a primeval substance which embodies creation itself, and faience not only recalls the regenerative forces of the universe[17] but comes to represent the sun itself. The erotic overtones of long hair, then, are combined with both the solar and creative significance of the materials from which the wig is made in order to insure the resurrection of the deceased. These figures need not be associated exclusively with male burials, since the concept here represented would be efficacious for women as well.[18] RSB

Bibliography. Hayes 1953, p. 219 and fig. 135.

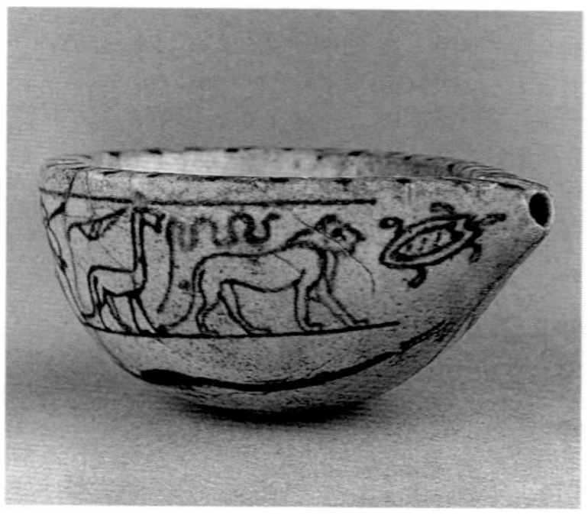

67 BABY'S FEEDING CUP PAGE 105

Middle Kingdom, late Dynasty 12 to Dynasty 13; Lisht, North Pyramid Cemetery, Surface, Basket 2
Faience, bright blue with black decoration; H. 3.5 cm; max. D. 8.0 cm

The Metropolitan Museum of Art, New York. Rogers Fund, 1944. 44.4.4

This small oviform cup was designed to assist a mother in feeding her infant. It has been carefully shaped with a hole at the narrow end to funnel a fine flow of liquid, even a very thin gruel, into a baby's mouth. A series of black strokes decorate the rim and black lines form irregular circles on the rounded base. There are also six small holes evenly spaced around the rim.[19]

The important element of decoration is the frieze, displaying a series of deities and demonic animals. Its central figure is a Bes-image, while two rows of identical figures move away from him towards the spout: Bes-images holding pairs of snakes; Tawerets; serpent-necked felines; snakes; lions; and turtles. These same gods and goddesses are repeatedly depicted on magic wands and rods. On the basis of the occasional inscriptions that accompany them, scholars have demonstrated that these figures provided protection for pregnant women and young children, whom ancient Egyptian society regarded as especially vulnerable to evil forces.[20]

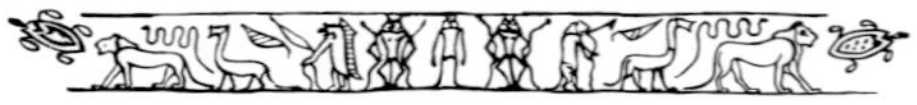

Fig. 48 Drawing of the decorative frieze.

Pottery feeding cups have been recognized among the ceramic finds at several Middle Kingdom sites, almost exclusively in the burials of very young children.[21] Most are simple cups or small jars whose rims have been pinched in one place to form a pouring lip.[22] One small bowl with an elongated spout is decorated with bands of red pigment, a more complex version of the type.[23] The material, style of decoration, and careful craftsmanship of the example displayed here, however, make it exceptional.

One possible explanation for the cup's manufacture in faience is because it was intended for burial and not for daily use like the pottery examples, and that the figures were to give the baby eternal protection. However, it was found in a basket alongside a small crocodile of Egyptian blue.[24] The basket was deposited just under the surface of debris in the cemetery west of the pyramid of Amenemhet I, with no sign of an accompanying burial. This circumstance suggests that a different function for this feeding cup must be considered. The fact that both objects in the basket had magical connotations and were found as an isolated deposit in a sacred area implies a more specialized use. The cup, with efficacious magic provided by the figures (and also quite possibly by its color), could have been used to give a specific type of drink, perhaps medicine, to a young child. The feeder's physical form would have contained the precious liquid, while the magical elements endowed the medicine with positive energy.

DCP

Bibliography. Scott 1944, fig. 30; Hayes 1953, p. 247; Fischer 1966, p. 168, fig. 9; Fischer 1968, pp. 16, 33, pl. 20; Charvát 1980, p. 46; Romano 1980, p. 48, n. 40.

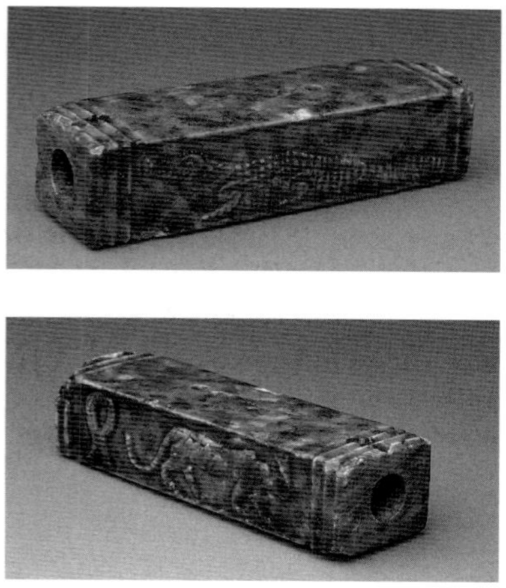

68 SECTION OF A MAGIC ROD PAGE 110

Middle Kingdom, late Dynasty 12 to Dynasty 13
Glazed steatite; H. 1.9 cm; W. 1.5 cm; L. 5.8 cm
Private Collection
Ex-Collection: Norbert Schimmel

Found in both settlements and cemeteries,[25] magic rods were designed to guard babies and new mothers from the threat of disease and the perils of everyday life. A *s3*-glyph signifying protection appears in carved relief on one side, accompanied by a stalking cat or panther. An alert crocodile is carved on the other side.[26] The full rod may have been used by a magician or even the woman herself to convert the fearsome power of the depicted beasts into benevolent aid.[27]

This section of a magic rod is only one piece of a larger, possibly four-segment rod, as seen in the complete example at the Metropolitan Museum of Art (MMA 26.7.1275). A drill hole through the center shows that further segments were attached at both ends, probably by means of a long pin.[28] The hole on the top, to receive a tenon, illustrates how a three-dimensional animal, such as a protective lion, frog, crocodile, or turtle, was affixed,[29] again demonstrated by the New York decorated rod.[30]

The rod shown here [68] is made not of faience but of green glazed steatite, the use of which preceded faience (see [1]) and continued, though less frequently than faience, in the millennia that followed. Certain magical objects like these rods were typically produced in glazed steatite, whose blue-green color, like that of faience, was deemed life-giving and protective. Magic knives formed another class of related objects to protect mothers and children. These were generally made of ivory, though one faience example exists in a private collection. Often the glaze on the magic rods has disappeared, unlike this well preserved example that retains its blue-green color. On steatite examples the glaze was applied to the stone surface, probably by dipping or brushing, while in faience production the colorant could be similarly applied but is more often mixed into the quartz paste.

FDF

Bibliography. Sotheby's 1992, Lot no. 81.

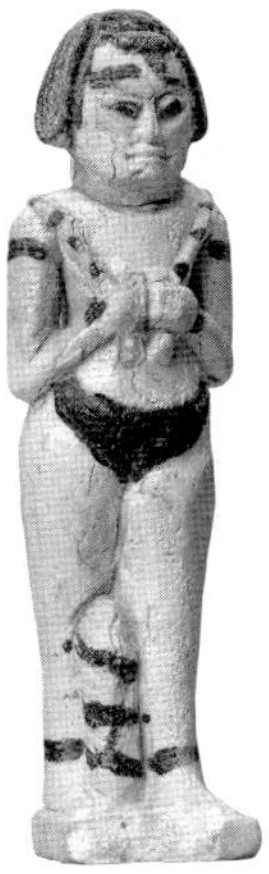

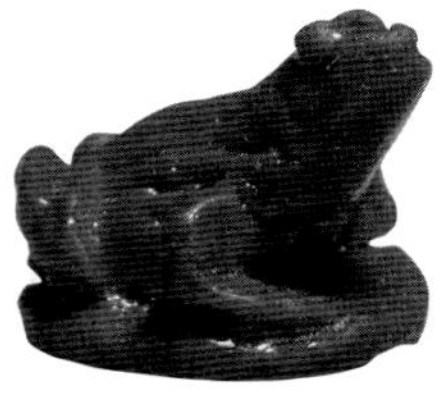

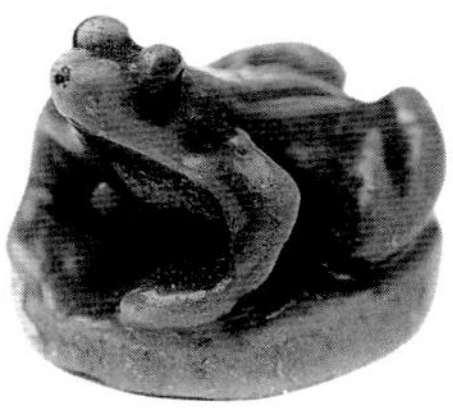

69 FEMALE STATUETTE PAGE 106

Late Period, Dynasty 25

Faience; H. 14.2 cm, W. 4.0 cm. Base, front to back 4.5 cm

Museum of Fine Arts, Boston. William Stevenson Smith Fund. 1984.168

Made for a magical purpose, this nude figure of a female standing on a square base carries an infant monkey on her back and has a second monkey seated behind her left foot. She also has a basket resting between her legs. The infant monkey rests in a backpack, the straps of which are spotted and held in the woman's hands joined on her chest. Black glaze painted on the pale green surface emphasizes her hairdo, eyes, pubic area, and jewelry as well as features on the basket and seated monkey. She has a distinctive four-part hairdo—with heavy bangs falling across her forehead—that is associated with Nubian women.[31] Her date is based on a similar hairdo on a statuette from el-Kurru in the Sudan.[32]

This object had a talismanic function and belongs to a larger group of figures that vary widely in appearance but share a similar magical purpose in Egyptian folk religion. Whether a figurine depicted the god Bes, the cat goddess Bastet, a monkey, or, as with this example, a Nubian woman, they were all made to protect women in childbirth and their nursing infants.[33] So popular were they that numbers of them have been found outside Egypt in ancient Kush[34] and throughout the Mediterranean, including Greece.[35]

In connection with its magical purpose, the figurine's various features were all selected for their efficacy. Unusually for this type, the figure carries an infant monkey rather than a human infant.[36] In ancient Egypt the monkey can play the role of nursemaid and in this context may have been placed both in the backpack and behind the left leg of this Nubian woman to assist her magically in her role as a wet-nurse.[37] The kneeling monkey eats what is probably the nut of a dom-palm, which also has magical properties associated with ideas of fertility and nurturing of the newborn.[38] The identification of the female as Nubian because of her special coiffure may associate her with a class of powerful goddesses such as Tefnut, Sekhmet, and Nekhbet: during the Late Period these goddesses were sometimes linked to Nubia in their roles as protectors of women in childbirth and of their newborn infants.[39]

Many of these figurines were intended to be worn as protective amulets and this example has a perforated lug at the back of its neck; others, however, have an opening on the underside of their bases, possibly for mounting on a handle, and may have been used in rituals. Small holes visible in the hair and ears of some of the main figures and infants suggest that thin metal objects (loops?) could have been threaded through them. The objects could then have been used as sistra (rattles): when the figurines were shaken during rituals surrounding childbirth and nursing, the jingling of the metal objects would scare off dangerous forces.[40] JWY

Bibliography. *The Boston Museum of Fine Arts Annual Report* 1983–84, p. 25; Brovarksi 1987, pp. 58–59; Bulté 1991, p 48, pl. 24 c–d.

70 FROG-SHAPED BEAD PAGE 116

New Kingdom, late Dynasty 18, *c.* 1380–1330 BC

Faience; L. 1.1 cm

The Cleveland Museum of Art. Gift of Cyril and Jessica Aldred. 1980.123

71 FROG-SHAPED BEAD PAGE 116

New Kingdom, late Dynasty 18, *c.* 1380–1330 BC

Faience; L. 0.8 cm

Musée du Louvre, Paris. AF 11514

The ancient Egyptians, especially women, believed that wearing frog-shaped beads and amulets brought them fertility. These little gems may be miniature representations of the frog-form goddess Heqat, who was worshiped as early as Predynastic times.[41] In the mid-Eighteenth Dynasty, in Queen Hatshepsut's famous temple at Deir el-Bahri, her artists portrayed the queen's pregnant mother being led into the birth chamber by Heqat, who was shown with a frog's head and a woman's body.

Frog beads and amulets, and indeed mummified frogs, were also placed with mummies to insure the deceased rebirth and everlasting life.[42] The frog image was also used after a deceased person's name as a hieroglyphic ideogram, or cryptogram, for the phrase *wehem ankh*, "repeating life,"[43] assuring the departed soul of renewal.

The Cleveland frog [70] is inscribed on the underside with the hieroglyph *nefer*, meaning "good" or "beautiful." The feminine suffix "*-t*" is lacking, and so perhaps this little frog belonged to a man. The purple-blue of this frog was a favorite color of Amenhotep III,[44] whose faience workshops regularly added details in contrasting colors, like the red eyes here. The lime green of the Louvre frog [71] was more popular during the next reign; however, images of animals were considered contrary to Akhenaten's monotheistic Atenism. These little mold-made frogs are especially charming because of their exquisite quality at a virtually microscopic size. Larger examples from the Eighteenth Dynasty are also known.[45] APK

Bibliography. [70]: Kozloff 1982, p. 6, no. 7.

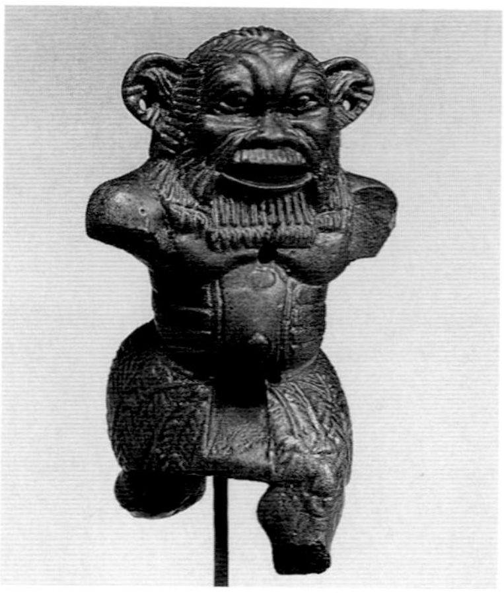

72 STATUETTE OF A BES-IMAGE PAGE 108

New Kingdom, Dynasty 18, reign of Akhenaten; Possibly from Amarna

Faience; H. 8.7 cm

Staatliche Museen zu Berlin - Preussischer Kulturbesitz Ägyptisches Museum und Papyrussammlung. 20484

Generations of museum visitors have marveled at the stately images of Egyptian deities with their formal poses, placid faces, and athletic physiques. One extraordinary image, however, invariably stands out from these "typical" gods. This figure, frequently identified as Bes, is shown with a huge head, a fierce or grimacing expression, muscular limbs, a distended abdomen, swollen buttocks, and a tail. In fact "Bes" is a convenient term for nearly a dozen individual deities, including Aha, Hayet, Menu, and Bes, all of whom have similar if not identical physical features. To avoid confusion, Egyptologists use the term "Bes-image" when the god's specific identity is not known.

The gods represented by the Bes-image seem to have been guardians of infants and new mothers. In the Middle Kingdom, for example, they appear on an infant's feeding cup [67] and on sickle-shaped objects called "magic knives" used to draw circles around sleeping children in the dirt floor to protect them during the perilous nighttime hours. Bes-images can also be seen in reliefs depicting the births of the Eighteenth Dynasty rulers Hatshepsut and Amenhotep III. In addition, they are found on a number of Nineteenth and Twentieth Dynasty painted limestone flakes (called *ostraca*) from Deir el-Medina that show scenes of post-partum rituals. Following birth, the new mother was removed to a temporary enclosure or arbor containing an elaborate bed on which she nursed her child. The legs of most of these beds were carved in the form of Bes-images, and some of these scenes also seem to contain statues of the god within the arbor.

Although this Bes-image is often said to have come from Amarna, the accession records of the Berlin Museum reveal that it was purchased in Cairo from the antiquities dealer Nicholas Tano and is only presumed to date to Akhenaten's reign. Nevertheless, several details can be paralleled on Bes-images from the Amarna Period. The cavities in the mouth and in the center of the god's kilt, for example, must have accommodated stone inlays; a treatment also found on a steatite cosmetic container excavated at Amarna.[46] Similarly, the unusual attitude, which suggests running or dancing, also appears on an *ostracon* from the Royal Tomb at Amarna.[47]

Because the god's attitude is best understood from the side, it is likely that the statuette was meant to be seen in profile rather than from the more familiar frontal position. A somewhat larger statuette in this pose appears on a maternity bower dating to the Nineteenth or Twentieth Dynasty.[48] It is possible that this example was used in a similar context during the Amarna Period. DCP

Bibliography. Schäfer 1913, 56, ill. 26; Werbrouck 1933, p. 30, fig. 1; Kozloff in Kozloff and Bryan 1992i, pp. 226–27, no. 35.

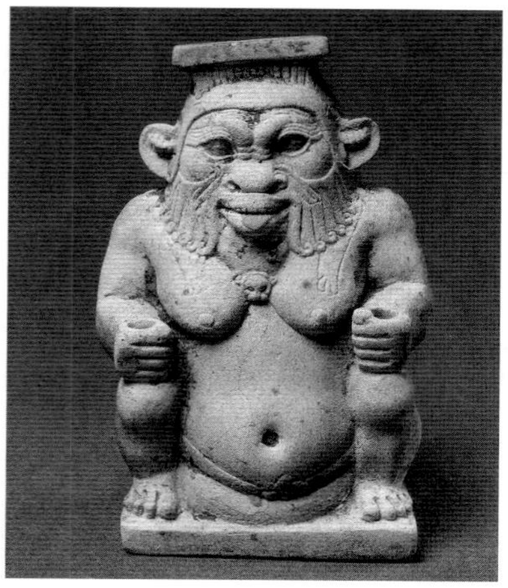

73 PERFUME JAR IN THE IMAGE OF THE GOD BES PAGE 108

Late Period, early to mid-Dynasty 26, 664–550 BC

Egyptian blue; H. 9.3 cm

The Cleveland Museum of Art. Purchase from the J.H. Wade Fund. 1995.13

This jar may have stood in a wealthy individual's household shrine,[49] where the popular domestic god Bes could not only dispense its contents but also watch over his owner's home and family. Romano suggests that such vessels contained either a pediatric remedy or a preparation for pregnant women or new mothers,[50] because Bes took care of matters close to home, guarding the hearth as well as protecting children and women in childbirth. At the owner's death, refilled to the crown, Bes could have become a tomb gift. Alternatively, he may have been purchased new as a donation to a favorite temple or sanctuary, in thanks for or in expectation of a favor from the god.

This Bes's main color is a grayish periwinkle-blue; bright yellow dots add color to his cheetah skin, and his tongue is red, just like the warts on his ears. The jar's mouth masquerades as the *modius* (platform) for Bes's crown of plumes; these are missing, but would have acted as the jar's stopper. Bes's two fists once held applicator sticks, probably either of wood or ivory. The eye sockets are hollow, having lost their inlays of glass or colored stone.

The figure was probably first modeled or molded around a core, with details touched up with a sharp instrument before firing. The red and yellow colors would also have been added at this stage, perhaps with a piping tube. The holes in the fists were drilled with a bow drill. The core was removed after firing.

Other examples of faience Bes cosmetic jars of similar date and material but without added colors include: 1) green, Museo Egizio, Turin, unpublished; 2) green, the Virginia Museum, 93.110;[51] 3) blue, Swiss collection, 1996;[52] 4) green with glass and carnelian inlays, Louvre, E 10929.[53] A similar faience jar on which Bes holds a lion is in the Louvre (EA 3311);[54] one in limestone holding a monkey is in Cairo (JE 28363).[55] Related faience *aryballoi*, clearly developments from the Cleveland type, on which Bes holds an antelope and the vessel rim and mouth are Corinthian-shaped, have been found on Samos in contexts dated 580–550 BC.[56] Finally, there are two small statuettes of Bes in blue faience with added red details in the Graeco-Roman Museum, Alexandria.[57] APK

Bibliography. Kozloff 1996, pp. 4–5 (illustrated front cover).

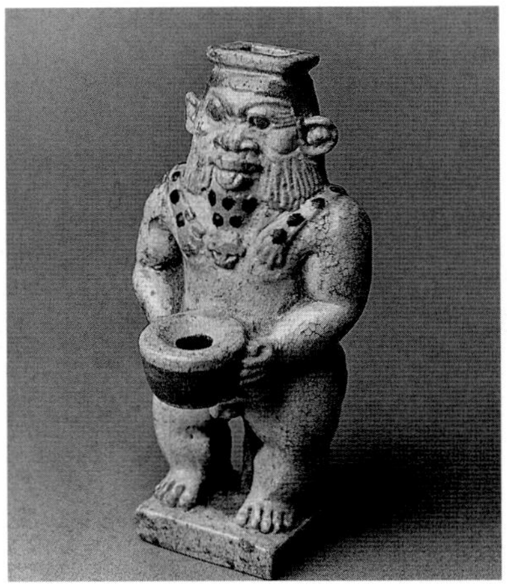

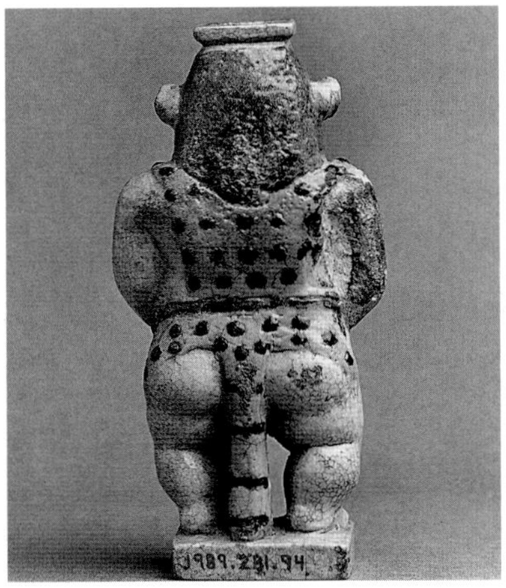

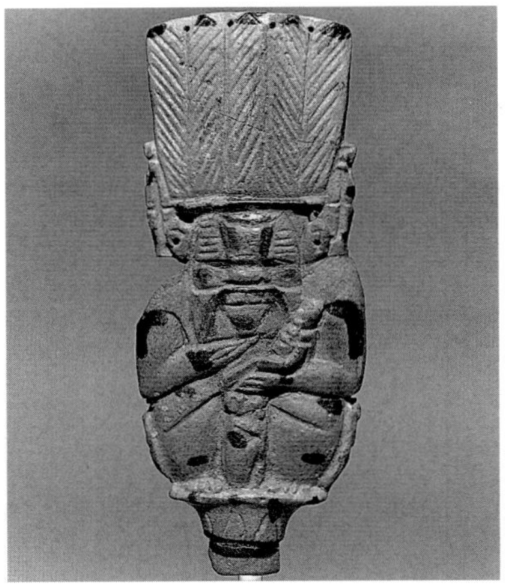

74 BES-IMAGE HOLDING A RING

PAGE 108

Late Period, Dynasty 27

Polychrome faience with traces of frit; H. 9.2 cm; W. 4.4 cm

The Metropolitan Museum of Art, New York. Gift of Norbert Schimmel Trust, 1989. 1989.281.94

Ex-Collection: Norbert Schimmel

By the Fifth Dynasty, Egyptian artisans were fashioning figures of demigods that combined the physical features of humans and lions. Over time this so-called Bes-image lost many of its original leonine traits, and by the Late Period only its rounded ears served to recall its ancient associations with lions. Despite dramatic changes in the Bes-image's iconography, however, it appears in a highly limited number of contexts: it is almost always found in scenes or on objects relating to fertility, sexual attraction, and the protection of infants and new mothers during the perilous hours after birth.

This Bes-image's striking appearance was probably even more dramatic in antiquity. In the plinth atop his head is a small square cavity containing a rich blue substance. Analysis by the Metropolitan Museum of Art's Conservation Department has determined that this material is Egyptian blue. During the Late Period Bes-images frequently wore feathered headdresses and the Egyptian blue in the cavity could have been the colorant in the adhesive securing the feathers—made from a separate faience piece—to the figure. Alternatively, the feathers themselves may have been fashioned of Egyptian blue. Certainly such blue plumes would have heightened the figure's visual impact while harmonizing with the blue-gray color of his hair.

Although the craftsmanship of the piece is superb, the iconography is essentially quite standard. One detail, however, distinguishes it from the thousands of Bes-images of Late Period date: the thick-banded ring he holds in front of his ample stomach. Scholars have focused on this unique detail to explain how the object functioned in antiquity. It has been suggested that the ring supported a stick used to apply kohl or some other cosmetic or that it served as the cap of a small cosmetic container that could be removed for easy filling.[58]

Other interpretations, however, are possible. If the Bes-image's ring did support a cosmetic applicator or act as a highly elaborate cap for a container, we would expect the ring to be parallel to the ground so that whatever was inserted into the opening would stand vertically. Instead, however, the god tips the ring slightly forward in a gesture signifying presentation, an orientation suggesting that whatever it held was meant to be seen but not necessarily used. One possible explanation for the piece then is that it served to hold a single lotus bud or small blossom whose stem rested in the ring but did not reach the ground. The lotus, an ancient symbol of birth and rebirth, would have been an appropriate "gift" for an expectant or new mother from the supreme birth god of ancient Egypt.[59] DCP

Bibliography. Cooney in Muscarella 1974a, no. 211; Settgast 1978, no. 241; Roehrig 1992c, pp. 33–34.

75 THE GOD BES AS A PROPHYLACTIC CHARM

PAGE 109

Third Intermediate Period to Late Period, Dynasty 21–25

Deep blue faience, dark speckled; H. 21.6 cm

Harer Family Trust

Although a flat, almost two-dimensional object, this representation of the god Bes should be viewed from all four sides because each side is decorated in relief. The principal image is Bes wearing a headdress of five plumes, the backs of which are decorated with the tied legs of an oryx. Five simians are incorporated into the composition: one each by Bes's ears, a third sitting in front of his legs and the fourth and fifth beside his thighs. The principal image of Bes offers an oval-shaped object in his right hand as nourishment to an infant, identified either as the child god Horus or another manifestation of Bes,[60] cradled in his left arm.

The object served as a terminal fixed into a short, papyriform scepter, much as a mirror's disk is attached to its handle. The holes in the ears and in the tops of the feathers seem to suggest the presence of other attributes in secondary materials that have been lost.

This particular object, among the finest of its type to have survived, is representative of the production of certain faience workshops thought to have been situated in the Eastern Delta during the Third Intermediate Period.[61] The various uses of such objects can be more narrowly defined only when their archaeological contexts are known, and since the present object has no recorded findspot, its interpretation can only draw on the plurality of meanings of its motifs. In general, these motifs are concerned with the successful and harmonious transition between threatened states or conditions, including, for instance, the calendrical change from the Old to the New Year, the birth of a child, and the annual flooding of the Nile. In ancient Egyptian thinking, these transitions could be aborted by the presence of malevolent forces of chaos, but these forces in turn were thought to be checked by the powers of Bes, each of which was positively reinforced by his various attributes. In his essay, Bulté discusses each of these elements and presents a synthesis of their meanings that, briefly stated, suggests that Bes is an appropriate prophylactic genius insuring smooth transitions from one state to another.

RSB

Bibliography. Bulté 1991, document 11.

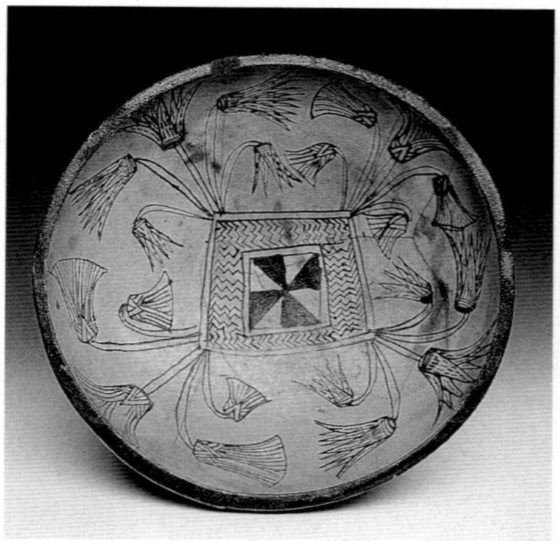

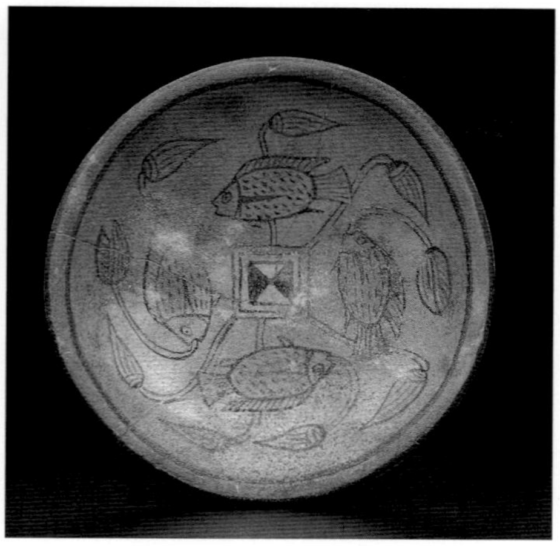

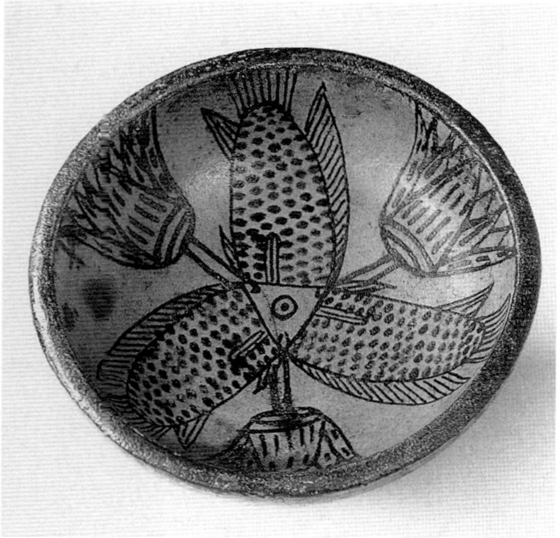

76 BOWL WITH POOL AND LOTUS MOTIFS PAGE 112

New Kingdom, early Dynasty 18

Faience; DIAM. 25.8 cm

The Trustees of the British Museum, London. EA 4790

Numerous fragments of decorated faience bowls have been found at temples and shrines dedicated to Hathor, where they served as votive offerings to the goddess;[62] a few are inscribed to Hathor.[63] The bowls' decoration typically consists of marshland imagery alluding to fertility: lotuses, papyrus umbels, buds, pools, and more overt Hathor symbols like sistra, *menats*, masks, and the goddess in her cow form.[64] The presence of marshland motifs has prompted one scholar to call these vessels "marsh bowls."[65] Their votive findspots, fertility/regeneration imagery, and examples inscribed to Hathor, link the bowls as a group to this goddess.[66]

Less frequently, marsh bowls were deposited in tombs, where intact examples such as this London vessel would have survived better than in a temple or shrine.[67] Expertly decorated in manganese, this bowl, probably a tomb offering, shows a rectangular pool from which emerge groups of blue lotus flowers, a frequent symbol of rebirth. The pool is decorated with a pinwheel design surrounded by wavy lines, which are the hieroglyphic sign for water.

The tombs in which such bowls have been excavated are non-royal and mostly female. In a burial context, the fertility imagery suggests rebirth and a desire for regeneration in the Beyond.[68] The predominant, though not exclusive, association of the bowls with women's graves is noteworthy: three bowls, for example, were found at the head end of a Theban female coffin.[69] Female associations are further emphasized by inscribed votive examples from Deir el-Bahri that mention, besides Hathor, queens or princesses but not kings.[70]

Did the London bowl—a very large example—contain anything? Virtually all bowls were found empty,[71] though one from Deir el-Medina contained a milky substance.[72] Contents might have ranged from libations (water, wine, milk), to flowers, perfumed fats, or food,[73] but evidence is scant and uses were probably multiple.[74] It seems clear, however, that this and related bowls were not tableware, as is often suggested.[75] This bowl (and [77–79]) was surely made over a hemispherical form, producing a smoother and more even interior than exterior.[76] FDF

Bibliography. Stead 1986, p. 42, fig. 57; Hugonot 1989, p. 220; Shaw and Nicholson 1995, p. 95.

77 BOWL WITH POOL AND FISH PAGE 112

New Kingdom, Dynasty 18

Faience; DIAM. 15.7 cm; H. 3.8 cm

Museum of Fine Arts, Boston.
William E. Nickerson Fund. 1977.619

This deep-blue bowl is decorated on the interior with four tilapia fish holding lotus buds in their mouths. In the center of the bowl is represented a deep artificial pool with more lotus buds rising from its four corners.[77] The bowl is very shallow, with no exterior foot, and is paralleled by both pottery dishes and faience bowl types that belong to the later Eighteenth Dynasty and Ramesside Period.[78] The whole decoration—the petals of the blue lotus (*Nymphaea caerulea*) on the exterior, the lotus buds on the interior and the tilapia fish (*Tilapia nilotica*)—represent rebirth and resurrection (see also [78]). The closing and opening of the lotus during the diurnal cycle of night and day indicated the renewal of life. The tilapia, which guards its young in its mouth, might have seemed to have been a case of spontaneous regeneration, and as such was another powerful image signifying eternal life.[79] Such symbolism indicates that this bowl, and others like it, were produced as funerary gifts and did not serve a function in daily life.[80] PL

Bibliography. Brovarski et al. 1982b, p. 143; Brovarski 1987, pp. 26–27.

78 BOWL WITH FISH AND LOTUS MOTIFS PAGE 113

New Kingdom, Dynasty 18

Faience; DIAM. 9.0 cm

Staatliche Museen zu Berlin - Preussischer Kulturbesitz Ägyptisches Museum und Papyrussammlung. 4562

Ex-Collection: Passalacqua, 1827

The principal motif of this bowl's decoration is a fish, the *Tilapia nilotica*, called *bulti* in Arabic,[81] one of the most frequently depicted fish in ancient Egyptian art.[82] The fish is stylized so that a single triangular head, with one round eye, serves to complete the three bodies. The fish are balanced by depictions of three blue lotuses (*Nymphaea caerulea*). The design and draftsmanship of this composition are among the best ever created in ancient Egypt.[83]

The meaning of the decoration revolves around themes of rebirth and regeneration, linked to the fish and flowers and reinforced by the color of the faience itself. The female tilapia, after laying her eggs, takes them up and stores them "in the buccal and pharyngeal cavities until they have hatched. Even after the young have hatched, they will return to the parent's mouth when frightened."[84] This trait of the tilapia probably contributed to its use as a motif suggesting birth and resurrection, a theme reinforced by the blue lotus, which opens when the rays of the sun's first light strike it at dawn.[85] RSB

Bibliography. Milward in Brovarski et al. 1982b, p. 143, cat. no. 140; Fay 1992, pp. 60–61; Kozloff in Kozloff and Bryan 1992b, p. 407, cat. no. 108, pl. 56.

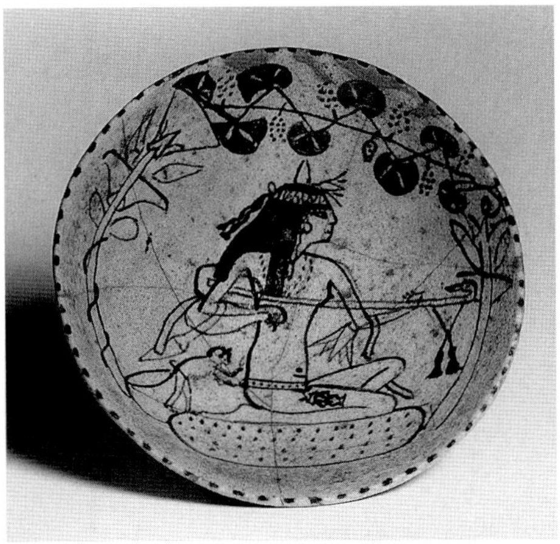

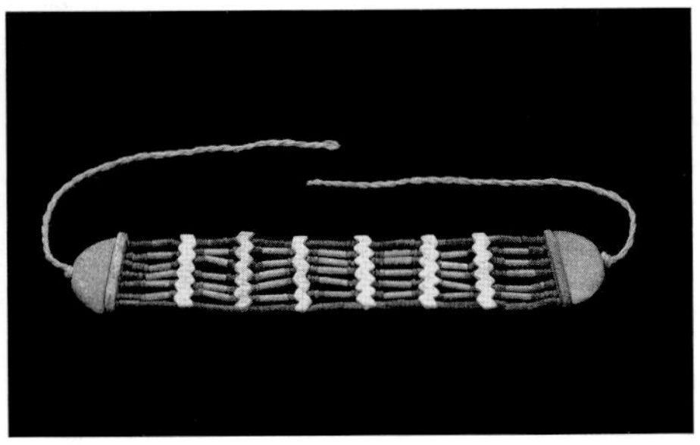

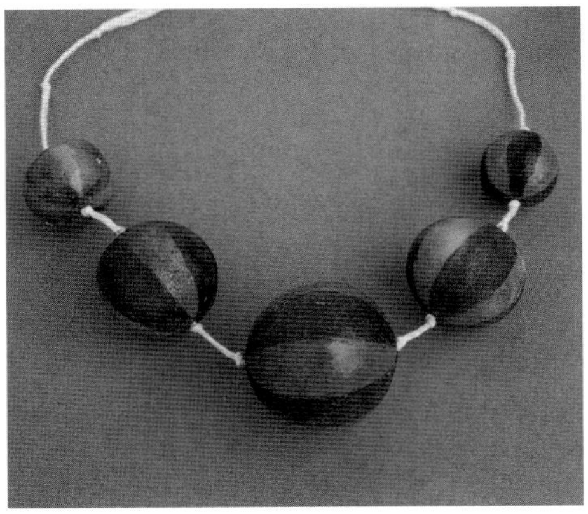

79 BOWL PAGE 113

New Kingdom, Dynasty 19–20

Light blue faience with black glaze details; DIAM. 14.0 cm

Rijksmuseum van Oudheden, Leiden. AD 14

This is without doubt the finest decorated vessel of its kind to have survived from ancient Egypt. The treatment of the bower in which the nude girl sits resting on a pillow playing an instrument, as well as the treatment of her body, strongly suggests a Theban provenance—probably the area of Deir el-Medina. The scantily clad figure has affinities with similar erotic figurines from the Middle Kingdom ([64] and [66]). The bowl's lack of damage has led at least one commentator to suggest, correctly to my mind, that it came from a tomb, thereby reinforcing the funerary overtones of the erotic imagery.[86]

This imagery includes a girdle about the waist, perhaps consisting of a stylized representation of cowrie shells which symbolize the female genitalia.[87] A baboon, which has a long history of erotic overtones in ancient Egypt,[88] seems to be playing with (untying?) the girdle in what may be a veiled rebus connoting fornication. Finally, there is a tattoo in the form of a Bes-image on the girl's thigh. Tattoos in ancient Egyptian culture seem to be confined to women, not men, and the Bes-image tattoo is habitually associated with erotic contexts.[89]

This combination of a nude girl, tattooed with a Bes-image and wearing a girdle, and set within a bower, finds its closest parallels in a fresco from Deir el-Medina.[90] Although the fresco when originally published was said to be a secular decoration in the house where it was found,[91] a reexamination of its context suggests that the room it was in was a birthing room.[92] The fresco was doubtless intended to promote fecundity and the successful delivery of newborns, whereas the bowl in Leiden was intended to revive the deceased's procreative abilities, thus linking him or her to the god Osiris and insuring resurrection in the Hereafter. Such scenes are about as sexually explicit as any in Egyptian art ever were: more graphic sexual images are confined to smaller statuettes, generally in limestone or faience, which seem to date to the Late Period.[93] RSB

Bibliography. Milward in Brovarski et al. 1982c, pp. 144–45, no. 143.

80 CHOKER PAGES 114–15

Old Kingdom, Dynasty 4, *c.* 2500 BC; Giza, Tomb G 4341A

Faience; L. 25.0 cm; H. 3.8 cm

Museum of Fine Arts, Boston. Harvard University-Museum of Fine Arts, Boston Expedition. 1924.1749

Although no examples have survived intact, the neck ornament known as the choker or dog collar appears frequently in Old Kingdom statues and paintings. This form of adornment was popular among women of all levels of society[94] during the Fourth through Sixth Dynasties (with or without an accompanying broad collar).[95] Later, it is featured on servant girls of the Middle Kingdom and on coffins of New Kingdom ladies.[96]

Representations of such chokers indicate that they consisted of several rows of beads strung between terminals, or end pieces, with a number of spacers in the form of perforated bars to keep the rows in alignment. The elements used in this reconstruction have two features of special interest: zigzag-shaped spacers and terminals in two separate parts. While zigzag spacers are often depicted on bracelets of the period,[97] indications that they existed on chokers are relatively rare.[98] This type of spacer has a straight, perforated bar on the underside, making stringing easy, with the wavy surface of the spacer overlying the rows of beads.

The terminal of a collar has two functions: to act as a spacer for the strings of beads to which it is attached and to bring together the strings holding the collar in place around the neck. Both functions are usually performed by a one-piece terminal. In this case a perforated bar acts as the spacer, and there is a separate hollow body through which the threads are gathered into a single unit for tying. The two-part terminal does not seem to be a development of the single-part variety, as many examples of the latter date to the Old Kingdom. The sections of the terminals shown here are of different colors, suggesting that they may have been intended as part of the overall decorative design. The space-bar of each terminal is black, complementing some of the beads, while the body of the terminal is buff-colored. It is possible that the body was originally this color, or that it was glazed in a color that has since disappeared, or that it was gilded.[99]

It is interesting that while neither the two-part terminal nor the zigzag spacer appear to be common elements of collars, other examples of chokers have been found at Giza that include both.[100] YJM & SBS

81 BALL BEADS PAGE 115

Middle Kingdom to New Kingdom, early Dynasty 18

Bichrome faience; max. DIAM. 5.1 cm

Trustees of the National Museums of Scotland. A.1965.275; A.1911.323; A.1956.126; A.1911.323A; and one unnumbered

Large, hollow ball beads of bichrome faience pierced for stringing have their origin in the Middle Kingdom. These spheres have alternating sectors of blue and black and may have been worn in a variety of ways, for instance singly or in multiples around the neck, strung with smaller beads fastened to the top of head,[101] or suspended from the bottom of a single plait of hair.[102]

Several beads of this type were excavated by Griffith in the vicinity of the Hathor Temple at Faras, a site on the Nile between the First and Second Cataracts in Nubia.[103] It has been suggested that this temple, dedicated to Hathor, Lady of Ibshek, was built by Sobekemhab during the Second Intermediate Period and later expanded during the reign of Ramesses II.[104] Jewelry, including hollow ball beads of faience, made up a significant percentage of the votive offerings at this and several other sites dedicated to Hathor.[105]

The method of manufacture of hollow faience balls has been the subject of speculation. Vergès has suggested that closed, hollow faience forms could be made using the "à noyau perdu" technique.[106] In this method a suitable vegetable material, such as reed, is compacted into the desired shape and then covered with a faience paste. On heating, the organic material is reduced to ash, leaving an essentially hollow core. Evidence of this technique can be found on the inner surface of broken beads where impressions of reed fibers are clearly visible (see also [190]).

YJM & SBS

Bibliography. Griffith 1921b, pp. 85–86; Aldred 1971a, pl. 23, pp. 184–85; Bourriau 1988a, pp. 132–33; Vergès 1992, pp. 36–37; Pinch 1993, p. 40.

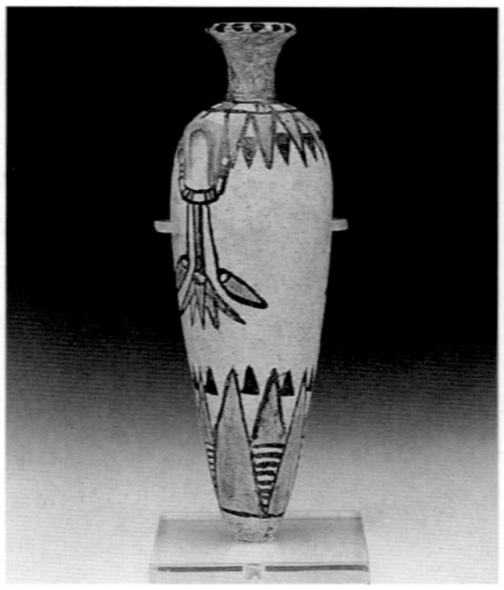

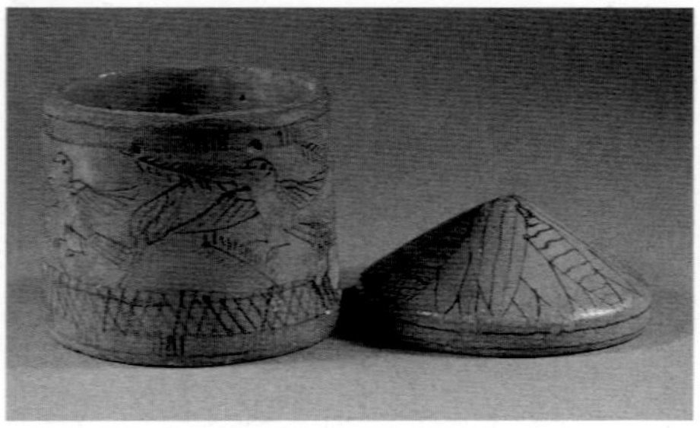

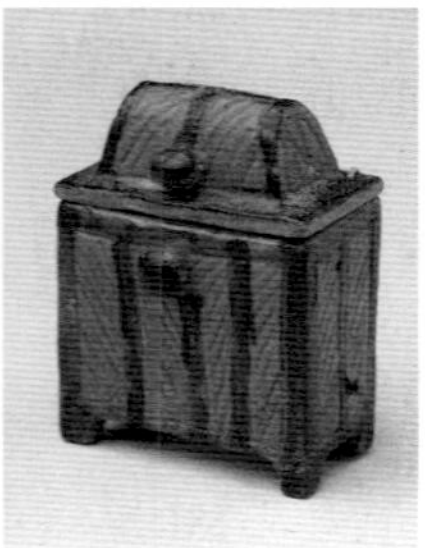

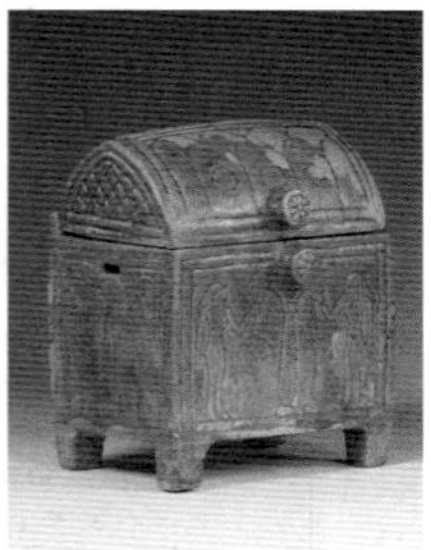

82 PERFUME VASE PAGE 119

New Kingdom, late Dynasty 18; Sesebi, Nubia

Faience; H. 14.5 cm

The Trustees of the British Museum, London. Donated by the Egypt Exploration Society, 1937. EA 64041

Perfume containers were often made of faience. This vessel in the form of a small amphora displays a light and delicate touch in its glaze-painted floral decoration and successfully imitates a shape already known for clay vessels and alabaster stoneware.[107]

The vessel is one of a group of three known examples that are almost identical in size and decoration. This London example was found without its neck (here restored) amidst the plundered debris of the Sesebi cemetery.[108] (During the New Kingdom, Egypt colonized an area to the south in Upper, i.e., southern, Nubia, where it established a walled settlement at this site.) The second was found at el-Ahaiwah in the Thinite nome near Abydos,[109] and the third is unprovenanced.[110] Despite different findspots, stylistic similarities suggest that they may all derive from the same workshop[111] from which they were exported to other sites.

Just as on the New Kingdom faience bowls [76–78], the decoration of this piece relies on the lotus motif, a symbol of resurrection found on numerous Egyptian objects in all media. But the treatment of the lotus is especially organic here, painted to conform to the shape of the vessel that is itself quite budlike. Against a white-glazed background, swags of buds and petals outlined in blue and black fall from a ringed decoration about the two handles, while petals drape from the shoulder and spring like an open flower from the base. FDF

Bibliography. Burlington Fine Arts Club 1922, p. 108, pl. XLI, no. 18; Blackman 1937, p. 151, pl. XVI, fig. 2. British Museum 1971, p. 199, fig. 75; Shaw and Nicholson 1995, p. 263.

83 PYXIS AND LID PAGE 110–11

Late Middle to New Kingdom (container); New Kingdom, Dynasty 18 (lid)

Faience; Container: H. 6.8 cm; DIAM. 7.5 cm. Lid: H. 3.5 cm; DIAM. 8.2 cm

Staatliche Sammlung Ägyptischer Kunst, Munich. ÄS 1575; ÄS 5631

This charming pyxis (box) and lid may have been used for storing cosmetics. Though not originally made together, container and lid reflect decorative motifs and forms found on faience objects from the Old to New Kingdom. The container's painted swamp scene, with birds flushed from a papyrus thicket, recalls the theme of fowling in the marshes[112] common from the Old to New Kingdom. Typically the birds are hunted with a clapnet,[113] and the crosshatched lines at the base of the Munich vessel may well be a reference not to water but to these nets. The swamp decoration shown here also recalls that found on the late Middle Kingdom hippos [142–45] and New Kingdom lotus bowls [76–78].

Like the Walter's lidded box [92], string was originally threaded through the holes of the container and fastened to the base of a lid, which would have had corresponding threadholes. FDF

Bibliography. Staatlich Sammlung Ägyptischer Kunst 1976, p. 108, no. 75; Arnold et al. 1978, p. 152, no. 223; Brovarski in Brovarski et al. 1982b, p. 151, no. 158; Wildung 1987, pp. 10ff., fig. 4; Schoske et al. 1992, p. 74, no. 6.

84 JEWELRY OR COSMETIC BOX PAGE 111

New Kingdom, Dynasty 18

Faience; Max. H. (with lid) 6.9 cm; H. of container 4.8 cm; H. of lid 2.1 cm

Musée du Louvre, Paris. E 1871

Ex-Collection: Clot Bey

85 JEWELRY OR COSMETIC BOX PAGE 110

Late Period, Dynasty 25

Faience; container H. 8.0 cm; W. 8.0 cm; L. 10.5 cm. H. with lid 12.5 cm

Staatliche Museen zu Berlin - Preussischer Kulturbesitz Ägyptisches Museum und Papyrussammlung. 16994

Ex-Collection: Passalacqua

Faience is often used to mimic other media and the black strips on this beautiful lidded box [84] simulate bands of ebony, while the incised diagonals on the panels between imitate a leafy vegetal material, possibly palm fronds. Like other Eighteenth Dynasty boxes,[114] this one has a knob on the lid and another just below on the container imitating mushroom-shaped handles typical on wooden boxes of the time. A cord could be wound around the knobs in a figure-eight pattern to secure the contents, with further protection given by a clay sealing if necessary. On the back of the lid threadholes at the two lower corners correspond to ones set diagonally below on the box: strings threaded through hinged the lid. The box was thus equipped for cherished trinkets or cosmetics, though no residue of the latter is present. The lid appears to be mold-made; the diagonal surface lines of lid and box imitating leaves were probably incised when the piece was damp. The bright blue glaze is very glossy and appears to have been applied. Though the inside of box and lid are unglazed, one can see a rim of painted glaze around the interior mouth of both.

From almost a millennium later, the little faience cosmetic or jewelry box from Berlin [85] illustrates the retention of the same basic design. Also with vaulted lid and double-knob fastening system,[115] this box was found in the tomb of a lady named Tadja. Unlike the Louvre box, this example is more elaborately decorated: in a framed front panel, women offer floral bouquets before a central papyrus umbel, and papyrus motifs decorate the sides and lid. FDF

Bibliography. [84]: Boreux 1932a, p. 591; Vandier d'Abbadie 1972, p. 49, OT 137. [85]: Wolf 1930, p. 60, fig. 1; Kaiser 1967, cat. no. 614, p. 58; Kayser 1969, p. 138, fig. 127; p. 136; Arnold et al. 1978, p, 110, cat. no. 127.

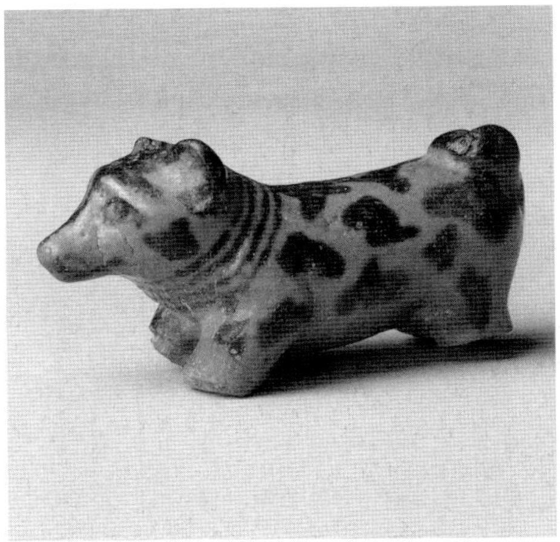

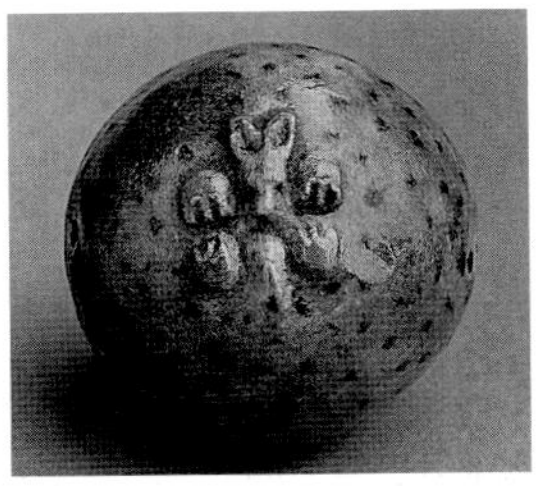

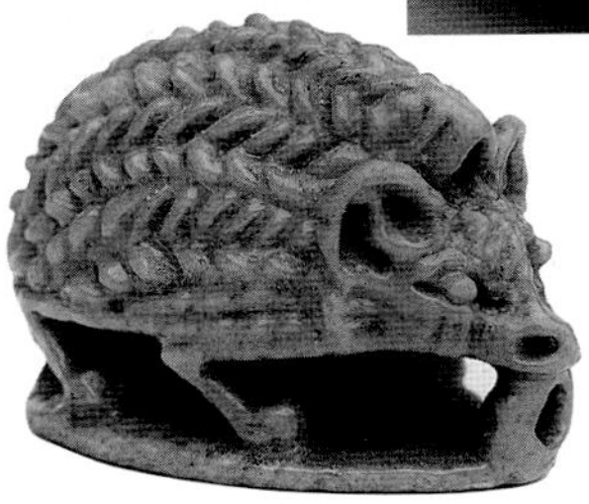

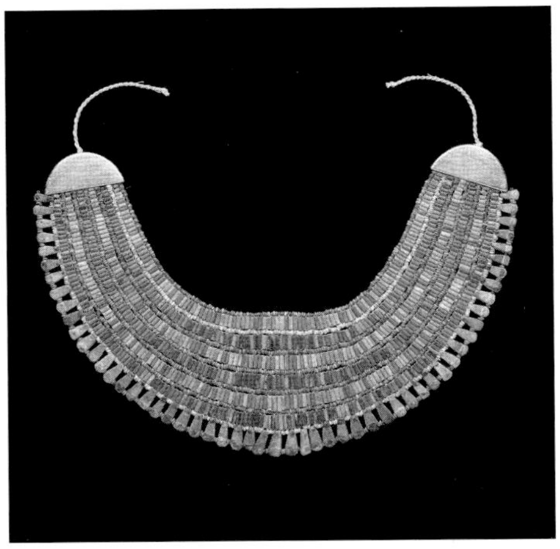

97 DOG PAGE 129

Middle Kingdom, late Dynasty 12 to early Dynasty 13

Faience; L. 5.2 cm

Staatliche Museen zu Berlin - Preussischer Kulturbesitz Ägyptisches Museum und Papyrussammlung. 15254

Poignant dog burials and accompanying texts show that the ancient Egyptians loved their canine companions as much as we do, and dogs are often represented in two- and three-dimensional Egyptian art.[18] A Middle Kingdom coffin painting contemporary with this faience figure, for example, shows the deceased in life carrying a stick in one hand and holding in the other the leash of his long-legged, black-and-white spotted dog named "He is a Shepherd."[19] But a contemporary wall painting from the tomb of Djehutyhotep at El-Berhseh gives the best two-dimensional parallel in a scene of offering bearers which is accompanied by exactly this type of squat little curly-tailed, spotted dog.[20]

Three-dimensional Middle Kingdom examples in faience, limestone, and clay depict individual dogs and owners set on a base, with the hound crouched expectantly, like this example, opposite his young master.[21] In a parallel composition the boy extends a stick in the age-old game of throw and fetch.[22] This dog, which has lost the lower part of its legs, was undoubtedly once attached to a base, and may have been part of such a group.[23]

Though it may have had a symbolic meaning (e.g., a watchdog in the afterlife[24]), the dog was most likely a treasured reminder of an ordinary person's pet[25] during life and thus included in the tomb as a keepsake, as perhaps were similar faience animals.[26]

The breed of dog is not clear. Its erect ears, curly tail and tapering muzzle point to the African Basenji, but its short legs militate against this. Archaeologists date the Basenji to 500 BC at the earliest,[27] so that this short-legged dog may represent a forerunner. That the Berlin dog, like his fellows in other materials, was a household pet is indicated by his collar, represented by painted (probably manganese) bands encircling the neck, allowing him to be leashed.

Just as with contemporary faience hippos, hedgehogs and other animals, the Egyptians were happy glazing their faience dogs in brilliant blue. The blue was intentional for reasons of ritual, or fashion, or both—that artisans were able to reproduce more natural tones is shown by the contemporary jerboa mice, glazed in naturalistic colors [146], [147]. FDF

Bibliography. Kaiser 1967, cat. no. 468.

98 HEDGEHOG PAGE 129

Middle Kingdom

Faience, blue glaze; DIAM. 6.0 cm

Trustees of the National Museums of Scotland. A.1965.245

99 HEDGEHOG PAGE 129

Third Intermediate Period

Faience, blue glaze; H. 1.5 cm

Musée du Louvre, Paris. AF 2302

Ancient Egyptian symbolism is elusive, and images that seem to signify one thing in one period or context may assume a quite different meaning in a later epoch or in different surroundings. The mixed messages such symbols convey can obscure their ancient meaning or meanings. This ambiguity is nowhere better demonstrated than in the various interpretations of the *Erinaceinae* hedgehogs, creatures which appear in Egyptian art from the Predynastic to the Late Period. They are found in desert hunting scenes, as decorative elements on the prows of Old Kingdom ships, as pottery vessels, statuettes, amulets, and as a type of "scarab" on which they replace the beetle. The hedgehog even served as the divine emblem of the goddess Abast at the Bahria Oasis in the Late Period.[28]

Ancient texts do not mention the animal's symbolic significance, but its frequent appearance on amulets implies that it served some magical function. This minuscule charm [99], with tiny, separately detailed spines, for example, is inscribed with an appeal to the goddess Bastet "to give life."[29] Perhaps it was the animal's behavior when threatened—curling itself into a ball, like [98], with a mass of spines—which made the Egyptians see it as a potent protective force. This behavior is a good paradigm for an apotropaic or protective symbol, and would thus explain the unusual form of this amulet.

Alternatively, the Egyptians may have associated the animal with a belief in eternal rebirth after death. No doubt they noticed that when food was scarce, hedgehogs retreat to their underground dens for long periods, re-emerging in times of abundance. The Egyptians may have believed that this aspect of its behavior had a religious counterpart in their notion of life coming forth after death.[30] The animal seems to have had another, far more prosaic significance. The Ebers Papyrus of the early Eighteenth Dynasty states that hedgehog spines, ground up and mixed with fat or oil, were a cure for baldness.[31] DCP

Bibliography. [98]: Droste zu Hülshoff 1980, p. 142, fig. 119, pl. 14. [99]: Droste zu Hülshoff 1980, no. 352, pl. 27.

100 BROAD COLLAR PAGE 122

Old Kingdom, late Dynasty 5, *c.* 2150 BC; Giza, Tomb G 2407 C

Blue-green, black and white faience; H. 10.5 cm; W. 33.0 cm

Museum of Fine Arts, Boston. Harvard University - Museum of Fine Arts, Boston Expedition. 1937.1314 (reconstruction by Suzanne E. Chapman)

The most frequently represented item of jewelry throughout Egyptian history was the broad or *weskhet* collar, worn by both genders as well as anthropomorphic deities. Broad collars of the Old Kingdom were beaded ornaments that fall into two categories. The first and most common is composed of multiple rows of densely spaced cylinder beads of steatite or faience. These are strung in an upright position and may or may not be separated by rows of small ring beads, with a bottom row of tear-shaped pendants. The second consists of units of strung beads interrupted by trapezoidal spacer elements that may be metal or beadwork.

Terminals, or end-pieces, bring together the material (linen) that the beads are strung on into one twist or braid for tying the collar around the neck.[32] Here, the terminals are modern gilded wood reproductions based on excavated examples from Giza.[33] They are hemispherical in shape and have seven holes along the flat side to accommodate the six rows of faience cylinder beads and one row of drop pendants.[34] Ring beads of white, blue-green, and black are woven between the rows of tubular beads, which are alternately black and blue-green faience. The cylindrical beads vary in length, the largest beads at the center tapering toward the smallest at the ends.
YJM & SBS

Bibliography. Harvard University and the Museum of Fine Arts, Boston, vol. 11, p. 1357.

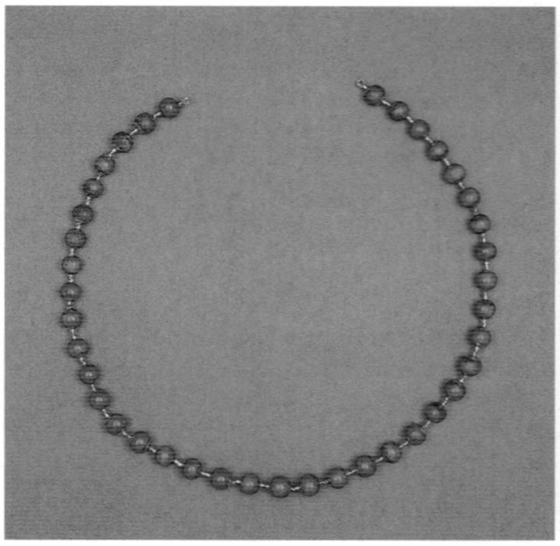

101 CAPPED BEADS WITH A REEF-KNOT CLASP

PAGE 123

Middle Kingdom

Blue faience, gold, silver, and copper; L. 72.8 cm; DIAM. of beads 15 mm

The Trustees of the British Museum, London. EA 3084

Necklaces of uniform spherical beads were fashionable during the Middle Kingdom. On occasion, individual beads were enhanced around the thread holes by caps of gold or silver. These caps were fabricated from hammered sheet metal cut into discs and then pierced in the center. Short, hollow cylinders of metal were then soldered to each disc and the whole cap secured to the bead by means of a copper tube threaded into the boring.[35]

The beads in this necklace are a bright blue faience and the caps are silver; the gold clasp in the form of a reef knot may or may not be original to the ornament. While reef-knot ornaments of gold wire originate in the First Intermediate Period, grooved "knot" clasps made in two sections do not appear until the Middle Kingdom.[36] The knot itself is amuletic, a symbol derived from the side panels of Old Kingdom thrones where the knot binds the antithetically placed and ideologically opposed figures of Horus and Seth as they pull on cords from the two plants symbolic of Upper and Lower Egypt. Hence the knot is an expression of unity, balance and cohesion.[37] YJM & SBS

Bibliography. Andrews 1981, no. 539, pl. 9, p. 40; Andrews 1990, p. 96, fig. 74a.

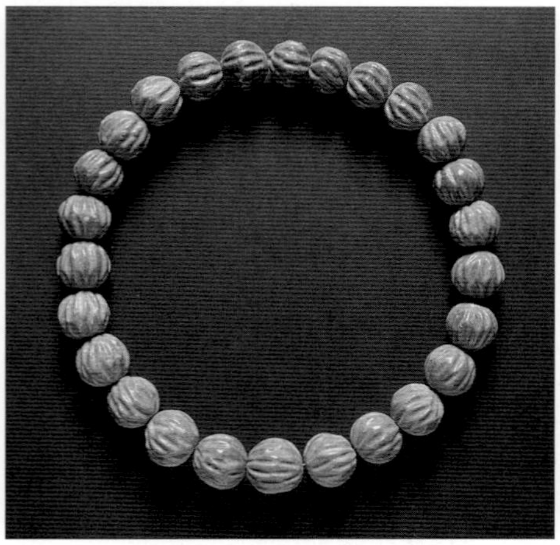

102 STRING OF RIBBED BALL BEADS

PAGE 123

Middle Kingdom; Abusir

Blue-green faience; L. 30.0 cm.; DIAM. of beads 10–15 mm

Staatliche Museen zu Berlin - Preussischer Kulturbesitz Ägyptisches Museum und Papyrussammlung. 16607

Ribbed or "melon" beads of blue faience are one of the bead types associated with the Middle Kingdom.[38] When incorporated into necklaces, they are typically strung in groups of uniform size or arranged in a graduated fashion. Single ribbed beads are also included in necklaces with beads and amulets of varying shapes, sizes, and materials.

While the form of these beads is thought to derive from the natural world, no specific fruit or seed has been identified. However, it has been suggested that their melon-like appearance endows them with powers of rebirth and rejuvenation.[39]

Necklaces of large, ribbed ball beads were popular in Nubia during the Second Intermediate Period.[40] Later, during the Napatan and Meroitic Periods, they were worn by kings, queens, and deities. YJM & SBS

Bibliography. Schoske et al. 1992, p. 223; Markowitz in Thomas et al. 1995a, p. 164.

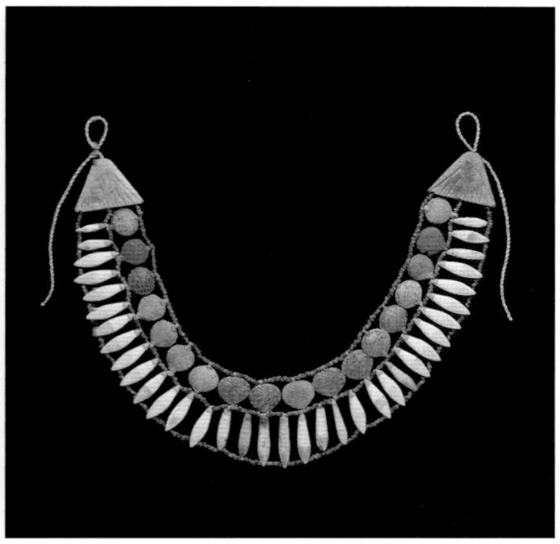

103 BROAD COLLAR

PAGE 122

New Kingdom, Dynasty 18

Polychrome faience; L. 27.0 cm

Museum of Fine Arts, Boston. Gift of C. Granville Way. 1955.1723 (reconstruction by Sheila Shear)

New Kingdom broad collars depart from earlier traditions by replacing dense, tightly strung beads with individual elements that derive from the natural world. Plant motifs, inspired by actual floral neck ornaments, were especially popular. Advances in faience technology, particularly in the use of metallic oxides as coloring agents, permitted an expanded color palette and the overall effect of these openwork necklaces is one of variety, delicacy, and dynamism.

This particular example is based on a real floral collar from the tomb of Tutankhamun, which was in an excellent state of preservation and consisted of two rows of sliced mandrake fruits and blue lotus petals.[41] The symbolism here, applicable in life as well as death, centers around concepts of sexuality and renewal.[42] A comparable broad collar from Thebes, with polychrome faience mandrake fruits, lotus petals, and lotus terminals, is now in Brussels.[43] In the Boston necklace, one of the blue lotus end-pieces is ancient, as are the ring beads and several of the mandrake pendants and lotus petals; the others are modern facsimiles. YJM & SBS

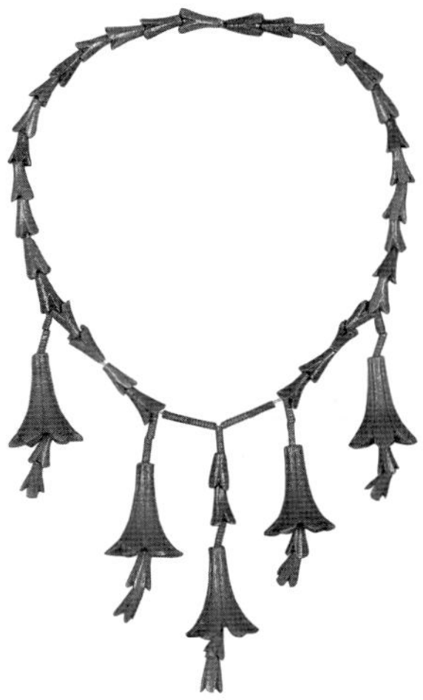

104 NECKLACE OF JASMINE BLOSSOMS

PAGE 123

New Kingdom, Dynasty 18

Faience; L. 38.0 cm

Staatliche Museen zu Berlin - Preussischer Kulturbesitz Ägyptisches Museum und Papyrussammlung. 9029

Beads of all sorts are common finds in Egypt but since they are often found as loose, unstrung elements, reconstructing their original arrangement can be difficult. In this case, ancient beads molded in the form of naturalistic three-dimensional blossoms have been attractively though inaccurately restrung: the five large trumpet-like beads would not have been hung as pendants nor would they have had smaller beads falling from within them. Such a modern arrangement, however, reflects the attraction of ancient faience jewelry for modern taste.

Both the large and small blossom beads[44] can be identified as jasmine, a fragrant flower used for perfume.[45] The same type of beads appears in another jasmine blossom necklace said to be from Malawi; its beads run in one continuous strand with the largest blossoms across the bottom,[46] possibly the original arrangement of this Berlin necklace. FDF

Bibliography. Priese 1991, p. 249, cat. no. 153; Schoske et al. 1992, p. 224, cat. no. 152.

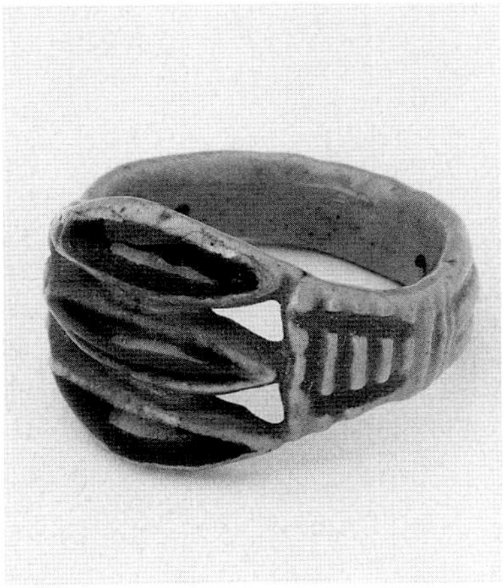

105 FINGER RING

PAGE 123

New Kingdom, Dynasty 18

Polychrome faience; H. (bezel) 1.3 cm; H. (shank) 0.5 cm; DIAM. 2.0 cm

The Trustees of the British Museum, London. EA 22594

While faience rings were mass-produced during the Eighteenth Dynasty, few are of the openwork type[47] and fewer still incorporate colored inlays. Color was of symbolic significance in Egypt and was used by the ancient craftsman to identify and define the essential nature of things.[48] It is clear that the colors used in the manufacture of this piece are not accidental. The brilliant yellow, a substitute for gold, was associated with the life-giving sun and the flesh of the gods. Blue, the color of the central inlay, was employed in lieu of lapis lazuli, a powerful stone symbolic of the heavens and cosmic waters. The vibrant red, the color of carnelian, was connected with concepts of birth and destruction.[49]

YJM & SBS

Bibliography. Andrews 1990, p. 60, pl. 45j; Wilkinson 1994, pp. 104–05.

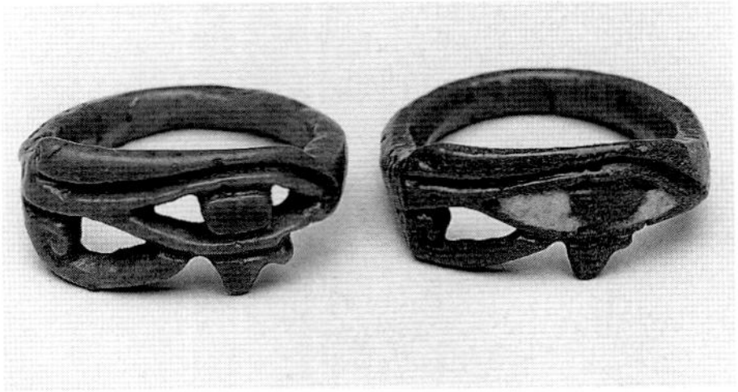

106 WADJET-EYE RING

PAGE 123

New Kingdom, late Dynasty 18

Mauve faience; DIAM. 2.3 cm

The Syndics of the Fitzwilliam Museum, Cambridge. E.473.1954

107 WADJET-EYE RING

PAGE 123

New Kingdom, late Dynasty 18

Cobalt blue faience; DIAM. 2.3 cm

The Syndics of the Fitzwilliam Museum, Cambridge. E.352.1939

These faience rings were manufactured from two separate clay molds, as evidenced by the hundreds recovered from the excavations at the site of Amarna.[50] Faience paste was pressed into separate molds for the bezel and the shank, and the resulting pieces were joined together with a slurry of the core material.[51] Glaze was then applied and the whole ring fired. The beautiful mauve color of one openwork ring represents an expansion of the palette available in faience production in the Eighteenth Dynasty, resulting from the introduction of new pigments.[52]

The *wadjet*-eye was one of the most ubiquitous and powerful amuletic symbols in ancient Egypt. A combination of the human eye and falcon markings of the sun-god Horus, it represented regeneration and restoration. Rings such as these were produced in great quantities as items of relatively inexpensive costume jewelry. SD'A

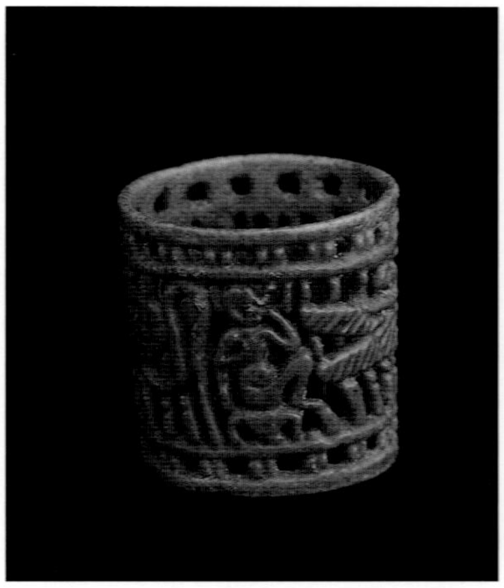

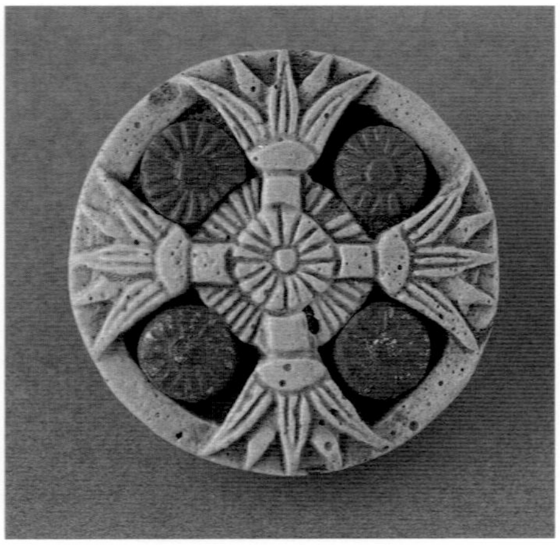

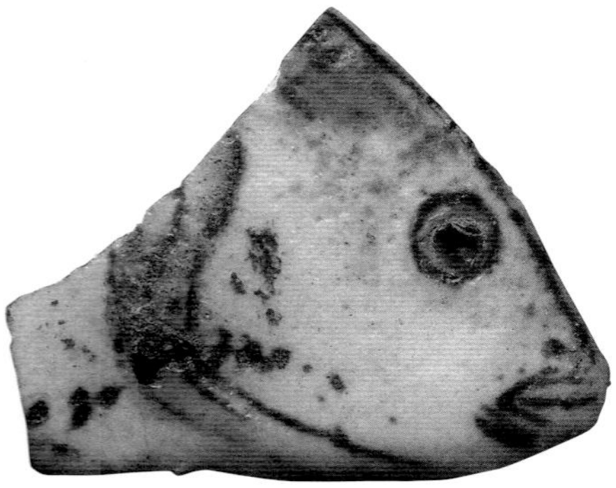

108 OPENWORK FINGER RING PAGE 123

Third Intermediate Period, Dynasty 21–22; probably from Tuna el-Gebel

Blue faience; H. 3.2 cm; DIAM. 2.4 cm

Myers Museum, Eton College, with Permission of the Provost and Fellows. Bequest of Major W. J. Myers, 1899. ECM 1482

Openwork finger rings constitute a subgroup of the flat-bezeled faience rings common in the New Kingdom.[53] Around the first millennium BC, a new shape of faience ring appeared, namely that of a wide band with a figured design pierced through the body. Wide band rings were already made in precious metals[54] and this ornament is arguably an attempt to provide a less costly substitute.

Rings of pierced faience of the Twenty-First and Twenty-Second Dynasties often feature images of the young Horus, winged cobras, and sacred flowers. In this delicate example, the young sun-god, with side-lock, uraeus, and finger to mouth, sits on a *nebew* sign. This is a variant of the sun-on-the-lotus motif—an iconographic representation associated with Hermopolis.[55] To his right is a cobra with outstretched wings, while a *djed*-pillar with disk, feathers, and flanking cobras is to his left. The figures are held in place with lace-like strut work (see also [46]).

Pierced rings, vessels, and plaques demonstrate the high level of skill achieved in faience manufacture during the Third Intermediate Period.[56] Rings could have been shaped around a metal tube, with the negative spaces cut out with a tool and the tube removed after drying. The final step would be firing in a kiln. YJM & SBS

Bibliography. Tait 1963, pp. 134–35.

109 ROUNDEL, PERHAPS FROM A HEADBAND PAGE 142

Late Period, Dynasty 25–26

Yellow and blue faience; DIAM. 4.0 cm

Musée du Louvre, Paris. Gift of L., I., and A. Curtis. E 22665

Four lotus blossoms emanating from a central marguerite form the principal design element of this roundel. The blossoms divide the circle into four quadrants with the spaces between filled with a separately molded blue marguerite. The elements appear to have been assembled before firing to judge by the inside edge of one marguerite, which seems to have been flattened while in its plastic state in order to fit it into the space it now occupies. The roundel is pierced longitudinally, and its dimensions and this suspension hole strongly suggest that it served as a jewelry element, perhaps for a headband.[57]

The dating of this piece is problematic. Whereas New Kingdom faience production often includes separately worked pieces inlaid into a matrix, in most examples the inlays fit snugly into the spaces cut out to accommodate them.[58] Openwork faience designs, on the other hand, appear to be restricted to the Third Intermediate Period[59] and, particularly in the case of amulets, seem to be the hallmark of Nubian faience from the Kushite Period, as the collection in the Tomb of Queen Tabiry, wife of Piankhy/Piye and daughter of Alara, reveals.[60] A marguerite replaces the expected sun-disk in many of these amulets. Also, the principal design of this roundel—four lotus blossoms radiating from a central marguerite—is exactly that found on a silver sheath dated to the reign of the Napatan king Aspelta.[61] To these examples may be added a pectoral in the shape of a falcon, formerly in the MacGregor Collection, reportedly found at Mendes and now in the Museum of Fine Arts, Boston.[62] This particular example is of yellow faience, very close in color to the roundel here, and was enhanced by blue faience inlays, only minute traces of which are still detectable.[63] The suggested date of the falcon-pectoral is the Twenty-Sixth Dynasty, a dating consistent with comparable faience material found in Nubian contexts. All these observations suggest a date for this roundel in the period between the seventh and sixth centuries BC.

Without its archaeological context, the significance of the motifs employed is unclear, but the resurrection symbolism inherent in the lotus may well be reinforced by the blue marguerites as well as by the solar associations of the color yellow. RSB

110 FRAGMENT OF A FISH PLAQUE PAGE 128

New Kingdom, possibly Dynasty 18; probably from Amarna

Polychrome faience; H. 3.8 cm; W. 4.2 cm; TH. 0.6 cm

Private Collection

This faience fragment showing the front portion of a tilapia (*bulti*) fish facing right is a particularly fine example of effective glaze use. Painted details were kept to a minimum in order to highlight the subtle but beautiful use of color. The outline and features of the fish are drawn in warm brown glaze paint, with fluid curving lines indicating the contours of the lips and semicircular lines below the mouth, the gills, and outline of the eye. The area around its wide brown pupil was incised and filled with a warm yellow glaze. A contrasting splash of translucent blue wash gives an almost three-dimensional effect edging the upper contour of the head. A second thin layer of blue streaking across the gill in a horizontal line emphasizes the side of the body, turning the yellow in the gill green at their intersection. These colors combine with the glistening surface of the faience to give the impression of a fish moving under water. On the underside, which is flat and slightly recessed along the base, there is a thick layer of glaze.

A parallel example from Amarna shows the right-facing head of a tilapia with minimal incised and painted details and a thick pool of glaze for the eye.[64] Other faience inlays in a more ornate style attest to the popularity of the tilapia and other varieties of fish at this site.[65] Their use as inlays is clear if they have an impression on the underside of the textile they were laid on during drying for efflorescence glazing.[66]

This fish plaque was probably made at Amarna, using the efflorescence process, but it was carefully elevated during drying to produce the attractive glaze on its underside.[67] At Amarna faience fish with glaze on all sides, with shallow cavities and fins curved out like handles, may have served as ointment dishes.[68] This flat faience fish plaque could possibly have been used as a lid for such a dish.[69]

A wide range of objects was made in this shape in various materials[70]—in addition to dishes, it is found in the form of bottles in glass and glazed steatite.[71] The tilapia's suggested connections with ideas of regeneration and resurrection[72] [77], [78] would have contributed to its popularity in the Eighteenth Dynasty, and equally so at Amarna. BC

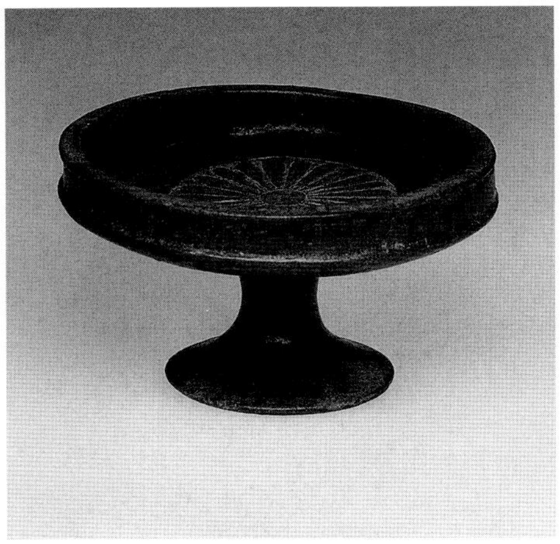

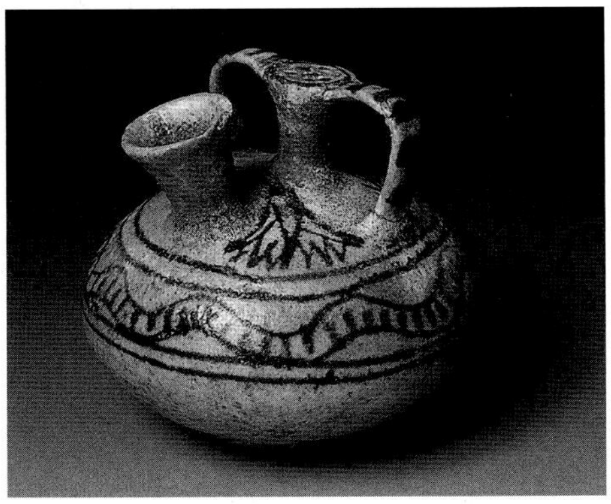

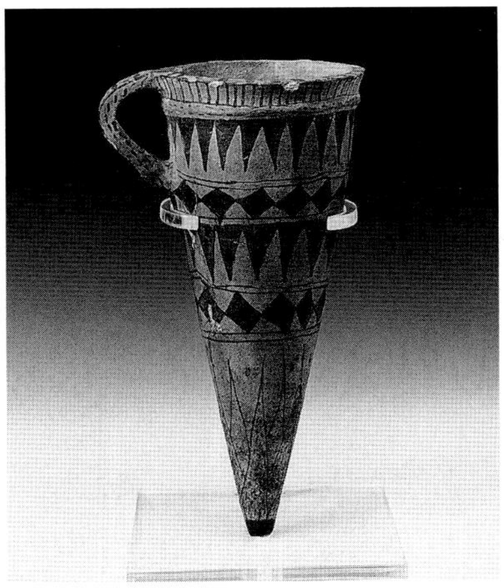

122 FOOTED DISH

PAGE 139

New Kingdom, Dynasty 18, possibly reign of Amenhotep III

Faience; H. of dish to point of insert: 2.7 cm; H. of base: 2.67 cm; total H. when dish inserted into base: 4.24 cm; DIAM. 7.65 cm

The Walters Art Gallery, Baltimore, Maryland. Acquired by Henry Walters, 1930. 48.1608a, b

This faience piece reveals how the form and decoration of larger vessels well known in the Eighteenth Dynasty in stone and pottery[135] were converted into a miniaturized faience version, just over 4 cm (about 1¾ in) in height. Looking much like a modern cake plate, this tiny, deep-blue, footed dish was made in two parts: a biconical foot whose top part opens to receive the dish and whose lower part flares to form the foot; and a dish, whose insertion point slips perfectly into the top of the base. A daisy motif at the dish's center is outlined in a now weathered white paste inlay.[136] On the bottom of the biconical foot are marks where the glaze was rubbed free when set down on kiln furniture. Extreme care has been taken to replicate in two interlocking parts a form that could more easily have been imitated in one. In addition, the precision of the craftsmanship and the quality of the glaze are exceptional, reflecting the artistry and kiln control of a royal workshop.

The even, glossy surface and saturated blue color could be the result of folding crushed glass into the faience paste.[137] Glass was at the height of its production at this time in the Eighteenth Dynasty, and such homogeneous, polished surfaces were as prized as gemstones.[138] A turquoise blue ribbed cup in the Metropolitan Museum of Art is the best glass comparison for this faience example.[139]

Theban tomb paintings reveal the purpose of the footed dish—servant girls apply unguents from such dishes for their banqueting owners, especially from the period of Amenhotep III;[140] ointment cones for the head were also carried in such vessels.[141] An ebony figure of a Nubian serving girl proffers just this sort of footed dish.[142] This example may have been a perfume holder during life or a tomb gift for banquets in the beyond. The dish has been dated to the reign of Amenhotep III on the basis of the daisy motif, which this king used frequently in sculpture and decorative art, and the placement of dots at the end of the daisy petals, a feature typical of work in his reign, but seen only intermittently here.[143] FDF

Bibliography. Spalinger in Brovarski et al. 1982, p. 149, cat. no. 153; Kozloff in Kozloff and Bryan 1992c, p. 406, cat. no. 107.

123 STIRRUP JAR

PAGE 137

New Kingdom, Dynasty 18

Blue faience with black glaze details; H. 6.5 cm

Private Collection

Egyptian craftsmen borrowed forms and motifs from neighboring cultures but adapted them to conform with strict pharaonic design tenets—a phenomenon well illustrated by this stirrup jar. In its proportions, particularly the height of its neck, spout, and handles, this vessel approximates to the classic form of a Late Helladic IIIB stirrup jar, produced in the Mycenaean world during the thirteenth century BC.[144] A date in the Late Eighteenth Dynasty is thus suggested for this example. The conical rather than cylindrical spout, however, betrays the hand of its Egyptian craftsman, as do its material and decoration in black glaze. Its floral elements and banded serpentine motif around the belly differ radically from the alternating bands found on contemporary Mycenaean vessels of this type.

Although the larger Mycenaean stirrup jars were doubtless intended to contain olive oil, the smaller ones, including these Egyptian faience imitations, seem to be for perfumed unguents or other precious liquids.[145] The shape and design of these jars made such substances easy to handle because it is "possible to stop the flow of the spout with the thumb, while the second and third fingers control the two sides of the stirrup handle."[146] RSB

Bibliography. Vermeule in Brovarski et al. 1982c, p. 146, cat. no. 165.

124 CONICAL RHYTON OR DRINKING CUP

PAGE 135

New Kingdom, Dynasty 18

Faience; H. 23.0 cm

The Trustees of the British Museum, London. EA 22731

This conical rhyton, with its tall sides, offset concave lip[147] and slightly crooked loop handle, is an Egyptian imitation of a form introduced on Crete during the late Middle Minoan Period.[148] It thus exemplifies again the characteristic of ancient Egyptian art already mentioned [123]: the adaptation according to pharaonic design tenets of objects and motifs characteristic of neighboring cultures.[149] This rhyton copies a Minoan form but is decorated with seven registers each containing abstract designs derived from the ancient pharaonic Egyptian repertoire of motifs. The designs are represented in dark blue with black outlines on a pale blue ground that contrasts with the rhyton's unglazed interior.

Of all the pharaonic Egyptian versions of the Minoan rhyton, this is the most famous and most frequently published. Its popularity with scholars resides no doubt in its demonstration that ancient Egyptian craftsmen had fully absorbed a foreign pottery typology into their local Egyptian production. The cosmopolitan Egyptians of the New Kingdom, doubtless aware of the opulence of Minoan Crete, adopted as their own a vessel used there primarily for ritual purposes. It is not known, however, whether this rhyton was employed in Egypt for similar ceremonies because judging from its excellent state of preservation it came from a tomb. RSB

Bibliography. Vermeule in Brovarski et al. 1982, p. 154, cat. no. 160.

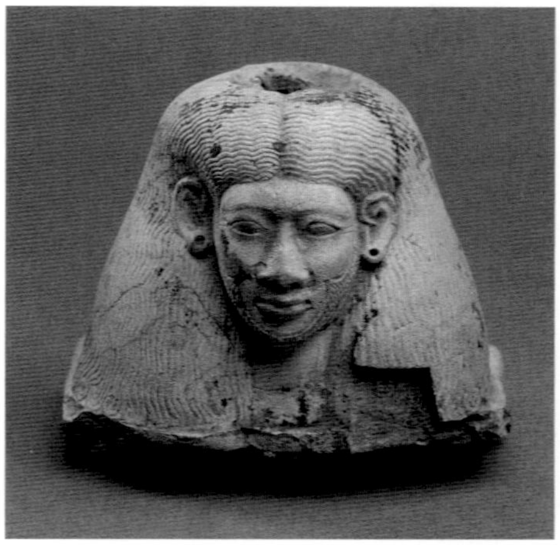

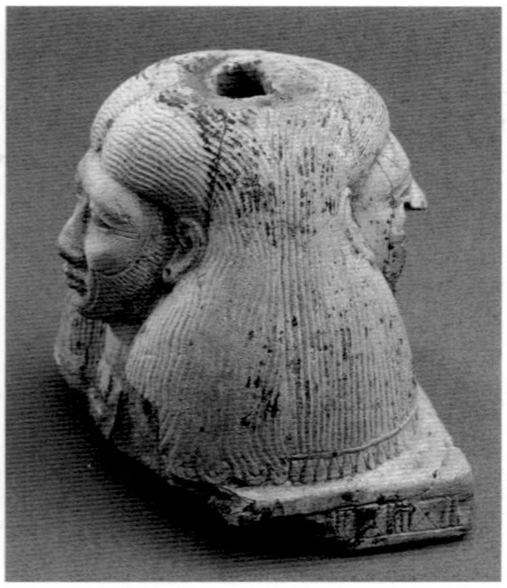

125 NECK FROM A PERFUME VASE

PAGES 140, 141

Late Period, Dynasty 26; Abydos
Faience, H. 10.0 cm
Musée du Louvre, Paris. E 11261

This vessel seems to have been made by joining together three separately cast elements: the fronts of two heads and the base upon which they rest. The heads were joined back to back in such a way that the hollow between them could become the neck of the *aryballos*,[150] or perfume vase, for which they formed the principal decoration. The better preserved head is a male with a closely cropped beard, the shape of which is delineated by a deep incision in the flesh of the cheeks. He wears an undulating wig, parted down the center.

The other head wears a long wig, the ends of the strands of which terminate in tear-drop shapes. This face has been tentatively identified as female,[151] although gender-specific attributes are absent. On both figures the ears are pierced, and they must have originally worn earrings, perhaps of metal.[152] The base is decorated with four vertical incisions forming a triglyph that alternate with a rectangle with an incised "X."

During the Third Intermediate Period a flourishing faience industry developed in Egypt that included the manufacture of anthropomorphic vessels in various shapes,[153] as well as *aryballoi*,[154] the forms of which were soon so successfully imitated by craftsmen in neighboring regions that it is often difficult to distinguish native Egyptian fabrics from Egyptianizing ones.[155] This vessel must be understood in terms of such developments, but can confidently be ascribed to an Egyptian workshop because of the nature of its fabric, findspot, and style.

The fabric appears to be that type of (originally) apple-green faience traditionally used for the manufacture of shabti, or funerary figurines, from the Twenty-Sixth to the Thirtieth Dynasty.[156] The style of the bearded face with its undulating wig is remarkably similar to images of Hathor, with their triangular faces, pronounced cheeks, and prominent noses with wings set off by incision, such as seen on a statue now in New York and dated by inscriptional evidence to the Twenty-Sixth Dynasty.[157] The beard seems to indicate that the male figure is intended to be a foreigner, inasmuch as native Egyptians are only infrequently shown with this sort of beard.

The figure may be a Persian, on the basis of Egyptian depictions of the Achaemenids.[158] That a Persian should be represented in Egyptian art during the Twenty-Sixth Dynasty is not unexpected because decidedly Achaemenid fashions were being depicted and presumably worn, in Egypt before the Persian occupation in 525 BC.[159] RSB

Bibliography. Vandier d'Abbadie 1972, pp. 96 and 97.

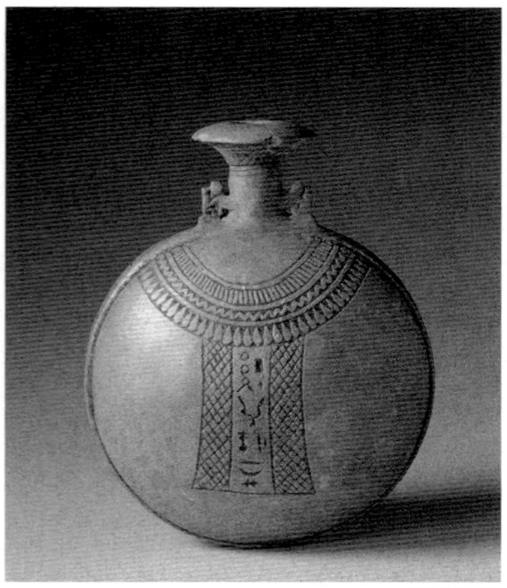

126 NEW YEAR'S FLASK PAGE 138

Late Period, Dynasty 26
Faience, H. 13.0 cm
Staatliche Museen zu Berlin - Preussischer Kulturbesitz Ägyptisches Museum und Papyrussammlung. 9480

127 NEW YEAR'S FLASK PAGE 138

Late Period, Dynasty 26
Faience, H. 13.4 cm
Staatliche Sammlung Ägyptischer Kunst, Munich. ÄS 2922

These two lentoid vessels, with round, narrow bodies resembling flasks, are approximately the same size and are similarly decorated. They are both topped by relatively tall necks crowned by flaring rims, which have been interpreted as stylized floral motifs, as has the garland, perhaps representing the lotus (*Nymphaea caerulea*), incised around the upper body.[160] Two pairs of baboons sit at the base of the neck, paws to mouth, in an attitude suggesting they are eating.[161] The narrow band running from baboon to baboon is inscribed with hieroglyphs, as were 85% of this type of faience vessel surveyed in one study.[162] The Munich flask is distinguished by an incised lion moving toward the right on a ground line, which appears at the bottom of what must be its principal side.

The inscriptions on the Munich vessel [127] may be translated "May the god Amun open the New Year for its Lord" and "May the god Shu open the New Year for its Lord"; that on the Berlin example [126] reads "May the god Ptah open a beautiful New Year for its Lord." The mention of the New Year accounts for the modern designation of this type of vessel; here the phrase "its Lord" is a circumlocution referring to their owners, who are not identified by name.

The ancient Egyptian New Year started in late summer, when the Nile began its annual flood. The transition between the years was considered fraught with dangers that threatened the cosmic stability of the land, and numerous rituals were developed in order to insure a harmonious transition.[163] It is within this context that these vessels are to be understood. The deities invoked are commonly Ptah and Amun, as here, as well as members of their triads, Sekhmet and Nefertum and Mut and Khonsu, respectively. The mention of Shu is exceptional, but may relate to the legend of the far-off goddess, often depicted in leonine form, whose fearsome nature is

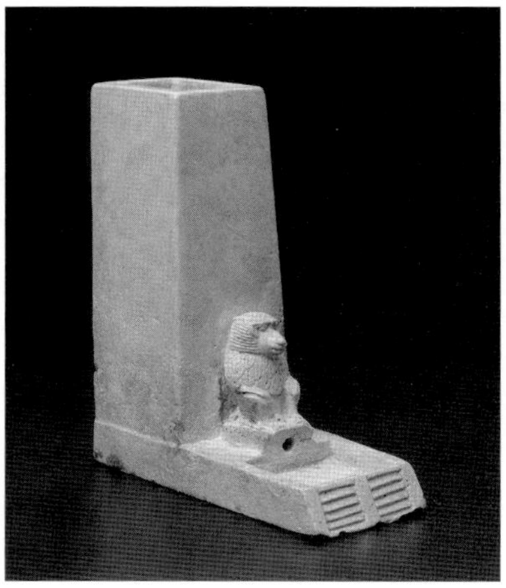

132 MODEL CLEPSYDRA, OR WATER CLOCK PAGE 145

Late Period, Dynasty 26 to Ptolemaic Period

Faience; H. 10.0 cm

William Kelly Simpson, New York

The clepsydra, or water clock—the ancient Egyptian word for this device is still a matter of speculation[184]—first appears in Egypt during the Eighteenth Dynasty[185] and is associated with a certain Amenemhat, who is credited with its invention.[186] Votive clepsydrae of the type depicted here generally consist of a base fronted by a single or a double flight of stairs. These stairs give the base the appearance of a dais whose profile resembles the hieroglyph for "truth,"[187] suggesting that whatever is thus supported is established on a place of truth. Rising from the dais is a reservoir for water in the form of a tall, tapering rectangle. A baboon squats on a narrow pedestal pressed up against the reservoir. In certain clepsydrae the baboon's phallus forms the conduit for the evacuation of the water from its reservoir,[188] but in this example the conduit is incorporated into the base on which the baboon squats. This design recalls the traditional, architectural lion-headed waterspouts that drain rainwater from temples via a conduit between or below the lion's paws rather than through its mouth—as inscriptions associated with the ritual of the lion-headed waterspout suggest. The conduit empties into a rectangular basin at the head of the stairs.

This clepsydra was probably a votive offering, but its precise significance cannot be determined due to the lack of archaeological context. Nevertheless, this example, one of the finest of its type,[189] can reasonably be dated to the Late Period, when such apple-green colored faience was in vogue. RSB

Bibliography. Brovarski 1977, no. 69, pp. 64, 70; Greenwich Library 1979a, no. 68, p. 19.

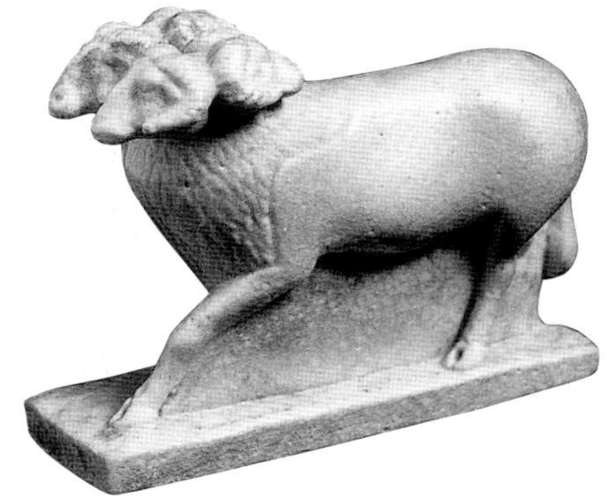

133 STRIDING FOUR-HEADED RAM PAGE 130

Late Period, Dynasty 30 to Ptolemaic Period

Faience; H. 4.9 cm; L. 6.5 cm; D. 2.3 cm

Private Collection

Ex-Collection: Béhague

Four-faced beings, either human or animal, are a striking feature of ancient Egyptian religious images, which Egyptian artists were expert at making appear almost natural. To this category belong certain representations of Hathor and Isis,[190] and also the ram, as seen in this pale blue example with two heads looking forward and two back, a work of exceptional detail and surface. Note the delicate bony structure of the hind leg and the even, lustrous glaze, possibly the result of adding ground glass to the faience paste.

Without accompanying inscriptions or an archaeological context it is difficult to identify which of the hypostases of the ram deity this image represents. It might be associated with the cult of the god known simply as "the Ram of Mendes," as summarized in the discussion of a very similar piece in the New York Bastis collection.[191] In the context of that cult, each head represents a specific *ba*, a complex concept that might be translated as a powered manifestation of a god or a natural force like the wind.[192] At Mendes, in this particular instance, the hypostases of the Ram god included the *Ba* of Osiris (hereafter), the *Ba* of Geb (earth), the *Ba* of Shu (sky), and the *Ba* of Ra (life). Elsewhere, the four-headed ram is associated with Osiris and Re as well as with other deities. Ba is also the name of the ram in ancient Egyptian, undoubtedly mimicking the animal's bleat.[193] RSB & FDF

Bibliography. Bothmer in Hall 1978a, pp. 73–74, cat. no. 26; Sotheby's 1987, p. 59, cat. no. 88.

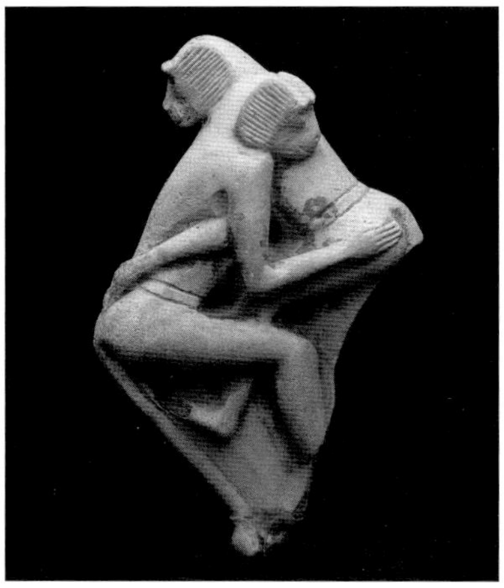

134 MONKEYS WRESTLING PAGE 144

Ptolemaic Period

Faience; H. 9.0 cm

William Kelly Simpson, New York

The protagonists in this composition, identifiable both by their characteristic green color[194] and distinctive heads, are monkeys [195] which appear to be wrestling.[196] This faience sculptural group is, to the best of my knowledge, unique in ancient Egyptian art, in that no parallels exist in any medium and depictions in the round of human wrestlers are very rare indeed.[197] Despite the lack of an archaeological provenance or accompanying inscriptions, an interpretation for this object might be sought among the recurring ancient Egyptian cyclical conflicts in which opposing cosmic forces are brought into equilibrium. This has been argued for the fablelike boxing match between a cat and a mouse depicted on an Egyptian terra-cotta of Roman date.[198] It might, therefore, be possible tentatively to link this statuette to phases of the moon and the myths of the *déesse lointaine*.[199]

Whatever its interpretation, this piece reaffirms an often overlooked characteristic of ancient Egyptian group sculptures. Most commentators dismiss sculptural groups as ineffective because the craftsmen habitually eschew representing the interaction of two or more figures in more than one plane[200] to produce what are called paratactic compositions. Group sculptures such as this, in which the individual members are intertwined on more than one plane, are consequently considered atypical. Such an assessment fails to take into consideration the fact that the extent to which figures in an ancient Egyptian group composition are intertwined is directly proportional to the size of the group: the larger the sculpture, the more likely it is to be designed syntactically. Thus, this statuette of wrestling monkeys follows accepted ancient Egyptian norms.[201] The relationship between this Ptolemaic Egyptian wrestling group and contemporary Hellenistic group sculptures of wrestlers identified as representations of Macedonian Greek rulers at Alexandria deserves further study.[202]

Although the surface of this piece has been considerably altered by weathering, its lively sculptural appearance remains unaffected. RSB

Bibliography. Greenwich Library 1979b, pp. 64 and 70, no. 68.

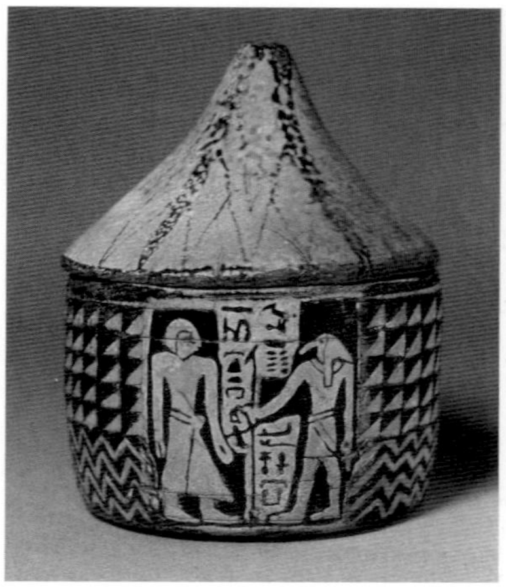

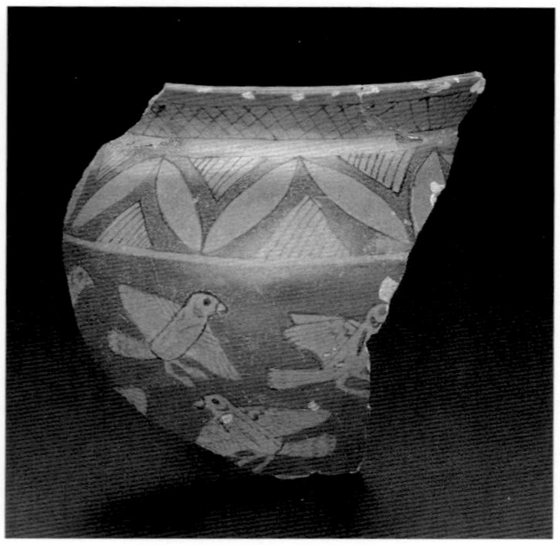

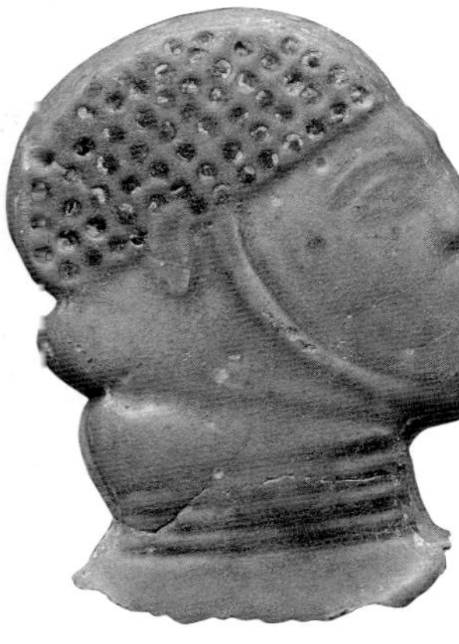

135 VESSEL IN THE SHAPE OF A BASKET WITH A CONICAL LID PAGE 134

Late Second Intermediate Period to New Kingdom, early Dynasty 18

Faience, H. 15.0 cm; DIAM. 11.9 cm

Musée du Louvre, Paris. E 3610

This vessel represents a wickerwork basket with a conical lid. A number of examples in faience have survived, several coming from Kerma, though the best parallel is a cartonnage example from Deir el-Medina. They show a range of treatment from very naturalistic—with a carefully ribbed outer surface—to more abstract renderings of the overall shape, as here.[203] Perhaps the product of a provincial workshop, this vessel is inscribed to the god shown on the right: "Thoth, Lord of Hermopolis, may he give goodness and life to the *ka* of the scribe of the harbor, Hori," the owner of the vessel, shown standing to the left. The diagonally divided squares and zigzag motifs are also common decorative devices of this period. PL

Bibliography. McDonald in Brovarski et al. 1982d, p. 151, cat. no. 159; Rigault in Phillips 1995, p. 90.

136 VESSEL FRAGMENT WITH FLYING BIRDS PAGE 136

Late Middle Kingdom; Kerma, Tumulus K XX

Faience, H. 10.3 cm

Museum of Fine Arts, Boston. Harvard University - Museum of Fine Arts, Boston Expedition. 1920.1235

Egyptian faience was exported in large quantities to Kerma, in Nubia, for recycling as inlay material and possibly to grind up for reuse in faience manufacture. This fragment from a wide-mouthed round jar with an outward-flaring rim is decorated with two rows of birds flying in opposite directions.[204] Above them is a register of zigzag lenticular elements alternating with hatched triangles. This decoration has been created in reserve against a dark manganese blue background, while the rim is embellished with a cross-hatch decoration of thin dark blue lines against light blue. The vessel from which this fragment comes represents the best Egyptian faience craftsmanship of the late Middle Kingdom and the motifs, particularly the flying birds and hatched triangles, are found on other vessels of this period.[205] PL

Bibliography. Reisner 1923, p. 162.

137 INLAY HEAD OF A NUBIAN PAGE 130

Nubian, Classic Kerma Period, *c.* 1600–1500 BC; Kerma, Chapel K II

Faience, H. 7.5 cm; W. 2.3 cm

Museum of Fine Arts, Boston. Harvard University-Museum of Fine Arts, Boston Expedition. 1920.1305

By the Late Classic Kerma Period (*c.* 1500 BC), faience was being manufactured at the Nubian site of Kerma itself and was used extensively in the decoration of the large brick funerary chapel, K II.[206] Like other tiles from this structure, this one is fairly thick with a deep blue vitreous glaze on the surface. This inlay head was part of a larger composition that included a set of arms tied behind the back of the figure. It either represented a prisoner or decorated the name of one of the enemies of the Kerma kingdom. The striations around the neck may represent ropes and the distinctive hairstyle perhaps suggests one of the other Nubian groups that vied with the Kerma kingdom for control of the middle Nile. PL

Bibliography. Reisner 1923, p. 152.

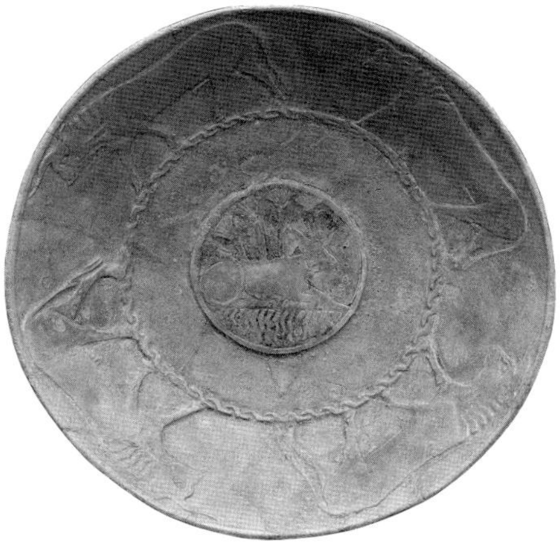

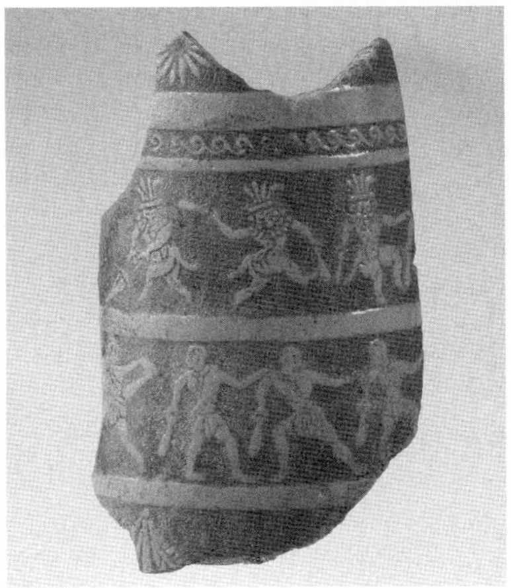

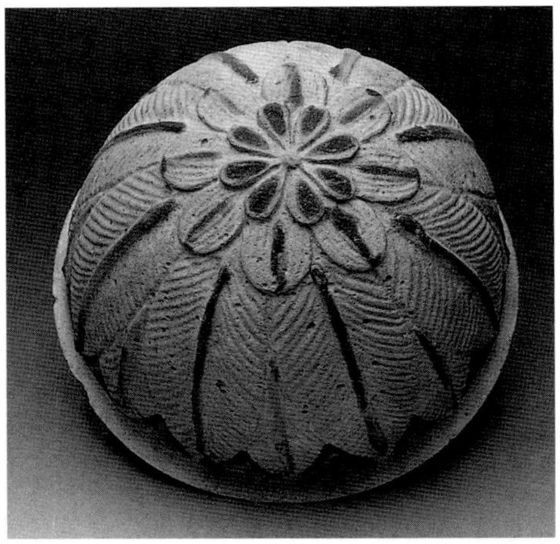

138 BOWL WITH CATTLE

PAGE 138

Third Intermediate Period; el-Kurru, Tomb K 55

Faience; H. 4.4 cm; DIAM. 16.4 cm

Museum of Fine Arts, Boston. Harvard University - Museum of Fine Arts, Boston Expedition. 1924.1089

As in the Second Intermediate Period, large quantities of Egyptian faience were exported to the Napatan kingdom to satisfy the desire of the Nubian court for exotic materials. This bowl was such an export item and was found in the burial chamber of a tomb at the royal cemetery site of el-Kurru, near the Fourth Cataract. No trace of a superstructure or chapel remained, but Reisner and Dunham suggested it might be the burial of a queen dating to the reign of Pi ('ankhy).[207] The bowl was one of two depicting a procession of four bulls below the rim. In the interior one of the bowls had a central rosette decoration while this one shows a cow lying in a papyrus marsh.[208] The pale, bichrome faience of these bowls is characteristic of a type that appears in the late Third Intermediate Period and continues into the early Ptolemaic era. While the bovine may have had special significance for the Nubians, a cow amidst papyri is common on faiences of the Third Intermediate Period in Egypt.[209] PL

Bibliography. Dunham 1950, 1955–65, pp. 2–3.

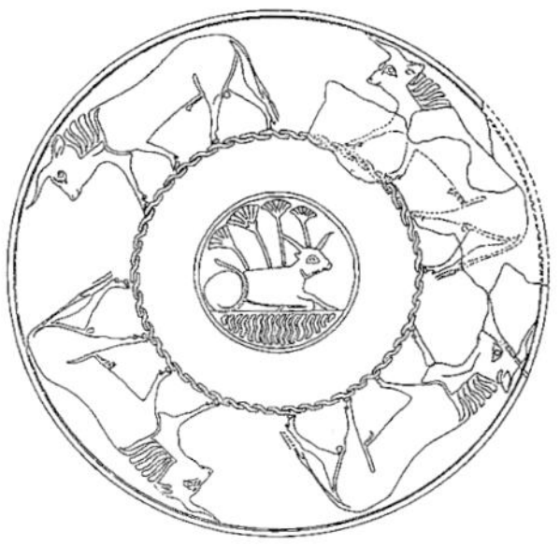

Fig. 52 Drawing of the faience bowl with cattle, possibly from the tomb of a wife of King Piye at el-Kurru. (Drawing by Suzanne E. Chapman.)

139 SHERD FROM A RHYTON OR DRINKING CUP WITH BES IMAGES[210]

PAGE 136

Ptolemaic Period, 3rd to 2nd century BC

Faience; H. 8.8 cm

Staatliche Sammlung Ägyptischer Kunst, Munich. ÄS 5980

When Ptolemy I Soter, a Macedonian Greek general in the army of Alexander the Great, eventually proclaimed himself pharaoh of Egypt in 305/304 BC, he followed a precedent established by Alexander himself and allowed native Egyptian bureaucrats to continue to serve in their hereditary capacities[211] and native Egyptian craftsmen to continue to produce traditional handicrafts.[212] At the same time, Greek craftsmen residing in Egypt began to appropriate pharaonic forms and motifs as their own. This vessel is one of those appropriations. The arrangement of figures in registers of shallow relief and the floral decoration, just barely preserved in the top and bottom registers, belong to the tradition of the chalices of the Third Intermediate Period.[213] On the other hand, the renderings of the Bes-images[214] and of the club-wielding male figures in the register below them boldly proclaim the hand of the craftsman well versed in Classical Greek forms of expression.

The Bes-images on this fragment share with their human counterparts below gyrating attitudes in which the body twists and turns as if to a frenetic tune[215] of war or in a ritualistic dance, to judge from the Heracles-clubs all seem to be wielding. Although one might wish to plumb the depths of Egyptian mythology in an attempt to adduce a tale upon which this depiction is based, the pitfalls of such an approach have been exposed elsewhere.[216] By consensus, most of the relief vessels of this type have been dated to the third and second centuries BC.[217] RSB

Bibliography. Müller 1974, pp. 220–21.

140 MOLDED BOWL

PAGE 143

Ptolemaic Period

Faience; H. 15.2 cm; DIAM. 10.3 cm

Private Collection

On the exterior of this deep, molded hemispherical bowl with everted rim is a decoration consisting of a series of overlapping relief ribbed petals radiating from a calyx of oval leaves at the center of the base, on top of which is superimposed a rosette. The leaves themselves are glazed a pale turquoise blue and emerge from a darker blue ground. Inside, the decoration is confined to a zone beneath the lip and consists of three register lines separating a wave pattern above from a reel pattern below, both patterns reserved in buff against a red ground. No molds are known for this particular type of vessel with its tripartite floral exterior,[218] but they would have differed little from the terra-cotta ones recovered from the industrial quarter of Pella, Greece, which date to the beginning of the first century BC.[219]

Deep hemispherical faience bowls with everted lips exhibit a wide variety of decoration including floral patterns as here, as well as zones with friezes of animals and scenes such as hunts, dances, and sacrifices.[220] Other examples are intentionally plain, with no decoration whatsoever.[221] The typology of such faience vessels from the Ptolemaic Period consists of a series of unique vases, suggesting that the molds from which they were cast were used only once.[222] Why such a practice should obtain for a craft characterized by mass production is uncertain, but may be related to the suggested Achaemenid inspiration for the type in general.[223]

The dating of Ptolemaic Period faience vessels is riddled with difficulties occasioned by the almost total lack of excavated examples in datable archaeological contexts,[224] and compounded by the imperfectly understood relationship between similar vessels in other materials common in the Mediterranean during the Hellenistic Period.[225] Correspondences between the decorative motifs of this particular bowl and those on precious metal vessels, particularly in silver,[226] are noteworthy enough to suggest that such faience vessels were in fact modeled on contemporary examples in plate, reaffirming their suggested Achaemenid inspiration. Certain Achaemenid craft forms, primary among them metal vessels, seem to have the singular distinction of being faithfully reproduced by craftsmen well after the demise of the Achaemenid Empire as a political entity—as the Achaemenid rhyton and vases in the tomb reliefs of Petosiris at Tuna el-Gebel in Middle Egypt would suggest.[227] The usual dating of vessels of this type to the second or first century BC[228] seems to gain support from correspondences to vessels in silver found in the Fayum and also dated to the second century BC.[229] This dating accords well with the observation that object types of the Hellenistic Period seem to be characterized by a periodicity of appearance and disappearance on the cultural horizons.[230] RSB

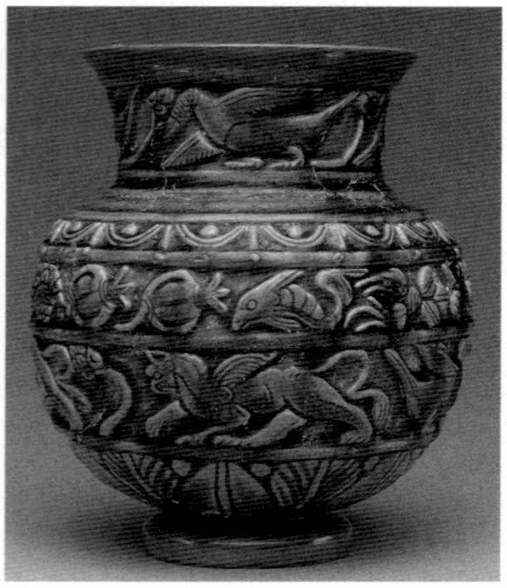

141 VESSEL WITH RELIEF DECORATION

PAGE 142

Roman Period, early 1st century AD; reportedly from Aulad el-Sheikh Ali

Faience, H. 17.0 cm

Brooklyn Museum of Art. The Charles Edwin Wilbour Fund. 70.89.3

This vase has thick walls, a globular body and a cylindrical neck.[231] The entire foot and that part of the lip above the red line have been restored; the surface has a number of cracks, and small, almost insignificant chips are missing from several places. Some of these areas have been masked by the modern application of paint, but despite this overpainting, the colors of the ancient glaze are still visible, ranging from light green and blue-green to yellow and green. Where it has accumulated in the contours and incised details of the decoration, the glaze is dark green, almost black (brown areas indicate deterioration of that dark-green glaze). The color of the interior is blue-green. In general, the vessel is in a remarkable state of preservation.

The five registers of relief decoration appear to have been worked into the fabric freehand, not cast from a mold.[232] On the neck, pine branches separate depictions of geese and ducks with outspread wings. Beneath the swags (probably representing textiles rather than floral motifs) on the body of the vessel are two figural registers. In the top register is an array of floral forms interspersed with marine animals. Below this, a taller register contains a frieze of animals separated by pine branches, including a feline about to prey on a fowl—the only two images that confront each other as the others are aligned in single file facing in the same direction. A register on the foot contains floral motifs, recalling the lotus forms in the same zone on chalices of the Third Intermediate Period.

A survey of all ancient Egyptian vessels with figural decoration in registers suggests that they developed from ones common in the Ptolemaic Period on which the decoration appears to be lightly incised, rather than rendered in bold contours as here.[233] The interpretation of the registers and the function(s) of such vessels are not known. RSB

Bibliography. Grimm 1972, pp. 71–100.

1 Petrie 19[illegible]4b, 2057, pls. IV, V; p. 10; now in the Manchester Museum.
2 British Museum EA 15667 and Myers Museum, Eton College ECM 494.
3 Areas with the most effective drying effloresce well and therefore glaze well during firing. The converse is also true, i.e., areas with less drying have less glazing.
4 McDonald in Brovarski et al. 1982c, p. 137, cat. no. 132; and see Hayes 1990 (1959), p. 205. I thank Stephen Harvey for this reference.
5 Thanks to Yunhui Mao, Mellon Intern in Conservation at the Walters Art Gallery, for the new stringing.
6 I thank Stephen Harvey for these observations and the following: "Clearly, the Egyptians were more interested in controlling access to the content than in ease of opening the basket. In our reconstruction of the likely ancient stringing, fourteen to sixteen 2-ply cords were strung through the holes around the rim of the lower part of the basket, and these were drawn together over the lid, where they were anchored to a short piece of cord in the center of the lid." Pers. comm., Oct. 1997. For examples of such stringing, Harvey notes Winlock 1932, pl. XXXVI, and fig. 20.
7 Sotheby, Wilkinson, and Hodge 1922, p. 37, no. 270.
8 Janssen and Janssen 1989, pp. 33–34 which also notes that pork never appears in temple offering lists either, though pigs were held as temple property for feeding lesser members of the temple personnel.
9 An early word for pig also meant "hippo" (Janssen and Janssen 1989, p. 33), and a possible conflation of Middle Kingdom faience animals may be at work here.
10 For New Kingdom cylindrical boxes, see the examples illustrated by Borchardt 1932, pp. 257–62; For a circular box of the Late Period, see Boston MFA 1970.571, in Brovarski 1987, p. 72 (illus.).
11 E.g., wood: New York, Metropolitan Museum of Art 12. 182.24 and 12.182.25: 1959, pp. 228–29, fig. 136; pottery: Brooklyn Museum of Art 37.342E & .343E: James 1974a, p. 117, nos. 265 and 266.
12 Nash 1898, pp. 266–69.
13 Houlihan 1986, pp. 65–74.
14 The tail of this duck, which might have assisted in species identification, is missing: although the markings have much in common with a pintail, it is not recognizable as an adult male of that species.
15 Hermann 1932, pp. 86–105.
16 Hermann 1932, pl. 9b; Davies 1930, pl. 18. If the Louvre piece belonged to a container of this type, its feather pattern might be explained as that of a juvenile.
17 Cairo no. 6036. Cf. Corteggiani 1979, pp. 168–69.
18 Fischer 1977 (1980), pp. 77–81.
19 Houlihan 1996, p. 80, fig. 57.
20 Newberry 1893–94, pls. XXIV, XXIX.
21 Hornemann 1951–69, vol. 5, pp. 1314–315 (MMA 24.1.46, faience; Berlin 13629, limestone); Garstang 1907, p. 146, fig. 144 (painted clay, Tomb 487, Beni Hasan, dimensions not available). For a contemporary object with dog and squatting man opposite on base, see Arnold 1995, pp. 61–62, no. 52; pl. 75, 52.
22 Schimmel collection "genre scene" (L. 9.5 cm; H. 4.1 cm): Cooney in Muscarella 1974d, no. 173; Sotheby 1992, lot 79.
23 As probably were those of Leo Mildenberg (Kozloff 1996, p. 79, no. III, 115; L. 7.2 cm; H. 5.38 cm) and a Swiss private collector (Page-Gasser in Page-Gasser and Wiese 1997, cat no. 53; L. 8.0 cm; H. 5.8 cm). Many Middle Kingdom faience animals were equipped with bases. See Hayes 1990 (1959), p. 224, fig. 140.
24 Canines were used as watchdogs (Janssen and Janssen 1989, p. 12).
25 Such Middle Kingdom faience figurines are not usually from wealthy burials (Kemp and Merrillees 1980, p. 168).

26 Cf. Kemp and Merrillees 1980, pp. 167–68.
27 Wade 1997, p. A12.
28 For a detailed discussion of the hedgehog and its symbolism, see Droste zu Hülshoff 1980.
29 See Droste zu Hülshoff 1980, no. 352 for a transliteration of the inscription.
30 Arnold 1995, pp. 22–23.
31 Riefstahl 1968, p. 94.
32 In excavated examples of beads with original stringing, multiple strands of threading material usually fill the lumen of the bead, providing evidence for the stringing technique used in this broad collar.
33 A pair of faience lunate terminals covered with gold foil, recovered by G.A. Reisner from Giza Tomb 7832 Z (31-1-347), served as models for the reconstructions.
34 For a description of the beads excavated by Reisner in 1936, see Harvard University and the Museum of Fine Arts, Boston vol. 11, p. 1357.
35 Andrews 1981, no. 539, pl. 9, 40.
36 Hayes 1953, p. 231–32.
37 Markowitz in Thomas et al. 1995a, no. 50, p. 142.
38 Andrews 1981, no. 514, p. 72, pl. 35.
39 Schoske et al. 1992, no. 151, p. 223.
40 Markowitz in Thomas et al. 1995b, no. 69, p. 164.
41 Carter 1927, pp. 191–92, pl. 36.
42 Wilkinson 1994, p. 182.
43 Eaton-Krauss in Brovarski et al. 1982, no. 308, pp. 234–35.
44 Except for the tiny disk beads that may not be original to this necklace.
45 Priese 1991, p. 224, cat. no. 152 maintains that these are pomegranate blossoms, noting jasmine is attested with certainty in Egypt only from the Ptolemaic Period. But a Twentieth Dynasty tomb painting points to the presence of jasmine in the New Kingdom (Spalinger in Brovarski et al. 1982, p. 43, cat. no. 13).
46 The Oriental Institute, The University of Chicago (532) in Spalinger in Brovarski et al. 1982, p. 43, cat. no. 13. Cf. another example in the Peabody Museum, Yale University (YAG 1941.307).
47 Andrews 1990, p. 60, pl. 45j.
48 Wilkinson 1994, p. 104-05.
49 Wilkinson 1994, p. 116.
50 Petrie 1894, p. 16, pp. 28–29.
51 Boyce in Kemp 1989, p. 162.
52 Kaczmarczyk and Hedges 1983, pp. 244ff.
53 For several *wadjet*-eye examples, see Eaton-Krauss in Brovarski et al. 1982, no. 346, p. 249.
54 Stierlin and Ziegler 1987b, pl. 37.
55 Tait 1963, pp. 134–35.
56 Riefstahl 1968, no. 51, pp. 104–05.
57 Cf. Andrews 1990, p. 107. The roundel seems too large to be an element in a necklace or a bracelet.
58 Cf. Brooklyn 49.8, identified as an architectural ornament said to be from Amarna; and Brooklyn 55.882, a floral frieze perhaps from the temple of Ramesses III at Tell el-Yahudiyah: Riefstahl 1968, pls. 29, no. 29; and 49 no. 48, respectively.
59 Cf. Brooklyn 49.30, an openwork spacer; Brooklyn 48.203 and 49.10, two openwork rings; and Brooklyn 44.175, an openwork bottle: Riefstahl 1968, pls. 57, no. 53; nos. 54-55; and 52, no. 51, respectively.
60 Dunham 1950, p. 87, and pl. XLIXa-b.
61 Dunham 1955, pp. 78-102, and pl. CV.A.
62 Boston 64.2179: Terrace 1968b, p. 121 and col. pl. 4.
63 Boston 64.2179: Terrace 1968b, p. 121 and col. pl. 4.
64 UC.472 (Samson 1972, pl. VII p. 90). The close similarity suggests that this fragment was produced here. A large number of faience fish plaques come from Amarna, e.g., Pendlebury 1951, pp. 31, 49, 66.
65 Tilapia: Berlin 25444 (Staatliche Museen zu Berlin 1991, no. 77, p. 126). For additional fish plaques from Amarna, see UC.476 (Samson 1972, pl. VII p. 91). Frankfort and Pendlebury 1933, p. 26, p. 54, pl. XXX.1; Pendlebury 1951, no. 56 a/b, p. 37, no. 64 a/b, p. 31, pl. LXXII.6.
66 Nicholson 1993: see UC.406, fig. 23, p. 32.
67 Nicholson 1993, p. 11: in the efflorescence method, a thick effloresced "crust," which on firing produces the glaze, builds up during drying and is thickest on those surfaces most exposed to air.
68 Müller 1964, A 122a, p. 85: a tilapia, probably from Amarna; several fragments of this type were found in the great palace (Petrie 1894, p. 28); see also UC.478 and UC.474. (Pendlebury 1951, p. 229).
69 Suggested for Müller 1964, A122c, p. 86, with reference to A 124 (K493 D) p. 88, an ivory fish of similar design that could have served as a lid.
70 Dambach and Wallert 1966, p. 284.
71 Brovarski et al. 1982, no. 155, p. 150 and no. 179 p. 165.
72 Milward in Brovarski et al. 1982d, no 138, p. 142; Gamer-Wallert 1970, pp. 109–13.
73 Weber 1969, 36–41; Helck 1982, cols. 656–58; and Cauville 1987a, pp. 185–87.
74 Holladay 1982, pp. 24–25, pl. XXI, fig. 31.
75 Redford in Holladay 1982, pp. 60–61. For a New Kingdom example of an inkwell in the form of two *sn* rings, see Schneider and Raven 1981, no. 110. For a Late Period one with *sn* rings, see Patch 1990, no. 69, p. 86.
76 Tait 1963, p. 101 speculated on the dating of the chalices while establishing the only effective, albeit hypothetical, sequence of style that others have since followed. Vandiver in Brovarski et al. 1982, pp. 147–48 gives further archaeological evidence for dating this chalice. E.g., the BM chalice has a narrow block border at the lip like Twenty-Second Dynasty relief chalices, while the horizontal lines at the V-shaped petal bases have parallels in depictions and remains of Eighteenth and Nineteenth Dynasty chalices, respectively.
77 For two others of almost comparable quality in the decoration of the cup, see Louvre E 11349 and Florence 3254, as noted by Tait 1963, p. 102, pl. XIII, 1 and 2.
78 Tait 1963, pp. 101–02.
79 Capart 1927, p. 63.
80 Pinch 1993, p. 307: "(i)t cannot be assumed that a particular type of vessel invariably had a single purpose." See Brovarski in Brovarski et al. 1982a, p. 146.
81 Brovarski in Brovarski et al. 1982a, p. 146 believes that the "blue-lotus chalices that do appear in ritual contexts probably represent larger chalices of alabaster, metal, or pottery."
82 E.g., Vernier 1927, p. 415, pl. 104, CG 53260; Montet 1952, pl. 67.
83 Predominantly calcite: e.g., Randall-MacIver and Mace 1902, pl. 51; Bissing 1907, pl. 6; Petrie 1937 (1957), pl. 32; Dunham 1978, pl. 31; Brovarski et al. 1982, p. 129, no. 119. Cf. Tait 1963, p. 96, n. 6 and p. 97.
84 E.g., Nolte 1985, jacket and pls. on pp. 11, 12, 16, 89.
85 Loret 1892, pp. 113–16; Keimer 1948, pp. 89–108; Keimer 1984, p. 35; Täckholm 1974, p. 144; Germer 1985, pp. 37–39; Moens 1984, pp. 11–53; Manniche 1989, pp. 126–27.
86 Steindorff 1935, 1937, II, pl. 91, 3–4. For the shape of the bowl of this example, cf. Bissing 1902, p. 78, CG 3851; Randall-McIver and Mace 1902, p. 46 (now British Museum EA 35616). For vessels of similar shape but with a higher bowl, cf. Bissing 1902, p. 22, CG 3678-3852; Pavlov and Khodzash 1959, p. 151, pl. 50. The relief decoration on the stem may be compared with that of the white lotus chalice British Museum EA 26227, published Capart 1927, p. 83a.
87 Bissing 1902, pp. 22 and 78, CG 3678 and 3852.
88 During his work in Sinai, Petrie recovered many fragments of such faience vessels, dating to the reign of Ramesses II, that had been destined for celebration of the cult of Hathor as tutelary goddess of mining expeditions: Petrie 1906, pp. 65–66.
89 Petrie 1891, pp. 16-17, pl. 17, 8. The contents of the pit had been burnt, perhaps suggesting that this deposit too may have had some ritual significance.
90 Strauss 1974, pp. 72–76; Derchain 1975b, pp. 65–86; Schlögl 1977; Weidner 1985.
91 *Pace* Montet 1937, p. 59; Montet 1949, p. 30.
92 The earliest excavated blue lotus chalices come from Abydos tomb no. D115, dated *temp.* Thutmose III–Amenhotep III (Boston MFA 01.7396). Cf. Brovarski in Brovarski et al. 1982a, p. 146, no. 145.
93 Tait 1963, pp. 93–138.
94 Cf. the Petrie Museum specimen (UC.15891) from the temple of Seth at Nubt: Petrie and Quibell 1896, p. 70 ("Probably of Ramesside date").
95 Tait 1963, p. 100.
96 Tait 1963, pp. 98–99.
97 Brovarski in Brovarski et al. 1982a, p. 146.
98 For a number of blue lotus chalice fragments found in a domestic context at El-Ashmunein, cf. Spencer 1993, p. 36, nos. 95–102.
99 Brovarski in Brovarski et al. 1982a, p. 147.
100 New York, the Metropolitan Museum of Art 07.228.20, a silver bowl from the Bubastis Treasure: Hayes 1990 (1959), pp. 238–360, and fig. 226.
101 Fazzini 1988, pp. 8–9.
102 See the comments for [78].
103 Bianchi 1996b, pp. 156–59.
104 [78]; Pinch 1993, pp. 321–22; Berlandini 1983, pp. 33–50.
105 Aldred 1973, p. 213, no. 153; Kozloff in Kozloff and Bryan 1992j, pp. 386–88, cat. no. 95: British Museum EA 55193: L. 14.5 cm; W. 7.0 cm; D. 3.2 cm.
106 Compare the Eighteenth Dynasty painted clay fish in the Brooklyn Museum (48.11).
107 The *heh*-sign, a small right-facing kneeling figure holding a bent palm frond in each hand and wearing a solar disk on his head, is a special variant of the sign representing a million. This sign is literally read as "millions and millions [of years]" (Erman and Grapow 1931 p. 154, 25) and is one way the Egyptians expressed the concept of eternity.
108 Quirke 1991, p.94.
109 For various other amulet types see, e.g., Dunham 1950, 1957, p. 80, nos. 22-1-5b, 21-12-137; p.143, pl. LXVII, no. 21-3-629; and passim.
110 Several centuries later, this town was to become the capital of the eponymous final Kingdom of Kush, the Meroitic Kingdom.
111 Two *ankh*-amulet handles are now in the collection of the Liverpool Museum (49.47.845), H. *c.* 10.5 cm and (49.47.846), *c.* 10.5 cm, and a complete amulet is in the Petrie Collection, London UC.43949 (Wellcome number A 15428, MacGregor lot 668). All were excavated in Meroë by Garstang 1911.
112 Al-Rayah 1981, pp. 132–33 noted that many of the objects found at this site had New Year dedications.
113 Goyon 1972.
114 Harvard University and the Museum of Fine Arts, Boston, Vol. 15, Giza, Part 4, p. 229. For a list of the finds from G 7510Z, see Museum of Fine Arts, Boston 1925, pp. 408–12.
115 The vessels are decorated with horizontal bands of demotic script, an everyday script used in Egypt during the seventh to fourth centuries BC. The texts designate the ceramics as embalming pots. See catalogue entry by Quirke in D'Auria et al. 1988b, pp. 182–83.
116 Nefertum is also represented as the son of Bastet and is sometimes associated with Mahes and Horus. See Grzymski 1994, pp. 200–01.
117 Zabkar 1975, p. 52.
118 Naville 1888, pl. 3-3, 7-3.
119 Andrews 1994, p. 18.

120 Steindorff 1946, pp. 125–26, pl. 83.
121 See contents of tombs W 508 and W 643 in Dunham 1950, 1965, p. 28, fig. 19h and p. 39, fig. 28a.
122 A recent list of known examples with provenances can be found in Grzymski 1994, p. 200.
123 Schoske et al. 1992, p. 127.
124 Schoske et al. 1992, pp. 201–02.
125 See, e.g., Vandier 1952, p. 321, fig. 223, no. 80.
126 See, e.g., Kelly 1976, pl. 2.12, 9; pl. 2.28, second row, left (unnumbered).
127 Petrie 1937 (1977), 99. 3-5, pls. II, VI-XII.
128 Petrie 1937 (1977), p. 5.
129 Petrie 1937 (1977), p. 5.
130 Egyptian blue versions of the cylindrical vessel also exist, e.g., Fitzwilliam E 275.1939.
131 See Petrie 1937 (1977), pp. 5; 134–42, pl. XII.
132 Hayes 1990 (1959), p. 84, fig. 46; p. 85, fig. 47.
133 Hayes 1990 (1959), pp. 66, 67, fig. 35.
134 Lilyquist 1995, cat. pt. 2, p. 115, fig. 139, P, S; pp. 51, 52.
135 For refs. see Kozloff in Kozloff and Bryan 1992c, p. 406, cat. no. 107, nos. 1–2.
136 Others state that the daisy is in a lighter turquoise (Spalinger in Brovarski et al. 1982, p. 149, cat. no. 153, and Kozloff in Kozloff and Bryan 1992c, p. 406, cat. no. 107), though its color appears to me to be the same deep blue as the body, a point confirmed by the Walters conservators. I thank Mimi Leveque for discussing the piece with me and noting the use of a paste inlay around the petals, a technique also used in the Ramesside rosettes [55, 56].
137 Other explanations include modification of the kiln environment or concentration of salts or fluxes. Additional glaze may have been applied prior to firing.
138 Russmann in Lilyquist 1983, p. 36, nos. 36, 37.
139 Russmann in Lilyquist 1983, p. 36, nos. 36, 37; Hayes 1990 (1959), p. 277; p. 278, fig. 170. Cf. also the Metropolitan Museum of Art's large faience version of the same footed dish form (MMA 18.2.6 a,b).
140 Freed in Brovarski et al. 1982, p. 204, cat no. 239; Kozloff in Kozloff and Bryan 1992c, p. 406, no. 107.
141 Schoske et al. 1990, p. 64, cat. nos. 9 and 10.
142 Petrie Museum of Egyptian Archaeology, UC.14210; illustrated in Kozloff in Kozloff and Bryan 1992, p. 362, cat. no. 88.
143 Kozloff in Kozloff and Bryan 1992c, p. 406, no. 107.
144 Museum of Fine Arts, Boston 72.1482: Vermeule in Brovarski et al. 1982c, p. 156, no. 165.
145 Vermeule in Brovarski et al. 1982b, p. 153.
146 Vermeule in Brovarski et al. 1982b, p. 153, and see n. 24 for pertinent literature.
147 The present discussion is based on the entry by Vermeule in Brovarski et al. 1982, p. 154.
148 Vermeule in Brovarski et al. 1982b, pp.152–53.
149 Bianchi et al. 1988b, pp. 63–65.
150 Vandier d'Abbadie 1972, p 96.
151 Vandier d'Abbadie 1972, p 96.
152 British Museum EA 37401, a Bes-image in faience with gold earrings and a silver nose ring.
153 See Bulté 1991.
154 Webb 1978, pp. 61–71.
155 Aldred et al. 1980, pp. 197–205.
156 Aldred et al. 1980, p. 215.
157 New York, the Metropolitan Museum of Art, 24.2.2: Davis 1981, p. 77.
158 Inter alia, Mathieson et al. 1995, pp. 23–41.
159 De Meulenaere 1987, p. 139.
160 Blanquet in Obsomer and Oosthoek 1992, p. 49.
161 Blanquet in Obsomer and Oosthoek 1992, p. 49.
162 Blanquet in Obsomer and Oosthoek 1992, p. 49.
163 Drioton 1959, pp. 555–56.
164 For example, Goyon 1972.
165 Goyon 1972, p. 52.
166 Goyon 1972, p. 52.
167 Houlihan 1986, p. 109.
168 Lythgoe 1927, p. 39; cf. Saleh and Sourouzian 1987, no. 260.
169 Hemiunu, Nefermaat's son, continued the practice on the base of his statue but it was then abandoned.
170 For glass inlays in wood from the Eighteenth Dynasty and later, see Lucas 1939, Bianchi 1983a, b.
171 Cf. the group of Thirtieth Dynasty faience inlays said to be from a wooden shrine in the Metropolitan Museum of Art (e.g., [161]); or the first century BC to first century AD glass inlays found amidst deteriorated wooden panels at Gumaiyima near Tanis, in Petrie 1888, pp. 39–40; for date, see Cooney 1976, p. 112, B Gumaiyima; or the Ptolemaic wooden box with vitreous paste inlays, in Roveri 1988b, p. 195, fig. 269.
172 The thickness of each element would have disappeared into the cell in which it was laid, unlike other object inlays which served as relief and sat on the surface of a piece. Additional application glaze has ensured that a lustrous, rich surface would be visible when each glyph was set in place.
173 There may originally have been three flagpoles, which, with the basket, would have read *nṯrw nbw*, "all the gods." But how the glyphs were originally arranged, and in conjunction with what missing elements, remains conjectural.
174 Cf. Cooney 1976, p. 113, no. 1167=Petrie 1888, pl. XVIII, lower center.
175 The surface is not perfectly smooth but undulates slightly like a honeycomb.
176 The crosshatched inlays have fallen out on two similar *nṯr* signs on the art market.
177 Saleh and Sourouzian 1987, no. 260.
178 Datable to the reign of Philip Arrhidaeus, late fourth century BC: Baines and Málek 1980, p. 127.
179 Roveri 1988b, p. 41.
180 Wolinski 1986, pp. 47–53.
181 Fischer 1986, pp. 139–40.
182 Fischer 1965, pp. 169–75; and Bothmer and de Meulenaere in Lesko 1986, p. 1.
183 The Brooklyn Museum of Art 44.175: Riefstahl 1968, no. 51, where the fabric is termed "lapis blue frit."
184 Devauchelle 1986, cols. 1156–157 and Sambin 1988, pp. 233–41 who demonstrates that this object is not a clepsydra as identified.
185 Devauchelle 1986, cols. 1156–157.
186 Nelson and Le Blanc in Desroches-Noblecourt et al. 1976, pp. 139–49. That the name of the inventor of the clepsydra was preserved is exceptional inasmuch as names of other inventors have rarely survived, save that of one of Amenemhat's near contemporaries, Senenmut, who was remembered as inventing composite hieroglyphs (see Fazzini et al. 1989, no. 34, n. 4).
187 Gardiner 1969, p. 541, Sign List Aa11.
188 Devauchelle 1986, cols. 1156–157.
189 Compared, e.g., with those illustrated by Capart 1937, p. 48, top, where these clepsydrae are confused with the object of Sambin's study, above, n. 184.
190 Aufrère 1991, p. 125.
191 Bothmer in Hall 1987a, pp. 73–74, no. 26.
192 For some of the issues involved, see Zabkar 1968.
193 Bothmer in Hall 1987a, p. 73, no. 26.
194 Compare a similar green monkey climbing the neck of a giraffe from the Tomb of Rekhmire ThT100: Eggebrecht 1984, p. 225, lower right. One should note, however, that ancient Egyptian craftsmen also preferred green for representations of baboons, for which see Aufrère 1983, p. 6.
195 See Arnold 1995, pp. 81–82 for images of monkeys, which are distinctly different from those of baboons.
196 Compare, e.g., the attitudes of two human wrestlers from the Tomb of Amenemhet (no. 2) at Beni Hasan with those of these monkeys: Decker 1992, p. 74, fig. 39, bottom register, second group from the left. As Decker points out on p. 71, the ancient Egyptian word for "wrestling" has yet to be identified, thereby once again attesting to the paucity of current knowledge of the ancient Egyptian lexicon.
197 Decker 1992, p. 77, and n. 42, where only four such sculptures of wrestling human beings are listed; they seem to be restricted to the Middle Kingdom.
198 Copenhagen, Ny Carlsberg Glyptotek, AEIN 449: Bianchi et al. 1988, pp. 246–47, no. 135.
199 Meeks in Luft 1992, p. 433.
200 The assessment of Russman 1989, p. 24 is an oversimplification of this characteristic of ancient Egyptian sculpture, which is more perceptively understood by Altenmüller 1991, pp. 11–19.
201 Compare the Brooklyn Museum of Art 58.13, a symplegma: Bianchi et al. 1988, pp. 241–42, no. 130.
202 Grimm 1990, p. 450.
203 McDonald in Brovarski et al. 1982d, p. 151; Rigault in Phillips 1995, p. 90; for basketware faience examples from Kerma, see Reisner 1923, pp. 154–55, 159–61.
204 Reisner 1923, p. 162.
205 Cf. Bourriau 1988, p. 132; Wildung 1987, pp. 10–11, pl. 4; Milward in Brovarski et al. 1982d, cat. no. 138, p. 142; MMA 11.151.12 etc.
206 Reisner 1923, p. 152.
207 Dunham 1950, pp. 2–3.
208 Named "Ferdinand," it was used by Dunham as the colophon for the Royal Cemeteries of Kush series.
209 Cf. Eggebrecht 1987, p. 208, no. 350, pl. 13; Webb 1978, pp. 36–60; Toledo 83.12, Brooklyn 49.133 and 74.98.1. For a late new Kingdom antecedent, see Wallis 1898, pl. 12, fig. 41, also Milward in Brovarski et al. 1982e, pp. 143–44. The pendant lotus petal decoration and rim ticking is paralleled by a faience beaker inscribed for Ramesses VIII in the Metropolitan Museum of Art, Hayes 1990 (1959), p. 375, fig. 235.
210 See [124], n. 147; and Nenna and Seif el-Din 1993, p. 584, for the rarity of this type among the vessels in this Alexandrian collection.
211 See the study by Samuel 1989.
212 Bianchi et al. 1988, pp. 55–80.
213 [72-75]; and Bianchi et al. 1988, p. 226.
214 See [72], n. 47, for a discussion of this image, to which must be added, in this context, the observations of Dasen 1993, pp. 55-83, in which she dismisses putative influences of this image on those of similar Greek composite mythological creatures.
215 Wildung 1976, p. 200 describes them as "dancing."
216 Bianchi et al. 1988, 218–19.
217 Bianchi et al. 1988, p. 226, and Reeder 1988, pp. 105 and 106.
218 Nenna and Seif el-Din 1993, p. 568.
219 Pella, Archaeological Museum 1981/37, 1981/236, and 1981/105: Florida International Museum 1996, 260.
220 Nenna and Seif el-Din 1993, p. 571.
221 Nenna and Seif el-Din 1993, p. 571.
222 Nenna and Seif el-Din 1993, p. 574.
223 Nenna and Seif el-Din 1993, p. 574.
224 For the problems of dating in general, see Nenna and Seif el-Din 1993, pp. 589–90.
225 See, for example, Parlasca 1955, p. 138.
226 Pfrommer 1987 and Pfrommer 1996, pp. 171–90.
227 Bianchi 1989, p. 67, fig. 34.
228 The consensus for this dating is found, for example, in Riefstahl 1968, pp. 80 and 111, no. 80.
229 E.g., Munich, Staatliche Antikensammlungen 4337: Pfrommer 1993, p. 55, fig. 43.
230 Bianchi 1993, pp. 35–44.
231 Grimm 1972, pp. 79–81, for this and the following statements about this vessel's physical condition.
232 Grimm 1972, p. 80.
233 Grimm 1972, pp. 76, 84, 90 and 92.

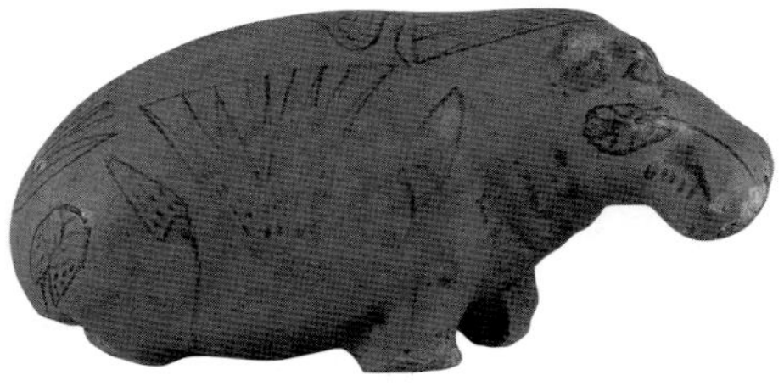

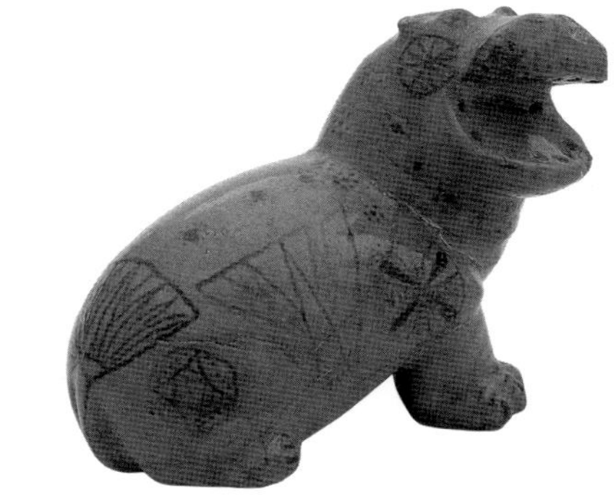

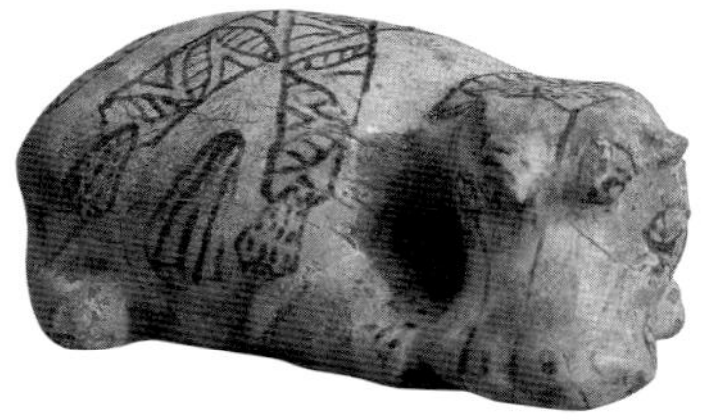

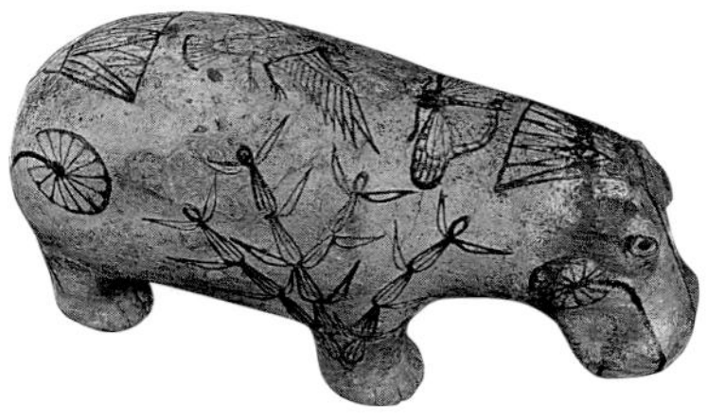

142 HIPPOPOTAMUS PAGE 149

Middle Kingdom, Dynasty 11–12

Faience; L. 12.8 cm

The Leo Mildenberg Collection

143 HIPPOPOTAMUS PAGE 148

Middle Kingdom, Dynasty 11–12; found in Tomb 416, Abydos, in 1907

Faience; L. 13.5 cm

The George Ortiz Collection

Ex-Collections: Rev. William MacGregor; Baron Maurice de Rothschild; Charles Gillet; Marion Schuster

It is hard to accept that these two blue faience hippopotami with their decorations of flowers and insects, charming as they are to the modern eye, represented evil forces in ancient Egyptian belief. Both their aquamarine hues and their aquatic floral decorations suggest that they are to be understood as submerged in the waters of the Nile. As denizens of the Underworld, they were associated with the evil god Seth—the antithesis of the good god Horus who was represented on earth by the living pharaoh.[1] One of Egypt's earliest kings was believed to have been killed by a hippo; perhaps in retaliation, many temple walls bear scenes of the falcon-headed Horus standing in a skiff and harpooning a partially or wholly submerged hippo. In the Old and New Kingdoms court officials also had themselves or their servants depicted on their tomb walls engaged in this activity; but Middle Kingdom officials did not.[2] Bourriau notes that since the statuettes have been found only in small burial chambers or in graves without relief decoration, they may be substitutes for the full pictorial scene.[3] The few faience hippos found in recorded excavations were placed behind the mummy's back or below its feet, perhaps as a device to place the deceased above or beyond the danger.

In ancient Egypt, the meaning of the "river-horse," like that of so many other animals, is ambivalent.[4] Because the hippo spends so much of its time in what the ancient Egyptians viewed as the primeval mud from which the world arose at creation, some scholars feel that the symbolism of the faience hippos also has a more positive side, so that as tomb gifts they could have been instruments for achieving rebirth into the Afterlife.[5] Most faience hippos have had their legs broken off, presumably deliberately, as if ritually to render them powerless, a fact which seems to support the first interpretation more than the second. This type of faience hippo statuette was only made during the Middle Kingdom, suggesting that the function it fulfilled in burial practices went out of fashion as quickly as it had appeared.

The Mildenberg hippo [142], now missing its legs, takes the most common of the four standard poses of the five dozen known faience hippos.[6] Facing forward, it was originally striding or swimming along the river bed. The modeling of face and neck is subtle and naturalistic, and the drawings of the pop-eyed frog and his intended prey, the cross-eyed butterfly, are both comical and deft.

The Ortiz hippo [143] strikes the posture of about 10% of the known hippos. In this version, the resting creature, obviously just aroused, sits up and turns to menace an intruder with its cavernous jaws and fearsome teeth. These last were probably made of ivory inlaid into what are now large, empty sockets. A gossamer dragonfly skims along the creature's back. The Ortiz hippo's head was broken off—apparently in antiquity—to render it harmless before placing it in the tomb. The head has been reattached and the hippo's blue-green glaze is still quite intact, while the Mildenberg hippo's finish has become somewhat matte with time. A fine green hippo of the Ortiz type, but less vigorous and lacking the tooth sockets, is in Berlin.[7]

The spirited execution of the Ortiz hippo's dynamic pose, the naturalistic modeling of the Mildenberg hippo, and the masterfully drawn details of dragonfly on the one and frog and butterfly on the other—each unusual in the corpus of Middle Kingdom hippo decoration[8]—make these two statuettes among the finest examples of their type known today. APK

Bibliography. [142]: Kozloff 1981, pp. 59–61, no. 46; Gehrig 1983 (German ed. of previous), pp. 46–47, 208, no. 46; Page-Gasser and Wiese 1997, p. 92, no. 56. [143]: Sotheby, Wilkinson, and Hodge, 1922, p. 34, no. 250, pl. IV; Ortiz 1994, no. 38; Ortiz 1996, no. 38; Page-Gasser and Wiese 1997, pp. 90–91, no. 55.

144 HIPPOPOTAMUS PAGE 148

Middle Kingdom, Dynasty 11–12

Faience; H. 5.3 cm; max. W. 6.2 cm; L. 11.7 cm

Staatliche Sammlung Ägyptischer Kunst, Munich. ÄS 6040

145 HIPPOPOTAMUS PAGE 148

Middle Kingdom, Dynasty 11–12

Faience; H. 9.7 cm; W. 7.4 cm; L. 20.3 cm

Museum of Art, Rhode Island School of Design, Providence. Museum Appropriation Fund. 29.119

The Munich hippo [144] is a docile beast, fashioned as though lying on the banks of the Nile, sleepy and a threat to no one. This especially appealing example is virtually intact, with the stubby legs held snug against the body. Though unusual in pose, like other hippos he displays painted images of Nilotic lotus flowers and buds across his body.

The Providence example [145] takes the faience hippo's more conventional stance. Still covered with the flora and fauna of the Nile (including a butterfly), he derives from some unknown person's burial, for which role his now-restored legs were cut off,[9] probably to render the beast harmless to the deceased in the afterlife. It is also possible, however, that such hippos, found in non-elite tombs,[10] were enjoyed as household objects before assuming a funerary function.[11]

Hippo statuettes were no longer made after the end of the Middle Kingdom, but their decoration and associated ideas continue in marsh images related to Hathor, as seen on New Kingdom bowls and Third Intermediate Period chalices (see [76–78] and [114–17]). FDF

Bibliography. [144]: Staatliche Sammlung Ägyptischer Kunst 1976, p. 67; Wildung 1987, cover; frontispiece; p. 12, fig. 5, top; p. 14; Schoske et al. 1992, p. 72, cat no. 4. [145]: Bull. RISD, vol. XIX, no. 1, 1931, p. 3; Bull. RISD, vol. XXVII, no. 1, 1939, p. 23; Capart 1939, p. 111.

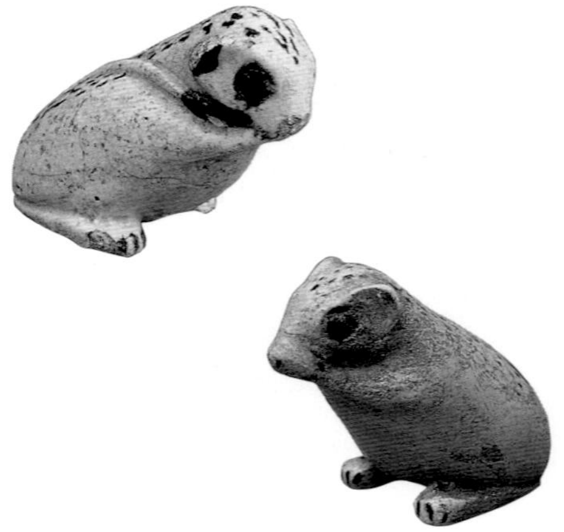

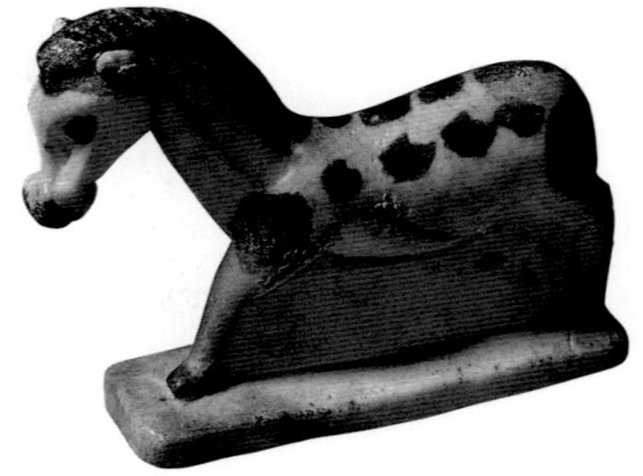

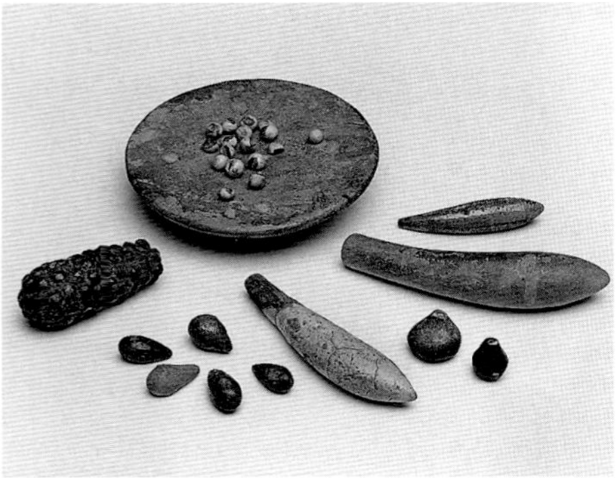

146 JERBOA MOUSE PAGE 149

Middle Kingdom, late Dynasty 12 or Dynasty 13; el-Matariya?

Faience, white glaze with brown details; H. 3.7 cm; W. 2.1 cm; L. 5.0 cm

The Metropolitan Museum of Art, New York. Purchase, Edward S. Harkness Gift, 1926. 26.7.899

147 JERBOA MOUSE PAGE 149

Middle Kingdom, late Dynasty 12 or Dynasty 13; el-Matariya

Faience, white glaze with brown details; W. 2.7 cm; L. 4.1 cm

The Syndics of the Fitzwilliam Museum, Cambridge. E.279.1939

Today, we generally view mice as pests because of their habit of eating stored food, but their small bodies dominated by large eyes and ears can make them attractive as well. Certainly the two jerboa mice here are visually appealing, crouched with their forepaws tucked under their chins and their very long tails wrapped closely around their bodies. Their eyes and ears are outlined in dark brown, as are the markings on their backs.

This pair of mice, along with two more in the collection of the Metropolitan Museum of Art and several other faience animals in other collections, are said to have been found together in a tomb near el-Matariya in the southeastern Delta, close to Heliopolis.[12] Faience animals were popular components of funerary equipment in non-elite tombs in the late Middle Kingdom, although mice are rare. In all likelihood they had a role in funerary ritual, although exactly what remains elusive. Jerboa mice live on the edge of the desert, an environment associated with instability. Perhaps the representation of the inhabitants of that environment bestowed protection from it. Another explanation derives from the jerboa's posture: seated with its paws raised, it resembles a person praying.[13] DCP

Bibliography. [146]: Morant 1938, p. 34; Phillips 1942, pl. 21; Hayes 1953, p. 224, fig. 140; Arnold 1995, p. 21, fig. 18. [147]: Keimer 1929a. pp. 49–50; Kemp and Merrillees 1980, pp. 163–64; Bourriau 1988b, no. 112; Bourriau in Vassilika 1995, pp. 40–41; Houlihan 1996, p. ix.

148 STRIDING HORSE OR PONY PAGE 149

New Kingdom, Dynasty 18

Faience; H. 6.6 cm; W. 9.3 cm; D. 2.6 cm

Private Collection

Ex-Collection: George Ortiz

Unlike figurines of baboons or scorpions in Early Dynastic temples or the menagerie of hippos and jerboa mice in Middle Kingdom tombs, the horse does not enter the Egyptian animal repertoire until the New Kingdom. Though first mentioned in texts relating to the Seventeenth Dynasty conflict between King Kamose and the Hyksos, it was not until the Eighteenth Dynasty reign of Thutmose I that the horse is first depicted.[14] Throughout the Eighteenth and Nineteenth Dynasties, the high point of the New Kingdom, the horse became the subject of some of Egypt's most sensitive animal portraits.[15]

The great love the ancient Egyptians felt for the horse is illustrated by a royal text of the Eighteenth Dynasty. Amenhotep II, in the so-called Great Sphinx Stela at Giza, is described as a great sportsman, who, while still a youth, "loved his horses and rejoiced in them...learning their natures...understanding their ways...[The horses] did not tire when he held the reins; they did not drip sweat in the gallop."[16]

In New Kingdom paintings and reliefs the noble horse that drew royal chariots and was the hunting steed of the wealthy is repeatedly shown with arched neck, pricked ears, and whinnying mouth, features taken up in this small-scale faience sculpture of a spirited horse or pony.[17] The function of this lively statuette remains unknown—it served no known protective purpose. A very fine white quartz is visible through the holes on the underside, however, indicating that a more costly material than coarser sand was lavished on this piece. Was the sculpture a memento in the tomb for a wealthy horse lover, perhaps in lieu of the actual burial of his beloved steed?[18]

Hand-modeled, with a cream body and brown spotted glaze applied before firing, the piece was intended to be attached to a rectangular base, as the holes on its underside reveal. The same stage-like platforms appear on some Middle Kingdom hippos (e.g., Louvre E 7770) and other animals, like the Berlin dog [97]. FDF

149 DISH WITH MODEL FOOD PAGE 151

Middle Kingdom, probably late Dynasty 12 to Dynasty 13; possibly from el-Matariya

Faience, glaze colors include dark blue, bright blue, green and white; Peas (A): DIAM. 0.8–0.9 cm; Melon or cucumber (C): L. 12.8 cm; DIAM. 2.9 cm; Melon or cucumber (D): L. 11.0 cm; DIAM. 2.35 cm; Melon or cucumber (G): L. 7.44 cm; DIAM. 1.7 cm; Bunch of grapes (I): H. 7.3 cm; DIAM. 3.0 cm; Figs (green) (K): H. 2.1–2.4 cm; W. 1.2–1.6 cm; Figs (brown) (L): H. 2.1–2.4 cm; W. 1.2–1.6 cm; Dish (M): H. 3.0 cm; DIAM. 12.8 cm

Musée du Louvre, Paris. E14188

An essential part of both funerary and cult rituals in ancient Egypt was the offering of sustenance. Providing the deceased or the god with perpetual food was the way to insure the continuance of eternal life. The most straightforward way of supplying food for cult purposes was by the offering of actual foodstuffs. In funerary and cult temples, the priests depended on this for their livelihood: after the edibles had been ritually consumed, they were handed out to the religious staff for their own consumption.

Tombs were furnished with actual containers of food as early as the Predynastic Period, but from the Early Dynastic and certainly by the Old Kingdom additional forms of food offerings were made: lists of foodstuffs and relief representations of heavily loaded offering tables were carved on tomb walls. In the early Middle Kingdom, some of the elite took to including wooden models of food preparation among their funerary equipment as another way of ensuring a permanent food supply. When this tradition died out, faience models of food became a customary features of the burial goods.[19]

The fruits and vegetables in this group are types often seen as model food. The bunch of grapes and the melons or cucumbers[20] are well known in both Middle Kingdom and New Kingdom contexts.[21] The remaining pieces are more difficult to identify because of their small size and less distinctive shapes, but the bigger ones may represent sycamore figs and *persea* fruit, and the small round ones, *nabk* berries or broad beans.[22] DCP

Bibliography. Keimer 1929a, pp. 49–50, pls. 5 and 7; *La vie au bord du Nil au temps des pharaons* 1980, pp. 70–71, nos. 128–30.

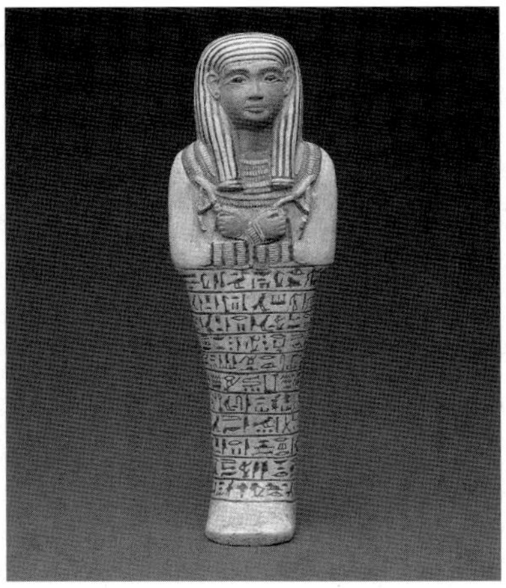

150 SHABTI OF LADY SATI PAGE 153

New Kingdom, Dynasty 18; possibly from Saqqara[23]

Faience; H. 25.0 cm

Brooklyn Museum of Art. Charles Edwin Wilbour Fund. 37.124E

Ex-Collections: Dr. Henry Abbott; New York Historical Society

Beginning in the First Intermediate Period, mummiform figures called shabtis (or ushabtis or shawabtis in different periods), were made in a variety of materials and included in burials. These early shabtis were prototypes for later ones (with Chapter 6 of the Book of the Dead) that acted as servants for the dead person with whose name they were inscribed.[24] Should the deceased be called upon to do manual labor in the Beyond, the shabti, typically equipped with agricultural implements, would answer "Here I am" and assume the duties.[25] By the New Kingdom, the complement of shabtis in a tomb numbered one for each day of the year plus 36 overseers. Shabtis are frequent and often crudely made, but this one is unusual both in terms of manufacture and quality.

At first glance it might be thought that the multiple colors of this shabti are painted, but most in fact are separate inlays. To produce this effect was both difficult and time-consuming, requiring the skills of the finest craftsmen—surely belonging to a royal workshop. Precise channels had to be made for the glyphs and hair striations, for example, before the body dried, and then the colored pastes were squeezed or pressed into them. The reds, yellows, and blues melted at slightly different temperatures, though not so different that the piece needed to be fired more than once: craftsmen apparently found a temperature range that accommodated all the colors. While many failures in this polychrome technique must have preceded triumphs like this shabti, a one-firing process was sufficient to leave the colors intact and fused almost perfectly with the white body. As a further credit to the craftsmen, note that when the different colored faience pastes were inserted into the channels they had little color, and none that approached their final hues; the true colors only appeared on firing. The craftsmen were thus in large part working blind, and only time and experience assured them of perfect results.

Made in two molds, one each for front and back—note the mold line along the side (fig. 53)—this shabti was produced for a non-royal woman named Sati, who, remarkably, has an almost identical companion shabti (37.123E). Though the two shabtis were made in the same molds, the inscriptions were cut separately by hand, resulting in eleven rows of text on this example and nine on the other. In both, Sati is given the incorrect male suffix pronoun in "He says," suggesting the work of a craftsman accustomed to inscribing male shabtis.[26]

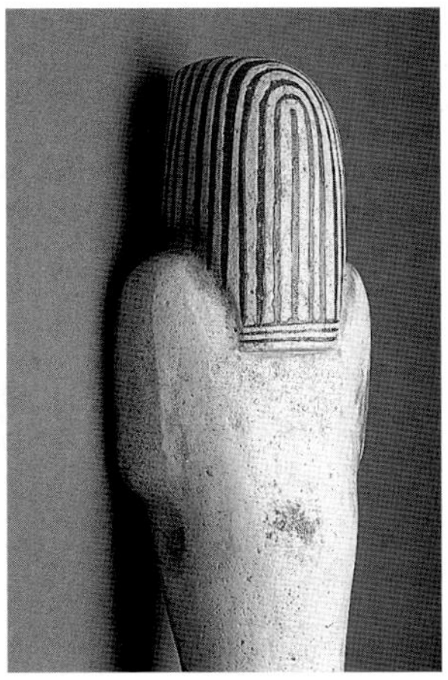

Fig. 53 The back of the shabti of Lady Sati, showing the mold line.

The meticulous craftsmanship of this figurine suggests that Sati was of sufficiently high standing in elite circles to command the talents of the best royal craftsmen, or, more probably, important enough to receive such a gift from the king. It was possibly made by the same craftsmen who created the inlaid faience for King Amenhotep III and his queen, Tiye, [23–25], including her recently found polychrome shabti,[27] and for their royal scribe, Huy.[28] A parallel contemporary inlaid shabti of Ptahmose, High Priest of Amen,[29] may, with the aforementioned royal examples, be the product of the same royal workshop.

On the basis of the two fat folds on the neck, the shape of the baskets and their location, Spanel dates the shabti between the reigns of Amenhotep III and Tutankhamun, with a preference for the former.[30]

FDF

Bibliography. Spanel 1988, pp. 86-89, no. 23 (with earlier bibliography); Fazzini et al. 1989, no. 47; Bryan in Kozloff and Bryan 1992a, pp. 328–29, no. 70; Thomas et al. 1995, pp. 83–84, cat. no. 5; Capel and Markoe 1996, pp. 149–51, cat. no. 75.

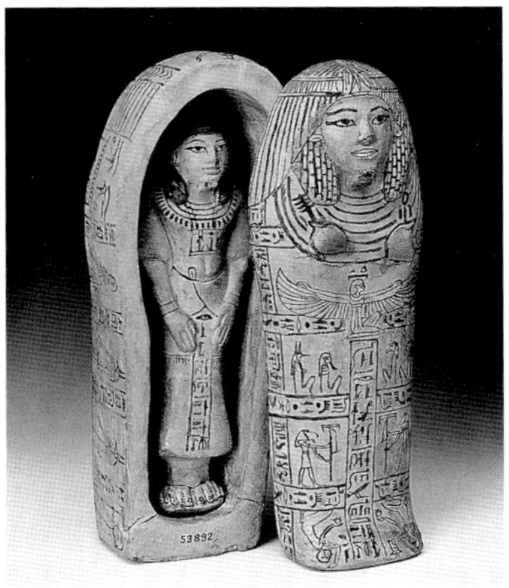

151 SHABTI WITH COFFIN INSCRIBED FOR AMENMES PAGE 152

New Kingdom, Dynasty 19 or 20; probably from Thebes

Faience; coffin: H. 7.0 cm; max W. 11.2 cm; L. 28.8 cm. Lid: H. 4.5 cm; L. 28.5 cm

The Trustees of the British Museum, London. EA 53892

The abundant tomb shabtis of the New Kingdom were often stored in wooden boxes, while other shabtis, of a type in vogue since the end of the Seventeenth Dynasty,[31] were placed in their own miniature anthropoid coffins. Most such shabtis with coffins were made of wood or clay,[32] but this exceptional example, belonging to a man of some administrative status, is in faience.[33] The absence of glaze in the recesses indicates that it was self-glazed.

Along the vertical band of the blue coffin, and similarly along the vertical band on the shabti's kilt, the owner's name and titles are painted in black (probably manganese): "fanbearer on the right of the king, royal scribe, overseer of the Great House, overseer of the treasury of the Temple of Amen, Amenmes of Thebes."[34] The style of Amenmes' linen dress, his curled duplex wig, and the position of his hands flat on the skirt[35] date the figure to the Nineteenth Dynasty.[36] Related monuments, however, inscribed with the name and titles of what appears to be the same man, would date his career to the reign of Ramesses III in the Twentieth Dynasty.[37]

Unlike the coffin, the shabti is not in the shape of a mummy (as in [150] and [152], [153]), and does not hold the usual agricultural implements for work in the Underworld. Instead he appears in the dress of daily life, perhaps to signal his rebirth as a *sah*. This is a form in which, free of the mummy's bandages, the deceased could leave the tomb, revivified by the sun's rays, and meet the living in the publicly accessible parts of the tomb such as the offering chapel and outer court.[38]

Amenmes is equipped for eternity by the protective texts running around his coffin. Four horizontal bands of text, a format introduced in the New Kingdom, wrap around the coffin like mummy bandages[39] and describe Amenmes as revered before a number of gods, including the Four Sons of Horus (see [157]). For eternal protection, his image on the coffin holds the *tyt*-girdle of Isis in his right hand, and the *djed*-pillar of stability of the god of the Underworld, Osiris, in his left—emblems especially characteristic of shabtis in the New Kingdom.[40]

Nut, the winged goddess of heaven, is painted across the chest of his coffin. This is a protective image later translated into faience mummy pectorals that were sewn into or laid within the mummy bandages (such as [159]).

The meaning of this coffined shabti is probably to be distinguished from that of the standard shabti that served until the late New Kingdom as a double of the deceased.[41] Neither figure nor coffin carry the usual shabti agricultural implements nor the typical shabti inscription, Chapter 6 of the Book of the Dead. Since the provenance of these coffined shabtis is generally unknown,[42] determining their meaning is difficult. Some examples have been found as votive deposits,[43] and Budge said of this piece in 1925: "There is reason to believe that the coffin and figure were not found in a tomb but on the ground under a large heap of sand near the entrance to the Valley of the Tombs of the Queens. They were probably votive offerings."[44]

Translation of the text on the shabti and coffin:

1. Words spoken by the Osiris, fanbearer on the right of the king, royal scribe, overseer of the Shrine [lit.: Great House], overseer of the treasury of the Temple of Amen, Amenmes of Thebes.

2. Revered before Imsety, the Osiris, overseer of the treasury, Amenmes of Thebes.

3. Revered before Anubis, foremost of the god's booth, the overseer of the treasury, Amenmes of Thebes.

4. Revered before Duamutef, the Osiris, overseer of the treasury of Amen, Amenmes of Thebes.

5. Words spoken: revered before Horus the mighty protector of his father, Amenmes of the Treasury.

6. Revered before Hapy, the Osiris, Amenmes.

7. Revered before Anubis the mighty who is in the place of embalming, the Osiris, overseer of the treasury, Amenmes.

8. Words spoken: revered before Kebeh-senuef, (Amen)-mes of Thebes.

9. Words spoken: revered before Thoth,the seat of Re, the Osiris (Amen)-mes.

Right line. Words spoken by Nut the great: He is (my) son, (the) Osiris, Overseer of the Shrine [Great House] in the Temple of Amen-mes of Thebes.

Left line. Words spoken by Geb: He is (my) son, the Osiris, Overseer of the Treasury, Amen-mese, (the) offspring of Geb, ruler of the two lands.[45]

FDF

Bibliography. British Museum 1922, pp. 143–44; Budge 1925 (1989), p. 258, pl XX; Porter and Moss 1964, p. 771; Aubert and Aubert 1974, pp. 121–22; Pomorska 1987, p. 205, no. 106; de Meulenaere 1989, p. 56.

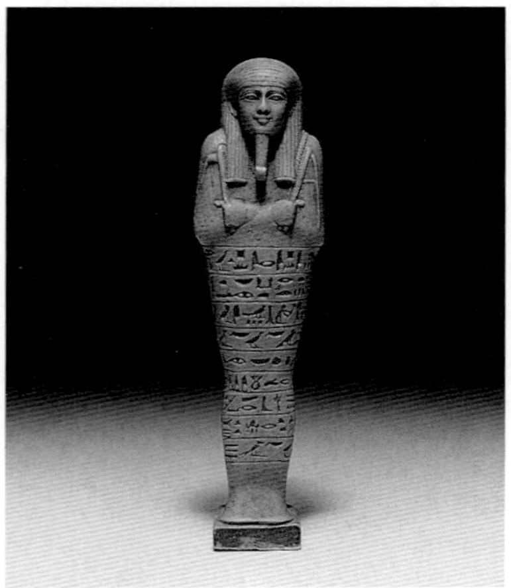

152 SHABTI OF A NOBLEMAN NAMED PSAMETIK

PAGE 155

Late Period, Dynasty 26

Faience, H. 18.4 cm; W. 7.1 cm; D. 3.8 cm

The Art Institute of Chicago. Gift of Mr. and Mrs. Theodore W. Robinson. 1942.647

In this bright blue funerary figurine, Psametik, son of Seba-rekhyet, is represented mummiform, with arms clasped across the chest, each hand holding a mattock (an agricultural implement for tilling the soil). A tripartite wig, without royal cobra (uraeus), and false beard complete his costume. The inscriptions around the body of the figure give a variant of Chapter 6 of the Book of the Dead, requesting that the funerary statuette substitutes for this official in the Hereafter whenever he might be called upon to perform specific duties.[46]

The text opens with the word *sehedj*, which has traditionally been translated as "the inspector" but in this context is better translated "the one who is illuminated." In this reading, the word conveys the solar associations necessary to identify the deceased with the sun-god and thus secure his hoped-for resurrection.[47] The sheen and gloss of the fabric of such statuettes, making manifest the sun's brilliance, reinforce that concept, and the bright blue color connotes concepts of rebirth and resurrection on analogy with perennial blue flowers. In a very tangible way, then, the anonymous theologians of ancient Egypt have harmoniously blended in this object two parallel concepts—solar symbolism and ability of plants to grow again from a dormant state. Such a wonderful integration of disparate elements around a central theme is one of the most salient features of the ancient Egyptian religion.

RSB

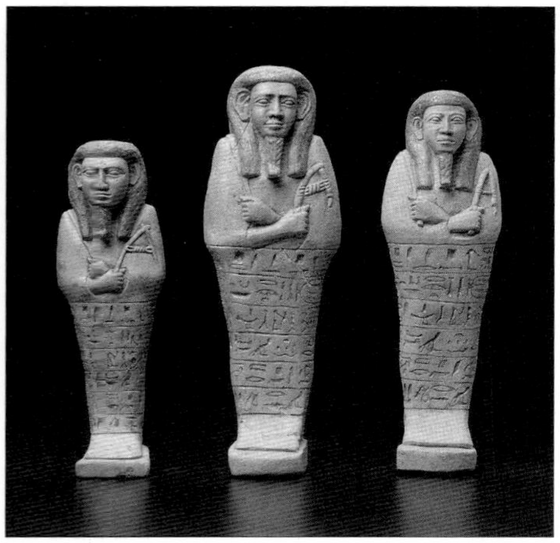

153 SHABTIS OF SENKAMENISKEN

PAGE 155

Kushite, Dynasty 25; Nuri

Faience, H. 15.8 cm; W. 5.2 cm; D. of foot 3.9 cm; H. 19.1 cm; W. 6.5 cm; D. of foot 4.1 cm; H. 17.8 cm; W. 5.6 cm; D. of foot 3.6 cm

Museum of Fine Arts, Boston. Harvard University - Museum of Fine Arts, Boston Expedition. 1921.2654; 2679; 2677

King Senkamenisken (643–623 BC) had more shabtis in his tomb than any other ruler, Nubian or Egyptian: an astonishing 1,277[48] shabtis, 410 of carved serpentine and 867 made of faience in two sizes, were found by G. Reisner in the king's pyramid tomb, Nuri 3.[49] The Museum of Fine Arts, Boston, holds approximately 218 examples of the smaller size, including the three featured here.

Although both are mummiform, the two sizes of faience shabtis form distinct types. The larger shabtis are adorned with the royal regalia of a *nemes* and double uraeus, while the smaller ones lack these royal attributes. They have a blue glazed body, with long tripartite wigs and plaited beards painted in black. Their arms are crossed, generally right over left, with some exceptions. In their right hand they hold a hoe while the left hand clasps the cord of a small bag slung over the right shoulder. These are representations of woven seed bags, primarily rectangular although two have a rounded bottom and a few have suspension loops.

Six vertical lines of incised, black text from Chapter 6 of the Book of the Dead encircle the body, with an additional column on the back pillar. The feet rest on a small rectangular base with a slightly rounded front.

The Kushites did not include shabtis in their burials until their contact with Egypt in the Twenty-Fifth Dynasty. At first glance it may seem that the Nubian shabtis are merely copies of Egyptian pieces; they are, however, unique creations. The Kushites did not adopt one specific type of shabti as a model, or even characteristics that are common to a single Egyptian chronological period. Rather, they adopted a blend of details and then added their own Nubian features (for instance the seed bags).[50]

Kushite royal shabtis are also distinguished from their Egyptian counterparts by their function as they were produced only for royal individuals. Also, by the time of Piye (750–712 BC), a particular burial arrangement had been established, with the shabtis laid against the tomb walls and along the sides of the

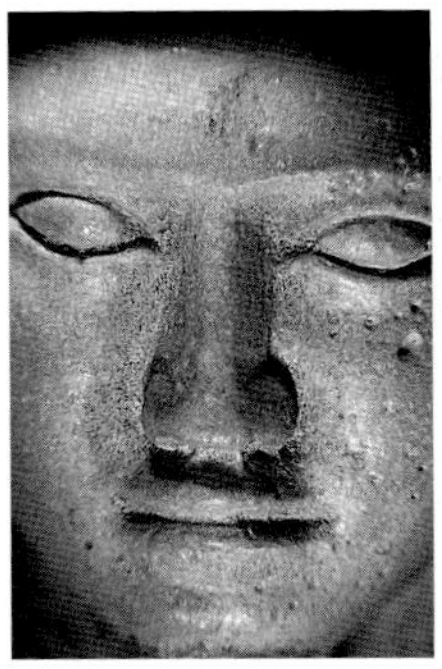

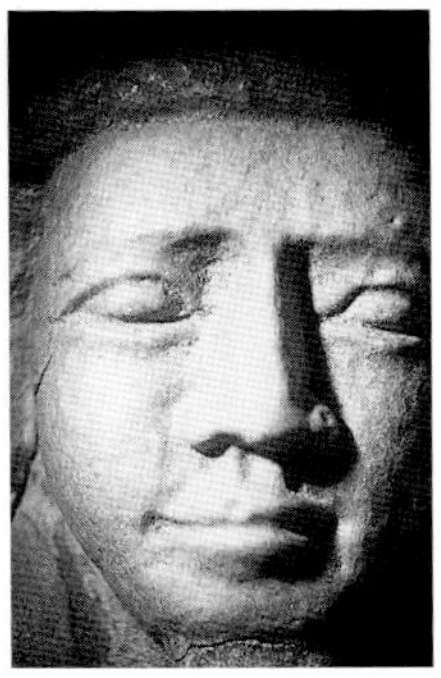

(*Left*) Figs. 54 and 55 Close-ups of the faces of 2654 and 2677, showing the individual facial characteristics of each.

(*Below*) Figs. 56 and 57 The intermediate zone (left) and glassy core (right) of a Senkenamisken shabti seen under the scanning-electron-microscope.

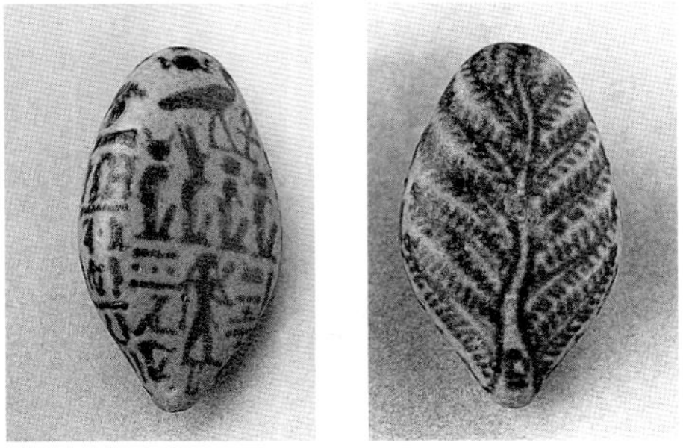

sarcophagus, in contrast to the varied placement of shabtis in Egyptian tombs.

It is generally assumed that when large numbers of similar faience objects were produced they were made in molds, as is the case with most Egyptian shabtis. And indeed the large shabtis from Senkamenisken's tomb all appear to have been made by that method and using the efflorescence technique of glazing, although surfaces are much altered by weathering during burial due to the waterlogging of the tomb. However, when all 218 smaller shabtis in Boston are laid out side by side, it is clear that no two are exactly alike. They vary in height from about 15 to 20 cm (6 to 8 in), with a similar range in the thicknesses and widths. There is also a tremendous individuality in facial features, tools, and hand positions; indeed, each is actually a unique work of art.

The uniqueness of these Senkamenisken shabtis poses the question of how they were manufactured. Could there have been a large number of molds, producing variations of the basic shape, with the separate details hand carved, or could they all have been individually shaped and modeled? X-rays of some of the shabtis revealed no variations in density that could be attributed to one technique or the other. Examination under magnification clearly shows that all the final features (the face, ears, hands, tools, and the text) were individually carved on each shabti prior to firing, but no indications of molds were discovered.

Why would it have been important to this king to have each figure individually carved? High aesthetic standards and available skilled, cheap labor no doubt played a role, but the individual shabtis must have had specific religious functions of which we are unaware. Perhaps the precursors of the Nubian shabtis were the retainers who were sacrificed to accompany the dead king in his burial. When the practice of placing shabtis in the tomb was introduced, human retainers ceased to be sacrificed. In the later Meroitic Period shabtis were no longer produced, and human retainers were once again included in the graves. Whether this observation has any bearing on the individuality of the shabtis deserves further consideration and research is currently being undertaken at the Museum of Fine Arts, Boston.

An additional unique feature of these smaller shabtis is their startling turquoise blue glassy core, seen in the cross-section of a number of broken pieces. Analysis has revealed that the core is a glass, with virtually no residual crystalline material, and a higher quartz content than glassy faiences.[51] The remainder of the body has a composition similar to other Egyptian faiences, although weathered. There appears to be no rational explanation for this glassy core. While some of the cores are oval, giving the impression that the glassy material could have been introduced as a rod, in other shabtis the distribution of the glassy material follows the contours of the piece, suggesting that the glass was added as a paste or powder and fired as an integral constituent. Examination of all the broken shabtis shows that their cross-sections range from a hard, dense white, seen in traditional faiences, to a uniform pale blue, a pale blue with a denser pale blue core, and a dark turquoise glassy core. Analysis of the pale blue faiences does not reveal any differences from the expected composition of weathered faiences glazed by the efflorescence technique. It is hoped that further analysis will help to elucidate this interesting phenomenon. JH & ML

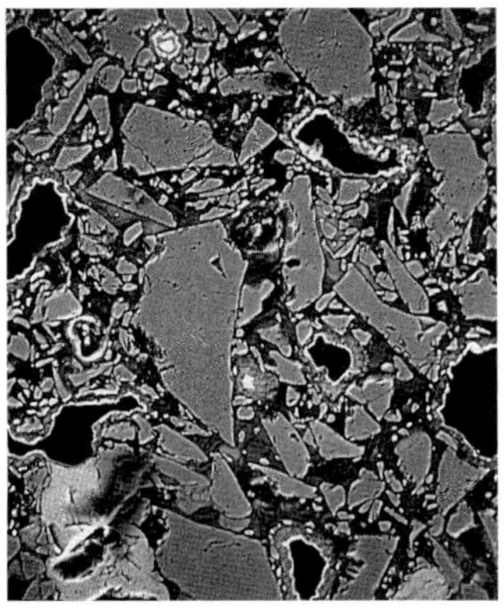

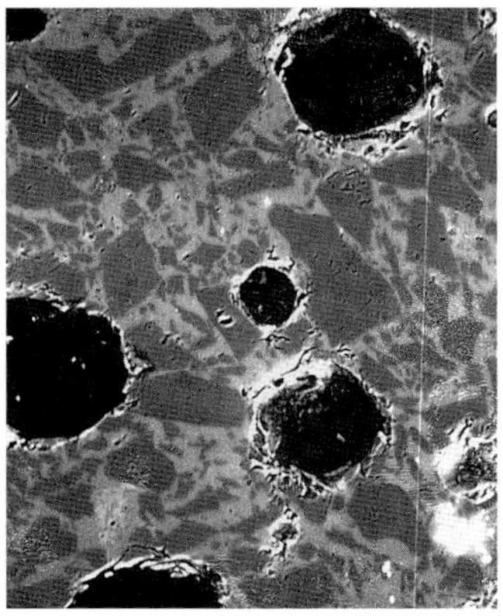

154 PENDANT IN THE FORM OF AN ISHED-TREE PAGE 150

New Kingdom, Dynasty 19–20

Faience; H. 4.1 cm; W. 2.3 cm

Musée du Louvre, Paris. Gift of L., I., and A. Curtis. E 22670

In shape this tiny object conforms to the outline of the spreading tree that is depicted on one side in black glaze, and is thus in keeping with ancient Egyptian two-dimensional depictions of trees, which traditionally adhere to a strict outline.[52] This same side also has the form of a leaf of the *ished*, the veins of which recall the spreading branches of the tree. Hieroglyphs on this side may be read *Djeser-ka-Re*, the prenomen of Amenhotep I, a reading supported by the fact that on the other side of this object is a scene of a train of deities, beneath which Amenhotep I is represented, identified by an inscription containing his nomen.

To understand this pendant's significance, it is helpful first to recall that the *ished*-tree, perhaps to be identified with the modern *persea*, was associated with kingship from the time of the New Kingdom. In a complex ritual the inscribing of the king's name on its leaves was linked to the prosperity of his reign and the posthumous perpetuation of his deeds.[53] During the Ramesside Period, Amenhotep I, together with his mother, Ahmose-Nofertari, were patron deities of the craftsmen at Deir el-Medina.[54] Inscribing the names of Amenhotep I on leaves of the *ished*-tree was meant to insure the perpetuation of his memory so that his benefactions might in turn be enjoyed by the individuals also named on this pendant, Ruru and Iniu.[55] By inscribing their own names and titles on the leaf of the *ished*-tree, in the form of this pendant, these individuals assured the perpetuation of their deed, thereby appropriating to themselves what had formerly been a royal prerogative.[56]

The turquoise-blue color of the pendant reinforces this theme of perpetuity and suggests that the pendant was funerary in nature, perhaps originally part of the panoply adorning one of the mummies of Ruru or Iniu. RSB

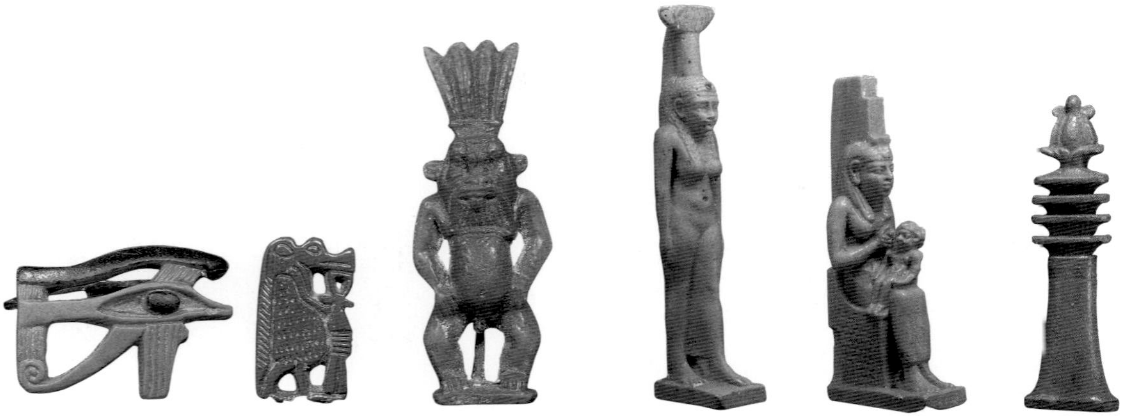

155 AMULETS PAGE 158

New Kingdom to Late Period
Faience
Dr. and Mrs. Jerome M. Eisenberg

Faience was a common material for amulets, which could be made in one- or two-part molds. Its intrinsic associations with light, rebirth, and fertility made it an appropriate material for objects intended to protect the dead—and often the living, as the following pieces illustrate.

Wadjet-eye, H. 3.8 cm

The *wadjet*- (*wḏ3t*, "the Sound One") eye is one of the most common amulets from ancient Egypt. It represents a human eye and eyebrow surmounting the distinctive markings found under the eye of the lanner falcon.[57] Originally the *wadjet*-eye was thought of as the eye of the sky-god Horus (who originally was distinct from Horus son of Osiris and Isis), which was wounded in his battle with the god Seth but restored to wholeness by the god Thoth. The *wadjet*-eye could be associated with both the sun and the moon. In a later myth, the *wadjet* is the eye of the sun-god Re, which abandons him in a fit of pique, travels to Nubia and has to be coaxed back to Egypt by Thoth. With the rise in popularity of Osiris and the myths surrounding him, the *wadjet*-eye became associated with Horus, son of Osiris, who was said to have restored Osiris to life by offering him his eye.

The *wadjet*-eye is first attested as an amulet in the Old Kingdom and continues in use through the Roman Period. It could be placed in various positions on the body of a mummy, but particularly on the chest.[58] It served to protect the deceased from the dangers of the afterlife and to assist in restoring the vitality of the body.

Taweret (Thoeris), H. 3.2 cm

Taweret (the Great One) was a goddess popular among women and was thought to protect them in childbirth. Her association with childbirth may derive from her unusual physique: she has the head and body of a hippopotamus, pendulous human breasts, the paws of a lion, and the tail of a crocodile. Here she is shown leaning on the hieroglyphs for protection (*sa*) and life (*ankh*), both of which could also serve as amulets. This particular example resembles others that have been dated to the New Kingdom.[59] Amulets of Taweret have been found placed on the diaphragm, stomach, and feet of mummies.[60]

Bes, H. 11.75 cm

The bandy-legged dwarf god Bes was thought to be a protector of children and women in childbirth, and often acted as a partner to Taweret. He is shown naked and a leonine face with a protruding tongue, wearing a plumed headdress and a lion's tail. Amulets of Bes are first attested in the Eighteenth Dynasty, and from the Third Intermediate Period on Bes heads alone are used as amulets.[61]

Nephthys, H. 14.3 cm

Amulets of deities could either place the wearer under the protection of that deity or enable him or her to "assimilate the person of the deity they represented and thus gain access to their particular powers or characteristics."[62] This amulet depicts the goddess Nephthys as a woman wearing the hieroglyphs of her name on her head (the basket, representing *Nb.t*, the rectangle under the basket being the *Hwt* sign, *Nebet Hut* meaning "mistress of the house"). Nephthys was the daughter of the earth-god Geb and the sky-goddess Nut and the sister of Osiris, Isis, and Seth. Nephthys is occasionally described as the consort of Seth, but a late tradition relates an affair she had with Osiris, the fruit of which was said to be the god Anubis. Nephthys and Isis are frequently depicted on each end of a funerary bier, mourning for the deceased Osiris. Nephthys also served as the protector of Hapy, one of the canopic deities who protected the lungs.[63] Amulets of Nephthys are common from the Twenty-Sixth Dynasty on, and frequently occur in rows of protective deities placed on the chests of mummies.[64]

Isis and Horus, H. 12.0 cm

The goddess Isis is shown seated on a throne, wearing the hieroglyph for her name on her head (*s.t*, "seat" or "throne") supporting her infant son Horus on her lap with her left hand, while her right hand cups her left breast, offering it to her child. Amulets similar to this one are known from the Ramesside Period, but become more numerous in burials of the Third Intermediate Period and later.[65] Such amulets would have been worn primarily by women and children.

Djed-pillar, H. 11.8 cm

The *djed*-pillar is one of the more enigmatic amulets from ancient Egypt. As a symbol it makes its first appearance in the Third Dynasty at the Step Pyramid complex of Djoser, but is not attested as an amulet until late in the Old Kingdom.[66] Exactly what it represents is uncertain. It has been described as "a tall broad shaft crossed near the top by four short horizontal bars."[67] Andrews notes that it may originally have been a stylized tree trunk. Other suggestions for its identity include a column of papyrus stems, a sheaf of bound cornstalks,[68] or the four pillars supporting the sky superimposed on one another.[69] By the New Kingdom, the *djed*-pillar had become associated with Osiris, representing his backbone. Its Osirian associations are emphasized by surmounting the pillar with the *atef*-crown, typical of this god, during the Late Period.[70]

In Egyptian *djed* (*ḏd*) meant "to endure, be stable," and the amulet was intended to impart the qualities of stability and endurance to its wearer. Pinch has suggested that an amulet should be understood as "a powerful or protective object worn or carried on a person," and is to be distinguished from a talisman, whose purpose is to "enhance a quality in the wearer or to promote success."[71] By this definition the *djed*-pillar would be a talisman rather than an amulet.

Chapter 155 of the Book of the Dead[72] provides instructions for placing a gold *djed*-pillar at the throat of the deceased. In this spell, the pillar is associated with the backbone of Osiris, and its possession is said to transform the deceased into an "equipped spirit" (*akh iqr*) in the necropolis in the entourage of Osiris. In spite of the instructions contained in this spell, the most common position for the *djed*-pillar is on the breast or stomach of a mummy, although some are found at the throat.[73]

SET & FDF

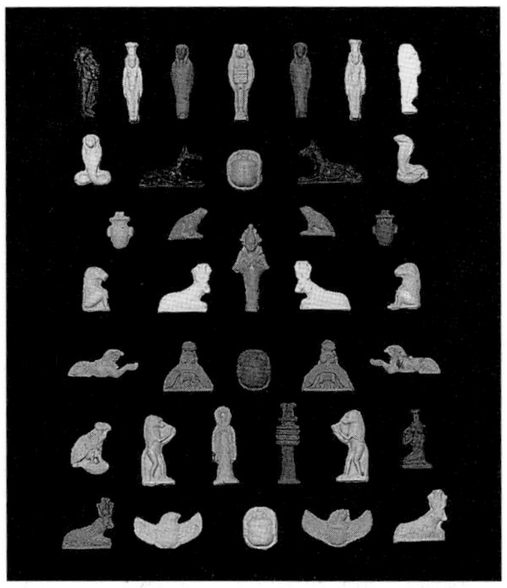

156 AMULETIC INLAYS PAGE 159

Late Period, Dynasty 27–31

Faience; H. of central Osiris 5.4 cm

Harer Family Trust

Many hieroglyphic inlays were used on wooden chests or other items of furniture (see also [129] and [61]). These particular inlays were probably intended for a wooden coffin which would thus have been covered with multicolored, dazzling images of protective faience deities, many of whom would also have appeared wrapped in the mummy bandages.

Horizontal rows, from right to left:

Row 1

1, 7 Imsety, one of the protective Four Sons of Horus (see [157]), holding linen for a mummy wrapping.

2, 6 Nephthys

See [155]

3, 5 Mummy

The act of mummification was a vital part of restoring life to the deceased. When a corpse was mummified, it was thought to have undergone the same treatment that the corpse of Osiris received at the hands of Anubis, Isis, and Nephthys—as a result of which Osiris's body received the energy necessary to father a son, Horus. The mummy provided a place for the *ba* to return to after its nightly travels (see below, p. 243). Amulets in the shape of a mummy guaranteed the benefits of mummification to the deceased. Although dating amulets is difficult, Eisenberg has suggested that amulets of mummies are first attested in the Ptolemaic Period.[74]

4 Anubis holding a *djed*-pillar

Anubis was the Egyptian god of cemeteries and embalming. He took the form of a jackal, perhaps derived from the tendency of dogs to inhabit areas around cemeteries. Anubis shares this form with other protectors of the necropolis such as Wepwawet and the early Khentiamentiu ("foremost of the westerners," who later merged with Osiris). Anubis was said to have embalmed the corpse of Osiris, and numerous scenes show Anubis bending over a sarcophagus tending to the deceased.[75] This image was reproduced as an amulet during the Ptolemaic Period.[76] Such amulets were placed on the chest, lower torso, and legs[77] of the mummy.

It is in this light that amulets showing Anubis holding the *djed*-pillar should be understood. By the New Kingdom the *djed*-pillar had become associated with Osiris. Scenes from Chapter 16 of the Book of the Dead include the *djed*-pillar, equipped with arms holding the crook and flail and flanked by the goddesses Isis and Nephthys.[78] Amulets depicting Anubis holding a *djed*-pillar are therefore semantically equivalent to those showing him attending to a mummy (Osiris) on a bier. This interpretation finds a parallel in a Late Period bronze statuette showing a standing Anubis holding a smaller figure of Osiris before him.[79]

Row 2

1 Lion-headed uraeus

Such amulets are first attested during the Saite Period and can represent the goddesses Sekhmet, Wadjet, or Tefnut. Sekhmet was a fierce lion-goddess who was associated with the destructive power of the sun. She was the daughter of Re, consort of Ptah and mother of the lotus-god Nefertum. Wadjet was most commonly depicted in the form of a cobra, and in this shape sat on the brow of the king as the uraeus. She was the protective goddess of Lower Egypt, and together with Nekhbet made up the deities in the "two goddesses" name of each king, one of the five elements in his titulary.[80] Tefnut was the daughter of the sun-god Atum, who together with her brother Shu (the air) was created when Atum masturbated on the primeval hill. She is thought to have personified moisture in the Heliopolitan ennead. She was also thought to be the eye of Re, and in a late myth she quarrels with her father Re and goes to Nubia. Thoth is then dispatched to coax her to return to Egypt. What all three goddesses represented by the lion-headed cobra have in common is that all could be thought of as the eye (uraeus) of the sun-god Re.

2, 4 Reclining dog

Amulets of reclining dogs (or jackals) with lop ears, perhaps intended to endow the wearer with swiftness, were worn during the late Old Kingdom and early First Intermediate Period, but seem to disappear after that.[81] They may represent the god Anubis or possibly Wepwawet, and if so would be primarily funerary in purpose. Anubis was the patron god of embalmers and was often depicted preparing the mummy. He also played a role in the judgment scene, as shown in New Kingdom and later papyri, where he has a dual role: he introduces the deceased before Osiris, and as master of the balance, assures an accurate weighing of the deceased's heart against the feather of Maat, calling out the scale reading to Thoth who writes it down.[82] Obviously, Anubis was a god whose favor the deceased wished to receive. He was always depicted in black, perhaps due to the black Nile silt (suggesting fertility) or from the color of the embalmed mummy.[83]

Wepwawet was another jackal-god of the dead. He is attested earlier than Anubis, appearing on the First Dynasty Narmer Palette.[84] His name means "Opener of the Ways," in which role he guided the dead along the paths of the Underworld.

3 Scarab

The scarab was undoubtedly the most common of all Egyptian amulets. The Egyptian word for scarab was *kheper*, meaning "to come into existence, develop," and the scarab was a symbol of rebirth and regeneration. It has been suggested that this symbolism derives from certain characteristics of the beetle itself, for instance the fact that female beetles lay their eggs underground in balls of dung, perhaps leading the Egyptians to believe that the beetles were produced by spontaneous generation. The beetle's practice of rolling a ball of dung to its hole found a place in the solar symbolism of Egypt, and the sun was often depicted as being rolled along its path by a scarab.[85] This amulet therefore enabled the wearer to partake in the regenerative power of the scarab and also to participate in the eternal circuit of the sun.

Scarab amulets are first attested during the Sixth Dynasty and continue in use until the Graeco-Roman Period. They were most commonly made of glazed steatite, but examples in such stones as amethyst, rock crystal, and feldspar are known, as well as glass.[86] Petrie notes that the most common location for small funerary scarabs like this example is within the body, while larger, winged examples are found on the chest.[87]

5 Uraeus on *nb*-basket

This is another form of Wadjet. We are not certain where this particular form of the uraeus would have been placed on a mummy. Other forms of uraeus-amulet are found on the forehead, neck, chest, stomach, and feet.[88]

Row 3

1, 4 *Ib*-heart

For the ancient Egyptians, the heart was the seat of emotion and thought. A person's fate in the afterlife was determined by weighing his or her heart against the feather of Maat, which embodied the Egyptian notion of proper conduct. If the heart balanced with Maat, the deceased was guaranteed access to a fortunate existence, while if it was heavier than Maat the offending heart would be gobbled up by the monster Ammet, thereby consigning the person to eternal non-existence.

Because of its importance to the deceased, the heart was left in place in the body and the Book of the Dead contained several spells intended to insure that the deceased kept possession of it.[89] An additional safeguard was the inclusion of heart amulets within the mummy-wrappings. These were usually positioned on the breast, and a mummy might be buried with several. One mummy was found to have nine such amulets in a row on its chest.[90]

2, 3 Squatting frog
Pliny the Elder reported that the Egyptians believed that frogs were produced by spontaneous generation from the Nile mud. The frog (and toad—the two were not distinguished in art) could symbolize regeneration for the dead and fertility for the living. Frog amulets were placed on the upper chest, groin, or upper arm of a mummy.[91] Pendants and rings depicting frogs were worn by living women to promote fertility as they may have been intended to represent the goddess Heqat, who played a significant role in the childbirth process. In the tale known as "Khufu and the Magicians," Heqat, along with Isis and Nephthys, assisted the wife of a priest of Re with the delivery of triplets.[92] Scenes depicting the birth of pharaoh, first attested in the Eighteenth Dynasty, give Heqat a role in the creation of the divine child. Images of frogs also appear on "magic knives" used to protect women during childbirth (see also [70], [71]).[93]

Row 4
1, 5 Thoth baboon (dog-headed ape), kneeling
One of the forms of the god Thoth was the dog-faced baboon (*Papio Cynocephalus*). Thoth was the god of wisdom and writing, and hence the patron god of scribes. As scribe to the gods, Thoth recorded their decrees and served as "court recorder" at the final weighing of the heart of the deceased.

2, 4 Hathor, Nut, Isis, or Mehetweret cow with horns, sun-disk, and *atef*-plumes
This amulet depicts a kneeling cow with horns and a sun-disk topped by two ostrich plumes typical of the *atef* crown. Exactly which goddess is intended is uncertain. It could be Hathor, the mother of the sun and mistress of love, music, and dance. Hathor also had a funerary character and was thought of as a guardian of the western necropolis of Thebes.[94] Other possibilities include Nut, daughter of Shu and Tefnut and consort of the earth-god Geb, who personified the sky; Mehetweret, the celestial cow who personified the watery abyss before creation and also was thought of as the mother of the sun-god Re; and Isis.[95] Such amulets were placed on the stomach or chest.[96]

3 Osiris
This amulet of Osiris shows him mummiform, wearing his typical *atef*-crown and carrying the crook and flail. According to Andrews, Osiris amulets are rare, with only a few glazed examples known, all of which date to the Late Period.[97] Osiris, son of Shu and Tefnut, ruled Egypt in earliest times. He was unjustly murdered by his brother Seth, either by drowning or bludgeoning, and his corpse was dismembered and scattered throughout Egypt. His sister-wife Isis collected the pieces of his body, reassembled them, and restored Osiris to life long enough for him to beget his heir, Horus, who grew up to avenge his father's death and wrest his rightful inheritance—the rule of Egypt—from Seth. Osiris became the ruler of the Underworld while his son became king of Egypt.

This is just one form of the Osiris myth, which underwent several transformations from Osiris's first appearance in Fifth Dynasty texts. There is no recorded narrative of the myth from ancient Egypt; all we have are scattered allusions to several episodes. It is to the Greek author Plutarch that we owe the only account of the story. The myth functioned on several levels. It legitimized the new king at the death of the old, with the old king becoming Osiris and the new king Horus. It also accounted for the resurrection of every individual, since from the First Intermediate Period on, every deceased person became an Osiris and hence benefited from Isis' efforts to revivify her husband. Osiris eventually became the judge of the dead, who were believed to appear before him in the Hall of Two Truths where their afterlife fate was determined.

Row 5
1, 5 Falcon-headed sphinx
The falcon-headed sphinx, called a Hieracosphinx, is first attested during the New Kingdom. The first examples of this shape of amulet were made of semi-precious stones such as carnelian and were inscribed on their bases, indicating that they served as seals.[98] Such amulets depict the Theban god Montu, a falcon-headed warrior god who rose to prominence with the rise to power of the Theban Eleventh Dynasty.

2, 4 Human-headed bird with sun-disk
After death, the Egyptians believed that an individual's continued existence involved several different aspects. One was the *ba*, often incorrectly translated as "soul." It has been defined as "the sum total of all the non-physical things that make each human being unique."[99] The *ba* had two main characteristics. The first was the freedom of movement. While the mummy remained in the tomb, the *ba* was free to roam the earth and to join the sun-god in his circuit. The *ba* returned to the body at times, however, and vignettes in the Book of the Dead show it entering and leaving the tomb and alighting on the corpse.[100]

The other major characteristic of the *ba* was its ability to transform into any desired shape: there are spells that allow the *ba* to become a golden falcon (Book of the Dead, Chapter 77), a lotus (Book of the Dead, Chapter 81A), and a heron (Book of the Dead, Chapter 83), among others. The most frequent method of depicting the *ba* was as a human-headed bird, as in this example. Amulets in the shape of a *ba* with outstretched wings are not attested before the period of Tutankhamun.[101] In each claw, the *ba* grasps the *shen*-symbol, which is related to the cartouche and refers to the eternal circuit of the sun-god (*shen* means "to encircle"). Amulets of the *ba* were commonly positioned at the throat and chest.[102]

3 Scarab

Row 6
1 Vulture on basket
Nekhbet, the protective goddess of Upper Egypt and companion of Wadjet, is usually represented as a vulture standing on a basket. Other goddesses, however, could also appear in the form of a vulture, such as Mut and Isis. Chapter 156 of the Book of the Dead[103] is for the positioning of a golden vulture amulet at the throat of the deceased for protection. This vignette, however, indicates that the amulet is that of a vulture with outspread wings.[104]

2, 5 Baboons in the attitude of praising
The Egyptians believed that the daily rebirth of the sun was attended by baboons praising the sun-god Re through their chattering and dancing. A text from the Third Intermediate Period temple of Taharka at Karnak states that "the baboons that announce Re when this great god is to be born again...are at both sides of this god until he rises in the eastern horizon of the sky. They dance for him, they jump gaily for him, they sing for him, they sing praises for him, they shout for him."[105] Vignettes depicting this scene are found accompanying Chapter 16 of the Book of the Dead.[106] Given their privileged position at the rebirth of the sun at dawn, it is no surprise that the deceased wished to become one of these baboons. In Book of the Dead Chapter 100, the deceased states that "I have sung and praised the sun-disk; I have joined the baboons and I am one of them."[107] Providing the deceased with amulets such as these was probably intended to facilitate his transformation into one of the baboons who praise the sun at his rising.

3 *Tyt*-amulet
The *tyt*-amulet, also known as the girdle of Isis, has been described as "an open loop of material from whose bound lower end hangs a long sash flanked by two folded loops."[108] Its name may derive from Egyptian *tayt*, meaning "shroud" or "curtain," and in origin may have been a cloth worn between the legs by women during pregnancy to prevent bleeding,[109] or during menstruation.[110] Such amulets are first attested during the New Kingdom.[111] Chapter 156 of the Book of the Dead provides for the placing of a *tyt*-amulet of red jasper at the throat of the deceased in order to provide him or her with protection by Isis.[112] While red is the preferred color of this amulet, examples in green are known[113] and although the neck is the location prescribed for the amulet, they are frequently found on the chest, and occasionally on the stomach and even the toes.[114]

4 *Djed*-pillar with *atef*-crown
The *djed*-pillar is associated with Osiris, and is sometimes said to represent his backbone (see [155]). The sign came to mean stability, an attribute every deceased desired to maintain after death. Emphasizing the association with Osiris, the pillar is equipped with an *atef*-crown.

6 Nephthys kneeling in mourning

Row 7
1, 5 Hathor, Nut, Isis, or Mehetweret cow with horns, sun-disk, and *atef*-plumes

2, 4 Winged scarab with falcon head
The scarab with falcon wings was known as Apy (from Egyptian *apy*, "flier"[115]). Apy was one of the forms of the falcon-god Horus of Edfu in the Graeco-Roman Period and it is this relationship that led to the mixed form of a scarab with falcon wings and head seen here.[116] In the myth of Horus of Edfu there is a series of episodes in which Horus takes the form of a winged sun-disk and defeats the enemies of his father Re.[117] At the conclusion of this text are instructions for its use: "a winged beetle in writing shall be made on his [the king's] breast when he sees trouble, just as Re-Harakhte did [when he saw] the trouble of the son of Re, its face being that of a falcon, <its> lips those of a vulture, and its body that of a beetle.... Let this utterance be recited when trouble occurs, and the king shall not be afraid, but his foes will be slain before him, and his heart will rejoice over them immediately, and [each] one will slay his fellow immediately, as befell the enemies of Re-Harakhte when Horus of Behdet [flew] against them as the great Winged Disk."[118]

An image or amulet of Horus of Edfu therefore could confer on its possessor the protection that Horus provided his father Re. In the light of this passage, it is possible that the amulet was placed on the chest of a mummy, though there is no firm evidence for this supposition.

3 Scarab

SET & FDF

Bibliography. Scott 1992, p. 183, cat. no. 131.

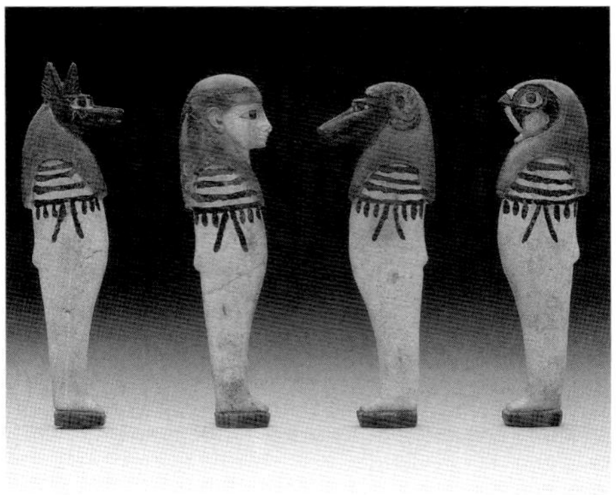

157 AMULETS: THE FOUR SONS OF HORUS

PAGE 155

Late New Kingdom to Early Third Intermediate Period (probably Dynasty 21)

Faience; Duamutef: H. 15.0 cm; Imsety: H. 14.4 cm; Hapy: H. 13.9 cm; Qebehsenuef: H. 14.1 cm

The Trustees of the British Museum, London. EA 26230

Mummified bodies were protected by numerous amulets, many made of faience that imparted light and rebirth to the deceased.[119]

The Four Sons of Horus were deities known from passages in the Pyramid Texts to help and protect Osiris, the great god of the Underworld; and just as they kept him from hunger and thirst and contributed to his resurrection, they could do the same for the deceased.[120] Each of the Four Sons protected and was identified with one of the deceased's internal organs—liver, lungs, stomach, and intestines—which before the Twenty-First Dynasty were placed in so-called canopic jars. Toward the end of the Eighteenth Dynasty and throughout the rest of the New Kingdom, the four canopic jars bore the heads of these mummiform Sons of Horus. Each embalmed organ, when placed in a jar, was both a representative of the whole person and equated with one of the Four Sons of Horus.[121] In the Twenty-First Dynasty the viscera were no longer placed in canopic jars, but were embalmed, placed in linen packages and returned to the body. At about the same time, the Four Sons of Horus, each correlated with one of the viscera, appear as amulets on the mummy.[122] Even when the organs were returned to the body, non-functional, empty canopic jars with the appropriate heads continued to equip some tombs.[123]

This is an especially beautiful mold-made set of the Four Sons of Horus, with details of the tripartite wigs, broad collars, and plinths painted in blue and black. Three sets of threadholes—at head, mid-section, and feet—appear on the back of each amulet, allowing them to be invisibly sewn to the mummy bandages. From left to right, these profile figures of the mummiform deities and the organs they protect are: the jackal-headed Duamutef, the stomach; the human-headed Imsety, the liver; the baboon-headed Hapy, the lungs; the falcon-headed Qebehsenuef, the intestines. While the viscera were protected by and equated with these gods, the gods were in turn protected by goddesses; finally, each group was associated with one of the four cardinal points,[124]

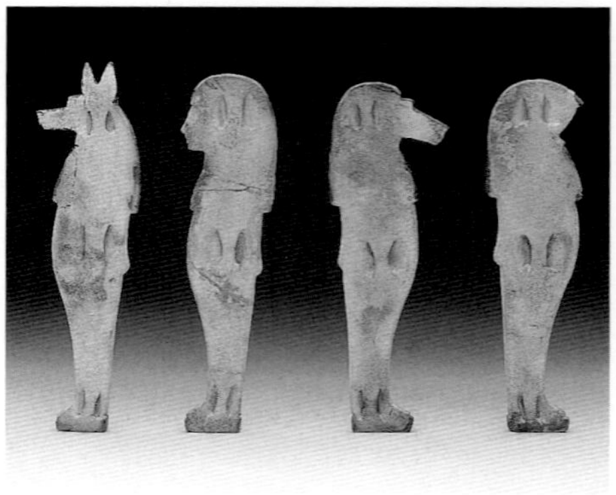

Fig. 58 Back view of the amulets of the Four Sons of Horus, showing the three sets of threadholes on each.

creating a sort of cosmic finale to this nesting of protective forces:

Stomach	Duamutef (Jackal)	Neith	East
Liver	Imsety (Human)	Isis	South
Lungs	Hapy (Ape)	Nephthys	North
Intestines	Qebehsenuef (Falcon)	Selket	West

FDF

Bibliography. Andrews 1984, p. 39, fig. 39; p. 37; Seipel 1989, p. 187, cat. no. 153 a–d.

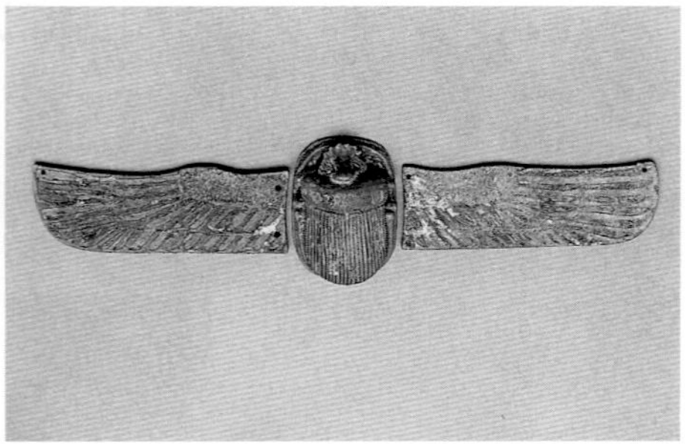

158 WINGED SCARAB PAGE 150

Late Period, Dynasty 26

Faience, with traces of gold foil; L. 26.0 cm

The Detroit Institute of Arts. Founders Society Purchase, Elizabeth and Allan Shelden Fund. 51.226

In ancient Egyptian culture the scarab has a long tradition in contexts associated with both the living and the dead.[125] The passage of the sun across the heavens was ascribed to the agency of an invisible beetle who pushed it across the firmament.[126] Holes in the three elements that make up this example indicate that its was originally sewn to the bandages of a mummy,[127] most probably over the chest. In this funerary context the aspirations of the deceased for rebirth and resurrection are linked to the diurnal rising of the sun, reinforced by the fact that the Egyptian word for the scarab, *kheper*, is a verb connected with concepts of coming into being—concepts then attributed to Khepri, a form of the sun god.[128] The colors of the faience reinforce these notions, as does the use of gold leaf, the color of which was simultaneously associated with the sun and with the flesh of Egypt's deities.

Such three-piece ensembles, consisting of the scarab's body and two wings, are usually dated to the Twenty-Sixth Dynasty.[129] In fact the wings of these scarabs bear a greater resemblance to the wings of a falcon or other bird of prey than of a beetle. This apparent lack of interest in a true representation of natural characteristics is consistent also with the total disregard for the actual color of the beetle—which is black, not blue, green, and gold as here. But this manipulation of nature is not capricious: the falcon was likewise associated with the sun, and the chosen colors reinforce the themes inherent in the scarab's funerary associations. This bringing together of several elements to produce a complex image replete with symbolism is typical of the polyvalent connotations of such animal depictions in ancient Egyptian art. In such depictions of fauna the ancient Egyptian craftsmen were not primarily interested in producing replications of nature's creatures. RSB

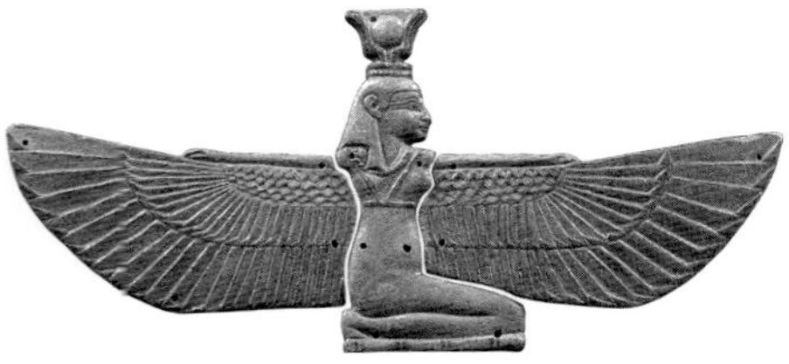

159 WINGED ISIS PECTORAL PAGE 158

Third Intermediate Period, Dynasty 21–22

Faience; L. 22.6 cm; W. 10.5 cm; D. 0.7 cm

Museum of Art, Rhode Island School of Design, Providence. Helen M. Danforth Acquisition Fund. 1996.73.1 a–c

This is the finest of the few such winged pectorals known.[130] Serving as a funerary amulet, it was sewn into the linen mummy bandages where the figure's wings spread across the chest of the deceased and embraced and protected him or her in the afterlife. High-relief figures of standing winged goddesses sometimes similarly enfolded the corners of royal stone sarcophagi to protect the deceased within.[131] Along with the face and hair, the chest was a special site of luminosity, expressed by the epithet *tjehen shenbet*, "with a scintillating chest," so that placing this amulet of *tjehnet*-faience on the chest imparted light and life to the deceased.[132]

Though the goddess wears the sun-disk and horns of Hathor on her head, she is to be identified with Isis, with whom Hathor was at this time conflated. Isis was the sister and wife of Osiris, the god of the Underworld, whom she helped and protected in life and death. In like manner, she ministers to every deceased, who at death becomes an Osiris.

This pectoral appears to have been made in three parts, possibly using one mold for the body and two for the wings. Alternately, the wings, which show no evidence of molding but only tool-marks, could easily have been made using templates, with all the feathering then impressed or incised by hand. The threadholes were made when the faience paste was almost dry, and some of the delicate feathering on the wings may have been reinforced at this time with a sharp tool before firing. The elegant horizontal sweep of the goddess's wings, unlike heavier curved wings of parallel examples, and the crisply detailed feathering make this the finest of such pieces. Its rich blue color is the result of effloresced copper oxide glaze with painted details applied in a darker blue, probably due to cobalt.[133] FDF

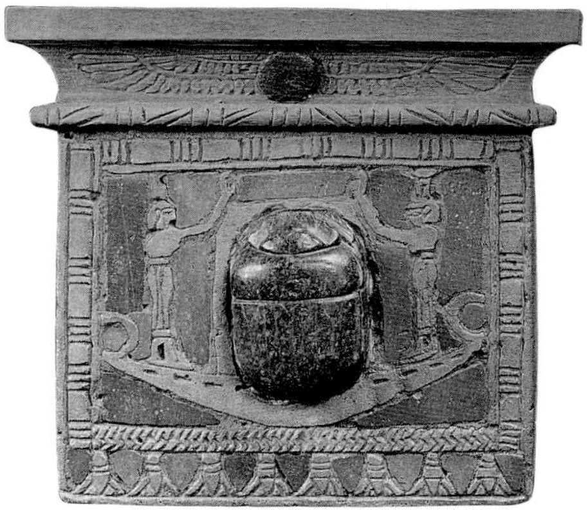

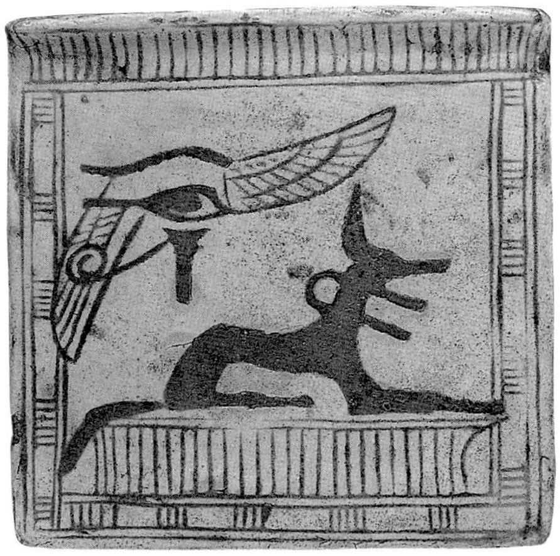

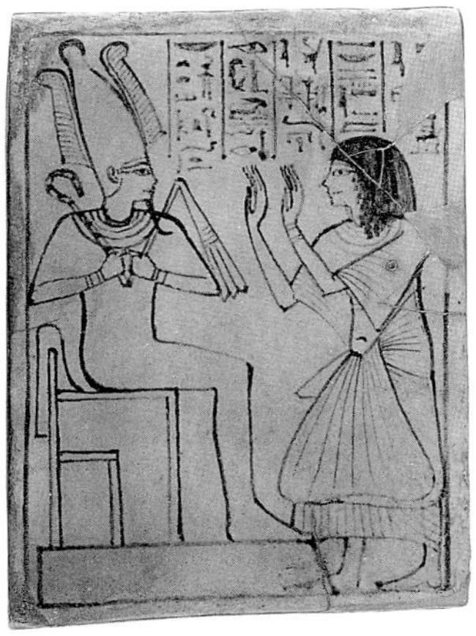

160 PECTORAL INSCRIBED FOR PANEHESI PAGE 161

Late Period

Faience inlaid with a colored stone; H. 10.5 cm; W. 9.0 cm

Staatliche Museen zu Berlin - Preussischer Kulturbesitz Ägyptisches Museum und Papyrussammlung. 1983

161 PECTORAL WITH ANUBIS PAGE 161

New Kingdom, Dynasty 19, reign of Ramesses II, *c.* 1250 BC

Blue and yellow faience; H. 10.7 cm; W. 10.6 cm

The Trustees of the British Museum, London. EA 7853

The earliest pectorals—ornaments for the upper chest—were associated with the office of pharaoh and were decorated with royal images. From the Middle Kingdom, however, pectorals began to be used in the funerary equipment of non-royals, and the images on these were almost exclusively concerned with rebirth and resurrection. These two examples are in the form of a pylon, or temple gateway. This trapezoidal shape recalls not only temple gateways but is also reflected in the design of certain pieces of furniture, particularly tables[134] when viewed from the side, and certain types of cabinets.[135]

The pectoral of Panehesi [160], reportedly found on his mummy,[136] has funerary images on both sides. On the front is a sacred barque conveying a scarab, or sacred beetle, flanked and thus protected by the divine sisters Isis and Nephthys. The symbolism is clear: the deceased wishes to be associated with Re, the sun-god, whose symbol is the scarab, and aspires to ride with him in his barque during his diurnal journey. On a second level, the deceased wishes to become identified with either Kheper, a form of the sun-god, or the phoenix to assure his hoped-for resurrection. On yet another level, Panehesi identifies himself with Osiris, the god of the dead, through the representation of Isis and Nephthys in their roles as protector of the deceased.

This Re-Osiris duality is a particular feature of ancient Egyptian religious beliefs in which the chthonic nature of the deceased interred in a tomb is transformed into a celestial element via the identification with Re—thus anticipating in some sense the Christian approach to death and resurrection.[137] The scene on the reverse of this pectoral depicts the veneration of Osiris, suggesting this very association.

The uninscribed pectoral in London [161] depicts the god Anubis as a jackal, with a winged *wadjet*, or sacred eye, in the upper left-hand corner. Anubis, as the god of embalming, is an appropriate deity in such funerary contexts, as is the sacred eye. The eye was injured during the struggle between Horus—intent on avenging his father—and Seth, his uncle, but was restored to health via the ministrations (according to one variant of the tale) of Thoth, god of wisdom. As a result, the injured eye was often symbolized by the waxing and waning of the moon, and both came to be regarded as images connoting resurrection. The color blue also connotes resurrection, as often remarked, and the color yellow alludes to the sun, itself a powerful symbol of resurrection.

RSB

Bibliography. [160]: Feucht 1971, p. 74, no. 43 C 3/a. [161]: Whyte 1892–93, p. 313, pl. 4; Feucht 1971, p. 106, no 144 F.

162 PLAQUE OF AMENEMOPET PAGE 156

New Kingdom to early Third Intermediate Period, Dynasty 20–21; from Thebes (?)

Faience; H. 16.5 cm; W. 12.3 cm; D. 1.4 cm

The Trustees of the British Museum, London. EA 6133

Though it looks like a stela, or funerary marker, this plaque may have had a different function—it was possibly framed in another material and, much like a pectoral, placed on the chest of a mummy.[138]

The decoration painted prior to firing in black (probably manganese oxide) shows a seated Osiris on the left, mummiform and holding the traditional crook and flail that are the symbols of his kingship of the Underworld. Opposite is Amenemopet, with arms upraised in an attitude of adoration. Above each figure are columns of text identifying them. In the two left columns (beginning with the right one) the text reads: "Osiris, Wenenefer, Lord of the West, Ruler of Eternity." Above Amenemopet the text faces toward Osiris, as Amenemopet himself does, and he is described as the royal scribe and overseer of the storehouse of the Lord of the Two Lands, Amenem(opet). The columns begin just above his left hand and move to the right.

The assured drawing of the figure of Amenemopet, as though alive and outfitted in the fine linen attire of the elite, is contrasted with the flat, outlined figure of Osiris with little interior detail.[139]

FDF

Bibliography. Wallis 1898, p. 47, fig. 97; British Museum 1922, p. 149, no. 38; Budge 1925, p. 450; Edwards 1964, p. 198; Seipel 1989, 239, no. 398, with fig. mistakenly pictured as 399.

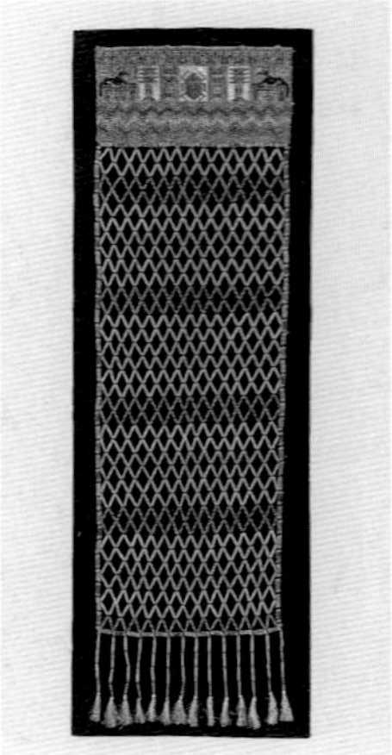

163 BEAD-NET SHROUD PAGE 160
Third Intermediate Period to Dynasty 30
Multicolored faience beads; H. 105.0 cm; W. 29.0 cm
Musée du Louvre, Paris. N 3078
Ex-Collection: Salt

Bead ensembles excavated from Old Kingdom contexts[140] are composed, as is this later example, of beads strung together in lozenge patterns but not attached to a fabric backing. Bead-nets of this kind were apparently worn over a tightly fitting sheath, recalling the fashion preserved on such well-known figures as the painted wooden female offering bearers from the tomb of Meketre.[141] Whether or not these ensembles reflect actual fashions of everyday life is debatable, because it is known that in certain contexts the tightly fitting sheath was reserved for funerary use.[142] The same may apply to a bead-net worn directly over the body as an independent garment, though this provocative fashion contributes to the titillating plot preserved in the famous episode of Khufu and his oarswomen in the Westcar Papyrus.[143] Whatever the function of the bead-net, with or without a sheath, whether an actual fashion or one reserved for tales and the tomb in the earlier periods of Egypt's history, by the time of the Third Intermediate Period the garment appears exclusively in funerary contexts.[144]

This example is particularly striking[145] and noteworthy for its excellent state of preservation, which includes the beaded frieze along the top. Here are depicted Anubis, or perhaps Wepwawet, on his shrine, clearly symbolizing a tomb, and framing *djed*-pillars flanking a single beetle. The dating of such bead-nets has not been precisely established,[146] particularly since the practice was apparently long-lived at Thebes. From the Third Intermediate Period on they were placed almost exclusively over outer mummy wrappings. One intrusive burial excavated on the side of Mentuhotep's court contained an actual fishnet, painted green and placed over the mummy.[147] I would propose a date for this example between the Twenty-First and Thirtieth Dynasty.

In the period of their greatest popularity, from the Third Intermediate Period on, these bead-nets seem to be found in both male and female burials. Their predominantly blue color imbues them with concepts of rebirth and resurrection, and their fringe, recalling the rays of the sun, contributes to the transformation of the deceased from a terrestrial into a solar being. RSB

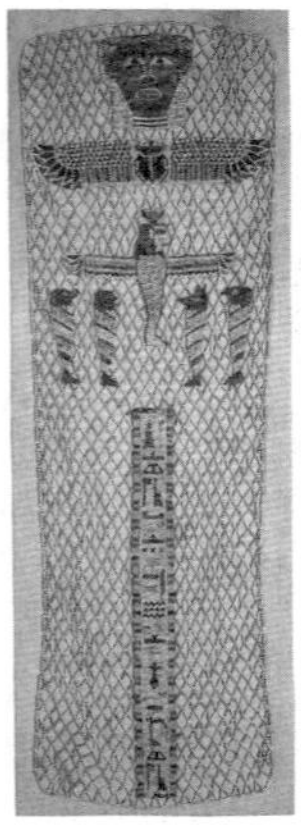

164 MUMMY BEAD NETTING PAGE 160
Nubian, Napatan Period, 7th to 6th century BC; Meroë, West Cemetery
Faience; H. 129.0 cm; W. 39.0 cm
Museum of Fine Arts, Boston. Harvard University - Museum of Fine Arts, Boston Expedition. 1927.443

From the earliest periods, the peoples of Nubia and Egypt practiced the art of threading ring beads to create textile-like pieces with designs worked in color. These pieces were then incorporated into ornaments, clothing, ceremonial items, and domestic objects.[148] Another type of beading—net-like arrangements of cylindrical beads usually separated by ring beads—was also used in various ways, of which the bead-net dress was perhaps the most frequently illustrated in paintings and statuary.[149] During the first millennium BC, the two techniques were combined to create the mummy bead-net which incorporated woven designs into a network. These designs consisted of one or more funerary motifs drawn from coffin decorations and other burial iconography. They included masks, collars, winged scarabs, winged goddesses, the Four Sons of Horus, Anubis figures, and hieroglyphic texts. The mummy bead-net was typically placed over the front of the wrapped mummy and then sewn or tied in place.[150] Since netting was included as part of the burial accouterments of all classes, the range of materials used varied greatly—from faience to stone and precious metals.[151]

This example is a modern reconstruction, made by Mrs. George Reisner in the 1920s, using beads found in various tombs of the West Cemetery at Meroë. She first made the woven pieces and then constructed the net around them. Although the beads from many networks were found at Meroë, the burials were badly disturbed and little remained of the original stringing. Good examples of the mask and the winged scarab can be seen in the excavation photographs. There is also mention in the records of a white strip along the legs. The red color of the face would indicate a male burial (yellow denotes a female burial), and the colors used for the features of the face and for the winged scarab are consistent with the excavation records.[152] There is some question whether the other elements are based on unpublished sources from Meroë or on the numerous extant Egyptian examples.[153] In any case, this well executed piece of work admirably represents the bead-nets common in Nubian and Egyptian burials in the middle of the first millennium BC. YJM & SBS

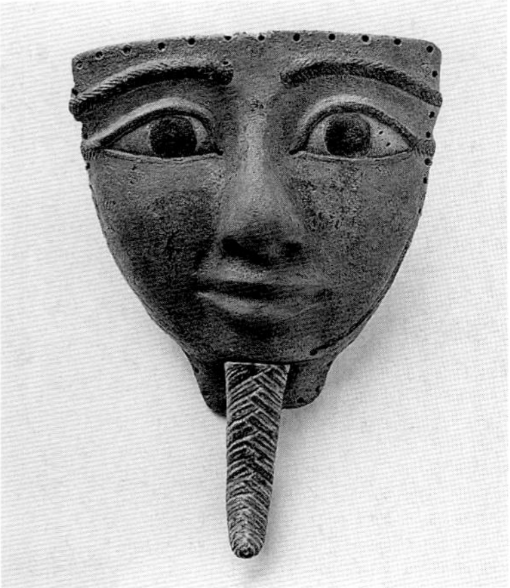

165 MASK FROM A MUMMY (?) PAGE 154
Middle Kingdom, Dynasty 12 to Second Intermediate Period
Multicolored faience; H. 16.5 cm; W. 11.8 cm
Musée du Louvre, Paris. E 1875
Ex-Collection: Clot Bey (C21 F568)

This miniature face, apparently unique among ancient Egyptian faience objects, was molded in one piece. Great attention was paid to the rope-like eyebrows and hieroglyphic eyes inlaid with a white paste(?), the painted blue and black colors of which contrast with the apple-green color of the flesh. When the face was in the collection of Clot Bey it had a beard, which subsequently became separated; later, another beard, apparently similar to the original, was discovered in the stores of the Louvre and attached to the object.[154]

The dating of this face is suggested by comparison with cartonnage mummy masks from the Nubian site of Mirgissa[155] with which this head has numerous stylistic affinities, foremost among them the distinctly triangular shape of the face and the thick eyebrows. These masks have generally been dated between the Middle Kingdom and the Second Intermediate Period, a date proposed for this faience face.[156]

Perforations around the circumference of the face suggest that it was once attached to the facial bandages of a mummy. Its height matches the average height of a human face from just above the eyebrows to the chin. Its relatively narrow width would have been enlarged by the addition of one or more separate pieces, perhaps also of faience, which doubtless included a headdress covering the forehead and perhaps even extended to the ears.

There is a tendency to regard such images over mummy faces as likenesses of the deceased because of their modern designation "mummy portrait." A survey of ancient Egyptian religious texts reveals, however, that these images were intended not to represent the features of the deceased, but rather to conceal the identity of the deceased from the nefarious demons of the Underworld.[157] If those demons could make a personal identification they might more readily gain their objective, namely the annihilation of the deceased en route to his/her aspired resurrection in the Hereafter. RSB

Bibliography. Letellier 1971, pp. 164–76, esp. pp. 175–76.[158]

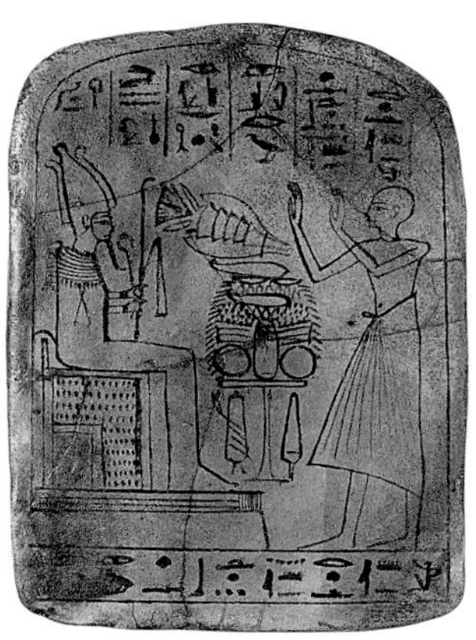

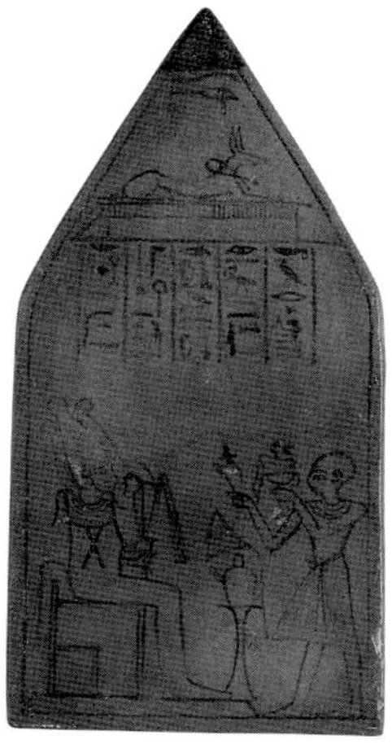

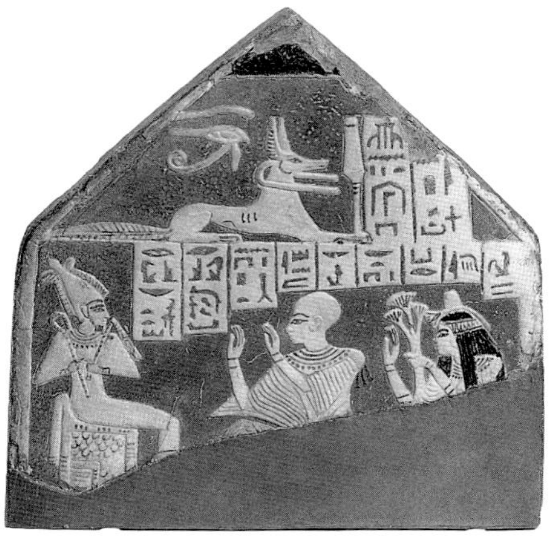

166 STELA OF REKHAMUN PAGE 156

New Kingdom, early Dynasty 19, reign of Ramesses II, *c.* 1295 BC; probably from Thebes[159]

Faience; H. 28.5 cm; W. 20.8 cm; D. 0.9 cm

Trustees of the National Museums of Scotland. A.1956.153

167 STELA OF KAR PAGE 156

New Kingdom, Dynasty 19; probably from Thebes

Faience; H. 28.6 cm; W. 14.0 cm; D. 1.3 cm

Trustees of the National Museums of Scotland. A.1956.152[160]

While stelae, or funerary markers, are ubiquitous in ancient Egypt, few were made in faience, and those few seem to be Ramesside innovations of the Nineteenth Dynasty. These two examples are similar enough stylistically in terms of the deftly drawn figures, black glyphs, and brilliant blue glaze to suggest that they come from the same workshop.[161] Compared to the more complex inlay work of the contemporary stela of Amenemheb from Saqqara [168], such painted faience examples were relatively easy to produce.

What is remarkable about the round-topped stela of Rekhamun [166], besides the fact that it is made of faience, is that it contains one of the few known names and titles of a faience worker. In the three vertical lines at the top right and across the base, he is called *Wsjr, jrw ḫsbḏ n Jmn, Rḫ-Jmn*, "the Osiris [i.e., deceased and united with the god, Osiris], the maker of [or worker in] faience for [the god] Amun, Rekhamun." The word *ḫsbḏ* literally means lapis lazuli but here denotes artificial lapis, that is blue faience,[162] the very material of which the stela is made. Rekhamun may have served in a faience workshop of the Amun temple at Thebes,[163] which is a logical production site of artificial lapis and may, according to a contemporary inscription, have been supervised by the royal treasury.[164]

Bald and dressed in a long Ramesside kilt, Rekhamun raises his hands in adoration to "Osiris, the lord of eternity, Wenenefer [a form of Osiris], Ruler of eternity," who sits on the throne to the left before a table of offerings.[165] Interestingly, a stylistically similar limestone stela from the end of the Eighteenth Dynasty names one Amunrekh (an inversion of "Rekhamun") as another craftsman, this time a sculptor. Amunrekh may be an earlier relative or possibly even the same man as the Rekhamun faience craftsman of the Edinburgh stela from the beginning of the next dynasty.[166]

The second faience stela from Edinburgh [167], dated on stylistic grounds to the same period as Rekhamun's, belongs to a certain Kar who is also shown adoring Osiris, god of the Underworld. This stela, however, has a pyramidal top with a protective *wadjet*-eye below it and a recumbent Anubis jackal atop a shrine. There are five vertical lines of inscription: one above the devotee names him as the servant (*b3k*) of Amun. Although a reference to personal piety,[167] this is hardly an elevated title and yet is the only one mentioned. Kar may not have been a man of substantial means, it appears, but he could still afford this faience stela. Three columns of text label the seated god to whom Kar is making offerings: Osiris, Wenenefer, the great god, Ruler of the West, Lord of Forever and Ever. FDF

Bibliography. [166]: Murray 1900, p. 29, no. 449, p. 55, no. XI, p. 67; Newberry 1914, p. 36, 9b; Porter and Moss 1964, I, pt. 2, pp. 803–04; Nolte 1968, p. 8; Luft 1977, pp. 48–49; Budischovsky and Genaille 1988, pp. 231–35. pl. II. [167]: Murray 1900, p. 29, p. 55, no. X; Royal Academy of Art 1962, pp. 25–26, cat. no. 115.

168 STELA OF AMENEMHEB AND HIS WIFE PAGE 157

New Kingdom, Dynasty 19–20; probably from Saqqara

Faience; H. 26.5 cm; W. 25.4 cm; D. 3.5 cm

Rijksmuseum van Oudheden, Leiden. AD 37

This remarkable stela shows Amenemheb and his wife to the right, adoring an enthroned Osiris, with the jackal god Anubis and a *wadjet*-eye in the triangular field at the top. It should be viewed within the development of multicolored faience, among the earliest examples of which are those discovered at Abusir by the Czech mission. These are associated with Raneferef and include the addition of gilded surfaces that may have used plaster as a fixative [21].[168] The technique was well established by the reign of Amenhotep III of the Eighteenth Dynasty, to judge from the accomplished objects dating to his reign, such as kohl-tubes[169] and book plates [24].[170] This well-established technique was used also for stelae at least as early as the Thirteenth Dynasty.[171]

According to the inscriptions on this stela Amenemheb served as an overseer of the artisans of Ptah, presumably at Memphis. In that capacity he may have had under his direct supervision the craftsmen who made this stela or he may have had access to other officials in charge of faience manufacture. The designer, whether Amenemheb himself or another, was working within well-established iconographic standards of the period: the egg-shaped head, the attitude of the figures, inclined at the waist, and the treatment of the garments are all within the expected repertoire encountered in the Ramesside Period.

Despite this traditional rendering, the stela has some interesting technical features. A shallow mold may have been used for the general design but the decoration appears to have been extensively handworked. This can best be seen in the sharp details produced by tooling on the head and arms of Amenemheb. A glaze slurry colored by copper oxide was painted over the entire surface. The glyphs were incised and filled with a thinned dark blue faience paste that was also painted over the background: dark blue strokes can be seen covering the turquoise glaze around the edges of many figures. Outlines were strengthened with a thin, sharp tool, in most cases removing the glaze. The black details were probably painted last. As overseer in a temple workshop, Amenemheb had the means to produce or commission this labor-intensive piece. RSB, ML & FDF

Bibliography. Rijksmuseum van Oudheden 1826, pp. 28–29; Boeser 1913, p. 11, no. 38

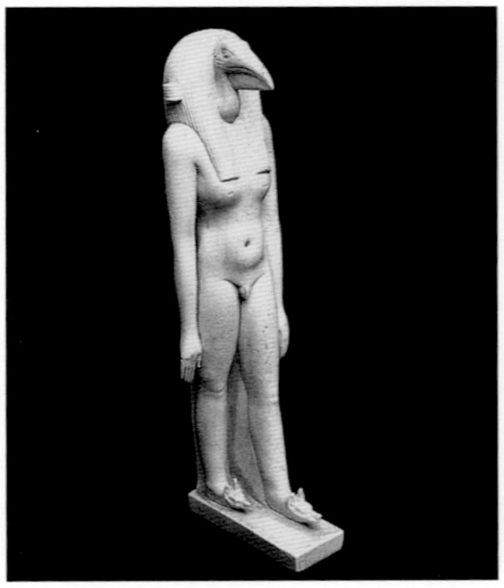

169 STATUETTE OF THE GOD THOTH

PAGE 146

Late Period, Dynasty 26–Ptolemaic Period

Faience; H. 13.0 cm

Myers Museum, Eton College, with Permission of the Provost and Fellows. ECM 1587

Thoth, the ibis-headed god who recorded the judgment of the dead in the Beyond, is shown here in the traditional attitude of the striding male with the left foot advanced[172] and arms held straight beside the body (see also [130]). As usual in ancient Egyptian art, the ibis head has been harmoniously integrated into the human torso.[173] The broad collar is a convention employed to conceal the point of transition between the two and is not to be taken, as has erroneously been argued,[174] as evidence that such animal-headed figures are representations of masked individuals.[175] The modeling of the male body, itself within an established Egyptian tradition for nudity,[176] is characterized by bi-partition.[177]

The most interesting iconographic feature of this statuette are the animal heads on the feet that have generally been interpreted as sandals or slippers.[178] Within the conventions of ancient Egyptian art, however, these attributes are not articles of clothing but deities in their own right, identified either as Wepwawet or the Bau.[179] They serve either to open the paths for Thoth or to protect him from dangers en route. RSB

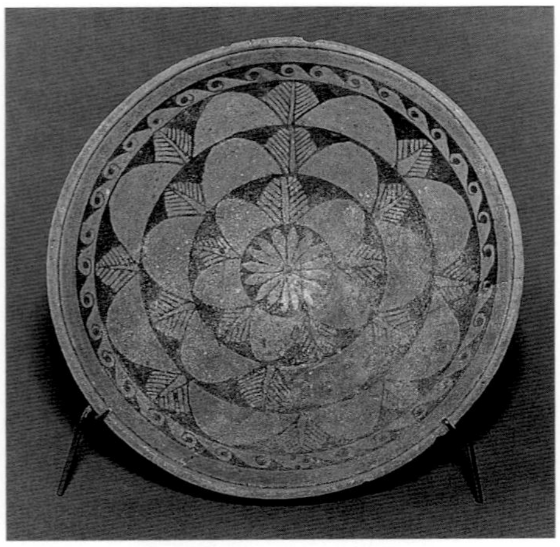

170 HEMISPHERICAL BOWL WITH FLORAL MOTIFS

PAGE 163

Ptolemaic Period, 3rd to 2nd century BC

Faience; DIAM. 16.9 cm

The Metropolitan Museum of Art, New York. Purchase, Lila Acheson Wallace Gift 1988. 1988.18

This vessel has been restored from four sections that fit together break to break with little appreciable loss. Its light turquoise color, the vessel's primary hue, contrasts pleasingly with the dark blue glaze used for the interstices and background.[180] The combination of these two glazes on the interior as well suggests that this bowl, like the few others with the same exterior and interior glazing combination, was manufactured in Egypt.

The floral motifs appear to be derived from the repertoire of pharaonic floral forms: the principal flower is the *nelumbo* lotus[181] and the central rosette has been convincingly interpreted as a stylized open lotus flower seen from above.[182] The two floral motifs have been combined with a third, with ribbed leaves, too stylized to identify. A Greek wave pattern occupies the topmost register just beneath the rim on the outer side. This combination of Hellenic and Egyptian motifs renders the exact interpretation of the symbolism difficult, but some general observations can be made.

The decoration of this vessel can be regarded as a descendant of the marsh bowls popular during the Eighteenth Dynasty (for instance [78]), while the inclusion of the Greek wave pattern demonstrates that the bowl was created for a Hellenistic Greek patron in Ptolemaic Egypt, since objects made for native Egyptians habitually eschew all foreign motifs and elements. The result is a synthesis of both traditions, whereby the underlying pharaonic significance of the floral forms was incorporated into the Hellenistic repertoire, with a possible shift in their symbolic value as a result. During the Graeco-Roman Period the cult of Isis absorbed the most salient characteristics of the cult of Hathor. Furthermore, Isis is the only pharaonic deity with Hathoric overtones to be associated by the Hellenistic Greeks with the sea. Such vessels were possibly employed in funerary and cultic practices[183] linked with Isis because the cult of Isis transcended both spheres of belief.[184] In addition the Isis cult was associated with the cults of the Ptolemaic queens. RSB

Bibliography. Arnold 1988, pp. 6–7.

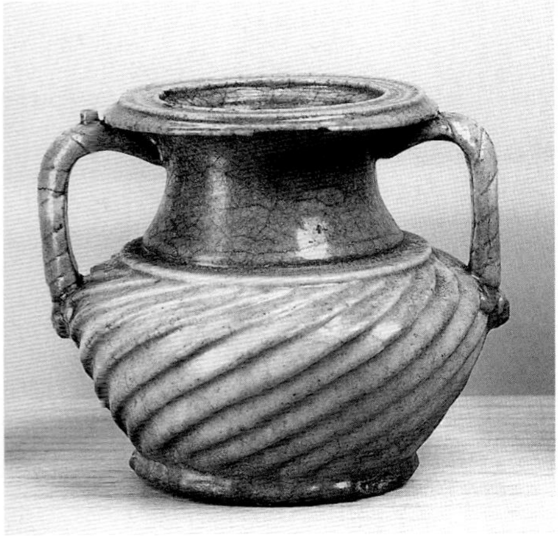

171 TWO-HANDLED URN

PAGE 162

Roman Period, 1st to 2nd century AD

Light blue faience with details in greenish-yellow; H. 23.1 cm; DIAM. of mouth 19.0 cm; DIAM. of base 16.0 cm

The Detroit Institute of Arts. City of Detroit Purchase. 40.49

Vessels of this sort, which were extremely popular during the Roman Imperial Period,[185] have a squat, broad-shouldered body, a neck of narrower diameter, a flaring lip, and strap handles. Although their decorative schemes do vary, the fluted decoration and handles of this vessel set it apart from others of its type. This decoration may be an imitation of the spiral flutes found on vessels made of glass, stone, and metal.[186] A prototype in metal seems the most likely because of the human-headed protome masking the join of the handle to the body of the vase, which has a long tradition in metalware.

The identification of the protome as a female figure seems assured by the flowing locks of hair to the left and right of the face. On the belly of the vase proper these are rendered in low relief, interrupting the spiral rhythm of the flutes. The treatment of the tresses as plastic masses, indicating wet hair, rather than as linearly defined striations, the expected rendering if serpents were intended, suggest an identification of the female not as a gorgon but as a goddess. That goddess is probably Aphrodite, who is perhaps the most frequently encountered Classical as opposed to pharaonic goddess, and one whose representation in Egypt in this period is commonly linked to her associations with the sea.[187] Aphrodite's popularity is attested by numerous examples of kneeling figures of the goddess with her hands to her hair.[188] It might therefore be reasonable to compare this vessel's spiral flutes and blue color to the waves of the sea. The suggestion that this was a cinerary urn[189] makes Aphrodite, with her association with immortality,[190] thematically appropriate. It might further be argued that the associations of the blue-green faience with pharaonic Egyptian conceptions of rebirth and resurrection are also important here.

When the vessel was fired it was supported by kiln furniture that touched its foot in at least five different places. The workshop must have been very similar to the one excavated by Petrie at Memphis in which vases of this type, though without the spiral fluting, were found. RSB

Bibliography. Reeves and Taylor 1992, p. 185.

1 Störk 1981, col. 504.
2 Bothmer 1951, p. 102.
3 Bourriau 1988b, p. 120.
4 Hornung and Staehelin 1976, p. 127.
5 Hornung and Staehelin 1976, p. 128.
6 See Hayes 1953, p. 226, who notes a rearing hippo; Hall 1927, p. 58, pl. XXIIIa illustrates a resting hippo.
7 Arnold et al. 1978, pp. 131–32, no. 176. L. 9 cm (3½ in).
8 Keimer 1929b, pp. 222–41.
9 Restored in 1939 at the Brooklyn Museum.
10 Kemp and Merrillees 1980, p. 168.
11 Kemp and Merrillees 1980, pp 167–68.
12 In all likelihood, the entire group of animals once attributed to a single tomb represents material from several burials (Bourriau 1988b, p. 120).
13 Arnold 1995, p. 21.
14 Störk 1982b, cols. 1009–10.
15 The wall painting of a pink horse from the tomb of Thanuny (TT 74) from the reign of Thutmose IV is one of the best examples. See Mekhitarian 1978, p. 99 (illus.); p. 96 (description).
16 Lichtheim 1976, pp. 41–42.
17 E.g., from the tomb of Nebamun (TT 146) in Janssen and Janssen 1989, p. 39, fig. 31.
18 Horse burials, though rare in Egypt, are attested, one from in front of the tomb chapel of Senenmut (TT 71) (Houlihan 1996, p. 35).
19 Bourriau in Quirke 1991, p. 12. Although this group is called a votive offering, it may very well have come from a funerary context.
20 Most discussions identify these as melons, but this is by no means clear and they are also referred to as marrows or courgettes (Darby et al. 1977, fig. 17.13; Keimer 1929b, pp. 92–93, pl. 7, fig. 2; Wilson 1988, pp. 22–24, fig. 21).
21 The simple shallow form of the faience bowl does not assist in the chronological placement of the group.
22 Sycamore figs: Keimer 1929a, pp. 50–57, pls. 1–3. *Nabk* berries are the fruit of the Christ's thorn tree and were eaten alone or put in a type of bread (Wilson 1988, pp. 18 and 32); Keimer 1929a, pp. 77–91, pl. 5.
23 Spanel, pers. comm., who also notes that shabtis bearing Chapter 6 of the Book of the Dead begin in the Middle Kingdom or Second Intermediate Period.
24 Bourriau 1988a, p. 100.
25 For a transcription of the text, see James 1974a, p. 121, pl. LXXI.
26 "True of voice," however, has the feminine ending on this shabti, unlike the masculine ending on 37.123E.
27 Discussed by Bryan in Kozloff and Bryan 1992a, p. 328.
28 JE 88902 in Saleh and Sourouzian 1987, cat. no. 151; Capel and Markoe 1996, p. 151, n. 24.
29 CG 48406 in Saleh and Sourouzian 1987, cat. no. 150.
30 Spanel 1988, p. 89. For further parallels and suggested dating to the early reign of Amenhotep IV, see Bryan in Kozloff and Bryan 1992a, pp. 328–29, no. 70. According to Spanel, however, baskets do not then appear on the front of non-royal shabtis (Spanel 1988, p. 89).
31 Hayes 1990 (1959), p. 34. For Middle Kingdom antecedents, see Hayes 1953, pp. 349–50; and Lacovara and Roth in D'Auria et al. 1988, p. 126, no. 55, and Bourriau 1988a, pp. 93–94, no. 74.
32 Newberry in Carnarvon and Carter 1912, pp. 19–21, pls. X, XI. For a steatite example, see Edwards 1939, pp. 42–43.
33 The level of care taken with the piece is underscored by the traces of gilding still evident on the coffin figure's beard (British Museum 1922, p. 144).
34 The *n w3st*, "of Thebes," in the inscription probably points to this town as Amenmes' home site (de Meulenaere 1989, p. 56), and may indicate the origin of the object. For comment on titles as indicators of rank, see Hamada 1947, p. 16, n. 1.
35 Schneider 1977, pt. II, pp. 209–10, VIB4, fig. 25, class VI, bottom right; Hand-key = H35, fig. 12; Stewart 1995, p.19 notes that the hands resting on the skirt are like that of Middle Kingdom statuary and are occasionally shown on post-Amarna shabtis.
36 Cf. Schneider 1977, pt.II, p. 105, 3.3.5.1; p. 106, 3.3.5.5; 3.3.5.6 and esp. 3.3.5.7, all on pl. 42.
37 De Meulenaere 1989, pp. 55–58, esp. p. 55, citing Cairo JE 87194 on which Amenmes is identified as the overseer of works in the mortuary temple of Ramesses III at Medinet Habu. Helck, however, still places Amenmes in the reign of Ramesses II (Helck 1960, p. 109).
38 Schneider 1977, pt. I, pp. 161–62.
39 As on full-scale New Kingdom coffins: Taylor 1989, p. 32.
40 Schnieder 1977, pt. I, p. 160.
41 For the change from double to slave, see Poole 1995, pp. 143–44.
42 Provenanced examples from the late Seventeenth Dynasty were found in niches within the west wall of a tomb court, recalling the place where the *sah* was understood to meet the living after emerging from the tomb. For discussion of these coffined examples, see Carnarvon and Carter 1912, pp. 5, 13, pls. II, XLIII; and Newberry in Carnarvon and Carter 1912, pp. 19–21, pls. X–XI.
43 Cf. Stewart 1995, p. 52.
44 Budge 1925 (1989), p. 258. For a Middle Kingdom alabaster shabti from Lisht, from the reign of Senusret I, that also bore Chapter 6 of the Book of the Dead and probably also served as a votive offering, see Aubert and Aubert 1974, p. 19.
45 Thanks to Stephen Thompson for this translation.
46 See Allen 1974, p. 8 and the Late Period variant thereof in Schneider 1977, fig. 5, section VIIB. I wish to acknowledge the research of Emily Teeter, which was adapted for this note, and for her reading of the name Seba-rekhyet.
47 Raven 1988, pp. 238–39; Assmann 1995, p. 112.
48 While the vast numbers of Nubian shabtis are frequently referred to, it is noteworthy that in fact only those of Senkamenisken, with 1,277, and Taharka, with 1,070 (all stone), were produced in vast numbers. In nearly all the rest of the Nuri tombs the numbers of shabtis were closer to an Egyptian norm, numbering from about 50 to 357.
49 Dunham 1950, 1955–65, p. 43.
50 For a complete discussion of Nubian shabti iconography, see Haynes and Leprohon 1987, pp. 18–32.
51 Newman 1997, unpublished analysis; Tite 1987.
52 Compare the depiction of trees in the Tomb of Nakht (ThT 52): Eggebrecht 1991, pp. 34–35, 40–41, 42–43, *passim*; as well as the reinterpretation of this New Kingdom convention by the craftsmen of the Late Period, Fazzini 1975, p. 114, who quotes a vignette in the earlier Tomb of Menena (ThT 69) and a second (Brooklyn 48.74) from the Tomb of Montuemhat (ThT 34).
53 Kákosy 1978 (1980), cols. 182–83.
54 Cerný 1927, pp. 159-203.
55 Both individuals bear the identical title, "chief draftsman," and neither is apparently known from other sources.
56 As Mýsliwiec 1980, pp. 349–56, points out in his expansion of the observations by Helck 1958, pp. 117–140, with an addendum on p. 146.
57 Andrews 1994, p. 43.
58 Taylor in D'Auria et al. 1988, p. 183.
59 Petrie 1914a, p. 47, pl. XL; Andrews 1994, pl. 39.
60 Petrie 1914a, p. 47.
61 Andrews 1994, pp. 39–40.
62 Andrews 1994, p. 15.
63 Hart 1986, p. 204.
64 Taylor in D'Auria et al. 1988, p. 182; Andrews 1994, p. 48.
65 Andrews 1994, 48.
66 Andrews 1994, p. 83.
67 Andrews 1994, p. 82.
68 Taylor in D'Auria et al. 1988, p. 181.
69 Eisenberg 1997, Plants, Inanimate Objects, p. 32, #4.
70 Andrews 1994, p. 83.
71 Pinch 1994, p. 105.
72 Allen 1974, pp. 154–55.
73 Taylor in D'Auria et al. 1988, p. 181.
74 Eisenberg 1997, Human Body Parts, p. 3, #10.
75 See the vignette to Book of the Dead Chapter 151, Naville 1886, vol. 1, CLXXIII–IV.
76 Andrews 1994, p. 69; for examples, see Reisner 1907, 1958, pp. 135–69 and Petrie 1914a, p. 87c, pl. VII.
77 Andrews 1994, p. 69.
78 Naville 1886, vol. 1, XXI, A.g.
79 Eisenberg 1997, Animal-headed Deities, p. 2, m.
80 Hart 1986, p. 170.
81 Andrews 1994, p. 62.
82 Seeber 1976, pp. 154–58.
83 Hart 1986, p. 22.
84 Most recently, Friedman 1995, pp. 5–6, fig. 3a.
85 Andrews 1994, pp. 50–52.
86 Andrews 1994, p. 50.
87 Petrie 1914a, pp. 23–24.
88 Petrie 1914a, p. 19.
89 Andrews 1994, pp. 72–73.
90 Taylor in D'Auria et al. 1988, p. 181.
91 Andrews 1994, p. 63.
92 Lichtheim 1973, 1975, p. 220
93 Koenig 1994, p. 93.
94 Hart 1986, pp. 76–82.
95 Andrews 1994, p. 20.
96 Petrie 1914a, p. 44.
97 Andrews 1994, p. 47.
98 Andrews 1994, p. 30.
99 Allen in D'Auria et al. 1988, p. 43.
100 Naville 1886, vol. 1, IV, p. e; CI; CIV.
101 Andrews 1994, p. 68.
102 Petrie 1914a, p. 14.
103 Allen 1974, p. 155.
104 Hüttner 1995, pp. 34-5.
105 Trans. te Velde 1988, p. 130.
106 Naville 1886, vol. I, XXI–XXII.
107 Trans. te Velde 1988, p. 129.
108 Andrews 1994, pp. 44–45.
109 Taylor in D'Auria et al. 1988, p. 182.
110 Andrews 1994, p. 45.
111 Andrews 1994, p. 44.
112 Allen 1974, p. 155.
113 Andrews 1994, p. 45.
114 Petrie 1914a, p. 23.
115 Altenmüller 1975, p. 338.
116 Bonnet 1952, p. 720.
117 Fairman 1935, p. 28.
118 Fairman 1935, p. 36.
119 Aufrère 1991, ch. 18.
120 Heerma van Voss 1977 (1980), pp. 52–53.
121 Spencer 1982, p. 158.
122 Andrews 1994, p. 45.
123 Bierbrier in D'Auria et al. 1988, p. 164, cat. no. 117.
124 Directional references can be somewhat loose, however; see illustration in Taylor 1989, p. 9, fig. 1.
125 Andrews 1994, pp. 50–52. It is important to

remember that the spheres of the living and the dead were not as strictly segregated as a modern observer might think. For another, more provocative example of the intersection of these two spheres, see Corcoran 1995, pp. 74–79.
126 Andrews 1994, pp. 50–51 for a succinct discussion of entomological issues involving the scarab and the balls of dung, and of the Egyptians' misunderstanding of the precise relationship of the one to the other.
127 Andrews 1994, p. 58, fig. 58a.
128 Andrews 1994, p. 51.
129 Andrews 1994, p. 58.
130 Wallis 1898, p. v (figure faces left); Sotheby's 1922, pl. II, 107 (figure faces left), now in the Gulbenkian Museum; pictured example in Kondeatis and Maitland 1996, inside cover (figure faces right); and Reeves 1989, p. 19 in Highclere Castle (figure faces left). For the last I thank Peter Lacovara.
131 Aldred 1980, p. 179, fig. 144.
132 Aufrère 1994, p. 533.
133 I thank Mimi Leveque for technical observations.
134 Brooklyn Museum of Art 37.41: see Der Manuelian in Brovarski et al. 1982, pp. 73-74, no. 45.
135 Musée du Louvre E 2773: see Killen 1994a, pp. 83–86.
136 Feucht 1971, p. 74.
137 Kurth 1990, pp. 17 and 67 for the latest phases of this belief system which are already in place during the New Kingdom, as Assmann 1995, pp. 7, 137, and 144–47. See too the Osirian solar rituals at the Temple of Dendera, neatly explained by Cauville 1990, pp. 68–84.
138 Seipel 1989, p. 239, no. 398 (mistakenly pictured as 399).
139 Seipel 1989, p. 239, no. 398 suggests that a sense of depth may even have been intentional.
140 Boston, Museum of Fine Arts 27.1548: Jick in D'Auria et al. 1988, pp. 78–79, no. 9.
141 Cairo, The Egyptian Museum JE 46725: Saleh and Sourouzian 1987, no. 74.
142 London, University College 31183: Hall and Barnett 1985, pp. 5-22.
143 Investigated by Janssen 1981, pp. 37–46.
144 Boston, Museum of Fine Arts 95.1407a: see Taylor in D'Auria et al. 1988, pp. 173–75, no. 125d.
145 See Gray 1966, pp. 1–19 for other examples still in place on their mummies.
146 On the dating problems, see, *inter alia*, Silvano 1980, pp. 83–97, as well as Pernigotti 1985, pp. 7–18.
147 New York, The Metropolitan Museum of Art Tomb Card 26.3.11: unpublished, but listed in Porter and Moss 1973, I, 2, p. 655; it is dated there to the Twenty-Sixth Dynasty, but see *supra* n. 146. I thank Dorothea Arnold for allowing me access to these files.
148 For examples, see Bosse-Griffiths 1975, pp. 115–18 and Reisner 1923, pp. 104–05.
149 For a discussion of the bead-net dress, see Jick in D'Auria et al. 1988, pp. 78–79.
150 For an explanation of this technique, see Bosse-Griffiths 1978, pp. 100–02.
151 For types of materials used, see Dunham 1963 (1950, 1955–65), p. 1, 366.
152 Dunham 1963, p. 11, fig. 8d; p. 45, fig. 30b; p. 61, fig. 45b.
153 For further examples, see Quibell and Hayter 1927, pl. VI, 4 and Petrie 1892, pp. 124–27
154 Letellier 1971, p. 175, n. 27.
155 Vila in Vercoutter et al., 1976, pp. 151ff.
156 Letellier 1971, pp. 175–76.
157 George 1981, pp. 15–38.
158 The organizers thank Peter Lacovara for this reference.
159 According to museum records, it was "presumably acquired at Thebes by A.H. Rhind in 1857," Rhind having worked and excavated at Thebes at that time.
160 1956.153 was broken in nine places, 1956.152 in four (NMS conservation report).
161 Cf. also Page-Gasser and Wiese 1997, p. 186, cat. no. 119; and Castel and Soukiassian 1985, p. 290, no. 557, pl. LXII from Gebel Zeit, where several faience stelae fragments have been found.
162 Nolte 1968, p. 8; Aufrère 1991, vol. II, p. 465. A related title appears on a false door stela from Memphis (Gaballa 1979, pp. 51–52). For mention of *ḥsbḏ*-lapis stelae (actually faience?) in an Amenhotep III inscription, see Breasted 1906, p. 360 (889) and Helck 1957, 1654, line 10. A Ramesside faience tile also refers to *mfk3t*-turquoise as a designation of faience made by one Pakeb (Anthes 1965, pp. 75–76; p. 77, fig. 6a, face A).
163 See n. 159.
164 Cf. Luft 1977, pp. 48–49 who cites related New Kingdom *ḥsbḏ*-titles of Hatiay, Ptahmose, and Qenenhor, the latter of whom, with the highest rank, was attached to the treasury (*pr-ḥḏ*). From their titles, plus Rekhamun's, Luft concludes that a ranking within the profession is possible, with Rekhamun on the lowest rung as a producer of the material, Hatiay and Ptahmose as master craftsmen, and Qenenhor as a supervisory official. (Like many scholars, however, Luft incorrectly calls the Edinburgh stela glass.)
165 The "bouquet of lettuce" is a diagnostic dating feature appearing from the reign of Thutmose IV to that of Ramesses II (Budischovsky and Genaille 1988, p. 233 with bibliography in n. 96). When this is taken together with the stylistic features of the figures and dress, the stela is dated to the start of Ramesses II's reign (Budischovsky and Genaille 1988, p. 234). For a parallel blue glazed example in Berlin (17276) of Paser, vizier under Ramesses II, see Budischovsky and Genaille 1988, pl. III and p. 234.
166 Budischovsky and Genaille 1988, esp. p. 235.
167 On this phrase, see Vernus 1975, pp. 109–10 (q) for a text of Ramesses VI, and Clère 1929, pp. 185–86, no. 5 for a text of period of Ramesses II.
168 Verner 1984, pp. 74–75, the better examples of which were featured in a temporary exhibition in Cairo, the Egyptian Museum JE 97317 and 97329: Egyptian Museum in Cairo 1984, unpaginated. For limestone backing used as a ground for gilding: [21].
169 Among others, Brooklyn Museum of Art 37.589E: Riefstahl 1968, p. 23, no. 21.
170 New Haven, Yale University Art Gallery 1936.100: see Scott 1986, p. 99, no. 50 for other examples as well, including London, British Museum 22878, upon which the reconstruction of the Yale object is based.
171 Castel and Soukiassian 1985, p. 290.
172 For the two-dimensional origin of this pose in sculpture in the round, see Bianchi 1996, pp. 50–51.
173 Fischer 1986, pp. 139–41
174 Wolinski in press.
175 Fischer 1986 and Bianchi in Celenko 1996a.
176 Cairo, The Egyptian Museum JE 46992, a Sixth Dynasty ebony statuette of Merire-hashetef; Saleh and Sourouzian 1987, no. 64.
177 See de Meulenaere 1962, p. 29, and n. 3, for a succinct survey of the literature on the male torso in Late Period art.
178 Goffoet in Obsomer and Oosthoek 1992, p. 124, citing a similar example in Brooklyn Museum 71.37.2. Andrews 1994, p. 27 states that this slippered Thoth form depicts the god as a Hermopolitan creator god.
179 Quaegebeur 1992, pp. 521–27.
180 Arnold 1988, p. 6 for a succinct discussion and relevant bibliography of the technique.
181 Arnold 1988, p. 6.
182 Keimer 1929a, pp. 238–40; see now Porter 1986, p. 125.
183 As Arnold 1988 already noted.
184 Bleeker 1963, p. 10.
185 Grimm 1972, pp. 71–100.
186 Reeves and Taylor 1992, p. 185.
187 Burkhalter 1990, pp. 51–60; Del Francia 1984, pp. 209–21; and Kyrieleis 1975, pp. 130–01.
188 Among others, New York, Collection of R.S. Bianchi: Royal-Athena Galleries 1988, p. 22, no. 103, which finds its closest parallel in similar figures decorating the shoulder of a pair of vessels of this classification in the Rockefeller Collection (unpublished).
189 Reeves and Taylor 1992, p. 185.
190 Grimal 1957, pp. 259–62. Störk 1981, col. 504.

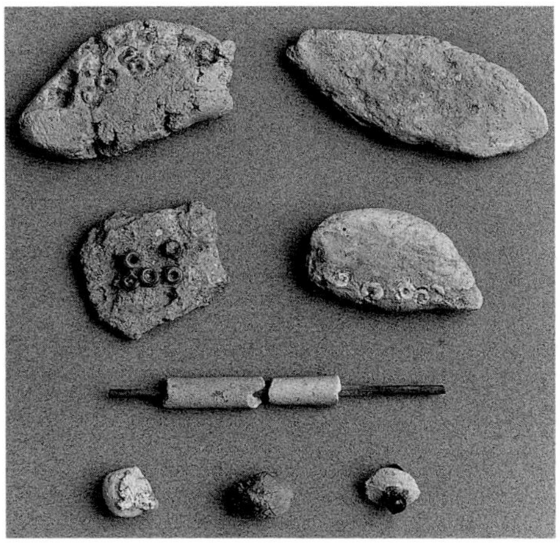

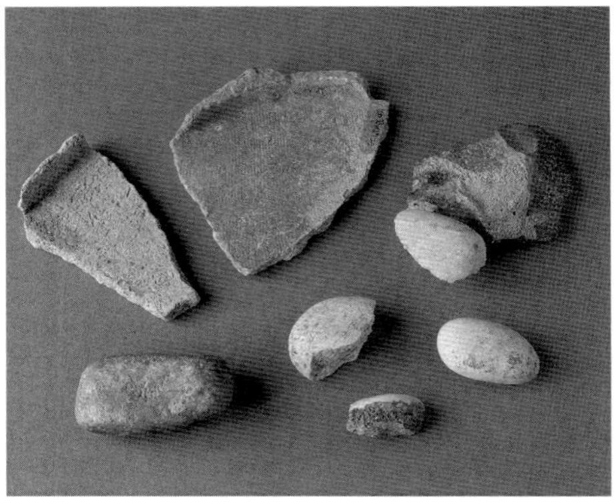

[173], [174], [175], [176], [177]

172 MATERIALS USED IN THE MANUFACTURE OF BEADS PAGE 166

Middle Kingdom, Dynasty 12; Lisht

Marl clay and faience; (top row) 22.1.1097: L. 3.0 cm; 22.1.1226 L. 3.6 cm; *(second row)* 22.1.1227 L.2.0 cm; 22.1.1225 L.2.4 cm; *(third row)* 22.1.1238 L. (of beads) 2.3 cm; *(bottom row)* 22.1.1937a–c DIAM. 0.5–0.7 cm

The Metropolitan Museum of Art, New York. 22.1.1097, 22.1.1226, 22.1.1227, 22.1.1225, 22.1.1238 and 22.1.1937a–c.

These objects come from the excavations of the Metropolitan Museum of Art at Lisht, south of Memphis, an important site in the early Middle Kingdom situated close to the as yet unidentified capital city of Itjtawy. Among the crafts carried out at Lisht was faience manufacture and there are numerous, if sometimes enigmatic, traces of the craft from the site.

The first four objects here are examples of such problematic pieces. A series of tiny blue faience ring beads can be seen impressed into or adhering to the surface of whitish clay objects. These objects are made from a calcareous "marl" clay which, as other finds from the site suggest, was commonly used in the production of kiln furniture. It may be that these beads somehow became pressed into unfired clay during firing. It is difficult to see in what other way they could have become incorporated since when unfired they would be very fragile and would probably have broken easily if subjected to any pressure.

Another object (22.1.1238) comprises two tubular beads on a piece of reed. These beads were presumably formed around a reed which was then withdrawn, or perhaps burned out during firing. If withdrawn, the pieces might be set to dry on a reed such as this one. It is not clear, however, whether this is how the pieces were actually found or whether they were threaded onto a piece of reed by the workmen at the time of their discovery.

The three clay balls have fragments of beads adhering to them. Similar small clay balls or pellets with beads either stuck to or embedded in them come from Amarna, of the Eighteenth Dynasty. Their function is far from clear. They may result from resting beads on a bed of small clay balls during firing (in which case it is hard to see how some became impressed into the clay) or may have some more important and as yet undeciphered role. The Lisht pieces are of calcareous (calcium-rich) clay and would not have survived repeated firings at high temperatures, though they may have been used several times before having to be discarded.[1] PTN

173 QUARTZ PEBBLES PAGE 166

New Kingdom, Dynasty 18; Amarna

Quartz; A: L. 4.6 cm; B: L. 4.7 cm

Petrie Museum of Egyptian Archaeology, University College London. UC.46179 A&B

174 QUARTZ PEBBLE WITH GLAZE PAGE 166

New Kingdom, Dynasty 18; Amarna

Quartz with soda-lime-silicate glaze; L.6.7 cm; W. 3.8 cm

Petrie Museum of Egyptian Archaeology, University College London. UC.46178

175 QUARTZ PEBBLE WITH ADHERING FRIT PAGE 166

New Kingdom, Dynasty 18; Amarna

Quartz with blue frit; L. 3.4 cm; W. 1.7 cm

Petrie Museum of Egyptian Archaeology, University College London. UC.36471

Finds of white quartz pebbles were fairly common in Petrie's excavations of glass and glazing works at Amarna, and he hypothesized that they made up the floor of the furnaces used in the production of these materials. Repeated heating and cooling of the furnaces would impart thermal shock to the pebbles, causing them to break up and making it easier to grind them to make a high quality silica for use in glass and faience manufacture.

The quartz frequently became glazed, perhaps as a result either of drips of glaze from vessels in the furnace or of glazing materials in the furnace atmosphere. Two of the quartz pebbles here ([173] *center and center right*) show signs of such glaze, imparting a slightly green colour to them. Another pebble ([174] *below, left*), however, is much more heavily glazed. This probably results from the same process, but the quartz perhaps spent longer in the furnace.

The fourth pebble ([175] *below, center*) has blue frit, probably rich in cobalt, adhering to it. This frit may be the raw material prepared for coloring glass or faience—recent analyses by Shortland and Tite suggest the latter. Presumably the frit was spilled onto the pebbles in the furnace, although whether such pebbles really served as the floor of the furnace is debatable; they may simply have served as supports for vessels. PTN

Bibliography. Petrie 1894, p.26 contra. Vandiver in Kaczmarczyk and Hedges 1983, p.A30; Vandiver et al. 1991, p. 614.; Shortland and Tite, pers. comm. 1997.

176 "PLASTER TRAYS" PAGE 166

New Kingdom, Dynasty 18; Amarna

Lime-rich plaster; A: L. 11.2 cm; W. 9.4 cm; B: L. 10.4 cm; W. 4.5 cm

Petrie Museum of Egyptian Archaeology, University College London. UC.40569

These plaster trays (*above, left and center*) come from Petrie's excavations at Amarna, although they are not mentioned in his account of the manufacture of faience or glass. Fragments of similar trays have been discovered in the recent excavations of the Egypt Exploration Society at Amarna, site O45.1.

The function of these objects still remains enigmatic—that Petrie found them puzzling is probably attested to by his omission of them from his report. The underside is usually flat and the interior frequently shows the impressions of linen cloth. The clay from which the trays are made is highly calcareous, suggesting that they cannot have been intended for any high temperature use since this would have burned out the lime, rendering them useless. Despite this, fragment B has a red-brown ceramic material adhering to its rim, suggesting that it was at some time attached to a fired plaster structure. This is the only example to show such a feature and may therefore be fortuitous.

On present evidence, the writer favors the view that these trays served for drying faience objects after they had been removed from their ceramic molds. Numerous faience objects, notably tiles and inlays, bear the impression of textiles on their flat surface, and it may be that this was the result of being placed in such trays. The porous nature of the trays would help to remove moisture from the faience paste as it dried in the same way that potters frequently use plaster of Paris molds or bats in their work.[2]

Objects such as these serve to emphasize how imperfectly we understand the stages of faience and glass production in ancient Egypt. As excavations at Amarna progress it is hoped that the proper archaeological context of such objects will be discovered and the technology of faience and glass production further elucidated. PTN

Bibliography. Petrie 1894; Nicholson 1995a, p. 15

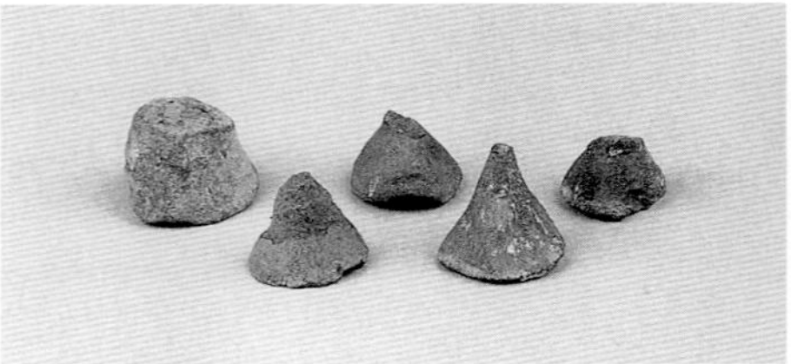

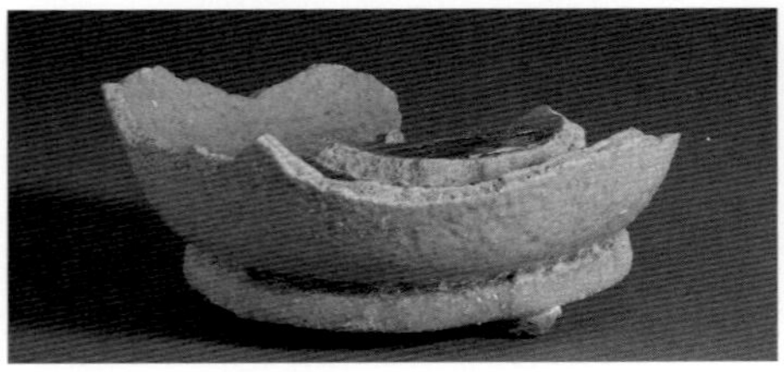

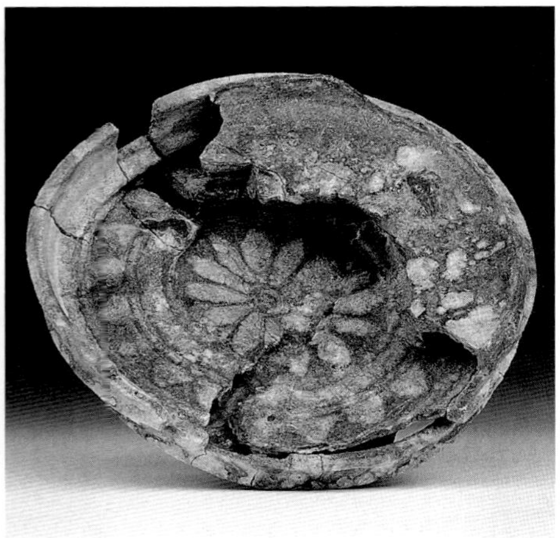

177 FRAGMENT OF "FRITTING PAN" WITH ADHERING QUARTZ PEBBLE
PAGE 166

New Kingdom, Dynasty 18; Amarna

Ceramic and quartz; L. 10.4 cm; W. 3.3 cm

Petrie Museum of Egyptian Archaeology, University College London. UC.40568

This object (*above, right*) comes from the excavations carried out by Flinders Petrie at Amarna in 1891–92, at which time he was assisted by the young Howard Carter. Between them they located the remains of what are described as "several glass and glazing works" which for over a century have been the source of our still limited understanding of the technological processes involved in the manufacture of ancient Egyptian glass and faience.

Petrie hypothesized that the furnaces or kilns used in the production of glass and faience (though he is less explicit about the latter) were floored with "cobbles" of white quartz pebbles. He believed that these would have provided a clean working surface for the crafts and at the same time the continual heating and cooling of the furnace would cause the quartz pebbles to fracture so that they could be more easily ground up for high quality silica for use in the making of faience bodies or glass.

This quartz pebble clearly has glaze adhering to it and is stuck to a potsherd by a glassy material, probably frit. It must be stressed that Petrie never discovered a faience or glass furnace and so his reconstruction of the process is hypothetical, and sometimes contradictory. For example, a sherd of "fritting pan" should not, according to his theory, be found adhering to quartz pebbles since he thought the pans were stood on cylindrical vessels which in turn, presumably, rested on the quartz pebbles. If so, this object would be the result of some accident and not part of the process. PTN

Bibliography. Petrie 1894, p. 26 contra. Vandiver in Kaczmarczyk and Hedges 1983, p. A30, Vandiver et al. 1991, p. 614.

178 KILN FURNITURE
PAGE 170

Roman Period; Memphis

Fired clay; H. 1.3–1.7 cm; DIAM. 1.5–2.2 cm

The Trustees of the British Museum, London. GR 1980.10–17.8–12

179 BOWL WITH ADHERING KILN SUPPORT
PAGE 170

Roman Period; Memphis

Faience with adhering fired clay; L. 13.0 cm; H. 6.0 cm

The Trustees of the British Museum, London. GR 1910.11–16.6

Kiln furniture is the name given to a whole range of stands and supports used in kilns in the making of pottery or faience items. Today the individual items of kiln furniture are products of specialized industries and are made in heat resistant (refractory) materials. But in antiquity they would have been made by the potters or faience workers themselves, and may even have been put into the kiln unfired, simply as little cones or rings of sun-dried clay.[3]

This series of such cones [178] would have been used to keep vessels apart during firing. Vessels were probably placed in the kiln upside down—as in much modern pottery production—so that the hot gases rising through the furnace would be trapped for a time inside them, helping to fire them thoroughly. It can be seen here that the widest surface of one of the cones has become stuck to the glaze on the base of a bowl [179]. The upper part of the cone has disappeared, but from the other examples it can be reconstructed as originally quite pointed. This upper part of the support would have come into contact with the interior surface of the bowl above it in the stack and would become stuck to the glaze. The cone's pointed shape would minimize damage to the interior of the vessel when the faience worker came to remove the support by snapping it off. Marks from these supports can often be seen on the bases and interiors of successfully completed vessels. PTN

Bibliography. Petrie 1909b, pp. 14–15; Petrie 1911 pl. xviii; Vandiver in Kaczmarczyk and Hedges 1983, p. A31.

180 PARTS OF THREE DISHES FUSED TOGETHER
PAGE 171

Roman Period; Memphis

Faience; L. 16.0 cm

The Trustees of the British Museum, London. GR 1980.10–17.1

By the Graeco-Roman Period the technologies of faience making and pottery production had become closely allied and some faience vessels were being wheel thrown as well as fired in saggars like certain types of pottery. These vessels come from Petrie's excavations near Kom Helul at the ancient city of Memphis in Lower Egypt, one of the most important sites for the later history of faience technology.

In firing, the vessels were stacked upside down, as in a pottery kiln, and usually separated by supports of some kind, as Petrie noted here. The supports served to prevent the vessels sticking together as the glaze sintered. As with the making of high quality pottery such as Roman Period *terra sigillata* or glazed pottery, the vessels were stacked inside saggars, closed vessels which prevented ash contaminating the glaze as well as keeping hot gases in contact with the vessels longer. In some cases the kiln, or parts of it, became too hot and vessels fused together inside the saggars as the clay supports softened, allowing the glazed vessels to come into contact with each other. This is what happened here and the vessels are firmly stuck together with hardened glaze.

Once the glaze has become hard it is virtually impossible to separate fused vessels without breaking them and they are invariably discarded as "wasters" in the area around the kilns or workshop. PTN

Bibliography. Petrie 1909b, pp. 14–15 and pl. xlix; Petrie 1911; Vandiver in Kaczmarczyk and Hedges 1983, p. A31.

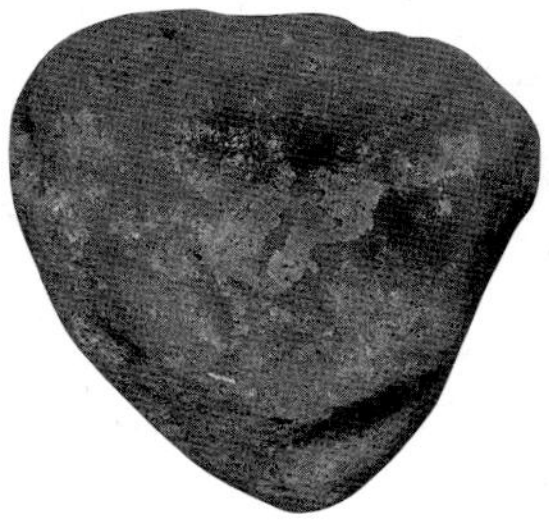

181 LUMP OF EGYPTIAN BLUE PAGE 167

New Kingdom, Dynasty 18; Amarna (?)
Egyptian blue; H. 8.9 cm; W. 8.3 cm; TH. 2.8 cm
The University of Pennsylvania Museum of Archaeology and Anthropology, Philadelphia.
29-85-482

This fragment of a cake of Egyptian blue is just as it came from the kiln: the curved outer edge retains the shape of the crucible in which it was made. The whole cake was broken up either for use in the workshop or during its burial in the ground—the blotchy discolorations are due to weathering of the surface and soil from burial.

To make Egyptian blue, the raw materials, similar to those for faience—silica, lime, and alkaline fluxes, plus copper oxide—are ground together and heated in a crucible until they begin to fuse. A second grinding and refiring produces a finer texture and lighter blue color than a single firing.[4] The resulting cake of Egyptian blue can then be ground up and mixed with a binder for use as a pigment or used to create three dimensional objects [73]. ML

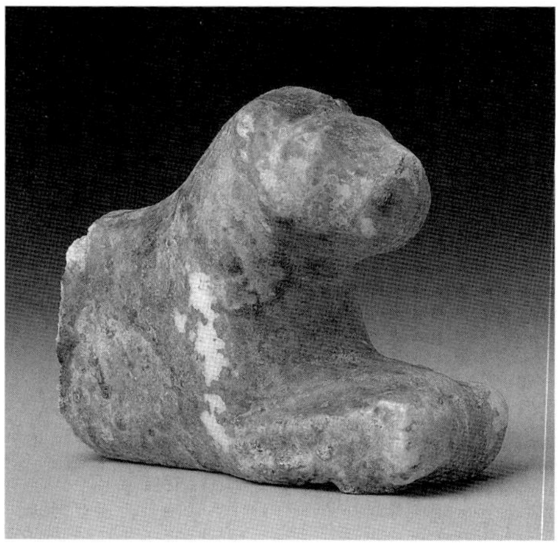

182 LION PAGE 169

Nubian, Classic Kerma Period, *c.* 1600–1500 BC; Kerma, Chapel K II
Glazed quartz; L. 12.0 cm
Museum of Fine Arts, Boston. Harvard University-Museum of Fine Arts, Boston Expedition.
1913.4229

Unlike faience and Egyptian blue, the production of glazed quartz seems to have been a Nubian innovation. As early as the A-Group Period, glazed quartz lion heads of remarkable sophistication were manufactured.[5] While glazed quartz plaques and beads are known from Egypt, they are uncommon and tend to be of southerly origin, suggesting importation from Nubia.[6] During the flowering of the Kerma Culture, contemporary with the late Second Intermediate Period in Egypt, large-scale production of glazed quartz took place.

This forepart of a lion is one of several glazed quartz animal figures to come from Kerma, and probably a mate to a complete recumbent lion of similar size found in the same context.[7] The lion's body is abstractly rendered in the hard milky quartz, with much of the deep blue original glaze surviving. An ancient drill hole on the underside suggests the lion was pegged into a base, either as a decoration on a piece of temple furniture, or simply to reattach it to the now missing rear half.

Although the precise technique of glazing quartz is not yet known, it seems unlikely that a liquid glaze slurry would be able to adhere to the smooth quartz surface. A paste similar to that used in the self-glazing technique has been proposed, mixed with an adhesive, like gum arabic, or a glazing powder could have been dusted onto a surface previously painted with a sticky substance such as gum arabic or honey.[8] PL & ML

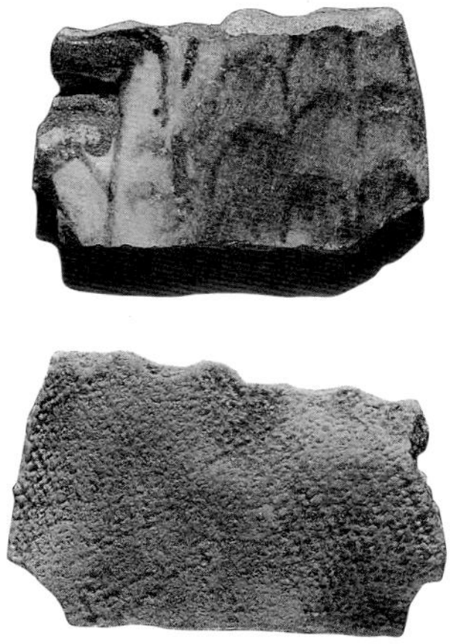

183 TILE FRAGMENT PAGE 166

New Kingdom, Dynasty 18; Amarna
Faience; L. 3.5 cm; W. 2.2 cm; TH. 0.6 cm
The University of Pennsylvania Museum of Archaeology and Anthropology, Philadelphia.
E 17897

This small fragment of a tile has delicately painted details of a bird wing on a white glazed ground. Light modeling with a fine tool helps create a sense of three dimensionality between some of the feathers. Unlike many other faience objects made in the New Kingdom this tile has a friable body, since there is no glaze on the back nor did it have added glass in the paste. However, it would have been adequately strong since it was intended to be fixed to a wall.[9] Like many other tiles found at Amarna [42], it has the impression of a textile on the back. Several suggestions have been proposed to explain this: it may have been due to placing the tile on a textile either for drying[10] or for keeping it sufficiently wet while working, or as a means to help key the tile into mortar on the wall, or it could have been placed to dry on a "plaster tray" that already bore a textile imprint [176]. ML

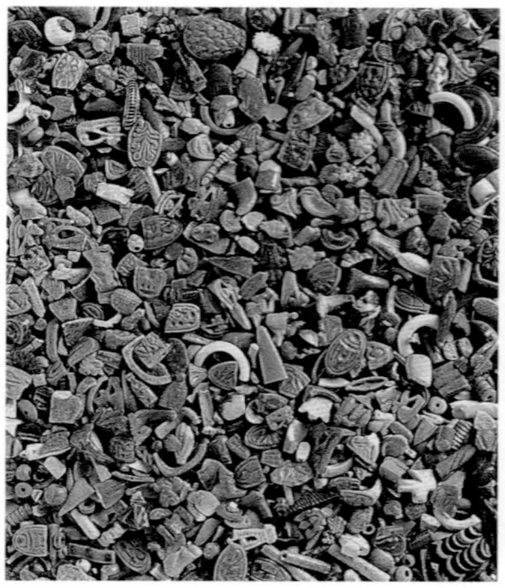

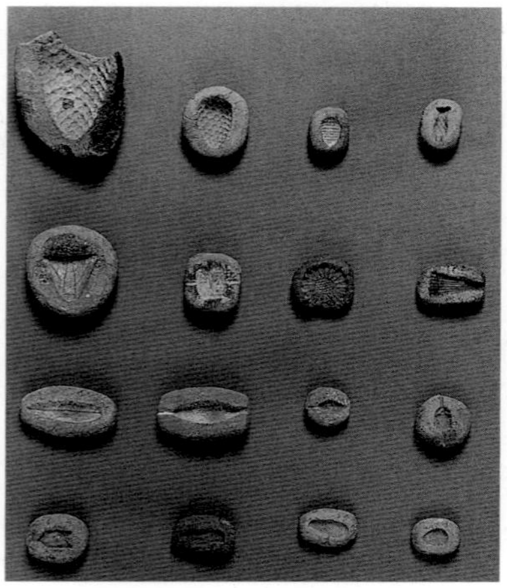

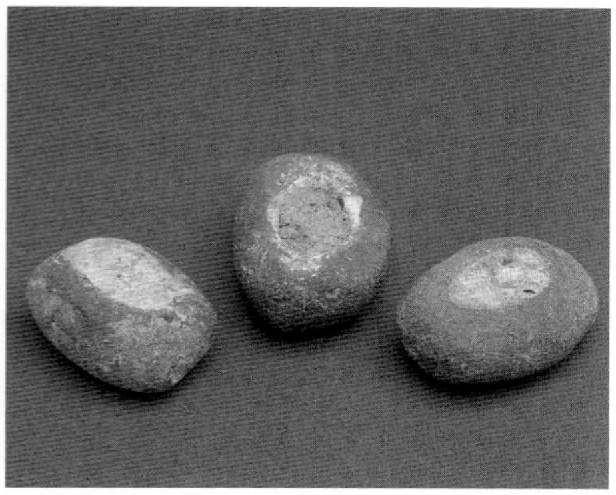

184 MISCELLANEOUS FAIENCE AND GLASS OBJECTS PAGE 164

New Kingdom, Dynasty 18, reign of Akhenaten; Amarna

Faience and glass

Julia Schottlander, London

This mass of brightly colored faience and glass objects mostly comprises the bezels and shanks of rings, although other items such as small beads are also present. Their bright colors reflect developments in glazing technology in the Eighteenth Dynasty when the color palette of the faience workers was expanded, perhaps as a result of the influence of glass workers. There are, in fact, several pieces of glass included in this collection, notably a fragment of vessel glass with trailed decoration. Such a mixture of glass and faience objects is typical of the finds from what Petrie describes as "glazing works" at Amarna, the area of Akhenaten's capital where glass and faience were manufactured as known from subsequent work at the site. This collection is believed to have come from the Egypt Exploration Society's excavations in 1926–27.

The many hundreds of faience ring fragments recovered from Amarna suggest that such rings were very widely worn. Numerous bezel fragments bear the name of Akhenaten or of the Aten and yet were certainly not royal signet rings. It has therefore been suggested that they might have been given out or sold at festivals as cheap "souvenir" jewelry.

That rings were made in faience at all reflects an improvement in technology. New Kingdom faience has an extensive glassy phase which some scholars have suggested is the result of mixing ground glass into the matrix, but which is more probably due to the addition of a higher proportion of glazing materials to the body paste producing a greater amount of interstitial glass. Bezels were made in separate molds from shanks and the two parts cemented together with faience paste before they dried completely. As a result there are examples where the shank and bezel are different colors. Some of the bezels, notably those in the form of *wadjet*-eyes are pierced. PTN

Bibliography. Petrie 1894, p. 28; Kühne 1969; Boyce in Kemp 1989.

185 MOLDS FOR FAIENCE PAGE 167

New Kingdom, Dynasty 18; Amarna

Clay; H. 2.5–8.0 cm; W. 2.2–6.5 cm; TH. 0.3–2.0 cm

The University of Pennsylvania Museum of Archaeology and Anthropology, Philadelphia. E671; E678B; E678C; E679; E685; E688; E690; E697; E717; E719; E721; E722; E735; E741; E743; E744; E785

The site of Amarna has yielded a tremendous number of small open molds for the manufacture of faience amulets and jewelry[11] made of fired, iron-rich Nile clay.[12] These molds, some of which yielded objects like those in [184] have shallow negative impressions of delightful floral motifs: rosettes, lotus blossoms, leaves, petals, and grapes, along with a cartouche of Akhenaten. Damp faience paste would have been pressed into a moistened mold and immediately removed to prevent it from sticking. Replication experiments have shown that no release agent was needed if the paste was at the right consistency and was removed at the right moment.[13] ML

Bibliography. Boyce in Kemp 1989, pp. 160–68; Nicholson 1995a, pp. 11ff.

186 THREE MOLDS FOR FAIENCE OBJECTS FILLED WITH PASTE PAGE 166

New Kingdom, Dynasty 18; Malkata

Fired clay with paste; 11.215.666: H. 2.0 cm; W. 4.0 cm; D. 3.0 cm. 11.215.667: H. 1.8 cm; W. 3.6 cm D. 2.7 cm. 11.215.668: H. 1.8 cm; W. 3.8 cm; D. 3.0 cm

The Metropolitan Museum of Art, New York. 11.215.666, 11.215.667 and 11.215.668

These three molds, slightly earlier than those in [185], come from excavations by the Metropolitan Museum of Art at Malkata, the site of the palace of Amenhotep III on the West Bank of the Nile at Thebes.

The court of Amenhotep III seems to have been one in which cosmopolitan ideas flourished and which supported new industries, such as glass making, as well as more traditional crafts, such as faience manufacture. As a result Malkata has become one of the few sites from which we have important technological evidence for the production of faience.

These particular molds, made of fired clay, are for the manufacture of small items such as amulets, probably in the shape of fruits. They are filled with a white or brownish paste, which has recently been analysed by Mark Wypyski of the conservation section of the Metropolitan Museum of Art (see Appendix). It was found to be a mixture of calcium, aluminium, silicon, iron, and other elements, but Wypyski regards these as more like a calcareous (calcium-rich) clay rather than a faience paste mixture.

Whether or not the material is original to the molds it clearly illustrates the appearance of the molds prior to the removal of their contents for final drying before firing. PTN

Bibliography. Petrie 1894, p. 28.

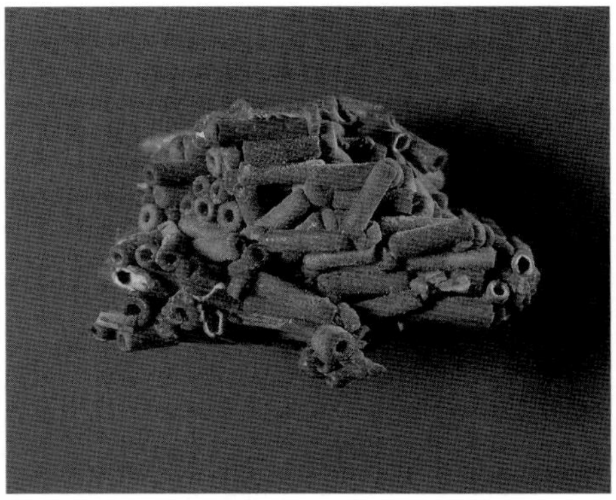

187 LUMP OF FUSED BEADS

PAGE 167

Roman Period; Memphis

Faience; H. 3.5 cm; L. 5.5 cm

The University of Pennsylvania Museum of Archaeology and Anthropology, Philadelphia. E 12501

One of the most common products made in faience, tubular and ring beads could be mass produced in one of two ways: either by squeezing and rolling the paste around a rod of organic material of the desired diameter (such as a reed); or by dipping a rod into a thinned faience mixture, like candle dipping, until it built up an adequate thickness.[14] Next, the beads could be cut to the right length; incomplete cuts often seen on tubular beads are evidence of this method. The beads could then have been left to dry on the rods, allowing a complete covering of the exterior surface by the efflorescing salts but preventing the interior from being glazed. They could be fired on a firing bed made of ashes or a glazing powder to prevent marring the glaze. If the organic rods were left in during firing, they would simply burn out.[15]

This mass of beads appears to have been strung together, alternating tubular and ring beads. It might have been intended as part of a bead network, as in a bead shroud [163], or as a broad collar [100]. It appears the beads were never used but were stored together, perhaps in a bag, as some of the beads have fibrous impressions in the accretions. During burial in the ground the thread disintegrated and the mass was fused together by the products of weathering.

ML

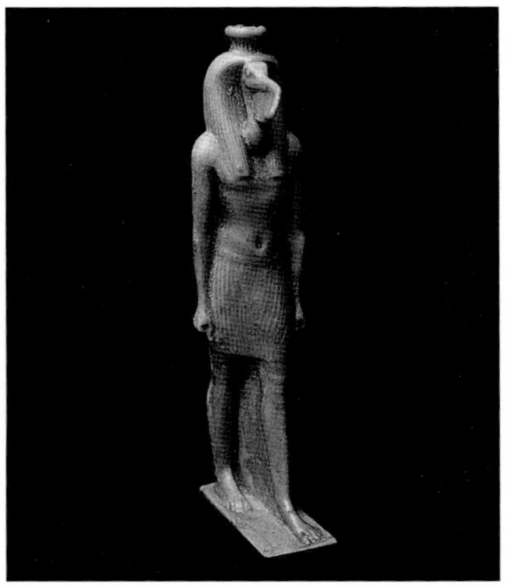

188 FIGURINE OF THOTH

PAGE 169

Late Period to Ptolemaic Period

Faience; H. 10.4 cm; W. 2.4 cm; D. 3.7 cm

Private Collection

Numerous problems in the manufacture of faience could occur before or during firing. This wonderfully detailed faience statuette of the god Thoth was made by pressing faience paste into a mold. Either at the point it was removed from the mold or at some time before it was completely dry the beak was knocked askew and never corrected, whether by intent or neglect. Hand tooling sharpened up the impression, and recesses of the design were filled with a fine slurry colored with cobalt, creating the subtle shading around the wig and crown. The turquoise glaze is the result of self-glazing (the efflorescence technique), although much of the present surface appearance is due to weathering during burial.

ML

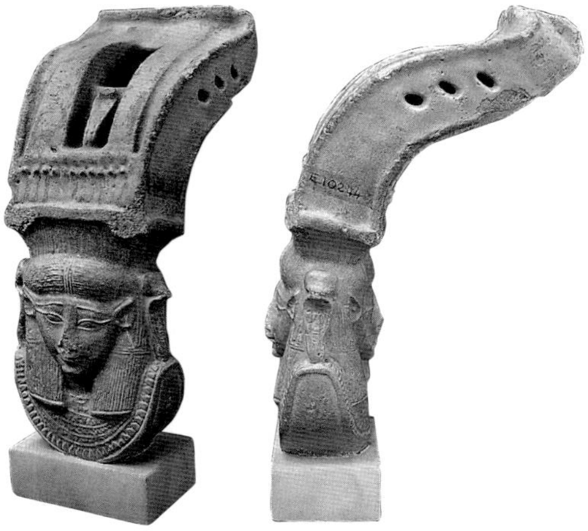

189 SISTRUM

PAGE 168

Late Period, Dynasty 26

Glassy faience; H. 16.5 cm; W. 6.2 cm; TH. 3.6 cm

Musée du Louvre, Paris. E 10244

Like the sistrum [91], this piece was molded from glassy faience. However, this example was affected by a fault in firing. Problems can occur at a number of points during this process, for example at 573°C, the quartz molecules undergo an inversion from the alpha to the beta form, expanding in volume by 2%. If this temperature is reached too soon the object can distort or crack apart. Objects can also warp if the temperature is uneven in the kiln, making them distort. And if the kiln is left too long at too high a temperature, the silicates begin to melt and flow, causing slumping.[16] This appears to have been the problem with this sistrum, causing its melted and blurry appearance.

ML

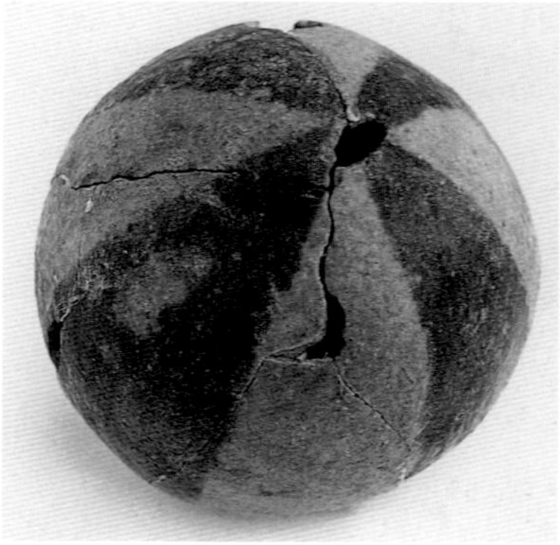

190 STRIPED BALL BEAD

PAGE 172

Middle Kingdom to early New Kingdom

Faience; DIAM. *c.* 4.0 cm

Musée du Louvre, Paris. AF 12531

Through examining the interior of this broken object, one can see how it was made. The simplest method of manufacture of hollow spherical beads is to fashion them around an organic core, such as straw, dung, etc., impressions of which can actually be seen on the interior of this fragment.[17] The pierced holes then serve the dual function of allowing gases to escape when the organic matter combusts and providing a means for subsequent stringing.

The paste used to make this bead is a straightforward copper-colored faience with black painted stripes, probably derived from manganese dioxide. It is glazed by the efflorescence (self-glazing) method.

ML

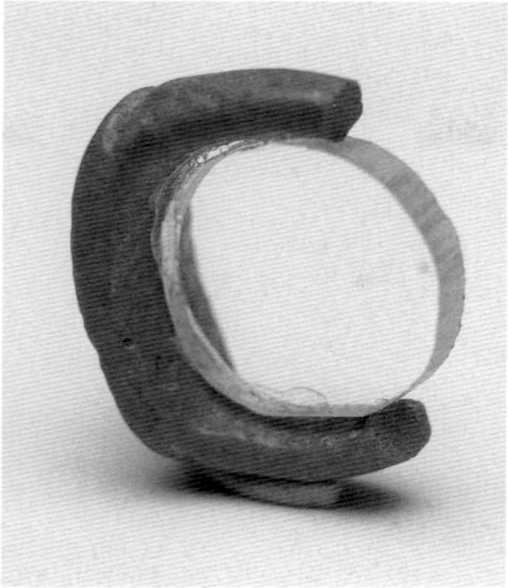

191 RING BEZEL WITH THE CARTOUCHE OF AMENHOTEP III

PAGE 175

New Kingdom, Dynasty 18, reign of Amenhotep III; Thebes

Faience; DIAM. 2.1 cm

The Syndics of the Fitzwilliam Museum, Cambridge. E.6.1920

This ring bezel with the cartouche of Amenhotep III is typical of a fashion for faience rings that sprang up in the Eighteenth Dynasty[18] (see also [106], [107]). In order to make a wearable ring from faience, the body composition needed to be altered to increase its strength. For these rings, finely powdered glass was incorporated into the body along with a small amount of lead oxide which both acted as a flux, allowing a lower firing temperature, and strengthened the final product.[19] New colorants were introduced at this time, including lead antimonate, that when added to copper oxide gave a wide range of greens.[20] The resulting paste was shaped in two small clay molds (see [185])—the bezel separately from the ring shank—and the parts joined with a small amount of faience slurry.

ML

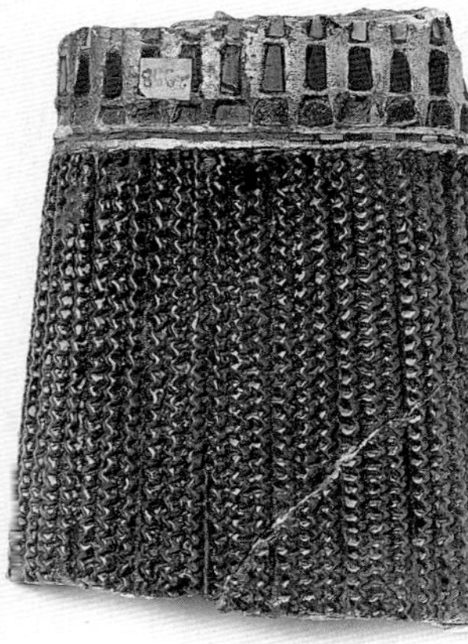

192 SIDELOCK FROM THE WIG OF A PRINCESS

PAGE 176

New Kingdom, end of Dynasty 18

Wood; gesso; blue, red, turquoise glass; blue faience; gilding; H 13.0 cm; W. 10.5 cm; D: 2.6 cm; TH. of faience 1.6 cm

Musée du Louvre, Paris. N 3364

This object is very complicated in its method of manufacture and decoration. Judging by its preserved width, this fragment of a sidelock would have belonged to a life-sized statue. The sidelock is a well-known symbol of youth in ancient Egypt. Such a high quality inlay for an exceptionally large statue raises the question of who the subject was. On the basis of the paste and glaze colors it may be dated to a series of reigns at the end of the Eighteenth Dynasty, the two longest being those of Amenhotep III and his son and successor, Amenhotep IV/Akhenaten.

The princesses who participated in the Jubilee ceremonies of their father, Amenhotep III, were adorned with this style of hairpiece, similarly depicted with tight fine zigzags.[21] Two of Amenhotep III's princesses, Isis and Sitamun, were raised to the rank of chief royal wife, and under this title were the subjects of important statues. In a beautiful fragmentary group held in a private collection, the princess Isis wears a sidelock with small zigzag waves that fall over her shoulders and follow her figure.[22] Similarly, during the reign of Akhenaten countless statues of the royal daughters,[23] often composite works, lent themselves perfectly to this type of inlay. None of these statues has survived intact, due to the complexity of their materials which made them particularly fragile.

The complex construction of this fragment becomes clear when it is turned over. At the back, remains of the wooden support of the sculpture, about 3 cm (just over 1 in) thick, can be seen at the top. On the front, a section of gesso was incised, creating cavities that were filled with colored mortar to hold glass inlays in place. The color of the mortar was coordinated with the inlays: blue for the turquoise glass in the top row, red for the glass in the middle row and blue again for the deep blue glass of the bottom row. Strangely, it seems that the gilding was applied after the application of the blue mortar and the insertion of the turquoise glass, as the gilding covers the mortar in some places. Below the vertical inlays, small canes of glass create a horizontal strip of alternating light and dark blue.

At the back, the wooden support has contracted and broken away and all that remains are splinters raised by the cement that held the hairpiece to the statue. The thickness is created by a wide prefabricated faience inlay with a bluish-gray paste, a color characteristic of pieces made with cobalt. Below 2 mm from the surface the core paste is crystalline, like sugar, while the upper 1 mm is vitrified, suggesting that the glaze was applied to the surface as it enfolds the sides for about 1 cm.[24] The color, a magnificent intense cobalt blue, and the brilliance are undimmed. GP-B

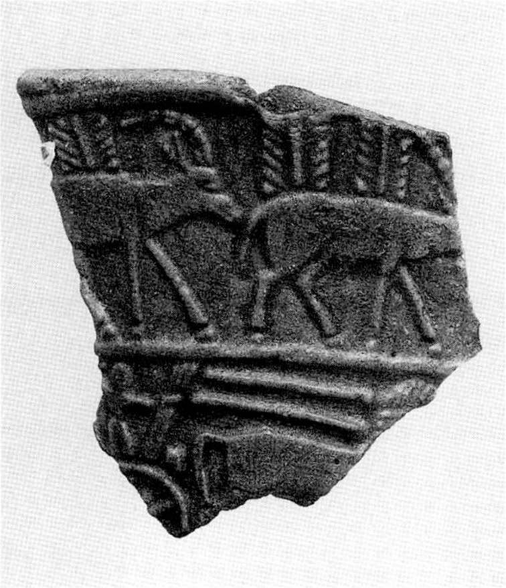

193 FRAGMENT OF A RELIEF CHALICE

PAGE 175

Third Intermediate Period

Faience; max. H. 5.4 cm; max. W. 4.9 cm; TH 0.4 cm

Museum of Art, Rhode Island School of Design, Providence. Gift of Peter Sharrer. 1996.56[25]

This charming fragment depicting a gazelle and an ibex strolling through tall plants comes from a relief chalice similar to the one from the Myers Museum, Eton College [116]. The complex manufacture of these chalices, which first appeared in the Eighteenth Dynasty,[26] is not yet completely understood, although most of the steps involved have been determined through technical examinations.[27] The chalice bowl was probably made using a mold, either concave, as used for the lotus chalice from the Museum of Fine Arts, Boston,[28] or convex, which could have supported the damp paste of the bowl during the later working. The stem would have been similarly molded.

The intricate carving of the relief figures was done by an artist carving directly into the body of the bowl before it had completely dried. To strengthen the faience paste for carving, it is possible that an organic binder, such as a glue or a gum, was added.[29] Since carving would have removed most of the efflorescing salts, a fresh coating of glaze—a slurry composed of finely ground quartz, fluxes, and colorants—was applied to the body and allowed to effloresce. Under low-power magnification this fine white layer can be clearly seen in the cross-section just below the glaze, following the contours of the relief and contrasting with the coarser, darker material of the main faience body. Final tooling would then have been added and, when dry, the vessel would have been fired to develop the rich green-blue glaze. ML

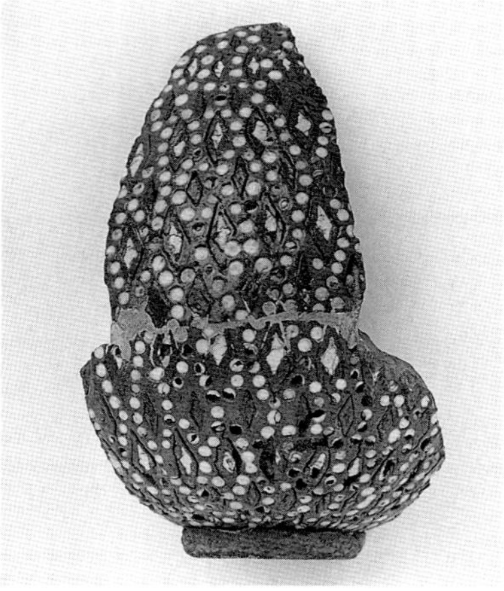

194 FRAGMENT OF A BOTTLE WITH POLYCHROMATIC GEOMETRIC DESIGN

PAGE 174

New Kingdom, end of Dynasty 18

Blue faience inlaid with red and white; H. 8.8 cm; W. 5.6 cm; max. orig. DIAM. *c.* 7.0 cm

Musée du Louvre, Paris. E10813

An especially interesting form of faience decoration is illustrated by this inlaid fragment, which is a small technical masterpiece. The body is a bluish gray, undoubtedly due to cobalt, very dense, without visible bubbles, and has a blue glaze derived from the paste; the entire surface is very glossy. Diamonds and dots a millimeter deep were incised into the damp body then inlaid with faience pastes colored red and white by the addition of glass.[30] Toward the bottom and top of the piece the diamonds and dots diminish in size, demonstrating the careful attention given to the placement of the design on the curved surface. The interior is regular in shape and was clearly molded around a form. The ring foot was applied to the underside with a slurry.

The diamond pattern is commonly found on basketry works, but its appearance on a vase is exceptional. It is known from wall paintings, probably depicting baskets, in the tombs of the Old Kingdom and the ceilings of Eighteenth Dynasty Theban tombs. A vase of Tiye has a similar pear-shaped swelling, but it is not certain that both vessels would have had the same overall shape since there were many innovations in the period when this vase was produced.

The only satisfactory date for this piece is late Eighteenth Dynasty, when the technique of inlaying faience into faience in small-scale objects reached its height. In fact, this fragment is a rare example of double inlaying: white in red in a blue background. The final result is superb since there is very little shrinkage between the colors, suggesting an excellent control of drying times. The white has fused on the surface with the blue, unlike the red which has slightly pulled away. The use of cobalt-tinted paste, the color chosen for the inner surface, is also characteristic of works of this period. A similar fragment[31] in the Ashmolean Museum, Oxford comes from a house in Amarna; another fragment can be found in the Petrie Museum, University College London. GP-B

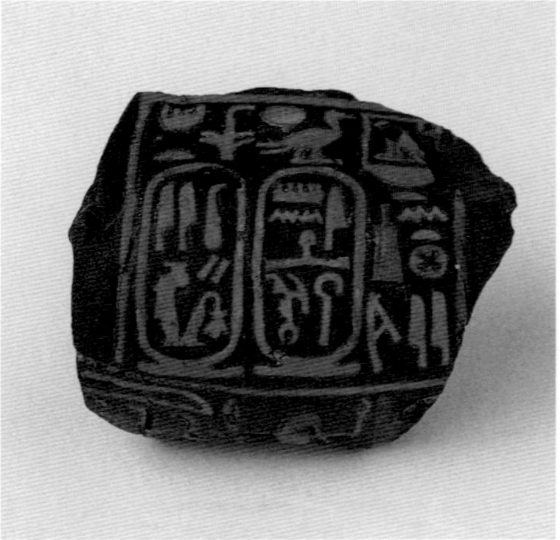

195 FRAGMENT OF A VASE WITH HANDLE

PAGE 174

New Kingdom, Dynasty 18, reign of Amenhotep III
Faience; original dimensions of the handle:
H. 7.0 cm; TH. 1.1 cm
Preserved dimensions: H. 5.7 cm; W. 6.8 cm
Musée du Louvre, Paris. Gift of L., I., and A. Curtis. E22662

Another form of New Kingdom decoration appears in this inlaid fragment of an unusually shaped handle joined to the body of a vase which originally was about 30.0 cm (12 in) in diameter. On the inside are ridges which are perhaps creases formed when material was shaped into a curve. The very dense and hard paste is an intense cobalt blue; the surface is glazed with the same color, less shiny on the outside of the handle than on the inside where it was more protected from weathering. The inlays can be seen in profile at the breaks. As is customary, the inlay paste is whitish and only superficially glazed in a bright turquoise blue. The source of this turquoise color was copper oxide, which creates a less stable blue than cobalt—there are areas of green which cobalt would never produce.

Faience paste colored throughout by cobalt is typical of the period at the end of the Eighteenth Dynasty, from the reign of Amenhotep III onward. In one of the traditional techniques of Egyptian faience—glazing by efflorescence—pigment is mixed into the paste and, after its salts have effloresced during drying, they mix with the silica, coloring it during the firing. Unlike copper, cobalt is such a powerful colorant that the entire paste remains imbued with blue, as is evident in the majority of blue-based objects from this period.

The fusion between the inlays and the body is well executed and there are very few areas of contraction between the two, for instance the man with uplifted arms. In those areas where the inlays have completely disappeared, no cement is visible and so the inlays must have been held in place by fusing when fired. The success of this technique is seen in many places in this piece.

The main framed section adorning the handle is almost entirely preserved. To the left the text "son of Re, Amenhotep ruler of Thebes, and the wife of the king, Tiye" faces the right column: "beloved of Hathor, mistress of Dendera." Within this frame is also a horizontal line of hieroglyphs that are twice as large; all that remains is "...great in years..." above the cartouche.

The size of the original vase, the technical and aesthetic quality of the inlaying, the superiority of the design, the wonderful interplay between the two shades of blue—everything points to the conclusion that the original was a masterpiece. In fact it belongs to a series of faience objects inlaid with faience of another color created during the reign of Amenhotep III, on which the name of the king is associated with a deity: (Ptah) Sokar,[32] Atum of Heliopolis[33], Neith of Sais,[34] and Amun-Re of Thebes.[35] Not all these pieces come from the region of Thebes; one comes from Heliopolis;[36] another[37] was discovered, along with fragments of a similar type, in the Temple of Hathor of Sinai. All share the same remarkable technology and must come from the same workshop. It may well be that these official products were distributed in temples across the entire country, as was the case with the scarabs of glazed stone.[38]

G P-B

Bibliography. Pierrat 1993, p. 49, fig. 51 and p. 52; Berlandini 1993, p. 26, n. 74 (quote).

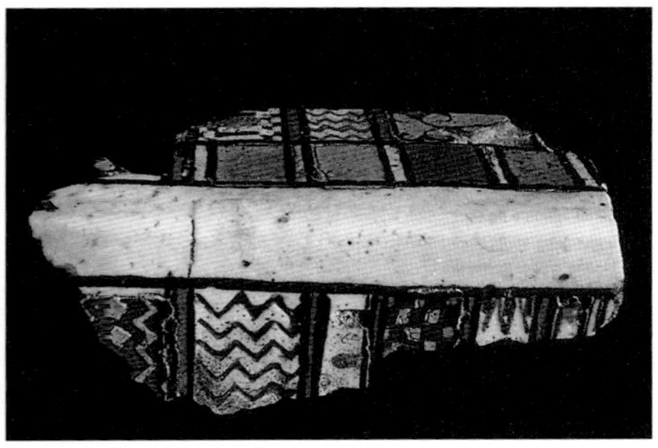

196 CORNER OF AN UNIDENTIFIED INLAID OBJECT

PAGE 172

New Kingdom, Dynasty 18
Faience; max. H. 2.2 cm; W. 4.8 cm; D. 1.2 cm
Private Collection

Although the exact purpose of the object from which this small, brilliantly colored fragment comes is unknown, it tells an extraordinary story of the level of complexity and sophistication of Eighteenth Dynasty faience technology. On two sides of a coarse faience core, recesses were cut for the insertion of faience pastes colored by the inclusion of finely powdered glass or frit. In turn, most of those inlays were themselves inlaid with patterns of contrasting color pastes or painted with fine glaze slurries. The timing of insertion of the inlays was critical in order to avoid serious cracking or insufficient adhesion of the inlays which could occur if either the body or the inlays were too wet or too dry. Although some cracking did occur, some of it may have been deliberate in order to produce the sharp outlines around the zigzags and other geometric shapes. This effect was achieved by allowing the incision in the inlay to dry slightly, so that when the next colored paste was inserted, it would shrink away from the sides.[39] The completed object must have been a masterpiece.

ML

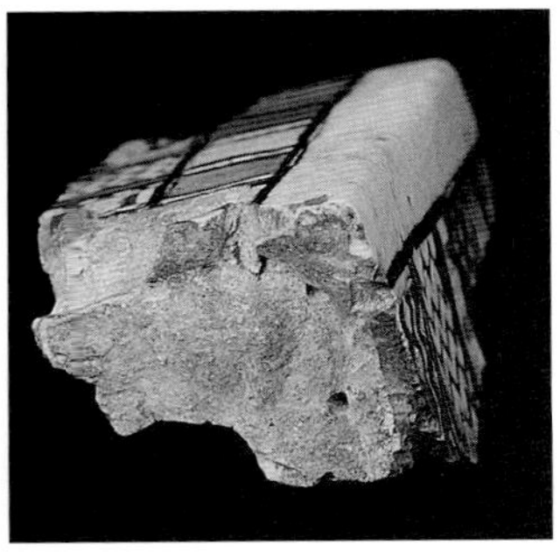

Fig. 59 Side view of the receptacle, showing the coarse core and the fine faience inlays.

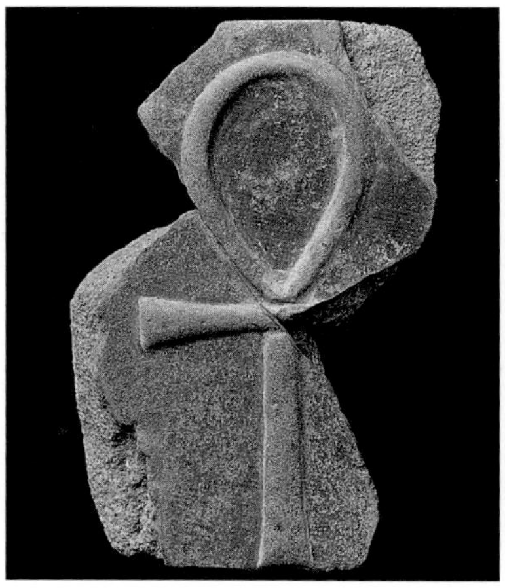

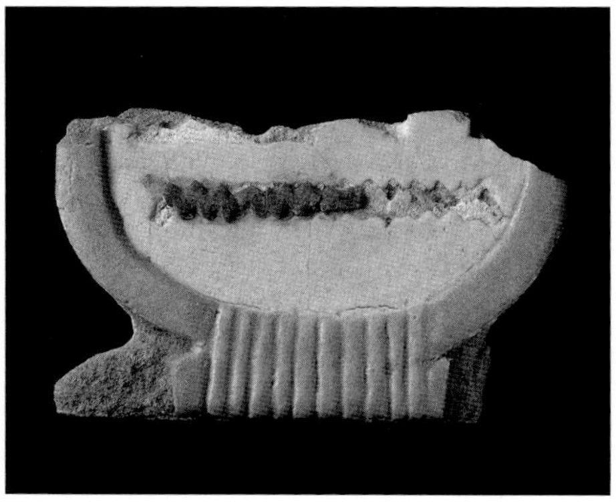

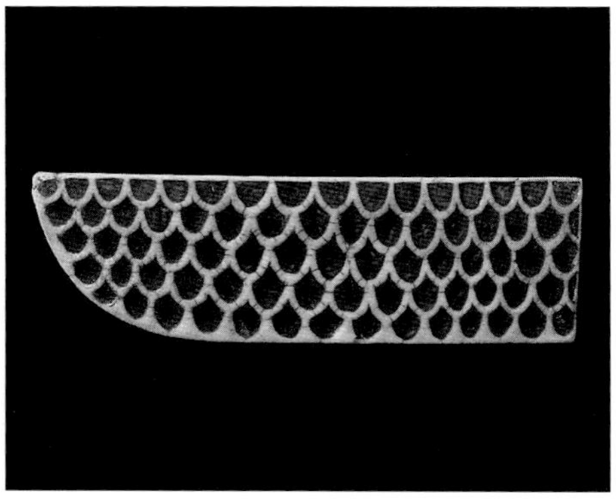

197 WALL TILE WITH FRAGMENT OF ANKH PAGE 173

New Kingdom, Dynasty 19, reign of Seti I

Faience; H. 9.9 cm; W. 5.0 cm; D. 2.0 cm

Musée du Louvre, Paris. E 11518

Here, a simpler method of decoration is illustrated. This wall tile fragment with an *ankh* in relief is covered in a luminous turquoise blue glaze, typical of faience made with a copper colorant. To create a very pure glaze a thin layer of fine white crushed quartz was sometimes applied over a base material colored by natural impurities. This practice has been noted at Qantir, where the faience core tends to be pinkish brown.[40] Such a layer was also used on this piece to produce the glaze above the coarse body of the tile and to form the *ankh* sign. Slight irregularities in the shape of the *ankh* suggest that it could have been modeled by hand rather than molded. A slurry of the body material wiped over the surface would have been sufficient to produce a vitreous blue glaze when fired. The glaze over the *ankh* appears to be lighter because it is raised and colored by a thicker deposit of the fine quartz. In some areas of the *ankh* the glaze has worn off, increasing this contrast. BC

198 CARTOUCHE FRAGMENT PAGE 173

New Kingdom, Ramesside

Polychrome faience; H. 9.1 cm; W. 14.2 cm; D. 2.2 cm

Musée du Louvre, Paris. AF 12532

This fragment of a tile in the shape of a cartouche was intended for architectural inlay.[41] The ring of the cartouche itself is a silvery blue and within it dark brown hieroglyphs have been set into a pure white background creating a bichrome effect. These colors may have been chosen deliberately to give the impression of precious metals.

The body of the tile was probably shaped with a mold or a template while the raised cartouche could have been added to the base either by means of a shallow mold or by applying the paste free-hand. The interior was filled with a white faience paste, and the details, such as the recesses for the glyphs and the vertical cartouche binding marks, were impressed. This sequence of fabrication is made evident by the easily visible tool marks that cross from the cartouche into the white paste. The glaze is probably the result of efflorescence, although an additional glaze slurry could have been applied to the cartouche to heighten the gloss. The hieroglyphs appear to have been formed separately from a denser material and, after firing, inlaid into a cement, traces of which are visible where the inlay is lost. BC & ML

199 INLAY IN THE SHAPE OF A WING PAGE 172

Late Period to Ptolemaic Period

Faience; H. 2.5 cm; W. 7.5 cm; D. 0.6 cm

Private Collection

This exquisite piece of late faience in the shape of a wing probably came from an inlay of a falcon used to decorate a wooden object.[42] Although it may initially been formed in a mold, or by use of a template, each feather was carved individually, as seen by irregularities in the shapes and the clear cutmarks between the cells. The recesses were filled with a faience paste colored with cobalt, contrasting beautifully with the lighter blue from copper of the outlines. It was glazed by the efflorescence (self-glazing) method. ML

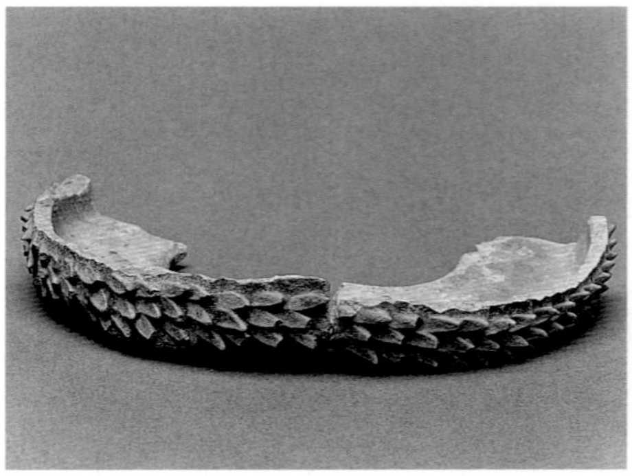

200 TWO FRAGMENTS OF RELIEF DECORATED VESSEL(S) PAGE 175

Roman Period; Memphis

Faience; A: L. 15.7 cm; W. 5.0 cm; B: L. 13.5 cm; W. 5.0 cm

Petrie Museum of Egyptian Archaeology, University College London. UC.40913 A & B

These fragments from Memphis are badly damaged but illustrate a form of relief decoration for vessels of the Roman Period.[43] Although both pieces are from the same type of vessel, minor differences in their diameter and in the size of the handle attachment (not visible in this photograph) might suggest that, since they do not appear to join, they are actually from different vessels of the same type (although variations in diameter on a single vessel[44] are common, since they are rarely truly circular).

This type of relief decoration, which represents a floral garland, is not uncommon in faience of this period. It would be difficult to make a vessel with high relief of this kind in a single mold and we can be fairly sure that either the leaves were made in separate "sprig" molds and attached before being hand finished, probably using a knife or similar tool, or—if made in one piece—had their decoration sharpened in the same way. Originally the garland would have run around the shoulder of the vessel, with the handle attached, in this case, just above it. The handle, which would have been attached in a separate operation, may have been one of a pair, making this a krater vase.

The glaze was probably added by the application method and was rich in copper, some of which is causing the bluish patches. Interestingly, the interior of the vessel is also glazed, suggesting that it was intended to hold liquids; glazing would prevent liquids from penetrating the vessel fabric. PTN

1 Replication experiments agree with this assumption. The shape of the balls minimizes contact with the beads, but they do leave small marks on the beads. ML

2 This would remove efflorescing salts from the under surface, preventing a glaze forming on the bottom, a desirable effect for tiles and inlays that needed a keyed surface to facilitate attachment to another surface, such as a wall or furniture. ML

3 This worked well in faience replication experiments.

4 Tite et al. in Bimson and Freestone 1992, pp. 42, 45–46. See another example in the Petrie Museum, UC.36457.

5 Nordström I 1972, p. 126; II pl. 195.

6 Cf. BMFA 1989.1014, from Hierakonpolis.

7 Reisner 1923, p. 53.

8 Vergès 1992, p. 24. Replication experiments at the RISD Museum suggest the latter is the most efficient technique.

9 Vandiver in Kaczmarczyk and Hedges 1983, p. A-109.

10 Nicholson 1995a, p. 15.

11 In his Amarna excavation report, Petrie notes that he "brought nearly 5,000 from Tell el-Amarna, after rejecting large quantities of the commonest" (quoted in Nicholson 1995a, p. 11) and in Griffith's 1923 excavation, small molds for faience accounted for ⅓ of the small finds (Boyce in Kemp 1989, p. 161).

12 Boyce in Kemp 1989, p. 163.

13 Vandiver in Kaczmarczyk and Hedges 1983, pp. A-24–25. Residue of the faience paste has been identified in some molds (see Appendix for analysis by Mark Wypyski at the Metropolitan Museum of Art, New York, NY, 1997), possibly due to tardy removal of the object from the mold.

14 Vandiver in Kaczmarczyk and Hedges 1983, p. A-112.

15 It is generally assumed that the rods are removed prior to drying, cf. Vandiver and Kingery 1987, pp. 19–34. Experiments to replicate such beads at the RISD Museum suggest that they are easier to manipulate if left on their sticks. An added benefit is that the reed ash adds an attractive thin glaze to the interior of the beads during firing making them easier to string.

16 A thorough explanation of firing effects can be found in Hodges 1964, pp. 39–41.

17 For further information see [81]. Vandiver in Kaczmarczyk and Hedges 1983, A-25; Vergès 1992, pp. 36–37. Following the suggestion in Vergès, a rolled section of a palm leaf was used in a replication experiment with considerable success.

18 Boyce in Kemp 1989, p. 160.

19 Vandiver in Kaczmarczyk and Hedges 1983, p. A-108.

20 Kaczmarczyk and Hedges 1983, p. 148.

21 Fakhry, 1943, fig. LIa.

22 Kozloff and Bryan 1992, no. 4, pp. 206–07.

23 For example, Louvre E 14715.

24 Examination of photographs of this object and a related piece in the Egyptian Museum, Turin, suggests that the wig locks may have been made from uncolored faience in small molds, each mold forming three strands of hair which were applied to the surface then glazed.

25 The fragment was originally given to the Minneapolis Institute of Arts in 1927 by Miss Lily Place, who lived until 1929 in Cairo, where she bought the piece. The MIA deaccessioned it in 1927, selling it to the Blumka family; it still bears on the back its MIA accession number (27.41.143), however. I thank Kenneth Krenz, MIA Registrar, for this information. the fragment was auctioned and later purchased by Peter Sharrer, who identifies it, on the basis of style and subject matter, as a companion to a chalice fragment once in Berlin (Berlin 16024) that was destroyed in World War II. For illustration, see Tait 1963, pl. XXII, fig. 2, chalice XXXVIII. The Berlin and Providence fragments were probably part of a very beautiful single chalice, other fragments of which may still exist somewhere.

26 Brovarski in Brovarski et al. 1982a, p. 145.

27 For a complete discussion of the manufacture of a lotus chalice see Kingery and Vandiver 1986, pp. 51–67; Vandiver and Kingery, 1992, pp. 79–90.

28 Kingery and Vandiver 1986, p.56

29 Vergès 1992, p.30, Kingery and Vandiver 1986, p.62.

30 For a full description of the technique of inlaying see Nicholson, and Vandiver in Kaczmarczyk and Hedges, 1983, pp. 1–117; A-121.

31 Oxford, Ashmolean Museum 1924, p. 114, published in Kaczmarczyk and Hedges 1983, fig. 40e.

32 Vase, Louvre E 25564 + AF 6533.

33 Vase, Turin 17136. It seems inaccurate to describe the vase as Egyptian blue, as it is in Kozloff and Bryan 1992, no. 106, p. 405. Actually, Egyptian blue can be distinguished from other materials by its completely crystalline state, the result of firing stopped before complete vitrification. This vase displays all the characteristics of the blue paste series "faience in faience" from the end of the Eighteenth dynasty, but displays a completely deglazed surface, undoubtedly a result of poor preservation conditions.

34 Bead, Louvre E 22630.

35 Badge-shaped plaque, Louvre E 3043.

36 Cf. n. 33.

37 Petrie Museum, University College London UC.35322.

38 For recent clarification on this subject, see Berman in Kozloff and Bryan 1992, p. 68.

39 Vandiver in Kaczmarczyk and Hedges 1983, p. A-117

40 Müller 1981, p. 341. This is faience "Variant A" in the categories established by Lucas and Harris 1962, pp. 161–62.

41 For the use of tiles like this in monumental New Kingdom architecture, see Hayes 1937, pp. 22–24, 27–30, pl. IX.

42 The shape of the wing suggests that its use may be related to that of the falcon from a wooden shrine from Ashmunein in the collection of the Metropolitan Museum of Art (26.7.991, Edward S. Harkness Gift, 1926).

43 These pieces have not been examined in person by the author.

44 Nenna and Seif el-Din 1993, p. 590 and pls. III:3 and III:4.

Contributing Authors

CA	Carol Andrews	JH	Joyce Haynes	DCP	Diana Craig Patch
RSB	Robert Steven Bianchi	APK	Arielle P. Kozloff	GP-B	Geneviève Pierrat-Bonnefois
BC	Brigit Crowell	PL	Peter Lacovara	NR	Nicholas Reeves
SD'A	Sue D'Auria	ML	Mimi Leveque	SBS	Sheila Shear
FDF	Florence Dunn Friedman	YJM	Yvonne Markowitz	SET	Stephen E. Thompson
CG	Carla Gallorini	PTM	Paul T. Nicholson	JWY	Janice W. Yellin

MAPS

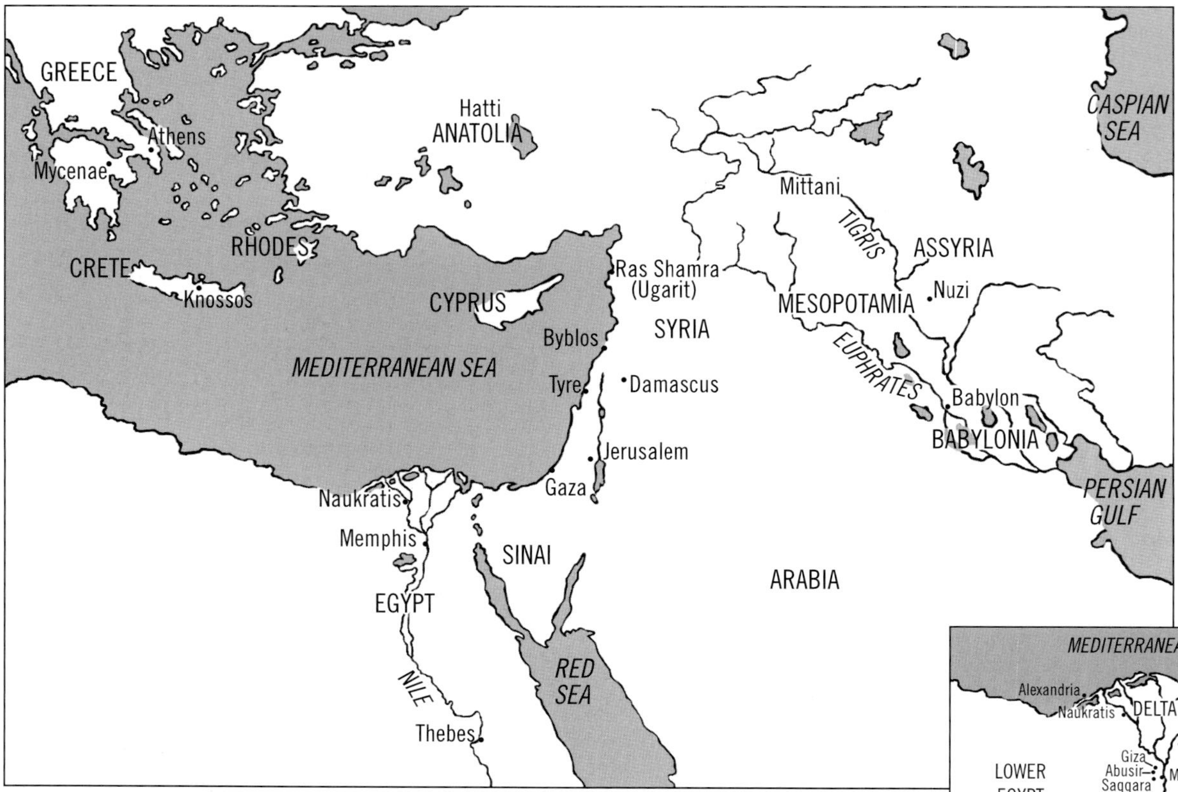

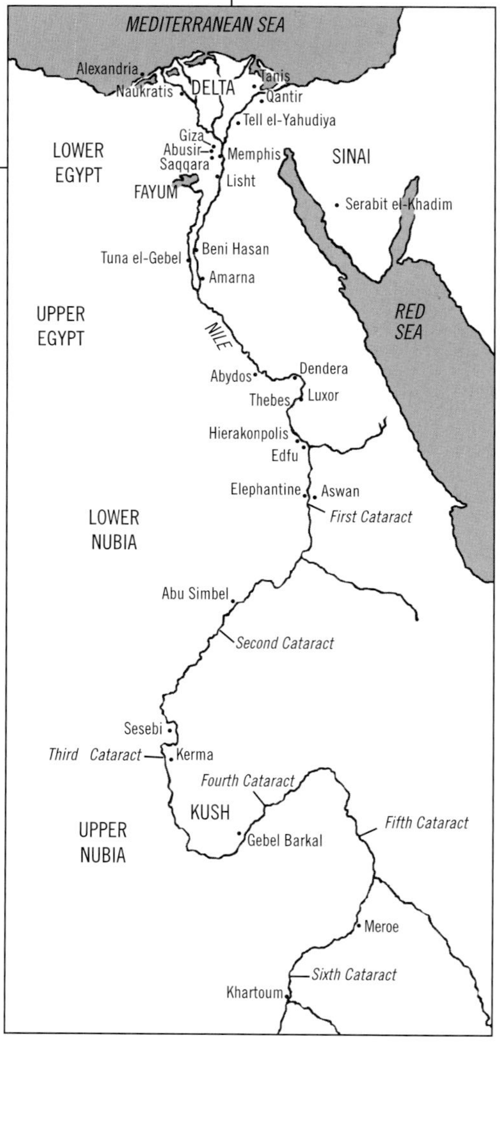

Map 1 (above) Egypt, the Near East and the Mediterranean world.
Map 2 (right) Egypt and Nubia.

APPENDIX

Five objects from the Metropolitan Museum of Art, selected by Dorothea Arnold, were analyzed to characterize the materials used. Micro-samples taken from the objects were analyzed using energy dispersive X-ray spectrometry (EDS) to determine the elemental compositions of the materials. (Kevex model Delta IV energy dispersive X-ray spectrometer, attached to an Amray modified model 1100 scanning electron microscope (SEM). Note: this model EDS does not detect elements below the atomic weight of sodium, such as carbon and nitrogen.)

The results and comments for each object are listed below. The table lists the quantitative analyses of the glassy phases (glaze layers) from three of the objects analyzed.

Mold from Malqata [186] (11.215.666)

The body of the mold was found to be a high iron clay containing a significant amount of phosphorus as well. This might be from a deliberate addition of calcium phosphate (from bone or ivory). The tan material inside the mold did not appear to be faience paste, as suspected, but was found to consist mainly of calcium, with some aluminum, silicon, iron, and other elements, including a trace of copper. This appears to consist of a mixture of lime (calcium carbonate) and clay. Some white powder on the surface, though, thought possibly to be salt efflorescence, was found to be nearly pure silica, with traces of sodium, aluminum, potassium, calcium, and iron. This looks like it could be faience core material, i.e. finely ground quartzite.

Lisht beads [172] (22.1.1097)

The small ring beads (approximately 2 mm across) were attached to a buff-colored base. The base appears to be very similar in composition to the tan colored powder from 11.215.666, that is, it appears to be a mixture of lime and clay. Samples of a turquoise bead and a dark purple bead were analyzed in cross-section (see table below). The compositions of the beads indicated that they were made of faience, rather than glass. No evidence of quartz cores was seen in the beads. The turquoise bead is colored with copper oxide, while the purple bead is colored with manganese oxide, with some copper oxide present also. (The low sodium values found, especially for the turquoise bead, are almost certainly due to loss of the alkali by weathering.)

Head of Augustus [63] (26.7.1428)

The body of the head of Augustus appears to be typical faience core material, i.e. over 90% silica, with very small amounts of other elements such as sodium, aluminum, potassium, calcium, and copper. The presence of a residual amount of copper in the core may be an indication that the piece was produced by efflorescence glazing. A sample of the glaze was also examined, but was found to be too weathered for accurate quantitative analysis. It appeared to be very similar to that found for the turquoise bead (2.1.1097), except for a smaller amount of copper oxide.

Amenhotep III as Sphinx [22] (1972.125)

The body of the sphinx appeared to be faience, similar to that of the head of Augustus, but with larger amounts of sodium and copper. The core was found to be a light blue in color, due to the presence of some copper oxide. The presence of a residual amount of copper and a relatively high amount of sodium in the core may be an indication that the piece was also produced by efflorescence glazing. Quantitative analysis of a sample of the turquoise glaze layer is shown in the table (the sodium value may be somewhat low due to weathering). The stone in the base of the sphinx was found to consist of calcium, presumably a form of calcite such as alabaster.

Ptolemaic Bowl [170] (1988.18)

The green and blue glazes on the bowl were found to be somewhat similar to the other faience glazes analyzed here, but also contained significant amounts of lead oxide, which is not found in most faience glazes (see quantitative analyses in the table). The green glaze was found to be colored by a mixture of copper oxide and a small amount of lead antimonate yellow. The blue glass appears to contain cobalt as well as copper as colorants. Analysis of the core material of the bowl indicated a typical faience body composition, along with the presence of small amounts of copper and lead. This, as well as the microstructure of the faience layers, indicates that this object was also efflorescence glazed.

Description: Faience glaze analyses

Cat. No.:	[170]		[22]	[172]*	
(Wt%)	Green	Blue	Turq	Turq	Purp
Na_2O	14.4	15.2	8.0	1.1	5.8
MgO	0.9	0.7	—	—	—
Al_2O_3	0.8	1.3	0.7	0.4	0.3
SiO_2	63.9	63.2	84.9	84.2	85.4
SO_3	—	—	0.2	0.3	—
Cl	1.5	1.7	0.7	1.5	0.4
K_2O	1.9	1.1	1.9	0.3	1.2
CaO	2.4	2.4	0.8	1.8	0.3
TiO_2	0.1	0.1	—	—	—
MnO	—	—	—	—	1.6
Fe_2O_3	0.7	1.3	0.3	0.3	0.6
CoO	—	0.1	—	—	—
CuO	2.2	3.4	2.4	6.6	1.6
Sb_2O_3	<0.6	—	—	—	—
PbO	<0.6	9.4	—	—	—

* The low sodium values, and low analytical totals indicate loss of alkali from weathering.
— = not detected. Also looked for, but not detected in any of these samples were: P_2O_5, NiO, ZnO, and SnO_2.

Mark T. Wypyski
Sherman Fairchild Center for Objects Conservation
The Metropolitan Museum of Art.

GLOSSARY Mimi Leveque

As many of the terms relating to the technology of the manufacture of faience, glass, and glazes used here will be unfamiliar to some readers, and in order to avoid redefining terms throughout the text, they are included in this glossary.

alkali Compounds including sodium, potassium, and other elements in the first column of the periodic table. In Egypt these are most commonly **soda**, Na_2O, found in **natron** and potassia, K_2O, found in plant ashes and in salt-water sources, like sea or brackish water. These substances are used as **fluxes** to lower the melting point of **silica** in **faience**, **glass** and **glaze** manufacture. The name derives from the Arabic *al khaly*, meaning soda.

alkaline earth Compounds of elements found in the second column of the periodic table, like **lime**, CaO, and magnesia, MgO; used as **fluxes** in **faience**, **glass** and **glaze** manufacture. Lime, in particular, helps to stabilize alkaline glazes and faience. Lime is found in Egyptian sand and some **alkali** sources; although critical to the stability of glassy materials, in ancient Egypt it was apparently introduced inadvertently (Tite et al. 1984, p. 218).

alumina Aluminum oxide, Al_2O_3, or hydroxide, $Al(OH)_3$, a substance found in clays, mica, and wood ash. It is helpful in **glaze** formation because it increases the viscosity of the glaze, preventing it from flowing off the surface to be glazed.

amorphous A property of matter in which the structure is not **crystalline** but has a random orientation. **Glass** is an example of an amorphous structure.

application A **glaze** can be applied to the surface of a **siliceous** body by dipping it into or painting on a glaze **slurry**. The slurry is made by **fritting** the raw materials of the glaze or using a **glass** finely ground into a powder and mixed with water. The use of this technique can often be recognized on faience objects by the fluid-looking, uneven glaze, which can have drip marks or pooled areas. Brush strokes can occasionally be seen; see [165] and [198].

binder, binding medium An organic substance used to hold together powdery materials, such as pigments. It is often a gum, like gum-arabic, or a resin, derived from plants, or a glue of animal origin.

cementation A glazing technique for faience that involves immersing the dried **siliceous** body in a glazing powder containing a high proportion of **lime** along with the **alkali** and metal salt **colorant**, most commonly a copper oxide (Wulff et al. 1968, p. 100; Vandiver 1992, p. 81). On firing, an interaction occurs between the silica body and the powder that creates a glazed surface and leaves a readily removable **sintered** powder around the object. Objects glazed by this technique have no marks of **kiln furniture**. The term derives from metallurgy, meaning a slow roasting process.

ceramics All types of fired **siliceous** wares, whether high- or low-fired, glazed or unglazed, made entirely from **clay**, like pottery, or of other siliceous materials, like **faience**. The word comes from the Greek *keramos*, "burnt material."

clay An extremely fine-particled material made of hydrated aluminum silicates that has plastic properties when wet, is rigid when dry and fires to a hard, water-insoluble substance. As a byproduct of the weathering of rocks, it is composed of a variety of mineral substances, primarily **silica** and **alumina**, along with impurities like iron, **alkalis**, and **alkaline earths** that modify its working properties.

colorant Color in a **glaze** of **faience** or a **glass** derives from the inclusion of small amounts of metal oxides, generally transition elements that are stable at higher temperatures, like copper, iron, cobalt, and manganese oxides. For example, in **glass** or **glazes**, copper produces a brilliant turquoise blue color when oxidized and greenish to red when reduced (see **oxidizing** and **reducing atmospheres** below); cobalt forms an intense dark blue. Blacks can be produced by manganese, iron, or both together. With the introduction of glass in Egypt, the color palette expanded to include a wide range of new colors, including yellows and yellow-greens by the addition of lead antimonate and white from calcium antimonate.

crawling A fault in glazing where the glaze pulls back exposing the surface. It can be the result of a number of problems, including an initially unclean surface and excessive shrinkage and cracking during drying. Alkaline and alkaline-lime glazes tend to crawl more than lead-silicate and lead-alkali-silicate glazes (Kingery and Vandiver 1986, p. 317) [196].

crystalline A property of matter, generally in solids, in which the atoms are arranged in a regular pattern.

devitrification The formation of crystals during the cooling of molten **glass**, generally too slowly. It can also occur on the surface of the glass as the result of an unstable composition. This term does not refer to deterioration of the glass due to burial or other environmental stress; this is called **weathering**.

efflorescence The most common **glazing** technique for **faience**. Also called "self-glazing," the process entails combining all the components of the faience—the **silica**, **lime**, **alkali**, and **colorant**—with water to become a **paste**. As the paste dries, the soluble salts, containing the **fluxes** and colorant, rise through the body and effloresce on the surface. When fired, the salts and silica body interact forming a glaze *in situ*. The thickness of the glaze is in part related to the rate of evaporation, so that recesses and hollows tend to have less glaze than more exposed parts of the piece (the reverse of objects glazed by **application** of a glaze **slurry**, where the glaze is thicker in deeper areas). Higher concentration of salts, higher firing temperature and a longer firing time also tend to increase glaze thickness (Vandiver 1997); see [48].

Egyptian blue Sometimes confused with **glass**, Egyptian blue is a synthetic polycrystalline material with **interstitial glass**; that is, it is made of mostly **crystalline** particles held together in an **amorphous** matrix. Without a surface **glaze**, it is colored blue throughout, having a structure of $CaO.CuO.4SiO_2$, identical to the rare native mineral, cuprorivaite. It has a higher **lime** and copper content than other Egyptian **vitreous** materials (Tite and Bimson 1987, p. 81; Tite et al. 1992, p. 40). The raw materials are fired together in a crucible at a temperature of 900–1000°C. Finer material can result from a regrinding and second firing (Tite et al. 1992, p. 42). "Egyptian blue" refers both to its bulk state for the manufacture of objects and to its use ground as a pigment. The earliest known use is from the Fourth Dynasty (Lilyquist, Brill, 1993, p. 5); see [181].

Egyptian faience An alternative, and less confusing, term for the glazed **siliceous** ware manufactured in Egypt in antiquity, often simply called **faience**. However, it was not exclusive to Egypt: during the Bronze Age, this material was used, with some technical variations, throughout the Mediterranean, Mesopotamia, eastward to the Indus Valley, and west as far as Britain. Egyptian faience is not **clay** but rather a manufactured, generally white-bodied **ceramic** made of ground **quartz** or sand (91–99% SiO_2), **lime** (1–5%), **soda** or other alkaline **fluxes** (0.5–3%) and colorants (1–1.5%) derived from metal salts, most commonly copper oxides, which yield a rich turquoise blue glaze upon firing (analyses: Tite 1987; Vandiver 1982, p. 167). Although black from iron or manganese oxides was used at an early stage, other colorants and additives, especially **glass**, were introduced only in the New Kingdom, expanding the color palette. The firing temperature range tends to be low: 800–1000°C. Even after firing, the interior often remains fairly friable, depending on the amount of **interstitial** (or interparticle) **glass**.

faience The term faience was originally used to describe a tin-glazed, white-bodied earthenware from Faenza, Italy (now usually known as majolica), but later applied to the ancient glazed **siliceous** ware due to similarities in appearance, although their techniques of manufacture are different. As many scholars feel that unqualified the word faience is too confusing, **Egyptian faience** is also used.

flux A substance used to promote the melting of materials such as **silica** which melts at a high temperature (1710°C) by lowering the melting point. Typical **fluxes** are **alkalis** like **soda** (Na_2O) or potassia (K_2O), **alkaline earths** like **lime** (CaO) and magnesia (MgO), as well as low-oxygen materials like lead oxide (PbO).

frit A confusing term because of its use in a variety of technical contexts. Lucas (1960, p. 156) uses it for powdered **quartz**; in glassmaking it refers to a first-stage process where the raw materials, the **silica** and **fluxes**, are melted together without complete fusion, and cooled, before being reground and resmelted. As the microstructure of such materials as **Egyptian blue** is similar to that of the melted frit in glassmaking, the term has been borrowed to describe ancient Egyptian glazeless **sintered** polycrystalline materials. Another type of Egyptian frit has a pale turquoise color and is primarily composed of a calcium silicate, wollastonite, $CaSiO_3$. Analysis has revealed that these materials have a higher proportion of copper, **alkali** and **lime** than **Egyptian faience**, ~75% SiO_2; 11–12% lime; ~6–7% alkali; ~6–7% CuO (Tite 1987, p. 27; Tite et al. 1992, p. 40). They are distinguished from Egyptian faiences as they have no surface **glaze** but are colored throughout their cross-section.

gesso A support or filling material for painting or gilding made from an inert powdery material, such as ground calcium carbonate ($CaCO_3$), mixed with an organic **binder**, such as a glue or a gum. The term originated in Italy to describe a ground made from gypsum plaster ($CaSO_4$) bound with rabbit-skin glue, but has now been extended to include all similarly bound supports. When properly prepared it can be smooth, hard and very durable; see [21].

glass A material composed of a glass-former (generally **silica**), along with **fluxes** (e.g. **alkalis** and **alkaline earths**) to lower the high melting temperature of the silica (1710°C) and colorants (metal oxides), which when melted and cooled form an **amorphous** solid. To describe its divergent properties, Brill called it "a fourth state of matter that combines the rigidity of a crystal with the largely random molecular structure of a liquid" (1963, pp. 126–27). Appearing at the end of the Second Intermediate Period or beginning of the New Kingdom, ancient Egyptian glass has a typical composition of 60–70% silica, 5–10% **lime**; 15–20% **soda**, 1–3% potassia, 2–5% magnesia.

glassy faience In a vague area between faience and **glass**, glassy faience is often confused with glass at first sight. To make it, **silica** and **fluxes** were combined with **fritted** material, fired and mostly **vitrified**, creating a hard, dense, opaque near-glass, which was colored throughout, and with a matte surface. Under high magnification a cross-section reveals **quartz** grains surrounded by a glassy matrix. It contains more **alkali** than typical faiences and this allows the extensive glass formation. Analysis reveals a composition of ~80% SiO_2, ~7% CaO; ~6% **alkali**, ~2% CuO (Tite 1987, p. 22); see [91].

glaze A glassy coating on a fired **silicate** body, generally composed of silicates, **fluxes** (e.g. **lime**, **alumina** and **alkali**) and **colorants**, metal salts like copper oxides. Glazes can be achieved by several methods, including: **application** as a **slurry** to the surface of a siliceous body as in most glazed **clay** wares and some **Egyptian faiences**; as a powder which the object is completely immersed in, as in Egyptian faiences made by the **cementation** technique; or self-glazed by materials derived from the faience paste itself (the **efflorescence** technique) efflorescing on the surface as the object dries. Glazes can be **amorphous** or partly **crystalline**.

glazed steatite Steatite, or soapstone, is a soft, easily carved stone that is a massive form of the mineral talc, a hydrated magnesium silicate. It can be carved into a desired shape, covered with an alkaline-based glazing compound and fired to form a hard core with a glazed surface. The magnesium silicate allows a range of workable firing temperatures; see [68].

inlay Any material set into the surface of a larger object. Glassy materials can be used as inlays in two ways: by shaping a cooled piece of **glass**, stone or **frit** and setting it into a prepared space in an object with an adhesive material, like a **gesso**—a technique often used for inlays in wooden or metal objects, see [192]; or by filling a prepared space with finely ground **frit** paste, with or without a **binder**, and firing it. Inlays of any color can be added to faience bodies using the second method; see [31] and [194].

interstitial glass A term used to describe an **amorphous** material (**glass**) found between grains of **crystalline** material or **quartz** in a fired **silicate** body. An alternate term is "interparticle" glass.

kiln An installation in which **ceramics** are baked, a process known as firing. Most kilns in Egypt appear to have been updraught, with the fuel placed below the material to be fired so that the heat and gases rise up through it and escape from the top. The typical temperature range is 800–1100°C. Ceramics fired in open pits, bonfires, or domestic firings are referred to as open firings (Nicholson 1993, p. 106).

kiln furniture Separators used during the firing of **glazed** materials to keep them from fusing together. Collectively known as kiln furniture, the most common separators, called **setters** by potters, were small pieces fired clay in a variety of shapes [178] designed to have the smallest surface area in contact with the glazed surface of the object, in order to leave the smallest traces; see [179]. Triangular shapes, called tripods, are also common. Fired **clay** pots were also used to protect glazed objects placed in them from the direct flame and debris during firing; such containers are generally called **saggars**.

lime Calcium oxide, CaO, made from the calcination of limestone, $CaCO_3$. It is a component of **glass**, **faience** and **glazes**, and occurs as an impurity in some **clays**.

mold A form from which many copies of an object can be made. Most faience molds were single-sided and made of fired **clay**, see [38], but more complex two- and three-part molds were also used, especially for the manufacture of shabtis; see [150].

mortise and tenon A technique of joinery in which a peg extends from the surface of a material to fit into a matching recess in another. It is especially common in Egyptian woodworking.

natron A naturally occuring evaporite salt composed of sodium carbonate and sodium bicarbonate with sodium chloride and sodium sulphate impurities. In ancient Egypt it had a variety of uses from mummification and incense manufacture to use as an **alkaline flux** in **glass**, **glazes** and **faience**.

network former; network modifier Glassmaking terms used to describe the random glass network *formed* by atoms of silicon and oxygen whose properties are *modified* by the addition of substances like sodium, calcium, potassium, magnesium, or lead. Those materials break the bonds between oxygen atoms, lowering the melting point of the glass (Greene 1961, pp. 95–96).

oxidizing atmosphere A **kiln** environment in which excess oxygen is available to react with the objects being fired, creating certain coloring effects. For example, under oxidizing conditions copper oxide as a **colorant** in a **glaze** will typically become a turquoise blue; see [22].

paste A white **ceramic** body; often used to describe **faience** body mixtures.

phase A physically distinct state of matter, with homogeneous composition and with a defined boundary.

plaster There are two primary types of plaster: lime plaster and gypsum plaster, commonly called plaster of Paris. Lime plaster is made by heating calcium carbonate ($CaCO_3$), from limestone, marble, or chalk, to drive off the carbon dioxide, producing **lime** (CaO). When combined with water, the lime rapidly converts to calcium hydrate, giving off considerable heat, hence the name "quicklime." Over time, the calcium hydrate, called "slaked lime," reconverts to calcium carbonate by absorbing carbon dioxide (CO_2) from the air. Gypsum plaster is made by heating hydrated calcium sulphate, gypsum ($2CaSO_4.H_2O$), to drive off some of the water. When the resulting plaster of Paris is made into a paste, it recombines with the water, giving off heat, to form a dense, hard, white surface.

quartz A common **crystalline** form of **silica**, SiO_2.

reducing atmosphere A **kiln** environment that is deprived of oxygen, often the result of using smoky or damp fuel or deliberately closing kiln vents, creating certain coloring effects. For example, colloidal copper oxide under reducing conditions becomes red cuprite ($CuO_2 \rightarrow Cu_2O$); see [21].

saggar A container used to protect a **glazed** object from direct exposure to the **kiln** environment. It is generally a fired **clay** vessel, although due to the scarcity of fuel in ancient Egypt, it is possible that, for the sake of economy, clay and **faience** vessels could have been fired simultaneously.

self-glazing A term used to describe the faience glazing technique by which the components of the body and the **glaze** are mixed together as a **paste** and the substances responsible for the glaze, the **alkali** and **colorants**, **effloresce** onto the surface as they dry. When the object is fired, the glaze forms directly on the surface; see [151].

setter Small pieces of fired **clay** used to prevent a glazed object sticking to the bottom of the **kiln** or to other objects when fired. They are hand formed, often with a roughly conical shape to have the smallest surface area touching the object; see [178].

silica, siliceous, silicate Silicon dioxide, SiO_2. It is the primary component of **glass**, **glazes**, **faience** and **ceramics**. The most prevalent sources of silica in Egypt are sand, **quartz**, and **clay**.

sintering The heating of particles to melting point, but stopping just short of complete melting, in order to drive off volatile reaction products. The end product is generally more dense. The term describes both a stage in firing and a first step in the manufacture of materials to be used for **glass** or **glazes**. In glassmaking it is also called **fritting**.

slurry A mixture of fine-particled materials in water; when consisting of **clay** it can be used as a slip; **glaze** components can also be applied as a slurry.

soda An alkaline oxide of sodium (Na_2O) used as a **flux** in vitreous materials. Unless properly balanced **lime**, such **glasses** or **glazes** would be unstable. Compounds containing **soda**, like **natron**, are found in abundance in the desert regions of Egypt, Nubian, and the Sudan.

vitreous, vitrified To make into or become a **glass** or glassy substance.

vitreous faience A dense variety of faience with a blue core and a brighter blue glaze. It was initially identified by Lucas as "Variant D" (Lucas and Harris 1962, pp. 163–64). Recent analysis has revealed that the body is high in cobalt, soda, and alumina with no discernible copper content and low in calcium with a great deal of **instersitial glass**. The lighter blue surface is due to an applied copper **glaze** (Tite and Shortland, in press).

waster A ceramic object, whether faience or pottery, damaged by a firing error in a **kiln** and discarded; see [178].

weathering Any change in the surface of a **glass** or **glaze**, like iridescence, increased opacity or color changes, that is the result of exposure to chemicals in the environment, whether from burial or exterior conditions. For example, blue **glass** or **glazes** tend to weather to green. Weathering can affect the analysis of glass, glazes or **faience** due to the leaching of some components; see [3].

BIBLIOGRAPHY

List of Abbreviations

ÄA	*Ägyptologische Abhanlungen*
AE	*Ancient Egypt (and the East)*
AJA	*American Journal of Archaeology*
ASAE	*Annales du Service des Antiquités de l'Égypte*
BASOR	*Bulletin of the American Schools of Oriental Research*
BdÉ	*Bibliothéque d'Étude*
BES	*Bulletin of the Egyptological Seminar*
BIFAO	*Bulletin de l'Institut française d'archéologie orientale*
BMFA	*Bulletin of the Museum of Fine Arts*
BMMA	*Bulletin of the Metropolitan Museum of Art*
CdÉ	*Chronique d'Égypte*
DAI	*Deutschen Archäologischen Instituts*
DE	*Discussions in Egypology*
GM	*Göttinger Miszellen*
HÄB	*Hildesheimer Ägyptologische Beitrage*
IFAO	*Institut française d'archéologie orientale*
JAOS	*Journal of the American Oriental Society*
JARCE	*Journal of the American Research Center in Egypt*
JEA	*Journal of Egyptian Archaeology*
JEOL	*Jaarbericht van het Vooraziatisch - Egyptisch Genootshcap 'Ex Oriente Lux'*
JGS	*Journal of Glass Studies*
JNES	*Journal of Near Eastern Studies*
JSSEA	*The SSEA Journal*
KMT	*KMT. A Modern Journal of Ancient Egypt*
LÄ	*Lexikon der Ägyptologie*
MÄS	*Münchner Ägyptologische Studien*
MDAIK	*Mitteilungen des Deutschen Archäologischen Instituts, Abteilung Kairo*
MDAIR	*Mitteilungen des Deutschen Archäologischen Instituts, Römische Abteilung*
MFAB	*Museum of Fine Arts, Boston*
MIFAO	*Memoires publiés par les membres de l'Institut française d'archéologie orientale du Caire*
MIO	*Mitteilungen des Instituts für Orientforschung*
PM	B. Porter and R.B. Moss, *Topographical Dictionary of Ancient Egyptian Hieroglyphic Texts, Reliefs and Paintings*
PSBA	*Proceedings of the Society of Biblical Archaeology*
RdÉ	*Revue d'Égyptologie*
REA	*Revue de l'Égypt Ancienne*
SAK	*Studien zur altägyptischen Kultur*
SAOC	*Studies in Ancient Oriental Civilization*
SSEA	*Society for the Study of Egyptian Antiquities*
TSBA	*Transactions of the Society of Biblical Archaeology*
ZÄS	*Zeitschrift für ägyptishce Sprache und Altertumskunde. Leipzig/Berlin*

Adams 1974. Barbara Adams. *Ancient Hierakonpolis.* Warminster, 1974.

Adams 1987. Barbara Adams. *The Fort Cemetery at Hierakonpolis: excavated by John Garstang.* (*Studies In Egyptology.*) London, 1987.

Adams 1995a. Barbara Adams. "Elite Graves at Hierakonpolis," in Spencer (ed.) 1995, pp. 1–15.

Adams 1995b. Barbara Adams. *Ancient Nekhen: Garstang in the City of Hierakonopolis.* Whitstable, Kent, 1995.

Al-Rayah 1981. Al-Rayah Sanhouri Al-Rayah. *The Napatan Kingdom (c. 860 BC to 310 BC).* Ph.D. thesis, Liverpool University. Liverpool, 1981.

Aldred 1971a. Cyril Aldred. *Jewels of the Pharaohs: Egyptian Jewelry of the Dynastic Period.* London, 1971.

Aldred 1971b. Cyril Aldred. "Egypt: The Amarna Period and the End of the Eighteenth Dynasty," in *Cambridge Ancient History Vol. II*, pp. 35–40. Cambridge, 1971.

Aldred 1973. Cyril Aldred. *Akhenaten and Nefertiti.* Exhibition catalogue. London, 1973.

Aldred 1975. Cyril Aldred. "Egypt: The Amarna Period and the End of the Eighteenth Dynasty," *Cambridge Ancient History.* 3rd ed. 2, part 2, pp. 49–97. Cambridge, 1975.

Aldred 1980. Cyril Aldred. *Egyptian Art in the Days of the Pharaohs, 3100–320 B.C.* Exhibition catalogue. New York, 1980.

Aldred 1988. Cyril Aldred. *Akhenaten, King of Egypt.* London and New York, 1988.

Aldred et al. 1980. Cyril Aldred, François Daumas, Christiane Desroches-Noblecourt and Jean Leclart. *L'Égypte du crépuscule: De Tanis à Méroé, 1700 av. J.-C. – 4e siècle apr. J.-C.* Paris, 1980.

Allan 1973. J.W. Allan. "Abu' L-Qasim's treatise on ceramics," *Iran* 11 (1973), pp. 111–20.

Allen 1974. T.J. Allen. *The Book of the Dead or Going Forth by Day.* (*SAOC* no. 37). Chicago, 1974.

Allen in D'Auria et al. 1988. James Allen. "Funerary Texts and their Meaning," in D'Auria et al. 1988, pp. 38–49.

Altenmüller 1965. Hartwig Altenmüller. *Die Apotropaia und die Götter Mittelägyptens.* 2 vols. Munich, 1965.

Altenmüller 1975. Hartwig Altenmüller. "Api," *LÄ* I (1975), col. 388.

Altenmüller 1991. Hartwig Altenmüller. "Papyrusdickicht unde Wüste: Überlegungen zu zwei Statuensembles des Tutanchamun," *MDAIK* 47 (1991), pp. 11–19.

Altenmüller in Verhoeven and Graefe 1991. Hartwig Altenmüller. "Ihy beim Durchtreib durch die Furt – Bemerkungen zu Gestalt und Person eines Gottes," in Verhoven and Graefe 1991, pp. 17–27.

Altmann 1980. Jeanne Altmann. *Baboon Mothers and Infants.* Cambridge, 1980.

Andreu et al. 1997. Guillemette Andreu, Marie Hélène Rutschowsaya and Christine Ziegler. *L'Égypte ancienne au Louvre.* Paris, 1997.

Andrews 1981. Carol Andrews. *Catalogue of Egyptian Antiquities in the British Museum.* 6: *Jewellery I.* London, 1981.

Andrews 1984. Carol Andrews. *Egyptian Mummies.* London and Cambridge MA, 1984.

Andrews 1990. Carol Andrews. *Ancient Egyptian Jewellery.* London, 1990.

Andrews 1994. Carol Andrews. *Amulets of ancient Egypt.* London and Austin, 1994.

Andronicos 1975. Manolis Andronicos, Manolis Chatzidakis and Vassos Karageorghis. *The Greek Museums.* Trans. Kay Cicellis et al. Athens, 1975.

Anthes 1965. Rudolf Anthes. *Mit Rahineh 1956.* Philadelphia, 1965.

Arnold 1988. Dorothea Arnold. "Egyptian Art" The Metropolitan Museum of Art: Recent Acquisitions: A Selection 1987–1988, *BMMA* 69, no. 2 (Fall 1988), pp. 6–7.

Arnold 1992. Dieter Arnold. *The Pyramid Complex of Senwosret I.* vol. 3: *The South Cemetries of Lisht.* (*The Metropolitan Museum of Art Egyptian Expedition* 25). New York, 1992.

Arnold 1994. Dieter Arnold. *Lexikon der ägyptischen Baukunst.* Zurich, 1994.

Arnold 1995. Dorothea Arnold. "An Egyptian Bestiary," *BMMA* 52, no. 4 (Spring 1995).

Arnold 1996. Dorothea Arnold. *The Royal Women of Amarna. Images of Beauty from Ancient Egypt.* Exhibition catalogue. New York, 1996.

Arnold et al. 1978. Dorothea Arnold. *Meisterwerke Altägyptischer Keramik: 5000 Jahre Kunst und Kunsthandwerk aus Ton und Fayence: 16. September bis 30 November 1978, Hohr-Grenzhausen, Rastal-Haus.* Höhr-Grenzhausen, 1978.

Arts Council of Great Britain 1962. Arts Council of Great Britain. *5000 Years of Egyptian Art.* Exhibition catalogue. London, 1962.

Assmann 1995. Jan Assmann. *Egyptian Solar Religion in the New Kingdom. Re, Amun and the Crisis of Polytheism.* Trans. Anthony Alcock. (*Studies in Egyptology.*) London, 1995.

Aubert and Aubert 1974. Jacques-F Aubert and Liliane Aubert. *Statuettes égyptienne: chaouabatis, ouchebtis.* Paris, 1974.

Aufrère 1983. Sydney Aufrère. "Études de lexicologie et d'histoire naturelle I–III," *BIFAO* 83 (1983), pp. 1–31.

Aufrère 1991. Sydney Aufrère. *L'univers minéral dans la pensée égyptienne.* 2 vols. (*IFAO: Bibliothèque d'Étude* 105.1 and 105.2). Cairo, 1991.

Aufrère 1994. Sydney Aufrère. *L'Egypte restituée. Tome II, Sites et temples des déserts, de la naissance de la civilisation pharaonique à l'époque gréco-romaine.* Paris, 1994.

Badawy 1961. Alexander Badawy. "The Stela Irtysen," *CdÉ* 36, no. 72 (July 1961), pp. 269–76.

Badawy 1972. Alexander Badawy. "A Monumental Gateway for a Temple of King Sety I: An Ancient Model Restored," in *Miscellanea Wilbouriana* 1 (1972), pp. 1–23.

Baer 1963. Klaus Baer. "An Eleventh Dynasty Farmer's Letters to his Family," *JAOS* 83 (1963), pp. 1–19.

Baines 1985a. John Baines. "Color Terminolgy and Color Classification: Ancient Egyptian Color Terminology and Polychromy," *American Anthropologist* 87, no. 2 (1985), pp. 282–97.

Baines 1985b. John Baines. "Theories and universals of representation: Heinrich Schäfer and Egyptian Art," *Art History* 8, no. 1 (March 1985), pp. 1–25.

Baines 1989. John Baines. "Communication and display: the integration of early Egyptian art and writing," in *Antiquity* 63, no. 240 (1989), pp. 471–83.
Baines 1990. John Baines. "Restricted knowledge, hierarchy, and decorum: modern perceptions and ancient institutions," *JARCE* 27 (1990), pp. 1–23.
Baines and Málek 1980. John Baines and Jaromir Málek. *Atlas of Ancient Egypt.* Oxford and New York, 1980.
Baines et al. 1988. John Baines et al. (eds.). *Pyramid Studies and other essays presented to I.E.S. Edwards.* London, 1988.
Banks 1939. Miriam A. Banks. "The Mummies of Nes-min," *Bulletin of the Museum of Art, Rhode Island School of Design* 27, no. 1 (July 1939), pp. 21–30.
Barag in Oppenheim et al. 1970. Dan Barag. "Mesopotamian core-formed glass vessels (1500–50 B.C.)," in Oppenheim et al. 1970, pp. 131–200.
Bard 1994. Kathryn Bard. *From Farmers to Pharaohs.* (*Monographs in Mediterranean Archaeology.*) Sheffield, 1994.
Barta 1970. Winifred Barta. *Das Selbstzeugnis eines altägyptischen Künstlers. (Stele Louvre C 14.)* (*MÄS* 22.) Berlin, 1970.
Baum 1988. N. Baum. *Arbres et arbustes de l'Égypte ancienne. La liste de la tombe thébaine d'Ineni (no. 81).* Hildesheim, 1969.
Becher 1985. Ilse Becher. "Augustus und der Kult der ägyptischen Götter," *Klio* 67, no. 1 (1985), pp. 61–64.
Beinlich 1984. Horst Beinlich. *Die "Osirisreliquien": zum Motiv der Korperzergliederung der altägyptischen Religion.* (*Ägyptologische Abhandlungen* 42.) Wiesbaden, 1984.
Bell 1990. Martha R. Bell. "An Armchair Excavation of KV 55," *JARCE* 27 (1990), pp. 97–137.
Bellion 1987. Madeleine Bellion. *Catalogue des manuscrits hiéroglyphiques et des dessins, sur papyrus, cuir, ou tissu, publiés ou signalés.* Pau, 1987.
Bénédite 1911. Georges Bénédite. *Catalogue général des antiquités égyptiennes du Musée du Caire.* v. 55: *Piegnes (nos. 44301–446638).* Cairo, 1911.
Beningson and Coplin 1992. Robin Beningson and Joseph Coplin, Antiquarium Ltd. *Myth and Majesty: Deities and Dignitaries of the Ancient World.* New York, 1992.
Berg 1990. David Berg. "Some Ramesside Fragments," *SAK* 17 (1990), pp. 75–106, pls. 1–4.
Berlandini 1983. Jocelyne Berlandini. "La déesse bucéphale: une iconograpie particulière de l'Hathor memphite," *BIFAO* 83 (1983), pp. 33–50, pls 1–2.
Berman and Letellier 1996. Larry M. Berman and Bernadette Letellier. *Pharaohs: Treasures of Egyptian Art from the Louvre.* Exhibition catalogue. Cleveland, 1996.
Berman in Kozloff and Bryan 1992a. Larry M. Berman. "Amenhotep III and His Times," in Kozloff and Bryan 1992, pp. 33–66.
Berman in Kozloff and Bryan 1992b. Larry M. Berman. "Bookplate of Amenhotep III," cat. no. 101, in Kozloff and Bryan 1992, p. 399.
Bernand 1981. Éttienne Bernand. *Receuil des inscriptions grècques du Fayoum.* 3: *La "Méris" de Polémôn.* (*IFAO: Bibliothèque d'Études* 30). Cairo, 1981.
Besques 1984. Simone Besques. "Un nouveau fragment d'oenochoé Ptolémaïque en faïence," in Nicola Bonacasa and Antonio di Vita (eds.). *Alessandria e il mondo ellenistico-romano,* pp. 273–76, pl. 48. (*Studi e Materiali* 5.) Rome, 1984.
Beyer 1982. Dominique Beyer, "Double Godet," no. 294 in *Naissance de l'écriture; cunéiform et hiéroglyphes,* p 346. Exhibition catalogue. Paris, 1982.
Bianchi 1980. Robert S. Bianchi in Kamal el-Mallakh, *Treasures of the Nile,* pp. 41–43. New York, 1980.
Bianchi 1983a. Robert S. Bianchi. "Those Ubiquitous Glass Inlays from Pharaonic Egypt: Suggestions about Their Functions and Dates," *JGS* 25 (1983), pp. 29–35.
Bianchi 1983b. Robert S. Bianchi. "Those Ubiquitous Glass Inlays, Part II," *BES* 5 (1983), pp. 9–29.
Bianchi 1992. Robert S. Bianchi. "Review of *The Canonical Tradition in Ancient Egyptian Art* by Whitney Davis, 1983," *JAOS* 112, no. 2 (1992), pp. 328–30.
Bianchi 1993. Robert S. Bianchi. "De Rogato Artium Elegantiorum Alexandrinarum," in *Bulletin de la Société archéologique d'Alexandrie* 45 (1993), pp. 35–44.
Bianchi 1995. Robert S. Bianchi. "Gods, State and People in Ancient Egypt," *Minerva* 6, no. 4 (1995), pp. 30–31.
Bianchi 1996a. Robert S. Bianchi. "Pharaonic Egyptian Elements in the Decorative Arts of Alexandria During the Hellenistic and Roman Periods," in The J. Paul Getty Museum. *Alexandria and Alexandrianism. Papers Delivered at a Symposium Organized by the J. Pual Getty Museum and The Getty Center for the History of Art and the Humanities and Held at the Museum April 22–25, 1993,* pp.191–202. Malibu, 1996.
Bianchi 1996b. Robert S. Bianchi. *Splendors of Ancient Egypt from the Egyptian Museum, Cairo.* Exhibition catalogue. London, 1996.
Bianchi 1996c. Robert S. Bianchi. "Faience and Glaze" in J. Turner (ed.) *The Dictionary of Art,* pp. 46–49. London, 1996.
Bianchi et al. 1988a. Robert S. Bianchi et al. *The Age of Cleopatra. The Art of Late Dynastic and Graeco-Roman Egypt.* Exhibition catalogue. New York, 1988.
Bianchi et al. 1988b. Robert S. Bianchi et al. *Cleopatra's Egypt: Age of the Ptolemies.* Exhibition catalogue. Brooklyn, 1988.
Bianchi in Celenko 1996a. Robert S. Bianchi. "The Case Against Extensive Masking in Egypt," in Celenko (ed.) 1996, pp. 75–77.
Bianchi in Celenko 1996b. Robert S. Bianchi. "Tattooing and Skin Painting in the Ancient Nile Valley," in Celenko (ed.) 1996, pp. 81–83.
Bianchi in Fazzini et al. 1989. Robert S. Bianchi. "Female Fecundity Figurine," cat. no. 26, in Fazzini et al. (eds.) 1989.
Bianchi in Johnson 1992. Robert Stephen Bianchi. "The Cultural Transformation of Egypt as Suggested by a Group of Enthroned Male Figures from the Faiyum." in Janet H. Johnson (ed.) *Life in a Multi-Cultural Society. Egypt from Cambyses to Constantine and Beyond,* pp. 15–214. Chicago, 1992.
Bianchi in Rubin 1988. Robert S. Bianchi. "Tattoo in Ancient Egypt," in Rubin (ed.) 1988, pp. 21–28.
Bienkowski and Southworth 1986. Piotr Bienkowski and Edmund Southworth. *Egyptian Antiquities in the Liverpool Museum.* 1: *A List of the Provenanced Ojects.* Warminster, 1986.
Bierbrier 1982. Morris L. Bierbrier. *The Tomb-Builders of the Pharaohs.* London and New York, 1982.
Bierbrier in D'Auria et al. 1988. Morris L. Bierbrier. "Set of canopic jars," cat. no. 117, in D'Auria et al. 1988, p. 164.
Bietak 1975. Manfred Bietak. *Tell el-Dab'a II.* Vienna, 1975.
Bietak 1981. Manfred Bietak. *Avaris and Piramesse: Archaeological Exploration in the Eastern Nile Delta.* Oxford, 1981.
Bigelow et al. 1991
D. Bigelow, E. Cornu, G.J. Landrey and C. van Horne (eds.). *Gilded Wood: Conservation and History.* Madison, Connecticut, 1991.
Bimson and Freestone 1987. M. Bimson and I.C. Freestone (eds.). *Early Vitreous Materials.* (*Occasional Paper (British Museum)* no. 56.) Oxford, 1987.
Binns et al. 1932. C.F. Binns, M. Klem and H. Mott. "An experiment in Egyptian blue glaze," *Journal of the American Ceramic Society* 15 (1932), pp. 271–72.
Bissing 1902. W. von Bissing. *Fayencegefäße.* Vienna, 1902.
Bissing 1907. W. von Bissing. *Steingefäße.* Vienna, 1907.
Bissing 1941. W. von Bissing. *Die Fussboden aus dem Palast des Königs Amenophis IV. zu el Hawara.* Munich, 1941.
Black 1987. James Black (ed.). *Recent Advances in Archaeological Conservation.* London, 1987.
Blackman 1937. A.M. Blackman. "Preliminary Report on the Excavations at Sesebi, Northern Province, Anglo-Egyptian Sudan, 1936–37," *JEA* 23 (1937), pp. 145–51, pls. 12–19.
Blanquet in Obsomer and Oosthoek 1992
Claire-Hélène Blanquet. "Typologie de la bouteille de nouvel an," in Obsomer and Oosthoek 1992, pp. 49–54.
Bleeker 1963. C.J. Bleeker. "Isis as a Savior-Goddess," in S.G.F. Brandon (ed.), *The Savior God. Comparative Studies in the Conception of Salvation presented to Edwin Oliver James.* Manchester, 1963, pp. 1–16.
Boeser 1913. P.A.A. Boeser. *Beschreibung der Aegyptischen Sammlung des Niederländischen Reichmuseums der Alterümer in Leiden. Die Denkmäler des Neuen Reiches. Dritte Abteilung. Stelen.* Haag, 1913.
Bonnet 1952. Hans Bonnet. *Reallexikon der ägyptischen Religionsgeschichte.* Berlin, 1952.
Borchardt 1897. Ludwig Borchardt. *Die aegyptische Pflanzensäule.* Berlin, 1897.
Borchardt 1909. Ludwig Borchardt. *Das Grabdenkmal des Königs Nefer-ir-ke-re.* Leipzig, 1909.
Borchardt 1932. Ludwig Borchardt. "Eine Holzschachtel mit Darstellung einer ländlichen Szene in Nubien," in S.R.K. Glanville (ed.). *Studies Presented to F. Ll. Griffith,* pp. 257–62. London, 1932.
Borchardt and Ricke 1980. Ludwig Borchardt and Herbert Ricke. *Die Wöhnhäuser in Tell el-Amarna.* Berlin, 1980.
Borchardt et al. 1913. Ludwig Borchardt et al. *Das Grabdenkmal des Königs Sa hu-re.* (Ausgrabungen der Deutschen Orient-Gesellschaft in Abusir, 1902–1908, vol. VII.) Leipzig. 1913.
Boreux 1932a. Charles Boreux. *Musée du Louvre – Antiquités égyptiennes – Catalogue-guide.* Paris, 1932.
Boreux 1932b. Charles Boreux. *Guide-catalogue sommaire. Département des Antiquités égyptiennes.* 2 vols. Paris, 1932.
Bosse-Griffiths 1975. Kate Bosse-Griffiths. "The Use of Disc-Beads in Egyptian Bead-Compositions," *JEA* 61 (1975) pp. 114–24.
Bosse-Griffiths 1978. Kate Bosse-Griffiths. "Some Egyptian Bead-Work Faces in the Wellcome Collection at University College, Swansea," *JEA* 64 (1978), pp. 90–106, pls. 15–16.
Bothmer 1951. Bernard V. Bothmer. "A Hippopotamus Statuette of the Middle Kingdom," *MFAB* 49 (1951), pp. 98–102.
Bothmer 1985. Bernard V. Bothmer. "The Brussels-Brooklyn Statue of Bakenrenef (Membra Dispersa

IV)" *Mélanges Gamal Eddin Mokhtar* I (BdÉ 97, 1), pp. 99–103. Cairo, 1985.
Bothmer in Hall 1987a. Bernard V. Bothmer. "Four-Headed Ram," cat. no. 26, in Emma Swan Hall (ed.), *Antiquities from the collection of Christos G. Bastis*, pp. 73–74. Mainz, 1987.
Bothmer in Hall 1987b. Bernard V. Bothmer. "Man of Experience." in Emma Swann Hall (ed.) *Antiquities from the Collection of Christos G. Bastis*, . pp. 93–94. Mainz, 1987.
Bothmer and de Meulenaere in Lesko 1986. Bernard V. Bothmer and Herman de Meulenaere. "The Brooklyn Statuette of Hor, son of Pawen (with an excursus on eggheads)," in Lesko 1986, pp. 1–15.
Bourriau 1981. Janine L. Bourriau. *Umm el-Ga'ab: Pottery from the Nile Valley before the Arab Conquest.* Exhibition catalogue. Cambridge, 1981.
Bourriau 1984. Janine L. Bourriau. "Museum Acquisitions, 1982," *JEA* 70 (1984), pp. 130.
Bourriau 1988a. Janine L. Bourriau. *Pharaohs and Mortals: Egyptian Art in the Middle Kingdom.* Exhibition catalogue. Cambridge, 1988.
Bourriau 1988b. Janine L. Bourriau. "Hippopotamus, Frog, and Jerboa," cat no. 112, in Bourriau 1988, pp. 120–21.
Bourriau in Brovarski et al. 1982. Janine L. Bourriau. "Dish on stand," cat. no. 120, in Brovarski et al. 1982, p. 129.
Bourriau in Quirke 1991. Janine L. Bourriau. "Patterns of change in burial customs during the Middle Kingdom," in Quirke 1991, pp. 3–20.
Bourriau in Vassilika 1995. Janine L. Bourriau. "Hedgehog and Jerboa," cat no.16, in Vassilika 1995, p. 40–41.
Boyce in Kemp 1989. Andrew Boyce. "Notes on the Manufacture and Use of Faience Rings at Amarna" in Kemp 1989, pp. 160–68.
Boyce in Kemp 1995. Andrew Boyce. "Collar and necklace designs at Amarna: A preliminary study of faience pendants," in Kemp 1995, pp. 336–71.
Breasted 1906. James Henry Breasted. *Ancient Records of Egypt.* 2: *The Eighteenth Dynasty.* New York, 1906.
Brewer and Friedman 1989. Douglas J. Brewer and Renée Friedman. *Fish and Fishing in Ancient Egypt.* Warminster, 1989.
Brill 1963. H. Brill. "Ancient Glass," *Scientific American* (Nov 1963), pp. 120–30.
British Museum 1922. British Museum. *A Guide to the Fourth, Fifth, and Sixth Egyptian Rooms, and the Coptic Room.* London, 1922.
British Museum 1971. British Museum. *A General Guide to the Egyptian Collections in the British Museum.* London, 1971.
Brooklyn Museum 1956. Brooklyn Museum. *Five Years of Collecting Egyptian Art 1951–1956.* John D. Cooney. Exhibition catalogue. Brooklyn, 1956.
Broucke in Matheson 1994. Pieter B.F.J. Broucke. "Tyche and the Fortune of Cities in the Greek and Roman World," in Matheson 1994, pp. 34–49.
Brovarski 1987. Edward Brovarski (ed.). *A Table of Offerings. Seventeen Years of Acquisitions of Egyptian and Ancient Art by William Kelly Simpson for the Museum of Fine Arts, Boston.* Boston, 1987.
Brovarski 1991. Edward Brovarski. "The Louvre Mastabas of Akhehotep and Lexicograhical Notes on Ancient Egyptian Jewellery," *ARCE, Annual Meeting, Boston: April 26–28, 1991, Programs and Abstracts*, pp. 32–33. Boston, 1991.
Brovarski et al. 1982. Edward Brovarski, Susan K. Doll and Rita E. Freed. *Egypt's Golden Age: The Art of Living in the New Kingdom 1558–1085 B.C.* Exhibition catalogue. Boston, 1982.
Brovarski in Brovarski et al. 1982a. Edward Brovarski. "Blue-lotus chalice," cat. no. 145, in Brovarski et al. 1982, p. 146.
Brovarski in Brovarski et al. 1982b. Edward Brovarski. "Blue-green pyxis with domed lid," cat. no. 158, in Brovarski et al. 1982, p. 151.
Brovarski in Brovarski et al. 1982c. Edward Brovarski. "Basket with lid," cat. no. 159, in Brovarski et al. 1982, p. 151.
Brunner-Traut 1955. Emma Brunner-Traut. "Die Wochenlaube," *MIO* 3 (1955) pp. 11–30.
Brunner-Traut and Brunner 1981. Emma Brunner-Traut and Hellmut Brunner. *Die Ägyptische Sammlung der Universität Tübingen.* 2 vols. Mainz, 1981.
Brunton 1937. Guy Brunton. *Mostagedda and Tasian culture: 1st and 2nd years 1928, 1929.* London, 1937.
Brunton and Caton-Thompson 1928. Guy Brunton and Gertrude Caton-Thompson. *The Badarian Civilisation and Predynastic Remains near Badari.* (*British School of Archaeology in Egypt* 46.) London, 1928.
Brunton and Engelbach 1927. Guy Brunton and Reginald Engelbach. *Gurob.* (British School of Archaeology, pub. 41.) London, 1927.
Bryan in Kozloff and Bryan 1992a. Betsy M. Bryan. "Shawabty of Lady Sati," cat. no. 70, in Kozloff and Bryan 1992, p. 328.
Bryan in Kozloff and Bryan 1992b. Betsy M. Bryan. "Head of Amenhotep III Wearing the Round Wig," cat. no. 8, in Kozloff and Bryan 1992, p. 159–61.
Bryan in Kozloff and Bryan 1992c. Betsy M. Bryan. "Head of Amenhotep III Wearing the Khepresh Crown," cat. no. 9, in Kozloff and Bryan 1992, p. 162–63.
Budge 1925 (1989). E.A. Wallis Budge. *The Mummy: A Handbook of Egyptian Funerary Archaeology.* 2nd ed. 1989, reprint of 1925 edition. New York, 1925 (1989).
Budischovsky and Genaille 1988. Marie-Christine Budi ovsky and Nicole Genaille. "Les stèles égyptiennes du Musée de Rennes (suite) Imen-Rekh," *Annales de Bretagne et des pays de l'ouest* 95, no. 3 (1988), pp. 225–46.
Bull 1942. Ludlow Bull. "An Egyptian Funerary Model of a Helmet," *BMMA* 37, no. 2 (Feb. 1942), pp. 41–42.
Bulletin RISD 1931. *Bulletin of the Rhode Island School of Design.* vol. XIX, no. 1, Jan. 1931.
Bulletin RISD 1939. *Bulletin of the Rhode Island School of Design.* vol. XXVII, no. 1, 1939.
Bulté 1991. Jeanne Bulté. *Talismans égyptiens d'heureuse maternité. Faïence bleu vert à pois foncés.* Paris, 1991.
Burkhalter 1990. Fabienne Burkhalter. "Les statuettes en bronze d'Aphrodite en Egypte romaine d'après les documents papyrologiques," *Revue archéologique* no. 1 (1990), pp. 51–60.
Burlington Fine Arts Club 1922. *Catalogue of an Exhibition of Ancient Egyptian Art.* Exhibition catalogue. London, 1922.
Burnham 1978. Robert Burnham, Jr. *Burnham's Celestial Handbook: An Observer's Guide to the Universe Beyond the Solar System.* New York, 1978.
Cambridge Ancient History 1973. *The Cambridge Ancient History.* 2, part 1: *History of the Middle East and Aegean Region c. 1800–1380 BC.* I.E.S. Edwards (ed.). Cambridge, 1973.
Cambridge Ancient History 1975. *The Cambridge Ancient History.* 2, part 2: *History of the Middle East and Aegean Region c.1380–1000 BC.* I.E.S. Edwards (ed.). Cambridge, 1975.
Caminos 1954. Ricardo A. Caminos. *Late-Egyptian Miscellanies.* Oxford, 1954.
Capart 1905. Jean Capart. *Primitive Art in Egypt.* London, 1905.
Capart 1927, 1931. Jean Capart. *Documents pour servir à l'étude de l'art égyptien.* 2 vols. Paris, 1927, 1931.
Capart 1937. Jean Capart. "Clepsydres égyptiennes," *CdÉ* 12 (1937), pp. 45–49.
Capart 1939. Jean Capart. "Hippotames en faience," *Bulletin des musées royal d'art et d'histoire* 11, no. 5 (Sept/Oct 1939), pp. 109–12.
Capart 1947. Jean Capart. *L'Art égyptien.* 4: *Les arts mineurs.* Paris, 1947.
Capel and Markoe 1996. Anne K. Capel and Glenn E. Markoe (eds.). *Mistress of the House, Mistress of Heaven: Women in Ancient Egypt.* Exhibition catalogue. New York, 1996.
Carnarvon and Carter 1912. G. Herbert, Earl of Carnarvon, and Howard Carter. *Five Years' Explorations at Thebes. A Record of Work Done 1907–1911.* London, 1912.
Carter 1927. Howard Carter. *The Tomb of Tut.ankh.Amen.* 2 vols. London, 1927.
Carter et al. 1904. Howard Carter, Percy E. Newberry and Gaston Maspero. *The Tomb of Thouthomsis IV.* London, 1904.
Castel and Soukiassian 1985. Georges Castel and Georges Soukiassian. "Dépôt de stèles dans le sanctuaire du Nouvel Empire au Gebel Zeit," *BIFAO* 85 (1985), pp. 285–93, pls. 40–44.
Castel and Soukiassian 1989. Georges Castel and Georges Soukiassian. *Gebel El-Zeit.* 1: *Les mines de galène (Égypte, IIe millénnaire av. J.-C.).* (*IFAO: Fouilles* 35.) Cairo, 1989.
Cauville 1987a. Sylvie Cauville. "À propos des désignations de la palette de scribe," *RdÉ* 38 (1987), pp. 185–87.
Cauville 1987b. Sylvie Cauville. "Les statues cultuelles de Dendera d'après les inscriptions pariétales," *BIFAO* 87 (1987), pp. 73–117, pls. 15–19.
Cauville 1990. Sylvie Cauville. *Le Temple de Dendera: guide archéologique.* (*IFAO: Bibliothèque générale* 12.) Cairo, 1990.
Celenko 1996. Theodore Celenko (ed.). *Egypt in Africa.* Indianapolis, 1996.
Cerny 1927. J. Cerny. "Le culte d'Amenophis Ier chez les ouvriers de la nécropole thébaine," *BIFAO* 27, no. 2 (1927), pp. 159–203, pls 1–9.
Charvat 1980. Petr Charvát. "The Bes Jug: Its Origin and Development in Egypt," *ZÄS* 107 (1980), pp. 46–52.
Chase and Pease 1942. George Henry Chase and Mary Zelia Pease. *Corpus Vasorum Antiquorum.* U.S.A. fasc. 8: *United States of America: Fogg Museum and Gallatin Collections.* Cambridge, MA, 1942.
Cheshire 1986. Wendy Cheshire. "Demotic writings of 'Tebtynis'," *Enchoria* 14 (1986), pp. 31–42.
Christie's 1992. Christie's. *The "Per-neb" Collection (Part I). Highly Important Egyptian Antiquities.* Auction catalogue. London, 1992.
Clark 1959. Kenneth Clark. *The Nude: a Study in Ideal Form.* London and New York, 1959.
Clayton 1994. Peter A. Clayton. *A Chronicle of the Pharaohs: the Reign-by-Reign Record of the Rulers and Dynasties of Ancient Egypt.* London and New York, 1994.
Clère 1929. J.J. Clère. "Monuments inédits des serviteurs dans la place de vérité," *BIFAO* 28 (1929) pp. 173–201.
Cline 1985. Eric Cline. "Amenophis III and the Aegean," *AJA* 89, no. 2 (April 1985), pp. 327–28.

Cline 1988. Eric Cline. "An Unpublished Egyptian Plaque from Mycenae," *AJA* 92 (1988), p. 254.
Cooney 1956. John D. Cooney. "Didactic Trivia of Egyptian Art," *The Brooklyn Museum Bulletin* 17, no. 2 (Winter 1956), pp. 3–10.
Cooney 1960. John D. Cooney. "Glass Sculpture in Ancient Egypt." *JGS* 2 (1960), pp. 11–43.
Cooney 1976. John D. Cooney. *Catalogue of the Egyptian Antiquities in the British Museum.* 4: *Glass.* London, 1976.
Cooney in Muscarella 1974a. John D. Cooney. "Bes as Attendant," cat. no. 211, in Muscarella 1974, unpaginated.
Cooney in Muscarella 1974b. John D. Cooney. "Architectural Tile," cat. no. 214, in Muscarella 1974, unpaginated.
Cooney in Muscarella 1974c. John D. Cooney. "Horus Falcon," cat. no. 216, in Muscarella 1974, unpaginated.
Cooney in Muscarella 1974d. John D. Cooney. "Genre Group." cat. no. 173, in Muscarella 1974, unpaginated.
Cooper 1972. Emanuel Cooper. *A History of World Pottery.* London, 1972.
Corcoran 1995. Lorelei H. Corcoran. *Portrait Mummies from Roman Egypt: (I–IV centuries A.D.).* (*SAOC* no. 56.) Chicago, 1995.
Corteggiani 1979. J.-P. Corteggiani. *L'Égypte des pharaons au musée du Caire.* Paris, 1979.
Coulson and Leonard 1981. William D.E. Coulson and Albert Leonard. *Cities of the Delta.* 1: *Naukratis: Preliminary Report on the 1977–1978 and 1980 Seasons.* Malibu, 1981.
Curto and Mancini 1968. Silvio Curto and M. Mancini. "News of Kha' and Meryt," *JEA* 54 (1968), pp. 77–81, pls. 12–13.
Curto in Roveri 1988c. Silvio Curto. "Concrete Space and Symbology: Ritual Architecture" in Roveri 1988c, pp. 14–97.
D'Amicone in Eggebrecht 1987. Elvira D'Amicone. "Fayenceshale," cat. no. 84, in Eggebrecht 1987, p. 169.
D'Auria et al. 1988. Sue D'Auria, Peter Lacovara and Catherine H. Roehrig. *Mummies and Magic: The Funerary Arts of Ancient Egypt.* Exhibition catalogue. Boston, 1988.
Dambach and Wallert 1966. M. Dambach and I. Wallert. "Das Tilapia-Motiv in der altägyptischen Kunst," *CdÉ* 41 (1966) p. 273–94.
Darby et al. 1977. William J. Darby, Paul Ghalioungui and Louis Grivetti. *Food: The Gift of Osiris.* 2 vols. New York, 1977.
Daressy 1905. M. Georges Daressy. *Catalogues générale des antiquités égyptiennes du Musée du Caire.* 28, 29: *Statues de Divintés (nos. 38001–39384).* Cairo, 1905.
Daressy 1911. M. Georges Daressy. "Plaquettes émaillées de Médinet-Habou," *ASAE* XI (1911) pp. 49–63.
Dasen 1993. Véronique Dasen. *Dwarfs in Ancient Egypt and Greece.* Oxford, 1993.
Daumas 1970. François Daumas. "Les objets sacrés de la déese Hathor à Dendera," *RdÉ* 22 (1970), pp. 63–78, pl. 5.
Davies 1902. Norman de Garis Davies. *The Rock Tombs of Deir el-Gebrâwi.* 2 parts. (*Archaeological Survey of Egypt* Memoirs 11 and 12.) London, 1902.
Davies 1905. Norman de Garis Davies. *The Rock Tombs of El Amarna* 2. London, 1905.
Davies 1906. Norman de Garis Davies. *The Rock Tombs of El Amarna* 4. London, 1906.
Davies 1908. Norman de Garis Davies. *The Rock Tombs of El Amarna* 6. London, 1908.
Davies 1923. Norman de Garis Davies. "Akhenaten at Thebes," *JEA* 9 (1923) pp. 132–52.
Davies 1930. Norman de Garis Davies. *The Tomb of Ken-Amun at Thebes.* 2 vols. (*Metropolitan Museum of Art Egyptian Expedition* 5.) New York, 1930.
Davies 1941. N. M. and N. de G. Davies. "Syrians in the Tomb of Amunedjeh," *JEA* 27 (1941) pp. 96–98.
Davies 1991. W. Vivian Davies (ed.). *Egypt and Africa: Nubia from prehistory to Islam.* London, 1991.
Davies and Gardiner 1926. Norman de Garis Davies and A. Gardiner. *The Tomb of Huy.* London, 1926.
Davies in Davies 1991. W. Vivian Davies. "Egypt and Africa in the British Museum," in Davies 1991, pp. 315–20, pls. 13–16.
Davis 1907. Theodore M. Davis. *The Tomb of Iouiya and Touiyou.* London, 1907.
Davis 1910. Theodore M. Davis. *The Tomb of Queen Tîyi.* London, 1910.
Davis 1981. Whitney Davis. "Egypt, Samos, and the Archaic Style in Greek Sculpture," *JEA* 67 (1981), pp. 61–81.
Davis 1989. Whitney Davis. *The Canonical Tradiition in Ancient Egyptian Art.* Cambridge, 1989.
Dayton 1978. J.E. Dayton. *Minerals, Metals, Glazing, and Man.* London, 1978.
de Meulenaere 1962. Herman de Meulenaere. "Une statue de prêtre héliopolitain," *BIFAO* 61 (1962), pp. 29–42, pl. 1.
de Meulenaere 1987a. Herman de Meulenaere. "Une statue de prêtre héliopolitain," *BIFAO.* Cairo, 1962, p. 29.
de Meulenaere 1987b. Herman de Meulenaere. "E pluribus una," *BIFAO* 87 (1987), pp. 135–40, pls. 21–22.
de Meulenaere 1989
Herman de Meulenaere. "Notes de prosopographie thébaine," *Cdé* 64 (1989), pp 169–75.
Decker 1992. Wolfgang Decker. *Sports and Games of Ancient Egypt.* Trans. Allen Guttmann. New Haven, 1992.
Decker and Herb 1994. Wolfgang Decker and M. Herb. *Bildatlas zum Sport im Alten Ägypten.* 2 vols. (*Handbook of Oriental Studies* 14.1 and 14.2.) New York, 1994.
Del Francia 1984. Loretta Del Francia. "Un tessuto copto con nascita di Afrodite," in *Alessandria e il mondo ellenistico-romano. Studi in onore di A. Adriani, 2.* Rome, 1984, pp. 209–21.
Delange and Ziegler 1980. Elisabeth Delange and Christiane Ziegler. *La Vie au bord du Nil au temps des pharaons.* Exhibition catalogue. Calais, 1980.
Delange in Eggebrecht 1987. Elisabeth Delange. "Pyramidion des Cha," cat. no. 299, in Eggebrecht 1987, p. 348.
Der Manuelian 1996. Peter Der Manuelian (ed.). *Studies in Honor of William Kelly Simpson.* 2 vols. Boston, 1996.
Der Manuelian in Brovarski et al. 1982. Peter Der Manuelian. "Table with splayed legs," cat. no. 45, in Brovarski et al. 1982, p. 73–74.
Derchain 1952. Philippe Derchain. "Bébon, le dieu et les mythes," *RdÉ* 9 (1952), pp. 23–47.
Derchain 1975a. Philippe Derchain. "La Perruque et le cristal," *SAK* 2 (1975), pp. 55–74.
Derchain 1975b. Philippe Derchain. "Le lotus, la mandragore et le perséa," *CdÉ* 50 (1975), pp. 65–86.
Derchain 1990. Philippe Derchain. "L'auteur du papyrus Jumilhac," *RdÉ* 41(1990), pp. 9–30.
Derchain in Martin 1981. Philippe Derchain. "Appendix K" in G.T. Martin, *The Sacred Animal Necropolis at North Saqqara.* London, 1981.
Desroches 1943. Christine Desroches. "Le papyrus," *La Feuille blanche* 3 (1943), pp. 1–3.
Desroches-Noblecourt 1961. Christiane Desroches-Noblecourt. *L'Art égyptien.* Paris, 1961.
Desroches-Noblecourt 1963. Christiane Desroches-Noblecourt. *Tutankhamun: Life and Death of a Pharaoh.* London and New York, 1963.
Desroches-Noblecourt and Kuentz 1968. Christiane Desroches-Noblecourt and Charles Kuentz. *Le petit Temple d'Abou Simbel.* 2 vols. Cairo, 1968.
Desroches-Noblecourt et al 1976. Christiane Desroches-Noblecourt et al. *Ramses le Grand.* Exhibition catalogue. Paris, 1976.
Devauchelle 1986. D. Devauchelle. "Wasseruhr," *LÄ* VI. 1986, cols. 1156–157.
Doll in Brovarski et al. 1982. Susan K. Doll. "Fish," cat. no. 155, in Brovarski, et al. 1982, p. 150.
Donadoni 1959. Sergio Donadoni. *Arte egizia.* Turin, 1959.
Donatelli in Roveri 1988a. Laura Donatelli. "Measuring Instruments, Tools, and Weapons," in Roveri 1988a, pp. 160–87.
Donatelli in Roveri 1988b. Laura Donatelli. "Small Objects in Ancient Egyptian Funerary Equipment," in Roveri 1988b, pp. 198–211.
Doran and Hodson 1975. J.E. Doran and F.R. Hodson. *Mathematics and Computers in Archaeology.* Cambridge, 1975.
Dorman et al. 1987. Peter Dorman, Prudence Olive Harpur and Holly Pitman. *The Metropolitan Museum of Art: Egypt and the Ancient Near East.* Exhibition catalogue. New York, 1987.
Drenkhahn 1967. Rosemarie Drenkhahn. *Darstellungen von Negern in Ägypten.* Hamburg, 1967.
Drenkhahn and Schmitz 1985. Rosemarie Drenkhahn and Bettina Schmitz. *Nofret – Die Schöne: die Frau im alten Ägypten.* Exhibition catalogue. Mainz, 1985.
Drenkhahn in Sasson et al. 1995. Rosemarie Drenkhahn "Artisans and Artists in Pharaonic Egypt," in Sasson et al. 1995, vol. 1, pp. 331–43.
Dreyer 1986. Günter Dreyer. *Elephantine.* VIII: *Der Tempel der Satet: die Funde der Frühzeit und des alten Reiches.* (*DAIK* 39.) Mainz, 1986.
Drioton 1959. É. Drioton. "Nouvel An (Fête du). I. Dans l'Égypte ancienne," in *Dictionnaire de la Bible, Supplément* fasc. 32 (1959), p. 555.
Droste zu Hülshoff 1980. Vera von Droste zu Hülshoff. *Der Igel im alten Ägypten.* (*HÄB* 11.) Hildesheim, 1980.
Dunbabin 1940. Thomas James Dunbabin (ed.). *Perachora: The Sanctuaries of Hera Akraia and Limenia. Excavations of the British School of Archaeology at Athens 1930–1933.* 2: *Pottery, Ivories, Scarabs, and Other Objects from the Votive Deposit of Hera Limenia excavated by Humphrey Payne.* Oxford, 1940
Dunham 1950, 1955–65. Dows Dunham. *The Royal Cemeteries of Kush.* 5 vols. 1: *El Kurru.* 2: *Nuri.* 4: *Royal Tombs at Meroe and Barkal.* 5: *The West and South Cemeteries at Meroe.* Cambridge, 1950–1965.
Dunham 1978. Dows Dunham. *Zawiyet el-Aryan. The Cemeteries Adjacent to the Layer Pyramid.* Boston, 1978.
Dunham 1982. Dows Dunham. *Excavations at Kerma* 6. Boston, 1982.
DuQuesne 1996. Terence DuQuesne. *Black and Gold God.* (*Oxfordshire Communications in Egyptology* 5). London, 1996.
Eaton-Krauss and Graefe 1990. Marianne Eaton-Krauss and Erhart Graefe (eds.). *Studien zur ägyptischen Kunstgeschichte.* (*HÄB* 29.) Hildesheim, 1990.

Eaton-Krauss in Brovarski et al. 1982. Marianne Eaton-Krauss. "'Jewelry' and jewelry entries," in Brovarski et al. 1982, pp. 227–50.
Edgar 1907. C.C. Edgar. "The treasure of Tell Basta in Le Musée Egyptien," *Recueil de monuments et de notices sur les fouilles d'Égypte. t. II.* 1907, pp. 93–108.
Edwards 1939. I.E.S. Edwards. "The Late Sir Robert Mond's Bequest," in *British Museum Quarterly* 13, no. 2 (1939), pp. 41–45, pls. 19–24.
Edwards 1964. I.E.S. Edwards (ed.). *A General Introductory Guide to the Egyptian Collections in the British Museum.* London, 1964
Edwards 1976. I.E.S. Edwards. *Tutankhamun's Jewelry.* London and New York, 1976.
Eggebrecht 1984. Arne Eggebrecht. *Das Alte Ägypten: 3000 Jahre Geschichte und Kultur des Pharaonen-reichs.* Munich, 1984.
Eggebrecht 1987. Arne Eggebrecht (ed.). *Ägyptens Aufstieg zur Weltmacht.* Exhibition catalogue. Mainz, 1987.
Eggebrecht 1991. Arne Eggebrecht. *Das Grab des Nacht. Kunst und Geschichte eines Beamtengrabes der 18. Dynastie in Theben-West.* Mainz, 1991.
Eggebrecht et al. 1993. Arne Eggebrecht et al. (eds.). *Pelizaeus-Museum Hildesheim: Die Ägyptische Sammlung.* Mainz, 1993.
Egypt Museum 1984. *The Czechoslovak Institute of Egyptology, Prague and Cairo, and Egyptian Antiquities Organization,* 25. Exhibition catalogue. Cairo, 1984.
Eisenberg 1997. Jerome M. Eisenberg. *Amulets.* Unpublished manuscript. 1997.
Eisenberg forthcoming. Jerome M. Eisenberg. *An Encyclopedia of Egyptian Antiquities.* New York, forthcoming.
El Mallakh and Brackman 1978. Kamal el Mallakh and Arnold Brackman. *The Gold of Tutankhamun.* New York, 1978.
Emery 1938. W.B. Emery. *Excavations at Saqqara: The Tomb of Hemaka.* Cairo, 1938.
Emery 1954. W.B. Emery. *Great Tombs of the First Dynasty.* 2 vols. London, 1954.
Emery 1961. W.B. Emery. *Archaic Egypt.* Harmondsworth, 1961.
Epigraphic Survey 1970. The Epigraphic Survey. *The Eastern High Gate with Translations of Texts.* Medinet Habu VIII, Oriental Institute Publications 94, Chicago 1970.
Erman and Grapow 1936. Adolf Erman and Hermann Grapow. *Royal Tombs at Meroe and Barkal.* (vol 4 of *The Royal Cemeteries of Kush.* Dows Dunham (ed.)). Boston, 1936.
Erman and Grapow 1931. Adolf Erman and Hermann Grapow (eds.). *Wörterbuch der Aegyptischen Sprache.* 5 vols. Leipzig, 1931.
Eton College 1990. Eton College. *Eton 1440–1990: Portrait, programme and catalogue.* Windsor, 1990.
Evers 1929. Hans Gerhard Evers. *Staat und Stein: Denkmäler Geschichte und Bedeutung der Ägptischen Plastick während des mittleren Reiches.* 2 vols. Munich, 1929.
Fairman 1935. H.W. Fairman. "The Myth of Horus at Edfu–I," *JEA* 21(1935), pp. 26–36.
Fakhry 1943. A. Fakhry. "A Note on the Tomb of Kherenuef at Thebes," *ASAE* LII. Cairo, 1943.
Fay 1990. Biri Fay. *Egyptian Museum Berlin.* 4th ed. Mainz, 1990.
Fay 1992. Biri Fay. *Egyptian Museum Berlin.* Mainz, 1992.
Fay 1995. Biri Fay "More Old Kingdom Sphinxes with Human Hands," *GM* 146 (1995) pp. 29–30.
Fazzini 1975. Richard A. Fazzini. *Images for Eternity: Egyptian Art from Berkeley and Brooklyn.* Exhibition catalogue. Brooklyn, 1975.
Fazzini 1988. Richard A. Fazzini. *Egypt: Dynasty XXII–XXV.* (*Iconography of Religions* section 16: Egypt fasc. 10). Leiden, 1988.
Fazzini et al. 1989. Richard A. Fazzini, Robert S. Bianchi, James F. Romano and Donald B. Spanel. *Ancient Egyptian Art in the Brooklyn Museum.* Brooklyn, 1989.
Feucht 1967. Erika Feucht. *Die königlichen Pektorale, Motive, Sinngehalt und Zweck.* Hamburg, 1967.
Feucht 1971. Erika Feucht. "Pektorale nichtköniglicher Personen." *ÄA* 22. Wiesbaden, 1971.
Firchow 1955. Otto Firchow (ed.). *Ägyptologische Studien.* (*Deutsche Akademie doer Wissenschaften zu Berlin* 29.) Berlin, 1955.
Firth 1927. C.M. Firth. *Archaeological Survey of Nubia: Report for 1910–1911* Cairo, 1927.
Fischer 1965. Henry George Fischer. "Anatomy in Egyptian Art," *Apollo* (September 1965), pp. 169–75.
Fischer 1966. Henry G. Fischer. "Egyptian Turtles," *BMMA* 24, no. 6 (Feb. 1966), pp. 193–200.
Fischer 1968. Henry G. Fischer. *Ancient Egyptian Representations of Turtles.* (*The Metropolitan Museum of Art Papers.* no. 13.) New York, 1968.
Fischer 1977 (1980). Henry G. Fischer. "Hunde," *LÄ* III, part 1. Wiesbaden, 1977 (1980), cols. 77–81.
Fischer 1986. Henry G. Fischer. *L'écriture et l'art de l'Égypte ancienne.* Paris, 1986.
Florida International Museum 1996. Florida International Museum. *Macedonians: The Northern Greeks.* Exhibition catalogue. Athens, 1996.
Forman and Quirke 1996. Werner Forman and Stephen Quirke. *Hieroglyphs and the Afterlife in Ancient Egypt.* London and Norman, Oklahoma, 1996.
Foster 1979. Karen P. Foster. *Aegean Faience of the Bronze Age.* New Haven, 1979.
Frankfort 1929. H. Frankfort. *The Mural Painting of El-Amarneh.* London, 1929.
Frankfort and Pendlebury 1933. Henri Frankfort and J.D.S. Pendlebury. *The City of Akhenaten.* Part 2: *The North Suburbs and the Desert Altars. The Excavations at Tell el Amarna during the Seasons 1926–1932.* (*Egypt Exploration Society* 40.) London, 1933.
Freed 1983. Rita. E. Freed *Ramesses the Great.* Memphis, 1983.
Freed 1987. Rita E. Freed. *Ramesses the Great.* Exhibition catalogue. Boston, 1987.
Freed in Brovarski et al. 1982. Rita E. Freed. "Wigs and Hair Accessories," in Brovarski et al. 1982, pp. 196–97.
Freeman 1997. Charles Freeman. *The Legacy of Ancient Egypt.* Advisory editor John D. Ray. New York, 1997.
Friedman 1995. Florence Dunn Friedman. "The Underground Relief Panels of King Djoser at the Step Pyramid Complex," *JARCE* 32 (1995), pp. 1–42.
Friedman in Der Manuelian 1996. Florence Dunn Friedman. "Notions of Cosmos in the Step Pyramid Complex," in Der Manuelian 1996, pp. 337–51.
Gaballa 1979. G.A. Gaballa. "False-door stelae of some Memphite personnel," *SAK* 7 (1979), pp. 41–52, pls. 1–3.
Galeries Nationales du Grand Palais 1982. Galeries nationales du Grand Palais. *Naissance de l'écriture: cunéform et hiéroglyphes.* Jean-Paul Boulanger and Genèviève Renisio. Exhibition catalogue. Paris, 1982.
Gamer-Wallert 1970. I. Gamer-Wallert. *Fische und Fischkulte im alten Agypten.* Wiesbaden, 1970.
Gardiner 1957. Alan Gardiner. *Egyptian Grammar, Being an Introduction to the study of Hieroglyphs.*(1st ed. 1927; 3rd ed. rev. 1957). London, 1957.
Gardiner 1969. Alan Gardiner. *The Admonitions of an Egyptian Sage from a Hieratic Papyrus in Leiden, Pap. Leiden 344 recto.* Hildesheim 1969.
Garstang 1907. John Garstang. *The Burial Customs of Ancient Egypt as Illustrated by the Tombs of the Middle Kingdom.* London, 1907.
Garstang 1911. John Garstang. *Meroë: The City of the Ethiopians.* Oxford, 1911.
Gehrig 1983. Ulrich Gehrig. *Tierbilder aus Vier Jahrtausenden: Antiken der Sammlung Mildenberg.* Mainz, 1983.
George 1980. Beate George. "Drei altägyptische Wurfhölzer," *Medelhavsmuseet Bulletin* 15 (1980), pp. 7–15.
George 1981. Beate George. "'Geheimer Kopf' – 'Kopf aus Lapislazuli'," in *Medelhavsmuseet Bulletin* 16 (1981), pp. 15–38.
Germer 1985. Renate Germer. *Flora des pharaonischen Ägypten.* (*MDAIK* 14.) Mainz, 1985.
Gessler-Löhr 1983. Beatrix Gessler-Löhr. *Die heiligen Seen ägyptischer Tempel. Ein Beitrag zur Deutung sakraler Baukunst im alten Ägypten.* Hildesheim, 1983.
Gitton 1976. Michel Gitton. "La résiliation d'une fonction religieuse: Nouvelle interprétation de la stèle de donation d'Ahmès Néfertary," *BIFAO* 76 (1976), pp. 65–89, pl. 14.
Gitton 1979. Michel Gitton. "Nouvelles remarques sur la stèle de donation d'Ahmès Néfertary," *BIFAO* 79 (1979), pp. 327–31.
Goedicke 1996. Hans Goedicke. "The So-called Ushebtis of King Merneptah," in *Bulletin de la société d'égyptologie de Genève* 20 (1996), pp. 19–27.
Goffoet in Obsomer and Oosthoek 1992. Jeanine Goffoet. "Notes sur les sandals et leur usage dans l'Égypte pharaonique," in Obsomer and Oosthoek 1992, pp. 111–23.
Gold 1983. D. Gold. "More than Mummies," *Horizon,* vol. 26, no 6 (1983), p. 4.
Goldstein in Brovarski et al. 1982. Sidney M. Goldstein. "Fish-shaped flask," cat. no. 179, in Brovarski et al. 1982, p. 165.
Goresy and Schiegl in DuQuesne 1996. Ahmed E. Goresy and Solveig Schiegl. "Annex 1. Ancient Egyptian Pigments and Faiences" in DuQuesne 1996, pp. 63–64.
Goring et al. 1997. Elizabeth Goring, Nicholas Reeves and John Ruffle (eds.). *Chief of Seers: Egyptian Studies in Memeory of Cyril Aldred.* London, 1997.
Goto 1968. S. Goto. *The Great Museums of the World. vol. I. Musée du Louvre.* Tokyo, 1968.
Goyon 1972. Jean-Claude Goyon. *La confirmation du pouvoir royal au novel an.* (*Bulletin des Études: IFAO* v. 52) Cairo, 1972.
Goyon 1974. Jean-Claude Goyon. *Confirmation du pouvoir royal au nouvel an.* (*Brooklyn Museum Papyrus 47.218.50.*) (*Bulletin des Études: IFAO* v. 52.) Cairo, 1975.
Goyon 1975. Jean-Claude Goyon. "Textes mythologiques II. Révélations du mystère des quatre boules," *BIFAO* 75 (1975), pp. 349–400.
Gray 1966. P.H.K. Gray. "Radiological Aspects of the Mummies of Ancient Egyptians in the Rijksmuseum van Oudheden, Leiden," *Oudheidkundige Mededelingen uit het Rijksmuseum van Oudheden te Leiden,* no. 47 (1966), pp. 1–30, pls 1–31.
Green 1993. L. Green. "More than a Fashion Statement: Clothing and Hairstyles as Indicators of Social Status in Ancient Egypt," *Bulletin of the Canadian Society for Mesopotamian Studies* 26 (1993), pp. 29–38.

Green in Arnold 1996. L. Green. "The Royal Women of Amarna: Who was Who," in Arnold 1996, pp. 7–15.

Greene 1961. Charles H. Greene. "Glass," *Scientific American*, vol. 204, no. 1 (January 1961), pp. 92–105.

Greenwich Library 1979a. Hurlbutt Gallery, Greenwich Library. *Divine, Domestic and Desert Animals in Ancient Egyptian Art.* Exhibition catalogue. Greenwich, Connecticut, 1979.

Greenwich Library 1979b. Greenwich Library. *The Face of Egypt.* Greenwich, Connecticut, 1979.

Grenier 1987. Jean-Claude Grenier. "Le protocole pharaonique des empereurs romains," *RdÉ* 38 (1987), pp. 81–104.

Griffith 1921a. F. Ll. Griffith. "Oxford Excavations in Nubia, part I," *Annals of Archaeology and Anthropology* 8, no. 1 (1921), pp. 1–18, pls. 1–5.

Griffith 1921b. F. Ll. Griffith. "Oxford Excavations in Nubia, continued," *Annals of Archaeology and Anthropology* 8, nos. 3 and 4 (1921), pp. 65–104, pls. 9–29.

Grimal 1957. Pierre Grimal. "Vénus et l'immortalité," *Homages à Waldena Deona.* (*Collection Latomus.* vol. 28.) 1957, pp. 258–62.

Grimal 1992. Nicholas Grimal. *A History of Ancient Egypt.* Trans. Ian Shaw. Oxford, 1992.

Grimm 1972. Günter Grimm. "Two Early Imperial Faience Vessels from Egypt," *Miscellanea Wilbouriana* 1. 1972.

Grimm 1990. Günter Grimm. "Repliken griechisher Meisterwerke und hellenistischer Herrscherporträts aus dem ptolemäischen Ägypten?," in *DAI, Akten des XIII. Internationalen Kongresses für klassische Archäologie Berlin 1988.* Mainz, 1990, p. 450.

Grzymski 1994. Krzystof Grzymski. "A Statuette of Nefertem on a Lion," *Homages à Jean Leclant: Nubie, Soudan, Éthiopie.* 2. (*IFAO: Bibliothèque d'Études.* vol. 106.2.) 1994, pp. 199–202.

Guidotti 1991. Maria Cristina Guidotti. *Vasi dall'epoca protodinastica al nuovo regno.* Rome, 1991.

Gurney 1990. O.R.Gurney. *The Hittites.* London, 1990.

Hall 1926. H.R. Hall. "An Egyptian Royal Bookplate: The Ex-Libris of Amenophis III and Teie," *JEA* 12 (1926), pp. 30–33.

Hall 1927. H.R. Hall. "Three Hippopotamus-Figures of the Middle Kingdom," *JEA* 13 (1927), pp. 57–58, pls. XXII–XXIII.

Hall 1981. Rosalind Hall. "Fish-Net Dresses in the Petrie Museum," in *GM*, no. 42 (1981), pp. 37–43 and pls. 1–2.

Hall 1987. Emma Swan Hall (ed.). *Antiquities from the Collection of Christos G. Bastis.* Exhibition catalogue. New York, 1987.

Hall 1995–1996. Rosalind Hall. "An Ancient Egyptian Erotic Fashion: Fishnet Dresses," *KMT* 6 (1995–1996), pp. 41–47.

Hall and Barnett 1985. Rosalind Hall and J. Barnett. "A Fifth Dynasty Funerary Dress in the Petrie Museum of Egyptian Archaeology: Its Discovery and Conservation," *Textile History* (1985), pp. 5–22.

Hamada 1947. A. Hamada. "Statue of the Fan-Bearer," *ASAE* 47 (1947), pp. 15–21, pls. 3–5.

Hamza 1930. Mahmud Hamza. "Excavations of the Department of Antiquities at Quantîr (Faqûs district)," *ASAE* 30 (1930), pp. 31–68, pls. 1–4.

Hanke 1978. R. Hanke. *Amarna-Reliefs aus Hermopolis, HÄB* 2. Hildesheim, 1978.

Hardin 1988. C.L. Hardin. *Color for Philosophers: Uweaving the Rainbow.* Indianapolis, 1988.

Hari 1985. Robert Hari. *New Kingdom Amarna Period. The Great Hymn to Aten.* Leiden, 1985.

Hart 1986. George Hart. *A Dictionary of Egyptian Gods and Goddesses.* London, 1986.

Harvard University and the Museum of Fine Arts, Boston a. Harvard University and the Museum of Fine Arts, Boston. *Giza.* (*Boston Expedition Diary* 15, part 4). Boston.

Harvard University and the Museum of Fine Arts, Boston b. Harvard University and the Museum of Fine Arts, Boston. *Egypt.* (*Boston Expedition Diary* 11). Boston.

Hassan 1932. Selim Hassan. *Excavations at Giza.* 1: *1929–1930.* Oxford, 1932.

Hatchfield and Newman in Bigelow et al. 1991. Pamela Hatchfield and Richard Newman. "Ancient Egyptian Gilding Methods," in Bigelow et al. 1991, pp. 27–47.

Hayes 1937. William C. Hayes. *Glazed Tiles from a Palace of Ramesses II at Kantir.* Metropolitan Museum of Art, Paper No. 3. New York, 1937.

Hayes 1953. William C. Hayes. *The Scepter of Egypt: A background for the study of the Egyptian antiquities in the Metropolitan Museum of Art.* Part 1: *From Earliest Times to the End of the Middle Kingdom.* Cambridge, 1953.

Hayes 1990 (1959). William C. Hayes. *The Scepter of Egypt: A background for the study of the Egyptian antiquities in the Metropolitan Museum of Art.: The Hyksos Period and the New Kingdom (1675–1088 BC).* 4th edition, revised. New York, 1990 (1959).

Haynes and Leprohon 1987. J.L. Haynes and R. Leprohon. "Napatan Shawabtis in the Royal Ontario Museum" *JSSEA 17*, no. 1–2. (1987), pp. 18–32.

Heerma van Voss 1977 (1980). Matthieu Heerma van Voss. "Horuskinder," *LÄ* III, cols. 52–53.Wiesbaden, 1977 (1980).

Helck 1957. Wolfgang Helck. *Urkunden der 18. Dynastie.* 20 Berlin, 1957.

Helck 1958. Wolfgang Helck. "Ramessidische Inschriften aus Karnak I. Eine Inschrift Ramses' IV," *Zeitschrift für Ägyptische Sprache und Altertumskunde* 82 (1958) pp. 117–40 with addendum on p. 146.

Helck 1960. Wolfgang Helck. *Materialien zur Wirtschaftsgeschichte des Neuen Reiches.* Mainz and Wiesbaden, *c.* 1960–*c.* 1970.

Helck 1982. Wolfgang Helck. "Palette (Screib-)," *LÄ* IV, no. 5, cols. 656–58, Wiesbaden, 1982.

Helck in Verhoeven and Graefe 1991. Wolfgang Helck. "Zu Ptah und Sokar," in Verhoeven and Graefe 1991, pp. 159–164.

Henein and Gout 1974. Nessim Henry Henein and Jean–François Gout. *Le verre soufflé en Égypte.* (*Bibliothèques des Études: IFAO* v. 63.) Cairo, 1974.

Hermann 1932. Alfred Hermann. "Das Motiv der Ente mit zurückgewendetem Kofpe im ägyptischen Kunstgewerbe," in *ZÄS* 68 (1932), pp. 86–105, pls. 7–11.

Hermsen 1981. Edmund Hermsen. *Lebensbaumsymbolik im alten Ägypten.* Cologne, 1981.

Herrmann 1985. Christian Herrmann. *Formen für ägyptische Fayencen.* Göttingen, 1985.

Hibbard 1980. Howard Hibbard. *The Metropolitan Museum of Art.* New York, 1980.

Hochfield and Riefstahl 1978. S. Hochfield and E. Riefstahl (eds.). *Africa in Antiquity, the Arts of Ancient Nubia and the Sudan.* Vol. I: *The Essays.* Exhibition catalogue. Brooklyn, 1978

Hoffman 1988. Michael Hoffman. *The First Egyptians: an exhibition.* Exhibition catalogue. Columbia, South Carolina, 1988.

Hölbl 1979. Günther Hölbl. *Beziehungen der ägyptischen Kultur zu Altitalien.* 2 vols. Leiden, 1979.

Holden in Brovarski et al. 1982. Lynn H. Holden. "Frog amulet," cat. no. 353, in Brovarski et al. 1982, pp. 251–52.

Holladay 1982. John S. Holladay. *Tell el-Maskhuta (Preliminary Report on the Wadi Tumilat Project 1978–1979).* Part 3: *Cities of the Delta.* William D.E. Coulson and Albert Leonard (eds.). (*American Research Center in Egypt Reports* 6.) Malibu, 1982.

Hölscher 1941. Uvo Hölscher. *The Excavation of Medinet Habu.* 3, part 1: *The mortuary temple of Ramses III.* (*University of Chicago Oriental Institute Publications* 54.) Chicago, 1941.

Hölscher 1951. Uvo Hölscher. *The Excavation of Medinet Habu.* 4, part 2: *The mortuary temple of Ramses III.* (*University of Chicago Oriental Institute Publications* 55.) Chicago, 1951.

Holthoer 1977. Rotislav Holthoer. *New Kingdom Pharaonic Sites: The Pottery.* (*The Scandinavian Joint Expedition to Sudanese Nubia* 5: 1.) Copenhagen, 1977.

Hornblower 1929. G.D. Hornblower. "Predynastic Figures of Women and their Successors," in *JEA* 15 (1929), pp. 29–47, pls. 6–10.

Hornemann 1951–69. Bodil Hornemann. *Types of Ancient Egyptian Statuary.* 7 vols. Copenhagen, 1951–1969.

Hornung 1990. Erik Hornung. *The Valley of the Kings: Horizon and Eternity.* Trans. David Warburton. New York, 1990.

Hornung and Staehelin 1976. Erik Hornung and Elisabeth Staehelin. *Skarabäen und andere Siegelamulette aus Basler Sammlungen.* Mainz, 1976.

Houlihan 1986. Patrick F. Houlihan. *The Birds of Ancient Egypt.* Warminster, 1986.

Houlihan 1996. Patrick F. Houlihan. *The Animal World of the Pharaohs.* London and Cairo, 1996.

Hoving 1975. Thomas Hoving. *The Chase, the Capture: Collecting at the Metropolitan.* New York, 1975.

Hugonot 1989. Jean-Claude Hugonot. *Le Jardin dans l'Égypte ancienne.* Frankfurt, 1989.

Hüttner 1995. Michaela Hüttner. *Mumienamulette im Totenbrauchtum der Spätzeit: eine Untersuchung an Objekten in der ägyptischen Sammlung des Kunsthistorischen Museums.* (*Beiträge zur Ägyptologie* 12.) 1995.

International Congress of Egyptology 1992. International Congress of Egyptology. *Sesto Congresso Internazionale di Egittolgia.* 2 vols. Turin, 1992.

Israelit-Groll 1990. Sarah Israelit-Groll (ed.). *Studies in Egyptology Presented to Miriam Lichtheim.* 2 vols. Jerusalem, 1990.

J.C. 1936. J(ean) C(apart). "Le sceptre en verre, de Sésostris," *CdÉ* 11, no. 2 (1936), pp. 484–87.

James 1962. Thomas Garnet H. James. *The Hekanakhte Papers and Other Early Middle Kingdom Documents.* New York, 1962.

James 1974a. Thomas Garnet H. James. *Corpus of hieroglyphic Inscriptions in the Brooklyn Museum.* 1: *From Dynasty I to the End of Dynasty XVIII.* (*Wilbour Monographs* no. 6.) Brooklyn, 1974.

James 1974b. Thomas Garnet H. James. *The Hekanakhte papers and other early Middle Kingdom documents.* (*Metropolitan Museum of Art Egypt Expedition* 19.) New York, 1974.

James 1979. Thomas Garnet H. James. *An Introduction to Ancient Egypt.* London, 1979.

James 1985. Thomas Garnet H. James. *Egyptian Painting and Drawing in the British Museum.* London, 1985.

James in Dunbabin 1940. Thomas Garnet H. James. "The Egyptian-Type Objects," in Dunbabin 1940. pp 191–202.

Janssen 1981. R. Hall Janssen. "Fish-net Dresses in the Petrie Museum," *GM* 42 (1981) pp. 37–46.
Janssen 1995–96. Rosalind Janssen. "An Ancient Egyptian Erotic Fashion: Fishnet Dresses," *KMT* 6, no. 4 (Winter 1995–96), pp. 41–47.
Janssen and Janssen 1989. Rosalind Janssen and Jack Janssen. *Egyptian Household Animals.* (*Shire Egyptology* 12). Aylesbury, 1989.
Jick in D'Auria et al. 1988. Millicent Jick. "Bead-net dress," cat. no. 9, in D'Auria et al. 1988, pp. 78–79.
Johnson 1992. Janet H. Johnson (ed.). *Life in a Multi-Cultural Society. Egypt from Cambyses to Constantine and Beyond.* (*SAOC* 51.) Chicago, 1992.
Johnson 1996. W.R. Johnson. "Amenhotep III and Amarna: Some New Considerations," *JEA* 82 (1996), pp. 65–82, pls. IV–VIII.
Jones and Uhl 1996. J. Jones and M. Uhl (eds.). *Under One Roof in the Royal Museum, Edinburgh.* Edinburgh, 1996.
Junge in Eaton-Krausss and Graefe 1990. F. Junge. "Anhang: Harmonia und Dissonant," in Eaton-Krauss and Graefe 1990, pp. 1–38.
Junker 1925. H. Junker. *Ermenne: Bericht über die Grabungen der Akademie der Wissenschaften in Wien.* Vienna and Leipzig, 1925.
Kaczmarczyk and Hedges 1983. A. Kaczmarczyk and R.E.M. Hedges (eds.). *Ancient Egyptian Faience: An Analytical Survey of Egyptian Faience from Predynastic to Roman Times.* Warminster, 1983.
Kaiser 1967. Werner Kaiser. *Staatliche Museen Preussischer Kulturbesitz. Ägypticher Museum Berlin,* Berlin, 1967.
Kákosy 1977a. László Kákosy. "Frosch," *LÄ* II, cols. 334–35. Wiesbaden, 1977.
Kákosy 1977b. László Kákosy. "Heqet," *LÄ* II, cols. 1123–124. Wiesbaden, 1977.
Kákosy 1978 (1980). László Kákosy. "Ischedbaum," *LÄ* III, part 2, cols. 182–83. Wiesbaden, 1978 (1980).
Kaplony 1975. Peter Kaplony. "Aha," *LÄ* I, cols. 94–96. Wiesbaden, 1975.
Kaplony 1977. Peter Kaplony. "Hedjwer," *LÄ* II, cols. 1078–80. Wiesbaden, 1977.
Katalog 1976. *Katalog, Staatliche Sammlung Ägyptischer Kunst,* 2. Munich, 1976.
Kayser 1969. Hans Kayser. *Ägyptisches Kusnthandwerk.* Braunschweig, 1969.
Kees 1958. H. Kees. "Die weisse Kapelle Sesostris I. In Karnak und das Sedfest," *MDAIK* 16, part 2 (1958), pp. 194–213, pl. 15.
Keimer 1924. Ludwig Keimer. *Die Gartenflanzen im alten Ägypten.* 2 vols. Hamburg, 1924.
Keimer 1929a. Ludwig Keimer. "Sur quelques petits fruits en faïence émaillée datant du moyen empire," *BIFAO* 28 (1929), pp. 49–97, pls. 1–8.
Keimer 1929b. Ludwig Keimer. "Nouvelles recherches au sujet du *Potamogeton lucens L.* dans l'Égypte ancienne et remarques sur l'ornamentation des hippopotames en faïence du moyen empire," *REA* 2 (1920), pp. 210–53.
Keimer 1944. Ludwig Keimer. "L'horreur des Égyptiens pour les démons du désert," *Bulletin de l'Institut d'Égypte* 26 (1944), pp. 135–47.
Keimer 1948. Ludwig Keimer. "La signification de l'hiéroglyphe rd...," *ASAE* 48 (1948), pp. 89–108.
Keimer 1984. Ludwig Keimer. *Die Gardenpflanzen im alten Ägypten* 2. Mainz, 1984.
Kelly 1976. Allyn Kelly. *The Pottery of Ancient Egypt.* Toronto, 1976.
Kemp 1968. Barry J. Kemp. "The Osiris Temple at Abydos," *MDAIK* 23 (1968), pp. 138–55.
Kemp 1987. Barry J. Kemp (ed.). *Amarna Reports 4.* London, 1987.
Kemp 1989a. Barry J. Kemp (ed.). *Amarna Reports 5.* London, 1989.
Kemp 1989b. Barry J. Kemp. *Ancient Egypt: Anatomy of a Civilization.* London, 1989.
Kemp 1995. Barry J. Kemp (ed.). *Amarna Reports 6.* London, 1995.
Kemp and Merrillees 1980. Barry J. Kemp and Robert S. Merrillees. *Minoan Pottery in Second Millennium Egypt.* Mainz, 1980.
Kendall 1978. Timothy Kendall. *Passing through the Netherworld: The Meaning and Play of Senet, an Ancient Egyptian Funerary Game.* Board game and booklet. Belmont, MA, 1978.
Kendall 1982. Timothy Kendall. *Kush, Lost Kingdoms of the Nile: a loan exhibition from the Museum of Fine Arts, Boston, September 1981–August 1984.* With historical introduction written in collaboration with Susan K. Doll. Brockton, MA, 1982.
Kendall in Brovarski et al. 1982a. Timothy Kendall. "Games," in Brovarski et al. 1982, pp. 263–66.
Kendall in Brovarski et al. 1982b. Timothy Kendall. "The House," in Brovarski et al. 1982, pp. 25–34.
Kiefer 1968. Charles Kiefer. "Les ceramiques bleues pharaoniques et leur procedé revolutionnaire d'émaillage," *Industrie Ceramique* (May 1968), pp. 395–402.
Kiefer and Allibert 1971. Charles Kiefer and A. Allibert. "Pharaonic blue ceramics: the process of self-glazing," *Archaeology* 24, no. 2 (April 1971), pp. 107–17.
Killen 1994a. Geoffrey Killen. *Ancient Egyptian Furniture.* 2: *Boxes, Chests and Footstools.* Warminster, 1994.
Killen 1994b
Geoffrey Killen. *Egyptian Woodworking and Furniture.* (*Shire Egyptology*) Prince's Risborough, 1994.
Kingery and Vandiver 1986
W. David Kingery and Pamela B. Vandiver. *Ceramic Masterpieces: Art, Structure, and Technology.* New York, 1986.
Kingery et al. 1976
W. David Kingery, H.K. Bowen and D.R. Uhlmann. *Introduction to Ceramics.* 2nd ed. New York, 1976.
Kiss 1984. Zsolt Kiss. *Études sur le portrait impérial romain en Égypte.* Warsaw, 1984.
Kitchen 1973. Kenneth A. Kitchen. *The Third Intermediate Period in Egypt (1100–650 BC).* Warminster, 1973.
Kitchen 1982
Kenneth A. Kitchen. *Pharaoh Triumphant, the Life and Times of Ramesses II.* Warminster, 1982.
Koenig 1994. Yvan Koenig. *Magie et magiciens dans l'Égypte ancienne.* Paris, 1994.
Kondeatis and Maitland 1996. Christos Kondeatis and Sara Maitland. *The Ancient Egypt Pack.* New York, 1996.
Kozloff 1974. Arielle P. Kozloff. "Three Ancient Near Eastern Celebrations and a Guest of Honor," in *Bulletin of the Cleveland Museum of Art* 61, no. 1 (1974), pp. 14–26.
Kozloff 1981. Arielle P. Kozloff (ed.). *Animals in Ancient Art from the Leo Mildenberg Collection.* Exhibition catalogue. Cleveland, 1981.
Kozloff 1982. Arielle P. Kozloff. "Frog Amulet," cat. no. 7, in Jenifer Niels (ed.) *The World of Ceramics: Masterpieces from the Cleveland Museum of Art.* 1982, p. 6.
Kozloff 1990. Arielle P. Kozloff. "A Capital Faience Cosmetic Box," *The Bulletin of the Cleveland Museum of Art* 77, no. 3 (March 1990), pp. 104–11.
Kozloff 1996. Arielle P. Kozloff. "Blue Bes," *The Cleveland Museum of Art Members Magazine* 36, no. 1 (January 1996), pp. 4–5.
Kozloff and Bryan 1992. Arielle P. Kozloff and Betsey M. Bryan (eds.). *Egypt's Dazzling Sun: Amenhotep III and his World.* With Lawrence Berman. Exhibition catalogue. Cleveland, 1992.
Kozloff in Goring et al. 1997. Arielle P. Kozloff. "The Malaqata/ El Amarna Blues: Favourite Colours of Kings and Gods," in Goring et al. 1997, pp. 78–192.
Kozloff in Kozloff 1981a. Arielle P. Kozloff. "Swimming Hippopotamus," cat. no. 46, in Kozloff 1981, pp. 59–61.
Kozloff in Kozloff 1981b. Arielle P. Kozloff. "Animals in Ancient Egypt," cat. nos. 45–66, in Kozloff 1981, pp. 59–77.
Kozloff in Kozloff and Bryan 1992a. Arielle P. Kozloff. "Bowl with Luteplayer and Monkey," cat. no. 109, entry in Kozloff and Bryan 1992, p. 408.
Kozloff in Kozloff and Bryan 1992b. Arielle P. Kozloff. "Bowl with Nile Fish and Lotuses," cat. no. 108, entry in Kozloff and Bryan 1992, p. 407.
Kozloff in Kozloff and Bryan 1992c. Arielle P. Kozloff. "Footed Dish," cat. no. 107, in Kozloff and Bryan 1992, p. 406.
Kozloff in Kozloff and Bryan 1992d. Arielle P. Kozloff. "Frog," cat. no. 120 in Kozloff and Bryan 1992, p. 431.
Kozloff in Kozloff and Bryan 1992e. Arielle P. Kozloff. "Glass Vessels," Kozloff and Bryan 1992, pp. 373–82.
Kozloff in Kozloff and Bryan 1992f. Arielle P. Kozloff. "King's Necklace Terminal in the Form of a Lotus Blossom," cat. no. 124, in Kozloff and Bryan 1992, p. 445.
Kozloff in Kozloff and Bryan 1992g. Arielle P. Kozloff. " Molded and Carved Vessels and Figurines," in Kozloff and Bryan 1992, pp. 393–97.
Kozloff in Kozloff and Bryan 1992h. Arielle P. Kozloff. "Ointment Flask Inscribed for Amenhotep III and Tiy," cat. no. 100, in Kozloff and Bryan 1992, p. 398.
Kozloff in Kozloff and Bryan 1992i. Arielle P. Kozloff. "Running or Dancing Bes," cat. no. 35, in Kozloff and Bryan 1992, pp. 226–27.
Kozloff in Kozloff and Bryan 1992j. Arielle P. Kozloff. "Perfume Bottle in the Shape of a Nile Fish," cat. no. 95, in Kozloff and Bryan 1992, pp. 386–88.
Kozloff in Kozloff and Bryan 1992k. Arielle P. Kozloff. "Tomb Decoration: Paintings and Relief Sculpture," in Kozloff and Bryan 1992, pp. 261–83.
Kuhlmann 1977. Klaus P. Kuhlmann. *Der Thron im alten Ägypten: Untersuchungen zu Semantik, Ikonographie und Symbolik eines Herrschaftszeichens.* Gluckstadt, 1977.
Kühne 1969. J. Kühne. *Zer Kenntnis silikatischer Werkstoffe und der Technologie ihrer Herstellung im 2. Jahrtausend vor unserer Zeitrechnung.* Berlin, 1969.
Kurth 1989. Dieter Kurth. "Zu ... in medizinschen Texten," *GM* 111 (1989), pp. 81–83.
Kurth 1990. Dieter Kurth. *Der Sarg der Teüris. Eine Studie zum Totenglauben im römerzeitlichen Ägypten.* Mainz, 1990.
Kyrieleis 1975. Helmut Kyrieleis. *Bildnisse der Ptolemäer.* 2 vols. (*DÄI* 2). Berlin, 1975.
La Rocca et al. 1976 (1981). Eugenio La Rocca, Arnold de Vos, and Mariette de Vos. *Guida archeologica di Pompei.* Milan, 1976.
Lacovara and Roth in D'Auria et al. 1988. Peter Lacovora and Ann Macy Roth. "Model coffin and shawabti," cat. no. 55, in D'Auria et al. 1988, p. 126.

Lacovara in D'Auria et al. 1988. Peter Lacovora. "Female Figurine," cat. no. 52, in D'Auria et al. 1988, p. 124.
Lacovara in Der Manuelian 1996. Peter Lacovora. "A Faience Tile of the Old Kingdom," in Der Manuelian 1996, pp. 487–91.
Lauer 1936. Jean-Philippe Lauer. *Fouilles à Saqqarah.* 5 vols. *La Pyramide à Degrés.* Cairo, 1936.
Lauer 1938. Jean-Philippe Lauer. "Restauration et transfert au Musée Égyptien d'un panneau ornés de faïences bleues, éxtrait de la pyramide à Degrés à Saqqarah," *ASAE* 38 (1938), pp. 551–65, pls. 50–51.
Lauer 1962. Jean-Philippe Lauer. *Histoire monumentale des pyramides d'Égypte.* 1: *Les Pyramides à Degrés (IIIe dynastie).* (*IFAO: Bibliothèque d'Étude* 39.) Cairo, 1962.
Lauer 1976. Jean-Philippe Lauer. *Saqqara: The Royal Cemetery of Memphis: excavations and discoveries since 1850.* London and New York, 1976.
Leclant 1980. Jean Leclant. *Ägypten II. Das Grossreich, 1560–1070 v. Chr.* Munich, 1980.
Leclant in Vercoutter et al. 1976. Jean Leclant. "Egypt, Land of Africa, in the Greco-Roman World," in Vercoutter et al. 1976, pp. 269–85.
Leospo in Roveri 1988a. Enrichetta Leospo. "Woodworking: Furniture and Cabinetry," in in Roveri 1988a, pp. 120–59.
Lesko 1986. Leonard H. Lesko (ed.). *Egyptological Studies in Honor of Richard A. Parker Presented on the Occasion of his 78th Birthday, December 10, 1983.* Hanover, New Hampshire, 1986.
Lesko 1994. Barbara Lesko. "Rank, Roles and Rights," in Leonard H. Lesko (ed.). *Pharaoh's Workers: The Villagers of Deir el Medina,* pp. 15–39. Ithaca, 1994.
Letellier 1971. Bernadette Letellier. "Découverte d'une tête colossale de Sésostris III à Karnak," *Kêmi* (1971), p. 175.
Letellier in Berman and Letellier 1996. Bernadette Letellier. "A Short History of the Louvre's Department of Egyptian Antiquities," in Berman and Letellier 1996, pp. 15–21.
Lewis 1881. T. Hayter Lewis. "Tel-el Yahoudeh." *TSBA* VII, pt. 2 (1881), pp. 177ff.
Lichtheim 1973, 1975. Miriam Lichtheim. *Ancient Egyptian Literature.* 1: *The Old and Middle Kingdoms.* (Paperback edition 1975). Berkeley, 1973.
Lichtheim 1976. Miriam Lichtheim. *Ancient Egyptian Literature.* 2: *The New Kingdom.* Berkeley, 1976.
Lichtheim 1980. Miriam Lichtheim. *Ancient Egyptian Literature.* 3: *The Late Period.* Berkeley, 1980.
Lilyquist 1995. Christine Lilyquist. *Egyptian Stone Vessels, Khian through Thutmosis IV.* New York, 1995.
Lilyquist and Brill 1993. Christine Lilyquist and R.H. Brill. *Studies in Early Egyptian Glass.* New York, 1993.
Lilyquist et al. in Lilyquist and Brill 1993. Christine Lilyquist, R.H. Brill and M.T. Wypyski. "Glassy Materials," in Lilyquist and Brill 1993, pp. 5–22.
Lilyquist in Hoving 1975. Christine Lilyquist. "The Acquisition of a Jewellike Sphinx," in Hoving 1975, pp. 107–10.
Loeben 1987. Christian E. Loeben. "A Throwstick of Princess Nfr-Nfrw-R', with Additional Notes on Throwsticks in Faience," *ASAE* 71 (1987), pp. 143–49, pl. 1.
Loret 1892. Victor Loret. *La flore pharaonique d'après les documents hiéroglyphiques et les spécimens découverts dans les tombes.* Paris, 1892.
Lucas 1939. A. Lucas. "Glass Figures," *ASAE* 39 (1939), pp. 227–35.
Lucas and Harris 1960. A. Lucas and J.R. Harris. *Ancient Egyptian Materials and Industries.* London, 1960 (4th edition 1989).
Lucas and Harris 1962 (1989). A. Lucas. *Ancient Egyptian Materials and Industries.* 4th edition, revised and enlarged by J.R. Harris. London, 1962.
Luft 1977. Ulrich Luft. "Das Totenbuch des Ptahmose," *ZÄS* 104 (1977), pp. 46–75, pls. 1–3.
Luft 1992. Ulrich Luft (ed.) *The Intellectual Heritage of Egypt: Studies Presented to László Kákosy by his Friends and Colleagues on the Occasion of his 60th Birthday.* Budapest, 1992.
Lythgoe 1927. Albert M. Lythgoe. "The Carnarvon Egyptian Collection," *BMMA* 22, no. 2 (Feb. 1927), pp. 31–40.
Macadam 1955. Miles F.L. Macadam. *The Temples of Kawa.* 2: *History and Archaeology of the Site.* London, 1955.
McDonald in Brovarski et al. 1982a. John K. McDonald. "Basket with lid," cat. no. 157, in Brovarski et al. 1982, p. 151.
McDonald in Brovarski et al. 1982b. John K. McDonald. "Baskets and basketry," in Brovarski et al. 1982, pp. 133–34.
McDonald in Brovarski et al. 1982c. John K. McDonald. "Elliptical basket with lid," cat. no. 132, in Brovarski et al. 1982, pp. 136–37.
McDonald in Brovarski et al. 1982d. John K. McDonald. "Rounded basket with conical lid," cat. no. 159, in Brovarski et al. 1982, p. 151.
McGovern et al. 1994. Patrick E. McGovern, Janine D. Bourriau, Garman Harbottle and Susan J. Allen. "The archaeological origin and significance of the Dolphin Vase as determined by neutron activation analysis," *BASOR* no. 296 (November 1994), pp. 31–43.
MacGregor 1922. W. MacGregor. *Catalogue of the MacGregor Collection of Egyptian Antiquities.* London, 1922.
Mackay 1921. E. Mackay. "Theban borders of lotus and grapes," *AE* (1921) pp. 39–41.
McNaught 1978. Lewis McNaught. "Henry Salt: His Contribution to the Collections of Egyptian Sculpture in the British Museum," *Apollo* 108, no. 200 (October 1978), pp. 224–31.
Malaise in Israelit-Groll 1990. Michel Malaise. "Bes et les croyances solaires," in Israelit-Groll 1990, pp. 680–729.
Manchester 1994. Karen Manchester. "The Queen's Vase: A Ptolemaic Oinochoe of Berenike II," *Re/Collections* 3, Merrin Gallery, New York, 1994.
Manniche 1989. Lise Manniche. *An Ancient Egyptian Herbal.* London and Austin, 1989.
Manniche 1991. Lise Manniche. *Music and Musicians in Ancient Egypt.* London, 1991.
Mariette 1870–1880 (1874). Auguste Mariette. *Dendéreh, Description générale du grande temple de cette ville.* 6 vols. 4: *Terrasses.* Paris, 1870–1880 (1874).
Markowitz in Thomas et al. 1995a. Yvonne Markowitz. "Reef Knot Bracelet," in Thomas et al. 1995, p. 142.
Markowitz in Thomas et al. 1995b. Yvonne Markowitz. "Ribbed Ball-Bead Necklace," entry in Thomas et al. 1995, p. 164.
Martin 1974. Geoffrey Thorndike Martin. *The Royal Tomb at El-Amarna. (The Rock Tombs of El-'Amarna).* 7 parts. 1: *The Objects.* (*Egypt Exploration Society, Archaeological Survey* Memoir 35). London, 1974.
Martin 1981. Geoffrey Thorndike Martin. *The Sacred Animal Necropolis at North Saqqâra. The Southern dependencies of the main complex.* (*Egypt Exploration Fund* Memoir 50). London, 1981.
Martin 1989. Geoffrey Thorndike Martin. *The Royal Tomb at El-Amarna II.* London, 1989.
Marucchi 1891. Horatius Marucchi. *Monumenta Papyracea Aegyptia Bibliothecae Vaticanae.* Rome, 1891.
Maspero 1914. Gaston Maspero. *Manual of Egyptian Archaeology and Guide to the Study of Antiquities in Egypt for the Use of Students and Travellers.* London, 1914.
Maspero 1915. Gaston Maspero. *Guide du visiteur au Musée du Caire.* 4th edition. Cairo, 1915.
Matheson 1994. Susan B. Matheson (ed.). *An Obsession with Fortune: Tyche in Greek and Roman Art.* New Haven, 1994.
Matheson in Matheson 1994. Susan B. Matheson. "The Goddess Tyche," in Matheson 1994, pp. 18–33.
Mathieson et al. 1995. Ian J. Mathieson, Elizabeth Bettles, Sue Davies and H.S. Smith. "A Stela of the Persian Period from Saqqara," *JEA* 1995, no. 1995 (81), pp. 23–41, pls. 5–6.
Meeks and Favard-Meeks 1996. Dimitri Meeks and Christiane Favard-Meeks. *Daily Life of the Egyptian Gods.* Trans. G.M. Goshgarian. Ithaca, 1996.
Meeks in Luft 1992. Dimitri Meeks. "Le nom du dieu Bès et ses implications mythologiques," in Luft 1992, pp. 423–36.
Mekhitarian 1978. Arpag Mekhitarian. *Egyptian Painting.* New York, 1978.
Mertens et al. 1992. Joan R. Mertens, Oscar White Muscarella, Catharine H. Roehrig, Marsha Hill and Elizabeth J. Milleker. "Ancient Art: Gifts from the Norbert Schimmel Collection," *BMMA* 49, no. 4 (Spring 1992), pp. 2–64.
Metropolitan Museum of Art 1952. Metropolitan Museum of Art. *Treasures from the Metropolitan Museum of Art.* New York, 1952.
Metropolitan Museum of Art 1973. *The Metropolitan Museum of Art Tomb Card 26.3.11.* unpublished but listed in *PM.* Oxford, 1973. p. 655.
Metropolitan Museum of Art Guide 1984. *The Metropolitan Museum of Art Bulletin.* V.41, no. 3. Winter, 1983–1984. New York, 1984.
Metzler in Matheson 1994. Dieter Metzler. "Mural Crowns in the Ancient Near East and Greece," in Matheson 1994, pp. 76–85.
MFA. Museum of Fine Arts, Boston. Object Register, Egypt, vol. XI, mixed dates.
MFA 1925. Museum of Fine Arts, Boston. Object Register, Egypt (Giza), vol. VI, 1925.
Michalowski 1938. K. Michalowski. *Tell Edfou.* Raport II. Chapter II, "Catalogue des objets," pp. 31–135. IFAO. Cairo, 1938.
Milward 1974. Angela J. Milward. *Die Nunschale–Eine Gefassegruppe des Neuen Reiches.* Munich, 1974.
Milward in Brovarski et al. 1982a. Angela J. Milward. "Bowl," cat. no. 139, in Brovarski et al. 1982, p. 143.
Milward in Brovarski et al. 1982b. Angela J. Milward. "Bowl," cat no. 140, in Brovarski et al. 1982, p. 143.
Milward in Brovarski et al. 1982c. Angela J. Milward. "Bowl," cat. no. 143, in Brovarski et al. 1982, pp. 144–45.
Milward in Brovarski et al. 1982d. Angela J. Milward. "Rilled cup," cat. no. 138, in Brovarski et al. 1982, p. 142.
Milward in Brovarski et al. 1982e. Angela J. Milward. "Bowl," cat. no. 141, in Brovarski et al. 1982, pp. 143–44.
Moens 1984. M.F. Moens. *The Ancient Egyptian Garden in the New Kingdom: a study of representations.* Louvain, 1984.

Montet 1937. Pierre Montet. *Les reliques de l'art Syrien dans l'Égypte du Nouvel Empire.* Paris, 1937.
Montet 1949. Pierre Montet. "Vases sacrées et profane du tombeau de Psousennès," in *Mon. Piot* 43 (1949), pp. 13–32.
Montet 1951. Pierre Montet. *La nécropole royale de Tanis.* 2: *Les constructions et le tombeau de Psousennès à Tanis.* Paris, 1951.
Montet 1952. Pierre Montet. *Psousennès.* Paris, 1952.
Moorey 1994. Peter R.S. Moorey. *Ancient Mesopotamian Materials and Industries: the archaeological evidence.* Oxford, 1994.
Morant 1938. Henry de Morant. "Jouets et poupées de l'ancienne Égypte," *La Nature* 66, no. 2 (1938), pp. 33–37.
Morant 1939. Henry de Morant. "Les objets de toilette dans l'ancienne Égypte," in *La Nature* no. 3053 (15 July 1939), p. 36.
Morenz in Firchow 1955. Siegfried Morenz. "Rote Stiere. Unbeachtetes zu Buchis und Mnevis," in Firchow 1955, pp. 238–43.
Morkot in Davies 1991. R.G. Morkot. "Nubia in the New Kingdom," in Davies 1991, pp. 294–301.
Müller 1961. Hans Wolfgang Müller. *Werke Altägyptischer und Koptischer Kunst aus der Sammlung Senator Dr. H. C. Wilhelm Esch, Duisburg.* Munich, 1961.
Müller 1964. Hans Wolfgang Müller. *Ägyptische Kunstwerke, Kleinfunde und Glas in der Sammlung E. und M. Kofler-Truniger.* (*MÄS* 5.) Berlin, 1964.
Müller 1974. Hans Wolfgang Müller. "Staatliche Sammlung Ägyptischer Kunst," *Münchner Jahrbuch der Bildenden Kunst,* Series 3, No. 25. (1974), pp.220–21.
Müller 1981. Hans Wolfgang Müller. "Bermerkungen zu den Kacheln mit Inschriften aus Qantir und zu den Rekonstruktionen gekachelter Palasttore," *MDAIK* 37 (1981), pp. 340–57.
Müller et al. 1961. Hans Wolfgang Müller, Klaus Wessel and Jürgen von Beckerath. *5000 Jahre Ägyptische Kunst.* Exhibition catalogue. Essen, 1961.
Munich 1995. "Staatliche Sammlung Ägyptischer Kunst." *Freundeskreis der Ägyptischen Sammlung München e.V.* Sonderdruck des Münchner Jahrbuchs der Bildenden Kunst. Munich, 1995. pp. 185–98.
Murray 1900. Margaret Murray. *Catalogue of the Egyptian Antiquities in the National Museum of Antiquities, Edinburgh.* Edinburgh, 1900.
Murray and Nuttall 1963. Helen Murray and Mary Nutall. *A Handlist to Howard Carter's Catalogue of Objects in Tut'ankhamun's Tomb.* Oxford, 1963.
Muscarella 1974. Oscar White Muscarella (ed.). *Ancient Art: The Norbert Schimmel Collection.* Exhibition catalogue. Mainz, 1974.
Musée d'Archéologie Méditerranéenne (Marseille) 1991
Musée d'Archéologie Méditerranéenne. *Jouer dans l'Antiquité.* Exhibition catalogue. Paris, 1991.
Musée du Louvre 1967. Musée du Louvre. *Vingt ans d'acquisitions au Musée du Louvre, 1947–1967.* Exhibition catalogue. Paris, 1967.
Musée du Louvre 1987. Musée du Louvre. *The Louvre. Seven Faces of a Museum.* Paris, 1987.
Museum of Fine Arts Boston 1984. "Egyptian and Near Eastern Art," *BMFA – Annual Reports. The Museum Year: 1983–84,* no. 108 (1984), pp. 24–25.
Museum of Fine Arts, Boston. Boston Museum of Fine Arts. *Object Register.* 11: *Egypt.* Unpublished, various dates.
Museum of Fine Arts, Boston 1920, 1930, 1935, 1947. Museum of Fine Arts, Boston. *Handbook of the Museum of Fine Arts.* 1920: 14th ed.; 1930: 22nd ed.; 1935: 23rd ed.; 1947: 28th ed. Boston, 1920, 1930, 1935, 1947.
Museum of Fine Arts, Boston 1925. Museum of Fine Arts, Boston. *Object Register.* 6: *Egypt: Giza.* Unpublished, 1925.
Mysliwiec 1976. Karol Mysliwiec. *Le portrait royal dans le bas-relief du Nouvel Empire.* (*Travaux du Centre d'Archéologie méditerranéenne de l'Acadamie polonaise de Sciences* no. 18). Warsaw, 1976.
Mysliwiec 1980. Karol Mysliwiec. "Die Rolle des Atum in der isd-Baum-Szene," *MDAIK* (1980), pp. 349–56.
Mysliwiec 1988. Karol Mysliwiec. *Royal Portraiture of the Dynasties XXI–XXX.* Mainz, 1988.
Nactergael 1981. Georges Nactergael. "La chevelure d'Isis," *L'Antiquité Classique* 50 (1981), pp. 584–606.
Naguib 1993. Saphinaz-Amal Naguib. *Miroirs du passé.* Geneva, 1993.
Nash 1898. Walter L. Nash. "An Ancient Egyptian Toilet-Box Belonging to W.L. Nash, F.S.A. with an Analysis of its Contents by W. Gowland, F.C.S., F.S.A.," *PSBA* 20, part 7 (November 1898), pp. 267–69.
Naville 1886. Édouard Naville. *Das ägyptische Totenbuch der XVIII bis XX Dysnastie.* 3 vols. Berlin, 1886.
Naville 1888. Édouard Naville. *The Shrine of Saft el Henneh and the land of Goshen (1885).* (*Egypt Exploration Fund* Memoir 5). London, 1888.
Needler 1953. Winifred Needler. "A Thirty-Square Draught-Board in the Royal Ontario Museum," *JEA* 39 (1953), pp. 60–75, pl. 4.
Nelson 1930. Harold H. Nelson. *Medinet Habu VIII; I. Earlier Historical Records of Ramesses III.* Chicago, 1930.
Nelson 1932. Harold H. Nelson. *Medinet Habu IX; II. Later Historical Records of Ramesses III.* Chicago, 1932.
Nelson and LeBlanc in Desroches-Noblecourt et al. 1976. M. Nelson and Ch. LeBlanc. "La Clepsydre de Karnak," in Desroches-Noblecourt et al. 1976, pp. 139–49.
Nenna and Seif el-Din 1993. Marie-Dominique Nenna and Merrat Seif el-Din. "La vaiselle en faïence du musée grèco-romain d'Alexandrie," *Bulletin de Correspondance Hellénique* 117, no. 2 (1993), pp. 565–602, pls 1–4.
Nenna and Seif el-Din 1994. Marie-Dominique Nenna and Merrat Seif el-Din. "La petite plastique en faïence du Musée grèco-romain d'Alexandrie," *Bulletin de Correspondence Hellénique* 118 (1994), pp. 291–320, pls. 1–4.
Newberry 1893. Percy E. Newberry. *Beni Hasan.* Parts 1 and 2. (*Archaeological Survey of Egypt:* Memoir 2). London, 1893.
Newberry 1893–1894. Percy E. Newberry. *El Berseh.* 1: *The Tomb of Tehuti-Hetep.* (*Archaeological Survey of Egypt:* Memoir 3). London, 1893–1894.
Newberry 1902. Percy E. Newberry. "Extracts from my Notebook," *PSBA* 24 (1902) pp. 245–48, pls. 1, 3, 4.
Newberry 1914. Percy E. Newberry. "Egyptian Historical Notes II," *PSBA* 36, no. 259 (January 1914), pp. 35–39, pls. 3–4.
Newberry 1920. Percy E. Newberry. "A Glass Chalice of Tuthmosis III," *JEA* 6, part 3 (July 1920), pp. 155–60, pl. 16.
Newberry in Carnarvon and Carter 1912. Percy E. Newberry. "The Funerary Statuettes from the Tomb of Teta-ky," in Carnarvon and Carter 1912, pp. 19–21, pls. 10–11.
Newman 1997. Richard Newman. Unpublished Analysis of the Senkamenisken Shabtis at the MFA, Boston. 1997.
Newton 1980. R.G. Newton. "Recent views on ancient glasses," *Glass Technology* 21, no. 4 (August 1980), pp. 173–83.
Newton and Renfrew 1970. R.G. Newton and Colin Renfrew. "British Faience Beads Reconsidered," *Antiquity* 44, no. 175 (September 1970), pp. 199–206.
Nicholson 1993. Paul T. Nicholson. *Egyptian Faience and Glass.* (*Shire Egyptology* 18). Princes Risborough, 1993.
Nicholson 1995a. Paul T. Nicholson. "Glassmaking and Glassworking at Amarna: some new work," *JGS* 37(1995), pp. 11–19.
Nicholson 1995b. Paul T. Nicholson. "The potters of Deir Mawas, an ethnoarchaeological study," in Barry J. Kemp (ed.) *Amarna Reports 6.* London, 1995, pp. 279–308.
Nicholson 1995c. Paul T. Nicholson. "Recent excavations at an ancient Egyptian glassworks: Tell el-Amarna," *Glass Technology* 36, no. 4 (1995), pp. 125–28.
Niemeyer and Docter 1993. Hans Georg Niemeyer and Roald F. Docter. "Karthago: Hamburger Grabung unter dem Decumanus Maximus," *MDAIR* 100 (1993), pp. 201–44.
Noble 1969. James Veach Noble. "The Technique of Egyptian Faïence," *AJA* 73 (1969), pp. 435–39, pls. 121–22.
Nolte 1968. Birgit Nolte. *Die Glasgefässe im alten Ägypten. MÄS 14.* Berlin, 1968.
Nolte 1977. Birgit Nolte. "Fayence," *LÄ* II, cols 138–42. Wisebaden 1977.
Nolte 1985. Birgit Nolte. *Egipto no kodai garasu.* Kyoto, 1985.
Nord in Brovarski et al. 1982. Del Nord. "Bottle," cat. no. 150, in Brovarski et al. 1982, p. 148.
Nordstöm 1972. Hans-Ake Nordström. *Neolithic and A-Group Sites.* (*The Scandinavian Expedition to Sudanese Nubia* 3, parts 1 and 2). Uppsala, 1972.
O'Connor 1990. David O'Connor: "The Nature of Tjemhu (Libyan) Society in the Later New Kingdom," in Anthony Leahy (ed.) *Libya and Egypt c. 1300–750 BC.* London, 1990, pp. 29–113.
O'Connor 1993. David O'Connor. *Ancient Nubia: Egypt's Rival in Africa.* Philadelphia, 1993.
Obsomer and Oosthoek 1992. Claude Obsomer and Ann-Laure Oosthoek (eds.). *Amoisades: Mélanges offerts au Professeur Claude Vandersleyen par ses anciens étudiants.* Louvain-la-Neuve, 1992.
Olin and Franklin 1992. Jacqueline S. Olin and Alan D. Franklin (eds.). *Archaeological Ceramics.* Washington D.C., 1982.
Oosthoek in Obsomer and Oosthoek 1992. Ann-Laure Oosthoek "Hittite ou pas Hittite? Trois Représentations à Caractère Hybride," in Obsomer and Oosthoek 1992, pp. 335–46.
Oppenheim et al. 1970. A. Leo Oppenheim, Robert H. Brill, Dan Barag and Axel von Saldern. *Glass and Glassmaking in Ancient Mesopotamia: An Edition of the Cuneiform Texts which Contain Instructions for Glassmaking with a Catalogue of Surviving Objects.* New York, 1970.
Ortiz 1994. George Ortiz. *In Pursuit of the Absolute: Art of the Ancient World from the George Ortiz Collection.* London, 1994.
Ortiz 1996. George Ortiz. *In Pursuit of the Absolute: Art of the Ancient World: The George Ortiz Collection.* exhibition catalogue. Bern, 1996.
Page-Gasser and Wiese 1997. Madeleine Page-Gasser and André B. Wiese. *Ägypten: Augenblicke der Ewigkeit: Unbekannte Schätze aus Schweizer Privatbesitz.* Exhibition catalogue. Mainz, 1997.
Painter and Whitehouse 1990. K. Painter and D. Whitehouse. "Early Roman Cameo Glasses," *JGS* 32 (1990), pp. 138–65.
Pantalacci 1987. Laure Pantalacci. "À propos de reliques osiriennes," *CdÉ* 62, fasc. 123–24 (1987), pp. 108–23.

Paris 1929. *Collection de feu Omar Pacha Sultan le Caire.* Exhibition catalogue. Paris, 1929.
Parlasca 1955. Klaus Parlasca. "Das Verhältnis der megarischen Becher zum alexandrinischen Kunsthandwerk," *Jahrbuch des Deutschen Archäologischen Instituts* 70 (1955), pp. 129–54.
Parlasca 1976. Klaus Parlasca. "Zur Verbreitung Ptolemäischer Fayencekeramik ausserhalb Ägyptens," *Jahrbuch des Deutschen Archäologischen Instituts* 91 (1976), pp. 135–56.
Parlasca 1984. Klaus Parlasca. "Neues zur ptolemäischen Fayencekeramik," *Alessandria e il Mondo ellenistico-romano. Studi in onore di Achille Adriani.* 2 vols. pp. 300–302 and pl. 54. Rome, 1984.
Partridge 1994. Robert Partridge. *Faces of Pharaohs: Royal Mummies and Coffins from Ancient Thebes.* London, 1994.
Passalacqua 1826. Joseph Passalacqua. *Catalogue raisonné et historique des antiquités découvertes en Égypte.* Paris, 1826.
Patch 1988. Diana Craig Patch. "Artifacts from Cemetery D, Abydos at the Carnegie Museum of Natural History," paper presented at the 39th Annual Meeting of the American Research Center in Egypt. Chicago, 1988.
Patch 1990. Diana Craig Patch. *Reflections of Greatness: Ancient Egypt at the Carnegie Museum of Natural History.* Exhibition catalogue. Pittsburgh, 1990.
Patch 1991/92. Diana Craig Patch. "Tutankhamun's Corselet: A Reconsideration of its Function," *BES* 11 (1991/92), pp. 57–77.
Pavlov and Khodzash 1959. V.V. Pavlov, and S.I. Khodzash. *Applied Arts of Ancient Egypt Illustrated from the Collection of the Pushkin Museum.* Moscow, 1959.
Payne 1993. Joan Crowfoot Payne. *Catalogue of the Predynastic Egyptian Collection in the Ashmolean Museum.* Oxford and New York, 1993.
Peden 1994a. A.J. Peden. *Egyptian Historical Inscriptions of the Twentieth Dynasty.* Jonsered, 1994.
Peden 1994b. A.J. Peden. *The Reign of Ramses IV.* Warminster, 1994.
Peet and Woolley 1923. Thomas E. Peet and C.I. Woolley. *The City of Akhenaten.* 1: *Excavations of 1921 and 1922 at el 'Amarneh.* (*Egypt Exploration Society.*) London, 1923.
Peltenburg 1986. E.J. Peltenburg. "Ramesside Egypt and Cyprus," in V. Karageorghis (ed.), *Acts of the International Archaeological Symposium "Cyprus Between the Orient and the Occident."* pp. 149–79. Nicosia, 1986.
Peltenburg in Bimson and Freestone 1987. E.J. Peltenburg. "Early faience: recent studies, origins and relations with glass," in Bimson and Freestone 1987, pp. 5–29.
Pendlebury 1931. J.D.S. Pendlebury. "Preliminary report of excavations at Tell El-'Amarnah, 1930–1," *JEA* 17 (1931), pp. 233–44.
Pendlebury 1951. J.D.S. Pendlebury. *The City of Akhenaten* 3. London, 1951.
Pernigotti 1985. Sergio Pernigotti. "Saitica, II," *Egitto e Vicino Oriente* 8 (1985), pp. 7–18.
Petrie n.d. William M. Flinders Petrie. *Mss Notebook no. 11.* London, n.d.
Petrie 1887. William M. Flinders Petrie. *Racial Types from Egypt* (album). London, 1887.
Petrie 1888. William M. Flinders Petrie. *Tanis: part 2: Nesbesheh (AM) and Defenneh (Tahpanhes).* (*Egypt Exploration Fund* Memoir 4). London, 1888.
Petrie 1891. William M. Flinders Petrie. *Illahun, Kahun and Gurob, 1889–1890.* London, 1891.
Petrie 1892. William M. Flinders Petrie. *Ten Years' Digging in Egypt (1881–1891).* London, 1892.
Petrie 1894. William M. Flinders Petrie. *Tell el Amarna.* London, 1894.
Petrie 1896. William M. Flinders Petrie. *Naqada and Ballas, 1895.* (*British Research Account* 1.) London, 1896.
Petrie 1900–01. William M. Flinders Petrie. *The Royal Tombs of the first dynasty, 1900–1901.* 2 parts. (*Egypt Exploration Fund* Memoir 18: 1900; Memoir 21: 1901.) London, 1900–1901.
Petrie 1902. William M. Flinders Petrie. *Abydos.* Part I. (*Egypt Exploration Society* Memoir 22.) London, 1902.
Petrie 1903. William M. Flinders Petrie. *Abydos.* Part II. (*Egypt Exploration Society* Memoir 24.) London, 1903.
Petrie 1906. William M. Flinders Petrie. *Researches in Sinai.* London, 1906.
Petrie 1909a. William M. Flinders Petrie. *The Arts and Crafts of Ancient Egypt.* London, 1909.
Petrie 1909b. William M. Flinders Petrie. *Memphis.* 1 (*British School of Archaeology in Egypt* no. 15.) London, 1909.
Petrie 1909c. William M. Flinders Petrie. *Qurneh.* (*British School of Archaeology in Egypt* 15.) London, 1909.
Petrie 1911. William M. Flinders Petrie. "The pottery kilns at Memphis," in E.B. Knobel, W.W. Midgeley, J.G. Milne, M.A. Murray and William M. Flinders Petrie. *Historical Studies.* (*British School of Archaeology in Egypt: Studies.* vol. 19.) pp. 34–37. London, 1911
Petrie 1914a. William M. Flinders Petrie. *Amulets.* London, 1914.
Petrie 1914b. William M. Flinders Petrie. *Tarkhan.* 2 (*British School of Archaeology in Egypt* 26.) London, 1914.
Petrie 1927. William M. Flinders Petrie. *Objects of Daily Use.* (*British School of Archaeology in Egypt* 42.) London, 1927.
Petrie 1937 (1977). William M. Flinders Petrie. *The Funeral Furniture of Egypt: Stone and Metal Vases.* (*British School of Archaeology at Athens* 59.) London, 1937 (1977).
Petrie and Gardner 1886–1888. William M. Flinders Petrie, and E. A. Gardner. *Naukratis.* 2 vols. (*Egypt Exploration Fund: Memoir* 3, 6.) London, 1886–1888.
Petrie and Quibell 1896. William M. Flinders Petrie and J.E. Quibell. *Naqada and Ballas. 1895.* London, 1896.
Pfrommer 1987. Michael Pfrommer. *Studien zu alexandrinischer and grossgriechischer Toreutik frühhellenistischer Zeit* (*DAI* 16). Berlin, 1987.
Pfrommer 1993. Michael Pfrommer. *Metalwork from the Hellenized East: Catalogue of the Collections.* Malibu, 1993.
Pfrommer 1996. Michael Pfrommer. "Roots and Contacts: Aspects of Alexandrian Craftsmanship," in The J. Paul Getty Museum. *Alexandria and Alexandrianism. Papers Delivered at a Symposium Organized by the J. Pual Getty Museum and The Getty Center for the History of Art and the Humanities and Held at the Museum April 22–25, 1993,* pp. 171–189. Malibu, 1996.
Phillips 1942. Dorothy W. Phillips. *Ancient Egyptian Animals.* Exhibition catalogue. New York, 1942.
Phillips 1994. J. Phillips. *Amarna Letters* 3 (1994), pp. 58–71.
Phillips 1995. Tom Phillips (ed.). *Africa: The Art of a Continent.* Exhibition catalogue. London, 1995.
Piccione 1990. Peter Piccione. *The Historical Development of the Game of Senet and its Significance for Egyptian Religion.* 2 vols. Ph.D. thesis, University of Chicago. Chicago, 1990.
Pierrat 1993. Genèviève Pierrat. "Les Arts du feu," *Connaissance des Arts,* no. 36, Paris, 1993, pp. 49, 52, fig. 51.
Pierret 1873. P. Pierret. *Catalogue de la Salle Historique de la Galerie Égyptienne.* Paris, 1873.
Pierret 1877. P. Pierret. *Catalogue de la Salle Historique de la Galerie Égyptienne. Musée du Louvre.* Paris, 1877.
Pinch 1993. Geraldine Pinch. *Votive Offerings to Hathor.* Oxford, 1993.
Pinch 1994. Geraldine Pinch. *Magic in Ancient Egypt.* London and Austin, 1994.
Pinch 1996. Geraldine Pinch. Unpublished manuscript. British Museum symposium, London, Summer 1996.
Pollini 1987–1988. John Pollini. "The Findspot of the Statue of Augustus from Prima Porta," *Bolletino della Commissione Archeologica Communale di Roma* 92.1 (1987–1988), pp. 103–08.
Pollini 1990. John Pollini. "Man of God: Divine Assimilation and Imitation in the Late Republic and Early Principate," in Kurt A. Raaflaub and Mark Toher (eds.). *Between Republic and Empire: Interpretations of Augustus and his Principate,* pp. 334–63. Berkeley, 1990.
Pomorska 1987. Irena Pomorska. *Les flabellifères à la droite du roi en Égypte ancienne.* Warsaw, 1987.
Poole 1995. Frederico Poole. "Slave or Double? A Reconsideration of the Conception of the Shabti in the late New Kingdom and the Third Intermediate Period," abstract *Seventh International Congress of Egyptologists: Abstract of papers,* pp. 143–44. Cambridge, 1995.
Porter 1986. Barbara A. Porter. *Egyptian Decorated Faience Bowls of Early Dynasty 18 from Thebes from the Excavations of the Metropolitan Museum of Art and Lord Carnarvon and Howard Carter.* M.A. thesis, Columbia University. New York, 1986.
Porter and Moss 1934. Bertha Porter and Rosalind L.B. Moss. *Topographical Bibliography of Ancient Egyptian Hieroglyphs, Texts, Reliefs, and Paintings.* 4: *Lower and Middle Egypt [Delta and Cairo, Asyût] (excluding Thebes).* Oxford, 1934.
Porter and Moss 1939. Bertha Porter and Rosalind L.B. Moss. *Topographical Bibliography of Ancient Egyptian Hieroglyphs, Texts, Reliefs, and Paintings.* 6: *Upper Egypt: Chief Temples (Excluding Thebes).* Oxford, 1939.
Porter and Moss 1964. Bertha Porter and Rosalind L.B. Moss. *Topographical Bibliography of Ancient Egyptian Hieroglyphs, Texts, Reliefs, and Paintings.* 2.1: *The Theban Necropolis: Royal Tombs and Smaller Cemeteries.* 2nd ed. London, 1964.
Porter and Moss 1972. Bertha Porter and Rosalind L.B. Moss. *Topographical Bibliography of Ancient Egyptian Hieroglyphs, Texts, Reliefs, and Paintings.* 2: *Theban Temples.* 2nd ed., revised by Jaromír Málek. London, 1972.
Porter and Moss 1973. Bertha Porter and Rosalind L.B. Moss. *Topographical Bibliography of Ancient Egyptian Hieroglyphs, Texts, Reliefs, and Paintings.* 1: *The Theban Necropolis.* Part 2: *Royal Tombs and Smaller Cemeteries.* Oxford, 1973.
Porter in D'Auria et al. 1988. Barbara A. Porter. "Bowl," cat. no. 76, in D'Auria et al. 1988, p. 138.
Priese 1991 Karl-Heinz Priese (ed.). *Ägyptisches Museum und Papyrussammlung. Staatliche Museen zu Berlin.* Exhibition catalogue. Mainz, 1991.
Pritchard 1958. James Bennett Pritchard. *The Ancient Near East: an anthology of texts and pictures.* 2 vols. Princeton, 1958.
Pusch 1979. Edgar Pusch. *Das Senet-Brettspiel im Alten Ägypten.* 2 vols. (*MÄS* 38.) Berlin, 1979.
Pusch in Eggebrecht et al. 1993. Edgar Pusch. "Pi-Ramesse-geliebt-von-Amun, Hauptquartier Deiner

Streitwagentruppen," in Eggebrecht. et al. 1993, pp. 126–43.
Quaegebeur 1983. J. Quaegebeur. "De l'origine égyptienne du griffon Némésis," *Visages du destin dans les mythologies. Mélanges Jacqueline Duchemin*, pp. 41–54. Paris, 1983.
Quaegebeur 1992. J. Quaegebeur. "Les pantoufles du dieu Thot," abstract *Sesto Congresso Internazionale di Egittologia*, pp. 521–27. Turin, 1992.
Quibell 1900. James Edward Quibell. *Hierakonpolis.* Part 1. (*Egyptian Research Account* Memoir 4.) London, 1900.
Quibell 1908. J.E. Quibell. *Tomb of Yuaa and Thuiu.* Cairo, 1908.
Quibell and Green 1902. J.E. Quibell and F. W. Green. *Hierakonpolis.* Part 2. (*English Research Account* Memoir 5.) London, 1902.
Quibell and Hayter 1927. J.E. Quibell, and A.G.K. Hayter. *Excavations at Saqqara: Teti Pyramid, North Side.* Cairo, 1927.
Quibell and Petrie 1902. J.E. Quibell and W.M.F. Petrie. *Hierakonpolis.* London, 1900–02
Quirke 1991. Stephen Quirke. "Royal Power in the 13th Dynasty," in Stephen Quirke (ed.) *Middle Kingdom Studies*, pp. 123–39. New Malden, 1991.
Quirke forthcoming. Stephen Quirke. "Figures of clay: toys or ritual objects?" in Stephen Quirke (ed.). *Lahun Studies.* New Malden, forthcoming.
Quirke and Spencer 1992. Stephen Quirke and Jeffrey Spencer (eds.). *The British Museum Book of Ancient Egypt.* London and New York, 1992.
Quirke in D'Auria et al. 1988a. Stephen Quirke. "Three embalming pots," cat. no. 182, in D'Auria et al 1988. pp. 227–28.
Quirke in D'Auria et al. 1988b. Stephen Quirke. "Set of amulets," cat. no. 129, in D'Auria et al 1988, pp. 180–83.
Randall-MacIver and Mace 1902. David Randall-MacIver and A.C. Mace. *El Amrah and Abydos 1899–1901.* (*Egypt Exploration Fund* Memoir 23.) London, 1902.
Raven 1988. Maartin J. Raven. "Magic and Symbolic Aspects of Certain Materials in Ancient Egypt," *Varia Aegyptiaca* 4, no. 3 (December 1988), pp. 127–242.
Redford in Holladay 1982. Donald B. Redford. "An Inscribed Inkwell from Tell-el-Maskhuta," in Holladay 1982. pp. 60–61.
Reeder 1988. Ellen D. Reeder. *Hellenistic Art in the Walters Art Gallery.* Baltimore, 1988.
Reeves 1989. Nicholas Reeves. *Ancient Egypt at Highclere Castle: Lord Carnarvon and the Search for Tutankhamen.* Newbury, 1989.
Reeves 1990a. Nicholas Reeves. *The Complete Tutankhamun: the King, the Tomb, the Royal Treasure.* London and New York, 1990.
Reeves 1990b. Nicholas Reeves. *Valley of the Kings: the Decline of the Royal Necropolis.* London, 1990.
Reeves and Spurr 1995. Nicholas Reeves and S. Spurr. "Ancient Egypt at Eton," *Egyptian Archaeology* 6 (1995), pp. 19–22.
Reeves and Taylor 1992. Nicholas Reeves and John H. Taylor. *Howard Carter: Before Tutankhamun.* London, 1992.
Reeves and Wilkinson 1996. Nicholas Reeves and Richard H. Wilkinson. *The Complete Valley of the Kings: Tombs and Treasures of Egypt's Greatest Pharaohs.* London and New York, 1996.
Reisner 1923a. George A. Reisner. *Excavations at Kerma.* 1–3 *(Harvard African Studies 5).* Cambridge MA, 1923.
Reisner 1923b. George A. Reisner. *Excavations at Kerma.* 4, 5 *(Harvard African Studies 6).* Cambridge MA, 1923.
Reisner 1907, 1958. George A. Reisner. *Catalogue générale des antiquités égyptiennes du Musée du Caire.* 2 vols: *Amulets: nos. 5218–6000, nos. 12528–13595* (23, 24). Cairo, 1907, 1958.
Reymond 1981. Eve A.E. Reymond. *From the Records of a Priestly Family from Memphis.* (*Ägyptologische Abhandlungen* 8.) Wiesbaden, 1981.
Reynders 1995. Marleen Reynders. "The Egyptian Sistrum: Names and Types," abstract *Seventh International Congress of Egyptologists: Abstracts of Papers* (1995), p. 150.
Rice 1987. Prudence Rice. *Pottery Analysis: A Sourcebook.* Chicago, 1987.
Ricketts 1918a. Charles Ricketts. "Bas-relief Figure of a King of the Ptolemaic Period in Blue Faience," *JEA* 5, no. 2 (1918), pp. 77–78, pl. 9.
Ricketts 1918b. Charles Ricketts. "Two faience chalices at Eton College from the collection of the late Major W.J. Myers," *JEA* 5, no. 3 (1918), pp. 145–47, pls. 23–25.
Riefstahl 1944. Elizabeth Riefstahl. *Patterned Textiles in Pharaonic Egypt.* Brooklyn, 1944.
Riefstahl 1968. Elizabeth Riefstahl. *Ancient Egyptian Glass and Glazes in the Brooklyn Museum.* (*Wilbour Monographs* 1). Brooklyn, 1968.
Rigault in Phillips 1995. Patricia Rigault, "Louvre E 3610," in Phillips 1995, p. 90, cat. no. 1.52.
Rijksmuseum van Oudheden 1826. *Egyptische Kunst en Beschaving in 'S Rijksmuseum van Oudheden. Gids voor Egyptische Afdeeling.* 'S-Gravenhage 1826.
Ritner 1993. Robert Kriech Ritner. *The Mechanics of Ancient Egyptian Magical Practice.* (*SAOC* 54). Chicago, 1993.
Roberts 1995. Alison Roberts. *Hathor Rising: Serpent Power of Ancient Egypt.* Totnes, Devon, 1995.
Robins 1990. Gay Robins. "Problems in Interpreting Egyptian Art," in *Discussions in Egyptology* 17 (1990), pp. 45–58.
Robins 1993. Gay Robins. *Women in Ancient Egypt.* London and Cambridge (MA), 1993.
Robins 1997. Gay Robins. *The Art of Ancient Egypt.* London and Cambridge (MA), 1997.
Roccatti in Roveri 1988a. Alessandro Roccatti. "The Art and Technique of Writing," in Roveri 1988a, pp. 20–45.
Roeder 1969. G. Roeder. *Amarna Reliefs aus Hermopolis. Ausgrabungen der Deutschen Hermopolis-Expedition in Hermopolis 1929–1939.* Vol. 2. Hildesheim, 1969.
Roehrig 1992a. Catharine H. Roehrig. "Hedgehog," in *BMMA* 49, no. 4 (Spring 1992), pp. 22–23.
Roehrig 1992b. Catharine H. Roehrig. "Ancient Art; Gifts from the Norbert Schimmel Collection," *BMMA* 49, no. 4 (Spring 1992).
Roehrig 1992c. Catharine H. Roehrig. "Cosmetic container in the form of a bes-image holding the cap of a kohl tube," in *BMMA* 49, no. 4 (Spring 1992), pp. 33–34.
Roehrig 1996
Catharine H. Roehrig. "Cult Figure of a Falcon-Headed Deity" in *Ancient Art from the Shumei Family Collection*, pp 4–7. Exhibition catalogue. New York, 1996.
Romano 1979. James F. Romano. *The Luxor Musem of Ancient Egyptian Art. Catalogue.* Cairo, 1979.
Romano 1980. James F. Romano. "The Origin of the Bes-Image," *BES* 2 (1980), pp. 39–56.
Romano and Bothmer 1979. James F. Romano and Bernard Bothmer. *The Luxor Museum of Ancient Egyptian Art: Catalogue.* (*American Research Center in Egypt)* Cairo, 1979.
Romano in Brovarski et al. 1982. James F. Romano. "Ointment spoon with double Bes-image," cat. no. 246, in Brovarksi et al. 1982, p. 209.
Romano in Capel and Markoe 1996. James F. Romano. "Vessel in form of Bes-image," cat. no. 18, in Capel and Markoe 1996, pp. 68–70, 196.
Romano in Eggebrecht 1987. James F. Romano. "Schale mit Nilszenen-Dekor," cat. no. 280, in Eggebrecht 1987, p. 327.
Rosati in Roveri 1988a. Gloria Rosati. "Precious Ornaments: Jewels and Amulets," in Roveri 1988a, pp. 218–31.
Rothenberg 1988. Beno Rothenberg. *The Egyptian Mining Temple at Timna.* London and New York, 1988.
Roveri 1988a. Anna Maria Donadoni Roveri (ed.). *Egyptian Civilization: Daily Life.* Milan, 1988.
Roveri 1988b. Anna Maria Donadoni Roveri (ed.). *Egyptian Civilization: Religious Beliefs.* Milan, 1988.
Roveri 1988c. Anna Maria Donadoni Roveri (ed.). *Egyptian Civilization: Monumental Art.* Milan, 1988.
Roveri in Roveri 1988a. Anna Maria Donadoni Roveri. "History of a Collection," in Roveri 1988a pp. 10–20.
Rowe 1908. L.E. Rowe. "Egyptian Portraiture of the XX Dynasty," *BMFA* 6 (1908), pp. 48–50.
Rowe 1931. L.E. Rowe. "An Egyptian Hippopotamus," in *Bulletin of the Rhode Island School of Design* 19, no. 1 (January 1931), pp. 3–4.
Royal Academy of Art 1962. Arts Council of Great Britain *5,000 Years of Egyptian Art.* Exhibition catalogue. London, 1962.
Royal Athena Galleries 1988. *The Age of Cleopatra. The Art of Late Dynastic and Graeco-Roman Egypt.* New York, 1988.
Rubin 1988. Arnold Rubin (ed.). *Marks of Civilization. Artistic Transformations of the Human Body.* Los Angeles, 1988.
Ruffle 1988. John Ruffle. *Collectors' Choice: ancient Egyptian antiquities from private collections in England.* Exhibition catalogue. Durham, 1988.
Russman 1989. Edna R. Russman. *Egyptian Sculpture: Cairo and Luxor.* Austin, 1989.
Russman in Lilyquist 1983. Edna R. Russman. "Egyptian Art" in Christine Lilyquist, *Notable Antiquities 1983*, Metropolitan Museum of Art Bulletin, Volume 41 #3, p.36, nos. 36, 37.
Saleh and Sourouzian 1987. Mohamed Saleh and Hourig Sourouzian. *The Egyptian Museum Cairo: Official Catalogue.* Mainz, 1987.
Sambin 1988. Chantal Sambin. *L'offrande de la soi-distant "clepsydre." Le symbole sbt / wnsb / wtt.* Budapest, 1988.
Samson 1972. Julia Samson. *Amarna, City of Akhenaten and Nefertiti: Key Pieces in the Petrie Collection.* London, 1972.
Samson 1973. Julia Samson. "Amarna Crowns and Wigs," in *JEA* 59 (1973), pp. 47–59 and pls. 26–29.
Samson 1978. Julia Samson. *Amarna, City of Akhenaten and Nefertiti: Nefertiti as Pharaoh.* 2nd ed. Warminster, 1978.
Samuel 1989. Alan Edward Samuel. *The Shifting Sands of History: Interpretations of Ptolemaic Egypt.* Lanham Maryland, 1989.
Sasson et al. 1995. Jack M. Sasson et al. *Civilizations of the Ancient Near East.* 4 vols. New York, 1995.
Sauneron 1982. Serge Sauneron. *Esna.* 8: *L'écriture figurative dans les textes d'Esna.* Cairo, 1982.
Save-Söderbergh 1957. T. Save-Söderbergh. *Four Eighteenth Dynasty Tombs.* Oxford, 1957.
Säve-Söderbergh 1989. T. Säve-Söderbergh. *Middle Nubian Sites: Scandanavian Joint Expidition to Sudanese Nubia 4:1.* Uppsala, 1989.

Schaden 1997. Otto J. Schaden. *Amenmesse Project KV-10. Summer Season 1997. Report Submitted to the Supreme Council of Antiquities, Cairo. 12 July 1997.* Cairo, 1997.
Schäfer 1910. Heinrich Schäfer (ed.). *Ägyptische Goldschmiedarbeiten unter Mitwirkung von Georg Moller und Wilhelm Schubat.(Mitteilung aus der Ägyptischen Sammlung* 1). Berlin, 1910.
Schäfer 1913. Heinrich Schäfer. "Ägyptische Abteilung – Ägyptische Fayencen," in *Amtliche Berichte aus den königlichen Kunstsammlungen* 34, no. 4 (1913), pp. 49–52.
Schäfer and Andrae 1925. Heinrich Schäfer and W. Andrae. *Die Kunst des Altes Orients.* Berlin, 1925.
Schiaparelli 1903–1927. Ernesto Schiaparelli. *Relazione sui lavori della Missione archeologica Italiana in Egitto.* 2 vols. Turin, 1903–1927.
Schildkraut and Solia 1992. Linda Schildkraut and Vicki Solia. *Egypt at the Merrin Gallery.* Exhibition catalogue. New York, 1992.
Schlick-Nolte 1968. Birgit Schlick-Nolte. *Die Glasgefässe im alten Ägyten.* (*MÄS* 14.) 1968.
Schlick-Nolte 1984. Birgit Schlick-Nolte . *Corpus antiquitatum Aegyptiacarum: Lose-Blatt-Katalog agyptischer Altertumer. Museen der Rhein-Main-Region.* Lieferung 1: Aegypiaca diversa, Teil I. Mainz, 1984.
Schlick-Nolte and Droste zu Hülshoff 1990. Birgit Schlick-Nolte and Vera Droste zu Hülshoff. *Liebieghaus—Museum Alter Plastik. Ägyptische Bildwerke.* 1: *Skarabaen, Amulette und Schmuck.* Melsungen, 1990.
Schliegl 1988. S. Schliegl. "Investigation on Faience Tiles from the Walls of Djoser's South Tomb in Saqqara: An Approach to Reveal the Technique of Their Manufacture," abstract *Fifth International Congress of Egyptologists*, pp. 242–43. Cairo, 1988.
Schlögl 1977. Hermann A. Schlögl. *Der Sonnengott auf der Blüte: eine ägyptische Kosmogonie des Neuen Reiches.* (*Aegyptiaca Helvetica* 5). Geneva, 1977.
Schlögl 1978. Hermann A. Shlögl (ed.). *Geschenk des Nil, Ägyptische Kunstwerke aus Schweizer Besitz.* Basel, 1978.
Schneider 1976. Beate Schneider. *Studien zu den kleinformatigen Kaiserportraits.* Ph.D. thesis. Munich, 1976.
Schneider 1977. Hans D. Schneider. *Shabtis: Introduction to the History of Ancient Egyptian Funerary Statuettes.* 3 vols Leiden, 1977.
Schneider and Raven 1981. Hans D. Schneider and Maarten J. Raven. *De Egyptische Oudheid.* The Hague, 1981.
Schoske and Wildung 1976. Sylvia Schoske and Dietrich Wildung. *Ägyptische Kunst München.* Munich, 1976.
Schoske and Wildung 1985. Sylvia Schoske and Dieter Wildung. *Ägyptische Kunst München: Katalog-Handbuch zur Staatlichen Sammlung Ägyptischer Kunst.* Munich, 1985.
Schoske and Wildung 1992. Sylvia Schoske and Dietrich Wildung. *Gott und Götter im alten Ägypten.* Exhibition catalogue. Mainz, 1992.
Schoske and Wildung 1993. Sylvia Schoske and Dietrich Wildung. *Egyptian Art in Munich.* Munich, 1993.
Schoske et al. 1985. Sylvia Schocke et al. *Ägyptische Kunst München, Katalog-Handbuch zur Staatlichen Sammlung Ägyptischer Kunst München.* Munich, 1985.
Schoske et al. 1990. Sylvia Schoske with Alfred Grimm and Barbara Kreißl. *Schönheit: Abglanz der Göttlichkeit.* Exhibition catalogue. Münich, 1990.
Schoske et al. 1992. Sylvia Schoske, Barbara Kreissel and Renate Germer. *"Anch." Blumen für das Leben: Pflanzen im alten Ägypten.* Exhibition catalogue. (*Scriften aus der Ägyptischen Sammlung* 6.) Munich, 1992.
Scott 1944. Nora Scott. *The Home Life of the Ancient Egyptians.* New York, 1944.
Scott 1986. Gerry D. Scott. *Ancient Egyptian Art at Yale.* New Haven, 1986.
Scott 1992. Gerry D. Scott. "Amuletic inlays," cat. no. 131, in *Temple, Tomb and Dwelling: Egyptian Antiquites from the Harer Family Trust Collections.* 1992, pp. 181, 183.
Seeber 1976. Christine Seeber. *Untersuchungen zur Darstellung des Totengerichts im alten Ägypten.* (*MÄS* 35.) Munich, 1976.
Seipel 1989. Wilfried Seipel. *Ägypten: Götter, Gräber, und die Kunst: 4000 Jahre Jenseitsglaube.* 1. Exhibition catalogue. Linz, 1989.
Seipel 1992. Wilfried Seipel. *Gott, Mensch, Pharao: Viertausend Jahre Menschenbild in der Skulptur des alten Ägypten.* Exhibition catalogue. Vienna, 1992.
Sesto Congresso Internazionale di Egittologia 1992. Sesto Congresso Internazionale di Egittologia, *Atti I.* Turin, 1992.
Settgast 1978. Jürgen Settgast (ed.). *Von Troja bis Amarna: The Norbert Schimmel Collection, New York.* Exhibition catalogue. Mainz, 1978.
Sety and El Zeini 1981. Omm Sety and Hanny El Zeini. *Abydos: Holy City of Egypt.* Los Angeles, 1981.
Shaw and Nicholson 1995. Ian Shaw and Paul Nicholson. *The British Museum Dictionary of Ancient Egypt.* London and New York, 1995.
Shedid 1991. Abdel Ghafor Shedid. *Das Grab des Nacht: Kunst und Geschichte eines Beamtengrabes der 18. Dynastie in Theben-West.* Mainz, 1991.
Silvano 1980. Flora Silvano. "Le reticelle funerarie nell'Antico Egitto: proposte di interpretazione," *Egitto e Vicino Oriente* 3 (1980), pp. 83–97.
Silverman in Brovarski et al. 1982 David P. Silverman. "Bookplate of Amenhoptep III and Queen Tiye," cat. no. 400, in Brovarski et al. 1982, p. 289.
Simpson 1977. William Kelly Simpson. *The Face of Egypt, Permanence and Change in Egyptian Art.* Exhibition catalogue. Dallas, 1977.
Skon 1977. Nancy Skon. "Votive *Aigyptiaka* from the Sanctuary of Athena at Ialysos on Rhodes." Archaeological Institute of America, *Abstracts of the Archaeological Institute of America General Meeting, 28–30 December 1977.* New York, 1977, p. 10.
Smith 1946. William Stevenson Smith. *A History of Egyptian Sculpture and Painting in the Old Kingdom.* London, 1946.
Smith 1965. William Stevenson Smith. *Interconnections in the Ancient Near East.* New Haven, 1965.
Smith 1942 (1952, 1960, 1961). William Stevenson Smith. *Ancient Egypt as Represented in the Museum of Fine Arts.* 4th ed. 1961. Boston, 1942 (1952, 1960, 1961).
Smith 1967. William Stevenson Smith. "Two Archaic Egyptian Sculptures," in *Boston Museum Bulletin* 45, no. 340 (1967), pp. 70–84.
Smith 1981. William Stevenson Smith. *Art and Architecture of Ancient Egypt.* 2nd rev. ed. with additions by W.K. Simpson. New York, 1981.
Smith et al. 1983. Harry S. Smith, David G. Jeffreys and Jaromir Málek. "Archaeological Survey at Mitrahina (1981): Kom Ravi'a and Kom Fakhri," *ASAE* 69 (1983), pp. 87–94, pls. 1–6.
Smith in Matheson 1994. Amy C. Smith. "Queens and Empresses as Goddesses: The Public Role of the Personal Tyche in the Graeco-Roman World," in Matheson 1994, pp. 86–105.
Sotheby, Wilkinson, and Hodge 1911. Sotheby, Wilkinson, and Hodge. Auction catalogue. London, 1911.
Sotheby, Wilkinson, and Hodge 1922. Sotheby, Wilkinson, and Hodge. *Catalogue of the MacGregor Collection of Egyptian Antiquities.* Auction catalogue. London, 1922.
Sotheby's 1987. Sotheby's. *Antiquités et Objets d'Art. Collection de Martine, Comtesse de Béhague provenant de la Succession du Marquis de Ganay.* Auction catalogue. Monaco, 1987.
Sotheby's 1988. Sotheby's. *Egyptian Antiquites from Eton: The Myers Museum Collection. A Loan Exhibition at Sotheby's.* Exhibition catalogue. London, 1988.
Sotheby's 1992. Sotheby's. *Antiquities from the Norbert Schimmel Collection.* Auction catalogue. New York, Dec. 16, 1992.
Spalinger in Brovarski et al. 1982. Gretchen L. Spalinger. "Footed dish," cat. no. 153, in Brovarski et al. 1982, pp. 149–50.
Spanel 1988. Donald Spanel. *Through Ancient Eyes: Egyptian Portraiture.* Exhibition catalogue. Birmingham, Alabama, 1988.
Spanton 1917. W.D. Spanton. "The Water Lilies of Ancient Egypt," *Ancient Egypt.* part 1. 1917, pp. 1–20.
Sparkes 1991. Brian A. Sparkes. *Greek Pottery: An Introduction.* Manchester, 1991.
Spencer 1980. A. Jeffrey Spencer. *Catalogue of Egyptian Antiquities in the British Museum.* 5: *Early Dynastic Objects.* London, 1980.
Spencer 1982. A. Jeffrey Spencer. *Death in Ancient Egypt.* London and New York, 1982.
Spencer 1984. A. Jeffrey Spencer. *Excavations at El-Ashmunein.* 3: *The Town.* (*Occassional Paper (British Museum)* no. 53). London, 1984.
Spencer 1993. A. Jeffrey Spencer. *Early Egypt: The Rise of Civilization in the Nile Valley.* London, 1993.
Spencer 1995. J. Spencer (ed.). *Aspects of Early Egypt.* London, 1995.
Staatliche Museen zu Berlin 1991. Staatliche Museen zu Berlin. *Ägyptisches Museum: Museumsinsel Berlin.* Mainz am Rhein, 1991.
Staatliche Sammlung Ägyptischer Kunst 1966. Staatliche Sammlung Ägyptischer Kunst. *Die Ägyptische Sammlung des Bayerischen Staates, Ausstellung in den Ausstellungsräumen der Staatlichen Graphischen Sammlung München, Meiserstrasse 10, Erdgeschoss vom 21. Juli bis 5. Oktober 1966.* Munich, 1966.
Staatliche Sammlung Ägyptischer Kunst 1976. Staatliche Sammlung Ägyptischer Kunst. *Staatliche Sammlung Ägyptischer Kunst.* 2nd ed. Exhibition catalogue. Munich, 1976.
Staatliche Sammlung Ägyptischer Kunst 1995. Staatliche Sammlung Ägyptischer Kunst. *Staatliche Sammlung Ägyptischer Kunst, München.* Sylvia Schoske and Alfred Grimm. Mainz, 1995.
Staehelin 1966. Elisabeth Staehelin. *Untersuchungen zur ägyptischen Tracht im Alten Reich.* (*MÄS* 8.) Berlin, 1966.
Staehelin 1978. Elisabeth Staehelin. "Zur hathorsymbolik in den ägyptischen Kleinkunst," *ZÄS* 105 (1978), pp. 76–84.
Stead 1986. Miriam Stead. *Egyptian Life.* London, 1986.
Stein and Rubino 1994. Victor Stein and Paul Rubino. *The Billiard Encyclopedia. An Illustrated History of the Sport.* New York, 1994.
Steindorff 1935, 1937. Georg Steindorff. *Aniba.* (*Mission archéologique de Nubie 1929–1934,* 2 vols.). Hamburg, 1935, 1937.
Steindorff 1946. Georg Steindorff. *Catalogue of the Egyptian Scultpure at the Walters Art Gallery.* Baltimore, 1946.
Steinmann 1984. Frank Steinmann. "Untersuchungen zu den in der handwerklich-

künstlerischen Produktion beschäftigten Personen und Berufsgruppen des neuen Reichs," *ZÄS* 111, no. 1 (1984), pp. 30–40.

Stern and Schlick-Nolte 1994. E. Marianne Stern and Birgit Schlick-Nolte. *Early Glass of the Ancient World, 1600 BC – AD 50: Ernesto Wolfe Collection.* Ostfildern, 1994.

Stewart 1995. Harry M. Stewart. *Egyptian Shabtis.* (*Shire Egyptology* 23). Aylesbury, 1995.

Stierlin and Ziegler 1987a. Henri Stierlin and Christiane Ziegler. *Tanis Trésors des Pharaons.* Munich, 1987.

Stierlin and Ziegler 1987b. Henri Stierlin and Christiane Ziegler. *Tanis, Vergessene Schätze der Pharaonen.* (trans. of Stierlin and Ziegler 1987a) Munich, 1987.

Stocks 1997. D. Stocks. "Derivation of ancient Egyptian faience core and glaze materials," *Antiquity* 71 (1997), pp. 179–82.

Stone and Thomas 1956. J.F.S. Stone and L.C. Thomas. "The use and distribution of faience in the Ancient Near East and Prehistoric Europe," *Proceedings of the Prehistoric Society* 22 (1956), pp. 37–84, pls. 5–6.

Störk 1981. Lothar Störk. "Nilpferd," *LÄ* IV, cols. 503–06, Wiesbaden, 1981.

Störk 1982a. Lother Störk. "Pavian," *LÄ* IV, cols. 915–20, Wiesbaden, 1982.

Störk 1982b. Lother Störk. "Pferd," *LÄ* IV, cols. 1009–113. Wiesbaden, 1982.

Strauss 1974. Elisabeth-Christine Strauss. *Die Nunschale–Eine Gefassgruppe des Neuen Reiches.* (*MÄS* 30.) Munich, 1974.

Strauss in Arnold et al. 1978. Ch. Strauss. "Fayenceproduktion im Alten Ägypten" in Arnold et al. 1978, pp. 42–48.

Stuart 1944. Meriwether Stuart. "A Faïence Head of Augustus," *AJA* 48, no. 2 (1944), pp. 171–75.

Täckholm 1974. Vivi Täckholm. *Students' Flora of Egypt.* 2nd ed. Beirut, 1974.

Tait 1963. G.A.D. Tait. "The Egyptian relief chalice," *JEA* 49 (1963), pp. 93–139, pls. 12–24.

Tait 1982. William J. Tait. *Game-Boxes and Accessories from the Tomb of Tut'ankhamun.* (*Tut'ankhamun's Tomb Series* 7.) Oxford, 1982.

Taylor 1989. John H. Taylor. *Egyptian Coffins.* (*Shire Egyptology* 11). Aylesbury, 1989.

Taylor in D'Auria et al. 1988. John H. Taylor. "Set of Amulets," cat. no. 129, in D'Auria. et al. 1988, pp. 180–83.

te Velde 1970. Herman te Velde. "The God Heka in Egyptian Theology," *JEOL* 21 (1970), pp. 175–86.

te Velde 1988. Herman te Velde. "Some remarks on the mysterious language of Baboons," in J.H. Kamstra, H. Milde and K. Wagtendonk (eds.), *Funerary symbols and religion*, , pp. 129–37. Kampen, 1988.

Tefnin 1983. Rolin Tefnin. "Une statue de reine British Museum et Karnak et les paradoxes du portrait égyptien," *JEA* 69 (1983), pp. 96–107, pls. 8–10.

Tefnin 1991. Rolin Tefnin. *Art et Magie au temps des Pyramides: l'enigme des têtes dites "de replacements."* Brussels, 1991.

Terrace 1962. Edward L.B. Terrace. *The Art of the Ancient Near East in Boston, Museum of Fine Arts.* Boston, 1962.

Terrace 1968a. Edward L.B. Terrace. "The Age of Empire and Rebellion: The New Kingdom in Boston," *Connoisseur* 169, no. 679 (September 1968), pp. 49–56.

Terrace 1968b. Edward L.B. Terrace. "The American Connoisseur. Urbanity and Verism: The Late Period in Boston," *Connoisseur* 169, no. 680 (October 1968), pp. 117–23.

Thomas et al. 1995. Nancy Thomas, Gerry D. Scott and Bruce G. Trigger (eds.). *The American Discovery of Ancient Egypt.* Exhibition catalogue. Los Angeles, 1995.

Thompson 1973. Dorothy Burr Thompson. *Ptolemaic Oinochoai and Portraits in Faience: Aspects of the Ruler-Cult.* Oxford, 1973.

Thompson 1979. Dorothy Burr Thompson. "Ptolemaic Cult Oinochoai," in Otto Morkholm and Nancy W. Waggoner (eds.). *Greek Numismatics and Archaeology: Essays in Honor of Margaret Thompson*, pp. 251–55. Wetteren, 1979.

Thompson 1988. Dorothy Burr Thompson. *Memphis under the Ptolemies.* Princeton, 1988.

Tite 1986. M.S. Tite. "Egyptian Blue, Faience and Related Materials Technological Investigations," in M. Jones and H. Catling (eds.). *Science in Archaeology: proceedings of a meeting held at the British School at Athens, January 1986.* (*Fitch Laboratory Occasional Paper.* vol. 2). 1986, pp. 39–41.

Tite 1987. M.S. Tite "Characterisation of Early Vitreous Materials" *Archaeometry* 29 no 1 (1987), pp 21–34.

Tite 1992. M.S. Tite. "Technology of early vitreous materials," paper presented at a Los Angeles symposium, unpublished, 1992.

Tite and Bimson in Black 1987. M.S. Tite and M. Bimson. "Identification of early vitreous materials," in Black 1987, pp. 81–86.

Tite et al. 1983. M.S. Tite, I.C. Freestone and M. Bimson. "Egyptian Faience: An Investigation of the Methods of Production," *Archaeometry* 25, no. 1 (February 1983), pp. 17–27.

Tite et al. in Bimson and Freestone 1992. M.S. Tite, M. Bimson and M.R. Cowell. "The Technology of Egyptian Blue," in Bimson and Freestone 1992, pp. 39–46.

Tite et al. forthcoming. M.S. Tite, A. Shortland, P.T. Nicholson and C.M. Jackson, "The use of copper and cobalt colorants in vitreous materials in ancient Egypt," in *La Couleur dans la peinture et l'émaillage de l'Égypte ancienne. Ravello 20–22 mars 1997.* Ravello, forthcoming.

Tokyo 1983. *Neferut net Kemet: Egyptian Art from The Brooklyn Museum.* Exhibition catalogue. Tokyo, 1983.

Török 1987. Laszlo Török. *The Royal Crowns of Kush: A Study of Middle Nile Valley Regalia and Iconography in the 1st Millennia BC and AD.* (*B.A.R. International Series* 38.) Oxford, 1987.

Trigger 1976. Bruce G. Trigger *Nubia Under the Pharaohs.* London, 1976.

Trigger in Hochfield and Riefstahl 1978. Bruce G. Trigger "Nubian, Negro, Black, Nilotic?" in Hochfield and Riefstahl 1978, pp. 27–35.

Tutundjian de Vartavan 1986. Christian Tutundjian de Vartavan. "The Origin, Evolution and Function of the *SHM*, Known as the Naos-Sistrum: Preliminary Researches," *Wepwawet* 2 (1986), pp. 26–29.

Tytus 1903. Robb de P. Tytus. *A Preliminary Report on the Re-excavation of the Palace of Amenhetep III.* New York, 1903.

Valbelle 1990. Dominique Valbelle. "L'artigano," in Sergio Donadoni (ed.). *L'Uomo Egiziano*, pp. 35–62. Rome, 1990.

Valbelle and Bonnet 1996. D. Valbelle and C. Bonnet. *Le sanctuaire d'Hathor, Maitresse de la turquoise Serabit el-Khadim au Moyen Empire.* Paris, 1996.

van Haarlem 1995. Willem M. van Haarlem. "Temple Deposits at Tell Ibrahim Awad – A preliminary report," *GM* 148 (1995), pp. 45–52.

Vandersleyen 1975. Claude Vandersleyen et al. *Das Alte Ägypten.* (*Propyläen Kunstgeschichte* 15). Berlin, 1975.

Vandier 1950. Jacques Vandier. "Acquisitions du département des Antiquités égyptiennes," *Musées de France* 15 no. 2 (1950), pp. 25–26.

Vandier 1952. Jacques Vandier. *Manuel d'archéologie égyptienne.* 1: *Les époques de formation.* Paris, 1952.

Vandier 1958. Jacques Vandier. *Manuel d'archéologie égyptienne.* Paris, 1958.

Vandier 1964. Jacques Vandier. *Manuel d'archéologie égyptienne.* 4: *Bas-reliefs et peintures: scénes de la vie quotidienne.* Paris, 1964.

Vandier 1967. Jacques Vandier. "Vingt ans d'acquisitions au Musée du Louvre, 1947–1967. Department des antiquités égyptiennes," *La revue du Louvre et des Musées de France* 17 no. 6 (1967), p. 308.

Vandier d'Abbadie 1937. Jeanne Vandier d'Abbadie. *Catalogue des ostraca figurés de Deir el Médineh (nos. 2256 à 2272).* (*IFAO: Documents des Fouilles* 2.) Cairo, 1937.

Vandier d'Abbadie 1938. Jeanne Vandier d'Abbadie. "Une fresque civile de Deir el Médineh," *RdÉ* 3 (1938), pp. 27–35, pl. 3.

Vandier d'Abbadie 1939. Jeanne Vandier d'Abbadie. *Deux Tombes de Deir el Médineh.* Cairo, 1939.

Vandier d'Abbadie 1972. Jeanne Vandier d'Abbadie. *Catalogue des objets de toilette égyptiens au Musée du Louvre.* Paris, 1972.

Vandiver in Olin and Franklin 1982. Pamela B. Vandiver. "Technological change in Egyptian faience," in Olin and Franklin 1982, pp. 167–79.

Vandiver forthcoming. Pamela B. Vandiver. "New Critieria for Production Technologies of Egyptian Faience," in *La Couleur dans la peinture et l'émaillage de l'Égypte ancienne. Ravello 20–22 mars 1997.* Ravello, forthcoming.

Vandiver and Kingery 1987. Pamela B. Vandiver and W. David Kingery. "Egyptian Faience: the First High-Tech Ceramic," in W. David Kingery (ed.), *High-Technology Ceramics: Past, Present and Future: the Nature of Innovation and Change in Ceramics Technology, Ceramics, and Civilization III,* Columbus OH 1987, pp. 19–34.

Vandiver and Kingery in Bimson and Freestone 1987
Pamela B. Vandiver and W. David Kingery. "The Manufacture of an Eighteenth Dynasty Egyptian faience chalice," in Bimson and Freestone 1987, pp. 79–90.

Vandiver et al. 1991. P. Vandiver, C. Swann and D. Cranmer. "A review of mid-second millennium BC Egyptian glass technology at Tell el-Amarna" in Vandiver, Durzik and Wheeler 1991, pp. 609–16.

Vandiver et al. forthcoming
P. Vandiver, A. Kaczmarczyk, P. Lacovara and Y. Markowitz. *The Faience Industry at Kerma* Forthcoming.

Vandiver in Brovarski et al. 1982. Pamela B. Vandiver. "Blue-lotus chalice," cat. no. 148, in Brovarski et al. 1982, pp. 147–48.

Vandiver in Kaczmarczyk and Hedges 1983
Pamela B. Vandiver. "Appendix A: Egyptian Faience Technology," in Kaczmarczyk and Hedges 1983, pp. A1–137.

Vandiver, Durzik and Wheeler 1991
P. Vandiver, J. Durzik and G.S. Wheeler (eds.). *Materials Issues in Art and Archaeology II.* London, 1991.

Vassilika 1995. Eleni Vassilika (ed.). *Egyptian Art.* (*Fitzwilliam Museum Handbooks)* Cambridge, 1995.

Vercoutter 1993. Jean Vercoutter. "Le rôle des artisans dans la naissance de la civilisation égyptienne," *CdÉ* 68 (1993), pp. 70–83.
Vercoutter et al. 1976. Jean Vercoutter et al. *Migrissa.* 3: *Les nécropoles. Deuxième partie: études anthropologiques, études archéologiques.* Paris, 1976.
Vergès 1992. Fabienne Lavenex Vergès *Bleus Égyptiens.* Louvain-Paris, 1992.
Verhoeven and Graefe 1991. Ursula Verhoeven and Erhart Graefe (eds.). *Religion und Philiospie im alten Ägypten.* (*Orientalia Lovaniensia Analecta* 39.) Louvain, 1991.
Vermeule 1981. Emily Townsend Vermeule. "Mycenaean Drawing, Amarna and Egyptian Ostraka," in William Kelly Simpson and Whitney M. Davis (eds.). *Studies in Honor of Dows Dunham on the Occasion of his 90th Birthday, June 1, 1980.* Boston, 1981, pp. 193–200.
Vermeule in Brovarski et al. 1982a. Emily Townsend Vermeule. "Conical rhyton," cat. no. 160, in Brovarski et al. 1982, p. 154.
Vermeule in Brovarski et al. 1982b. Emily Townsend Vermeule. "Egyptian imitations of Aegean Vases," in Brovarski et al. 1982, pp. 152–53.
Vermeule in Brovarski et al. 1982c. Emily Townsend Vermeule. "Mycenaean Stirrup Jar," cat. no. 165 in Brovarski et al. 1982, p. 156.
Verner 1984. Miroslav Verner. "Excavations at Abusir: season 1982 preliminary report," *ZÄS* 111, no. 1 (1984), pp. 70–78.
Verner 1986. Miroslav Verner. "Nouvelles découvertes des égyptologues tchécoslovaques," *Solidarité* 4 (1986), pp. 20–21.
Verner 1994. Miroslav Verner. *Forgotten Pharaohs, Lost Pyramids: Abusir.* Prague, 1994.
Vernier 1927. Émile Vernier. *Catalogue générale des antiquités égyptiennes du Musée du Caire.* 4 vols: *Bijoux et orfevreries. (nos. 52001–53855.* 38, 48, 80, 84). Cairo, 1927.
Vernus 1975. P. Vernus. "Un texte oraculaire de Ramsès VI." *BIFAO* 75 (1975) pp. 103–10.
Vierneisel and Zanker 1979. Klaus Vierneisel and Paul Zanker. *Die Bildnisse des Augustus: Herrscherbild und Politik im kaiserlichen Rom.* Exhibition catalogue. Munich, 1979.
Vila in Vercoutter et al. 1976. Andé Vila. "Les masques funéraires," in Vercoutter, et al. 1976, pp. 151–268, pls. H.-T. 1 – H.-T. 4.
Villa Hügel 1961. Villa Hügel. *5000 Jahre Ägyptische Kunst, 15. Mai bis 2. August in Villa Hügel, Essen.* Essen, 1961.
Vitruvius 1914. Vitruvius. *The Ten Books of Architecture.* Trans. M.H. Morgan. Cambridge, 1914.
von Beckerath 1984. J. von Beckerath. "Handbuch der Ägyptischen Königsnamen," *MÄS* 20 (1984).
Wade 1997. Nicholas Wade. "Man has older friend than thought," *The New York Times* (Friday, June 13, 1997), p. A: 12.
Wainwright 1962. G. Wainwright, "The Meshwesh," *JEA* 48 (1962), p. 94.
Walker 1996. Alan S. Walker (ed.). *Animals in Ancient Art from the Leo Mildenberg Collection.* Part III. Mainz, 1996.
Walker and Burnett 1981. Susan Walker and Andrew Burnett. *The Image of Augustus.* London, 1981.
Wallis 1898. Henry Wallis. *Egyptian Ceramic Art. The MacGregor Collection: A Contribution Towards the History of Egyptian Pottery.* London, 1898.
Wallis 1900. Henry Wallis. *Egyptian ceramic art: typical examples of the art of the Egyptian potter portrayed in colour plates.* London, 1900.
Ward-Perkins and Claridge 1976. John Ward-Perkins and Amanda Claridge. *Pompeii, AD 79: treasures from the National Archaeological Museum Naples and the Pompeii Antiquarium.* 2 vols. London, 1976.
Weatherhead 1992. Fran Weatherhead. "Painted Pavements in the Great Palace at Amarna," *JEA* 78 (1992), pp. 179–94.
Weatherhead and Buckley in Kemp 1989a. Fran Weatherhead and A. Buckley. "Artist's pigments from Amarna," in Kemp 1989a, pp. 202–40.
Webb 1978. Virginia Webb. *Archaic Greek Faience.* Warminster, 1978.
Weber 1969. Manfred Weber. *Beiträge zur Kenntnis des Schrift- und Buchwesens der alten Ägypter.* Ph.D. thesis, University of Cologne. Cologne, 1969.
Weidner 1985. Stephan M. Weidner. *Lotos im alten Ägypten.* Pfaffenweiler, 1985.
Wenig 1978. S. Wenig. *Africa in Antiquity II: The Catalog.* Brooklyn, 1978.
Werbrouck 1933. Marcelle Werbrouck. "À propos du dieu Bès," in Samuel A.B. Mercer (ed.). *Egyptian Religion.* 1. New York, 1933.
Whyte 1892–93. E. Towry Whyte. "Notes on Pectorals" *PSBA* 15 (1892–3), p. 313, pl. 4.
Whyte 1896. E. Towry Whyte. "Some Remarks on the Sepulchral Figures usually called Ushabti," *PSBA* 18, no. 134 (April 1896), pp. 138–145, pls. 1–10.
Wild 1960. Henri Wild. "Statue d'un noble medésien du règne de Psamétik Ier aux musées de Palerme et du Caire," *BIFAO* 60 (1960), pp. 43–67, pls. 1–5.
Wildung 1976. Dietrich Wildung, *Staatliche Sammlung Ägyptischer Kunst.* Munich, 1976.
Wildung 1980. Dietrich Wildung. *Fünf jahre. Neuerwerbungen der Staatliches Sammlung Ägyptischer Kunst München 1976–1980.* Mainz, 1980.
Wildung 1987. Dietrich Wildung. *Nilpferd un Krokodil, Das Tier in der Kunst des alten Ägypten.* (*SÄS* 4.) Munich, 1987.
Wildung and Schoske 1984. Dietrich Wildung and Sylvia Schoske. *Nofret – die Schone.* Mainz, 1984.
Wilkinson 1971. Alix Wilkinson. *Ancient Egyptian Jewellery.* London, 1971.
Wilkinson 1994. Richard H. Wilkinson. *Symbol and Magic and Egyptian Art.* London and New York, 1994.
Williams 1930. C.R. Williams. "Wall Decorations at el 'Amarneh," *Metropolitan Museum Studies II 1929–30.* New York, 1930.
Williams 1986
B. Williams. *The A-Group Royal Cemetery at Qustul: Cemetery L: The University of Chicago Oriental Institute Nubian Expedition 3* Chicago, 1986.
Wilson 1947
John Wilson. "The Artist of the Egyptian Old Kingdom," *JNES* 6 (1947), pp. 231–49.
Wilson 1988. Hilary Wilson. *Egyptian Food and Drink.* (*Shire Egyptology.*) Aylesbury, 1988.
Winlock 1932. Herbert E. Winlock. *The Tomb of Queen Meryet-Amun at Thebes.* New York, 1932.
Winlock 1939. Herbert E. Winlock. "New Galleries of Egyptian Art," *BMMA* 34, no. 1 (1939), pp. 118–22.
Winlock 1948. Herbert E. Winlock. *The Treasure of Three Egyptian Princesses.* New York, 1948.
Wolf 1930. Walther Wolf. *Ägyptisches Kunstgewerbe.* Berlin, 1930.
Wolinski 1986. Arlene Wolinski. "Ancient Egyptian Ceremonial Masks," in *DE* 6 (1986), pp. 47–53.
Wolinski in press. "The Case for Ceremonial Masking" in Theodore Celenko (ed.), *Egypt in Africa.* Indianapolis, in press.
Wulff et al. 1968. Hans E. Wulff, Hildegard S. Wulff and Leo Koch. "Egyptian Faïence: a Possible Survival in Iran," *Archaeology* 21, no. 2 (April 1968), pp. 98–107.
Yakata 1983. Teisuke Yakata. *Neferut net Kemit: Egyptian Art from the Brooklyn Museum.* Exhibition catalogue. Tokyo, 1983.
Yoyotte 1983. Jean Yoyotte. "Sekhmet hier, Ouadjyt aujourd'hui. Le bilan annuel des péchés et la conjuration de périls de l'année dans l'Égypte ancienne," *Revue de l'Histoire des Religions* 200 (1983), pp. 263–65.
Zabkar 1968. Louis V. Zabkar. *A Study of the Ba Concept in Ancient Egyptian Texts.* Chicago, 1968.
Zabkar 1975. Louis V. Zabkar. *Apedemak, Lion God of Mercë: a study in Egyptian-Meroitic syncretism.* Warminster, 1975.
Ziegler 1979. Christiane Ziegler. *Catalogue des instruments de musique égyptienne au Musée du Louvre.* Paris, 1979.
Ziegler 1990. Christiane Ziegler. *The Louvre: Egyptian Antiquities.* Paris, 1990.
Zivie 1985. A.-P. Zivie. "Tell el Jahudija," *LÄ* VI, cols. 331–35, Wiesbaden, 1985.
Zoffili 1992. Ermano Zoffili. *Kleidung und Schmuck im alten Ägypten.* Frankfurt, 1992.

PHOTOGRAPHIC CREDITS

© 1996 The Art Institute of Chicago [152]

Delmont Bogart, Providence:
Brooklyn Museum of Art [49];[51]; [141]; [150]
W.K. Simpson [134]
Museum of Art, RISD [91]; [159]

P.J. Bonhof:
Rijksmuseum van Oudeheden, Leiden [79]; [168]

Copyright, The Trustees of the British Museum, London: [13]; [14]; [15]; [16]; [19]; [28]; [31]; [32]; [46]; [48]; [54]; [76]; [82]; [101]; [105]; [114]; [119]; [124]; [151]; [157]; [161]; [162]; [178]; [179]; [180]

Margarete Büsing
Staatliche Museen zu Berlin – Preussischer Kulturbesitz Ägyptisches Museum und Papyrusammlung [34]; [35]; [72]; [78]; [85]; [97]; [102]; [126]

Christie's:
The George Ortiz Collection [64]

© The Cleveland Museum of Art [70]; [73]; [87]

Prudence Cumming:
Julia Schottlander, London [44]; [45]; [184]

© 1997 The Detroit Institute of Arts:
[55]; [158]; [171]
Collection of Dr. Irving F. Burton [18]
Collection of William H. Peck [17]

Dr. and Mrs. Jerome M. Eisenberg [155]

Michael Fredericks, Ghent, New York (Museums retain copyright):
The Syndics of the Fitzwilliam Museum, University of Cambridge [3]; [8]; [9]; [10]; [20]; [58]; [106]; [107]; [121]; [147]; [191]
Musée du Louvre, Paris [23]; [24]; [29]; [33]; [60]; [71]; [84]; [94]; [95]; [96]; [99]; [109]; [111]; [112]; [125]; [135]; [149]; [154]; [163]; [165]; [188]; [189]; [190]; [192]; [194]; [195]; [197]
The Metropolitan Museum of Art, New York [22]; [25]; [61]; [63]; [66]; [67]; [74]; [90]; [117]; [130]; [146]; [170]
Museum of Art, Rhode Island School of Design [118]; [145]; [193]
Myers Museum, Eton College, with Permission of the Provost and Fellows [43]; [65]; [108]; [115]; [116]; [169]
Petrie Museum of Egyptian Archaeology, University College London [1]; [2]; [5]; [6]; [7]; [12]; [37]; [38]; [42]; [173]; [174]; [175]; [176]; [177]; [200]
Trustees of the National Museums of Scotland, Edinburgh [59]; [81]; [93]; [98]; [166]; [167]
Private Collection [26]; [39]; [40]; [56]; [68]; [110]; [123]; [129]; [133]; [140]; [148]; [188]; [196]; [199]
Private Collection [21]
Private Collection, Dallas [131]

The J. Paul Getty Museum, Los Angeles, California [62]

Shawn Kenney: figs. 4; 27; 40; 42–43; 47; 48; 49; maps

Jürgen Liepe:
Staatliche Museen zu Berlin – Ägyptisches Museum und Papyrussammlung. [104]

M. Robert Markowich:
Harer Family Trust [75]; [156]

Courtesy, Museum of Fine Arts, Boston:
[11]; [41]; [52]; [53]; [69]; [77]; [80]; [86]; [89]; [100]; [103]; [113]; [120]; [128]; [136]; [137]; [138]; [153]; [164]; [182]

William Kelly Simpson, New York [88]; [132]
Clare Niggli:
The Leo Mildenberg Collection [142]

The University of Pennsylvania Museum of Archaeology and Anthropology: [181]; [183]; [185]; [187]

Copyright, Justin Van Soest 1997:
Brooklyn Museum of Art [30]

The Walters Art Gallery, Baltimore, Maryland [57]; [92]; [122]

Dietrich Wildung:
Staatliche Sammlung Ägyptischer Kunst, Munich [4]; [47]; [50]; [83]; [127]; [139]; [144]

CONCORDANCE OF OBJECTS IN CATALOGUE BY LENDER

The Art Institute of Chicago
AIC 1942.647 [152]

British Museum
EA 38010 [13]
EA 68151 [14]
EA 38025 [15]
EA 37282 [16]
EA 66830 [19]
EA 2280 [28]
EA 65817 [31]
EA 34213 [32]
EA 14556 [46]
EA 22818 [48]
EA 12337 [54]
EA 4790 [76]
EA 64041 [82]
EA 3084 [101]
EA 22594 [105]
EA 26226 [114]
EA 54412 [119]
EA 22731 [124]
EA 53892 [151]
EA 26230 [157]
EA 7853 [161]
EA 6133 [162]
GR1980.10-17.8–12 [178]
GR1910.11-16.6 [179]
GR1980.10-17.1 [180]

Brooklyn Museum of Art
BMA 49.56a,b; 49.57.1-13 [30]
BMA 52.54 [49]
BMA 55.182 a–i [51]
BMA 70.89.3 [141]
BMA 37.124E [150]

Collection of Dr. Irving F. Burton
[18]

The Cleveland Museum of Art
CMA 1980.123 [70]
CMA 1995.13 [73]
CMA 1987.127 [87]

The Detroit Institute of Arts
90.1S12593.1; 90.1S12821.1; .3; .4; .5 [55]
51.226 [158]
40.49 [171]

Dr. and Mrs Jerome Eisenberg
[155]

The Syndics of the Fitzwilliam Museum, University of Cambridge
E.91.1898 [3]
E.11.1898 [8]
E.18.1898 [9]
E.21.1898 [10]
EGA.xxxx.1943, etc. [20]
E.6. 1969 [58]
E.473.1954 [106]
E.352.1939 [107]
E.274.1939 [121]
E.279.1939 [147]
E.6.1920 [191]

The J. Paul Getty Museum, Malibu, California
96.A.I.58 [62]

The Harer Family Trust
[75]
[156]

Metropolitan Museum of Art, New York
1972.125 [22]
26.7.954 [25]
26.7.996 [61]
26.7.1428 [63]
15.10.90 [66]
44.4.4 [67]
1989.281.94 [74]
26.7.1175 [90]
26.7.971 [117]
26.7.860 [130]
26.7.899 [146]
1988.18 [170]
22.1.1097;1226;1227;1225; 1238;1937a–c [172]
11.215.666; 667; 668 [186]
1924.1749 [80]
1970.571 [86]
1996.108 [89]
1937.1314 [100]
1965.1723 [103]
1982.150 [113]
1927.1014 [120]
1971.773 [128]
1920.1235 [136]
1920.1305 [137]
1924.1089 [138]
1921.2654; 2679; 2677 [153]
1927.443 [164]
1913.4229 [182]

The Leo Mildenberg Collection
[142]

Musée du Louvre, Paris
E 4877 [23]
E 3043 [24]
AF 2436 [29]
E 17357 [33]
E 22634 [60]
AF 11514 [71]
E 1871 [84]
E 11061 [94]
E 10857 [95]
N 3043; N4265 A, B, C [96]
AF 2302 [99]
E 22665 [109]
E 10482 [111]
N 3035 [112]
E 11261 [125]
E 3610 [135]
E 14188 [149]
E 22670 [154]
N 3078 [163]
E 1875 [165]
E 10244 [189]
AF 12531 [190]
N 3364 [192]
E 10813 [194]
E 22662 [195]
E 11518 [197]
AF 12532 [198]

Museum of Art, Rhode Island School of Design
1995.050 [91]
1996.73.2 [118]
29.119 [145]
1996.73.1a–c [159]
1996.56 [193]

Museum of Fine Arts, Boston
1898.1832a-v [11]
1988.339 [41]
1903.1569 [52]
1903.1570 [53]
1984.168 [69]
1977.619 [77]

Myers Museum, Eton College, with Permission of the Provost and Fellows
ECM 1887 [43]
ECM 1843 [65]
ECM 1482 [108]
ECM 1581 [115]
ECM 1582 [116]
ECM 1587 [169]

The George Ortiz Collection
[64]
[143]

Collection of William H. Peck
[17]

Petrie Museum of Egyptian Archaeology, University College London
UC.9250 [1]
UC.35976 [2]
UC.15012 [5]
UC.11001 [6]
UC.11005 [7]
UC.14893 [12]
UC.23267 [37]
UC.1703 [38]
UC.509 [42]
UC.46179 A, B [173]
UC.46178 [174]
UC.36471 [175]
UC.40569 A, B [176]
UC.40568 [177]
UC.40913 A, B [200]

Private Collection
[26]
[39]
[40]
[56]
[68]
[110]
[123]
[129]
[133]
[140]
[148]
[188]
[196]
[199]

Private Collection
[21]

Private Collection, Dallas
[131]

Rijksmuseum van Oudheden, Leiden
AD 14 [79]
AD 37 [168]

Julia Schottlander, London
[44]
[45]
[184]

William Kelly Simpson, New York
[88]
[132]
[134]

Staatliche Museen zu Berlin-Ägyptisches Museum und Papyrussammlung
22726 [27]
30552 [34]
30541 [35]
21971 [36]
20484 [72]
4562 [78]
16994 [85]
15254 [97]
16607 [102]
9029 [104]
9480 [126]
1983 [160]

Staatliche Sammlung Ägyptischer Kunst, Munich
ÄS 1511 [4]
ÄS 7121 [47]
ÄS 5535 [50]
ÄS 1575; 5631 [83]
ÄS 2922 [127]
ÄS 5980 [139]
ÄS 6040 [144]

Trustees of the National Museums of Scotland
A.1956.1485 [59]
A.1965.275; A.1911.323; A.1956.126; A.1911.323A; 1 unnumbered [81]
A.1951.292 [93]
A.1965.245 [98]
A.1956.153 [166]
A.1956.152 [167]

The University of Pennsylvania Museum of Archaeology and Anthropology
29-85-482 [181]
E 17897 [183]
E 671; E 678B; E 678C; E 679; E 685; E 688; E 690; E 697; E 717; E 719; E 721; E 722; E 735; E 741; E 743; E 744 [185]
E 12501 [187]

The Walters Art Gallery, Baltimore, Maryland
48.412 [57]
48.426a, b [92]
48.1608a, b [122]

INDEX

Page numbers in **bold** indicate color plates. Page numbers in *italic* indicate other illustrations. Catalogue numbers are given in square brackets [ ].